Node.js

Rheinwerk Computing

The Rheinwerk Computing series from Rheinwerk Publishing offers new and established professionals comprehensive guidance to enrich their skillsets and enhance their career prospects. Our publications are written by leading experts in the fields of programming, administration, security, analytics, and more. Each book is detailed and hands-on to help readers develop essential, practical skills that they can apply to their daily work. For further information, please visit our website: *www.rheinwerk-computing.com*.

Philip Ackermann
JavaScript: The Comprehensive Guide
2022, approx. 982 pp, paperback and e-book
www.rheinwerk-computing.com/5554

Christian Ullenboom
Java: The Comprehensive Guide
2022, approx. 1258 pp, paperback and e-book
www.rheinwerk-computing.com/5557

Johannes Ernesti, Peter Kaiser
Python 3: The Comprehensive Guide
2022, approx. 1078 pp, paperback and e-book
www.rheinwerk-computing.com/5566

Bernd Öggl, Michael Kofler
Git: Project Management for Developers and DevOps Teams
2023, approx. 415 pp, paperback and e-book
www.rheinwerk-computing.com/5555

Sebastian Springer

Node.js

The Comprehensive Guide

Editor Megan Fuerst
Acquisitions Editor Hareem Shafi
German Edition Editor Patricia Schiewald
Translation Winema Language Services, Inc.
Copyeditor Julie McNamee
Cover Design Graham Geary
Photo Credit Shutterstock: 1940821471/© banjongseal956
Layout Design Vera Brauner
Production Graham Geary
Typesetting III-satz, Germany
Printed and bound in Canada, on paper from sustainable sources

ISBN 978-1-4932-2292-6
© 2022 by Rheinwerk Publishing, Inc., Boston (MA)
1st edition 2022
4th German edition published 2021 by Rheinwerk Verlag, Bonn, Germany

Library of Congress Cataloging-in-Publication Control Number: 2022023980

Contents at a Glance

Dear Reader,

Fun fact about us: Rheinwerk Publishing has branches in both Bonn, Germany, and Boston, Massachusetts. The benefit of this international setup is that we can publish both German-language books and English-language books—the challenge is translating them.

When our colleagues at Rheinwerk Verlag in Bonn publish a book that we would also like to provide to English-speaking readers, or vice versa, the manuscript undergoes the translation process. This means that either the author, or a third party, must translate every sentence, diagram, and piece of code. However, receiving the translated manuscript several months later isn't the end of the story. Both the author and the editor must review and fine-tune the manuscript: the author ensures no errors have been introduced, and the editor realigns any variations in our formatting standards. Then, the copyeditor edits each chapter line-by-line to polish the grammar and style in the book's new language.

Node.js: The Comprehensive Guide is one of these translations, brought to you from its fourth German edition. Ironically, the topic of this book, Node.js, is the solution for this "translation" process in the programming world. Node.js allows your client- and server-side scripts to be written in a single language: JavaScript. In these pages, you'll find the instructions and practical examples you need to make the most of the Node.js environment for unified web application development.

What did you think about *Node.js: The Comprehensive Guide*? Your comments and suggestions are the most useful tools to help us make our books the best they can be. Please feel free to contact me and share any praise or criticism you may have.

Thank you for purchasing a book from SAP PRESS!

Megan Fuerst
Editor, SAP PRESS

meganf@rheinwerk-publishing.com
www.rheinwerk-computing.com
Rheinwerk Publishing · Boston, MA

Contents

4   Node.js Modules   101

5   HTTP   137

6   Express

11 GraphQL

12 Real-Time Web Applications

15   Node on the Command Line

16 Asynchronous Programming

17 RxJS

18   Streams

20   Socket Server

21   Package Manager

24   Security

25   Scalability and Deployment

26   Performance

Foreword

My first contact with Node.js was twelve years ago. In 2010, I worked on a software to evaluate websites regarding aspects such as accessibility, search engine optimization, corporate identity, and web compliance in general. The software had been implemented as a pure Java desktop application in the first version using the Swing GUI framework and later migrated to version 2 as a client-server web application based on web services.

Without a doubt, the software was stable, but as time went on, we realized that we were increasingly reaching the limits of Java. The websites to be evaluated with the software were for the most part no longer static websites, but single-page applications, which in turn required them to be rendered on the server side to perform a meaningful evaluation. Because the possibilities offered by Java at that time were far from satisfactory, we looked for alternatives and found them in the headless browser, PhantomJS, a browser without a graphical user interface (GUI) that can be controlled via JavaScript.

With this first step from Java toward JavaScript, one thing led to another, and we decided, with a view to version 3 of the software, to first rewrite individual components and, in the course of the subsequent refactoring, almost all components in JavaScript. However, the decisive point for this was not PhantomJS, but another, new player in the JavaScript universe, the Node.js runtime environment, which made it possible to run JavaScript efficiently on the server in the first place. For precisely this reason, Node.js is also significantly responsible for the renewed success of JavaScript.

Both the success of JavaScript and the success of Node.js continue unabated whether in the realm of web apps, mobile apps, Internet of Things (IoT) apps, desktop apps, or as part of the build process. The same is true whether on a traditional server, in the cloud, or on a mini-computer such as Raspberry Pi. Node.js now plays an important role in all areas and is thus, in combination with JavaScript, a serious competitor for the "big languages": Java, C#, or PHP. Recent surveys, trends, and the popularity of Node.js projects on GitHub are just a few indicators, along with the large community and the abundance of open-source projects. For example, the official Node.js package registry currently lists more than 1,700,000 packages. In addition, Node.js applications are considered to be extremely performant, excellently scalable thanks to nonblocking input and output, and—from a project management perspective—desirable in that, in the best-case scenario, the same JavaScript developers who develop the frontend can also develop the backend.

But how and where should you start as a budding Node.js developer? Which application programming interfaces (APIs) are available, and which libraries? How do you structure Node.js projects, and what do you look for in general? This book provides answers to these and many other questions. Sebastian Springer not only helps you with basic questions but also shows you how to solve various practical use cases with Node.js. What I particularly appreciate is the didactic structure of the book: the topics build on each other both within individual chapters and across chapters, but are nevertheless neatly separated from each other. For example, you'll learn step by step how to build a web application using Node.js, implement a representational state transfer (REST) API, set up a microservice architecture, and connect to both relational and NoSQL databases. Sebastian not only goes into details of the standard Node.js API, but he also uses numerous practical examples to show you how to use popular and proven libraries and frameworks such as Express and Nest. In my opinion, this valuable knowledge makes the book a perfect introduction to the world of Node.js.

I hope you enjoy reading this book, working through the source code, and then having fun in the world of Node.js.

Philip Ackermann
Rheinbach, Germany

Preface

Node.js has been with me for many years now as a server-side development platform and also in the form of this book, which is now in its fourth edition in German and debuting with this first edition in English. Over time, the JavaScript world, and also Node.js itself, has changed a lot. Node.js has now grown up and is part of the main-stream. In contrast to the early days, when you had to convince funders, decision mak-ers, and coworkers to use Node.js, it has become much easier now. In some cases, Node.js is already used as the base platform in projects. One aspect that has contributed decisively to this success story is the flexibility of the platform. You can use Node.js in small command-line tools, for building rapid prototypes, and also for large-scale server applications in an enterprise context. This book is intended to accompany you on your journey into the world of Node.js, to help you get started developing applications based on Node.js, and to serve as a reference in your daily work.

In this book, you'll learn the basics of Node.js, learn more about how the platform is built, and work with the various interfaces that Node.js makes available to you.

Note that to work with this book, you should have a solid basic knowledge of JavaScript. While I do cover some language features throughout this book, such as destructuring, promises, and the module system, the focus is on Node.js, and so you should take a look at the Mozilla Developer Network (*https://developer.mozilla.org/de/*), which compre-hensively explains all aspects of JavaScript. I would also like to take this opportunity to recommend Philip Ackermann's *JavaScript: The Comprehensive Guide* (SAP PRESS, 2022, *www.rheinwerk-computing.com/5554*).

Server-side JavaScript with Node.js differs in some aspects from developing client-side applications with HTML, CSS, and JavaScript, so you usually don't have direct visual feedback like you are used to in the browser. The architecture and design patterns you use on the server side also differ to some extent from those on the client side. Other patterns and paradigms are the same on both sides. Thus, Node.js is event-driven in many places, similar to the browser. This means that you have a lot to do with asyn-chronous operations because your application in Node.js usually runs in a single pro-cess, and performance bottlenecks can easily occur here if different operations block each other.

Node.js uses the same JavaScript engine as the Chrome browser: the V8 engine. Since the Node.js development team always keeps the engine up to date, you can develop modern JavaScript with Node.js and also have access to the latest language features. In addition to the engine, Node.js provides you with an extensive collection of core modules that you can use to solve your problems relatively close to the system level. However, you'll usually use external packages because, for most problems, there are already established solutions that you only need to adapt for your application. The module system of

Node.js takes a prominent position here. A lot has happened in this area in recent years, and the platform has taken a big step forward in adapting the ECMAScript module system. Throughout this book, you'll learn more about the different layers of the module system and how you can use it to build your application.

As already mentioned, Node.js has been with me for a few years now in my development work. I started with web development under PHP, and like most web developers, I couldn't escape the influence of JavaScript. In addition to the aspect of implementing application logic in the frontend, I've also been primarily concerned with quality assurance in the area of JavaScript. The Node.js platform, along with the possibility to use JavaScript on the server as well, piqued my interest quite early. Like so many other developers, I was faced with the question: Can Node.js already be used productively in applications? I approached the answer to this question step by step in the past. Initially, the focus was on implementations of various sample applications in Node.js and testing out the toolset available for Node.js. Tooling requirements for Node.js range from the availability of a development environment to tools such as debuggers and platforms for continuous integration. In the first project, I used Node.js in combination with other programming languages. Node.js took care of the real-time communication in this case. After it had been shown over a longer period of time that Node.js can be used stably in such an environment, nothing stood in the way of its further use in other projects as well, so now I use Node.js on quite a few projects.

Nearly all examples in this book use the ECMAScript module system, which significantly modernizes the source code as a whole. Due to the new features of JavaScript, but also of Node.js, the source code has become more compact and also more readable than in the past. However, don't be put off by the new features and the multitude of packages. When working with JavaScript, it's important to learn about patterns and architectures so that you can evaluate new paradigms and packages and then deploy them with a manageable learning curve. Many of the patterns and best practices you're currently working with have been in place in a similar form since the earliest versions of Node.js. When working with Node.js, understanding the core of the platform is essential, and you acquire this best by experimenting with the platform. I invite you to follow the examples in the course of this book, to extend them, and to try out different tactics. In this book, you'll find both extensive connected examples, such as in Chapter 6 through Chapter 10, in which you implement a web application based on Express, and small, self-contained examples, such as in Chapter 17 on RxJS.

Structure of the Book

This book is roughly divided into four sections with thematically-related chapters.

The first part of the book covers the basics of Node.js and the general structuring of applications based on Node.js. Here we take a look at the development history of the platform and the installation. You'll also receive a practical introduction to the module system.

Node.js is primarily a platform for web development, which the second part of this book is devoted to covering. Here you'll learn how to implement a secure web server and also how to program extensive web applications with numerous components and modules. Numerous frameworks such as Express or libraries and template engines such as Pug offer assistance. The connection of various databases should also not be missing at this point. Here, with Node.js, you have a flexible and versatile platform as the basis for your application. The strength of a Node.js application is the combination of many small specialized individual parts. You'll learn different aspects of web development, including implementation with Node.js using practical examples and developing different types of web applications. You'll also learn about GraphQL, an alternative to the widely used REST interfaces. With Nest, you'll explore another framework for web backends that puts even more emphasis on structure and architecture than Express does.

JavaScript and asynchronicity go hand in hand. The third part of the book deals with different approaches to asynchronous programming. You'll learn both how to handle promises and child processes and how to use data streams in development. In this context, you won't be limited to your local system but can also communicate between different systems via TCP and UDP.

The last part of the book deals with problems beyond pure programming and is intended to give you important tips for dealing with Node.js in everyday life as a developer. This concerns topics that take place directly in the course of development, such as dealing with Node Package Manager (npm) as a package manager and handling quality assurance of applications by implementing tests, and also code analysis and debugging. Another very important topic is application security. In a separate chapter, you'll learn more about attack possibilities and how you can counter them to protect yourself and the users of your application. The following chapters are dedicated to the deployment and scalability of Node.js applications, in which you'll learn more about the performance of applications as well as the use of Node.js in a microservice architecture. The last chapter introduces you to Deno, the biggest competitor with Node.js. In that chapter, you'll also learn why it's still worth your while to get involved with Node.js, despite the competition.

Downloading the Code Samples

All code samples used in this book are available for download from the website at *www.rheinwerk-computing/5556*.

If you have any problems with the implementation or if I've overlooked an error despite careful checking, please feel free to contact me at *node@sebastian-springer.com*.

Acknowledgments

Finally, I would like to thank all the people involved in this book, especially Philip Ackermann, who contributed many valuable comments and tips.

I would also like to thank Sibylle Feldmann for proofreading and fine-tuning the language of my book.

A big thank you also goes to the entire team at Rheinwerk Verlag, especially Patricia Schiewald.

Finally, I would like to express my heartfelt thanks to my wife Alexandra and my daughter Emma for their patience and support.

Sebastian Springer
Aßling, Germany

Chapter 1
Basic Principles

All beginnings are difficult.
–Ovid

Bringing more dynamics into web pages was the original idea behind JavaScript. The scripting language was intended to compensate for the weaknesses of HTML when it came to responding to user input. The history of JavaScript dates back to 1995 when it was developed under the code name Mocha by Brendan Eich, a developer at Netscape. One of the most remarkable facts about JavaScript is that the first prototype of this successful and globally used language was developed in just 10 days. Still in the year of its creation, Mocha was renamed to LiveScript and finally to JavaScript in a cooperation between Netscape and Sun. This was mainly for marketing purposes, as at that time it was assumed that Java would become the leading language in client-side web development.

Node.js ES2015 Support — Learn more — kangax's compat-table applied only to Node.js

	Nightly! 11.0.0	10.1.0	9.11.1	8.9.4	8.6.0	8.2.1	7.10.1	7.5.0	6.14.2	6.4.0	5.12.0	4.9.1	0.12.18	0.10.48
optimisation														
proper tail calls (tail call optimisation)														
direct recursion	Error	Error	Error	Error	Error	Error	Flag	Flag	Flag	Error	Error	Error	Error	Error
mutual recursion	Error	Error	Error	Error	Error	Error	Flag	Flag	Flag	Error	Error	Error	Error	Error
syntax														
default function parameters														
basic functionality	Yes	Yes	Yes	Yes	Yes	Yes	Yes	Yes	Yes	Yes	Error	Error	Error	Error
explicit undefined defers to the default	Yes	Yes	Yes	Yes	Yes	Yes	Yes	Yes	Yes	Yes	Error	Error	Error	Error
defaults can refer to previous params	Yes	Yes	Yes	Yes	Yes	Yes	Yes	Yes	Yes	Yes	Error	Error	Error	Error
arguments object interaction	Yes	Yes	Yes	Yes	Yes	Yes	Yes	Yes	Yes	Yes	Error	Error	Error	Error
temporal dead zone	Yes	Yes	Yes	Yes	Yes	Yes	Yes	Yes	Yes	Yes	Error	Error	Error	Error
separate scope	Yes	Yes	Yes	Yes	Yes	Yes	Yes	Yes	Yes	Yes	Error	Error	Error	Error
new Function() support	Yes	Yes	Yes	Yes	Yes	Yes	Yes	Yes	Yes	Yes	Error	Error	Error	Error
rest parameters														
basic functionality	Yes	Yes	Yes	Yes	Yes	Yes	Yes	Yes	Yes	Yes	Flag	Flag	Error	Error
function 'length' property	Yes	Yes	Yes	Yes	Yes	Yes	Yes	Yes	Yes	Yes	Flag	Flag	Error	Error
arguments object interaction	Yes	Yes	Yes	Yes	Yes	Yes	Yes	Yes	Yes	Yes	Flag	Flag	Error	Error
can't be used in setters	Yes	Yes	Yes	Yes	Yes	Yes	Yes	Yes	Yes	Yes	Flag	Flag	Error	Error
new Function() support	Yes	Yes	Yes	Yes	Yes	Yes	Yes	Yes	Yes	Yes	Flag	Flag	Error	Error
spread (...) operator														
with arrays, in function calls	Yes	Yes	Yes	Yes	Yes	Yes	Yes	Yes	Yes	Yes	Yes	Flag	Error	Error
with arrays, in array literals	Yes	Yes	Yes	Yes	Yes	Yes	Yes	Yes	Yes	Yes	Yes	Flag	Error	Error
with sparse arrays, in function calls	Yes	Yes	Yes	Yes	Yes	Yes	Yes	Yes	Yes	Yes	Yes	Flag	Error	Error
with sparse arrays, in array literals	Yes	Yes	Yes	Yes	Yes	Yes	Yes	Yes	Yes	Yes	Yes	Flag	Error	Error
with strings, in function calls	Yes	Yes	Yes	Yes	Yes	Yes	Yes	Yes	Yes	Yes	Yes	Flag	Error	Error
with strings, in array literals	Yes	Yes	Yes	Yes	Yes	Yes	Yes	Yes	Yes	Yes	Yes	Flag	Error	Error
with astral plane strings, in function calls	Yes	Yes	Yes	Yes	Yes	Yes	Yes	Yes	Yes	Yes	Yes	Flag	Error	Error
with astral plane strings, in array literals	Yes	Yes	Yes	Yes	Yes	Yes	Yes	Yes	Yes	Yes	Yes	Flag	Error	Error
with generator instances, in calls	Yes	Yes	Yes	Yes	Yes	Yes	Yes	Yes	Yes	Yes	Yes	Flag	Error	Error
with generator instances, in arrays	Yes	Yes	Yes	Yes	Yes	Yes	Yes	Yes	Yes	Yes	Yes	Flag	Error	Error
with generic iterables, in calls	Yes	Yes	Yes	Yes	Yes	Yes	Yes	Yes	Yes	Yes	Yes	Flag	Error	Error
with generic iterables, in arrays	Yes	Yes	Yes	Yes	Yes	Yes	Yes	Yes	Yes	Yes	Yes	Flag	Error	Error
with instances of iterables, in calls	Yes	Yes	Yes	Yes	Yes	Yes	Yes	Yes	Yes	Yes	Yes	Flag	Error	Error
with instances of iterables, in arrays	Yes	Yes	Yes	Yes	Yes	Yes	Yes	Yes	Yes	Yes	Yes	Flag	Error	Error
spreading non-iterables is a runtime error	Yes	Yes	Yes	Yes	Yes	Yes	Yes	Yes	Yes	Yes	Yes	Flag	Error	Error

Figure 1.1 Support for JavaScript Features in Node.js (http://node.green)

Convinced by the success of JavaScript, Microsoft also integrated a scripting language into Internet Explorer 3 in 1996. This was the birth of JScript, which was mostly compatible with JavaScript, but with additional features added.

Today, the mutual vying of the two companies is known as the "browser wars." The development ensured that the two JavaScript engines steadily improved in both feature set and performance, which is the primary reason for JavaScript's success today.

In 1997, the first draft of the language standard was created at Ecma International. The entire language core of the script language is recorded under the cryptic designation ECMA-262 or ISO/IEC 16262. The current standard can be found at *www.ecma-international.org/publications/standards/Ecma-262.htm*. Due to this standardization, vendor-independent JavaScript is also referred to as ECMAScript. Until a few years ago, the ECMAScript standard was versioned in integers starting at 1. Since version 6, the versions are also provided with year numbers. ECMAScript in version 8 is therefore referred to as ECMAScript 2017. As a rule, you can assume that the manufacturers support the older versions of the standard quite well. You must either enable newer features by configuration flags in the browser or simulate them via polyfills (that is, recreating the features in JavaScript). A good overview of the currently supported features is provided by kangax's compatibility table, which can be found at *http://kangax.github.io/compat-table/es6/*. A version adapted for Node.js can be reached at *http://node.green/*.

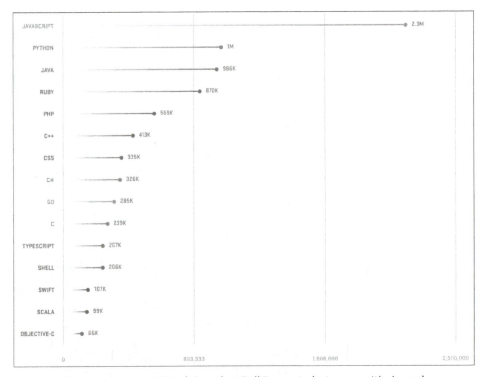

Figure 1.2 Top Languages in GitHub Based on Pull Requests (octoverse.github.com)

JavaScript is lightweight, is relatively easy to learn, and has a huge ecosystem of frameworks and libraries. For these reasons, JavaScript is one of the most successful programming languages in the world. This success can be backed up by numbers: Since 2008, JavaScript has been in the top two spots in GitHub's language trends. In 2021, JavaScript was passed by Python in the number one spot and is now in second place in language trends.

Node.js is based on this successful scripting language and has had a meteoric rise itself. This chapter will serve as an introduction to the world of Node.js, showing you how the platform is built, and where and how you can use Node.js.

1.1   The Story of Node.js

To help you better understand what Node.js is and how some of the development decisions came about, let's explore the history of the platform.

1.1.1   Origins

Node.js was originally developed by Ryan Dahl, a PhD student in mathematics who thought better of it, abandoned his efforts, and instead preferred to travel to South America with a one-way ticket and very little money in his pocket. There, he kept his head above water by teaching English. During this time, he got in touch with PHP as well as Ruby and discovered his affection for web development. The problem with working with the Ruby framework, called Rails, was that it couldn't deal with concurrent requests without any workaround. The applications were too slow and utilized the CPU entirely. Dahl found a solution to his problems with Mongrel, a web server for applications based on Ruby.

Unlike traditional web servers, Mongrel responds to user requests and generates responses dynamically, where otherwise only static HTML pages are delivered.

The task that actually led to the creation of Node.js is quite trivial from today's point of view. In 2005, Dahl was looking for an elegant way to implement a progress bar for file uploads. However, the technologies available at the time only allowed unsatisfactory solutions. Regarding file transfers, HTTP was used for relatively small files, and File Transfer Protocol (FTP) was used for larger files. The status of the upload was queried using long polling, which is a technique where the client sends long-lived requests to the server, and the server uses the open channel for replies. Dahl's first attempt to implement a progress bar took place in Mongrel. After sending the file to the server, it checked the status of the upload using a large number of Asynchronous JavaScript and XML (AJAX) requests and displayed it graphically in a progress bar. However, the downside of this implementation was Ruby's single-threaded approach and the large number of requests that were required.

Another promising approach involved an implementation in C. Here, Dahl's options weren't limited to one thread. However, C as a programming language for the web has a decisive disadvantage: only a small number of developers are enthusiastic about this field of application. Dahl was also confronted with this problem and discarded this approach after a short time.

The search for a suitable programming language to solve his problem continued and led him to functional programming languages such as Haskell. Haskell's approach is built on nonblocking input/output (I/O), which means that all read and write operations are asynchronous and don't block the execution of a program. This allows the language to remain single-threaded at its core and doesn't introduce the problems that arise from parallel programming. Among other things, no resources have to be synchronized, and no problems are caused by the runtime of parallel threads. However, Dahl still wasn't fully satisfied with this solution and was looking for other options.

1.1.2   Birth of Node.js

Dahl then found the solution he was finally satisfied with—JavaScript. He realized that this scripting language could meet all his requirements. JavaScript had already been established on the web for years, so there were powerful engines and a large number of developers. In January 2009, he began working on his implementation for server-side JavaScript, which can be regarded as the birth of Node.js. Another reason for implementing the solution in JavaScript, according to Dahl, was the fact that the developers of JavaScript didn't envision this area of use. At that time, no native web server existed in JavaScript, it couldn't handle files in a file system, and there was no implementation of sockets to communicate with other applications or systems. All these points spoke in favor of JavaScript as the basis for a platform for interactive web applications because no determinations had yet been made in this area, and, consequently, no mistakes had yet been made either. The architecture of JavaScript also argued for such an implementation. The approach of top-level functions (i.e., functions that aren't linked to any object, are freely available, and can be assigned to variables) offers a high degree of flexibility in development and enables functional approaches to solutions.

Thus, Dahl selected other libraries in addition to the JavaScript engine, which is responsible for interpreting the JavaScript source code, and put them together in one platform.

In September 2009, Isaac Schlueter started working on a package manager for Node.js, the *Node Package Manager* (*npm*).

1.1.3   Breakthrough of Node.js

After Dahl integrated all the components and created the first executable examples on the new Node.js platform, he needed a way to introduce Node.js to the public. This also became necessary because his financial resources shrank considerably due to the development of Node.js, and he would have had to stop working on Node.js if he didn't find any sponsors. He chose the JavaScript conference JSConf EU in November 2009 in Berlin as his presentation platform. Dahl put all his eggs in one basket. If the presentation was a success and he found sponsors to support his work on Node.js, he could continue his involvement; if not, almost a year's work would have been in vain. In a rousing talk, he introduced Node.js to the audience and showed how to create a fully functional web server with just a few lines of JavaScript code. As another example, he introduced an implementation of an Internet Relay Chat (IRC) chat server. The source code for this demonstration comprised about 400 lines. Using this example, he demonstrated the architecture and thus the strengths of Node.js while making it tangible for the audience. The recording of this presentation can be found at *www.youtube.com/watch?v=EeYvFl7-li9E*. The presentation didn't miss its mark and led to Joyent stepping in as a sponsor for Node.js. Joyent is a San Francisco-based software and services provider offering hosting solutions and cloud infrastructure. With its commitment, Joyent included the open-source software Node.js in its product portfolio and made Node.js available to its customers as part of its hosting offerings. Dahl was hired by Joyent and became a full-time maintainer for Node.js from that point on.

1.1.4   Node.js Conquers Windows

The developers made a significant step toward the spread of Node.js by introducing native support for Windows in version 0.6 in November 2011. Up to that point, Node.js could only be installed awkwardly on Windows via Cygwin.

Since version 0.6.3 in November 2011, npm has been an integral part of the Node.js packages and is thus automatically delivered when Node.js is installed.

Surprisingly, at the start of 2012, Dahl announced that he would finally retire from active development after three years of working on Node.js. He handed over the reins of development to Schlueter. The latter, like Dahl, was an employee at Joyent and actively involved in the development of the Node.js core. The change unsettled the community, as it wasn't clear whether the platform would continue to develop without Dahl. A signal that the Node.js community considered as being strong enough for solid further development came with the release of version 0.8 in June 2012, which was primarily intended to significantly improve the performance and stability of Node.js.

With version 0.10 in March 2013, one of the central interfaces of Node.js changed: the Stream application programming interface (API). With this change, it became possible to actively pull data from a stream. Because the previous API was already widely used, both interfaces continued to be supported.

1.1.5   io.js: The Fork of Node.js

In January 2014, there was another change in the project management of Node.js. Schlueter, who left Node.js maintenance in favor of his own company (called npmjs), the host of the npm repository, was succeeded by TJ Fontaine. Under his direction, version 0.12 was released in February 2014. A common criticism of Node.js at the time was that the framework had still not reached the supposedly stable version 1.0, which prevented numerous companies from using Node.js for critical applications.

Many developers were unhappy with Joyent, which had provided maintainers for Node.js since Dahl, and so the community fractured in December 2014. The result was io.js, a fork of Node.js that was developed separately from the original platform. As a result, the independent Node.js Foundation was founded in February 2015, which was responsible for the further development of io.js. At the same time, version 0.12 of the Node.js project was released.

1.1.6   Node.js Reunited

In June 2015, the two projects io.js and Node.js were merged into the Node.js Foundation. With version 4 of the project, the merger was completed. Further development of the Node.js platform is now coordinated by a committee within the Node.js Foundation rather than by individuals. As a result, we see more frequent releases and a stable version with long-term support (LTS).

1.1.7   Deno: A New Star in the JavaScript Sky

Since the merger of io.js and Node.js, things have become quieter around Node.js. The regular releases, the stability, and also the integration of new features, such as worker threads, HTTP/2 or performance hooks, keep up the good mood within the community. And just when things were starting to get almost too quiet around Node.js, an old acquaintance, Dahl, took the stage again in 2018 to introduce a new JavaScript platform called Deno during his talk, "10 Things I Regret about Node.js."

The idea behind Deno is to create a better Node.js, untethered from the backwards compatibility constraints that prevent revolutionary leaps in development. For example, Deno is based on TypeScript by default and adds a fundamentally different module system. Deno's core is also quite different from Node.js, as it's written almost entirely in Rust.

Nevertheless, there are also some common features. For example, Deno is based on the tried and tested V8 engine, which also forms the heart of Node.js. And you don't have to do without the huge number of npm packages either. For this purpose, Deno provides a compatibility layer. You can read more about Deno in Chapter 28.

1.1.8 OpenJS Foundation

In 2015, the Node.js Foundation was established to coordinate the development of the platform. The foundation was a subordinate project of the Linux Foundation. In 2019, the JS Foundation and the Node.js Foundation then merged to form the OpenJS Foundation. In addition to Node.js, it includes a number of other popular projects such as webpack, ESLint, and Electron.

1.2 Organization of Node.js

The community behind Node.js has learned its lessons from the past. For this reason, there are no longer individuals at the helm of Node.js, but a committee of several people who steer the development of the platform.

1.2.1 Technical Steering Committee

The technical steering committee (TSC) is responsible for further developing the platform. The number of members of the TSC isn't limited, but 6 to 12 members are targeted, usually selected from the contributors to the platform. The tasks of the TSC are as follows:

- Setting the technical direction of Node.js
- Performing project and process control
- Defining the contribution policy
- Managing the GitHub repository
- Establishing the conduct guidelines
- Managing the list of collaborators

The TSC holds weekly meetings via Google Hangouts to coordinate and discuss current issues. Many of these meetings are published via the Node.js YouTube channel (*www.youtube.com/c/nodejs+foundation*).

1.2.2 Collaborators

Node.js is an open-source project developed in a GitHub repository. As with all larger projects of this type, a group of people, called collaborators, have write access to this repository. In addition to accessing the repository, a collaborator can access the continuous integration jobs. Typical tasks of a collaborator include supporting users and new collaborators, improving Node.js source code and documentation, reviewing pull requests and issues (with appropriate commenting), participating in working groups, and merging pull requests.

Collaborators are designated by the TSC. Usually the role of a collaborator is preceded by a significant contribution to the project via a pull request.

1.2.3 Community Committee

As the name implies, the Community Committee (CommComm) takes care of the Node.js community with a special focus on education and culture. The CommComm coordinates in regular meetings, which are recorded in a separate GitHub repository (*https://github.com/nodejs/community-committee*). The CommComm exists to give the community a voice and thus counterbalance the commercial interests of corporations.

1.2.4 Work Groups

The TSC establishes various work groups to have specific topics addressed separately by experts. Examples of such work groups include the following:

- **Release**
  This work group manages the release process of the Node.js platform, defining the content of the releases and taking care of LTS.

- **Streams**
  The streams work group is working to improve the platform's Stream API.

- **Docker**
  This work group manages the official Docker images of the Node.js platform and ensures that they are kept up to date.

1.2.5 OpenJS Foundation

The OpenJS Foundation forms the umbrella for Node.js development. Its role is similar to that of the Linux Foundation for the development of the Linux operating system. The OpenJS Foundation was founded as an independent body for further developing Node.js. Its list of founding members includes companies such as IBM, Intel, Joyent, and Microsoft. The OpenJS Foundation is funded by donations and contributions from companies and individual members.

1.3 Versioning of Node.js

One of the biggest points of criticism concerning Node.js before the fork of io.js was that its development was very slow. Regular and predictable releases are an important selection criterion, especially in enterprise usage. For this reason, after merging Node.js and io.js, the developers of Node.js agreed on a transparent release schedule with regular releases and an LTS version that is provided with updates over a longer period of time. The release schedule provides for one major release per half year.

Table 1.1 shows the release schedule of Node.js.

Release	Status	Initial Release	Active LTS Start	Maintenance LTS Start	End of Line
https://nodejs.org/download/release/latest-v14.x/	Maintenance LTS	4/21/2020	10/27/2020	10/19/2021	4/30/2023
https://nodejs.org/download/release/latest-v16.x/	Active LTS	4/20/2021	10/26/2021	10/18/2022	4/30/2024
https://nodejs.org/download/release/latest-v17.x/	Current	10/19/2021		4/1/2022	6/1/2022
https://nodejs.org/download/release/latest-v18.x/	Pending	4/19/2022	10/25/2022	10/18/2023	4/30/2025
v19	Pending	10/18/2022		4/1/2023	6/1/2023
v20	Pending	4/18/2023	10/24/2023	10/22/2024	4/30/2026

Table 1.1 Node.js Release Schedule

As you can see from the release schedule, versions with an even version number are LTS releases, while odd ones are releases with a shortened support period.

1.3.1   Long-Term Support Releases

A Node.js version with an even version number is transitioned to an LTS release as soon as the next odd version is released. The LTS release is then actively maintained over a period of 12 months. During this time, the version receives the following:

- Bug fixes
- Security updates
- npm minor updates
- Documentation updates
- Performance improvements that don't compromise existing applications
- Changes to the source code that simplify the integration of future improvements

After this phase, the version enters a 12-month maintenance phase during which the version will continue to receive security updates. In this case, however, only critical bugs and security gaps are fixed. In total, the developers of the Node.js platform support an LTS release over a period of 30 months.

1.4 Benefits of Node.js

The development history of Node.js shows one thing very clearly: it's directly connected to the internet. With JavaScript as its base, you have the ability to achieve visible results very quickly with applications implemented in Node.js. The platform itself is very lightweight and can be installed on almost any system. As is common for a scripting language, Node.js applications also omit a heavyweight development process, so you can check the results directly. In addition to the fast initial implementation, you can also react very flexibly to changing requirements during the development of web applications. Because the core of JavaScript is standardized by ECMAScript, the language represents a reliable basis with which even more extensive applications can be implemented. The available language features are well documented extensively both online and in reference books. In addition, many developers are proficient in JavaScript and able to implement even larger applications using this language. Because Node.js uses the same JavaScript engine as Google Chrome—the V8 engine—all language features are also available here, and developers who are proficient in JavaScript can familiarize themselves with the new platform relatively quickly.

JavaScript's long history of development has produced a number of high-performance engines. One reason for this development is that the various browser manufacturers were always developing their own implementations of JavaScript engines, so there was healthy competition in the market when it came to running JavaScript in the browser. On one hand, this competition led to the fact that JavaScript is now interpreted very quickly, and, on the other hand, it led to manufacturers agreeing on certain standards. Node.js as a platform for server-side JavaScript was designed as an open-source project since the beginning of its development. For this reason, an active community quickly developed around the core of the platform and deals mainly with the use of Node.js in practice, but also with the further development and stabilization of the platform. Resources on Node.js range from tutorials to help you get started to articles on advanced topics such as quality assurance, debugging, or scaling. The biggest advantage of an open-source project such as Node.js is that the information is available to you free of charge, and questions and problems can be solved quite quickly and competently via a wide variety of communication channels or the community itself.

1.5 Areas of Use for Node.js

From a simple command-line tool to an application server for web applications running on a cluster with numerous nodes, Node.js can be used anywhere. The use of a technology strongly depends on the problem to be solved, personal preferences, and the developers' level of knowledge. For this reason, not only should you know the key features of Node.js, but you should also have a feel for working with the platform. You can only fulfill the second point if you either have the opportunity to join an existing

Node.js project or gain the experience in the best case with smaller projects that you implement.

But let's now turn to the most important framework data:

- **Pure JavaScript**
  When working with Node.js, you don't have to learn a new language dialect because you can fall back on the JavaScript language core. Standardized and well-documented interfaces are available for accessing system resources. However, as an alternative to JavaScript, you can also write your Node.js application in TypeScript, translate the source code to JavaScript, and run it with Node.js. You'll find more information about this topic in Chapter 13.

- **Optimized engine**
  Node.js is based on Google's V8 JavaScript engine. Here, you benefit above all from the constant further development of the engine, where the latest language features are supported already after a very short time.

- **Nonblocking I/O**
  All operations that don't take place directly in Node.js don't block the execution of your application. The principle of Node.js is that everything the platform doesn't have to do directly is outsourced to the operating system, other applications, or other systems. This gives the application the ability to respond to additional requests or to process tasks in parallel. Once the processing of a task is complete, the Node.js process receives feedback and can process the information further.

- **Single-threaded**
  A typical Node.js application runs in a single process. For a long time, there hasn't been any multithreading, and concurrency was initially only provided for in the form of the nonblocking I/O already described. Thus, all the code you write yourself potentially blocks your application. For this reason, you should pay attention to resource-saving development. If it still becomes necessary to process tasks in parallel, Node.js offers you solutions for this in the form of the `child_process` module, which enables you to create your own child processes.

To develop your application in the best possible way, you should have at least a rough overview of the components and how they work. The most important of these components is the V8 engine.

1.6 The Core: V8 Engine

For you, as a developer, to assess whether a technology can be used in a project, you should be sufficiently familiar with the characteristics of that technology. The sections that follow now dive deep into the internal details of Node.js to show you the components that make up the platform and how you can use them to the advantage of an application.

The central and thus most important component of the Node.js platform is the V8 JavaScript engine developed by Google (for more information, visit the V8 Project page at *https://code.google.com/p/v8/*). The JavaScript engine is responsible for interpreting and executing the JavaScript source code. There isn't just one engine for JavaScript; instead, the different browser manufacturers use their own implementations. One of the problems with JavaScript is that each engine behaves slightly differently. Standardization to ECMAScript attempts to find a reliable common denominator so that you, as a JavaScript application developer, have less uncertainty to worry about. The competition among JavaScript engines resulted in a number of optimized engines, all with the goal of interpreting JavaScript code as quickly as possible. Over time, several engines have established themselves on the market: Mozilla's JaegerMonkey, Apple's Nitro, and Google's V8 engine, among others. Microsoft meanwhile uses the same technical basis as Chrome for its Edge browser, so it also uses the V8 engine.

Node.js uses Google's V8 engine. This engine has been developed by Google since 2006, mainly in Denmark, in collaboration with Aarhus University. The engine's primary area of use is Google's Chrome browser, where it's responsible for interpreting and executing JavaScript code. The goal of developing a new JavaScript engine was to significantly improve the performance of interpreting JavaScript. The engine now fully implements the ECMAScript standard ECMA-262 in the fifth version and large parts of the sixth version. The V8 engine itself is written in C++, runs on various platforms, and is available under the Berkeley Source Distribution (BSD) license as open-source software for any developer to use and improve. For example, you can integrate the engine into any C++ application.

As usual in JavaScript, the source code isn't compiled before execution; instead, the files containing the source code are read directly when the application is launched. Launching the application starts a new Node.js process. This is where the first optimization by the V8 engine takes place. The source code isn't directly interpreted, but is first translated into machine code, which is then executed. This technology is referred to as just-in-time (JIT) compilation and is used to increase the execution speed of the JavaScript application. The actual application is then executed on the basis of the compiled machine code. The V8 engine makes further optimizations in addition to JIT compilation. Among other things, these include improved garbage collection and an improvement in the context of accessing object properties. For all the optimizations that the JavaScript engine makes, you should keep in mind that the source code is read at process startup, so the changes to the files have no effect on the running application. For your changes to take effect, you must exit and restart your application so that the customized source code files are read again.

1.6.1 Memory Model

The goal of developing the V8 engine was to achieve the highest possible speed in the execution of JavaScript source code. For this reason, the memory model has also been optimized. Tagged pointers, which are references in memory that are marked as such in a special way, are used in the V8 engine. All objects are 4-byte-aligned, which means that 2 bits are available to identify pointers. A pointer always ends on 01 in the memory model of the V8 engine, whereas a normal integer value ends on 0. This measure allows integer values to be distinguished very quickly from memory references, which provides an extremely significant performance advantage. The object representations of the V8 engine in memory each consist of three data words. The first data word consists of a reference to the hidden class of the object, which you'll learn more about in later sections. The second data word is a pointer to the attributes, that is, the properties of the object. Finally, the third data word refers to the elements of the object. These are the properties with a numeric key. This structure supports the JavaScript engine in its work and is optimized in such a way that elements in the memory can be accessed very fast so that little wait time arises from searching objects.

1.6.2   Accessing Properties

As you probably know, JavaScript doesn't know classes; the object model of JavaScript is based on prototypes. In class-based languages such as Java or PHP, classes represent the blueprint of objects. These classes can't be changed at runtime. Prototypes in JavaScript, on the other hand, are dynamic, which means that properties and methods can be added and removed at runtime. As with all other languages that implement the object-oriented programming paradigm, objects are represented by their properties and methods, where properties represent the state of an object, and methods are used to interact with the object. In an application, you usually access the properties of the various objects very frequently. In addition, methods in JavaScript are also properties of objects that are stored with a function. In JavaScript, you work almost exclusively with properties and methods, so access to them must be very fast.

Prototypes in JavaScript

JavaScript differs from languages such as C, Java, or PHP in that it doesn't take a class-based approach but instead is based on prototypes, such as the Self language. In JavaScript, every object normally has a `prototype` property and thus a prototype. In JavaScript, as in other languages, you can create objects. For this purpose, however, you don't use classes in conjunction with the `new` operator. Instead, you can create new objects in several different ways. Among other things, you can use constructor functions or the `Object.create` method. These methods have in common that you create an object and assign the prototype. The prototype is an object from which another object inherits its properties. Another feature of prototypes is that they can be modified at application runtime, allowing you to add new properties and methods. By using prototypes, you can build an inheritance hierarchy in JavaScript.

Normally, accessing properties in a JavaScript engine is done through a directory in the memory. So, if you access a property, this directory is searched for the memory section of the respective property, and then the value can be accessed. Now imagine a large application that maps its business logic in JavaScript on the client side, and in which a large number of objects are held in parallel in the memory, constantly communicating with each other. This method of accessing properties would quickly turn into a problem. The developers of the V8 engine have recognized this vulnerability and developed a solution for it—the hidden classes. The real problem with JavaScript is that the structure of objects is only known at runtime and not already during the compilation process because such a process doesn't exist with JavaScript. This is further complicated by the fact that there isn't just one prototype in the structure of objects, but they can rather exist in a chain. In classical languages, the object structure doesn't change at application runtime; the properties of objects are always located in the same place, which significantly speeds up accessing them.

A hidden class is nothing more than a description in which the individual properties of an object can be found in the memory. For this purpose, a hidden class is assigned to each object. This contains the offset to the memory section within the object where the respective property is stored. As soon as you access a property of an object, a hidden class is created for that property and reused for each subsequent access. So for an object, there is potentially a separate hidden class for each property.

In Listing 1.1, you can see an example that illustrates how hidden classes work.

```
class Person {
  constructor(firstname, lastname) {
    this.firstname = firstname;
    this.lastname = lastname;
  }
}
const johnDoe = new Person("John", "Doe");
```

Listing 1.1 Accessing Properties in a Class

In the example, you create a new constructor function for the group of person objects. This constructor has two parameters—the first name and the last name of the person. These two values are to be stored in the firstname and lastname properties of the object, respectively. When a new object is created with this constructor using the new operator, an initial hidden class, class 0, is created first. This doesn't yet contain any pointers to properties. If the first assignment is made, that is, the first name is set, a new hidden class, class 1, is created based on class 0. This now contains a reference to the memory section of the firstname property, relative to the beginning of the object's namespace. In addition, a class transition is added to class 0, which states that class 1 should be used instead of class 0 if the firstname property is added. The same process takes place when the second assignment is performed for the last name. Another hidden class, class 2, is created based on class 1, which then contains the offset for both the `firstname` and `last-name` properties and inserts a transition indicating that class 2 should be used when the `lastname` property is used. If properties are added away from the constructor, and this is done in a different order, new hidden classes are created in each case. Figure 1.3 clarifies this process.

When the properties of an object are accessed for the first time, the use of hidden classes doesn't yet result in a speed advantage. However, all subsequent accesses to the property of the object then happen many times faster, because the engine can directly use the hidden class of the object and this contains the reference to the memory section of the property.

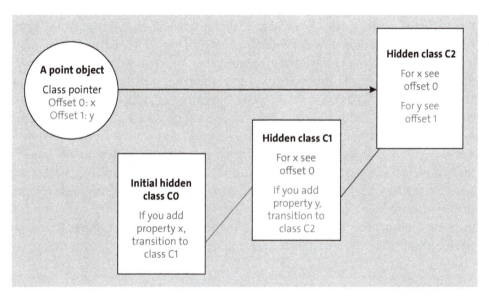

Figure 1.3 Hidden Classes in the V8 Engine (https://github.com/v8/v8/wiki/Design%20 Elements#fast-property-access)

1.6.3   Machine Code Generation

As you already know, the V8 engine doesn't directly interpret the JavaScript application source code, but performs a JIT compilation into native machine code to increase execution speed. No optimizations are made to the source code during this compilation. The source code written by the developer is thus converted one to one. In addition to this JIT compiler, the V8 engine has another compiler that is capable of optimizing the machine code. To decide which code fragments to optimize, the engine maintains internal statistics about the number of function calls and how long each function is executed. Based on this data, the decision is made regarding whether the machine code of a function requires optimizing.

Now you're probably wondering why the entire source code of the application isn't compiled with the second, much better compiler. There is a very simple reason for this:

a compiler that doesn't perform optimizations is much faster. Because the source code is compiled JIT, this process is very time critical because any wait times caused by a compilation process that takes too long can have a direct impact on the user. Therefore, only code sections that justify this additional effort are optimized. This machine code optimization has a particularly positive effect on larger and longer-running applications and on those in which functions are called more often than just once.

Another optimization the V8 engine performs is related to the hidden classes and internal caching already described earlier. After the application is launched and the machine code is generated, the V8 engine searches for the associated hidden class each time a property is accessed. As a further optimization, the engine assumes that the objects used at this point will have the same hidden class in the future, so it modifies the machine code accordingly. The next time the code section is traversed, the property can be accessed directly with no need to search for the associated hidden class first. If the object used doesn't have the same hidden class, the engine detects this, removes the previously generated machine code, and replaces it with the corrected version. There is a critical problem with this approach: Imagine you have a code section where two different objects with different hidden classes are always used in alternation. Then the optimization with the prediction of the hidden class would never take effect at the next execution. In this case, various code fragments are used, which can't be used to find the memory section of a property as quickly as with just one hidden class, but the code in this case is many times faster than without the optimization because it's usually possible to select from a very small set of hidden classes. The generation of machine code and the hidden classes in combination with the caching mechanisms creates possibilities that are familiar from class-based languages.

1.6.4 Garbage Collection

The optimizations described so far mainly affect the speed of an application. Another very important feature is the garbage collector of the V8 engine. *Garbage collection* refers to the process of clearing up the application's memory area in the main memory. Elements that are no longer used are removed from memory so that the space freed up becomes available to the application again.

If you're wondering why you need a garbage collector in JavaScript, the answer is quite simple: Originally, JavaScript was intended for small tasks on web pages. These web pages, and thus the JavaScript on this page, had a fairly short lifetime until the page was reloaded, completely emptying the memory containing the JavaScript objects. The more JavaScript is executed on a page and the more complex the tasks to be performed become, the greater the risk that memory will be filled with objects that are no longer needed. If you now assume you have an application in Node.js that has to run for several days, weeks, or even months without restarting the process, the problem becomes clear. The V8 engine's garbage collector comprises a number of features that allow it to perform its tasks very quickly and efficiently. Basically, when the garbage collector is running, the engine stops the execution of the application completely and resumes it as soon as the run is finished. These application pauses are in the single-digit millisecond range so that the user normally doesn't feel any negative effects due to the garbage collector. To keep the interruption by the garbage collector as short as possible, the complete memory isn't cleaned up, but only parts of it. In addition, the V8 engine knows at all times where in the memory which objects and pointers are located.

The V8 engine divides the available memory into two areas—one area for storing objects and another area to keep the information about the hidden classes and the executable machine code. The process of garbage collection is relatively simple. When an application is executed, objects and pointers are created in the short-lived area of the V8 engine's memory. If this memory area is full, it's cleaned up. Objects that are no longer used are deleted, and objects that are still needed are moved to the long-lived area. During this shift, the object itself is shifted, and the pointers to the object's memory location are corrected. The partitioning of memory areas makes different types of garbage collection necessary.

The fastest variant is represented by the scavenge collector, which is very fast and efficient and deals only with the short-lived area. Two different garbage collection algorithms exist for the long-lived memory section, both based on mark-and-sweep. The entire memory is searched, and elements that are no longer needed are marked and later deleted. The real problem with this algorithm is that it creates gaps in the memory, which causes problems over a longer runtime of an application. For this reason, a second algorithm exists that also searches the elements of the memory for those that are no longer needed, marks them, and deletes them.

The most important difference between the two is that the second algorithm defragments the memory; that is, it rearranges the remaining objects in the memory so that afterwards, the memory has as few gaps as possible. This defragmentation can only happen because V8 knows all objects and pointers. For all its benefits, the garbage collection process also has a drawback: it takes time. The fastest the scavenge collection can run is about 2 ms. This is followed by the mark-and-sweep process without optimizations at 50 ms and finally the mark-and-sweep with defragmentation with an average of 100 ms.

In the following sections, you'll learn more about the other elements used in the Node.js platform besides the V8 engine.

1.7   Libraries around the Engine

The JavaScript engine alone doesn't make a platform yet. For Node.js to handle all requirements such as event handling, I/O, or support functions such as Domain Name System (DNS) resolution or encryption, additional functionality is required. This is implemented with the help of additional libraries. For many tasks that a platform such as Node.js has to deal with, ready-made and established solutions already exist. For this reason, Dahl decided to build the Node.js platform on top of a set of external libraries and fill in the gaps he felt weren't adequately covered by any existing solution with his own implementations. The advantage of this strategy is that you don't have to reinvent the solutions for standard problems; you can fall back on tried and tested libraries.

A prominent example that is also built on this strategy is the Unix operating system. In this context, developers should stick to the following principle: focus only on the actual problem, solve it as well as possible, and use existing libraries for everything else. Most command-line programs in the Unix area implement this philosophy. Once a solution has established itself, it can be used in other applications for similar problems. This in turn has the advantage that improvements in the algorithm only have to be made at one central point. The same applies to bug fixes. If an error occurs in DNS resolution, it's fixed once, and the solution works in all places where the library is used. But that also leads to the flip side of the coin: the libraries on which the platform is built must exist. Node.js solves this problem in that it's built on only a small set of libraries that must be provided by the operating system. But these dependencies rather consist of basic functions such as the GNU Compiler Collection (GCC) runtime library or the standard C library. The remaining dependencies, such as zlib or http_parser, are included in the source code.

1.7.1 Event Loop

Client-side JavaScript contains many elements of an event-driven architecture. Most user interactions cause events that are responded to with appropriate function calls. By using various features such as first-class functions and anonymous functions in JavaScript, you can implement entire applications based on an event-driven architecture. The term *event-driven* means that objects don't communicate directly with each other via function calls; instead, events are used for this communication. Event-driven programming is therefore primarily used to control the program flow. In contrast to the classical approach, where the source code is run through linearly, here functions are executed when certain events occur. A small example in Listing 1.2 illustrates this approach.

```
myObj.on('myEvent', (data) => {
    console.log(data);
});
myObj.emit('myEvent', 'Hello World');
```

Listing 1.2 Event-Driven Development in Node.js

You can use the on method of an object that you derive from events.EventEmitter, a component of the Node.js platform, to define which function you want to use to respond to each event. This pattern is referred to as a publish-subscribe pattern. Objects can thus register with an event emitter and then be notified when the event occurs. The first argument of the on method is the name of the event in the form of a string to respond to. The second argument consists of a callback function that is implemented as an arrow function in this case, which is executed once the event occurs. Thus, the function call of the on method does nothing more than register the callback function the first time it's executed. Later in the script, the emit method is called on myObj. This ensures that all callback functions registered by the on method are executed.

What works in this example with a custom object is used by Node.js to perform a variety of asynchronous tasks. However, the callback functions aren't run in parallel, but sequentially. The single-threaded approach of Node.js creates the problem that only one operation can be executed at a time. Time-consuming read or write operations in particular would block the entire execution of the application. For this reason, all read and write operations are outsourced using the event loop. This allows the available thread to be exploited by the application's code. Once a request is made to an external resource in the source code, it's passed to the event loop. A callback is registered for the request that forwards the request to the operating system; Node.js then regains control and can continue executing the application. Once the external operation is complete, the result is passed back to the event loop. An event occurs and the event loop ensures that the associated callback functions are executed. Figure 1.4 shows how the event loop works.

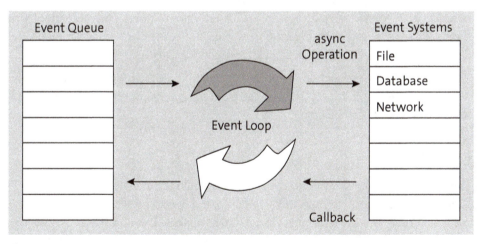

Figure 1.4 Event Loop

The original event loop used in Node.js is based on libev, a library written in C that stands for high performance and a wide range of features. libev is based on the approaches of libevent but has a higher performance rate, as evidenced by various benchmarks. Even an improved version of libevent—libevent2—doesn't match the performance of libev. However, for compatibility reasons, the event loop was abstracted to achieve better portability to other platforms.

1.7.2   Input and Output

The event loop alone in combination with the V8 engine allows the execution of JavaScript, but there is still no possibility of interacting with the operating system directly in the form of read or write operations on the file system. In the implementation of server-side applications, accesses to the file system play an important role. For example, the configuration of an application is often outsourced to a separate configuration file. This configuration must be read by the application from the file system. However, templates, which are dynamically filled with values and then sent to the client, are also usually available as separate files. Both reading and writing information to files is often a requirement for a server-side JavaScript application. Logging within an application is another common area of usage of write accesses to the file system. Here, different types of events within the application are logged to a log file. Depending on where the application is executed, only fatal errors, warnings, or even runtime information is written. Write accesses are also used for persisting information. During runtime of an application, usually through the interaction of users and various computations, information is generated that needs to be captured for later reuse.

Node.js uses the C library `libeio` for these tasks. It ensures that the write and read operations can take place asynchronously, and thus the library works very closely with the event loop. However, the features of `libeio` aren't limited to write and read access to the file system; rather, they offer considerably more possibilities to interact with the file system. These options range from reading file information (e.g., size, creation date, or access date) to managing directories (i.e., creating or removing them) to modifying access rights. Similar to the event loop, during the course of its development, this library was separated from the actual application by an abstraction layer.

To access the file system, Node.js provides its own module, the file system module. This module enables you to address the interfaces of `libeio` and thus represents a very light-weight wrapper around `libeio`.

1.7.3   libuv

The two libraries you've encountered so far are related to Linux. However, Node.js was supposed to become a platform independent of the operating system. For this reason, the `libuv` library was introduced in version 0.6 of Node.js. This library is primarily used to abstract differences between different operating systems. Consequently, using `libuv` makes it possible for Node.js to run on Windows systems as well. The structure without `libuv`, as it was used in Node.js up to version 0.6, looks like this: the core is the V8 engine; it's supplemented by `libev` and `libeio` with the event loop and the asynchronous file system access. With `libuv`, these two libraries are no longer directly integrated into the platform, but are abstracted.

For Node.js to work on Windows, it's necessary to provide the core components for Windows platforms. The V8 engine isn't a problem here; it has been working in the Chrome browser for many years on Windows without any problems. However, it gets more difficult with the event loop and asynchronous file system operations. Some components of libev would need to be rewritten when running on Windows. In addition, libev is based on native implementations of the operating system of the select function, but, on Windows, a variant optimized for the operating system is available in the form of IOCP. To avoid having to create different versions of Node.js for the different operating systems, the developers decided to include an abstraction layer with libuv that allows libev to be used for Linux systems and IOCP for Windows. With libuv, some core concepts of Node.js have been adapted. For example, we no longer speak of events, but of operations. An operation is passed to the libuv component; within libuv, the operation is passed to the underlying infrastructure, that is, libev or IOCP, respectively. Thus, the Node.js interface remains unchanged regardless of the operating system used.

libuv is responsible for managing all asynchronous I/O operations. This means that all access to the file system, whether read or write access, is performed via libuv's interfaces. For this purpose, libuv provides the uv_fs_ functions, as well as timers, that is, time-dependent calls, and asynchronous Transmission Control Protocol (TCP) and User Datagram Protocol (UDP) connections run via libuv. In addition to these basic functionalities, libuv manages complex features such as creating and spawning child processes and thread pool scheduling, an abstraction that allows tasks to be completed in separate threads and callbacks to be bound to them. Using an abstraction layer such as libuv is an important building block for the wider adoption of Node.js and makes the platform a little less dependent on the system.

1.7.4   Domain Name System

The roots of Node.js can be found on the internet. When you're on the internet, you'll quickly encounter the problem of name resolution. Actually, all servers on the internet are addressed by their IP address. In Internet Protocol version 4 (IPv4), the address is a 32-bit number represented in four blocks of 8 bits each. In IPv6, the addresses have a size of 128 bits and are divided into eight blocks of hexadecimal numbers. You rarely want to work directly with these cryptic addresses, especially if a dynamic assignment via Dynamic Host Configuration Protocol (DHCP) is added. The solution to this is the Domain Name System (DNS). The DNS is a service for name resolution on the web that ensures domain names are converted into IP addresses. There is also the possibility of reverse resolution, where an IP address is translated into a domain name. If you want to connect a web service or read a webpage in your Node.js application, DNS is used here as well.

Internally, Node.js doesn't handle the name resolution itself but passes the respective requests to the C-Ares library. This applies to all methods of the dns module except for dns.lookup, which uses the operating system's own getaddrinfo function. This exception is caused by the fact that getaddrinfo is more constant in its responses than the C-Ares library, which, by itself, is a lot more performant than getaddrinfo.

1.7.5   Crypto

The crypto component of the Node.js platform provides you with several encryption options for development purposes. This component is based on OpenSSL. This means that this software must be installed on your system if you want to encrypt data. The crypto module allows you to encrypt data with different algorithms as well as create digital signatures within your application. The entire system is based on private and public keys. The private key, as the name implies, is for you and your application only. The public key is available to your communication partners. If content is to be encrypted, this is done with the public key. The data can then only be decrypted with your private key. The same applies to the digital signature of data. Here, your private key is used to generate such a signature. The recipient of a message can then use the signature and your public key to determine whether the message originated from you and hasn't been changed.

1.7.6   Zlib

When creating web applications, as a developer, you need to take into consideration the resources of your users and your own server environment. For example, the available bandwidth or free memory for data can be a limitation. To address such cases, the Node.js platform contains the zlib component. With its help, you can compress data and decompress it again when you want to process it. For data compression, you can use two algorithms, Deflate and Gzip. Node.js treats the data that serves as input to the algorithms as streams.

Node.js doesn't implement the compression algorithms itself, but instead uses the established zlib and passes the requests on in each case. The zlib module of Node.js simply provides a lightweight wrapper for the underlying Gzip, Deflate/Inflate, and Brotli algorithmns and ensures that I/O streams are handled correctly.

1.7.7   HTTP Parser

As a platform for web applications, Node.js must be able to handle not only streams, compressed data, and encryption but also HTTP. Because parsing HTTP is a laborious procedure, the HTTP parser handling this task has been outsourced to a separate project and is now included by the Node.js platform. Like the other external libraries, the HTTP parser is written in C and serves as a high-performance tool that reads both HTTP requests and responses. As a developer, this means you can use the HTTP parser to read, for example, the various information in the HTTP header or the text of the message itself.

The primary goal of developing Node.js is to provide a performant platform for web applications. To meet this requirement, Node.js is built on a modular structure. This allows the inclusion of external libraries such as the previously described libuv or the

HTTP parser. The modular approach continues through the internal modules of the Node.js platform and extends to the extensions you create for your own application.

Throughout this book, you'll learn about the different capabilities and technologies that the Node.js platform provides for developing your own applications. We'll start with an introduction to the module system of Node.js.

1.8   Summary

For many years now, Node.js has been an integral part of web development. In this context, Node.js isn't just used to create server applications but also is the basis for a wide range of tools—from the bundler webpack to tools such as Babel and the compiler for CSS preprocessors. The success of the platform is based on several very simple concepts. The platform is based on a collection of established libraries, which together create a very flexible working environment. Over the years, the core of the platform has always been kept compact, offering only a set of basic functionalities. For all other requirements, you can use the npm to integrate a wide variety of packages into your application.

Although Node.js has now been proven in practice for several years, you may still frequently hear the following question: Can I safely use Node.js for my application? In the versions prior to 0.6, this question could not be answered in the affirmative in good conscience because the interfaces of the platform were subject to frequent changes. Today, however, Node.js is much more mature. The interfaces are kept stable by the developers. The LTS version was created for use in enterprises. This is a Node.js version that is supported by updates for a total of 30 months. This increases the reliability of the platform and takes the pressure off companies to always update to the latest version.

A thoroughly exciting chapter in the development history was the separation of io.js because the development of Node.js had lost its momentum, and no innovations entered the platform for a long time. This event was a crucial turning point for the development of Node.js. The Node.js Foundation was formed, and responsibility for development was transferred from an individual to a group. As a result, release cycles and versioning were standardized, signaling both reliability and continuous further development to users of the platform.

By deciding to delve deeper into Node.js, you'll be in good company with numerous enterprises large and small around the world that are now strategically using Node.js for application development.

Chapter 2
Installation

The tallest towers start with the foundation.
—*Thomas Alva Edison*

The components of Node.js were developed in C++. This means that the entire platform is basically independent of the operating system on which it runs. This platform independence ensures that you can install Node.js on Unix-based systems, such as Linux or macOS, as well as on Windows. Originally, Node.js was developed to be installed and used on Unix-based systems. You can still notice this origin because some functionalities aren't available on Windows. For example, you can't access various functions of the process module on Windows. Another difference can be observed in the fs module that encapsulates the file system functionality for Node.js. The watch functionality is based on the interfaces provided by the operating system, so it behaves somewhat differently on different systems. In addition, the interfaces aren't 100% consistent. In summary, Node.js works stably and reliably on all three platforms mentioned. However, when using the various features, as a developer, you should always consult the application programming interface (API) documentation at *http://nodejs.org/api/* to ensure that the respective functionality is also available on your target system in the expected manner.

Regarding versioning, Node.js follows the classic semantic versioning approach, *semver* (*http://semver.org*). This means that a Node.js version number consists of three parts: the major release, minor release, and patch level. The name of a Node.js package, as available on the Node.js website, appears as *node-v <major>.<minor>.<patch>*, usually followed by information about the operating system and the target architecture. For example, for a Linux system with a 64-bit processor, you get the following name: *node-v10.6.0-linux-x64.tar.xz*. A major release increase means that, in our case, Node.js has undergone serious changes, also referred to as *breaking changes*, and there's no guarantee that existing applications will be able to run without extensive modifications. This part of the version number also has an additional meaning: even numbers indicate that it's a long-term support (LTS) release with extended support, whereas odd versions have a shorter life span. The minor version is reserved for enhancements and improvements that don't contain breaking changes, if the Node.js version can be updated easily. The patch level is increased quite often, and it simply tells you that the version used contains the smallest updates and bug fixes.

After all these rather theoretical explanations so far, the following sections deal with the installation of the Node.js platform. By the end of this chapter, you'll have a working installation of Node.js on your system, whether you're running Linux, macOS, or Windows.

In the course of this chapter, you'll be guided step by step through the installation process. We'll primarily cover the installation of the packages for your particular operating system. You'll also learn how to compile the source code and install it on your system.

2.1   Installing Packages

The easiest way to install Node.js on your system is to use existing packages for your system. The advantage here is that you can use your system's package manager, which does most of the work for you during the installation phase. You don't need to worry about resolving dependencies here, so you can install Node.js on your system with just a few lines on the command line or a few clicks, depending on which operating system you're using. Node.js is an open-source project, so it's available free of charge from *https://nodejs.org/en/download/current/*. There you have the choice between the LTS version, which is recommended for most users, and the current version, which contains the latest features. You can also download the packages for different operating systems and computer architectures to your computer using the respective links. The table in Figure 2.1 shows the different versions available for download.

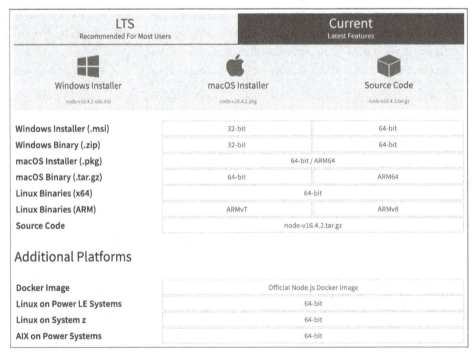

LTS Recommended For Most Users		Current Latest Features	
Windows Installer node-v16.4.2-x86.msi		**macOS Installer** node-v16.4.2.pkg	**Source Code** node-v16.4.2.tar.gz
Windows Installer (.msi)	32-bit		64-bit
Windows Binary (.zip)	32-bit		64-bit
macOS Installer (.pkg)	64-bit / ARM64		
macOS Binary (.tar.gz)	64-bit		ARM64
Linux Binaries (x64)	64-bit		
Linux Binaries (ARM)	ARMv7		ARMv8
Source Code	node-v16.4.2.tar.gz		
Additional Platforms			
Docker Image	Official Node.js Docker Image		
Linux on Power LE Systems	64-bit		
Linux on System z	64-bit		
AIX on Power Systems	64-bit		

Figure 2.1 Downloads from Node.js

Each of the following sections covers the installation of packages for a particular operating system. It's usually sufficient to read through the appropriate section for your system and then move on to Chapter 3. If you want to compile and install Node.js from the source code, you can proceed directly to Section 2.2, which provides a detailed description of this process.

2.1.1 Linux

This section describes how you can install Node.js on a Linux system. In this context, you have two different options for installing Node.js. The first one consists of installing the Linux binaries that you can download from *http://nodejs.org*. The use of the package manager of the operating system represents the second option.

Installing the Linux Binaries

In the first installation variant, the distributions don't differ because the Linux binaries package already contains the executables, and the package only needs to be unpacked and correctly integrated into the system. According to the Filesystem Hierarchy Standard (FHS) for Unix systems, the */opt* directory serves as a container for additional software, so this directory is a suitable location for the Node.js Linux binaries. The installation of the packages is described in Listing 2.1.

```
$ cd ~
$ wget https://nodejs.org/dist/v16.8.0/node-v16.8.0-linux-x64.tar.xz
--2021-09-03 11:34:59--  https://nodejs.org/dist/v16.8.0/node-v16.8.0-linux-
x64.tar.xz
Resolving nodejs.org... 104.20.23.46, 104.20.22.46
...
$ cd /opt
$ sudo tar xvf  ~/node-v16.8.0-linux-x64.tar.xz
[sudo] password for <username>:
node-v16.8.0-linux-x64/
...
$ sudo ln -s node-v16.8.0-linux-x64 nodejs
$
```

Listing 2.1 Installing the Node.js Linux Binaries

Listing 2.1 shows you how to download the Node.js Linux binaries package without a graphical user interface (GUI). To do this, you use the wget command-line tool. It downloads the package from the web server *http://nodejs.org*. After that, it will be unpacked in the */opt* directory. To install software in this directory, you need a root permission, which, in this case, you can obtain via the sudo command. In the final step, a symbolic link with the name *nodejs* to the directory is created, so you'll save some typing work in the further course and avoid mistakes when writing the complete directory name. At this point, you can already use Node.js on the command line by addressing the *node* executable with its absolute or relative path specification. However, this in turn means that you have to enter a disproportionately long command each time you call it, depending on where it's stored. In addition, it's easy for errors to creep in. The goal now is to call Node.js directly by entering the node command, which you can easily do by including the *bin* directory within the Node.js installation in the system's search path. Listing 2.2 shows the command lines required to expand the search path accordingly.

```
$ PATH=$PATH:/opt/nodejs/bin
$ export PATH
```

Listing 2.2 Extending the Search Path under Linux

After typing the two lines shown in Listing 2.2 in your command-line tool, you can use Node.js. The only problem now is that you have to reenter these commands for each shell session because the search path extension isn't persistent. The solution to this is to include these lines in one of the system-wide configuration files. Because you're making adjustments to an environment variable in this case, the */etc/profile* file is recommended at this point. Here, you just add the two lines to the end of the file, and Node.js is available on the command line every time you log in to the system. Finally, to activate the change in the current shell, you must enter the source /etc/profile command, which ensures that the file will be retrieved again.

Installation via Package Manager

The second, better option of installing Node.js on Linux systems depends on the package manager of the respective distribution. Listing 2.3 shows how to install Node.js on an Ubuntu system with just a few steps.

```
$ sudo apt-get install nodejs
```

Listing 2.3 Installing Node.js via the Ubuntu Package Manager

The command in Listing 2.3 uses the version that is stored in the default repositories. If you install Node.js in this method, the advantage is that the software is automatically updated as soon as a new version becomes available in the repository. The disadvantage of this type of installation is that the versions are updated quite slowly so the latest version is rarely available. However, you can include an additional repository that provides you with the latest version of Node.js as a package and can be updated automatically if a new version is released. Listing 2.4 shows the individual steps you need to perform to include the repository and install Node.js from it.

```
$ curl -fsSL https://deb.nodesource.com/setup_16.x | sudo -E bash -
$ sudo apt-get install -y nodejs
```

Listing 2.4 Integrating the Node.js Repository for Ubuntu

As with most operations involving package manager, you need to have `root` permissions again, and the easiest way to obtain this is using the `sudo` command.

There is one drawback to installing Node.js via the system's internal package manager: there is only one version of Node.js available to you. If you want to test your application on different versions of Node.js, you can either use Node.js via the Linux binaries or use a tool such as Node Version Manager (nvm; *https://github.com/creationix/nvm*), which allows you to run multiple versions in parallel. Apart from that, the only way left is to use several self-compiled versions of the platform.

Once you've successfully completed these steps, you'll have a fully functional installation of the Node.js platform on your system and can start developing your own applications. To check if the installation completed successfully, you should retrieve the version information of your Node.js installation. Listing 2.5 shows how to call Node.js to retrieve the version information.

```
$ node -v
v16.8.0
```

Listing 2.5 Retrieving Version Information of Node.js on Linux

If you see the correct version number, it means that the installation was successful, and you can start using Node.js.

The next sections deal with installing the Node.js platform on other systems. You can also skip those sections and proceed directly to Chapter 3, where the initial practical examples under Node.js are presented.

Uninstalling

The way you remove Node.js from your system depends predominantly on how you installed the platform. For the Linux binaries, you should delete the directory that you unpacked during the installation and remove the entries from the */etc/profile* file.

If you installed Node.js via your system's package manager, you can also use this tool to remove it. On Ubuntu systems, you must run the commands shown in Listing 2.6.

```
$ sudo apt-get remove --purge nodejs
$ sudo apt-get clean
```

Listing 2.6 Uninstalling Node.js on Linux

The `apt-get` command with the `remove` option ensures that the Node.js installation on your system is deleted. With `--purge`, you can also remove any configuration files created during the installation from the system. The next command, `apt-get` with the `clean` option, is responsible for flushing the package cache and thus freeing the occupied space. The package cache contains the packages that were downloaded for installation. Thus, Node.js can be completely removed from the system.

2.1.2   Windows

Originally, Node.js was only available on Linux. If you wanted to install it on Windows, you had no choice but to run it using Cygwin. This project can be found at *www.cygwin.com*. Cygwin provides a Linux-like environment on Windows to run Linux software there. As of version 0.6, however, a lot of things have changed in terms of support for different platforms. With the introduction of the libuv library and the concurrent abstraction of libev and libeio, it became possible to run Node.js natively on Windows without any further workaround or additional software. The Node.js download page provides both an executable binary package of Node.js and an *.msi* package for installing Node.js. Node.js can run on almost any Windows platform. Support ranges from Windows 2000 to Windows 10 for desktop systems. However, Node.js can also be installed on Windows server systems. In addition, Node.js is available on the Microsoft Azure cloud platform, making cloud applications with Node.js possible.

Binary Package

The easiest way to run Node.js on Windows is to use the binary package. You just need to download it and then use it without any further installation. Node.js can then be launched in two different ways, either by double-clicking the *node.exe* file or via the command line. Listing 2.7 shows how you can check whether or not Node.js runs on your system. Here it's assumed that the *node.exe* file is located directly in the root directory on your hard disk. However, you can also place the file in any other directory.

```
C:\>node.exe -v
V16.8.0
```

Listing 2.7 Viewing Node.js Version Information on Windows

Using the binary version of Node.js on Windows has some significant drawbacks. For example, you can't start Node.js from anywhere in the command line with just the node command. To achieve this, you must manually extend the system's search path or place the file in a directory that is already included in the search path. Another disadvantage of this option is that you can only use the Node.js platform with the binary, but not npm, which you can find at *https://npmjs.com*. You can get around these disadvantages by using the second method of running Node.js on Windows.

Microsoft Software Installer

On the download page of *https://nodejs.org*, there is also a Microsoft Software Installer (i.e., *.msi*) package available in addition to the binary package, which you can use to install Node.js. In just a few steps, you're guided through the installation, and then you can start using Node.js on your system.

After double-clicking on the Node.js installer package, the interactive installer will launch, and you'll be in the welcome window shown in Figure 2.2.

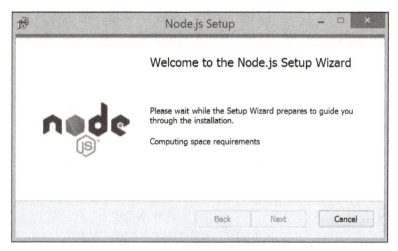

Figure 2.2 First Step in the Installation of Node.js on Windows

The **Next** button takes you to the second step of the installation. Here you're presented with the license information for Node.js, which you must accept by checking I **accept the terms in the License Agreement**.

At this point, you have the option to print the license information, go back to the first step, or accept the license conditions, as shown in Figure 2.3. (By the way, you can cancel the installation process at any time by clicking the **Cancel** button.)

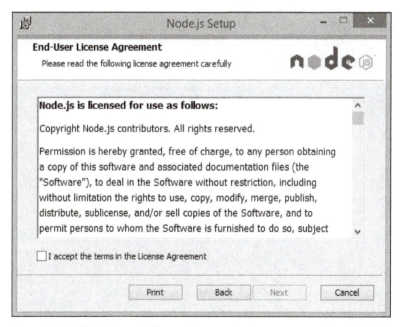

Figure 2.3 Node.js License Information on Windows

Once you've checked the box, use the **Next** button to select the target directory for the installation. The default value here is *C:\Program Files\nodejs*. Once you've set the installation target, you can select the components to install, with the default selection including all required components. Then click the **Install** button to start the actual installation of Node.js as shown in Figure 2.4. This involves copying the necessary files to the right locations in the system and registering the software so that you can use Node.js on your system.

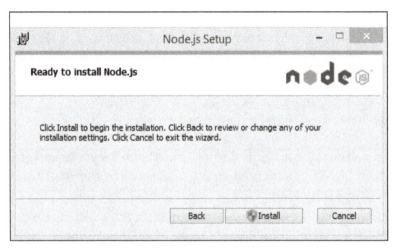

Figure 2.4 Installing Node.js on Windows

Once all the tasks required for you to run Node.js on Windows have been completed, the display switches to the final step of the installation. Then you can finish installing Node.js via the **Finish** button as shown in Figure 2.5.

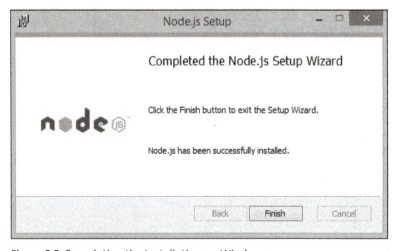

Figure 2.5 Completing the Installation on Windows

When the setup window is closed, you can open the command prompt window (*cmd.exe*) and check whether the installation of Node.js on your system was successful. For this purpose, as shown in Listing 2.8, you must run the node command along with the -v option to retrieve the version information.

```
C:\>node -v
v16.8.0
```

Listing 2.8 Viewing Node.js Version Information on Windows

If you installed Node.js using the *.msi* package, you should note that Node.js is now available to you system-wide on the command line, and you don't need to customize any environment variables. This means you can start implementing your first application with Node.js.

Uninstalling

If at any time you want to remove Node.js from your system, that's no problem either. Depending on how you proceeded with the installation, you can choose one of two ways to delete Node.js from your Windows system. If you use the Windows binaries of Node.js, you only need to remove the *node.exe* file from your system. If you've installed Node.js on your system using the *.msi* package, you can use Windows Package Manager to uninstall Node.js.

You can get to the control panel in Windows via Windows Explorer by selecting **Computer** on the left and then **Computer** on the menu bar. After that, you must click on **Control Panel**. There, the **Uninstall program** link under the **Programs** item will take you to an overview where you can select the **Uninstall program** item under **Programs and Features** to get a list of all installed software components on your system. In this list, select the **node.js** entry, and then click **Uninstall** to remove Node.js from your system.

The rest of the chapter deals with installing Node.js on macOS and compiling Node.js from source files. If you want to jump right into development with Node.js, you can skip ahead to Chapter 3.

2.1.3   macOS

As is the case for Windows, a binary package and an installer package for installation are available as downloads for macOS systems.

Binary Package

The easiest way to run Node.js on macOS is to use the binary package. The package is available as a zipped tar archive, and all you have to do is unzip it on the command line, as shown in Listing 2.9.

```
$ wget https://nodejs.org/dist/v16.8.0/node-v16.8.0-darwin-x64.tar.gz
$ tar xvzf node-v16.8.0-darwin-x64.tar.gz
$ cd   node-v16.8.0-darwin-x64
$ bin/node -v
v16.8.0
```

Listing 2.9 Installing the Node.js Binary Package on macOS

As you can see in Listing 2.9, Node.js can be used directly after unpacking. Using the -v option, you can display the version information and thus check whether it's the correct version and whether Node.js will basically work. The big disadvantage of installing the binary package is that Node.js won't be available system-wide via the command line. But there's a solution to this problem: using the installer.

Installer Package

To start the installation, you must double-click the downloaded *.pkg* file. You'll then be guided through a multistep interactive process that results in a working installation of Node.js. Figure 2.6 shows the first step of the installation, which tells you that Node.js and npm will be installed into the */usr/local/bin* directory. Click **Continue** to move on with the installation.

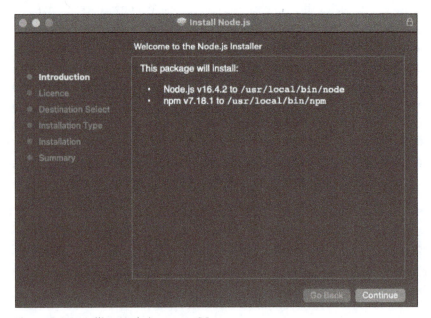

Figure 2.6 Installing Node.js on macOS

In the subsequent step of the installation, you'll be presented with the Node.js license terms. Here, as you can see in Figure 2.7, you can choose different languages in which the corresponding information will be displayed to you. You can also print the license terms or save them to your system.

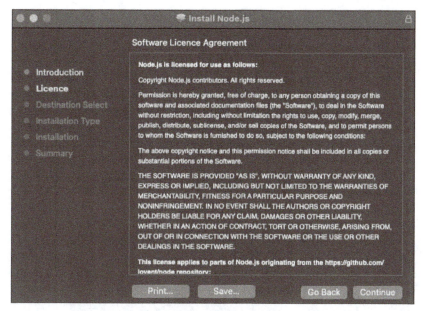

Figure 2.7 Node.js for macOS License Terms

As you move through the installation process, you can always return to the previous installation step by clicking the **Go Back** button. After clicking **Continue**, a separate popup window prompts you to agree to the license terms and proceed with the installation. You have the choice to either agree—by clicking the **Agree** button—and thus continue the installation process, or disagree and thus cancel the installation.

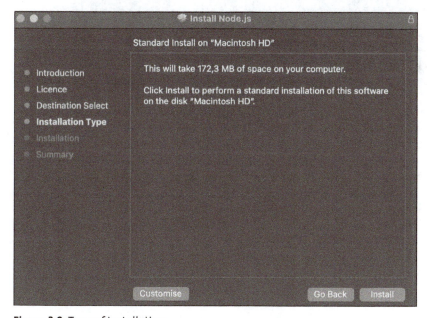

Figure 2.8 Type of Installation

Once you've accepted the license terms, the next question you'll be asked is about the partition you want to install Node.js on. The **Continue** button will take you to the next step, where you'll select the type of installation. To proceed with the standard installation, click **Install**.

At this point, you need to enter your user name and the corresponding password so that the software can be installed correctly on your system. Once you've provided and confirmed these details, the actual installation of Node.js will begin, and the files will be copied from the installer package to the system. From this point on, you can no longer return to a previous step via **Go Back**.

When all the files are copied, the installation is complete, and you'll get a short summary similar to the one shown in Figure 2.9.

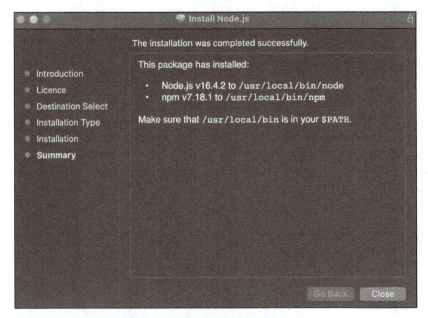

Figure 2.9 Completing the Node.js Installation on macOS

Now you find out where Node.js and npm were installed and which directory you need to include in your PATH variable so that you can use Node.js on the command line with the node command without having to include the full path. By default, the */usr/local/ bin* directory is in the system search path, as shown in Listing 2.10.

```
$ echo $PATH
/usr/bin:/bin:/usr/sbin:/sbin:/usr/local/bin:/usr/X11/bin
```

Listing 2.10 Querying the "PATH" Variables on macOS

If you've followed the steps of installing Node.js as described, you can now use the platform. To make sure that you've really installed the latest version and that Node.js works correctly, you can retrieve the version information via the command line, as shown in Listing 2.11.

```
$ node -v
v16.8.0
```

Listing 2.11 Querying the Version Information of Node.js on macOS

Uninstalling

If you want to remove Node.js from your system, you can simply delete the previously unpacked directory again, provided you use the binary package.

If you've installed Node.js via the installer, when uninstalling, you'll benefit from the fact that the pkg installer logs the files that are copied to your system. You can find that information under */var/db/receipts/* in the files *org.nodejs.node.npm.pkg.bom* and *org.nodejs.pkg.bom*. The *.bom* file extension stands for bill of material. These files record the location of the files relative to the location of the installation. Because all pieces of information, such as the file list and also the location of the installation, are in binary format, you can use the pkgutil tool to output the information. The pkgutil tool uses the names of the respective packages. The name of your Node.js package is *org.nodejs.pkg*. As shown in Listing 2.12, the metadata can be viewed using the --pkg-info option.

```
$ pkgutil --pkg-info org.nodejs.node.pkg
package-id: org.nodejs.node.pkg
version: v16.8.0
volume: /
location: /
install-time: 1526228155
```

Listing 2.12 Metadata about the Node.js Package on macOS

Listing 2.12 shows that you've installed Node.js on the / volume via the *usr/local* path. This path represents the prefix for the file list you can obtain from the *.bom* file, as shown in Listing 2.13.

```
$ pkgutil --lsbom org.nodejs.node.pkg
.
./usr
./usr/local
./usr/local/bin
./usr/local/bin/node
./usr/local/include
...
```

Listing 2.13 List of Installed Files on macOS

In previous versions, pkgutil could use an option called --unlink to completely delete a package. This option has been removed in newer versions because removing a package can affect other installed software applications on your system. For this reason, you should act with extreme caution if you want to remove software that was installed using the pkg installer. In the simplest case, you should remove the installed files manually or create a shell script that iterates across the file list and removes the files. Once you've removed the files of the package, you can also remove the package information using pkgutil, as shown in Listing 2.14.

```
$ sudo pkgutil --forget org.nodejs.pkg
```

Listing 2.14 Removing the Package Information on macOS

Installing Node.js via a prebuilt package has many advantages. First of all, you're dealing with a hassle-free installation process and don't have to consider any dependencies. In addition, you can remove these packages from the system again afterwards. But there is yet another installation option available: download the source code of Node.js, compile it yourself, and install it on the system. The next sections describe how to get from source files to an operable version of Node.js.

After following the installation steps, you now have a running version of Node.js that you can use to develop your own applications. In Chapter 3, we'll guide you step-by-step to code your first application under Node.js based on your installation. The remaining part of this chapter deals with the manual compilation and installation of Node.js from the source code. If this isn't an option for you, you can proceed directly to Chapter 3.

2.2   Compiling and Installing

In this section, you'll learn how to operate Node.js not by using binary packages or by installing it using an installer for your system, but by creating a customized installation from the source files for your system. The following sections describe how you can compile Node.js on a Linux system. This explanation is based on the assumption of a standard Ubuntu desktop installation in version 20.04.2.0 LTS. The first step of the installation is that you need to download the Node.js source code. This is available as a zipped tar archive in the download area on *https://nodejs.org/en/download/*. Before you can start compiling Node.js, you should make sure that you have a compiler. By default, this isn't the case with the desktop variant of Ubuntu. However, you can install the compiler via the system's package manager, as shown in Listing 2.15.

```
$ sudo apt-get install g++
```

Listing 2.15 Installing the GNU Compiler Collection on Ubuntu

Once this requirement is met, you can unpack the source code package and go to the resulting directory, as shown in Listing 2.16.

```
$ tar xvzf node-v16.8.0.tar.gz
$ cd node-v16.8.0
```

Listing 2.16 Unpacking the Node.js Source Code

The first step of the actual compilation process consists of creating a makefile. This file will later serve as the basis for the make command to compile Node.js. However, you don't need to create the makefile manually; instead, you can use the configure program. You can pass additional information that's relevant to the installation to this command. The available options include --without-npm to avoid installing the Node.js package manager as well, or --without-ssl to build Node.js without Secure Sockets Layer (SSL). Another option is to include different libraries such as V8, OpenSSL, or zlib as shared libraries instead of linking them statically. The --dest-cpu= option allows you to select the target architecture; possible values here are arm, ia32, and x64. You can also select the operating system for which Node.js will be built. In this case, pass the --dest-os= option the values win, mac, or linux, among others.

An important option for configure is --prefix. It specifies the location where Node.js should be installed. If you don't use this option, the default *usr/local* will be used. Relative to this path, all files from Node.js are copied to the system. You can use this option to maintain the possibility of installing multiple versions of Node.js on your system. By using the ./configure --help command, you'll get a list of all available configuration options, including short explanations.

Listing 2.17 shows the next steps in the process.

```
$ ./configure --prefix=/opt/node/node-v16.8.0
...
$ make
...
$ sudo make install
...
```

Listing 2.17 Compiling and Installing Node.js on Ubuntu

The first command in Listing 2.17—configure—is used to create the makefile for Node.js, as mentioned earlier. You can use the --prefix=/opt/node/node-v16.8.0 option to install Node.js in a separate directory. This information is recorded in the makefile. The next command, make, builds on the information in the makefile and searches for the first target in it, that is, the description of what is to be done. Then it builds the project, in this case, Node.js, according to the information it finds there. The goal of this process step is to get an executable version of Node.js but still in the directory you're currently in, which is the unpacked source code. Finally, the last command—make install—ensures that the compiled files are copied to the correct location in the system. For this reason, you must also run make install with root permissions because a user should not normally have permissions to write to /opt, that is, to your current installation target.

Once these steps have been completed, you should see a new directory called *node* in the */opt* directory in your system. This is where your Node.js now resides. You can already test this in the *node-v16.8.0/bin* subdirectory by executing the node command with the -v option. The output you get is the version number of your Node.js installation. If this test has worked, you can remove the directory along with the unpacked source code from your system, as you no longer need either. As with the binary packages on Linux, the problem of this installation option is that you can't execute Node.js system-wide from the command line, but must always specify the complete path to the executable file. The next section of this chapter goes into further detail about this problem.

Installing Node.js in the */opt* directory enables you to run multiple versions of Node.js in parallel on your system. If you develop an application that should work on different versions of Node.js and want to test this application, such an approach is a good idea. For example, you can run a version of each major version of Node.js and test your application in that environment. Normally, however, you probably want to have the latest version of Node.js available globally on your system. The easiest and fastest way to accomplish this is to create a symbolic link to the version of Node.js you want to have available globally and include that symbolic link in your system's search path. This procedure allows you to switch to another version of Node.js by customizing this link. Listing 2.18 demonstrates how you can create the link.

```
$ ln -s /opt/node/node-v16.8.0 /opt/node/node
```

Listing 2.18 Creating a Symbolic Link

In a final step, you need to extend the search path with an entry in the */etc/profile* file, as shown in Listing 2.19.

```
PATH=$PATH:/opt/node/node/bin
export PATH
```

Listing 2.19 Extending the Search Path on Linux

You now have a working installation of Node.js and can easily test it by entering the node command with the -v option in the command line. The output is the version number of the Node.js installation. You can now start developing your own applications with Node.js. As mentioned, Chapter 3 provides a first introduction to developing with Node.js and shows how you can implement your first application in a step-by-step process.

2.3   Node Version Manager

As you've seen, it's not straightforward to install multiple versions of Node.js in parallel on your system. Particularly if a library or an application should be executable on different systems, you need several parallel versions of the platform for testing. One solution to that is the Node Version Manager (nvm) command-line tool for Unix systems, which allows you to install and update Node.js. nvm works on Unix systems, macOS, and Windows Subsystem for Linux (WSL), and it enables you to switch between multiple versions on one system. The alternatives for Windows users are nodist, nvs, and nvm-windows.

Listing 2.20 shows the required command to run the installation of nvm.

```
$ wget -q0- https://raw.githubusercontent.com/nvm-sh/nvm/v0.38.0/
install.sh | bash
```

Listing 2.20 Installing nvm

The installation routine also automatically inserts a source code snippet into the startup file of your user profile shell to load nvm correctly. In Listing 2.21, you can see the corresponding code block.

```
export NVM_DIR="$([ -z "${XDG_CONFIG_HOME-}" ] && printf %s "${HOME}/
.nvm" || printf %s "${XDG_CONFIG_HOME}/nvm")"
[ -s "$NVM_DIR/nvm.sh" ] && \. "$NVM_DIR/nvm.sh" # This loads nvm
```

Listing 2.21 Configuring nvm

The first step in using nvm is to install a Node.js version. The nvm install 16 command installs the latest version of Node 16 on your system. nvm switches to this version when the installation is complete.

nvm has an important feature when dealing with globally installed npm packages. Each installed Node.js version has its own global npm packages. To transfer the packages to the next version, you can use the --reinstall-packages-from option. To this option, you specify the version number of the Node.js installation in which you installed the desired global npm packages.

Use the nvm use 16 command to switch from the currently used Node.js version to the latest installed Node 16 version on your system. You can use the nvm list command to list the installations available on your system. You can also use the nvm list-remote command to display all installable versions.

2.4   Node and Docker

In addition to the installation options presented in this chapter, you can also run Node.js in a Docker container. You can use this during development if you don't want to install Node.js on your system, as well as for production use in a scalable environment.

In the Node.js technical steering committee (TSC), there is a work group that takes care of the official Docker images and builds, manages, and continuously improves them. The work group is also responsible for making sure that images of the latest versions of Node.js are always available.

In the Docker images, which you can find at *https://hub.docker.com/_/node*, the npm and Yarn package managers are installed in addition to Node.js. For more information about working with Docker, see Chapter 25.

2.5 Summary

To develop Node.js applications, you should always use the latest version of the platform. In this context, you can be pretty sure that the vast majority of available packages are executable and tested. You'll also get bug fixes and security updates as well as access to the latest features. In most cases, it's not worth compiling Node.js from the source code itself because ready-made packages already exist for most operating systems. The advantage of an installed package is that it can be easily updated and easily removed from the system.

If it isn't possible to use the latest version in your application because major updates aren't readily available, you can access the LTS versions of Node.js. In these versions, the supply of updates and bug fixes is ensured for a longer period of time.

With tools such as nvm, it's also possible to run multiple versions of Node.js simultaneously on one system. This becomes particularly relevant when you're creating libraries for Node.js to support multiple versions of the platform.

If you do get Node.js from the Node.js download page, make sure you don't just download the *node.exe* file. This doesn't include the package manager you'll need in most cases to develop your application. You should always use the appropriate installer for your system.

Chapter 3
Developing Your First Application

Even the longest journey begins with a first step.
—*Confucius*

By the time you get here, you should already have a working installation of the Node.js platform on your system. To run the examples in this chapter, you must use the command line of your operating system. It doesn't matter whether you use Windows, Linux, or macOS. The examples work independently of the operating system. You can use Node.js in two different ways. For simple experiments, you can use the interactive shell. Alternatively, you can run an application by passing the name of the initial file to the node command. In this case, no further user interaction is usually required.

3.1   Interactive Mode

You can reach the interactive mode of Node.js, as you can see in Listing 3.1, by entering the node command in the command line.

```
$ node
>
```

Listing 3.1 Interactive Mode of Node.js

In interactive mode, you can directly enter JavaScript code on the command line and execute it. This type of user interface is referred to as *read-eval-print loop (REPL)*, which means that commands are read on the command line and evaluated, and then the result is output on the command line. The mode isn't intended to implement and run complete applications. Instead, this interface of Node.js is used to test the behavior and functionality of individual code snippets. Figure 3.1 shows how the interactive mode works.

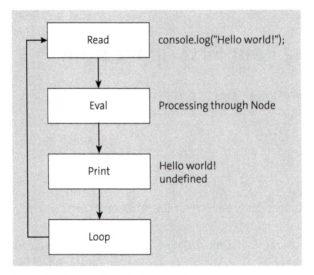

Figure 3.1 Interactive Mode of Node.js

3.1.1   General Use

Listing 3.2 shows how you can issue commands in the Node.js REPL.

```
$ node
> console.log('Hello World!');
Hello world!
undefined
>
```

Listing 3.2 Executing Commands in the Node.js REPL

The JavaScript commands also end with a semicolon in the Node.js REPL. A line break ends the input of the current command and sends the command to the JavaScript engine. In the example, the console.log method with the Hello World! argument is evaluated, and the Hello World! result is output to the command line. As you can see in Listing 3.2, the value undefined is output in addition to the expected Hello World!. This is because the return value of the console.log function is represented; in this case, it's undefined. Apart from executing output, in REPL, you can also execute all JavaScript commands available under Node.js, as shown in Listing 3.3.

```
> function greet(name) {
... console.log(`Hello ${name}`);
... }; greet('world');
Hello world
undefined
>
```

Listing 3.3 Definition of a Simple Node.js REPL Function

Listing 3.3 shows how to define a function in Node.js REPL that gets a name as a parameter and how to output it to the console as the function progresses. After the definition, the function greet is called with the argument world as name. The output consists of Hello world and undefined. If you want to run different commands in the Node.js REPL that build on each other, you can easily do so because the context is preserved within a session. For example, if you define functions or perform a variable assignment, these will be preserved even after the command line is evaluated. In Listing 3.4, you can see how this works in concrete terms.

```
$ node
> const sayHello = 'Hello world!';
undefined
> console.log(sayHello);
Hello world!
undefined
>
```

Listing 3.4 Interdependent Command Lines

In the example in Listing 3.4, you assign a value to the sayHello constant. This constant is used again in the output in the subsequent statement. Among the most important features of the Node.js REPL is the auto-completion function. If you press the ⌨Tab key without entering anything else, you'll get a list of all available objects. If you use the auto-complete function in conjunction with one or more letters, only the matching suggestions will be displayed. Another feature worth mentioning is the multiline commands. As you can see in Listing 3.3, the function code isn't entered on a single line but on several lines. An uncompleted command is indicated by three dots instead of the greater-than sign as the command prompt. Multiline commands can be achieved, for example, by unfinished code blocks or a plus operator for calculation or string concatenation at the end of the line.

3.1.2 Other REPL Commands

One of the special features of the Node.js REPL is that it provides you with a few more commands to control the REPL in addition to the JavaScript command set. The commands always start with a period and don't have to end with a semicolon. Table 3.1 contains an overview of these commands.

Command	Description
.break	Terminates the current input. .break is especially useful for multiline commands.
.clear	Serves as alias for .break.

Table 3.1 Available REPL Commands

Command	Description
.exit	Terminates the Node.js REPL.
.help	Outputs a list of available commands.
.load <file>	Loads a saved session from a file into the current REPL.
.save <file>	Saves the commands of the current REPL session to a file.
.editor	Opens the editor mode where you can define a block of instructions. Ctrl+D executes the block, and Ctrl+C exits the editor mode without executing anything.

Table 3.1 Available REPL Commands (Cont.)

There are two options available to exit the REPL: using the .exit command or pressing Ctrl+D, which will also terminate the process immediately. Alternatively, you can press Ctrl+C twice.

The .break and .clear commands are used when the command line is blocked by incorrect input. Listing 3.5 shows a use case for these commands.

```
> function greet(name) {
... .break
>
```

Listing 3.5 Use of ".break"

In the example in Listing 3.5, you've started to formulate a function, but you don't want to finish writing it, you would rather cancel the entry. You can't terminate the current input by pressing the Enter key, as this would merely insert a line break. If you find that you've made a similar mistake in your input, you can terminate the current input by using the .break command and enter your command again. The same effect can be achieved via the shortcut Ctrl+C. The Node.js REPL provides the option to navigate through the history of the most recent commands. With this feature, you don't have to retype your command, but you can use the Up and Down arrow keys to navigate through the history of entered commands, retrieve the corresponding command line, correct it, and enter it again.

3.1.3 Saving and Loading in the REPL

If you want to run more extensive tests in REPL or record the results, you can use the .save and .load commands to save the previously executed commands to a file or load a file with JavaScript instructions into the current REPL.

Listing 3.6 shows how you can use the .load and .save commands. To illustrate their usage, you should first enter the console.log command. After that, the current session is saved to the *myShell.js* file. This file then contains the command line as you entered it in the REPL, but not the associated output. Next, you must load this file back into the session using the .load statement. The file is read line by line, each command is executed, and the corresponding output gets displayed. You can also use the .load command to prepare a specific initial situation for an experiment. For this purpose, you can formulate a set of commands in a file, for example, to define variables or functions that you need in the course of a session in the Node.js REPL.

```
> console.log('Hello World!');
Hello world!
undefined
> .save myShell.js
Session saved to:myShell.js
> .load myShell.js
> console.log('Hello World!');
Hello world!
undefined
>
```

Listing 3.6 Using ".load" and ".save"

3.1.4 Context of the REPL

As is common in JavaScript, the Node.js REPL provides a global context that you can access anywhere in your program. In the REPL, some variables are already registered at the beginning in this global context, which facilitate your work as a developer. This way, all Node.js core modules are available to you without having to load them separately via the module system. For example, you can use http.STATUS_CODES to print the predefined list of HTTP status codes. Besides these modules, you can load files or Node Package Manager (npm) packages via the module system by using the require function. In the global scope of the Node.js REPL, the _ variable provides you with another special feature: this variable always contains the value of the most recent command. For example, if you enter the command 1 + 1, _ will contain the value 2 afterwards. If you call a method such as process.uptime(), _ contains its return value afterwards.

3.1.5 REPL History

The Node.js REPL has some special environment variables. Two of them concern historicizing entries. You probably already know this feature from the command prompt of your operating system. In the case of Bash on Unix systems, there is a file called *.bash_history*, which stores all the commands that were entered. A similar functionality exists for the Node.js REPL. In the default configuration, the input is stored in the *.node_repl_history* file in the user's root directory. You can use two environment variables from your operating system to control the history functionality. With NODE_REPL_

HISTORY, you can change the location of the history. If no value is specified, the default is used. The second environment variable, NODE_REPL_HISTORY_SIZE, determines how many lines the history file can hold before overwriting older commands. The default value is 1000.

3.1.6   REPL Mode

You can use the NODE_REPL_MODE environment variable to determine in which mode you want to run the Node.js REPL. The three possible values are as follows:

- sloppy
  The REPL is set to nonstrict mode. The rules of JavaScript strict mode are overridden. This is the default mode for running the REPL.

- strict
  The strict value activates the strict mode. In this case, for example, you can no longer create multiple properties with the same name in an object, and changing a constant returns an error. A very good and detailed description of the strict mode can be found at *https://developer.mozilla.org/en-US/docs/Web/JavaScript/Reference/Strict_mode*.

- magic
  This value is now deprecated and is used as an alias of sloppy.

You can also run Node.js directly in strict mode via the --use_strict command-line option. In most cases, this makes sense because you can save the use strict specifications, and strict mode prohibits many antipatterns in JavaScript.

Using the Node.js REPL as a tool, you can easily test source code to interactively see how the Node.js platform behaves in certain situations. The Node.js REPL isn't suitable for extensive applications. In this case, a different way of running Node.js is used.

3.1.7   Searching in the REPL

The Node.js REPL allows you to not only navigate within the history using the arrow keys, but also to search for specific lines. You can use Ctrl+R and Ctrl+S to perform backward and forward search runs in the history.

You access this feature mainly when you want to execute a certain line again but don't want to enter it a second time. The search finds the entered code whether it occurs at the beginning or anywhere within the line. A found match is displayed at the command prompt, and you have the option to adjust the code and then execute it by pressing the Enter key. If a certain text is found several times, you can jump to the next hit by pressing the respective shortcut again or go to the previous hit by pressing the other shortcut.

3.1.8   Asynchronous Operations in the REPL

JavaScript provides various means of handling asynchrony, such as *callbacks* or *promises*. A few years ago, the `async-await` concept was introduced, which will be discussed in greater detail later in this book. You can use the `await` keyword to wait for an asynchronous operation without registering a callback function. The engine pauses the execution of the current code block until the result is available. The rest of the application remains responsive and can continue its work undisturbed.

Normally, you must mark a function in which you want to use the `await` keyword with the `async` keyword. Newer versions of the ECMAScript standard provide for a feature called *top-level await*, which allows you to use `await` even at the top level of your application and thus without a surrounding `async` function. This feature is also available in the Node.js REPL, and, since version 16.6, it's also enabled by default and no longer hidden behind the `--experimental-repl-await` flag.

Listing 3.7 shows the example of a `promise` object created with `Promise.resolve` to demonstrate how you can launch REPL with the `--experimental-repl-await` option and how you can use the `await` keyword. `Promise.resolve` is one of the simplest ways to simulate an asynchronous operation by creating a `promise` object and resolving it immediately.

```
$ node
Welcome to Node.js v16.8.0.
Type ".help" for more information.
> await Promise.resolve('Hello world');
'Hello world'
```

Listing 3.7 Using a Top-Level Await in the REPL

3.2   The First Application

When you create applications using Node.js, the source code of that application is contained in one or more files. When launching the application, you specify the name of the initial file as an option in the command line. From this file, you then load the rest of the components of your application via the Node.js module system. The entire source code is read in and optimized by the JavaScript engine. As a consequence, changes to the source code don't directly affect the running application. This means you need to exit and restart it for the changes to become active. Listing 3.8 shows how you can run an application with Node.js.

```
$ node server.mjs
Hello world!
$
```

Listing 3.8 Running Node.js Applications

The *server.mjs* file contains only the `console.log('Hello world!')` line. The advantage of this method of running an application is that you can run the application as many times as you want, and all you need to do is run the command line from Listing 3.8. In addition, you can easily run the source code on other systems or make the application available to other users as open-source software.

> **Node.js Module Systems**
>
> Currently, Node.js supports two different module systems. The previous implementation—the CommonJS module system—uses `module.exports` to export elements and the `require` function to load elements. This module system has been part of the Node.js platform from the beginning.
>
> Meanwhile, another module system—the ECMAScript module system—has also been included in the standard ECMAScript. This system uses the `import` and `export` keywords and isn't compatible with the CommonJS module system.
>
> For several years now, Node.js has been in a transition phase away from the CommonJS module system and toward the ECMAScript module system. For the ECMAScript modules to work, it's required that the files have the *.mjs* extension. Throughout this book, we'll use the ECMAScript module system. However, in Chapter 4, you'll also learn more about the CommonJS module system and how you can work with both systems.

Note that the output of `Hello world!` doesn't yet represent an application. However, with Node.js, you can create dynamic web applications without the need for a separate web server because Node.js allows you to create your own web server via the `http` module. The following sections will guide you step by step through the classic example of a Node.js application: a very lightweight web server.

3.2.1   Web Server in Node.js

The web server you develop in this example should be able to accept requests from browsers and respond to them with a correct HTTP response and the output of the `Hello world` string. You start with a basic framework and extend it until the application meets the requirements. Listing 3.9 contains the basic structure of the application. You should save this code in a separate file named *server.mjs*.

```
import { createServer } from 'http';

const server = createServer();
server.listen(8080, () => {
  console.log(
    `Server is listening to http://localhost:${server.address().port}`,
  );
});
```

Listing 3.9 Structure of a Web Server in Node.js

Template Strings

With *template strings*, such as those used in Listing 3.9, there is a third way to define strings in JavaScript besides single and double quotes. However, this is a special form whose processing is somewhat slower than that of simple strings. With template strings defined with the backtick character (`` ` ``), you can use ${} to replace variables or evaluate the JavaScript expressions within a string. It's also possible to insert line breaks without concatenating the string with the + operator.

Actually, a JavaScript engine such as V8 doesn't have the capabilities to provide a web server in a simple way. For this reason, modules exist for Node.js that extend the functionality of the Node.js platform. In this example, you need the functionality of a web server. A separate module exists for Node.js for this purpose and to solve other tasks related to HTTP. The functionality from the various modules of Node.js is automatically available to you. As a developer, all you need to do is load the modules you need for your application before using them. Loading modules and other files in Node.js is done via the import keyword. As you can see in the example, you can directly address the parts of the interface of the respective module that you need for your application.

var, let, and const

In JavaScript, there are now three ways available to define variables. Each of these ways has an impact on the way you develop your applications. If you define your variables by prefixing them with the var keyword, this has the effect that the variable is valid in the current function and all subfunctions. For a long time, this was the only available option.

The let keyword enables you to define variables at the block level. For example, if you define a counter variable in a for loop with let, this variable is valid only within the loop. A variable defined with let in a function has the same properties as one defined with var. let has the same range of functions as var except that you have even better control over the scope. So, there are actually hardly any reasons to continue using var. However, be careful not to mix var and let within your application, as this can easily lead to errors that are difficult to locate.

The third way to define a variable is with the const keyword. Such variables aren't variables in the true sense, but constants, which means that you can't change the value of the variable after the initial assignment. The fact that JavaScript works with references for nonprimitive values such as objects or arrays puts the whole thing into perspective again. With a const object, you can no longer change the reference, but you can change the properties of the object itself. Try to use const as much as possible during development to avoid overwriting variables by mistake. If you actually need variables, you should use let.

Using the http module, you can create a client to query other web servers in addition to the initial server. However, for your web server application, you only need the server. You can create this with the imported createServer function of the http module. The return value of this method is the HTTP server, which is available to you as an object for later use. The newly created server object currently has no functionality, nor is a connection opened to the outside world.

The next step is to open this very connection toward the clients so that they can connect to the server and retrieve data. The server provides you with the listen method, a way to specify a port and an IP address through which your users can connect to the server. You can pass the port number and the IP address to which the server should be bound to the listen method. Normally, however, you should at least specify the port number, as otherwise any free port will be assigned. The port number is specified as an integer, which must be between 0 and 65,535. There are two things to keep in mind when choosing a port for your web server: The port used must not already be taken by another application, and it should not be in the range of system ports between 0 and 1,023. If you use a port 1,024 or higher, you can run your Node.js script as a normal user; for ports below that value, you need admin privileges. You should always run tests and examples as a normal user because as an administrator you have considerably more privileges and can seriously damage the system. You can specify the IP address as a string, for example, '127.0.0.1'. If you don't specify any address, the IPv6 address :: or the IPv4 address 0.0.0.0 will be used by default. This means that the server is bound to all interfaces of the system. So, for example, you can reach your server using the name localhost.

In addition to specifying the address and port, calling the HTTP server's listen method opens the connection and makes the server wait for incoming requests. You can also pass a callback function to the listen method as the last argument. This is executed as soon as the server is bound. In the example, this function outputs the information that the server is ready to operate and at which address you can reach it. If you don't take care of such an output yourself, Node.js doesn't display any further information. Now you should save the script under the name *server.mjs*. You can run the web server on your system and test the result already. Listing 3.10 shows what the result of the test looks like.

```
$ node server.mjs
Server is listening to http://localhost:8080
```

Listing 3.10 Running the Web Server on Node.js

If you get the error create Server: listen EADDRINUSE :::8080 when running your application, it means that the port is already taken by another application, and you need to choose another port for your Node.js application.

The node command with the file containing the source code of the web server as an option causes a Node.js process to be started that connects to the specified combination of address and port and then waits for incoming connections that it can serve. By executing the script, the command line is blocked, and you can't make any further entries to it. Due to the architecture of Node.js, which is based on the event-driven principle, very little load is created by the web server script because Node.js doesn't block when it has nothing to do. If you want to cancel the script, you can do this via the [Ctrl]+[C] shortcut, which returns a command prompt. Now you can test the web server with your browser by entering "http://localhost:8080" in the address bar.

The problem is that although your web server is bound to the correct address and port, it has no logic to handle incoming requests. This primarily causes you to get no output when testing, and, if you leave your browser window open long enough, a time-out error. For this reason, you'll insert source code in the next step to ensure that incoming requests are also served in a meaningful way.

The web server you create here in Node.js differs seriously in some features from other implementations in dynamic scripting languages such as PHP. Here, each request is served separately, and the necessary source code is read in the process. With Node.js, the application's code is read once and then remains in the memory. The application runs permanently. This is where an important aspect of Node.js comes into play: asynchronous task processing. The web server responds to events, in this case, to the clients' requests. For this purpose, a function is defined—a callback—which is executed as soon as a request is received. Although this code is defined in a block, as in other languages, the source code responsible for handling the requests isn't executed until such a request is received.

3.2.2   Extending the Web Server

In Listing 3.11 you can see the extended source code from Listing 3.9. This version of the web server can also handle requests correctly.

```
import { createServer } from 'http';

const server = createServer((request, response) => {
  response.writeHead(200, { 'content-type': 'text/plain; charset=utf-8' });
  response.write('Hello ');
  response.end(' World\n');
});

server.listen(8080, () => {
  console.log(
    `Server is listening to http://localhost:${server.address().port}`,
  );
});
```

Listing 3.11 Web Server with Callback

The only adaptation of the example from Listing 3.9 takes place in the call of the createServer function. Here, Node.js receives the callback that specifies what should happen when a request from a client reaches the server. In this simple example, you first just output the string Hello world in the client's browser.

To achieve this output, you should first look at the structure of the callback function. It has two parameters, a request and a response object, representing the client's request and the server's response, respectively. In this example, you should first disregard the client's request and focus on the server's response. The first step is to prepare the HTTP header information that will later be sent back to the client. This is done using the writeHead method. The first argument of this function consists of a number representing the HTTP status code. The second argument is an object that contains the actual HTTP header. The key values of the object, such as the content-type value in the example, should be written in lowercase according to convention. In the example, you can see the specification of the content type, which in this case is set to text/plain to indicate to the client that the server's response contains only text. Because some browsers such as Firefox return error messages if the character coding isn't specified correctly, the content type is extended by the information charset=utf-8 to inform the browser that the HTTP body is UTF-8 encoded.

You can create the response visible to the user—the HTTP body—using the write method. When this method is called, fragments of the response, called *chunks*, are sent. You can call this method several times in a row, which will result in the individual parts being joined together. However, you should make sure that before calling write, the correct HTTP headers are always sent with writeHead. If you don't call the writeHead method, the Node.js HTTP server implicitly sends an HTTP header with a status code of 200 and a content type of text/plain, so a response without explicitly providing header information is also valid. Calling write ensures that parts of the response are sent to the client. However, in this case, the client doesn't know when the server is finished sending the response. You, as the developer, must take care of this by using the end method of the response object. You can optionally provide a string as an argument. In this case, end behaves in the same way as write as it sends the specified chunk to the client and then terminates the response.

The write method has two other features worth mentioning. For one thing, not only can you pass strings as arguments but also as buffer objects. A buffer object consists of binary data that greatly facilitates the streaming of data. This class of objects primarily comes into play when streams are used. The second feature consists of specifying the coding of the string, namely, via the second parameter of the write method. This is optional, and, if omitted, Node.js uses utf-8 as the default coding method. Possible other values are utf16le, ascii, or hex. UTF-8 as the coding method is permitted in this example, which is why it's also not necessary to specify a character coding. As an alternative to combining multiple write calls and one end call, you can also store the entire response to the client in a variable and send it in a single call of the end method.

For the example to work correctly, you need to make sure that you restart the web server so that the custom source code from Node.js is read correctly. For this purpose, it's best to terminate the possibly still running instance of the first example via the shortcut <kbd>Ctrl</kbd>+<kbd>C</kbd> and restart the web server by calling the node command again with the name of the file of your source code. Figure 3.2 shows the result of the request.

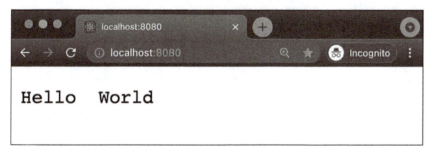

Figure 3.2 Response from the Web Server to the Client

In this example, you've seen how it's possible, with just a few lines of JavaScript code, to create a functional web server that responds to a client's request with a correct HTTP response.

3.2.3   Creating an HTML Response

In reality, however, you rarely have to deal with responses from web servers in plain text. Thus, we'll now extend the example so that the server responds with a response in HTML, just as a normal web server would. Listing 3.12 shows the adjustments you need to make for this.

```
import { createServer } from 'http';

const server = createServer((request, response) => {
  response.writeHead(200, { 'content-type': 'text/html; charset=utf-8' });

  const body = `<!DOCTYPE html>
    <html>
      <head>
        <meta charset="utf-8">
        <title>Node.js Demo</title>
      </head>
      <body>
        <h1 style="color:green">Hello World</h1>
      </body>
    </html>`;

  response.end(body);
```

```
});
server.listen(8080, () => {
  console.log(
    `Server is listening to http://localhost:${server.address().port}`,
  );
});
```

Listing 3.12 Web Server HTML Response

The only change you need to make to the source code of the example is to adjust the content type, which is now `text/html` instead of `text/plain`. In addition, the `write` was dropped, and the HTTP body is sent entirely using the `end` method. The value passed to the `end` method contains an HTML string that reflects the structure of the web page to be displayed. Because this string is quite large, it's best to outsource it to the separate `body` constant and use a template string to create a clear multiline string with simple means. Finally, you must pass the `body` constant to the `end` method. Once you've made these changes, all you need to do is restart the Node.js process running your web server for the changes to take effect. When you reload the page in your browser now, you should see a similar result to the one shown in Figure 3.3.

Figure 3.3 Output of an HTML Page

Up to this point, you've predominantly been concerned with the `response` object, that is, the response to the client. Now it's time to take a closer look at the `request` object, which is the actual request. This object allows you to read the information sent by the client and include it in the response generation.

3.2.4   Generating Dynamic Responses

In classic web applications, information is sent from the browser using the HTTP methods GET and POST. Mostly this is done via forms or parameters that are coded in the URL. You'll now extend the example and display a string specified by the user in the URL on the output page.

You can use the source code from Listing 3.12 as a basis. The adapted source code is shown in Listing 3.13, followed by the corresponding explanations of the changes.

```
import { createServer } from 'http';

const server = createServer((request, response) => {
  response.writeHead(200, { 'content-type': 'text/html; charset=utf-8' });

  const url = new URL(request.url, 'http://localhost:8080');

  const body = `<!DOCTYPE html>
    <html>
      <head>
        <meta charset="utf-8">
        <title>Node.js Demo</title>
      </head>
      <body>
        <h1 style="color:green">Hello ${url.searchParams.get('name')}</h1>
      </body>
    </html>`;

  response.end(body);
});
server.listen(8080, () => {
  console.log(
    `Server is listening to http://localhost:${server.address().port}`,
  );
});
```

Listing 3.13 Manipulating Web Pages via Parameters

The most important adaptation of the source code is that you read the URL the client has requested in the source code and write parts of it in the response. In the request object, the information about which URL the user specified in their browser is present in the url property. For example, if you assume that the user typed the URL *http://localhost:8080/?name=Besucher* in the address bar of their browser, the url property of the request object contains the value /?name=visitor.

Your goal now is to output the Hello visitor string. To do this, you need to extract the string, in this case visitor, from the url property. You can do this, for example, by splitting the string with the JavaScript string function split at the equal sign and using the second element of the resulting array. However, this variant only works as long as the user passes only one parameter in the URL or this parameter is in the first position in the case of several parameters.

A better way to handle URLs is to use the WHATWG URL API, which is now a native part of the Node.js platform; therefore, no separate import is required for the URL class. Among other things, this API enables you to parse URLs and thus break them down into their individual components. To do this, you must create a new instance of the URL class and pass the constructor the relative path of the call contained in the `url` property of the `request` object and the base URL of your application, in this case, `http://local-host:8080/`. The newly created object represents the requested URL with all of its components. You can find the individual query parameters that were transferred in the `searchParams` property. You can read these using the `get` method and transfer the desired parameter name. In our example, this is the `name` string. Here, the number and order of the parameters in the URL no longer play any role either because you can access the value via the name of the parameter. Thus, you can then access the string the user has entered in the address bar of the browser via `url.searchParams.get('name')`. This means you have all the components you need to achieve your goal.

After you've made the adjustments to the source code and restarted the web server, you can test the result by calling the page again. Figure 3.4 shows the result you get when you call the page *http://localhost:8080/?name=user*.

Figure 3.4 The First Dynamic Website on Node.js

3.3   Debugging Node.js Applications

Even when implementing smaller applications, sooner or later, you'll reach the point at which you need to find and fix a bug in your own source code. Most of these errors are caused by incorrectly assigned variables or logic errors within the application. For this reason, when troubleshooting, you're usually concerned with the values of certain variables and the flow of the application logic.

In the simplest case, you insert `console.log` statements at certain points in the source code, which helps you output the values of the variables and check the individual flow steps of your source code. In Listing 3.14, you can see what the web server example can look like with such debug outputs. In addition, as you can see in the code, `console.log` is quite flexible. You can pass either one or more arguments to this method. If you pass multiple arguments, `console.log` takes care of the joining and the output.

```
import { createServer } from 'http';

console.log('createServer');
const server = createServer((request, response) => {
  console.log('createServer callback');

  response.writeHead(200, { 'content-type': 'text/html; charset=utf-8' });

  const url = new URL(request.url, 'http://localhost:8080');

  console.log(url);
  console.log('Name: ', url.searchParams.get('name'));

  const body = `...`;

  response.end(body);
});

console.log('listen');
server.listen(8080, () => {
  console.log(
    `Server is listening to http://localhost:${server.address().port}`,
  );
});
```

Listing 3.14 Debugging with "console.log"

When you run the source code from Listing 3.14, you'll see that first createServer, listen, and the string Server is listening to http://localhost:8080 are output to the console. As soon as you start a query with your browser, the createServer callback string, the URL object, and the name from the query string are output.

This way of debugging an application has several problems at the same time. To receive output, you need to actively edit the source code and include the statements in the relevant places. This means that you'll have to make additional adjustments to the source code for error analysis, and for this reason, you'll have to modify it further, which makes it vulnerable for additional problems. Another difficulty of this method of debugging is that by using the console.log statements, at runtime of the application, you don't get an image of the whole environment but only of a very specific section, which can be even further distorted by certain influences.

The Node.js debugger provides a remedy for these problems. The advantage of the debugger is that it's an integral part of the Node.js platform, so you don't need to install any other software. To start the debugger, save your source code to a file, which in this example is the *server.mjs* file, with the source code from Listing 3.13, and run the node inspect server.mjs command in the command line. Listing 3.15 shows the output of the command.

```
$ node inspect server.mjs
< Debugger listening on ws://127.0.0.1:9229/63f3a320-4d08-48ab-847f-300688e54760
< For help, see: https://nodejs.org/en/docs/inspector
<
connecting to 127.0.0.1:9229 ... ok
< Debugger attached.
<
Break on start in server.mjs:1
> 1 import { createServer } from 'http';
  2
  3 const server = createServer((request, response) => {
debug>
```

Listing 3.15 Debugging with Node.js

If you add the inspect option when calling your application, the application will start in interactive debug mode. The first information you get is that the debugger is waiting for incoming connections via a WebSocket connection. Furthermore, the display tells you in which file and line the debugger has interrupted the execution. Finally, the first three lines of the application code are output. The statement at which the debugger stopped is highlighted in green.

3.3.1   Navigating in the Debugger

The debug> prompt signals that the debugger is now waiting for your input. You can see which commands are available to you in Table 3.2.

In the example shown in Listing 3.15, you use the n or next command, respectively, to jump to the next statement with the debugger. This is marked by the fact that the createServer function is highlighted in green in line 3.

Command	Description	Description
c	Continue	Continues the execution of the application until the next breakpoint
n	Step next	Skips a subroutine
Add	Step in	Jumps to a subroutine

Table 3.2 Commands for the Debugger

Command	Description	Description
o	Step out	Jumps back from a subroutine to the next higher level
pause	Pause	Pauses the execution

Table 3.2 Commands for the Debugger (Cont.)

3.3.2 Information in the Debugger

If you jump further in the debugger to the second line, you can display the value of the http constant. To do so, you must enter the repl command in the debugger. This command launches an interactive shell from which you can access the debugger environment. For example, you can then enter the string http and get the structure of this variable. The shortcut Ctrl + C enables you to switch from the interactive shell back to the debugger. After that, you can use the commands from Table 3.2 for navigation purposes as usual.

If you've created an output in the interactive shell and then jumped back to the debug mode, you can no longer see where you are in your source code. The list command helps you to solve this problem. This function ensures that the debugger shows you the currently executed line of source code and a certain number of lines before and after this line. You can specify the number of lines you want to see as an argument. If you don't specify a number, the value 5 is assumed. Listing 3.16 shows an example of how to use the list command.

```
debug> list(1)
> 1 import { createServer } from 'http';
  2
```

Listing 3.16 "list" Function of the Debugger

Another function the debugger offers you is the output of a backtrace. This is especially helpful if you've jumped to various subroutines using the s command and now want to find out how you got to the current location. The backtrace function, or its shorter variant bt, enables you to display the backtrace of the current execution. Listing 3.17 shows the output of the backtrace in case you've jumped into the callback function of the createServer function in the web server example.

```
debug> bt
#0 (anonymous) server.mjs:4:2
#1 emit node:events:394:27
#2 parserOnIncoming node:_http_server:924:11
#3 parserOnHeadersComplete node:_http_common:127:16
```

Listing 3.17 Backtraces with the Debugger

When you run through the source code of your application with the debugger, you're usually interested in the values of certain variables. You can easily determine these values via the repl command and the interactive shell. However, in many cases, this variant isn't very handy because you have to switch back to the shell each time and can only read the values there. Another way to find out the values of variables is to use the watch function of the debugger. In this case, you pass the name of the variable whose value you want to observe as a string to this function. If you now step through your application, you'll see the value of this variable in each step.

Listing 3.18 shows how you can use the watch function. The output of the structure in this case only provides the hint that the watch expression is the createServer function. However, you can not only monitor native structures but also observe any variables during debugging. But if you set a watcher on a more extensive object with many properties, the output isn't structured. Watchers therefore offer an advantage mainly for variables with scalar values or small objects. For more extensive objects, we recommend using the repl command.

```
debug> watch('createServer')
debug> n
break in server.mjs:3
Watchers:
  0: createServer = [Function: createServer]

  1 import { createServer } from 'http';
  2
> 3 const server = createServer((request, response) => {
  4   debugger;
  5   response.writeHead(200, { 'content-type': 'text/html; charset=utf-8' });
debug>
```

Listing 3.18 Watcher with Node.js

In addition to the watch function, there are two other functions you can use for monitoring structures. The unwatch function allows you to remove watchers that have already been set. For this purpose, you only have to pass the name of the variable as a string to the function, and the watcher will be removed. The second watchers function takes no arguments and lists the existing watchers and the associated values of the corresponding variables. Table 3.3 summarizes the debugger commands for you again.

Command	Description
repl	Opens an interactive shell in the debugger
list, list(n)	Displays the current source code of the debugger
backtrace, bt	Outputs the backtrace of the current execution

Table 3.3 Commands in the Debugger

Command	Description
watch(exp)	Displays the value of the specified expression at each debugger step
unwatch(exp)	Removes a watcher
watchers	Lists all active watchers

Table 3.3 Commands in the Debugger (Cont.)

3.3.3   Breakpoints

With the current state, it's only possible for you to go through the source code of your application step by step from the beginning to the point where you suspect a problem. This can be difficult with extensive applications, as it may take a long time to get to the relevant location. For these cases, the Node.js debugger provides the breakpoints feature. A breakpoint represents a marker in the source code at which the debugger automatically stops.

With the setBreakpoint function (or sb in the short form) of the debugger, you can define a breakpoint. In the case of Listing 3.19, you use setBreakpoint to set a breakpoint in line 7 at the start of the run. You can use the c command to continue execution, which then stops at the breakpoint.

setBreakpoint allows you to set breakpoints in several different ways. As you've already seen, you can specify a particular line in which you want to set the breakpoint. If you don't specify a value, the breakpoint is set in the current line. In addition, you can specify a function as a string at whose first statement the execution will stop. Finally, in the last variant, you specify a file name and a line number. When the execution of the application reaches this file and line, the execution will be interrupted. The clearBreakpoint or cb command enables you to remove a set breakpoint by specifying the file name and the line number.

```
$ node inspect server.mjs
< Debugger listening on ws://127.0.0.1:9229/92b7f273-d2ec-4134-a700-a4b69e90a4f2
< For help, see: https://nodejs.org/en/docs/inspector
<
connecting to 127.0.0.1:9229 ... ok
< Debugger attached.
<
Break on start in server.mjs:1
> 1 import { createServer } from 'http';
  2
  3 const server = createServer((request, response) => {
debug> setBreakpoint(8)
  3 const server = createServer((request, response) => {
  4   response.writeHead(200, { 'content-type': 'text/html; charset=utf-8' });
```

```
   5
   6    const url = new URL(request.url, 'http://localhost:8080');
   7
>  8    const body = `<!DOCTYPE html>
   9      <html>
  10        <head>
  11          <meta charset="utf-8">
  12          <title>Node.js Demo</title>
  13        </head>
debug> c
< Server is listening to http://localhost:8080
<
break in server.mjs:8
   6    const url = new URL(request.url, 'http://localhost:8080');
   7
>  8    const body = `<!DOCTYPE html>
   9      <html>
  10        <head>
debug>
```

Listing 3.19 Breakpoints in Node.js

Alternatively, you can set a breakpoint directly in your source code by inserting the
debugger statement. However, the disadvantage is that you have to modify your source
code for debugging. In any case, you must make sure to remove all debugger statements
after debugging. Listing 3.20 shows how you can use the debugger statement in the web
server example.

```
import { createServer } from 'http';

const server = createServer((request, response) => {
  response.writeHead(200, { 'content-type': 'text/html; charset=utf-8' });

  const url = new URL(request.url, 'http://localhost:8080');
  debugger;
  const body = `<!DOCTYPE html>
    <html>
      <head>
        <meta charset="utf-8">
        <title>Node.js Demo</title>
      </head>
      <body>
        <h1 style="color:green">Hello ${url.searchParams.get('name')}</h1>
      </body>
    </html>`;
```

```
    response.end(body);
});
server.listen(8080, () => {
  console.log(
    `Server is listening to http://localhost:${server.address().port}`,
  );
});
```

Listing 3.20 Using the "debugger" Statement

If you start your script now, as shown in Listing 3.21, and continue the execution using the c command, the application is ready to accept requests from clients.

```
$ node inspect server.mjs
< Debugger listening on ws://127.0.0.1:9229/5a149c3f-d4c3-4529-bc84-045a72f49357
< For help, see: https://nodejs.org/en/docs/inspector
<
< Debugger attached.
<
 OK
Break on start in server.mjs:1
> 1 import { createServer } from 'http';
  2
  3 const server = createServer((request, response) => {
debug> c
< Server is listening to http://localhost:8080
<
break in server.mjs:7
  5
  6    const url = new URL(request.url, 'http://localhost:8080');
> 7    debugger;
  8    const body = `<!DOCTYPE html>
  9      <html>
debug>
```

Listing 3.21 Running an Application in Debug Mode

If you now access the web server via a web browser using the URL *http://localhost:8080/?name=user*, the execution will be interrupted within the callback function. Then the familiar features of the debugger will be available.

If you start your application in debug mode, it will run until the debugger hits the first breakpoint. During initial execution, you thus only have the option of setting a breakpoint via a debugger statement in the code. The --inspect-brk option provides help here by ensuring that the debugger stops at the first line; you can then connect to your developer tools, set breakpoints, and run the application.

3.3.4 Debugging with Chrome Developer Tools

The V8 inspector is integrated in the Node.js debugger and is responsible for opening a WebSocket to the outside world through which you can connect various tools to your debugging session. This makes it possible for you not only to debug on the command line but also to use graphical tools. The most convenient variant is to use Chrome in this context. The connection is established via the *Chrome DevTools Protocol*.

Instead of starting the debugger via the `inspect` option as before, you must use the `--inspect` option for remote debugging. Listing 3.22 shows the corresponding output.

```
$ node --inspect server.mjs
Debugger listening on ws://127.0.0.1:9229/53dc01a4-d65e-47a9-bb88-bc38b4e059d5
For help, see: https://nodejs.org/en/docs/inspector
Server is listening to http://localhost:8080
```

Listing 3.22 Remote Debugging

As you can see in the output, the application doesn't stop; it just waits for incoming debugging connections as well as regular client requests. To be able to connect your browser to the running debug process, you should now enter "chrome://inspect" in the address bar of the browser. You'll then see an overview of all available remote targets, as shown in Figure 3.5.

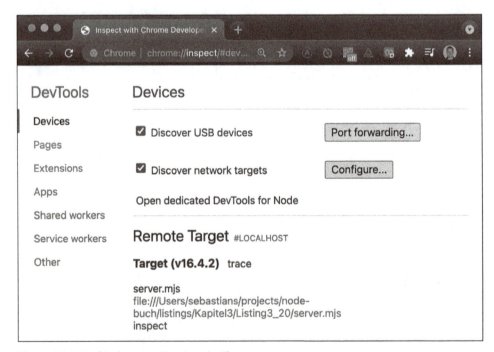

Figure 3.5 List of Debugging Sessions in Chrome

When you now click on the **inspect** link, another browser window will open, consisting only of the developer tools. These are associated with your Node.js process. You'll now see all console messages in the **Console** tab of the Chrome DevTools as well. To inspect your source code, go to the **Sources** tab. There you can make selections from the files of your application in the left-hand pane. Clicking on one of these files displays the source code. At this point, you can set breakpoints by clicking on the corresponding line number. As soon as the execution of the application reaches this line, the process stops, and you have control over the runtime environment. Figure 3.6 shows an example of such a debugging session.

In this mode, just like on the console, you can create watch expressions, navigate through your application with the debugger, or manipulate the environment via the console. You also have access to all available variable scopes and the current backtrace. In addition to these functions, you can use the profiler to create CPU profiles and use the **Memory** tab to analyze the memory utilization of your application.

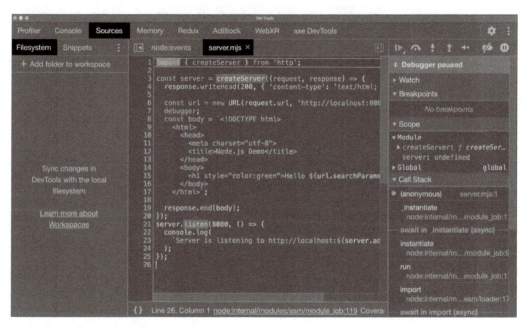

Figure 3.6 Active Debugging Session

3.3.5 Debugging in the Development Environment

However, the actual development process takes place neither on the command line nor in the browser, but in your development environment. Most development environments used in web development, such as Visual Studio Code or the development environments of JetBrains (e.g., WebStorm), help you debug Node.js applications. The corresponding plug-ins are either included by default or can be easily installed later. For information on how to configure the debugger in your development environment, you should refer to the documentation for your development environment, which usually contains detailed step-by-step instructions.

If you use the debugger in your development environment, you can access the same features of the debugger as has already been possible on the command line. Thus, you can skip subroutines or dive deeper into the structures. But you also have the option to set breakpoints or to read the values of certain variables.

These features, combined with the capabilities of a graphical development environment, increase the level of convenience during the development and maintenance of Node.js applications.

3.4   nodemon Development Tool

While developing a Node.js application, you'll regularly come across a specific problem: you must get your customized source code into the running process for your changes to take effect. In the simplest case, you write a block of code, save it, switch to the command line, abort the current process using the shortcut $\boxed{\texttt{Ctrl}}$+$\boxed{\texttt{C}}$, and restart it. Then you switch to the browser and check the effect of your changes. If the frequency of changes is high, you'll go through these steps many times. At this point, it's important to reduce the operations to be performed to a minimum. Restarting the process especially offers the potential for automation. Today, there's a large number of tools available that can do this job for you. One of the most popular is nodemon.

> **Warning! Don't Use Nodemon in Production Mode**
> Note that tools such as nodemon should only be used during development, but never in production. An accidental restart while users are connected to your application can cause severe problems.

You can install nodemon via npm using the npm install -g nodemon command. This will make nodemon globally available for use on your system. In the simplest case, to run your application, you should replace the node command with nodemon. Listing 3.23 shows the execution of the web server example via nodemon.

```
$ nodemon server.mjs
[nodemon] 1.19.3
[nodemon] to restart at any time, enter `rs`
[nodemon] watching dir(s): *.*
[nodemon] watching extensions: js,mjs,json
[nodemon] starting `node server.mjs`
Server is listening to http://localhost:8080
```

Listing 3.23 Running an Application with "nodemon"

As soon as nodemon is started, and you modify a file in your project—in this case, the *server.mjs* file—the process will automatically restart. When using nodemon, however, you should keep in mind that such a restart will cause the current state, that is, all variable assignments, to be lost.

As is stated in the output of nodemon, you don't necessarily have to save a file to cause a restart. You can also enter "rs" in the console where nodemon is running. In addition to this direct control option, you can also manipulate the behavior of nodemon via a configuration file. In this context, it's recommended to name that file *nodemon.json*. This file is passed with the --config nodemon.json option. Listing 3.24 contains an example of such a configuration file.

```
{
  "verbose": true,
  "ignore": ["*.spec.js"],
  "execMap": {
    "rb": "ruby"
  }
}
```

Listing 3.24 Configuring "nodemon"

The verbose property activates an additional log output on the command line. With ignore, you can specify files whose modification should not lead to an automatic restart of the process. Finally, execMap is a feature that allows you to automatically start not only JavaScript, but any other scripts, such as Ruby in this case. The execMap property contains a mapping from the file extension to the executing program. For example, if you call nodemon index.rb with this configuration, the script will be executed in Ruby.

As an alternative to the *nodemon.json* file, you can also store the nodemon configuration directly in the *package.json* file of your project under the nodemonConfig key.

Last but not least, nodemon also supports the debugging of Node.js applications. You can use the --inspect or --inspect-brk options for remote debugging or inspect for interactive debugging on the command line.

3.5 Summary

In this chapter, you learned how to use the REPL to launch interactive sessions with Node.js to run lightweight experiments. You know how to launch regular Node.js applications on the command line by passing the file name of the initial file. You've also been introduced to the http module in the form of a simple web server and used it to develop your first application.

The built-in debugger of the Node.js platform enables you to troubleshoot within a running application. You can use it both interactively on the command line and remotely via the Chrome DevTools or a development environment.

With nodemon, you finally got to know a tool that automatically restarts your application to let changes to the source code take effect.

Chapter 4
Node.js Modules

The whole is more than the sum of its parts.
—Aristotle

The structure of Node.js is inspired by the Unix philosophy. In essence, this philosophy states that software should consist of components that focus on completing only one specific task. These components work together via interfaces to form the overall system. This idea runs through the entire structure of Node.js—from the core libraries to your own application. This chapter is designed to help you understand the Node.js module system and how you can use it when building your applications.

4.1 Modular Structure

You can compare the structure of Node.js to an onion. The platform is made up of several layers, each of which serves a specific purpose. Figure 4.1 illustrates this structure.

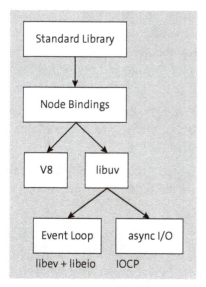

Figure 4.1 Structure of Node.js

The core of Node.js is the *V8 engine* and some additional libraries such as libuv or openssl. This layer represents the execution environment and is written in C++. Most developers working with Node.js don't come into direct contact with these components.

The layer that surrounds the core of the platform is referred to as *node bindings* and represents the transition between C++ and JavaScript. This part of the platform makes it possible that parts of Node.js itself are implemented in JavaScript and can also be used directly when you implement applications.

The final layer of the actual Node.js platform—the *standard library*—consists of the core modules. With this interface, you work directly in the development of your applications. The task of the core modules is to give you access to the interfaces of your system, so that you can access the file system or the network, for example. Besides modularization, another goal of Node.js developers is to keep the platform relatively small, o Node.js is just a tool that provides the basic functionality for your application. You have to take care of everything else yourself, which means, for example, you would have to implement access to a database or the WebSocket protocol yourself. But this contradicts the philosophy of Node.js, which envisions many small and reusable components. For this reason, package managers exist for Node.js—most notably Node Package Manager (npm), which is very closely tied to the platform.

The package managers or the external packages form another layer in the Node.js architecture and provide you with almost all conceivable modules you need when implementing an application. In the broadest sense of the word, a *module* is a library in Node.js that can be loaded via the module system and then used in an application. A *package* consists of one or more modules that have been combined into one package. This package can then be installed via a package manager. The range of available packages extends from auxiliary libraries such as *lodash* and database drivers to complete application frameworks or content management systems (CMSs). And if you don't find the package you need, you can always write and publish it yourself. See Chapter 21 to learn how to do that.

Finally, the last layer is your own application. Here, you should also take a modular approach. This means that your application consists of many small self-contained parts that interact with each other via defined interfaces.

Figure 4.2 contains an example for the structuring of an application. You should pay particular attention to the meaningful naming of directories and files, which makes it much easier to find source code.

Application Structure

Modularization is the key to a maintainable and extensible application. However, this doesn't mean that every Node.js application has to be a composite of microservices. Instead, you should choose an appropriate architectural form for each problem. A monolith with a modular structure can also be a valid solution strategy for a clearly defined problem.

When modularizing, you should make sure that each module is in its own file and contains only a manageable number of functions or exactly one concrete object or class. You should also make sure that the content of a module is always thematically very similar and solves only one very specific task at a time. Give your module structures meaningful names that are consistent across your entire application. You can then further arrange the individual files in a directory structure, where a directory should again contain modules from the same theme.

To keep an application organized, you shouldn't place too many files in a single directory. As a safe guideline, you can use 7–10 files per directory. If there are more, you should create subdirectories.

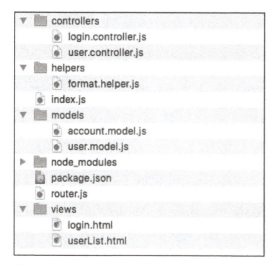

Figure 4.2 Structure of an Application

Modularization in software development has some decisive advantages:

- Reusability of subcomponents
- Better testability due to small, self-contained components
- Parallelizability during development due to the independence of the components
- Interchangeability of individual components through defined interfaces

At the core of Node.js, the modular design allows developers to continuously modernize the platform by marking individual features or modules as deprecated or adding new modules. The following sections describe which modules make up this core.

4.2   Core Modules

The basic building blocks of an application are the core modules such as the HTTP or file system module. You can find documentation on these modules at *https://*

nodejs.org/api/. This link refers to the documentation of the current Node.js version and covers all interfaces, describes how to use them, and gives you numerous concrete code examples. The documentation is managed using the source code of the platform. You can also download it directly and get access to the description of older versions. Alternatively, you can view these older versions using the **View another version link** in the header of the documentation page.

If this information isn't sufficient for you and research on the internet doesn't provide the expected result, you can still access the source code of the respective module directly. This can be found in the GitHub repository of the Node.js project at *https:// github.com/nodejs/node* in the *lib* directory. In addition to the source code itself, you can also access a large number of unit tests that further describe the use of the respective interfaces using concrete test cases.

In the early days of Node.js, interfaces changed very frequently, and there were also frequent *breaking changes*, that is, changes to interfaces that caused problems for existing applications. Meanwhile, developers try to avoid this phenomenon as much as possible. For a list of changes in a release, you must check the project's changelog at *https:// github.com/nodejs/node/blob/master/CHANGELOG.md*.

4.2.1   Stability

The modular approach in the structure of Node.js also supports the stability of the overall system and helps to avoid errors. If one of the modules contains a malfunction, all other modules can still continue to work. Of course, this doesn't apply to central components such as the V8 engine. But, in general, backward compatibility and platform support are very important.

Due to the continuous further development of Node.js, the question arises as to which modules can be used without hesitation, which should no longer be used, and which are better left to wait a while before going live.

For a better overview of the modules and their degree of stability, the stability index was created. You can find the stability of a module in the application programming interface (API) documentation. For each module, the table of contents and the heading of a documentation page are followed by a colored bar indicating the index value. Originally, this value consisted of six levels, then it was reduced to four levels, then to three, and, currently back to four levels, which you'll find briefly described in Table 4.1.

Index	Name	Color code	Description
0	Deprecated	Red	These modules should no longer be used. They will be removed from future versions. When using these features, warnings may be issued. Backward compatibility of these modules isn't guaranteed.

Table 4.1 Stability Index

Index	Name	Color code	Description
1	Experimental	Orange	Modules with this index value are actively developed further, but production use isn't recommended. Changes are to be expected. They aren't subject to semantic versioning; breaking changes can also occur in minor updates.
2	Stable	Green	There will be hardly any changes in these modules. Compatibility is interrupted only in rare cases. The developers place great emphasis on compatibility with the npm ecosystem.
3	Legacy	Blue	The use of these features isn't recommended. They are subject to semantic versioning and will continue to be part of the platform in the near future.

Table 4.1 Stability Index (Cont.)

An example of a *deprecated* module is the domain module. It was an attempt to create an error domain for handling errors in one area of an application. This module has proven to be unhelpful over several years and will no longer be supported in the future. The **Deprecated** status is also applied to numerous methods of existing modules. For example, you shouldn't use the exists method of the fs module in the future. In most cases, the documentation will give you tips about functionality that you can use instead.

Of the existing functionalities, only the JavaScript Object Notation (JSON) output of the documentation has **Experimental** status for a longer period of time. New features, such as the async_hooks module or the diagnostics_channel module, are marked as experimental until they are stabilized.

Most modules in the Node.js platform have the index status **Stable**. This means that while the API may change, developers pay special attention to backward compatibility with older versions. Typical examples of **Stable** status modules are the stream, http, and fs modules.

An important goal in Node.js development is to keep the platform organized and manageable. For this reason, there is only a comparatively small number of core modules.

4.2.2   List of Core Modules

Table 4.2 provides an overview of the core modules of the Node.js platform.

Module	Description
assert	This is the testing module of Node.js used to cover the platform itself with unit tests.

Table 4.2 Overview of the Node.js Modules

Module	Description
async_hooks	This module allows and simplifies the tracking of asynchronous resources during their lifecycle.
buffer	This module helps to handle binary data for the file system or network operations.
child_process	This module allows you to create and control child processes and communicate between processes.
cluster	This module is an extension of the child_process module for dynamic load balancing between processes.
console	This module represents a wrapper around the standard output.
crypto	This module provides encryption under Node.js.
dgram	This module enables you to establish User Datagram Protocol (UDP) connections and communicate through them.
dns	This module resolves names via Domain Name System (DNS).
domain	This module deals with grouping operations and handling errors that occur.
events	The events module provides the infrastructure for registering and triggering events.
fs	The fs module is used to gain both read and write access to the system's file system.
http	This module helps you create HTTP clients and servers.
http2	With this module, the HTTP/2 protocol is now natively supported by Node.js. HTTP/2 represents a further development of HTTP.
https	This module enables encrypted communication both as HTTP client and server.
inspector	This module represents the interface to the V8 inspector.
modules	With this module, the Node.js module system is itself implemented as a module.
net	This module is the basis for network servers and clients.
os	This module allows you to read information about the operating system.
path	This module contains all the important operations for handling directory paths.

Table 4.2 Overview of the Node.js Modules (Cont.)

Module	Description
perf_hooks	This module allows you to make highly accurate time measurements in your application.
process	What the os module is to the operating system, the process module is to the current Node.js process.
punycode	This module deals with the standard-compliant conversion of Unicode characters to ASCII characters.
querystring	This module greatly simplifies the handling of query strings in URLs.
readline	Due to this module, a stream can be consumed line by line.
repl	This module represents the read-eval-print loop (REPL), which is the command line of Node.js.
stream	This module API provides different types of data streams.
string_decoder	This module can be used to convert buffer objects into strings.
timers	This module contains all time-based functions.
tls	This module is the interface to the public/private key infrastructure for secure communication.
trace_events	With this module, tracing information from the V8 engine, the Node platform as well as customized tracing information from the user can be processed centrally.
tty	This module represents the connection to the terminal, for example, the standard input and output.
url	This module is used to generate or parse URLs.
util	This module collects helpful functions such as type queries, formatting, and the like.
v8	This module enables you to work directly with the V8 engine.
vm	This module provides an environment for executing JavaScript code.
wasi	This module can be used to integrate WebAssembly modules or entire applications into Node.js. The module represents an implementation of the WebAssembly system interface specification.
worker_threads	In addition to the child_process module, this module helps to offload routines from the main process. The focus of the worker_threads module is on CPU-intensive calculations.
zlib	This module deals with the compression and decompression of information.

Table 4.2 Overview of the Node.js Modules (Cont.)

Some of the modules presented here serve as an interface to the operating system, such as the net or fs modules. Others implement protocols or define commonly used structures such as the http modules or the events module. The latter are often used by Node.js itself to build other core modules. Parts of the fs module, for example, use the stream module to map data streams; this module in turn is based on the events module.

4.2.3   Loading Core Modules

The core modules of Node.js are loaded through the platform's module system, with some exceptions. Currently, the platform is in a state of transition, as the previously used CommonJS module system is being switched to the ECMAScript modules. Of course, such a drastic change takes time, which is why the transition to the new modular system has already taken years. In the course of this book, we'll mainly use the ECMAScript module system. However, in this section, you'll get to know both module systems and their respective characteristics.

Loading Core Modules via the CommonJS Module System

The original Node.js module system uses the require function to load structures. Listing 4.1 shows an example of loading the os module to display the uptime of the system.

```
// Loading the entire module
const os = require('os');
console.log(os.uptime());

// Loading the module and extracting certain functions by means of destructuring
const { uptime } = require('os');
console.log(uptime());
```

Listing 4.1 Loading Core Modules

Each of the core modules exports an object through which you can use the functionality of the respective module. Normally, you assign the return value of the require function to a variable that has the same name as the module and then call the respective required functions. In the code example, you can see both this variant and how you can directly extract the required interfaces with a *destructuring* statement.

> **Destructuring**
>
> If you want to store individual properties of objects or elements from arrays in several variables, several operations are necessary, as you can see in Listing 4.2.
>
> ```
> const person = {
>   name: 'Lisa',
>   age: 32
> };
> ```

```
const name = person.name;
const age = person.age;
```

Listing 4.2 Variable Assignment of Object Properties

For both objects and arrays, you can combine such operations by using destructuring. This feature has been part of the standard version since ECMAScript 2015 and is now available in all modern browsers. You can write the code from Listing 4.2 in a more compact way using destructuring, as shown in Listing 4.3.

```
const person = {
  name: 'Lisa',
  age: 32
};

const { name, age } = person;

console.log('Name: ', name); // Output: Name: Lisa
console.log('Age: ', age); // Output: Age: 32

const person2 = ['John', 17];
const [name2, age2] = person2;

console.log('Name: ', name2); // Output: Name: John
console.log('Age: ', age2); // Output: Age: 17
```

Listing 4.3 Destructuring Statement

The code example also shows that you can use square brackets instead of curly brackets for arrays and thus assign the individual elements to variables. You can also apply destructuring to deeper levels and combine destructuring for objects and arrays as you wish. However, you should be careful not to overdo it, as it can easily get very confusing.

Loading Core Modules via the ECMAScript Module System

The official module system of JavaScript takes a slightly different approach than the previously used ECMAScript module system. With regard to loading structures, the most important change is that the import keyword replaces the require function. The core modules of Node.js have a default export that is broadly similar to the behavior of the old module system. In addition, each module exports its public interface as named exports, which you can compare to the destructuring statement we used earlier. Listing 4.4 shows how you can use the default export of the core modules.

```
import os from 'os';

console.log(os.uptime());
```

Listing 4.4 Including Core Modules with a Default Import

Listing 4.5 shows the second variant; that is, using named exports.

```
import { uptime } from 'os';

console.log(uptime());
```

Listing 4.5 Including Core Modules with a Named Import

It's up to you which of the two variants you use in your application, but make sure to implement your source code as consistently as possible and use the same variants throughout, as this significantly increases the readability of the source code.

ECMAScript Module System

Currently, the CommonJS module system is still the standard for Node.js. Although this will change in the future, keep that in mind if you want to work with the ECMAScript module system. There are three ways to enable the ECMAScript module system:

- **File extension .mjs**
  You've already learned about this variant. If a file name ends with *.mjs*, Node.js automatically ensures that the ECMAScript module system is activated.

- **type field in the package.json file**
  Alternatively, you can set the type field in the *package.json* file to the module value. If you do that, your files can keep the usual *.js* extension.

- **--input-type flag**
  The third variant is to start your Node.js process with the command-line option --input-type=module. Again, if you decide to do that, you can keep using the *.js* file extension.

---

package.json File

You can use the type field in the *package.json* file to enable the ECMAScript module system. But this file can do much more, as you'll learn in the course of this book. At this point, the only important thing for you to know is that this is the central description file for your application. You store information in it, such as the name or version number of your application. In addition, the file contains a list of all dependencies that your application requires.

You can have npm create a *package.json* file on the command line by running the npm init command. You'll then be asked a series of questions about your project. In addition, you can use the -y option to have these questions answered with the default answers.

Besides the core modules that you must load explicitly, there are some globally available structures you can use in your application. There are also some differences here between the CommonJS module system and the ECMAScript module system, which we'll describe in more detail in the following section.

4.2.4   Global Objects

The developers of Node.js have chosen to make individual objects and functions available globally and within the scope of a module, respectively, for several reasons. For some, it's simply necessary that they are there because without them, you wouldn't be able to develop your application. This includes, for example, the modular system. Other objects and functions are also globally available in the browser and have been adopted in Node.js, such as the console object and the timing functions. The third category provides commonly used functionalities, such as the __filename constant. Table 4.3 provides an overview of the global objects in Node.js.

Variable Name	Variable Name
__dirname	__filename
Buffer	clearImmediate()
clearInterval()	clearTimeout()
console	Event
EventTarget	exports
global	MessageChannel
MessageEvent	MessagePort
module	performance
process	queueMicrotask()
require()	setImmediate()
setInterval()	setTimeout()
TextDecoder	TextEncoder
URL	URLSearcchParams
WebAssembly	

Table 4.3 Global Objects in Node.js

In addition to these Node.js-specific objects, numerous other classes and objects are included in the JavaScript standard, for example, the string and array classes.

In the following sections, we'll briefly introduce the individual global objects and their possible uses.

File and Directory Name

Two variables that are very useful in application development are __filename and __dirname. As the names of these variables already suggest, both contain information about the location of the file, which stores the source code of the currently executed script. The string in __filename is the absolute path and file name of the script. __dirname is just the path.

You get the name of the file or directory where the variable is used, even if it's included elsewhere via the module system.

When used in the REPL, note that neither __filename nor __dirname is defined, as there is no script in this case. Accessing these variables will result in a ReferenceError.

The same restriction applies to the ECMAScript module system. If you try to access these two variables, the system will return a ReferenceError. However, there is a way to obtain the information of the current file and directory name, as shown in Listing 4.6.

```
import { dirname } from 'path';
import { fileURLToPath } from 'url';

const __filename = fileURLToPath(import.meta.url);
const __dirname = dirname(__filename);

console.log(__filename);
console.log(__dirname);
```

Listing 4.6 Simulating __filename and __dirname for the ECMAScript Module System

You can use the import.meta.url property to display the absolute file name of the current script. Here, however, Node.js adds the protocol at the beginning—in this case, the file:// string. To obtain the pure absolute path, you must use the fileURLToPath function from the url module. You get the directory name by passing the absolute file name to the dirname function from the path module.

Buffer

The buffer class is also available globally because you deal with this type of object very often in Node.js. Buffer objects are used whenever binary data handling is involved. Listing 4.7 contains an example that shows how you can come into contact with buffer objects—sometimes unintentionally.

```
import { readFile } from 'fs';

readFile('input.txt', (err, data) => {
```

```
    console.log(data); // Output: <Buffer 48 61 6c 6c 6f 20 57 65 6c 74>
    console.log(data.toString()); // Output: Hello world
});
```

Listing 4.7 Buffer Objects When Reading Files

In this example, you read the contents of the *input.txt* file and write it to standard output. However, because you haven't specified any character encoding here, Node.js reverts to the default handling, which means that it considers the data as a buffer. The most important methods of buffer objects are the toString method for converting to a string and the write method for writing information to the buffer. So, if you want to output the contents of the buffer object to the console, you can use the data.toString method, as shown in the example.

Timing Functions

The timing functions setTimeout, setInterval, and setImmediate aren't part of the ECMAScript language standard. In the browser, they are part of the window object. Because these functions are essential for implementing time-based features, they have been ported to Node.js and are available globally. setTimeout allows you to have a callback function executed after the specified number of milliseconds has elapsed. The setInterval function executes the specified callback function periodically at intervals, and setImmediate runs the callback function at the end of the current event loop cycle. The return value of these three functions can be used in conjunction with the respective clear function, for example, clearTimeout, to abort the corresponding operation.

In Listing 4.8, you first create a counter variable and then start an interval that generates an output every second. Without any further termination condition, the script would continue to run until you finally terminate it manually on the console. To prevent this effect, you must define a termination condition that ensures that processing is terminated after three runs.

```
let counter = 1;
const interval = setInterval(() => {
  console.log(`${counter} iteration`);
  if (counter++ > 2) {
    clearInterval(interval);
  }
}, 1000);
```

Listing 4.8 Using the "setInterval" Function

console

Another functionality you already know from client-side JavaScript—the console object—is also available as a global object and is mainly used for output on the command line during development. Besides the well-known console.log method, there are numerous other helpful methods in the console object. Table 4.4 provides a list of the most important methods.

Method	Description
debug, info, warn, error	These methods represent different logging priorities.
group, groupEnd	These methods are used to visually group console outputs.
time, timeEnd	These methods allow for a simple time measurement. With time, you can set a marker, while timeEnd ends the time measurement and outputs the result.
trace	This method outputs the current stack trace.

Table 4.4 Most Important Methods of the "console" Object

Global Event API

The two classes, EventTarget and Event, are implementations of the client-side event API. In the broadest sense, you can compare EventTarget to, for example, a button element in the browser that a user has clicked. The biggest difference is that the element structure in the browser is hierarchical, which isn't the case in Node.js. This means that the events aren't passed through an element tree, but are only triggered at EventTarget. Listing 4.9 shows an example of how you can use the two event classes.

```
const target = new EventTarget();

target.addEventListener('customEvent', (event) => {
  console.log(`${event.type} was triggered`);
    // Output: customEvent was triggered
});

const event = new Event('customEvent');

target.dispatchEvent(event);
```

Listing 4.9 Using the Event API

In the example, you first create an EventTarget instance on which you register an event handler for the customEvent type via the addEventListener method. You can choose these event types yourself. Then you create an event object of the customEvent type and trigger it via the dispatchEvent method of the EventTarget.

Later in this book, you'll learn about yet another way to handle events in Node.js via the EventEmitter class from the events module. This class forms the basis for numerous internal and external modules in Node.js.

CommonJS Module System

You can also access the Node.js-specific functions and objects of the module system from anywhere within your module. The require function enables you to load external dependencies, while exports or the module object are used to make information available outside your module. You can also use this object to control other aspects of the module system. We'll introduce the module system of Node.js in more detail later in Section 4.3. More recent versions of Node.js provide the ECMAScript module system with the import and export keywords too.

global: Global Scope

In client-side JavaScript, you have the global scope for variables in addition to the block, function, and closure scopes. Node.js doesn't contain anything like that. If you define a variable in a file, you can only access it within this file, so the variable is only valid within the module. If you add a new property to the global object, it will be available as a global property in your entire application, that is, even across file boundaries. Listing 4.10 illustrates how you can use the global object.

```
function createGlobal() {
  global.myName = 'Peter';
}
createGlobal();
console.log(myName);
```

Listing 4.10 Using the "global" Object

In Listing 4.10 you first create a function in which you set the global variable. Then the function is called, and the content of the global variable is output. On a larger scale, setting and accessing global variables also works across file boundaries.

> **Avoid Using Global Variables!**
> At this point, we strongly advise against the use of global variables. They lead to potential name conflicts with local variables and generally make your application harder to read and more error-prone.

Message System for Communicating with Worker Processes

You can use three classes, MessageChannel, MessageEvent, and MessagePort, for the communication between worker processes. The MessagePort class represents the end of a bidirectional communication channel, which in turn is represented by the MessageChannel class. The implementation is based on the MessagePort implementation of the browser.

As you can see in Listing 4.11, the MessageChannel class creates a new object with the two properties port1 and port2, each of which is an instance of the MessagePort class and represent the two endpoints of the communication channel. You can now use these objects to send messages between both ports. Chapter 16 provides further information about worker processes.

```
const { port1, port2 } = new MessageChannel();

port1.on('message', (message) => {
  console.log(message);
});

port2.postMessage({ data: 'Hello world' });
```

Listing 4.11 Using the MessageChannel Class

performance

The performance object is a reference to the perf_hooks module that you can use to measure performance in your application. For more information on this interface and other performance aspects, see Chapter 26.

process

The global process object isn't a full-fledged Node.js module; its source code isn't located in the *lib* directory of the Node.js platform. The process object is your interface to the current Node.js process running your application. For example, you access standard output, standard input, and standard error output via process.stdout, process.stdin, and process.stderr.

You can also use the process object to terminate your application in a controlled manner. For example, with a call of the exit method, to which you optionally pass a status code, you can end the current process, as is shown in Listing 4.12.

```
$ node
> process.exit(42);
$ echo $?
42
```

Listing 4.12 Return Value of Node.js Applications

With echo $?, you can query the return value of the last application on the Unix shell. A value other than 0 means that an error occurred during execution. Depending on how you choose this value, you can use it to encode more information.

The abort method is a little more drastic than process.exit. Here, the shutdown no longer happens in a controlled manner. Besides these two methods, you can also use the kill method, which accepts a process ID as the first argument and a signal to be sent as the second, optional argument. Normally, this is SIGTERM, which leads to the termination of the process. Listing 4.13 shows how you can use the kill method.

```
$ node
> process.kill(process.pid, 'SIGKILL');
Killed: 9
$ echo $?
137
```

Listing 4.13 Ending Processes with "kill"

You can use the argv property of the process object to access the command-line call of your application. Assuming you call your application via the node server.js --env= debug command line, argv contains an array of three elements. The first element is the node command itself, the second is the absolute path and name of the JavaScript file, and the third is the specified --env=debug option.

The env property provides the environment variables of the current Node.js process. Part of the information is, for example, the user's name, the PATH variable, and the user's home directory.

You can use the process object to read the versions of the Node.js platform. process.version returns the version of Node.js itself. process.versions also contains the version information of additional libraries, such as libuv, zlib, openssl, or the V8 engine. In Figure 4.3, you can see the output of these versions.

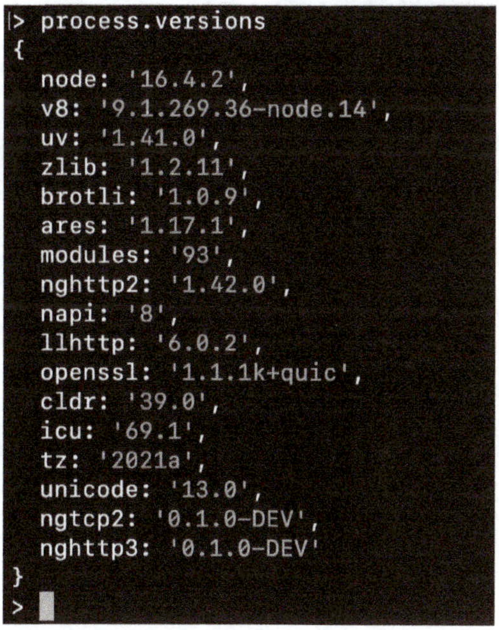

```
> process.versions
{
  node: '16.4.2',
  v8: '9.1.269.36-node.14',
  uv: '1.41.0',
  zlib: '1.2.11',
  brotli: '1.0.9',
  ares: '1.17.1',
  modules: '93',
  nghttp2: '1.42.0',
  napi: '8',
  llhttp: '6.0.2',
  openssl: '1.1.1k+quic',
  cldr: '39.0',
  icu: '69.1',
  tz: '2021a',
  unicode: '13.0',
  ngtcp2: '0.1.0-DEV',
  nghttp3: '0.1.0-DEV'
}
>
```

Figure 4.3 Output of Node.js Versions

With the process object, you can also actively manipulate the current process. For example, you can change the user under which the current process is running via process.setuid. To do that, however, you need the permission to change the user; otherwise, you'll receive an error message. You can obtain the currently set user ID by using the process.getuid method. Similar to the user ID, you can also use the two methods, process.setgid and process.getgid, with the group ID.

The object exported through the process module also represents an EventEmitter. This means that in certain situations, the module triggers events that you can subscribe to. Table 4.5 contains an overview of the events with a short description of each.

Event	Description
beforeExit	This event is triggered when the event loop has no further work, causing the application to be terminated.
disconnect	This event is triggered when the communication channel between a parent and its child process is interrupted.
exit	This event is triggered when the process is about to finish.
message	You can create child processes via the child_process module. You can communicate between the individual processes via messages. As soon as a process receives a message, the message event is triggered.
multipleResolves	This event is triggered when a promise has been resolved or rejected more than once, or when it has been resolved again after a reject or rejected again after a resolve. The triggering of this event is an indicator of potential error sources in the application.
rejectionHandled	This event is triggered if a promise is rejected and this is intercepted by a handler function.
uncaughtException	If an exception is launched in your application, it usually causes the process to terminate. By handling this event, you can manipulate the default behavior.
unhandledRejection	This event acts similarly to the rejectionHandled event, except that it's triggered for promises that don't have rejection handlers.
warning	This event is triggered when a warning is launched in your application.
worker	This event is triggered after a worker process has been created. The argument you get is a reference to the created worker process in the event handler function.

Table 4.5 Events of the "process" Module

When dealing with asynchronicity in the context of promises, one of these events is particularly helpful. The unhandledRejection event is triggered when a promise failure isn't handled in your application. Listing 4.14 contains a code example for this.

```
process.on('unhandledRejection', (error) => {
  console.error('unhandledRejection'); // Output: unhandledRejection
  console.error(error);                 // Output: Whoops, an Error occurred
});

function withPromise() {
  return Promise.reject('Whoops, an Error occurred');
}

withPromise().then(() => {
  console.log('Promise resolved');
});
```

Listing 4.14 Unhandled Promise Rejection

queueMicrotask

Asynchronicity is ubiquitous in JavaScript, and thus also in Node.js. Chapter 16 describes these aspects of implementing JavaScript applications in great detail. At this point, we want to give you an outlook on the topic and the context of the execution sequence. There are different types of asynchroncity in Node.js. These mainly concern the order of execution. One of the core components of Node.js is the event loop, which is responsible for registering and executing event handlers. The individual runs of the event loop are divided into different phases, as demonstrated in Listing 4.15.

```
setTimeout(() => {
  console.log('setTimeout');
}, 0);
Promise.resolve().then(() => {
  console.log('Promise');
});
queueMicrotask(() => {
  console.log('queueMicrotask');
});
process.nextTick(() => {
  console.log('nextTick');
});

// Output:
// nextTick
```

```
// Promise
// queueMicrotask
// setTimeout
```

Listing 4.15 Asynchronous Operations in Node.js

In Listing 4.15, you can see that the output doesn't correspond to the order of registration of the respective callback functions. The process.nextTick method is the smallest unit you can use. To be precise, it's not part of the event loop, but it's executed between the different phases of the event loop. Node.js first executes the microtasks—these include directly resolved promises as well as callback functions that you register with the queueMicrotask function. Then the asynchronous tasks are executed, which you can register for example with the timing functions, setImmediate, setTimeout, or setInterval.

TextEncoder and TextDecoder

The TextEncoder and TextDecoder classes are intended for working with TypedArrays in JavaScript. These are data structures that work with binary raw data. The instances of the Node.js buffer class are also instances of Uint8Array and TypedArray. There are minor incompatibilities between the buffer and TypedArray classes, but in general both behave in a very similar way and are used to exchange data within an application. In Listing 4.16, you can see how you can convert a string into a Uint8Array and then decode it again.

```
const textEncoder = new TextEncoder();
const encodedString = textEncoder.encode('Hello World');
console.log(encodedString); // Output: Uint8Array(11) [72,101,108,108,
                            //   111,32,87,111,114,108,100]

const textDecoder = new TextDecoder();
const decodedString = textDecoder.decode(encodedString);
console.log(decodedString); // Output: Hello World
```

Listing 4.16 Using TextEncoder and TextDecoder

URL and URLSearchParams

In Node.js, you often deal with URLs, which is why the platform provides you with the URL class as well as URLSearchParams globally (see Listing 4.17), so you don't have to load them separately.

```
const url = new URL('/dist/latest-v16.x/docs/api/', 'https://nodejs.org');

console.log(url.href); // Output: https://nodejs.org/dist/
                       //   latest-v16.x/docs/api/
```

```
const searchParams = new URLSearchParams();
searchParams.set('name', 'john');
searchParams.set('age', 42);
console.log(searchParams.toString()); // Output: name=john&age=42
```

Listing 4.17 Working with URLs in Node.js

The URL class represents the various aspects of a URL, such as the protocol, host name, or path. You can use the URLSearchParams class either implicitly along with a URL instance and the searchParams property, or explicitly as a standalone instance.

WebAssembly

The WebAssembly object controls access to the WebAssembly interfaces of the V8 engine. Using this interface, you can work with WebAssembly within your Node.js application and, for example, outsource performance-critical components.

4.3   JavaScript Module Systems

You already got to know the module systems of Node.js in the approach when we looked at the core modules of Node.js. In the following sections, we'll take a closer look at the module systems, and you'll learn how to split your application into multiple files in both the CommonJS and ECMAScript module systems, as well as how the module systems work together.

4.3.1   CommonJS

In Node.js, a module is a self-encapsulated scope for variables. This means that you can define variables at the top level in a file, and they are valid only in the module. This avoids the accidental definition of global variables. However, this also means that without the module system, you have no way to use functionality from your module in your application. A module never stands for itself; instead, it's a component of a larger application. With the exports or module.exports object, you can define the interface of your module, which you can then use in other modules. Listing 4.18 contains an example of an export of a simple function.

```
module.exports = function(a, b) {
  return a + b;
};
```

Listing 4.18 Exporting a Function (add.js)

The CommonJS module system provides that you load modules represented by files using the require function. This function returns an object representing the public

121

interface of the file. You can use the functionality of the module via this object. Listing 4.19 shows how you can include the previously exported function.

```
const add = require('./add');

const result = add(1, 2);
console.log('result: ', result);
```

Listing 4.19 Using Modules (index.js)

In Listing 4.19, it's assumed that you've saved the source code from Listing 4.18 in a file named *add.js*. You can choose the names of your modules as well as their location. Just make sure that the path specification for the import is correct. When importing, you pass the path to the file you want to include to the require function. In this context, you can choose between absolute and relative paths. An absolute path starts from the root of the file system; a relative path starts from the current file. Specifying the file extension during import is optional. When loading modules via the require method, the module loader looks not only for the specified file but also for the file name. If no file extension is specified, the module loader appends the extensions *.js*, *.json*, and *.node*.

4.3.2 ECMAScript Modules

The basic principle of ECMAScript modules is similar to that of CommonJS modules. The biggest difference between both module systems can be found in the syntax. As of version 8.5 of Node.js, the ECMAScript modules are part of the platform. Meanwhile, they have reached stability index 2, that is, *stable*, and you can thus use them without hesitation. As you already know, the CommonJS module system is still currently the default in Node.js, so you need to explicitly enable the ECMAScript module system. You can achieve this by using one of the following measures:

- File extension *.mjs*
- type field in *package.json* with the module value
- --input-type option on the command line with the module value

The scope of variables remains limited to the module level, as is the case with CommonJS modules. You can use the export keyword to specify that an object, class, or function can be used from outside the module. Listing 4.20 contains the source code of a module that exports a function.

```
export function add(a, b) {
  return a + b;
}
```

Listing 4.20 Export of a Function (add.mjs)

You can import this function using the `import` keyword. For the code in Listing 4.21 to work, you must save the `add` function from Listing 4.20 in a file named *add.mjs*.

```
import { add } from './add.mjs';

const result = add(1, 2);
console.log('result: ', result);
```

Listing 4.21 Import of a Function (index.mjs)

As with the CommonJS modules, the file name and location are arbitrary, and you can use absolute and relative paths. However, you should prefer relative paths for your application in both cases, as this provides better reusability of your application on other systems.

The ECMAScript module system offers a slightly higher degree of flexibility than CommonJS does. Table 4.6 summarizes the different export variants for you.

Export Statement	Type
export {var1, var2 as alias}	Named
export let var1, var2;	Named
export default <expression>	Default
export * from 'filename'	Default
export {var1, var2 as alias} from 'filename'	Named

Table 4.6 Exports in ECMAScript

As you can see in Table 4.6, there are two types of exports. Named exports allow you to export variables, functions, or classes. With a default export, you export any expression. There can be only one default export per module, but there can be any number of named exports. For named exports, the `as` keyword also enables you to change the name of the exported object. A module can have both a default export and one or more named exports—this means you can also combine the two. Imports provide a similar kind of flexibility as exports. Table 4.7 contains an overview of the different variants.

Import Statement	Type
import * as moduleContent from 'filename';	Named
import {var1, var2 as alias} from 'filename';	Named
import 'filename';	Named

Table 4.7 Imports in ECMAScript

Import Statement	Type
import defaultVar from 'filename'	Default
import defaultVar as aliasVar from 'filename';	Default
import * as defaultVar from 'filename';	Default

Table 4.7 Imports in ECMAScript (Cont.)

With regard to imports, a general distinction is made between a named import and a default import. The first three rows of the table refer to named imports, and the last three rows refer to default imports. If a module contains a default export and a named import, you can combine the second and fourth rows of the table, as shown in Listing 4.22.

```
import divide, {add} from './module.mjs';

console.log(divide(4, 2));
console.log(add(2,2));
```

Listing 4.22 Default and Named Imports (index.mjs)

You can find the corresponding exports in Listing 4.23.

```
export function add(a, b) {
  return a + b;
}

export default function(a, b) {
  return a / b;
}
```

Listing 4.23 Module with Default and Named Exports (module.mjs)

You can use both ECMAScript and CommonJS modules in your application. However, you can't load ECMAScript modules using the require function. In that case, you'll have to use the import function. But the ECMAScript module system does allow you to load CommonJS modules. If you import such a module, it behaves as if it were an ECMAScript module with a default export. This applies to both your own modules and npm modules.

4.4   Creating and Using Your Own Modules

If you're working on a Node.js application, you should make it as modular as possible; that is, divide your source code into several files. One of the most important reasons for this type of structuring is clarity. In a file of several thousand lines of source code, finding specific code sections becomes increasingly difficult. It also makes it nearly impossible to reuse code blocks across applications. But reusability within an application is also much more convenient with self-contained modules, each in its own file. Once your application becomes more extensive and complex, and areas with self-contained functionality begin to emerge that can be communicated with via uniform interfaces, the time is right to outsource this source code and integrate it as a module. A sure sign to start modularizing is when you start copying entire blocks of code. In this case, you should swap out the code block and generalize it so that it can be used in multiple places.

4.4.1   Modules in Node.js: CommonJS

For your Node.js application, this principle should be followed: one structure, one file. This means that all logical units of your application are located in their own files. The advantage here is that each file deals with only one topic and has only one defined interface to the rest of the application, so the different parts of your application can be located quickly and easily.

Loose Coupling, Tight Cohesion

This type of modularization uses the principle of *loose coupling*, which means that the structures (i.e., functions, objects, or classes) of an application are only loosely connected via interfaces. This in turn has the benefit that you can replace individual modules without having to rebuild the entire system.

The components of the individual modules must be closely related to each other, which is referred to as *tight cohesion*. This means that only the logic actually belonging to the topic of the module is placed in a module. Everything else is swapped to a separate module and addressed via interfaces.

As a result, you have an application that consists of numerous manageable modules, which ultimately leads to improved maintainability, greater parallelizability of tasks, better testability of the source code, and better responsiveness to changing requirements.

Normally, when you build your application, you group your modules according to topics. When outsourcing blocks of code that are used multiple times, the trick is to find the right balance between generalization and effort. As a guideline here, you should keep in mind to always primarily solve your current problem and only ever generalize as much as is necessary for your application. If you write code that is too generic, it automatically becomes more complex, harder to read, and more expensive to implement.

In practice, your modules usually export either classes that you instantiate in other modules or functions and objects you can interact with directly. A good example is provided by the modules that Node.js makes available to you.

4.4.2   Custom Node.js Modules

In the following example, you'll implement a function to count the frequency of words in a sentence. This function is exported via the module system. The first variant shows the implementation in the CommonJS module system, and the second shows it in the ECMAScript module system.

First, in Listing 4.24, a period and comma are stored in a regular expression to ignore these characters during processing. The space character as word separator is also stored in a constant. The wordCount function itself accepts a string in which you first replace periods and commas with an empty string. The string prepared in this way is converted to lowercase to ignore case sensitivity. Then you use the split method to convert the string into an array of words. The actual counting of words is carried out in the reduce method. An empty object is used as the start value. The individual words are used as keys in the object. For each word, either an existing value is increased by one or the initial value is set to one if the word doesn't yet exist as a key in the object.

```
const ignore = /[\.,]/g;
const separator = ' ';
module.exports = function wordCount(sentence) {
  return sentence
    .replace(ignore, '')
    .toLowerCase()
    .split(separator)
    .reduce((prev, current) => {
      prev[current] = prev[current] + 1 || 1;
      return prev;
    }, {});
};
```

Listing 4.24 Implementing the "wordCount" Function as a CommonJS Module (word-count.js)

The function is made available as an interface of the module using the module.exports object, so you can include it in your application using the require function.

The source code from Listing 4.25 shows how you can use the module you just created. Use the wc = require('./word-count') statement to include the module in the current application. This assumes that you've saved the source code from Listing 4.24 in a file named *word-count.js*. All functions and objects that you've assigned as properties to the module.exports object in the module are available.

```
const wc = require('./word-count');
const sentence = 'Where there is much light, there is also much shadow.';
const wordCount = wc(sentence);
console.log(sentence);
for (let i in wordCount) {
```

```
    console.log(wordCount[i] + ' x ' + i);
}
```

Listing 4.25 Using the "wordCount" Module (index.js)

Naming Files and JavaScript Structures

Unlike JavaScript, not all file systems are case sensitive. To prevent problems in this context, you should only use lowercase letters when naming your files. If a file or directory name consists of several words, separate them with a hyphen. The CamelCase designation, on the other hand, is now much more common. Here, the individual words in the file name are introduced with a capital letter.

Note that you can't use hyphens in variable names in JavaScript. This is possible via the array notation when accessing object properties, but you should still avoid it. JavaScript objects and functions begin with a lowercase letter. Otherwise, you can use the CamelCase notation. Only class names start with a capital letter.

As you've seen in Listing 4.25, only the contents and interfaces of a module that are made available through the exports object are published. All other variables, functions, or classes defined within a module are only available in that module. So, in this case, you don't have to worry about keeping the global scope of your application clean.

4.4.3   Modules in Node.js: ECMAScript

So far, we've used the *.mjs* file extension for ECMAScript modules in all examples. In this example, we use the type field in the *package.json* file to activate the ECMAScript module system. To do this, you must first run the npm init -y command in the directory where you want to create your initial file. This command creates a standard *package.json*. Then you must insert the type field, as shown in Listing 4.26.

```
{
  "name": "node-book",
  "version": "1.0.0",
  "description": "",
  "main": "index.js",
  "type": "module",
  "scripts": {
    "test": "echo \"Error: no test specified\" && exit 1"
  },
  "keywords": [],
  "author": "",
  "license": "ISC"
}
```

Listing 4.26 "package.json" with "type" Field

With this preparation, you can transfer the previous example to the ECMAScript module system with only a few adjustments. In Listing 4.27, you can find the customized source code of the wordCount module. By making adjustments to the *package.json* file, you can also keep the *.js* file extension.

```
const ignore = /[\.,]/g;
const separator = ' ';
export function wordCount(sentence) {
  return sentence
    .replace(ignore, '')
    .toLowerCase()
    .split(separator)
    .reduce((prev, current) => {
      prev[current] = prev[current] + 1 || 1;
      return prev;
    }, {});
}
```

Listing 4.27 "wordCount" Module as ECMAScript Module (word-count.js)

The change here is that instead of assigning it to module.exports, you use the export keyword. In this case, you create a named export that you can use in your application. The customization in Listing 4.25 is also limited to just one line, as you can see in Listing 4.28.

```
import { wordCount as wc } from './word-count.js';
const sentence = 'Where there is much light, there is also much shadow.';
const wordCount = wc(sentence);
console.log(sentence);
for (let i in wordCount) {
  console.log(wordCount[i] + ' x ' + i);
}
```

Listing 4.28 Integrating the "wordCount" Module

In Listing 4.28, you import the wordCount function from the *word-count.js* file using the import keyword. Because this name is already used in the source code, the function is renamed to wc using the as keyword. The remainder of the source code remains unchanged.

> **Required File Name Extension**
>
> As you've seen in the examples in this chapter, specifying the file name extension is mandatory when loading modules in the ECMAScript module system. This applies to both absolute and relative path specifications.
>
> If you omit the extension, Node.js returns a corresponding error.

4.4.4   Exporting Different Types of Data

When using the Node.js module system, you're not limited to just using functions, as you can export any type of data. So it's possible that you export classes or objects or just provide simple values like a string or a number.

Listing 4.29 contains an example in which an object with several functions is exported.

```
function add(a, b) {
  return a + b;
}

function subtract(a, b) {
  return a - b;
}

module.exports = { add,  subtract };
```

Listing 4.29 Exporting Objects

Listing 4.30 shows the same functionality, but in ECMAScript module syntax.

```
function add(a, b) {
  return a + b;
}

function subtract(a, b) {
  return a - b;
}

export { add, subtract };
```

Listing 4.30 Exporting Objects in ECMAScript Modules

In the examples shown in Listing 4.29 and Listing 4.30, you can see that implementation and export are separated processes. This is a best practice to make the source code clearer. You should always place the exports at the end of the file so that all developers working with your code will know where to find the module's interface definition. Another unique feature about this example is that it uses the shorthand notation introduced with ECMAScript 2015 for object properties, where the property name and the variable containing the value have the same designation.

There are cases when you need to manipulate the behavior of a module from the outside. You can do this by exporting a function that receives arguments from outside and generates a return value based on them. The source code from Listing 4.31 clarifies the example.

```
export default function(DEBUG) {
  return {
    options: {
      outputStyle: DEBUG ? 'expanded' : 'compressed',
      sourceMap: DEBUG,
      sourceMapEmbed: true,
    },
    files: {
      'style/style.css': 'style/style.scss',
    },
  };
};
```

Listing 4.31 Manipulating Modules

In Listing 4.31, you transfer a Boolean value that affects the returned object. This is the swapped configuration of parts of a grunt configuration for the CSS preprocessor, Sass.

4.4.5   The modules Module

The modules module represents the CommonJS module loader. This module shouldn't be used in conjunction with ECMAScript modules.

The two most important components of the modules module are the exports or module.exports object, which you can use to publish modules, and the require function, which you can use to include the module. In addition to these two core features, however, this module offers you a number of other functionalities that can be very helpful in the development and operation of modules. For this purpose, the Node.js platform provides you with the module object globally. If you use the ECMAScript module system, then this isn't the case, and the module variable isn't defined. You can use this object to query various information about the current module. First and foremost, the module.id and module.filename properties should be mentioned here. These two properties normally specify the absolute file name of the module. If you want to use this information as a basis, you should use the second variant, that is, module.filename. The module.id property contains the value . when you access it outside of a module, such as in the main file of your application. You can also use these two properties of the module object in the Node.js REPL. In this case, the id property has the value repl, and the filename has the value null.

You can use the loaded property of the module object to find out if the current module has already been loaded. In this case, the value is true. If the current module hasn't been loaded yet or is still in the load process, the value of this property is false.

When a Node.js application is launched, the require.main property is automatically populated with the module object of the initial file. Therefore, you can access the file name of the file that serves as the entry point to your application in each module via `require.main.filename`.

In addition to this information, the `modules` module also contains data about the relationships between the modules, that is, which module was loaded by which other module or which modules are loaded by a particular module. The `parent` property of the `module` object provides information about the module that loaded the current module. Again, this information comes in the form of a `module` object, which means you have access to the `id` or `filename` properties of the parent module, among others. The `children` property contains an array of modules that the current module loads via `require`. However, this only applies to your own modules. The core modules aren't listed in the `children` array. The objects in this data structure have the same structure as the `parent` object.

4.4.6 Module Loader

The inclusion of modules is done either via the `require` function or via the `import` statement. For this purpose, you should commit the name of the file that contains the source code of the module. You can specify the file name both as an absolute name and relative to the current file.

Assuming a directory structure like the one in Listing 4.32, that is, the two JavaScript files *word-count.js* and *index.js*, where *index.js* is the entry point to your application, your application is launched via the `node index.js` command. You can then include the `word-count` module either through a relative path using `require('./word-count')` or `import wordCount from './word-count'`, or via the absolute path, that is, using `require('/srv/node/word-count/word-count')` or `import wordCount from '/srv/node/word-count/word-count'`. As already mentioned, you should use the relative variant, which allows you to run the application on other systems or make it available to other people.

```
$ ls /srv/node/word-count
word-count.js index.js package.json
```

Listing 4.32 Directory Listing of the "wordCount" Application

Resolving Node Package Manager Modules

When searching for npm modules, the CommonJS module loader and the ECMAScript module loader behave in the same way. You can load npm modules by not prefixing `/` or `./` to the module you want to load. In this case, the module loader either looks for a Node.js core module, or it searches for a package with the corresponding name in the *node_modules* subdirectory of the current directory. If the package isn't found there, an attempt is made one level higher to resolve the package name. In the directory structure from Listing 4.32 this means that the search will first take place in the */srv/node/word-count/node_modules* directory, then in */srv/node/node_modules*, and so on until the module loader has reached the root directory. If the module loader can't find the package in this directory structure, it searches in the directories specified in the NODE_PATH environment variable. It also searches in the *<home>/.node_modules*, *<home>/.node_libraries*, and *<install-prefix>/lib/node* directories. This way of searching for modules allows you to install different versions of npm packages on your system and control which version the module loader should load via the placement of each package. This allows you to avoid version conflicts caused by another application or library requiring a different version of a package.

Depending on where you store the packages, you can influence the speed of the load process. Best practice has been to install packages in the root directory of the application, if possible. Packages placed in the local *node_modules* directory are loaded fastest, avoiding a lengthy search process.

The following list briefly summarizes again in which directories packages are searched for in the example:

- */srv/node/word-count/node_modules*
- */srv/node/node_modules*
- */srv/node_modules*
- */node_modules*
- */home/<username>/.node_modules*
- */home/<username>/.node_libraries*
- */usr/local/lib/node_modules*

On this system, the NODE_PATH environment variable is empty, so this doesn't add an additional path.

Importing Directories

With the CommonJS module loader of Node.js, there is yet another way to include modules in your application. Instead of specifying the name of a module, you can also specify an entire directory. The reason is that libraries are often stored in their own directory structures. For those modules, there is a defined naming convention on how to name the files so that the module loader can find the source code and include it in a correct way. If, instead of a file name, you pass a directory to the module loader, it tries to find a *package.json* in the first step. You can use this file to point to the entry point of a module within a directory. To demonstrate this case, we must adjust the word counter example slightly. First, you need to create a directory named *word-count*. This directory should contain your module later. In this directory, you must again create a subdirectory named *lib*, and then you must copy the *word-count.js* file from Listing 4.24 into it. Next, you must create a file named *package.json* in the *word-count* directory. The content of this file corresponds to the source code from Listing 4.33.

```
{
  "name": "word-count",
  "main": "./lib/word-count.js",
}
```

Listing 4.33 "package.json" for the "wordCount" Module

The last adjustment must be implemented in *index.js* from Listing 4.25, that is, in the entry point of the application. Here, you just have to make sure that the wordCount module is included via the const wc = require('./word-count') command. If you specify a directory when you want to load a module and that directory doesn't have a *package.json* file with a valid main field, the module loader alternatively searches for the *index.js* and *index.node* files as entry points to the module.

Module Cache

Within your application, you can load a module not only once at the beginning of a source code file, or even only in a single file, but also as often as you like, at different places, and thus also multiple times. To avoid having to read these modules from the file system multiple times, both the CommonJS and ECMAScript loaders perform an optimization by caching the module in memory. This means that the module only needs to be loaded and run the first time. The remaining require or import calls with the name of the module are then provided from the cache. As a result, this feature makes sure that the source code is only executed at the first require or import call. If you want to get a side effect on every call, you have to force this via other functions. In Listing 4.34 and Listing 4.35, you can see how this behavior can be re-created.

```
console.log('myModule called');
```

Listing 4.34 "my-module.js"

```
require('./my-module');    // Output: myModule called
require('./my-module.js'); // no output
```

Listing 4.35 "index.js"

When you run the source code via the node index.js command, you get the output myModule called only once because the second require call is provided directly from the cache, and the *my-module.js* file isn't run a second time. The same result occurs if you customize the *index.js* file as shown in Listing 4.36 and use the ECMAScript module system.

```
import './my-module.js'; // Output: myModule called
import './my-module.js'; // no output
```

Listing 4.36 Multiple Imports of the Same Module in the ECMAScript Module System

Like the CommonJS module system, the ECMAScript module system has a local cache. However, both caches are independent of each other. Another difference is that you can manipulate the CommonJS module cache much more easily.

There are several ways to achieve a multiple effect when loading a module. For example, you can load the module, clear the module cache, and load the module again. The better variant, however, is to dispense with any side effect when loading a module and encapsulate it in a function instead. This way, you only have to load the module once and can call the returned function as often as you like. Listing 4.37 and Listing 4.38 show what this looks like for the CommonJS module system, and Listing 4.39 and Listing 4.40 show the same for the ECMAScript module system.

```
module.exports = function () {
  console.log('myModule called');
};
```

Listing 4.37 Exported Function in CommonJS (my-module.js)

```
const myModule = require('./my-module');

myModule(); // Output: myModule called
myModule(); // Output: myModule called
```

Listing 4.38 Multiple Calls of the Exported Function in CommonJS (index.js)

```
export default function () {
  console.log('myModule called');
}
```

Listing 4.39 Exported Function in ECMAScript (my-module.js)

```
import myModule from './my-module.js';

myModule(); // Output: myModule called
myModule(); // Output: myModule called
```

Listing 4.40 Multiple Calls of the Exported Function in ECMAScript (index.js)

require Functionality

The structure of CommonJS module loader of Node.js is relatively simple. Nevertheless, it can be difficult to keep track of applications with many modules. It's also challenging to deal with different versions of certain modules in one system. The caching mechanism of the module loader can also become a problem under certain circumstances. In addition to the functionalities of the Node.js module system presented so far, there are other features that can make it easier for you to work with modules.

The resolve method of the require object enables you to find out in which file a certain module is located. For this purpose, you only have to provide the method with the information as to which module you want to load. The naming scheme is similar to the one used in the regular load operations. The resolve method also performs the same search operations as the actual require method, the only difference being that the module isn't loaded, but the absolute path of the file in which the module is located is returned as a string. For core modules, resolve returns only the name of the module. Moreover, this functionality is not only available in applications but also in the Node.js REPL.

You've already learned about the Node.js module cache. You can read and edit this cache via the cache property of the require object. The cache object is a normal JavaScript object in which the information is stored. The keys consist of the absolute file names of the respective modules where in each case the value is the module object of the module. Thus, you can use the cache object to check whether a module has already been loaded within your application. However, there is one important aspect you need to keep in mind: no core modules are listed in the cache. In the module cache example in Listing 4.34 and Listing 4.35, you saw that a module is evaluated only once and provided from the cache on the second call. The cache object allows you to change this behavior.

If you delete the cache entry for the module after the first require call, as shown in Listing 4.41, the module will be completely removed from the cache, causing it to be reloaded and evaluated the next time it's called, and any side effect that the module is intended to have will occur again. You can manipulate not only the cache but also the way Node.js loads the modules you include via require. For this purpose, the require module has the extensions property. The value is an object where the keys consist of various file extensions, and the associated values consist of the functions used to load the files with the corresponding extensions. Now, if you want to add support for another file extension, all you need to do is extend the extensions object with a key that has the name of the file extension and then add a function that is responsible for loading the files. The easiest way to do this is to simply use one of the existing functions. In a later chapter, you'll implement a slightly more extensive application where you can see the various aspects of Node.js in action.

```
require('./my-module'); // Output: myModule called
delete require.cache[require.resolve('./my-module')];
require('./my-module'); // Output: myModule called
```

Listing 4.41 "app.js"

4.5 Summary

This chapter has introduced you to the core components of Node.js and highlighted the differences between the various module levels. You've seen which modules are included in the platform and how you can use them.

An important component of Node.js is the module system, which enables you to divide your application into smaller, independent sections that interact with each other via defined interfaces. Node.js is undergoing a major revamp at the moment in terms of the module system. For many years, developers have based their efforts on the CommonJS module system, whereas now Node.js is gradually moving to the ECMAScript module system. Meanwhile, the new module system is so stable that you can use it in a production application without any problem. However, the CommonJS module system still represents the default, so you need to enable the new module system via a special file extension, an entry in the *package.json* file, or a command-line flag.

Chapter 5
HTTP

No one serves another of his own free will, but if he knows that he is serving himself, he does it gladly.
—Johann Wolfgang von Goethe

One of the most well-known and also most important modules of Node.js is the http module. This module enables you to create a web server with Node.js. What is important for you to know at this point is that this is a full-fledged web server that you can run independently from other server applications such as Nginx or Apache. With a Node.js web server, you can respond to incoming HTTP requests and send an appropriate response back to your users' browsers. However, the http module can do much more than just send HTML structures to a user's browser. The http module and its secure variant, the https module, allow you to respond to different types of requests, accept file uploads, and also take on the role of a browser yourself and send requests to other web servers. In addition to the http module for the first version of the HTTP protocol, Node.js contains a separate module for HTTP/2—the http2 module.

In this chapter, you'll learn about the numerous facets of http modules. A practical example will demonstrate how you can solve various tasks with relatively little source code.

5.1 Web Server

In the first part of this chapter, you'll learn more about Node.js in the role of an http server. In a step-by-step process, you'll implement a simple address book where you can create, read, update, and delete records.

5.1.1 Server Object

In Chapter 3, you were able to gain some initial experience with implementing a web server in Node.js. You've also seen that the platform already does some of the work for you in this respect. Before you start with the actual implementation, you must first create a *package.json* file in a new directory using the npm init -y command, as shown in Listing 5.1.

```
{
  "name": "node-book",
  "version": "1.0.0",
  "description": "",
  "main": "index.js",
  "type": "module",
  "scripts": {
    "start": "node index.js"
  },
  "author": "",
  "license": "ISC"
}
```

Listing 5.1 The package.json File of the Address Book

The two changes to the default version of *package.json* shown in Listing 5.1 are the activation of the ECMAScript module system via the type property and the start entry
under scripts. The latter is a Node Package Manager (npm) script that allows you to
launch the application on the console using the npm start command instead of entering
node index.js. The advantage here is that you can customize and add options to the
startup script as you wish, but for those who want to use your application, the command to launch it always remains the same. Listing 5.2 contains the source code of the
startup file named *index.js*, which serves as the basis for the example in this chapter.

```
import { createServer } from 'http';

createServer((request, response) => {
  response.writeHead(200, { 'content-type': 'text/html' });
  const responseBody = `<!DOCTYPE html>
    <html>
      <head>
        <title>Address book</title>
      </head>
      <body>
        <h1>Address book</h1>
      </body>
    </html>`;
  response.end(responseBody);
}).listen(8080, () => {
  console.log('Adress book reachable via http://localhost:8080');
});
```

Listing 5.2 Getting Started with the Web Server with Node.js (index.js)

In Listing 5.3, you can see what Node.js does with the code in this example.

```
import { Server } from 'http';

const server = new Server();

server.on('request', (request, response) => {
  response.statusCode = 200;
  response.setHeader('content-type', 'text/html');
  const responseBody = `<!DOCTYPE html>
<html>
  <head>
    <title>Address book</title>
  </head>
  <body>
    <h1>Address book</h1>
  </body>
</html>`;
  response.write(responseBody);
  response.end();
});

server.on('listening', () => {
  console.log('Adress book reachable via http://localhost:8080');
});

server.listen(8080);
```

Listing 5.3 The Web Server in Detail (index.js)

If you start the server process and then access it from the browser via the address *http://localhost:8080/*, you should see a view like the one shown in Figure 5.1. The source code from the examples in Listing 5.2 and Listing 5.3 has the same functionality with the only difference being that care has been taken in Listing 5.3 to make the individual steps happening in the background clearer for you.

- **createServer**
  This function creates an instance of the server class. You can also do this yourself by creating a new instance using the server constructor of the http module and the new operator. The callback function you pass to the createServer method is bound to the server's request event.

- **listen**
  With the listen method of the server object, you instruct your server to listen for incoming connections on the specified Transmission Control Protocol (TCP) port and an Internet Protocol (IP) address.

- **write**

  The write method allows you to write only a part of the body. You can call this method several times per response. Calling the write method causes the specified content to be sent as a chunk, that is, as part of the message to the client. Optionally, you can pass the encoding of the string as the second argument and a callback function as the third argument. This function is called as soon as the chunk has been sent.

- **end**

  The write method sends only a part of the message but keeps the response open for further parts. If you want to signal to the client that it has received the entire message with a particular data packet, you must use the end method. If you don't do this, the client terminates the connection itself after a preconfigured period of time and evaluates this as a time-out. The end method has the same signature as the write method. You can use it to send the last chunk of a message. After calling the end method, the response is completed. You can't send any further chunks.

Figure 5.1 Initial View of the Address Book

In the simplest case, you merely pass a TCP port to the listen method. The server is then bound to all available IPv6 interfaces on the specified port. If IPv6 isn't available, IPv4 is used. If the port number is 0, the server is bound to a random port that you can identify using the address function of the server object. You can also specify an IP address or a host name, and then the server will be bound to this address.

The third optional argument of the listen method allows you to specify the size of the queue for incoming connections. The standard value is 511.

If you specify a function last, regardless of the number of arguments, it will be executed as soon as the server is successfully connected. This callback function is bound to the listening event of the server. It's often used to generate console output, signaling to a user that the server is waiting for incoming connections. If you don't provide an output, the console prompt disappears without another message.

Once you've bound the server by calling the listen method, it waits for requests. You can stop this process by calling the close method on the server object. This ensures that the server doesn't accept any new requests.

Both write and end accept strings and buffer objects as their first argument. The default value for the encoding is utf8. If you haven't yet called writeHead (i.e., the method to prepare for sending the header information) before calling write, then write will do this for you and also send the implicit header information to the client. If the write method returns true, it means that the message was successfully passed to the kernel. The value false, on the other hand, means that the message has been queued. When the buffer is freed up again, the drain event gets triggered. Before you finalize the message by calling the end method, you can use the message trailer to add more metadata to the message. The addTrailers method allows you to specify an object with the appropriate information, which is then sent to the client.

Arrow Functions

Arrow functions are a feature of ECMAScript 2015. This syntax is a shorthand notation for functions with some handy effects. Listing 5.4 shows an example of such an arrow function.

```
const arr = [1, 2, 3];
const mappedArr = arr.map((el) => {
  return el * 2;
});
console.log(mappedArr); // Output: [ 2, 4, 6 ]
```

Listing 5.4 Arrow Function in Connection with the Array "map" Function

The code in the example applies the arrow function to each array element and creates a modified copy of the original array. After that, the copy will be output. A special feature of arrow functions is that the parentheses of the parameter list are optional if there is only one parameter. In addition, if there is only one expression, the return value is returned directly. As a result, you get a very abbreviated notation, as you can see in Listing 5.5.

```
const arr = [1, 2, 3];
const mappedArr = arr.map(el => el * 2);
console.log(mappedArr); // Output: [ 2, 4, 6 ]
```

Listing 5.5 Shortened Arrow Function

Another special feature concerns the value of this in an arrow function. In a normal callback function used inside an object, as in Listing 5.6, the value of this is the global object. This behavior can be changed by specifying the use strict string. In strict mode, this then has the value undefined. The situation is made even more error-prone by the fact that you can bind a function to another context via the bind method and thus additionally influence the value of this.

```
const myObj = {
  myMethod() {
    setTimeout(function() {
```

```
      console.log(this); // Output: Timeout { ... }
    });
  },
};


myObj.myMethod();
```

Listing 5.6 Callback Function

This fact is especially relevant for asynchronous operations in objects. In this case, you can access the object context by storing it in a separate variable or binding the callback function to the correct context. Alternatively, you can also use an arrow function, as shown in Listing 5.7.

```
const myObj = {
  myMethod() {
    setTimeout(() => {
      console.log(this); // Output: { myMethod: [Function: myMethod] }
    });
  },
};


myObj.myMethod();
```

Listing 5.7 Arrow Functions as Callback

Arrow functions are mainly used where short functions are used, such as most array functions. As soon as a function becomes more extensive, you should no longer write it inline, but consider using a normal function.

5.1.2   Server Events

As you've seen from the callbacks of the `request` and `listening` events, when building the web server, the event-driven architecture of Node.js also runs through the `http` module. In your implementation, you can draw on a set of events that help you respond asynchronously to various incidents.

Table 5.1 shows the most important events of the HTTP server. The `listening` event isn't part of the `http` server itself, but originates from the `net` module and the `server` class, which serves as the parent class of the `http` server.

Event	Description
request	This represents an incoming client request.
connection	A connection with a client has been established.

Table 5.1 Server Events

Event	Description
close	The server is terminated.
checkContinue	This occurs when a request is sent with an Expect: 100-continue header. The server should respond with a 100 status code.
checkExpectation	This is triggered when a request is received with an Expect header whose value isn't 100-continue. If you don't implement this function, the server responds with a 417 Expectation Failed.
connect	A client sends a request to the server using the HTTP method CONNECT.
upgrade	A client requests an HTTP upgrade.
clientError	A client has sent an error message.

Table 5.1 Server Events (Cont.)

In the callback functions of the individual events, you have access to different objects. These are provided to you as arguments and contain details about the event in question so that you can respond accordingly.

Delivery of the Address Book

At this point, your address book consists only of a heading. To change this and make the result more dynamic, the first step is to take care of data management. For the address book, we use a simple JavaScript object that holds the state of the application. The disadvantage of this is that all information is lost as soon as you restart the server. Listing 5.8 contains the customized code of the address book.

```
import { createServer } from 'http';

const addresses = [
  {
    id: 1,
    firstname: 'James',
    lastname: 'Bond',
    street: '12 Millbank',
    city: 'London',
    country: 'United Kingdom',
  },
  {
    id: 2,
    firstname: 'Sherlock',
    lastname: 'Holmes',
    street: '221b Baker St',
    city: 'London',
```

```
      country: 'United Kingdom',
  },
];

createServer((request, response) => {
  response.writeHead(200, { 'content-type': 'text/html' });
  const responseBody = `<!DOCTYPE html>
    <html>
      <head>
        <title>Address book</title>
      </head>
      <body>
        <h1>Address book</h1>
        <table>
          <thead>
            <tr>
              <th>Id</th>
              <th>First Name</th>
              <th>Last Name</th>
            </tr>
          </thead>
          <tbody>
            ${addresses.map(createRow).join('')}
          </tbody>
        </table>
      </body>
    </html>`;
  response.end(responseBody);
}).listen(8080, () =>
  console.log('Address book reachable at http://localhost:8080'),
);

function createRow(address) {
  return `<tr>
    <td>${address.id}</td>
    <td>${address.firstname}</td>
    <td>${address.lastname}</td>
  </tr>`;
}
```

Listing 5.8 Extended Address Book (index.js)

The most important changes consist of defining the information to be displayed in the addresses array and extending the HTML code. Within the template string, the table is built using the map function. To keep the source code as clear and manageable as possible, the task of generating the individual rows was outsourced to the createRow function. After that, you must join the returned array into a string using the join method. You then pass the string you want to use for joining the individual array elements to this method as a parameter. In the example, an empty string is used so that the elements are appended directly to each other. The result of the extension displays in the browser as shown in Figure 5.2.

Figure 5.2 List View of the Address Book

5.1.3 Request Object

In the next step, you must add the possibility to delete addresses from the list. Your web server must then perform two different tasks: display the address list and delete data. Therefore, it can no longer respond to all requests in the same way. The way in which the server responds determines the URL requested by the client. To identify that URL, you need to evaluate the request. This can be done via the request object, which contains all the information you need on the server side to answer the request accordingly.

Structure of a Request

An HTTP request normally consists of two parts: the header and the message body. Figure 5.3 contains a graphical representation of this structure.

The header contains metadata such as what format the server's response should be in. It consists of a set of key-value pairs defined in the HTTP standard. The message body (or just body for short) contains the use data of the request. Depending on the type of the request, the body doesn't necessarily have to contain any data. A request without a body occurs when, for example, you inform a web server that you want to see a particular page or delete a resource on the server. In this case, the header contains all the relevant information.

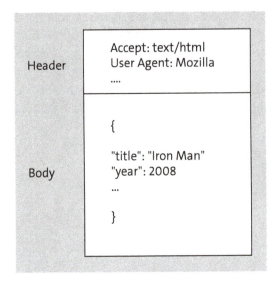

Figure 5.3 Structure of an HTTP Request

The situation is different with regard to sending forms. Here you have to submit data to the server. The form data usually resides as key-value pairs in the body of the message. Another example where you submit data to the server via requests are file uploads. Depending on what kind of data you're uploading, this case can also generate very large amounts of data that you need to handle correctly on the server side.

Restructuring the Address Book

To help you implement the additional functionality in your address book, you should make use of the Node.js module system and divide your application into multiple sections. The *index.js* file is the entry point. It contains the setup of the web server. Listing 5.9 contains the source code of the file.

```
import { createServer } from 'http';
import data from './data.js';
import { getList } from './list.js';

createServer((request, response) => {
  response.writeHead(200, { 'content-type': 'text/html' });
  const responseBody = getList(data.addresses);
  response.end(responseBody);
}).listen(8080, () =>
  console.log('Address book reachable at http://localhost:8080'),
);
```

Listing 5.9 Getting Started with the Address Book (index.js)

The getList function and the array that holds the data are swapped out into separate modules. In the *list.js* file that generates the HTML structure, you can add one more column per line that contains a link to delete the entry. Listing 5.10 shows the customized source code.

```javascript
export function getList(addresses) {
  return `<!DOCTYPE html>
    <html>
      <head>
        <title>Address book</title>
        <meta charset="utf-8">
      </head>
      <body>
        <h1>Address book</h1>
        <table>
          <thead>
            <tr>
              <th>Id</th>
              <th>First Name</th>
              <th>Last Name</th>
              <th>delete</th>
            </tr>
          </thead>
          <tbody>
            ${addresses.map(createRow).join('')}
          </tbody>
        </table>
      </body>
    </html>`;
}

function createRow(address) {
  return `<tr>
    <td>${address.id}</td>
    <td>${address.firstname}</td>
    <td>${address.lastname}</td>
    <td><a href="/delete/${address.id}">delete</a></td>
  </tr>`;
}
```

Listing 5.10 List Display (list.js)

You must add the additional column in both the getList and createRow functions. In the latter, the table cell contains a link pointing to the address */delete/<id>*, where id identifies the particular data record.

What you can also see in this code example is that not only can you collect a central export at the end of a file, but you can directly tag the structures you want to make available as an interface to the outside world using the export keyword, like the getList function here. The final part of the application extension is the *data.js* file, which represents the data storage.

```
export default {
  addresses: [
    {
      id: 1,
      firstname: 'James',
      lastname: 'Bond',
      street: '12 Millbank',
      city: 'London',
      country: 'United Kingdom',
    },
    {
      id: 2,
      firstname: 'Sherlock',
      lastname: 'Holmes',
      street: '221b Baker St',
      city: 'London',
      country: 'United Kingdom',
    },
  ],
};
```

Listing 5.11 Data Management in the Application (data.js)

In this case, you export an object to make it easier to modify the data later.

In general, you can also solve the import of data by importing a JavaScript Object Notation (JSON) file. Unlike the CommonJS module system, the ECMAScript module system doesn't currently support such imports. This feature is still in experimental status and must first be enabled via the --experimental-json-modules flag. Alternatively, you can read a JSON file with the file system module or use module.createRequire to access the CommonJS module system. Due to the adjustments to the source code, the link to delete a record is now also visible in the browser after a restart of the server process, as shown in Figure 5.4.

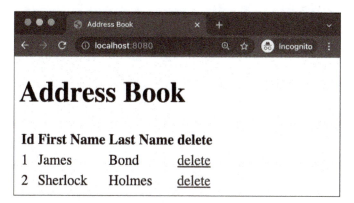

Figure 5.4 Possibility to Delete Records

Properties of the Request Object

The request object is the means by which the client tells the server what to do. The header information of the request is directly available as properties of the request object, and the message body is processed as a stream of one or more data packages. You should treat the request object as a read-only object, or the information received could be corrupted. The most important properties of the request object are as follows:

- method
  The HTTP method specifies what to do with the requested resource. The value of this property is a string that can assume the value GET, POST, PUT, DELETE, HEAD, PATCH, TRACE, or OPTIONS, for example. In web development, GET and POST are most commonly used.

- url
  In a request, the URL represents the resource the client wants to use. If in the browser, you click the link to delete the first record, and the url property assumes the value /delete/1. If you specify a query string in addition to the path, the url property will contain that string as well.

- header
  Metadata about the request is transmitted as key-value pairs via the HTTP header. For example, the accept header with the value application/json defines that the client expects a JSON structure from the server. However, the HTTP header is relevant not only for the server but also for caches located along the way. For example, you use the cache-control header to control caching behavior. In total, the W3C specifies more than 40 different header directives for HTTP. You can find further details on this topic at *www.ietf.org/rfc/rfc2616.txt*.

- trailers
  Trailers serve as the counterpart to the header information . You can access them in a similar way to the headers, namely, via the trailers property.

- **httpVersion**
  This property contains the HTTP version that was used for the request. You can access the individual components of the version number via `httpVersionMajor` or `httpVersionMinor`.

- **connection**
  Finally, this property provides access to a socket object that represents the connection between client and server.

Deleting Records

In the initial file of your application, you must now decide what to do based on the requested URL. If the client requests the URL */*, you must display the address list; if the client calls */delete/1*, the record with id 1 gets deleted. First, you must implement a function that deletes an element from the `addresses` array. You should outsource this function to a separate module with the file name *delete.js*. The source code of this module is shown in Listing 5.12.

```
export function deleteAddress(addresses, id) {
  const parsedId = parseInt(id, 10);
  const filteredAddresses = addresses.filter(
    (address) => address.id !== parsedId,
  );
  return filteredAddresses;
}
```

Listing 5.12 Deleting an Address (delete.js)

When implementing the `deleteAddress` function, you must make sure that the information coming from the client—in this case, the `id`—is a string, not a number. For this reason, you must first explicitly convert it to a number before you can perform a strict check for equality with three equal signs. There are several ways to remove an element from an array in JavaScript, including filtering it out using the `filter` method shown here or using the `splice` method.

Equality in JavaScript

If you want to check in JavaScript whether two values match, you should always do so with three equal signs. Similarly, you should check for inequality with an exclamation point and two equal signs. This prevents the JavaScript engine from changing the type of the values. Such a strict comparison returns `false` if you compare string 1 with number 1. With two equal signs, this comparison would return `true`. If you always use the strict variant for comparisons, you can exclude this source of error. If the types don't match, you should take typecasting into your own hands. This makes your source code easier to understand.

In the request callback function in the initial file of your application, you decide which action to perform based on the URL. In case of a delete operation, you must execute the `deleteAddress` function and then forward the request back to the list using the `request` function. This ensures that the updated list is displayed to the user. Listing 5.13 shows the customized *index.js* file.

```javascript
import { createServer } from 'http';
import data from './data.js';
import { getList } from './list.js';
import { deleteAddress } from './delete.js';

createServer((request, response) => {
  let responseBody;
  const parts = request.url.split('/');
  if (parts.includes('delete')) {
    data.addresses = deleteAddress(data.addresses, parts[2]);
    redirect(response, '/');
  } else {
    response.writeHead(200, { 'content-type': 'text/html' });
    responseBody = getList(data.addresses);
    response.end(responseBody);
  }
}).listen(8080, () =>
  console.log('Address book reachable at http://localhost:8080'),
);

function redirect(response, to) {
  response.writeHead(302, { location: '/', 'content-type': 'text/plain' });
  response.end('302 Redirecting to /');
}
```

Listing 5.13 Adjustments to the Initial File (index.js)

The user is redirected in the `redirect` function, which sets the status code 302 and the `location` header to /. This information signals the browser to request this address, which results in an updated list display.

HTTP Status Codes

The status code signals the status of the request to the browser. The status codes 200 and 302 have already been introduced in two examples. The status codes can be divided into five groups, each of which has its own meaning:

- 100–199: Information is provided by the request.
- 200–299: Feedback is provided on the success of the request.

- 300–399: The client must take further actions (redirection).
- 400–499: A client-side error has occurred.
- 500–599: A server-side error has occurred.

Not only are the categories of status codes standardized, but the individual codes are also subject to strict rules. Node.js provides a way to resolve the individual status codes into strings with the http.STATUS_CODES object.

The easiest way to formulate a correct response header is to use the writeHead method, which normally requires two arguments. The first argument consists of a number representing the status code, while the second consists of an object with header information. You can use this method only once; after that, you can't make any modifications to the header. You must also call this method before using write or end to send the body of the message.

You can also set the header information of the response object individually using the statusCode property and the setHeader method. To set the status code, you must assign a valid number to the property. To set the header information, you must pass the name of the field you want to set to the setHeader method as the first argument, and the corresponding value as the second argument. For example, you use location as the field name and / as the value. To modify a header information, you can read the value using the getHeader method and set it via setHeader. The removeHeader method enables you to remove individual fields from the header.

5.1.4 Handling the Request Body (Update)

The last two operations that are still to be done for your address book are creating and modifying data records. Both operations apply similar structures, so you can combine most of the steps.

Delivering the Form

First, you need an HTML form that you deliver to the client to create or modify the data records. The required structures can be found in Listing 5.14.

```
export function getForm(addresses, id) {
  let address = {
    id: '',
    firstname: '',
    lastname: '',
    street: '',
    city: '',
    country: '',
  };
  if (id) {
```

```
      address = addresses.find((adr) => adr.id === parseInt(id, 10));
  }
  const form = `<!DOCTYPE html>
<html>
  <head>
    <title>Address book</title>
    <meta charset="utf-8">
  </head>
  <body>
    <form action="/save" method="POST">
      <input type="hidden" id="id" name="id" value="${address.id}" />
      <div>
        <label for="firstname">First Name</label>
        <input type="text" id="firstname" name="firstname" ⤸
          value="${address.firstname}" />
      </div>
      <div>
        <label for="lastname">Last Name</label>
        <input type="text" id="lastname" name="lastname" ⤸
          value="${address.lastname}" />
      </div>
      <div>
        <label for="street">Street</label>
        <input type="text" id="street" name="street" value="${address.street}" /
>
      </div>
      <div>
        <label for="city">City</label>
        <input type="text" id="city" name="city" value="${address.city}" />
      </div>
      <div>
        <label for="country">Country</label>
        <input type="text" id="country" name="country" value=
"${address.country}" />
      </div>
      <div>
        <button type="submit">save</button>
      </div>
    </form>
  </body>
</html>`;
  return form;
}
```

Listing 5.14 Form for Creating and Editing Addresses (form.js)

If you want to edit an existing data record, you must pass the array of addresses and the ID to be edited. Otherwise, you don't have to transfer anything. The form itself is in a template string, which ensures that the values are correctly inserted into the form elements. Finally, you can return the completed form.

Customizing the Router

The next step is to include your form in the *index.js* file of your application. The source code of this file is shown in Listing 5.15.

```
const http = require('http');
let addresses = require('./data');
const getList = require('./list');
const deleteAddress = require('./delete');
const getForm = require('./form');

http
  .createServer((request, response) => {
    const parts = request.url.split('/');
    if (parts.includes('delete')) {
      addresses = deleteAddress(addresses, parts[2]);
      redirect(response, '/');
    } else if (parts.includes('new')) {
      send(response, getForm());
    } else if (parts.includes('edit')) {
      send(response, getForm(addresses, parts[2]));
    } else {
      send(response, getList(addresses));
    }
  })
  .listen(8080, () =>
    console.log('Address book reachable at http://localhost:8080'),
  );

function send(response, responseBody) {
  response.writeHead(200, { 'content-type': 'text/html' });
  response.end(responseBody);
}

function redirect(response, to) {
  response.writeHead(302, { location: '/', 'content-type': 'text/plain' });
  response.end('302 Redirecting to /');
}
```

Listing 5.15 Getting Started with the Application (index.js)

To avoid duplicates in the code, the actual task of sending the response to the client was swapped out to the send function. Restart the server process, and then call the address *http://localhost:8080/new*; you'll see the form for creating new data records.

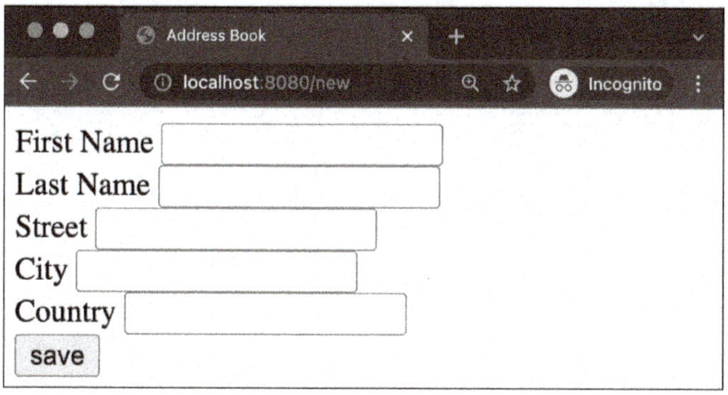

Figure 5.5 Form for New Data Records

Responding to the Form Submission

The actual logic can be found in the callback function of the createServer method. The task of this function is to decide which function to call to create the response; thus, it performs the task of a very simple router in the application. The form is sent to /save using the POST method. Currently, the server still responds to the call of this address by delivering the list. However, you can change that by extending your routing functionality. In this case, you can extend the decision for an action to the HTTP method used. Listing 5.16 contains the customized source code of the createServer callback function.

```
import { parse } from 'querystring';
import { saveAddress } from './save.js';
...
createServer((request, response) => {
  const parts = request.url.split('/');
  if (parts.includes('delete')) {
    data.addresses = deleteAddress(data.addresses, parts[2]);
    redirect(response, '/');
  } else if (parts.includes('new')) {
    send(response, getForm());
  } else if (parts.includes('edit')) {
    send(response, getForm(data.addresses, parts[2]));
  } else if (parts.includes('save') && request.method === 'POST') {
    let body = '';
    request.on('readable', () => {
      const data = request.read();
      body += data !== null ? data : '';
    });
```

```
    request.on('end', () => {
      const address = parse(body);
      addresses = saveAddress(data.addresses, address);
      redirect(response, '/');
    });
  } else {
    send(response, getList(data.addresses));
  }
}).listen(8080, () =>
  console.log('Address book reachable at http://localhost:8080'),
);
...
```

Listing 5.16 Saving Addresses (index.js)

In contrast to the header information of the request, the body isn't available as a property, but must be received via a data stream. The request can be transmitted in one or more parts, called chunks. As soon as a part of the request is available, the readable event gets triggered. In the handler function, you can retrieve the data using the read method and merge it into a variable. Once the request is completely accepted, the end event gets triggered. At this point, you can use the querystring module of Node.js to process the URL. The parse method ensures that the address formatted as querystring is converted into an object.

Saving the Information

For the change in Listing 5.16 to work properly, you must implement and load the saveAddress function. If you save the function in a file named *save.js*, the import is done via import { saveAddress } from './save.js'; in the *index.js* file. Listing 5.17 shows the implementation of the function.

```
export function saveAddress(addresses, address) {
  if (address.id) {
    const index = addresses.findIndex((adr) => {
      return adr.id === parseInt(address.id, 10);
    });
    address.id = parseInt(address.id, 10);
    addresses[index] = address;
  } else {
    const nextId = Math.max(...addresses.map((address) => address.id)) + 1;
    address.id = nextId;
    addresses.push(address);
```

```
  }
  return addresses;
}
```

Listing 5.17 Implementing the "saveAddress" Function (save.js)

In the `saveAddress` function, you distinguish between creating and updating data records depending on whether the passed data record has an `id` field. For a new data record, you must identify the next free `id` before inserting it. To do this, you should use the `map` method to extract the `id` properties of the address records, apply the result to the `Math.max` method using the spread operator, and add the value 1 to the result.

5.1.5 Delivering Static Content

So far, you've only delivered dynamic content with your web server. For purely static content such as HTML, CSS, or image files, it makes little sense to store them in a JavaScript template string. For this purpose, you can either use existing packages such as `node-static` or write the implementation yourself. For example, to style the address list with CSS, you must first create a stylesheet. Listing 5.18 contains its source code, which you must save in the *public* subdirectory in the *style.css* file of your application.

```
table {
  border-spacing: 0;
}

td {
  width: 80px;
}

tr:first-child th {
  font-weight: bold;
  text-align: left;
}

tr:nth-child(2n) td {
  background-color: lightgrey;
}
```

Listing 5.18 Stylesheet (public/style.css)

In the subsequent step, you must add the following line in the `head` section in the list template of the *list.js* file: `<link rel="stylesheet" href=" style.css" />`. After that, you just need to make sure that the server delivers the stylesheet correctly. Listing 5.19 shows the adjustments to the `createServer` callback function.

```
...
import { readFile } from 'fs';

createServer((request, response) => {
  const parts = request.url.split('/');
  if (parts.includes('delete')) {
    data.addresses = deleteAddress(data.addresses, parts[2]);
    redirect(response, '/');
  } else if (parts.includes('new')) {
    send(response, getForm());
  } else if (parts.includes('edit')) {
    send(response, getForm(data.addresses, parts[2]));
  } else if (parts.includes('save') && request.method === 'POST') {
    let body = '';
    request.on('readable', () => {
      const data = request.read();
      body += data !== null ? data : '';
    });
    request.on('end', () => {
      const address = parse(body);
      data.addresses = saveAddress(data.addresses, address);
      redirect(response, '/');
    });
  } else if (request.url === '/style.css') {
    readFile('public/style.css', 'utf8', (err, data) => {
      if (err) {
        response.statusCode = 404;
        response.end();
      } else {
        response.end(data);
      }
    });
  } else {
    send(response, getList(data.addresses));
  }
}).listen(8080, () =>
  console.log('Address book reachable at http://localhost:8080'),
);
...
```

Listing 5.19 Adjustments to the "createServer" Callback Function (index.js)

The last else if statement is particularly interesting here. Here, you use the readFile function from the fs module to read the requested file from the file system and send it to the client. Unlike in the previous implementations, you send the response to the client asynchronously in this case. This means that your web server will wait until the contents of the file are available before sending the response. After restarting the server, you'll see a slightly nicer form of the address list at *http://localhost:8080/*.

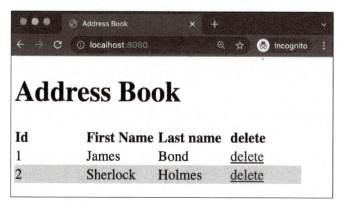

Figure 5.6 Address List with Stylesheet

When delivering static files, you should always make sure to strictly limit the files a client can request to avoid security problems on your server. The more dynamics you insert at this point, the greater the risk to your system. You should make sure that one directory is shared with your clients at most and that requests from there can't break out by jumping up the directory tree. In the example, you work around the problem by delivering only that one file when you request the *style.css* file. However, such a single implementation works only for very few static files. In the next chapter, you'll learn even more about static file delivery when we take a look at the Express framework.

5.1.6 File Upload

Your application is now capable of delivering dynamic and static information as well as handling form input. So far, all features could be implemented with integrated Node.js tools. Next, you should implement a way to upload files. You can implement this yourself and should make use of an already existing functionality. An example of this is the `for-midable` package. If you haven't yet created a *package.json* file for your application, now would be a good time to do so, namely, before you install the package. You can create a standard *package.json* file using the `npm init -y` command. After this step, you must use the `npm install formidable` command to install the package. Then the source code of `for-midable` will be downloaded and unpacked into a directory named *node_modules*. In addition, the package is entered as a dependency in the *package.json* file in the `dependen-cies` section, and a *package-lock.json* is created, which contains detailed information about the dependencies of your application. For more information, refer to Chapter 21.

To support file uploads, you need to make adjustments in a few places. The first adjustment concerns the form. Here, you must insert a new `input` element of the `file` type. Furthermore, the form additionally receives the attribute `enctype="multipart/form-data"`. Listing 5.20 shows the sections of the form that are affected by the changes.

```
const form = `<!DOCTYPE html>
...
  <form action="/save" method="POST" enctype="multipart/form-data">
...
    <div>
      <label for="upload">file</label>
      <input type="file" id="upload" name="upload" />
    </div>
    <div>
      <button type="submit">save</button>
    </div>
...
</html>`;
```

Listing 5.20 Upload Element in the Form (form.js)

After adjusting the source code, the **Choose file** button will display in the form view after a server restart.

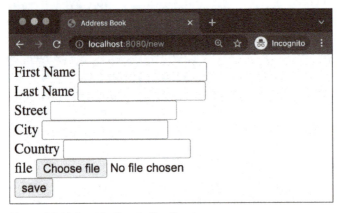

Figure 5.7 Upload Button in the Form

The biggest change concerns the *index.js* file. In it, you must adjust the area responsible for saving the data. Moreover, you must ensure that the uploaded files are delivered statically.

```
import formidable from 'formidable';
...

  } else if (parts.includes('save') && request.method === 'POST') {
    const form = new formidable.IncomingForm();
    form.parse(request, (err, address, files) => {
      if (files.upload) {
        rename(files.upload.path, `public/assets/${files.upload.name}`, () => {
          address['file'] = `/assets/${files.upload.name}`;
```

```
    });
  }
  data.addresses = saveAddress(data.addresses, address);
  redirect(response, '/');
  });
} else if (parts.includes('assets')) {
  readFile(`public${request.url.replaceAll('%20', ' ')}`, (err, data) => {
    if (err) {
      response.statusCode = 404;
      response.end();
    } else {
      response.end(data);
    }
  });
} else {
  send(response, getList(data.addresses));
}
}).listen(8080, () =>
  console.log('Address book reachable at http://localhost:8080'),
);
...
```

Listing 5.21 Adjusting the index.js File

Best Practice in Handling node_modules

When you install dependencies in a Node.js application, they and all their subdependencies are stored in the local *node_modules* directory. This directory is usually not included in the version control system; instead, the complete *node_modules* directory is ignored. When you download the code of a Node.js application for the first time, no dependencies are installed, and the application isn't functional. For this reason, you need to install the dependencies in the first step. You can do so via the npm install command in the root directory of your application, where the *package.json* file is usually located. The *package-lock.json* file must be included in the version control system that specifies which packages are installed in which version.

Using formidable simplifies the handling of the form. The parse function extracts both the form data and the submitted files from the request. Finally, you must use the rename method from the fs module to make sure that the file gets moved to its destination. Besides handling the files, you also need to make sure that they are delivered. The corresponding section is similar to the one that delivers the stylesheets, except for the fact that binary data and not text data is delivered here. To support spaces in the file names of the requested files, you should use the replaceAll method and replace the string %20, which represents a space character with a real space character when reading the file. For the code example to work smoothly, you should create a subdirectory named *assets* in the *public* directory. In the final step, you only need to display the image files in the list. For this purpose, you must insert a new column in the table and display an img element with the file as its source. For data records without an image, no image will be displayed.

```js
function getList(addresses) {
  return `<!DOCTYPE html>
...
      <th>Image</th>
      <th>Id</th>
      <th>First Name</th>
      <th>Last Name</th>
      <th>delete</th>
      <th>edit</th>
...`
function createRow(address) {
  const img = address.file
    ? `<img src="${address.file}" height="20" width="20">`
    : '';

  return `<tr>
    <td>${img}</td>
    <td>${address.id}</td>
...`
```

Listing 5.22 Display of the Uploaded Image in the List (list.js)

If you create a new record, including image upload after restarting the server, you can see the image in a thumbnail view, as shown in Figure 5.8.

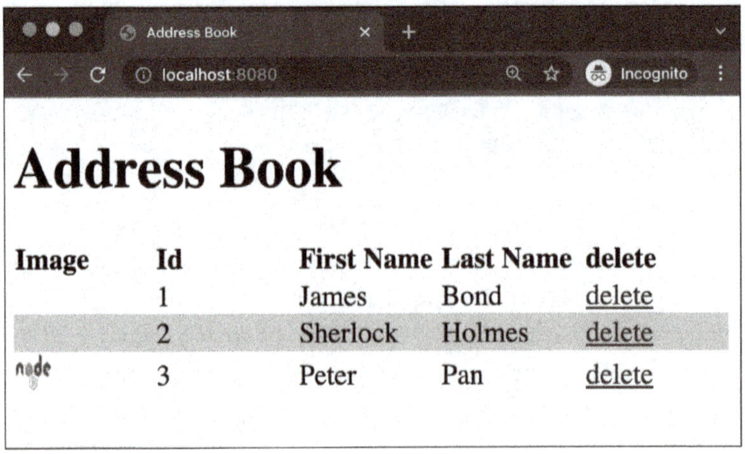

Figure 5.8 Displaying the Image

Before we move on to Section 5.2, let's make a few small changes to the application to make it a bit more usable.

5.1.7 Fine-Tuning the Frontend

To create and edit records, you currently need to adjust the URL manually. To make the application even easier to use, you should add links to the *list.js* file to make both features accessible directly from the browser. The required changes can be found in Listing 5.23.

```
export function getList(addresses) {
  return `<!DOCTYPE html>
...
      <table>
        <thead>
          <tr>
...
            <th>delete</th>
            <th>edit</th>
          </tr>
        </thead>
        <tbody>
          ${addresses.map(createRow).join('')}
        </tbody>
      </table>
      <a href="/new">create new data record</a>
    </body>
  </html>`;
}

function createRow(address) {
...
  return `<tr>
...
    <td><a href="/delete/${address.id}">delete</a></td>
    <td><a href="/edit/${address.id}">edit</a></td>
  </tr>`;
}
```

Listing 5.23 Links to Edit and Delete Records (list.js)

The HTTP server enables you to respond to the requests from clients. However, if you want to retrieve data from other web servers, for example, via a web service, the HTTP server is of little use. This is where the HTTP client comes into play.

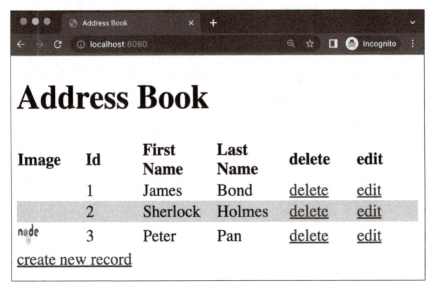

Figure 5.9 Extended List Display

5.2 Node.js as HTTP Client

The client allows you to formulate requests to servers and have all aspects of the request under your control, from the header to the body. In the following sections, Node.js plays the role of the client and interacts with the address book you created earlier. In this context, there are different options available to you to formulate a request. You can either use the http module of Node.js itself or install an additional module.

5.2.1 Requests with the http Module

The request function of the http module allows you to send requests to any web server. The advantage of this method is that you don't need to install any additional packages, whereas its disadvantage is a somewhat inconvenient interface. To generate a request, you must pass a configuration object and a callback function to the request function, which is executed as soon as the response is received. For a simple request like the one that's sent to the address book, you can use a URL object instead of an option object. In Listing 5.24, you can see the source code for this.

```
import { request } from 'http';

const options = new URL('http://localhost:8080/');

request(options, (response) => {
  let body = '';
  response.on('data', (chunk) => (body += chunk));
```

```
  response.on('end', () => {
    console.log(body);
  });
}).end();
```

Listing 5.24 Querying the Address Book Using the HTTP Request (index.js)

The URL object contains all the important information for the request, such as the server, port, and path. For all other information, such as the HTTP method, use the default values, in this case, GET. Handling the server's response is similar to the HTTP server implementation. The response is considered as a data stream consisting of one or more parts. You consume this by means of the data event. When the response is over, the end event gets triggered. The actual processing of the response then takes place at this point.

A prerequisite for this example to work is that the web server you developed earlier has been launched. If you run the example shown in Listing 5.24, you'll get the HTML code of the server's response on the command line.

Instead of the request function, you can also use the get function of the http module. That function is similar to the request function, but it provides a better description of your intention.

5.2.2   The request Package

A very widely used alternative to the request function of Node.js is the request package. This is an open-source project managed on GitHub and distributed via npm. It's installed via the npm install request command.

Read Accesses

After the installation, you can send read requests to a web server by using just a few lines. Listing 5.25 shows the request of the address book example.

```
import request from 'request';

request('http://localhost:8080/', (err, response, body) => {
  console.log(body);
});
```

Listing 5.25 Read Request Using the "request" Package (index.js)

The prerequisite for this example to work is that the previously implemented web server has been launched. As shown earlier in Listing 5.24, the server's response will be output to the command line.

As you can see, specifying the destination URL as a string is sufficient in this case. The handling of the response is also made much easier because it's directly available as a variable.

Write Accesses

In addition to read accesses, you can also use the request package to create data records in the address book. The source code shown in Listing 5.26 creates a new record, including the associated file upload.

```
import request from 'request';

import { createReadStream } from 'fs';

const formData = {
  firstname: 'Jason',
  lastname: 'Bourne',
  street: '1000 Colonial Farm Rd',
  city: 'Langley',
  country: 'USA',
  upload: createReadStream('./bild.png'),
};

request.post(
  { url: 'http://localhost:8080/save', formData },
  (err, response, body) => {
    if (err) {
      console.error(err);
    } else {
      console.log(body);
    }
  },
);
```

Listing 5.26 Creating New Entries on the Server (index.js)

The post function of the request package generates a POST request to the server. To this request, you must pass an object with the URL to which the information should be sent and the form data. For the key-value combination of formData: formData, you can use the standardized JavaScript shorthand notation formData. You should specify the information to be transmitted as an object. For the file upload, you must pass a readableStream as the value, which you can create via the createReadStream function from the fs module. In the callback function, which is executed after the response arrives, you have access to an error object, the representation of the response, and its body.

5.2.3   HTML Parser

In the previous examples, you retrieved HTML pages from the server and displayed their contents on the console. However, you normally use Node.js HTTP clients to read information from a page and process it further. This means that you locate and extract specific data within the HTML structure. This section introduces you to the cheerio package, a tool that allows you to work with HTML structures in a similar way to the browser. In addition to this package, there are many other HTML parsers available for Node.js such as the htmlparser2 package or jsdom.

You can install cheerio using the npm install cheerio command. For the following example, you also need the request package. In Listing 5.27, a read request is sent to the server, as in the previous example shown in Listing 5.25. For this purpose, you should make sure that the server is up and running.

```
import request from 'request';
import cheerio from 'cheerio';

request('http://localhost:8080/', (err, response, body) => {
  const addresses = [];

  const $ = cheerio.load(body);
  const tr = $('tr');
  tr.each((index, element) => {
    if (index === 0) {
      return;
    }
    addresses.push({
      id: element.children[3].children[0].data,
      firstname: element.children[5].children[0].data,
      lastname: element.children[7].children[0].data,
    });
  });

  console.log(addresses);
});
```

Listing 5.27 Using the HTML Parser (index.js)

Once the server's data is available to you, you must use the load method of cheerio to load the HTML string. After that you can use selectors to select and use the individual Document Object Model (DOM) nodes. The address data is available in a table structure. This means you need access to the individual table rows, which you get via the tr selector. In the resulting object, the each method is defined, which you can use to iterate across all found elements. In the callback function, you have access to the index as well as the representation of the object. You can use the index to ignore the first line containing the headings. The line contains alternating td nodes and space characters caused by the indentions in the code. The td nodes in turn contain the text nodes that contain the actual information. You must extract these into an object and insert this object into an array, which you finally output to the console. You can see the output of the script in Listing 5.28.

```
$ npm start

> node-book@1.0.0 start
> node index.js

[
  ID '1', firstname: 'James', lastname: 'Bond' },
  ID '2', firstname: 'Sherlock', lastname: 'Holmes' },
  ID '3', firstname: 'Peter', lastname: 'Pan' },
  ID '4', firstname: 'Jason', lastname: 'Bourne' }
]
```

Listing 5.28 Output of the "cheerio" Script (index.js)

5.3 Secure Communication with HTTPS

HTTP is an unencrypted protocol that poses the risk of a potential attacker eavesdropping on the communication between client and server and thus gaining possession of sensitive data. For this reason, most browsers also show in the address bar when a form is delivered over HTTP, especially with password entry. To switch a Node.js server from HTTP to HTTPS, only a few adjustments are required. In the following sections, you'll learn how to secure the address book example step by step.

5.3.1 Creating Certificates

First, you need a certificate for encryption. For a product application, you should obtain a certificate from a trusted certificate authority. Alternatively, you can use a Let's Encrypt certificate. Let's Encrypt is a free and open certification authority. However, for the example, you can also issue a self-signed certificate yourself. In this case, you need the command-line tool openssl. Listing 5.29 contains the commands needed to create a certificate for your web server.

```
openssl genrsa -out localhost.key 2048
openssl req -new -x509 -key localhost.key -out localhost.cert -days 9999 -subj
/CN=localhost
```

Listing 5.29 Generating Certificates

Using these two commands, you've created two files: *localhost.key* and *localhost.cert*.

5.3.2   Using HTTPS in the Web Server

For secure communication, you need to use the https module of Node.js instead of http. Both are application programming interface (API) compatible, so changes are kept to a minimum. You can see the necessary changes in Listing 5.30.

```
import { createServer } from 'https';
import { readFile, readFileSync, rename } from 'fs';
...
const options = {
  key: readFileSync('./localhost.key'),
  cert: readFileSync('./localhost.cert'),
};

createServer(options, (request, response) => {
  ...
}).listen(8080, () =>
  console.log('Address book reachable at https://localhost:8080'),
);
...
```

Listing 5.30 Secure Communication via HTTPS

When you create the server, you pass a configuration object that contains the key and the certificate. You can read both files from the file system using the readFileSync function of the fs module. In this case, synchronous processing is fine because it only happens once when the application starts. Finally, you should adjust the output on the command line after the server starts so that the correct protocol is displayed to the user.

Figure 5.10 Security Warning in Chrome

When you start your server now, you can access the address book through your browser via URL *https://localhost:8080*. Because the certificate is self-signed and therefore untrusted, you'll receive a warning in the browser that you must acknowledge before you can access the page.

5.4 HTTP/2

Since version 8.4, the http2 module is shipped with Node.js and supports the new protocol version for both the server and the client. The handling is slightly different from the http module. Furthermore, HTTP/2 provides some interesting additional features. First, HTTP/2 should no longer be used in the unencrypted version. Originally, it was planned that HTTP/2 should only exist in an encrypted variant, but the standardization consortium didn't come to a uniform solution here, so HTTP/2 can be used both encrypted and unencrypted. However, because most browser developers now display warnings for unsecured connections, this shouldn't be an option for you.

5.4.1 HTTP/2 Server

The interface of the http2 module is slightly different from that of the http module. The new module also builds on an event-based model, so the basic approach to development remains the same. You must import the createSecureServer function from the http2 module and use it instead of the createServer function. The rest of the code remains unchanged. The interaction with external libraries such as formidable also continues to work without any problems. Listing 5.31 shows the necessary adjustments to the source code.

```
...
import { createSecureServer } from 'http2';

const options = {
  key: readFileSync('./localhost.key'),
  cert: readFileSync('./localhost.cert'),
};

createSecureServer(options, (request, response) => {
...
```

Listing 5.31 Using the HTTP/2 Protocol (index.js)

If you want to use the more modern variant of the http2 module, you have to modify your initial file significantly more. In this case, you can't use the request event as usual, but the stream event. In Listing 5.32, you can see a shortened variant of the initial file, which only ensures that the list gets displayed.

```javascript
import { constants, createSecureServer } from 'http2';
import data from './data.js';
import { getList } from './list.js';
import { parse } from 'querystring';
import { readFile, readFileSync } from 'fs';

const {
  HTTP2_HEADER_PATH,
  HTTP2_HEADER_STATUS,
  HTTP2_HEADER_METHOD
} = constants;

const options = {
  key: readFileSync('./localhost.key'),
  cert: readFileSync('./localhost.cert'),
};

const server = createSecureServer(options);

server
  .on('stream', (stream, headers) => {
    const parts = headers[HTTP2_HEADER_PATH].split('/');
    if (headers[HTTP2_HEADER_PATH] === '/style.css') {
      readFile('public/style.css', 'utf8', (err, data) => {
        if (err) {
          stream.respond({
            'content-type': 'text/plain',
            [HTTP2_HEADER_STATUS]: 404,
          });
          stream.end();
        } else {
          stream.end(data);
        }
      });
    } else if (parts.includes('assets')) {
      readFile(
        `public${headers[HTTP2_HEADER_PATH].replaceAll('%20', ' ')}`,
        (err, data) => {
          if (err) {
            console.log(err);
            stream.respond({
              [HTTP2_HEADER_STATUS]: 404,
            });
            stream.end();
```

```
        } else {
          stream.end(data);
        }
      },
    );
  } else {
    send(stream, getList(data.addresses));
  }
})
.listen(8080, () =>
  console.log('Address book reachable at https://localhost:8080'),
);

function send(stream, responseBody) {
  stream.respond({
    'content-type': 'text/html',
    [HTTP2_HEADER_STATUS]: 200,
  });
  stream.end(responseBody);
}
```

Listing 5.32 List Display via HTTP2 (index.js)

The most important difference is that the HTTP/2 server supports the stream event in addition to the request event, which is largely compatible with the http and https modules. This event is triggered when a request is made through an HTTP/2 session and is similar to the request event—the only difference being that this is a socket connection. In the event handler, you have access to the stream representation and the headers. For example, you can use the stream to formulate the response to the client. The headers provide access to the URL path or the requested HTTP method. The header information is read via constants defined in the http2 module. In the example, the HTTP2_HEADER_PATH constant is used to access the URL path. Using the respond method of the stream, you can send a part of the response. The constants of the http2 module are also used to generate the response. The specification of [HTTP2_HEADER_STATUS]: 404 is a *computed property*, that is, a computed property name, which ensures that the value behind the constant is used as an object property. Calling the end method completes the response. Once you've made the adjustments to the source code, you can start the server and test your application.

In Figure 5.11, you can see the application delivered via HTTP/2. When you open the developer tools of your browser, you'll see **h2** entries in the **Protocol** column of the **Network** section. These entries represent the HTTP/2 protocol.

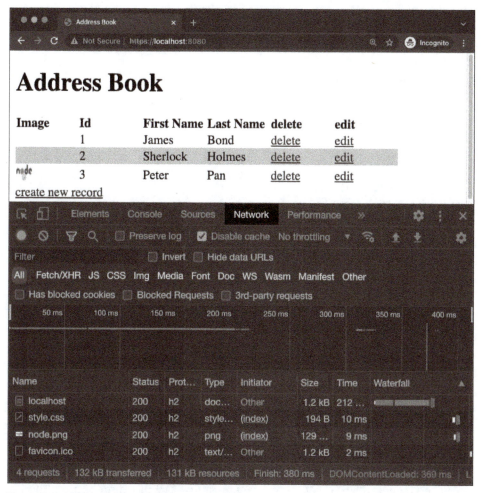

Figure 5.11 Delivery of the Application via HTTP/2

5.4.2 HTTP/2 Client

Like the http module, the http2 module can assume the role of an HTTP client and query other servers. For the following example, you must start the HTTP/2 server you created in Listing 5.32. Then you must create the HTTP/2 client using the source code from Listing 5.33.

```
import { connect, constants } from 'http2';
import { readFileSync } from 'fs';
import cheerio from 'cheerio';

const client = connect('https://localhost:8080', {
  ca: readFileSync('./localhost.cert'),
});
```

```
client.on('error', (err) => console.error(err));

const req = client.request({ [constants.HTTP2_HEADER_PATH]: '/' });

req.setEncoding('utf8');
let body = '';
req.on('data', (chunk) => {
  body += chunk;
});
req.on('end', () => {
  const addresses = [];
  const $ = cheerio.load(body);
  const tr = $('tr');
  tr.each((index, element) => {
    if (index === 0) return;
    addresses.push({
      id: element.children[3].children[0].data,
      firstname: element.children[5].children[0].data,
      lastname: element.children[7].children[0].data,
    });
  });

  console.log(addresses);
});
req.end();
```

Listing 5.33 HTTP/2 Client for Querying the Address List

To make a request to an HTTP/2 server, you must first establish a connection. This can be done via the connect method to which you pass the target server. In the example, self-signed certificates are used, which usually leads to the termination of the connection. For this reason, you must define the ca key in the second argument and pass the server certificate.

You can start the actual request using the request method. In this context, you must pass an object with the computed property HTTP2_HEADER_PATH from the HTTP/2 constants and the value /. On the data stream thus generated, you must then bind a handler to each of the data and end events. In the data handler, you collect the data that you receive from the server as a response. In the end handler, you process this data with the cheerio package; read the id, firstname, and lastname information from the table, as shown earlier in Listing 5.27; and output it to the console.

5.5 Summary

The Node.js HTTP server is one of the reasons for the success of Node.js. In just a few lines, you can implement a web server capable of delivering static content to a client. Add a few more lines, and you already have a dynamic solution that can handle data from the client and generate output based on it.

If you work directly with the http module, you should definitely make the extra effort and choose the secure variant with the https module. All you need to do that is a valid certificate. This means that communication between client and server is encrypted, which both increases your users' trust in your application and improves search engine ratings.

With the http2 module, the Node.js platform has been enriched by another module. This module enables contemporary applications with secure connections.

However, the http modules are in most cases only the entry point to web development with Node.js. They don't offer enough features for implementing extensive applications, which means you have to implement a lot of things yourself. A classic example of a library that you should include in this case is the request package.

With regard to productive web applications, it's also better to use frameworks such as Express. These are based on the http module or allow the integration of https and http2, and they enrich their functionality with additional useful features.

Chapter 6

Express

The future was better in the past too!
– Karl Valentin

Express has been the most popular web application framework for Node.js for many years. The open-source project was launched in June 2009 by T. J. Holowaychuk, and its purpose is to help you develop web applications. The focus of Express is on speed, manageable scope of the core framework, and an easily extensible interface. The well-thought-out architecture makes it possible to maintain until today, and thus the framework has become an almost indispensable companion when it comes to the development of web server applications based on Node.js. Frameworks such as Express exist because web development often involves solving standard tasks. For example, in PHP, there is the Symfony framework; in Python, you can use Django; and Ruby on Rails offers a solution for web applications under Ruby. You can implement your application completely in the respective language (in this case, Node.js) without the help of further libraries and frameworks, but you lose a lot of time with the implementation of the basic infrastructure. Just remember the `createServer` callback function from the previous chapter where you had to take care of parsing the URL and performing the corresponding action yourself.

In addition to handling requests and resolving URLs, other standard tasks such as session handling, authentication, or file uploads need to be taken care of. There are already established solutions for all these tasks, which have been combined into a framework under the leadership of Express. Because of its stability over the years and its extensible architecture, Express serves as the foundation for a variety of other libraries and frameworks, such as Nest, which we'll look at in more detail in Chapter 14.

6.1 Structure

Express is a compact framework with a manageable range of functions. However, it can be easily extended with middleware components. The structure of Express, much like Node.js itself, is layered, as you can see in Figure 6.1.

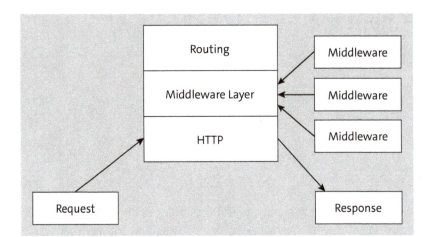

Figure 6.1 Express Structure

The http module of Node.js serves as the foundation for Express. The http module cre-ates the server process on which Express is based. In addition, the request and response objects are available to access the request information and create the response to the client, respectively. Internally, for example, Express makes use of the URL the user has entered in the browser to implement the routing process within the application.

The second layer of the Express architecture is the middleware layer. In the context of Express, a middleware is a function located between the incoming request and the server's response to the client. Multiple middleware functions can be chained together to perform specific actions based on the client's request. Prior to the third version of Express, Connect formed this middleware layer. In version 4, the developers aban-doned this additional dependency and developed a standalone layer, which remains mostly compatible. The third layer of the Express architecture is the router. This com-ponent of Express controls which function should be executed depending on the called URL to generate a response to the client. When routing, both the HTTP method and the URL path are considered.

In this chapter, you'll create a web application that allows you to manage a movie data-base. Before you start working on the application, you must first initialize it and install Express.

6.2   Installation

Express follows the Node Package Manager (npm) package standard: It's freely avail-able as an open-source project, subject to the MIT License and developed on GitHub. The Express package is available through a package manager of your choice, for exam-ple, npm. Before installing Express in your application, you must use npm init -y on the command line to generate the *package.json* file for your application and add the type field with the module value to use the ECMAScript module system. Then you must install Express via the npm install express command. After that, you can test the functionality of the framework with a simple application. Listing 6.1 shows the source code of this first step. You save the source code in a file named *index.js*.

```
import express from 'express';

const app = express();

app.get('/', (req, res) => {
  res.send('My first express application');
});

app.listen(8080, () => {
  console.log('Movie database accessible at http://localhost:8080');
});
```

Listing 6.1 First Express Application (index.js)

In the first step, you include the express package. The default export of the package is a function that you use to create the base for your application via the app object. The get method of the app object creates a route, in this case, for the path /. In the last step, you bind your application to Transmission Control Protocol (TCP) port 8080. Internally, a server is created at this point using the http module of Node.js and bound to the specified port. Once you've started the application via the node index.js command, you can access and test it in the browser using the URL *http://localhost:8080*. The results are displayed in Figure 6.2.

Figure 6.2 Output of the Express Application in the Browser

Based on this working foundation, you can now proceed to extend this example step by step to a fully functional application.

6.3 Basic Principles

The process by which an Express application works always has the same pattern. The Express server receives a request from a client. Based on the chosen http method and

URL path, a suitable route is chosen, and one or more callback functions are executed. Within this callback function, you can access the request and response objects, as is the case with the http module. These two objects, along with the router and middleware components, are the heart of an application.

6.3.1   Request

The request object is the first argument of the Express routing callback functions and represents the user's request. You can extend this object by using middleware components such as the body parser and the cookie parser, for example, so that you can manage cookies or other aspects of the communication with the client more conveniently. But even in standard mode, it contains a lot of helpful information. Table 6.1 introduces you to some of the most important properties of the request object.

Characteristic	Description
method	Contains the HTTP method used to send the request to the server.
originalUrl	Contains the original request URL. This allows the url property, which contains the same information, to be modified for in-application purposes.
params	Contains the value that consists of the variable parts of the URL. You'll learn how to define and use them in Express later in this chapter.
path	Enables you to access the URL path.
protocol	Contains the protocol of the request, such as HTTP or HTTPS.
query	Accesses the query string is a part of the URL.

Table 6.1 Key Properties of the "request" Object

In addition to the properties, you also have access to some methods that allow you to read more information about the incoming request. The get method enables you to read header fields from the request. For example, if you're interested in the Content-Type field, the call is req.get('Content-Type'). It doesn't matter whether you use uppercase or lowercase letters with this method.

6.3.2   Response

The response object, which you can access via the second argument of the routing function, represents the response to the client. Because you mainly write to this object, it also provides significantly more methods than properties. The most important property of the object is headersSent. This Boolean value tells you whether the HTTP headers of the response have already been sent. If this is the case, you can no longer modify it. Table 6.2 provides an overview of the most important methods of the response object.

method	Description
get(field)	Reads the specified header field of the response.
set(field[, value])	Sets the value of the specified header field.
cookie(name, value[, options])	Sets a cookie value.
redirect([status,]path)	Forwards the request.
status(code)	Sets the status code of the response.
send([body])	Sends the HTTP response.
Json([body])	Sends the HTTP response. The passed object is converted to a JavaScript Object Notation (JSON) object, and the correct response headers are set.
end([data][, encoding])	Sends the HTTP response. You should use this method primarily if you don't send user data such as HTML structures. Otherwise, you should use the send method.

Table 6.2 Key Methods of the "response" Object

After this brief introduction to the request and response handling elements, the following sections deal with the setup and architecture of an Express application.

6.4 Setup

As a general best practice in dealing with Express, it has emerged that an application should be divided into separate components as far as possible, each of which is stored in separate files. Although you create a lot of files with this strategy, depending on the size of your application, you'll still be able to locate the files quickly due to a well-structured directory hierarchy. A file contains only one component and thus a self-contained unit. For structuring an Express application, a classic model-view-controller (MVC) approach is the best choice.

MVC: The Model-View-Controller Pattern

The MVC pattern is used to structure applications, especially in web development, where it has become an important standard. This pattern describes where certain parts of an application should be stored and how these parts interact. The name MVC already contains the three components of the pattern:

- **Model**
  The models of an MVC application are used for data management. Models encapsulate all operations related to the data of your application. This concerns both the

creation and the modification or deletion of information. Typically, a model encapsulates database accesses. In addition to the pure data and the associated logic for handling it, models also encapsulate the business logic of your application.

■ **View**
The task of views consists of displaying information. The views of an Express application are mostly HTML templates populated with the dynamic data of your application before delivery to the client. In modern applications that are application programming interface (API) heavy, this aspect of the MVC architecture is increasingly taking a back seat, as templates are rarely rendered, and, instead, JSON objects are often sent from the server to the client.

■ **Controller**
A controller contains the control logic of your application. The controller brings models and views together. You should make sure that your controllers don't become too large. If the controller contains too much logic, you should outsource it to support functions or models.

When building your application, it's critical that you follow a consistent convention when structuring the file and directory hierarchy to maintain maintainability and extensibility over the lifecycle of the application.

6.4.1   Structure of an Application

The choice of directory structure depends very much on the scope of your application. Avoid making the structure unnecessarily complex at the very start because when you start working on an application, you usually don't know exactly what it will look like in the end. The more complex the structure becomes, the more time-consuming its adjustments become. Start with as flat a hierarchy as possible, and restructure the directories and files as needed. The module system of Node.js and modern development environments support you in this continuous refactoring process by easily moving files and directories and automatically adjusting import statements. An application usually consists of the following components: models, views, controllers, routers, and helpers.

Structure for Small Applications

For very small applications, you should create one file per component and place it in a directory. An example of such a structure is given in Figure 6.3.

This structuring approach only works for very manageable applications or small prototypes. As soon as your project has more than three or four separate endpoints, you should switch to the next larger variant or start with it directly, as migrating the structure in this case will only become unnecessarily time-consuming.

Figure 6.3 Directory Structure for Small Applications

Structure for Medium-Sized Applications

Web applications that have 10 to 15 independent endpoints, that is, separate routes, fit into the category of medium-sized applications. This structuring variant is a good starting point for normal web applications. In this structure, the different components—models, views, and controllers—are stored in separate directories. All structures are located in their own files and are named accordingly. To make it easier to locate the structures in the development environment, it has become best practice to include the type of structure in the file name. For example, a controller that is responsible for the login process of your application is then located in a file named *login.controller.js* in the *controllers* directory. The structure of such an application could look like the one shown in Figure 6.4.

Figure 6.4 Structure for Medium-Size Applications

The advantage of this structuring variant is that all structures are stored separately from each other and also within the respective component; for example, in the case of models, a thematic separation takes place at the file level. This decouples the different areas of the application and keeps the number of files per directory low. For small- and medium-sized applications this is a very good approach.

Structure for Large Applications

As far as the scope of your application is concerned, you're hardly limited when using Express. However, when developing the file and directory structure of large-scale applications, you should take an approach that allows you to thematically separate the modules of your application. Such a strategy allows you to develop your application in parallel with several teams and manage the individual modules independently. This also greatly simplifies the localization of code locations. Figure 6.5 shows an example of such a structure.

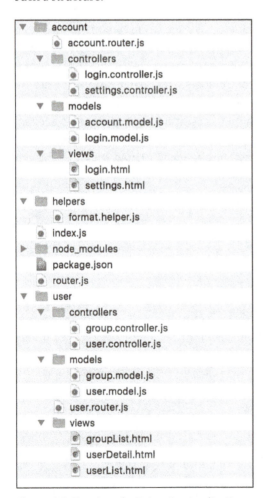

Figure 6.5 Structure for Extensive Applications

As you can see in Figure 6.5, there are separate directories for each subject area of the application. The selection and delineation of these areas depend entirely on you and the requirements of your application. Typically, modules are chosen to cover a topic in its entirety. This approach enables clean interfaces to the other parts of the application. The available options here range from logical units within an endpoint to groups of multiple thematically related endpoints. Each module in turn contains subdirectories, each of which contains the module's models, views, and controllers. In addition, each module defines its own router. Now that you have an overview of the structuring options for your application, you can move on to extending your first sample application in the next step.

6.5   Movie Database

A movie database will serve as a sample application for Express. This covers all essential aspects of a typical application. You can add movies to the database, view the existing records, update them if necessary, and also delete them. In addition, further functionalities such as ratings can be implemented. This application also serves as a basis for the following chapters when it comes to integrating template engines, connecting different databases, or authenticating users.

For the sample application, we chose the structure of a large application, although it will initially consist of only one module. The reason is that this structure offers the highest degree of flexibility, allowing you to get to know more features of Express.

The first step in the implementation of the application consists of the initialization. For this purpose, you should create a directory named *movie-db* and go to this directory via the command line. After that, you must run the `npm init -y` command to create a *package.json* file. Once you've created the file, you must add the `type` field with the `module` value to be able to use the ECMAScript module system. You're relatively free to choose a name, but you should select a unique name in case you want to publish your application. Note that the name must be written in lowercase letters and consist of only one word. However, it may contain hyphens and underscores. Then you must install Express using the `npm install express` command. Listing 6.2 shows the *package.json* file of the application.

```
{
  "name": "node-book",
  "version": "1.0.0",
  "description": "",
  "main": "index.js",
  "type": "module",
  "scripts": {
    "start": "node index.js"
  },
```

```
  "keywords": [],
  "author": "",
  "license": "ISC",
  "dependencies": {
    "express": "^4.17.1"
  }
}
```

Listing 6.2 Initial Configuration of the Application (package.json)

The two changes you need to make manually to the file are the type field and a startup script that allows you to conveniently start your application using the npm start command.

In the final step of initialization, you must create an *index.js* file in the root directory of your application as the entry point to your application. During development, you should make sure that this file is only responsible for initializing the application and doesn't perform any other tasks. The preliminary source code of this file is shown in Listing 6.3.

```
import express from 'express';

const app = express();

app.listen(8080, () => {
  console.log('Server is listening to http://localhost:8080');
});
```

Listing 6.3 Getting Started with the Application (index.js)

6.5.1   Routing

In the first step, you want your application to output a simple list of movie titles. For this purpose, you must first define a module, that is, a unit in your application that covers all aspects related to movies in the application. Based on the default guidelines for the structure, you first need a directory with the name of the module, in this case, *movie*. In this directory, you create a file named *index.js*. The file is the entry point to the module. If you integrate it into your application at a later point in time, this file ensures that all other relevant parts of the module are loaded so that the integration causes as little effort as possible.

The index file of your module exports the router object you later include in the index file of your application. In addition to creating the router object, this file currently takes care of managing the data and the response to the request in the callback function of the route. Listing 6.4 contains the source code of the file.

```
import { Router } from 'express';

const router = Router();

const data = [
  { id: 1, title: 'Iron Man', year: '2008' },
  { id: 2, title: 'Thor', year: '2011' },
  { id: 3, title: 'Captain America', year: '2011' },
];

router.get('/', (request, response) => {
  response.send(data);
});

export { router };
```

Listing 6.4 Router File of the Movie Module (movie/index.js)

Before you can display the data in the browser, you must integrate the router into your application. This is done in the *index.js* file in the root directory of your application, as shown in Listing 6.5.

```
import express from 'express';
import { router as movieRouter } from './movie/index.js';

const app = express();

app.use('/movie', movieRouter);

app.get('/', (request, response) => response.redirect('/movie'));

app.listen(8080, () => {
  console.log('Server is listening to http://localhost:8080');
});
```

Listing 6.5 Integrating the Router (index.js)

When loading the router, you must specify the name of the file in the ECMAScript module system, that is, *index.js*, as Node.js doesn't use this automatically when specifying a directory. This is different from the CommonJS module system. To make the code a bit more meaningful, you should rename the router to movieRouter on import. The use method specifies that the movieRouter is responsible for the /movie path. Currently, users of your application need to know that the movie list can be found at *http://localhost:8080/movie*. By using the get route for the / path and then redirecting to /movie, you enable users to also access the list via *http://localhost:8080*. This way, you've defined the entry point for your application. If you start your application via the npm start or node index.js commands, you can open it in your browser and get a display similar to the one shown in Figure 6.6.

Figure 6.6 Movie List in the Browser

Patterns in Routes

Static routes, as you've come to know them so far, cover most use cases in a web application. However, there are use cases where you reach the limits due to little flexibility. For this reason, it's possible to formulate dynamic routes in Express.

Patterns	Example	Path	Description
?	/ab?c	/abc or /ac	Sign may occur, but doesn't have to.
+	/ab+c	/abc or /abbc	Character occurs once or multiple times.
*	/a*c	/ac or /aABCc	Any character string.

Table 6.3 Patterns in Routes

In addition to the patterns listed in Table 6.3, you can create groups of characters by means of parentheses and apply the multipliers to these groups. Thus, a route from /a(bc)?d applies to both /ad and /abcd. If these options are still not sufficient to cover your use case, you can also specify routes as regular expressions. Listing 6.6 shows an example of such a route, which is responsible for all paths that contain the string /movie somewhere in the path.

> **Route Dependency**
>
> Note that a route in Express can cause other routes to stop running, depending on where you place it in your application. Express always uses the first suitable route it can find. If it sends its response to the client, the middleware chain is broken, and Express doesn't perform any further functions for this request.

```
app.get(/.*\/movie.*$/, function (request, response) {
  response.send('Movie Route');
});
```

Listing 6.6 Regular Expressions as Routes

If you formulate your routes with regular expressions, you have maximum flexibility. However, this often makes the routes less legible, which makes troubleshooting more difficult. For this reason, you should use regular expressions sparingly in this case and rather as an exception when the normal route definitions are no longer sufficient.

6.5.2   Controller

At this point, your router still implements the complete MVC pattern on its own. This isn't desirable because readability suffers with increasing functionality, so in the next step, you must outsource everything except the actual route definition to a controller. The controller has the task of merging the view and the model. In addition, at this point, the information is usually extracted from the request, and the response to the client is formulated. As to the naming of routing callback functions, it has become standard in many web frameworks to refer to these functions as actions. A controller can contain several of these action functions. Listing 6.7 shows the implementation of the controller for the list view.

```
const data = [
  { id: 1, title: 'Iron Man', year: '2008' },
  { id: 2, title: 'Thor', year: '2011' },
  { id: 3, title: 'Captain America', year: '2011' },
];

export function listAction(request, response) {
  response.send(data);
}
```

Listing 6.7 Controller (movie/controller.js)

Export and implementation are linked in this case. However, at this point, you may as well collect all exports at the end of the file. There is no right or wrong here; the only important thing is to stay consistent and always use the same type of export. Typically, you use the combination of export and definition in files that contain only a few exports. In general, you should make sure that a file doesn't export too many structures, as this can quickly become confusing and indicate that the file hosts too many structures.

The controller is included in the router, where a reference to the listAction method of the controller is entered instead of the routing callback function. The source code of the customized router is shown in Listing 6.8.

```
import { Router } from 'express';
import { listAction } from './controller.js';

const router = Router();
```

```
router.get('/', listAction);
```

```
export { router };
```

Listing 6.8 Including the Controller Action in the Router (movie/index.js)

When extending the router, you must import listAction and use it in the get method of the router. With this modification, you've separated the routing of your module and the handling of request and response. However, model, view, and controller are still quite tightly connected. The next step is to resolve this.

6.5.3   Model

The movie database data has the form of a simple array of objects. The model encapsulates this array and provides a function to read the data and later further methods to modify this data structure. You're not yet working with a database or other external system for data storage in your application. But to make the source code of the application a bit more realistic, you should implement the interfaces of the model with promises and, thus, asynchronously.

Promises

A *promise* is an object that represents the fulfillment of an asynchronous operation in JavaScript. Unlike callback functions, you can work much better with promises and also bind multiple operations to the fulfillment of such a promise object.

Promises are a language feature of JavaScript and part of the standard, so they are supported on both the client side and server side. You can create a promise object either with the promise constructor or with Promise.resolve or Promise.reject. Listing 6.9 shows a simple example of a function that works with promises.

```
function asyncFunction() {
  return new Promise((resolve, reject) => {
    setTimeout(() => {
      resolve('Hello world!');
    }, 1000);
  });
}

const promise = asyncFunction();
promise.then((value) => {
  console.log(value);
});
```

Listing 6.9 Using Promises

> You pass a callback function to the promise constructor in the asyncFunction function. This function has access to the resolve and reject arguments. You can use these functions to indicate a success or failure of an asynchronous operation by calling the respective function. Here, you can pass any value that represents something like the return value of the asynchronous operation.
>
> The promise object that the asyncFunction returns has the then, catch, and finally methods. Each of these methods accepts a callback function that will be executed in case of success, error, or both, respectively, and will be passed the value you passed when calling resolve or reject. The then method is a special case because here you can specify a second callback function for the case of an error.

The data of the model is in the scope of the file and can't be modified directly from outside. The getAll method returns a promise object that you can create using the Promise.resolve method (see Listing 6.10). This promise object is resolved with a reference to the data. This is a problem at first because the information could be changed via this reference. At a later date, this data structure will be exchanged for a fully-fledged database, so there's currently no need to worry about this problem. After you've created the basis for the model, you still need to integrate it into your application. The controller is the place to go for this. Listing 6.11 shows the adjustments you need to make to your code.

```
const data = [
  { id: 1, title: 'Iron Man', year: '2008' },
  { id: 2, title: 'Thor', year: '2011' },
  { id: 3, title: 'Captain America', year: '2011' },
];

export function getAll() {
  return Promise.resolve(data);
}
```

Listing 6.10 Implementing the Model (movie/model.js)

```
import { getAll } from './model.js';


export async function listAction(request, response) {
  const data = await getAll();
  response.send(data);
}
```

Listing 6.11 Adapting the Controller to Integrate the Model (movie/controller.js)

If you implement the listAction function as an async function as in our example, you can use the await keyword within this function to wait for the promise to resolve. This whole task is done asynchronously, that is, nonblocking, making the source code much more readable than if you were using callback functions. Express supports this type of asynchronicity directly and without additional configuration.

6.5.4 View

The final component of your MVC application with Express is the view. This part is responsible for the display. The output of a JavaScript object isn't a particularly appealing form of presentation. Therefore, it's better to use HTML as the output format at this point. You have several options for the display. For example, you can save the HTML code in a separate HTML file, read it with JavaScript, and replace the appropriate sections. You can either do this replacement directly using the replace method of the HTML string, or you can use an HTML parser such as Cheerio. A simpler variant is to use JavaScript template strings, as you'll see later in this section. Another option is to use a template engine. The next chapter describes this topic in greater detail. Listing 6.12 contains the movie list view.

```
export function render(movies) {
  return `
<!DOCTYPE html>
<html lang="en">
<head>
  <meta charset="UTF-8">
  <title>Movie list</title>
</head>
<body>
  <table>
    <thead><tr><th>Id</th><th>Title</th></tr></thead>
    <tbody>
      ${movies
        .map(movie => `<tr><td>${movie.id}</td><td>${movie.title}</td></tr>`)
        .join('')}
    </tbody>
  </table>
</body>
</html>
  `;
};
```

Listing 6.12 Displaying the Movie List View (movie/view.js)

The view in this case consists of a render function that receives the data to be displayed as an argument. Within the HTML structure, each entry is transformed into a table row using the map method. You connect this structure with the join method into a character string, which is then output at the correct position within the template string. The task of the controller is to bring the model and view together. Listing 6.13 contains the customized code of the controller.

```
import { getAll } from './model.js';
import { render } from './view.js';

export async function listAction(request, response) {
  const data = await getAll();
  const body = render(data);
  response.send(body);
}
```

Listing 6.13 View Integration in the Controller (movie/controller.js)

The listAction function loads the list of movies in the first step. This is passed to the view in the second step. In the last step, you send the HTML structure to the client. When you restart your application via the command line using the npm start command now, you'll get an output like the one shown in Figure 6.7.

Figure 6.7 Display of the Movie List after the View Conversion

When implementing your application, make sure that you move as little logic as possible into the view. Iteration, as you've implemented here, or simple conditions to hide or show parts are recommended options. You should definitely outsource more extensive logic to your models.

6.6   Middleware

A key design feature of Express is the middleware concept, which makes the framework a very flexible tool. Simply put, middleware here refers to a function that stands between the incoming request and the outgoing response. You can put as many of these functions in succession as you like. There are already numerous predefined middleware functions that you can include in your application and that perform specific tasks for you. If all this doesn't provide any solution to your problem, you can even write such a function yourself.

6.6.1   Custom Middleware

You can use a middleware function to extract information from the incoming request and store it, such as with a logger. However, you can also enrich the response based on information from the request. A middleware function must have a specific signature so that it doesn't break the chain of middleware functions. Suppose you wanted to define a logger for your application that writes each request to the console. To do this, you must adjust the contents of your application's initial file according to Listing 6.14.

```
import express from 'express';
import { router as movieRouter } from './movie/index.js';

const app = express();

function log(request, response, next) {
  console.log(request.url);
  next();
}
app.use(log);

app.use('/movie', movieRouter);

app.get('/', (request, response) => response.redirect('/movie'));

app.listen(8080, () => {
  console.log('Server is listening to http://localhost:8080');
});
```

Listing 6.14 A Simple Logger (index.js)

As you can see in Listing 6.14, the signature of a middleware function is similar to that of an ordinary routing function. A middleware function always has the three parameters: request, response, and a callback function. The request and response parameters provide access to the request and response, just like in the controller actions. The request object is used in the example to output the requested URL to the console. The passed callback function, which by convention is named next, ensures that the next middleware function in the chain is called when the function is called. If you don't perform this callback function, usually no response is sent to the client, and the client receives a time-out error. You can register your middleware using the use method of your application. As the first argument, this method optionally accepts a URL path to which the middleware should be applied. If you only pass a callback function, the middleware will be executed on every request. The order in which you register your functions is important. If you first register a regular routing method that doesn't call the next callback function, your middleware component, which is registered afterwards, won't be executed. If your middleware is to perform calculations or modifications you need later in the call chain of the functions, you can cache this information in the request object or, better yet, in the response object within a property. These objects are available to all functions as a reference and can therefore also be used to transport information.

Especially for standard tasks, such as the creation of an access log, there are prefabricated components that you only have to install and integrate. For a list of middleware components, see *http://expressjs.com/en/resources/middleware.html*.

6.6.2   Morgan: Logging Middleware for Express

Logging incoming requests is a standard problem for which there are established solutions. Morgan is one of the most popular middleware components available that does this work for you. Use the npm install morgan command to install the package in your application. At its core, Morgan consists of a function that accepts a format for the log entries and additional options. This means you can replace your current logger implementation with Morgan in the next step, as shown in Listing 6.15.

```
import express from 'express';
import morgan from 'morgan';
import { router as movieRouter } from './movie/index.js';

const app = express();

app.use(morgan('common', { immediate: true }));

app.use('/movie', movieRouter);

app.get('/', (request, response) => response.redirect('/movie'));

app.listen(8080, () => {
  console.log('Server is listening to http://localhost:8080');
});
```

Listing 6.15 Morgan Middleware

Concerning the format, you can choose from a number of predefined formats such as combined, short, or dev. The common format used in the example is similar to the format used by the Apache web server in the access log. As an alternative to the predefined formats, you can also define a format yourself. For example, if you want to record only the date, HTTP method, URL, and status code, the corresponding format looks like this: `':date :method :url :status'`. The third variant for defining a format consists of using a function instead of a character string. Irrespective of the variant you decide on, you must pass it to the `morgan` function as the first argument. The `option` object, which you pass as the second argument to Morgan, allows you to manipulate the behavior of the logger. With the `immediate` key used in the example, you specify whether the log entry should be written immediately or only when the response is sent to the client. The `stream` property allows you to specify a writable stream to which the log entries are written. This allows you to write the log entries to not only the console but also a file.

In Listing 6.16, you can see how to use the `createWriteStream` function from the `fs` module to open a data stream that writes to the *access.log* file and pass it to Morgan using the `stream` property of the configuration object. This results in a new entry being written to the file each time it's accessed. The configuration object of the `createWriteStream` function with the `flags` property and the a value ensures that new entries are appended and the existing content isn't overwritten. Furthermore, the file gets created, if it doesn't already exist.

The `skip` property allows you to specify a function that can access the request and response and whose return value determines whether an entry is written to the log or not. If the `skip` function returns the `false` value, the entry won't be written.

```
import express from 'express';
import morgan from 'morgan';
import { createWriteStream } from 'fs';
import { router as movieRouter } from './movie/index.js';

const app = express();

const accessLogStream = createWriteStream('access.log', { flags: 'a' });
app.use(morgan('common', {
  immediate: true,
  stream: accessLogStream
}));

app.use('/movie', movieRouter);

app.get('/', (request, response) => response.redirect('/movie'));

app.listen(8080, () => {
  console.log('Server is listening to http://localhost:8080');
});
```

Listing 6.16 Writing Log Entries to a File (index.js)

6.6.3 Delivering Static Content

Web applications that you implement with Express usually not only consist of dynamic content but also require static files. For this reason, HTML, JavaScript, CSS, and image files must be loaded. Although you can use the fs module to read the contents of these files and send them to the client as a response, this task becomes much easier if you use the static middleware. Unlike Morgan, that is a component of Express, so you don't need to install any additional packages. If you take a look at the movie list in your browser, you won't be presented with a particularly attractive sight. However, this can be changed with a little bit of CSS. The CSS code shown in Listing 6.17 makes the table look slightly more appealing.

```css
table {
  border-spacing: 0
}
th {
  background-color: black;
  font-weight: bold;
  color: lightgrey;
  text-align: left;
  padding: 5px;
}
td {
  border-top: 1px solid darkgrey;
  padding: 5px;
}
tbody tr:hover {
  background-color: lightgrey;
}
```

Listing 6.17 Styling the List (public/style.css)

To apply the styling to the movie list, you must adjust your application in two places. First, you need to make sure that the server delivers the CSS file and that the browser actually loads it. The delivery is carried out via the already mentioned static middleware. As was the case with the logger or the router, you include the static middleware via the use method of the app object. Listing 6.18 shows the customized initial file of your application.

```javascript
import express from 'express';
import morgan from 'morgan';
import { dirname } from 'path';
import { fileURLToPath } from 'url';
import { router as movieRouter } from './movie/index.js';
```

```
const app = express();

app.use(express.static(`${dirname(fileURLToPath(import.meta.url))}/public`));

app.use(morgan('common', { immediate: true }));

app.use('/movie', movieRouter);

app.get('/', (request, response) => response.redirect('/movie'));

app.listen(8080, () => {
  console.log('Server is listening to http://localhost:8080');
});
```

Listing 6.18 Integrating the "static" Middleware (index.js)

When you call the static middleware, you pass the name of the directory where the static content resides. For the movie list, this is the *public* directory in the root of your application. In the next step, you can now reference the CSS file via a link tag in the HTML code of the list, as shown in Listing 6.19.

```
export function render(movies) {
  return `
<!DOCTYPE html>
<html lang="en">
<head>
  <meta charset="UTF-8">
  <title>Movie list</title>
  <link rel="stylesheet" href="style.css" />
</head>
<body>
  <table>...</table>
</body>
</html>
  `;
}
```

Listing 6.19 Embedding the CSS File into the HTML Code (movie/view.js)

If you modify the list view source code according to Listing 6.19 and restart your application, you'll get a view similar to the one shown in Figure 6.8.

Figure 6.8 List View with CSS

6.7   Extended Routing: Deleting Data Records

Until now, the functionality of your application is limited to the display of data. In the next step, you provide your users with the option to delete data, as shown in Listing 6.20. To do this, you must first insert one link per record in the frontend. This link leads to a route on the server that takes care of deleting the record. After the deletion is done, you must redirect the user to the list so that the view gets updated.

```
<table>
  <thead><tr><th>Id</th><th>Title</th><th></th></tr></thead>
  <tbody>
    ${movies
      .map(
        movie => `
        <tr>
          <td>${movie.id}</td>
          <td>${movie.title}</td>
          <td><a href="/movie/delete/${movie.id}">delete</a></td>
        </tr>`,
      )
      .join('')}
  </tbody>
</table>
```

Listing 6.20 Extending the Template with a Delete Link (movie/view.js)

The routing functions in Express support all available HTTP methods, including, for example, the DELETE method. This should normally be the preferred way of deleting data, as each HTTP method has a specific meaning. In classic web applications, however, the only method you can invoke through a link is GET. For this reason, you must add an appropriate get route to your router for deleting data records. In Chapter 10, when you implement a representational state transfer (REST) server, the situation is different. When you take a look at the delivered source code, you'll notice that each link in the table looks different because you specify the ID of the record you want to delete. This leads to a peculiarity in specifying the path in the router link. In this case, the link contains a variable portion representing the ID you can access through the request object. You must mark such a variable in the specification of the path of the routing function by a colon followed by the name of the variable. Listing 6.21 shows the modification at the router.

```
import { Router } from 'express';
import { listAction, removeAction } from './controller.js';

const router = Router();

router.get('/', listAction);
router.get('/delete/:id', removeAction);

export { router };
```

Listing 6.21 Extending the Router with a Delete Route (movie/index.js)

In the removeAction of the controller, you can access the variables of the route via the params object of the request. In this case, you can reach the ID passed by the user via request.params.id. Here you should note that Express interprets the transmitted values as strings. To be able to continue using the ID later, you should convert it to a number via the parseInt function. Listing 6.22 contains the source code of the controller.

```
import { getAll, remove } from './model.js';s
import { render } from './view.js';

export async function listAction(request, response) {...}

export async function removeAction(request, response) {
  const id = parseInt(request.params.id, 10);
  await remove(id);
  response.redirect(request.baseUrl);
}
```

Listing 6.22 "removeAction" of the Controller (movie/controller.js)

Once you've converted the ID, you can call the remove method of the model, which will make sure that the corresponding record in the data source gets deleted. This operation is also asynchronous and works with promises, so put async/await here. After the operation is complete, you must redirect the user to the list using the response.redirect method. Here you can see another feature of the modular structure of an application:

instead of redirecting directly to "/movie/" in the `redirect` method, the `baseUrl` property of the `request` object is used in this case. The reason for this is that the movie module itself doesn't know the base URL for which it's responsible. To avoid a tight coupling between the embedding location and the module here, you must use the `baseUrl` property that contains the information. This allows you to change the `baseUrl` in the *index.js* file at a later stage without having to modify the module.

Finally, the `remove` method of the model filters out the data record to be deleted from the data source and overwrites the data source with the updated information. Listing 6.23 shows the corresponding implementation.

```
let data = [...];

export function getAll() {
  return Promise.resolve(data);
}


export function remove(id) {
  data = data.filter(movie => movie.id !== id);
  return Promise.resolve();
}
```

Listing 6.23 Customization on the Model (movie/model.js)

Note that in the model implementation, to clear the data, you must change the `data` array from a constant to a variable via `let`.

6.8   Creating and Editing Data Records: Body Parser

You can only transmit a few data records via variables in the URL, and especially for forms this isn't a practicable solution. As a rule, data is also sent using HTTP POST. You can benefit from this fact when extending your application. In the next step, you'll implement a way to create new records and edit existing ones. You start this customization again in the frontend of your application by adding a link to the list display, which allows your users to create new records. Furthermore, you should add a link in the table for each entry to edit the records. Listing 6.24 contains the source code of the view.

```
export function render(movies) {
  return `
<!DOCTYPE html>
<html lang="en">
<head>
  <meta charset="UTF-8">
```

```
    <title>Movie list</title>
    <link rel="stylesheet" href="style.css" />
</head>
<body>
    <table>
        <thead><tr><th>Id</th><th>Title</th><th></th><th></th></tr></thead>
        <tbody>
            ${movies
              .map(
                (movie) => `
              <tr>
                <td>${movie.id}</td>
                <td>${movie.title}</td>
                <td><a href="/movie/delete/${movie.id}">delete</a></td>
                <td><a href="/movie/form/${movie.id}">edit</a></td>
              </tr>`,
              )
              .join('')}
        </tbody>
    </table>
    <a href="/movie/form">new</a>
</body>
</html>
    `;
}
```

Listing 6.24 Customizing the View (movie/view.js)

Both links of the view point to the same route, once to /movie/form and once to /movie/form/:id. In Express, you can define optional parameters. If you attach a question mark to the parameter, it will be marked as optional, and you won't have to define two separate routes. You can see the updated router configuration in Listing 6.25.

```
import { Router } from 'express';
import { listAction, removeAction, formAction } from './controller.js';

const router = Router();

router.get('/', listAction);
router.get('/delete/:id', removeAction);
router.get('/form/:id?', formAction);

export { router };
```

Listing 6.25 Customizing the Router Configuration (movie/index.js)

The controller is responsible for reading information from the model based on the information from the request, if necessary, and for rendering the view. The crucial point here is to distinguish whether the user passed an ID to edit a data record or to create a new one. As you can see in Listing 6.26, a data record is passed to the view in each case.

```javascript
import { getAll, remove, get } from './model.js';
import { render } from './view.js';
import { render as form } from './form.js';

export async function listAction(request, response) {...}

export async function removeAction(request, response) {...}

export async function formAction(request, response) {
  let movie = { id: '', title: '', year: '' };

  if (request.params.id) {
    movie = await get(parseInt(request.params.id, 10));
  }

  const body = form(movie);
  response.send(body);
}
```

Listing 6.26 "formAction" in the Controller (movie/controller.js)

The implementation of this view is based on the implementation of the list. Listing 6.27 contains the source code.

```javascript
export function render(movie) {
  return `
<!DOCTYPE html>
<html lang="en">
<head>
  <meta charset="UTF-8">
  <title>Movie list</title>
  <link rel="stylesheet" href=" /style.css" />
</head>
<body>
  <form action="/movie/save" method="post">
    <input type="hidden" id="id" name="id" value="${movie.id}" />
    <div>
      <label for="title">Titel:</label>
```

```
          <input type="text" id="title" name="title" value="${movie.title}" />
        </div>
        <div>
          <label for="id">Year:</label>
          <input type="text" id="year" name="year" value="${movie.year}" />
        </div>
        <div>
          <button type="submit">save</button>
        </div>
      </form>
    </body>
    </html>
    `;
};
```

Listing 6.27 Form View (movie/form.js)

The form uses the action="/movie/save" and method="post" attributes to ensure that
the HTTP POST method data entered by the user is sent to the server. Based on the presence of an ID value, the server can distinguish whether the request is a creating or modifying operation. The values that are passed during editing are inserted into the
individual form fields as value attributes via template substitutions. To be able to edit
a record, you still need to implement the get method in the model, which you use to
load the data record from the data source. In this application, it's sufficient to call the
find method of the data array to load the data record based on its ID. Listing 6.28 shows
the corresponding source code.

```
let data = [...];

export function getAll() {...}

export function get(id) {
  return Promise.resolve(data.find((movie) => movie.id === id));
}

export function remove(id) {...}
```

Listing 6.28 Extending the Model with the "get" Method (movie/model.js)

When reloading your application, you can reach the form either via the **New** or the **Edit**
links in the list. The results are shown in Figure 6.9.

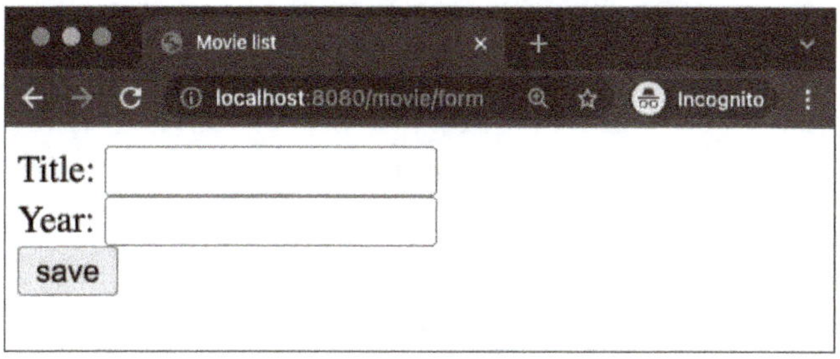

Figure 6.9 Form for Creating Data Records

6.8.1   Handling Form Input: Body Parser

To save your users' input, you must be able to access the form data. The most convenient way to do so is to use the body parser middleware. The body parser package has had a troubled past. Originally, middleware was an integral part of Express, similar to static middleware. However, with version 4, it was moved out into a package of its own, and with version 4.16, it was incorporated back into the core of Express. So, if you're using a recent version of Express, you don't need to install any additional packages to request body processing.

The body parser provides you with the two functions, json and urlencoded for JSON- and URL-encoded requests, respectively, which you can access directly via the express object. You can see the middleware integration in the *index.js* file of your application in Listing 6.29.

```
import express from 'express';
import morgan from 'morgan';
import { dirname } from 'path';
import { fileURLToPath } from 'url';
import { router as movieRouter } from './movie/index.js';

const app = express();

app.use(express.static(`${dirname(fileURLToPath(import.meta.url))}/public`));

app.use(morgan('common', { immediate: true }));

app.use(express.urlencoded({ extended: false }));

app.use('/movie', movieRouter);

app.get('/', (request, response) => response.redirect('/movie'));
```

```
app.listen(8080, () => {
  console.log('Server is listening to http://localhost:8080');
});
```

Listing 6.29 Integrating the Body Parser Middleware (index.js)

As already mentioned, the body parser middleware supports various parsers. If you're processing an ordinary HTML form, as in the example, you should use the urlencoded parser. If your frontend sends the information in JSON format instead, the JSON parser comes into play. Other parsers include the raw parser, which parses the body as a buffer, and the text parser, which interprets the body of the request as text. However, these two are only available as of Express version 4.17. You can also use the different parsers in parallel, for example, both the urlencoded and the JSON parser at the same time. After the inclusion, you must extend the router of your movie module to support the */movie/save* URL path.

As you can see in Listing 6.30, the extension follows the scheme we've been using until now. The saveAction of the controller passes the information to the model. For better control, the controller extracts the required properties from the request.body property provided by the body parser. This property contains all the data of the form as object properties.

```
import { Router } from 'express';
import
  listAction,
  removeAction,
  formAction,
  saveAction,
} from './controller.js';

const router = Router();

router.get('/', listAction);
router.get('/delete/:id', removeAction);
router.get('/form/:id?', formAction);
router.post('/save', saveAction);

export { router };
```

Listing 6.30 Extending the Router with the Save Route (movie/index.js)

A separate view isn't needed in the controller because saveAction redirects to the list. Again, as with deleting data records, the baseUrl property of the request object comes into play. Listing 6.31 shows the customized controller.

```
import { getAll, remove, get, save } from './model.js';
import { render } from './view.js';
import { render as form } from './form.js';

export async function listAction(request, response) {...}
export async function removeAction(request, response) {...}
export async function formAction(request, response) {...}

export async function saveAction(request, response) {
  const movie = {
    id: request.body.id,
    title: request.body.title,
    year: request.body.year,
  };
  await save(movie);
  response.redirect(request.baseUrl);
}
```

Listing 6.31 "saveAction" of the Controller (movie/controller.js)

The controller doesn't know whether the current operation is a new creation or an update of a data record. This decision is left to the model. For this reason, the model code is also a bit more extensive at this point, as you can see in Listing 6.32.

```
let data = [...];

function getNextId() {
  return Math.max(...data.map((movie) => movie.id)) + 1;
}

function insert(movie) {
  movie.id = getNextId();
  data.push(movie);
}

function update(movie) {
  movie.id = parseInt(movie.id, 10);
  const index = data.findIndex((item) => item.id === movie.id);
  data[index] = movie;
}

export function getAll() {...}

export function get(id) {...}
```

```
export function remove(id) {...}

export function save(movie) {
  if (movie.id === '') {
    insert(movie);
  } else {
    update(movie);
  }
  return Promise.resolve();
}
```

Listing 6.32 Implementing the "save" Method in the Model (movie/model.js)

In the save function of the model, the id property of the transferred data is used to decide whether it's a new or an existing data record. For new records, the hidden input field of the form isn't filled or has an empty character string as its value. To keep the method clear and manageable, the insert and update functionality are swapped out into separate helper functions. The insert function uses the getNextId function, which searches for the next free ID in the data source. Normally, this task is assumed by the database; in our case, the highest ID of the data in the array is searched and incremented by one. Then the new ID is assigned to the record, and the information is pushed into the data array. When updating the data, you must first convert the ID of the record to a number because all information arrives from the client as character strings, and the ID is stored as a number for the calculation of the next higher ID in the data source. This change allows you to find the index of the affected record in the data source and adjust the array by overwriting the old record with the new information.

After restarting the process, you can now view, delete, edit, and create new movies in your database.

6.9   Express 5

The development of Express has lost some momentum. A clear sign of this is that there hasn't been a major release in quite some time. In the summer of 2021, version 5 of the framework was still in alpha stage. Version 4 of Express was released in April 2014. Since then, the framework has received numerous minor updates. For web developers, however, this has a decisive advantage as well: Express is a very stable and thousand-times field-tested basis for your application, where you don't have to fear that the API will change seriously.

For Express 5, the developers have announced that there will be no serious changes. Some methods that have proven to be impractical or misleading over time are removed. A classic example is the send method with which you could send a string or a number. If a number is passed, it's sent to the user as a status. For example, an

Unauthorized message can be sent in a quick way. However, this has the disadvantage that you have no way to send a regular number to the client. With Express 5, you accomplish this with the `sendStatus` method.

Express 5, as long as it hasn't yet been released, can be installed using the command `npm install express@5.0.0-alpha.8`.

6.10   HTTPS and HTTP/2

Because Express is based on the HTTP module of Node.js, the framework is quite flexible when it comes to exchanging the communication protocol.

6.10.1   HTTPS

Instead of HTTP, you can also use the secure HTTPS variant recommended for productive applications. For this, you don't need to do anything more than pass the `app` object you created by calling the `express` function to the `createServer` method of the `https` module.

Listing 6.33 contains the necessary customizations to deliver your movie database with HTTPS. The example assumes that you've issued yourself a self-signed certificate and saved the files in the *cert* directory as in Chapter 5, Section 5.3. When you restart the server after these adjustments, you can reach your application at *https://localhost:8080*.

```
import { createServer } from 'https';
import { readFileSync } from 'fs';
import express from 'express';
import morgan from 'morgan';
import { dirname } from 'path';
import { fileURLToPath } from 'url';
import { router as movieRouter } from './movie/index.js';

const app = express();

app.use(express.static(`${dirname(fileURLToPath(import.meta.url))}/public`));

app.use(morgan('common', { immediate: true }));

app.use(express.urlencoded({ extended: false }));

app.use('/movie', movieRouter);

app.get('/', (request, response) => response.redirect('/movie'));
```

```
const options = {
  key: readFileSync('./cert/localhost.key'),
  cert: readFileSync('./cert/localhost.cert'),
};

createServer(options, app).listen(8080, () => {
  console.log('Server is listening to https://localhost:8080');
});
```

Listing 6.33 Express with HTTPS

6.10.2   HTTP/2

The integration of HTTP/2 works similar to HTTPS. However, the problem here is that Express version 4 isn't compatible with the HTTP/2 module of Node.js. Therefore, you have to switch to the spdy module at this point. Native support is planned for version 5.

You can install the spdy module using the npm install spdy command. The name of this module is somewhat misleading, as it not only supports SPDY but also HTTP/2. SPDY is a protocol developed by Google to replace HTTP in version 1. The HTTP/2 protocol picks up some concepts from the SPDY protocol.

The spdy module is API compatible with the http and https modules of Node.js, so it combines well with Express. With regard to the integration, you can proceed in a similar way as you did before with the HTTPS integration. As you can see in Listing 6.34, instead of importing the https module, you must import the spdy package and call the spdy.createServer function instead of the createServer function of the https module.

```
import spdy from 'spdy';
import { readFileSync } from 'fs';
import express from 'express';
import morgan from 'morgan';
import { dirname } from 'path';
import { fileURLToPath } from 'url';
import { router as movieRouter } from './movie/index.js';

const app = express();

app.use(express.static(`${dirname(fileURLToPath(import.meta.url))}/public`));

app.use(morgan('common', { immediate: true }));

app.use(express.urlencoded({ extended: false }));

app.use('/movie', movieRouter);
```

```
app.get('/', (request, response) => response.redirect('/movie'));

const options = {
  key: readFileSync('./cert/localhost.key'),
  cert: readFileSync('./cert/localhost.cert'),
};

spdy.createServer(options, app).listen(8080, () => {
  console.log('Server is listening to https://localhost:8080');
});
```

Listing 6.34 HTTP/2 in Express

You can verify that the switch to the HTTP/2 protocol worked by opening your browser's developer tools and making sure that, as in Figure 6.10, the **h2** protocol is used for loading each resource.

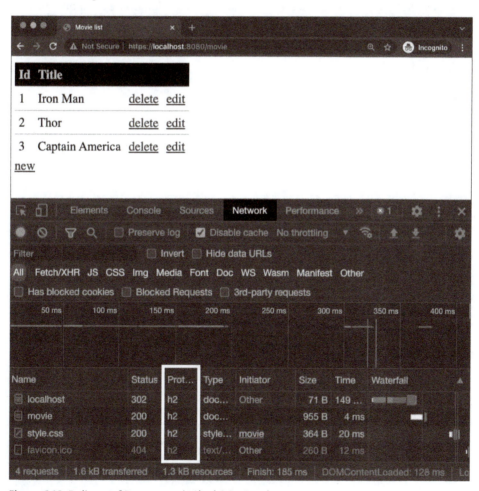

Figure 6.10 Delivery of Resources via the h2 Protocol

6.11 Summary

In this chapter, you learned about Express, the most widely used web application framework for Node.js. Unlike the http module of Node.js, it's much more convenient by either completely relieving you of numerous tasks or at least making them much easier. Express is a lightweight framework that is well suited for use in both small- and large-scale applications.

The Express framework provides a router that can be used to define combinations of http methods and URL paths and then bind callback functions to them. Routes in Express can have static and dynamic parts.

The middleware components provide you with a flexible plug-in system. A middleware refers to a function that is located between the incoming request and the outgoing response. You can use these functions to implement additional features, such as logging or request body processing, and use them to process, enrich, or log the request.

To extend your application, you can either use existing middleware components, such as Morgan or the body parser, or write your own components.

Due to its modular design, Express can be operated not only with HTTP but also with HTTPS and HTTP/2.

Chapter 7
Template Engines

If you want to enjoy the whole, you must see the whole in the smallest.
—Johann Wolfgang von Goethe

This chapter builds on the previous chapter and uses an Express application as the basis. Throughout this chapter, you'll learn about different template engines and their respective advantages and disadvantages. All the template engines presented aren't tied to use with Express, but they are often used in combination. However, we'll also introduce you to stand-alone use with each framework. But before we dive into the topic of template engines, let's take a quick look at what a template engine is and what it can do for you.

Simply put, a template is a static structure, usually an HTML document, with markers that are replaced by concrete values by the template engine at a later point in time. Template engines offer a number of advantages that justify their use in web applications. These include the following, for example:

- **Separation of logic and markup**
  Mixing HTML and JavaScript code in an application degrades the readability of the source code on both sides and thus also impacts the maintainability of the entire application. For this reason, it makes sense to separate the representation from the application logic as much as possible. Template engines contribute to this by giving you, the developer, a way to write templates without logic and insert the dynamic parts via markers.

- **Reusability**
  Many template engines have features that allow you to subdivide templates to define blocks, called partials, and then dump them into separate files. Partials can thus be used multiple times in your application. This reusability ensures that you can make changes to the appearance of your application more quickly and conveniently.

- **Parallelization of work**
  With a template engine, you can separate the work on the frontend and the backend of your application and parallelize the work. If a feature needs to be implemented, one developer can deal with the controllers and models that need to be implemented. In the meantime, other developers can already take care of implementing

the templates and frontend logic. Both teams coordinate at the controller-template interface and agree on which variables are available.

Along with the advantages of using a template engine, the processing of the templates by the application, that is, searching and replacing the markers, requires time and resources. However, there are solutions to this problem as well, namely, in the form of precompiling and caching. Before we introduce you to Pug, the first template engine in this chapter, let's take a quick look at the previous chapter.

7.1   Custom Template Engine

In Chapter 6, you've already implemented a very lightweight template engine yourself. This was used for both the list view and the form. Let's take the *movie/view.js* file as an example. This file is responsible for rendering the list and, at its core, consists of a function that provides the HTML structure. Listing 7.1 shows the source code of the view.

```
export function render(movies) {
  return `
<!DOCTYPE html>
<html lang="en">
<head>
  <meta charset="UTF-8">
  <title>Movie list</title>
  <link rel="stylesheet" href="style.css" />
</head>
<body>
  <table>
    <thead><tr><th>Id</th><th>Title</th><th></th><th></th></tr></thead>
    <tbody>
      ${movies
        .map(
          (movie) => `
        <tr>
          <td>${movie.id}</td>
          <td>${movie.title}</td>
          <td><a href="/movie/delete/${movie.id}">delete</a></td>
          <td><a href="/movie/form/${movie.id}">edit</a></td>
        </tr>`,
        )
        .join('')}
    </tbody>
  </table>
  <a href="/movie/form">new</a>
</body>
```

```
</html>
  `;
}
```

Listing 7.1 Custom Template Engine Based on Template Strings

The solution you've implemented in the movie database represents a simple type of template engine. It enables you to insert variables into your HTML structure, and, thanks to the functionality of JavaScript template strings, you can also formulate simple loops or conditions. In this case, you use the `map` and `join` methods to put an array into the appropriate form and integrate it into your template. The result is the list of movies present in the data source, displayed in an HTML table.

Instead of using template strings, you can also implement such a template engine by using markers in your template and then replacing them with dynamic content using the string `replace` method. Markers in this case are specially marked strings. Usually, special characters such as curly brackets are used here, resulting in markers such as `{{movie}}`.

Basically, you should keep two things in mind about template engines:

- Template editing takes time and resources in itself, whether you use your own implementation or an existing engine. The templates must be processed.
- Template engines are anything but simple. The example shown in Listing 7.1 only covers a simple loop and variable substitution. Neither considerations about escaping or security nor about troubleshooting and performance have been included. So, you probably get an idea of the scope of the established template engines.

After this short excursion into the implementation of template engines, in the following sections, you'll learn how to use a template engine based on the example of Pug.

7.2   Template Engines in Practice: Pug

Given the quality of the available template engines, it doesn't make sense to write another implementation yourself. A very widely used template engine for Node.js is called Pug and was known as Jade for a long time. Due to trademark issues, the engine was renamed from Jade to Pug. In the following sections, you'll learn about the most important features of such an engine and its practical use in an application, using Pug as an example. In this chapter, we'll also go into more detail about the architecture and design of template structures. But first you need to install the engine on your system.

7.2.1   Installation

Pug is installed using the `npm install pug` command. Like so many other Node Package Manager (npm) packages, Pug is an open-source project maintained on GitHub. You can find the source code at *https://github.com/pugjs/pug*. The project site, including extensive documentation, can be reached at *https://pugjs.org*.

7.2.2   Pug and Express: Integration

Using the source code from Chapter 6 and having Pug installed in your application, you now can integrate Pug with your application. To do this, you must first expand the initial file as shown in Listing 7.2.

```
import express from 'express';
import morgan from 'morgan';
import { dirname } from 'path';
import { fileURLToPath } from 'url';
import { router as movieRouter } from './movie/index.js';

const app = express();

app.set('view engine', 'pug');

app.use(express.static(`${dirname(fileURLToPath(import.meta.url))}/public`));

app.use(morgan('common', { immediate: true }));

app.use(express.urlencoded({ extended: false }));

app.use('/movie', movieRouter);

app.get('/', (request, response) => response.redirect('/movie'));

app.listen(8080, () => {
  console.log('Server is listening to http://localhost:8080');
});
```

Listing 7.2 Integrating Pug with Express

Calling app.set('view engine', 'pug') causes the default template engine to be set from Express to Pug. This allows you to use the render method of the response object for rendering your templates.

By default, the render method expects the templates to be located in a *views* directory. By calling app.set('views', './templates'), you can change this behavior and adjust the default directory to *templates*, for example. In a modularized application like the movie database, however, a central default directory for the templates makes little sense. In this case, the templates are located in the respective modules.

The connection of a template engine to Express takes place through a method named __express in the respective template engine. Thus, Pug implements this method and then calls its own renderFile method. If you want to connect to another template engine, you just need to make sure that such a method is implemented, so you're not limited to Pug.

As a first view, you should change the list view to Pug. You can do this by changing it into a static version as a first step with a hard-coded data record. To do this, you must create a *views* subdirectory in the *movie* directory and create a file named *list.pug* there. Express expects the *.pug* file extension for template files in combination with Pug. In Listing 7.3, you can see that Pug uses its own syntax for creating templates.

```
doctype html
html(lang="en")
  head
    meta(charset="UTF-8")
    title Movie list
    link(rel="stylesheet" href="/style.css")
  body
    table
      thead
        tr
          th Id
          th Title
          th Year
          th
          th
      tbody
        tr
          td 1
          td Iron Man
          td 2008
          td
            a(href="/movie/delete/1") delete
          td
            a(href="/movie/form/1") edit
    a(href="/movie/form") new
```

Listing 7.3 Pug Template for the List View (movie/views/list.pug)

Pug changes the structure of the file considerably, which means the angle brackets of the tags are dropped and so are the closing tags. The first word in a line is interpreted as a tag. The indention of the lines reflects the nesting in the Document Object Model

(DOM). The attributes of an element are written in parentheses after the tag name, followed by the textual content of a node. To use this template in your application, you should use the render method instead of the send method of the response object in the listAction of the controller. Listing 7.4 contains the corresponding source code.

```
import { dirname } from 'path';
import { fileURLToPath } from 'url';
import { getAll, remove, get, save } from './model.js';
import { render } from './view.js';
import { render as form } from './form.js';

export async function listAction(request, response) {
  const data = await getAll();
  response.render(`${dirname(fileURLToPath(import.meta.url))}/views/list`);
}

export async function removeAction(request, response) {...}
export async function formAction(request, response) {...}
export async function saveAction(request, response) {...}
```

Listing 7.4 Rendering the List Template (movie/controller.js)

Specifying `${dirname(fileURLToPath(import.meta.url))}/views/list` ensures that the local views directory of the module is used instead of the default views directory of Express. The *.pug* file extension is added automatically by Express. You can now start your application via the npm start command, and you'll see in your browser the list with a static entry, as shown in Figure 7.1.

Figure 7.1 List View

If you take a look at Figure 7.2, which shows the delivered source code of the page, you'll notice that the result of template processing by Pug is standards-compliant HTML.

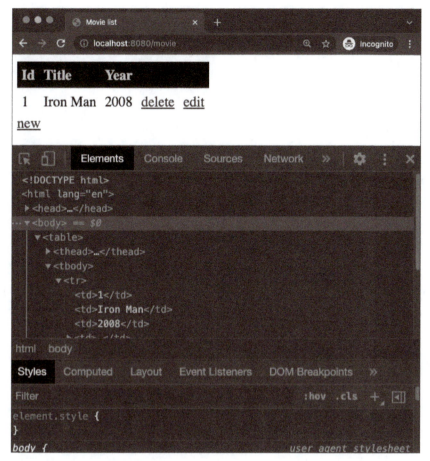

Figure 7.2 HTML Source Code of the List Display

7.2.3   Variables in Pug

As you've seen in the previous examples, by using Pug, you can deliver static HTML files just as well and generate less overhead. The use of template engines becomes really useful when you use dynamic elements or assemble a page from several parts. Like many other template engines, Pug supports the use of variables in templates. This allows you to pass an object to the render method, which you can access in the template.

The source code shown in Listing 7.5 ensures that you can access the movie object in the template. In the template, you can then access the object via interpolation. To do this, you must use the #{<variable>} syntax, where <variable> corresponds to the name of the variable you want to access. You're not limited to just reading variables but can also have any JavaScript expressions evaluated. However, you should refrain from doing this because logic within the template worsens the maintainability of your application.

```
export async function listAction(request, response) {
  const data = await getAll();
  response.render(`${dirname(fileURLToPath(import.meta.url))}/views/list`, {
    movie: data[0],
  });
}
```

Listing 7.5 Passing an Object to the Template (movie/controller.js)

In addition to interpolation, Listing 7.6 also shows how you can use variables in attributes via the href attribute. In this case, you don't need to use any special syntax, but you can access the variables directly and join the target path by string concatenation.

```
doctype html
html(lang="en")
  head
    meta(charset="UTF-8")
    title Movie list
    link(rel="stylesheet" href="/style.css")
  body
    table
      thead
        tr
          th Id
          th Title
          th Year
          th
          th
      tbody
        tr
          td #{movie.id}
          td #{movie.title}
          td #{movie.year}
          td
            a(href="/movie/delete/" + movie.id) delete
          td
            a(href="/movie/form/" + movie.id) edit
    a(href="/movie/form") new
```

Listing 7.6 Using Variables in the Template (movie/views/list.pug)

When using variables in Pug, you should note that the template engine escapes the values to be displayed for security reasons to prevent malicious code from being introduced. For example, the < and > characters are masked so that you can't insert tags in the variables. If you want to bypass this filtering, you must use the character combination !{} instead of #{}. And that wasn't even the only specific feature of the Pug template engine.

7.2.4   Specific Features of Pug

One of the most important differences of Pug compared to other template engines such as Handlebars is the formulation of templates. Whereas in other cases you resort to HTML, in Pug, you write the templates in a specific syntax. As you've already seen in the examples, this syntax isn't at all reminiscent of HTML. The word at the beginning of the line is automatically interpreted as a tag. This notation forces a developer to better and more clearly structure the templates. Too deep a nesting will be noticed very quickly here, as you'll have to indent nested tags. For indention, you can choose either two or four spaces. However, you should maintain this standard consistently for the entire project.

Because Pug interprets the beginning of a line as an HTML tag, it becomes difficult to insert multiline blocks. There are several ways to solve this. First, Pug interprets any line that starts with a < character as text. This means, for example, that regular HTML tags can be written without any problem. Another option is to have a period directly follow the tag that is to be followed by the text. A third variant is to place a | symbol at the beginning of the line. Even then, Pug interprets this line as text.

To organize your HTML code and also to apply CSS, HTML classes and IDs are used in most cases. A class is introduced by a . and an ID by a # character; each directly follows the tag. You can combine classes, IDs, and also multiple classes by simply concatenating them. In Pug, you can use any attributes besides the class and id attribute. All you have to do is write them in parentheses after the tag. Table 7.1 summarizes the most important statements in Pug.

Statement	Description
tag.myClass	This sets the HTML class attribute to the value myClass.
tag#myId	This sets the HTML id attribute to the value myId.
tag(href="www.google.com")	The href attribute is set to the value www.google.com.
tag text | more text	The | indicates that the text in the second line still belongs to the previous tag.
${1 + 1}	The expression is interpreted as JavaScript code, and the result is output in the template.
- for (var i = 0; i < 10; i++)	Everything that follows a - after the beginning of the line is interpreted as JavaScript code; the result isn't output.
// Comment	Everything that follows // is interpreted as an HTML comment. You can also form blocks by indention.

Table 7.1 Most Important Statements in Pug

7.2.5 Conditions and Loops

As you already know, you should avoid having program logic in your templates. However, there are some exceptions to this rule. These exceptions are the reason elements such as loops or conditions exist in template engines. Currently, your application displays only the first entry from the database. To be more flexible in this context, you can use a loop to iterate over the individual entries. To do this, you must first ensure that the controller passes all records to the view. Listing 7.7 shows the customized controller code and how you can use the object shortcut notation. For this to work, you still need to rename the data variable to movies.

```
export async function listAction(request, response) {
  const movies = await getAll();
  response.render(`${dirname(fileURLToPath(import.meta.url))}/views/list`, {
    movies,
  });
}
```

Listing 7.7 Assigning the Data Records to the View (movie/controller.js)

In the template, the changes are limited to inserting the loop into the table. To include JavaScript code in a Pug template, you must precede the expression with a hyphen. For the loop, you can omit the curly brackets because the block limitation in Pug is implemented by indenting the code. Listing 7.8 contains the customized code of the template.

```
doctype html
html(lang="en")
  head
    meta(charset="UTF-8")
    title Movie list
    link(rel="stylesheet" href="/style.css")
  body
    table
      thead
        tr
          th Id
          th Title
          th Year
          th
          th
      tbody
        - for(let movie of movies)
          tr
            td #{movie.id}
```

```
            td #{movie.title}
            td #{movie.year}
            td
              a(href="/movie/delete/" + movie.id) delete
            td
              a(href="/movie/form/" + movie.id) edit
    a(href="/movie/form") new
```

Listing 7.8 Implementing a Loop in Pug (movie/views/list.pug)

Inside the loop, you can access the Pug template syntax as usual. You can also use the local variable movie here. However, template engines such as Pug have a number of other functionalities that allow you to make your templates more maintainable and reusable.

7.2.6   Extends and Includes

Extends and includes allow you to create reusable blocks and then combine them into larger templates. The extends feature starts from a base template in which certain blocks are overwritten. The includes feature works in exactly the opposite way—integrating other subtemplates into one template.

But let's first take a look at how the extends feature works. You should use this feature mainly if you have a base template that is to be used for multiple pages within your application—if the page title and logo, for example, should always remain the same, while only the content area varies. You can see an example of such a base template in Listing 7.9. Save this source code to a file named *base.pug* in the *templates* directory.

```
doctype html
html(lang="en")
  head
    meta(charset="UTF-8")
    title Movie list
    link(rel="stylesheet" href="/style.css")
  body

  img.logo(src="logo.png" height="50")

  block content
    div No content
```

Listing 7.9 Base Template (templates/base.pug)

The only special feature in your base template is the block markup. You can overwrite it in a template that extends the base template. Optionally, you can specify placeholders

223

that will be displayed if the block isn't overwritten. For the example to work properly, you need the logo of your application as a PNG file named *logo.png* in the *public* directory. You should also adjust your stylesheet a little. The code from Listing 7.10 ensures that the logo is displayed in the upper-right corner.

```
...
img.logo {
  position: absolute;
  top: 0;
  right: 10px;
}
```

Listing 7.10 Stylesheet (public/style.css)

To use the base template, you still need to customize the list template of your application. Listing 7.11 contains the corresponding source code.

```
extends ../../templates/base

block content
  h1 movie database
  table
    thead
      tr
        th Id
        th Title
        th Year
        th
        th
    tbody
      - for(let movie of movies)
        tr
          td #{movie.id}
          td #{movie.title}
          td #{movie.year}
          td
            a(href="/movie/delete/" + movie.id) delete
          td
            a(href="/movie/form/" + movie.id) edit
  a(href="/movie/form") new
```

Listing 7.11 Extending the Base Template (movie/views/list.pug)

First, you bind the base template by using the extends keyword followed by the file name of the base template, in this case, base. After that, you just need to fill the blocks with content. The base template has only one block. You address this block using block content and define the content of the page there. Markup outside the defined blocks or blocks not defined in the base template are ignored. You can see the result of this example in Figure 7.3.

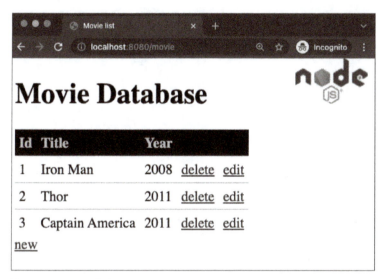

Figure 7.3 Extends in Pug

When using extends, it's assumed that the basic structure of several pages is similar. However, if you want to use the same blocks on several pages, you should use include instead. Note that includes are not only used to reuse sections of templates but also to simplify and better structure templates by separating sections into separate files. The source code in Listing 7.12 allows you to outsource the structure of the individual list entries to a separate file.

```
tr
  td #{movie.id}
  td #{movie.title}
  td #{movie.year}
  td
    a(href="/movie/delete/" + movie.id) delete
  td
    a(href="/movie/form/" + movie.id) edit
```

Listing 7.12 Includes in Pug (movie/views/list-item.pug)

The partial template from Listing 7.12 doesn't have a valid structure for an HTML page because it contains only the table row, but neither a doctype nor html, head, or body tags. This is already a first indication that this template is used elsewhere. The next step is to include the table row in the list template. Listing 7.13 shows how you can do this.

```
extends ../../templates/base

block content
  h1 movie database
  table
    thead
      tr
        th Id
        th Title
        th Year
        th
        th
    tbody
      - for(let movie of movies)
        include ./list-item
  a(href="/movie/form") new
```

Listing 7.13 Embedding Templates in Pug (movie/views/list.pug)

As you've seen in Listing 7.12 and Listing 7.13, you can access variables of the including template from within an include. The problem with this type of inclusion is that you must rely on the outer template to provide the appropriate variables. Furthermore, it isn't obvious at first glance which variables are required for such an include to function. Includes are therefore better suited for independent subtemplates. If the template needs to be integrated into an environment with certain variables, the mixins presented next are more suitable.

7.2.7 Mixins

A mixin is very similar to a function. You must first define a mixin, and then you can call it as often as you like. The result of such a call is a template block. Like a function, a mixin can also be parameterized. A mixin allows you to create a dynamic HTML block relying on a defined interface, namely, the mixin's signature. In the case of the list display, you can outsource the display of the list entries to a mixin. To do this, you must first modify the source code of the listItem template, as shown in Listing 7.14.

```
mixin listItem(movie)
  tr
    td #{movie.id}
    td #{movie.title}
    td #{movie.year}
    td
```

```
    a(href="/movie/delete/" + movie.id) delete
  td
    a(href="/movie/form/" + movie.id) edit
```

Listing 7.14 Defining a Mixin in Pug (movie/views/list-item.pug)

To use this mixin, you must first include the file in your list template and then address the mixin. Listing 7.15 contains the necessary changes.

```
extends ../../templates/base
include ./list-item

block content
  h1 movie database
  table
    thead
      tr
        th Id
        th Title
        th Year
        th
        th
    tbody
      - for(let movie of movies)
        +listItem(movie)
  a(href="/movie/form") new
```

Listing 7.15 Using the Mixin (movie/views/list.pug)

As you can see in Listing 7.15, you define a mixin via the mixin keyword followed by the mixin name. Optionally, you can also specify a parameter list that you access within the mixin. You then use the mixin through its name preceded by a + sign. Mixins become particularly interesting when you combine them with includes. Specifically, this means that you can either swap out individual mixins or a collection of mixins into a separate file, include it via includes, and then use it. With such a strategy, you achieve maximum reusability of your mixins. It's also sometimes helpful to group frequently used mixins together in some kind of library that you can then use in multiple applications.

Mixins are the last of the important features of Pug you should be aware of. You should now have a rough overview of how the template engine works and know how to write concise and reusable templates. At this point, we'll discuss how you can use Pug without Express in your application.

7.2.8   Using Pug without Express

Basically, Pug isn't bound to Express. After installing the package, you can use Pug directly to render templates. In this context, you can access all the features already presented. In Listing 7.16, the render method of Pug is used to render a template that is a JavaScript string.

```
import pug from 'pug';

const template = 'h1 Hello World';

const output = pug.render(template);

console.log(output);
```

Listing 7.16 Direct Rendering with Pug

After you include Pug via the module system, you can access one of several variants to render a character string. The simplest way to do that is the render method shown in Listing 7.16. You pass it the template string and optionally an object with substitutions you want Pug to make. What you get in return is the transformed character string. If you run the example on your command line, you'll get the string <h1>Hello World</h1> as output.

In addition to the render method, there is also the renderFile method, which allows you to swap out the template to a separate file. Basically, it works like the render method, except that instead of passing it a template string, you pass it the name of the template file.

Finally, we'll briefly introduce how Pug internally handles templates to optimize the runtime.

7.2.9   Compiling

To load the templates, Pug currently uses the readFileSync method. This function blocks the execution of the remaining source code because it waits for the completion of the read process. However, with Pug, this isn't a big deal, especially when templates are used several times, because the template engine keeps a cache of previously used templates. Pug divides the template processing process into two parts. First, the template is prepared in the compile process. The placeholders are then inserted into this compiled template. Pug performs the compile operation only once for each template. All further uses of the templates are served from the cache. You can also address this feature directly, for example, by using the compileFile method. To demonstrate this feature, it's best to use a simple template like the one shown in Listing 7.17.

```
h1 Hello #{name}
```

Listing 7.17 Sample Template for the Compile Process (templates/compile.pug)

In the next step, you compile the template using the `compileFile` method. For the source code to work, you should save the template in the *compile.pug* file within the *templates* directory.

As you can see in Listing 7.18, the `compileFile` method returns a function. This function represents the prepared template to which you still need to pass the placeholders, in this case, an object with the `name` key. You can call this function as often as you like and with different values. In the example, the compiled template is used in a web server. For each request, only the template function is called with the values, and the result is sent to the client.

```
import { createServer } from 'http';
import pug from 'pug';

const fn = pug.compileFile('templates/compile.pug');
createServer((req, res) => {
  let output = fn({ name: 'World' });
  output += fn({ name: 'Node.js' });

  res.end(output);
}).listen(8080);
```

Listing 7.18 Compiling Templates

As mentioned earlier, Pug isn't the only template engine for Node.js. An alternative, for example, is the more lightweight Handlebars.

7.3 Handlebars

To give you a better idea of working with template engines in Node.js, this chapter covers not only Pug but also Handlebars. The following sections are intended to show you that features similar to those in Pug are available in other template engines and that you're relatively free to choose which tools you want to use.

What is noticeable from the first contact with Handlebars is that the templates are written in HTML and not in a custom markup language. The advantage of this is that you don't have to learn a new markup language, but can work directly with the familiar HTML. Furthermore, numerous tools are available for editing HTML that make your work easier. Another difference from Pug is that the core of Handlebars is deliberately kept small, and the template engine itself has relatively little functionality, so it focuses on the essentials, which doesn't tempt a developer to swap out too much logic to the templates.

7.3.1 Installation

Like Pug, Handlebars is an open-source project maintained in the GitHub repository at *https://github.com/wycats/handlebars.js/*, and you can install it via npm. The project site with comprehensive documentation and numerous code samples can be found at *https://handlebarsjs.com/*. To use Handlebars in your application, you just need to run the `npm install handlebars` command. Once you've done that, you can include the library using the Node.js module system.

7.3.2 Integration with Express

As you already know, a template engine only needs to implement an __express method to be used with Express. Handlebars doesn't implement this method directly, but there is a package called express-handlebars that does it for you. You can install it via npm using the `npm install express-handlebars` command. If you use this package, you don't need to install Handlebars itself because it's installed as a dependency of express-handlebars. Listing 7.19 shows what you need to do to integrate Handlebars into your application instead of Pug.

```
import express from 'express';
import morgan from 'morgan';
import { dirname } from 'path';
import { fileURLToPath } from 'url';
import { router as movieRouter } from './movie/index.js';
import expressHandlebars from 'express-handlebars';

const app = express();

app.engine('handlebars', expressHandlebars());
app.set('view engine', 'handlebars');
app.set('views', [`${dirname(fileURLToPath(import.meta.url))}/views/list`]);

app.use(express.static(`${dirname(fileURLToPath(import.meta.url))}/public`));

app.use(morgan('common', { immediate: true }));

app.use(express.urlencoded({ extended: false }));

app.use('/movie', movieRouter);

app.get('/', (request, response) => response.redirect('/movie'));

app.listen(8080, () => {
  console.log('Server is listening to http://localhost:8080');
});
```

Listing 7.19 Including Handlebars in Express (index.js)

With `app.engine`, you register the `express-handlebars` function, that is, the actual template engine with Express. You then use the `app.set` method and the `view engine` value to set `express-handlebars` as the template engine for the `render` calls of Express. Finally, the `app.set` call with `views` tells `express-handlebars` to look for templates in the *movie/views* directory.

When used in Express, Handlebars is hardly different from Pug. However, you should note that `express-handlebars` accepts files with the extension *.handlebars* as templates by default. This behavior can be customized, if necessary, with the `extname` configuration directive that you pass to the `express-handlebars` function. Initially, as with Pug, you display only one record. This means that you also need to adjust the controller slightly.

As you can see in Listing 7.20, the `render` method behaves similarly to Pug when using Handlebars. You pass the name of the template and an object to fill the placeholders. `express-handlebars` finds the *list.handlebars* file in the *movie/views* directory by specifying the `list` template.

```
import { getAll, remove, get, save } from './model.js';
import { render as form } from './form.js';

export async function listAction(request, response) {
  const movies = await getAll();
  response.render('list', {
    layout: false,
    movie: movies[0]
  });
}
...
```

Listing 7.20 Customizing the Controller (movie/controller.js)

As the second argument, you pass an object that contains both the values for the placeholders in the template and additional configuration. For example, the `layout: false` option tells Handlebars not to use the default template. You can find the code of the template in Listing 7.21.

```
<!DOCTYPE html>

<html>

<head>
  <title>Handlebars example</title>
</head>

<body>
```

```
    <table>
      <thead>
        <tr>
          <th>Id</th>
          <th>Title</th>
          <th>Year</th>
        </tr>
      </thead>
      <tbody>
        <tr>
          <td>{{movie.id}}</td>
          <td>{{movie.title}}</td>
          <td>{{movie.year}}</td>
        </tr>
      </tbody>
    </table>
  </body>

</html>
```

Listing 7.21 Handlebars Template (movie/views/list.handlebars)

When you start your server process after these adjustments and access the URL *http:// localhost:8080*, you'll get the familiar list view as a result.

The variables in Handlebars are enclosed in double curly brackets. The replaced values are escaped for security reasons, so that no attacks can occur against the users of your application. If you want to prevent escaping, you must use triple curly brackets instead of double ones.

7.3.3 Conditions and Loops

You can extend the functionality of Handlebars using helpers, which are functions you can execute from within your templates. Some of the most important helpers form an integral part of Handlebars, such as the each helper, which allows you to iterate over data structures. You should now reset your controller to its original state, as shown in Listing 7.22, so that it passes the entire array of movie objects to the template, and all the data displays again.

```
import { getAll, remove, get, save } from './model.js';
import { render } from './view.js';
import { render as form } from './form.js';

export async function listAction(request, response) {
  const movies = await getAll();
```

```
    response.render('list', { layout: false, movies });
}
...
```

Listing 7.22 Customization on the Controller (movie/controller.js)

You address the each helper via the each keyword, as shown in Listing 7.23.

```html
<!DOCTYPE html>

<html>

<head>
  <title>Handlebars example</title>
</head>

<body>
  <table>
    <thead>
      <tr>
        <th>Id</th>
        <th>Title</th>
        <th>Year</th>
      </tr>
    </thead>
    <tbody>
      {{#each movies}}
      <tr>
        <td>{{this.id}}</td>
        <td>{{this.title}}</td>
        <td>{{this.year}}</td>
      </tr>
      {{/each}}
    </tbody>
  </table>
</body>

</html>
```

Listing 7.23 Iterations in Handlebars (movie/views/list.handlebars)

Like the variables, the helper is enclosed in double curly brackets and is preceded by a # character. Then follow the name of the helper—in this case, it's the keyword each—and finally other options such as the data structure to iterate over. The this keyword provides access to the respective active element within the iteration, which you can then output.

In addition to the each helper, you can use the `if` helper to formulate conditions within your templates, for example. For a list of other helpers, visit *https://handlebarsjs.com/ guide/builtin-helpers.html*.

7.3.4   Partials

A concept you already know from Pug's includes are partials, that is, parts of templates you can reuse in several places in your application. In Handlebars, you register the partials via the `registerPartial` method in the JavaScript code and then access them from your template. In `express-handlebars`, you can either store your partials in a directory so that `express-handlebars` automatically finds and registers them, or you can perform the registration manually. We'll use this manual registration for the list entries of the film database. For this purpose, you first need a template for the partial. You can find the source code in Listing 7.24.

```
<tr>
  <td>{{this.id}}</td>
  <td>{{this.title}}</td>
  <td>{{this.year}}</td>
  <td>
    <a href="/movie/delete/{{this.id}}">delete</a>
  </td>
  <td>
    <a href="/movie/form/{{this.id}}">edit</a>
  </td>
</tr>
```

Listing 7.24 Partial Template (movie/views/list-item.handlebars)

When implementing the partial template, you assume that it will be used within the each helper. For this reason, you also use the `this` keyword here to access the information of the `movie` object. The integration in the controller is a bit more complex than with Pug, as you can see in Listing 7.25.

```
import { getAll, remove, get, save } from './model.js';
import { render } from './view.js';
import { render as form } from './form.js';
import handlebars from 'handlebars';
import { readFileSync } from 'fs';
import { dirname } from 'path';
import { fileURLToPath } from 'url';

const listItem = handlebars.compile(
  readFileSync(
    `${dirname(fileURLToPath(import.meta.url))}/views/list-item.handlebars`,
```

```
    'utf-8',
  ),
);

export async function listAction(request, response) {
  const movies = await getAll();
  response.render('list', { layout: false, movies, partials: { listItem } });
}
```

Listing 7.25 Using Handlebars Partials in Express (movie/controller.js)

In preparation for using the partial, you must first prepare it separately from the listAction function by reading the partial file *list-item.handlebars* with the readFileSync
function of the fs module. You then compile the contents of the file using the compile
function of Handlebars and get the compiled partial as the result, which you can then
continue to use. The advantage of this procedure is that the template doesn't have to be
read and compiled again each time listAction is called, but only once at the start of the
server process.

In the controller, you also pass the name of the template and an option object to the
render method, as before. This method receives a reference to the movie list in the form
of the movies variable, the layout property, and a partials property. Here, the partials
are registered on the render level. You then pass the previously compiled partial from
under the name listItem. Finally, the use of the partial template takes place in the list
template. Listing 7.26 shows the necessary adjustments.

```
<!DOCTYPE html>

<html>

<head>
  <title>Handlebars example</title>
</head>

<body>
  <table>
    <thead>
      <tr>
        <th>Id</th>
        <th>Title</th>
        <th>Year</th>
      </tr>
    </thead>
    <tbody>
      {{#each movies}} {{>listItem}} {{/each}}
```

```
      </tbody>
    </table>
</body>
```

Listing 7.26 Integration (movie/views/list.handlebars)

As you can see, you access the respective partial template via {{> followed by the name of the partial. From the partial, you have access to all variables that are also available to you in the template itself. You can also parameterize a partial by assigning a value to an internal placeholder inside the curly brackets.

7.3.5   Custom Helpers

In addition to the provided helpers, you can define your own helpers and use them in Handlebars. These are functions you can call from within the template. In Listing 7.27, you create a custom helper named uc that converts a passed string to uppercase.

```
import express from 'express';
import morgan from 'morgan';
import { dirname } from 'path';
import { fileURLToPath } from 'url';
import { router as movieRouter } from './movie/index.js';
import expressHandlebars from 'express-handlebars';

const app = express();

app.engine(
  'handlebars',
  expressHandlebars({
    helpers: {
      uc: (data) => data.toUpperCase(),
    },
  }),
);
app.set('view engine', 'handlebars');
app.set('views', [`${dirname(fileURLToPath(import.meta.url))}/movie/views`]);

app.use(express.static(`${dirname(fileURLToPath(import.meta.url))}/public`));

app.use(morgan('common', { immediate: true }));

app.use(express.urlencoded({ extended: false }));

app.use('/movie', movieRouter);
```

```
app.get('/', (request, response) => response.redirect('/movie'));

app.listen(8080, () => {
  console.log('Server is listening to http://localhost:8080');
});
```

Listing 7.27 Custom Helper in Handlebars (index.js)

Similar to partials, helpers are registered either when the render method is called or, as in this case, globally, when express-handlebars is initialized. You can use the helper after registering it in your template by listing the name in double curly brackets before the variable to be output. In Listing 7.28, you use the uc helper to output the column headers in uppercase letters.

```
<!DOCTYPE html>

<html>
<head>
  <title>Handlebars example</title>
</head>

<body>
  <table>
    <thead>
      <tr>
         <th>{{uc 'Id' }}</th>
         <th>{{uc 'Title'}}</th>
         <th>{{uc 'Year'}}</th>
      </tr>
    </thead>
    <tbody>
      {{#each movies}} {{>listItem}} {{/each}}
    </tbody>
  </table>
</body>

</html>
```

Listing 7.28 Using the "uc" Helper (movie/views/list.handlebars)

If you don't use express-handlebars, you must register your helpers using the register-Helper method of Handlebars. This method receives the name of the helper and a callback function.

7.3.6   Handlebars without Express

For Handlebars, the same applies as for Pug. You can also use the template engine separately from Express. To do this, you must first install the package via npm install handlebars. You can then use it in the context of a web server, for example. In Listing 7.29, you create a web server that returns a rendered Handlebars template.

```
import { createServer } from 'http';
import { readFile } from 'fs';
import hbs from 'handlebars';

createServer((req, res) => {
  readFile('templates/index.hbs', 'utf-8', (err, data) => {
    const template = hbs.compile(data);
    const result = template({ name: 'Handlebars' });
    res.end(result);
  });
}).listen(8080);
```

Listing 7.29 Rendering Templates with Handlebars (index.js)

Listing 7.29 shows how you can process a template with Handlebars. First you need to import the Handlebars package. After that, you need the template as a character string. Again, you shouldn't place your templates directly in the JavaScript source code, but rather swap them out to a separate file. The source code of the template for this example is shown in Listing 7.30, and you save it in the *templates* directory in the *index.hbs* file.

```
<!DOCTYPE html>
<html lang="en">
<head>
  <meta charset="UTF-8">
  <meta http-equiv="X-UA-Compatible" content="IE=edge">
  <meta name="viewport" content="width=device-width, initial-scale=1.0">
  <title>Document</title>
</head>
<body>
  <h1>Hallo {{name}}</h1>
</body>
</html>
```

Listing 7.30 Template File in Handlebars (template/index.hbs)

The process of template processing consists of two steps, as was the case with Pug. First, you must prepare the template by passing it to the compile method. In the second step, you execute the resulting template function and pass it the placeholders to be inserted into the template. The result of this operation is a character string containing the finished HTML.

With Handlebars and Pug, you now know two of the most popular template engines for Node.js and should have an idea of their features and areas of use. This knowledge can be applied to most other template engines because they all work in a similar way.

7.4   Summary

7

In addition to the Pug and Handlebars engines presented here, numerous other implementations exist for Node.js. Another template engine also frequently encountered is Embedded JavaScript (EJS). As the name suggests, this is a comparatively simple yet flexible engine that has a flatter learning curve than Pug and is slightly more flexible than Handlebars. Like Handlebars, EJS uses HTML as a template language. Instead of the double curly brackets, <% and %> are used here as markers. The integration with Express is similarly smooth as with Pug. You can find the EJS project site at *https://ejs.co*.

Template engines are an indispensable tool that allows you to separate the view from the logic of your application. Templates not only encapsulate HTML but also allow you to insert dynamic content. By dividing your application into smaller components in an intelligent manner, you can achieve reusability in your templates, which significantly increases the maintainability of your application and can greatly reduce the effort required to create new pages. Many template engines also offer additional features such as mixins or helpers, which you can use to extend your application with your own tools that you can in turn combine into libraries and also use across application boundaries.

If you only need the basic functionality of a template engine in your application, such as support for variables, loops, and conditions, you should consider using a lightweight engine such as Handlebars. However, as soon as you want to map more extensive templates and more complex structures, you should use an engine such as Pug, which leaves almost no wishes unfulfilled when it comes to template engines.

Plug-ins for development environments such as WebStorm or Visual Studio Code exist for most common template engines, so you're supported here in terms of autocompletion and syntax highlighting.

Chapter 8
Connecting Databases

I know that I know nothing.
—Socrates

As you've already seen in the previous chapters, when you implement applications, you also need to store data all the time. Node.js only provides you with the `fs` module for persisting data. The drawback of storing data directly in the file system is that this method isn't optimized for directly accessing specific information in large data sets. In the worst case, you'll have to search an entire file for the information you need, which can be very time-consuming depending on the file size. This is one reason you should use databases to persist information in your application. They also offer additional features such as scalability or transaction security.

In most cases, databases aren't accessed directly, but rather through a driver that serves as an interface to the database and implements the database's communication protocol. These drivers aren't integral components of the Node.js platform. Either the drivers are provided by the database manufacturer, or they are a product of the open-source community. They are usually available as Node Package Manager (npm) modules and can be installed if required.

Today, there is a driver for Node.js available for almost every database. For example, the supported systems include the relational databases MySQL, MSSQL, SQLite, PostgreSQL, OracleDB, and many others. A large number of nonrelational databases such as Redis, CouchDB, and MongoDB are also supported.

In this chapter, you'll learn more about connecting various databases to your Node.js application. In particular, you'll use MySQL, SQLite, Redis, and MongoDB. You'll include each of these databases in the movie database and implement both read and write access.

You'll also learn more about the areas of use and the pros and cons of the individual databases. To reproduce the examples in this chapter, you have several options, including installing the respective database systems locally on your development system or running the database in a container, which is the better alternative. The advantage of this method is that you don't need to install all possible databases. For this reason, in the respective sections, we'll show you how you can launch such a database container. This requires that you have Docker installed on your system. For more information on Docker, see *https://docker.com/*, as well as Chapter 25 and Chapter 27.

8.1 Node.js and Relational Databases

Relational databases have established themselves over the years as the database standard in the IT world. This type of database is based on a structure of tables in which the data is stored. In this context, a table defines the structure of individual data records.

You can think of a table in a relational database as just an ordinary table. The rows represent the individual records, and the columns represent the respective properties. This means that all data records in a table have the same structure. The aggregate of all tables and their structure finally represents the schema of the database.

In relational databases, you can define almost any number of tables. You can then use *foreign keys* to establish a relationship between the tables. For the example of the movie database, this means you can store the movie data in one table and the user ratings for the individual movies in another. Another example is storing the information about the movie studio in another table. This process is called *normalization* and is used to avoid duplicates in the database. You can create a relationship between the records from both tables using a foreign key.

Structured Query Language (SQL) has become the language of choice for formulating database queries. SQL has been standardized by International Organization for Standardization (ISO) and International Electrotechnical Commission (IEC), with each specific implementation adding its own extensions to this standard. You can find more information at *https://en.wikipedia.org/wiki/SQL*.

The sections on the individual databases always follow the same structure. You'll get to know some details about the database and the respective pros and cons. This is followed by the installation of the driver for the database and a concrete example of how to use the database within the movie database application.

The first part of this chapter deals with the connection of a MySQL database.

8.1.1 MySQL

MySQL is one of the most widely used databases on the web. You can access this database with almost all major programming languages. The connection of Node.js to MySQL can be realized via a special database driver.

MySQL has already proven itself as a database for many years, even in very large applications. Not only does the system have a simple server component, but it also allows you to run a database on multiple servers in a primary-secondary compound structure. The benefit of this is that you can distribute the requests across several systems and thus ensure resilience.

In addition, for very large data volumes, a database can be partitioned and distributed across multiple systems, which offers further opportunities in terms of performance improvements. MySQL has many other useful features, including triggers (functions that are executed when certain operations are performed), and transactions. A *transaction* is a group of operations that may only be performed in their entirety or not at all.

Another advantage of MySQL is that this database is available on a large number of different operating systems, such as Linux, Windows, and macOS. The availability and widespread use have led to a very active community that you can call on if you have any questions or problems. There are also forks of MySQL, such as MariaDB, which offer similar functionality.

One of the drawbacks of MySQL is that it can't quite keep up with the big SQL databases such as Oracle or DB2 in terms of its feature set. However, the advanced development of the database is increasingly compensating for this disadvantage.

In general, there are two different approaches to connecting to a MySQL database. For one thing, there is a driver that directly implements the MySQL protocol and is written entirely in JavaScript. No other software is needed for this driver, and it can be used directly to work with a database.

Another variant of MySQL drivers is based on the MySQL client libraries. These have the advantage of being slightly more performant than drivers implemented entirely in JavaScript. However, they have the disadvantage that the MySQL client libraries must be installed on the system running the Node.js application.

MySQL in a Container

As mentioned earlier, you don't need to install MySQL on your development system. Especially for experimenting, running the database in a container is a viable alternative. But containers are also becoming increasingly popular for day-to-day development operations, as this approach allows both the configuration to be shared between developer systems and the container configuration to be versioned along with the rest of the application's source code. You can launch the MySQL container using the command shown in Listing 8.1.

```
docker run
  --name mysql
  -v db-data:/etc/mysql/conf.d
  -e MYSQL_ROOT_PASSWORD=topSecret
  -e MYSQL_ROOT_HOST=% -p 3306:3306
  -d
  mysql:latest
```

Listing 8.1 Launching the MySQL Container with Docker

The docker run command creates a new container from the image named mysql:latest. The mysql image is officially provided by MySQL on Docker Hub (*https://hub.docker.com/*), which is downloaded by the command in the specified version—here :latest—that is, the latest version. The --name option assigns a name to the container so that it's easier to manage and doesn't need to be addressed by its ID. You can use the -v option to specify that a local directory is mounted as a volume in the container, so that the database files are located on the host system rather than in the container. The subsequent -e option sets environment variables for the container, which MySQL uses in this case to set the root password and allow the root user to log on from outside the container. Finally, you use -d to specify that the container should run in the background. When you execute the command, you'll get a cryptic-looking character string as a result. This is the ID of the container, which you can also use to manage the container in addition to the name. Once you've launched the container, you can use MySQL on your system.

> **The Most Important Docker Commands at a Glance**
>
> Table 8.1 contains an overview of the most important commands for the Docker command line. A comprehensive list of all commands, including descriptions and all available options, can be found in the official documentation at *https://docs.docker.com/engine/reference/commandline/cli/*.

Command	Description
docker run <image>	Creates and runs a new container
docker rm <container>	Deletes the specified container
docker rmi <image>	Deletes the specified image
docker ps	Displays a list of all containers
docker stop <container>	Stops the container
docker start <container>	Starts a stopped container

Table 8.1 Most Important Docker Commands

Installation

The MySQL driver for Node.js is available as an npm module and can be installed from the command line using the npm install mysql2 command. The driver implements the MySQL protocol entirely in JavaScript, so it doesn't require you to install any other external libraries or perform any compilation steps during the installation process.

Once the installation is complete and you have a MySQL database available, you can access the MySQL database from your application.

Database Structure

To reproduce the examples in this chapter, you need a running instance of a MySQL database with a data structure to work on. Listing 8.2 contains the required SQL commands to create a database with the two tables, Movies and Ratings, and to fill the database with initial values. Once you've executed these statements, you can start implementing the sample application in the next step. To create the structure, you must either use the mysql command locally on the console of your system, or, if you're running the database in a Docker container, you should use the docker exec -it mysql mysql -p command to execute the mysql command in the container named mysql. Then you can execute the statements shown in Listing 8.2.

```
CREATE DATABASE `movie-db`;
USE `movie-db`;
CREATE TABLE `Movies` (
  `id` int(11) NOT NULL AUTO_INCREMENT,
  `title` varchar(255) DEFAULT NULL,
  `year` int(11) DEFAULT NULL,
  PRIMARY KEY (`id`)
) ENGINE=InnoDB DEFAULT CHARSET=utf8;
INSERT INTO `Movies` (`title`, `year`) VALUES
('Iron Man', 2008),
('Thor', 2011),
('Captain America', 2011);
```

Listing 8.2 MySQL Database Structure

Establishing the Connection

In any application that uses a database, before using this database, a connection must first be established through which the commands are sent to the database system and the information from the database can flow back to the application. The application is based on the source code from Chapter 7, and it uses the Pug template engine. The database connection is established in the *movie/model.js* file. Listing 8.3 shows how you can do this in the source code.

```
import mysql from 'mysql2/promise';

const connection = await mysql.createConnection({
  host: 'localhost',
  user: 'root',
  password: 'topSecret',
  database: 'movie-db',
});

await connection.connect();

export async function getAll() {}
export async function get(id) {}
```

```
export async function remove(id) {}
export function save(movie) {}
```

Listing 8.3 Establishing a Database Connection (movie/model.js)

After including the promise interface of the mysql2 module, you can use the createConnection function to configure the connection and then use the connect method of the connection object to connect to the database. Much of the driver's functionality in this case is based on promises. For the createConnection function, it returns a promise object that you can wait to be resolved using the await keyword. You can also terminate an open connection by calling the end method. The connect method also returns a promise object. You can use the catch method of this object to implement error handling related to the connection establishment. Alternatively, you can use the await keyword and perform error handling with try-catch.

The connection can also be established implicitly by calling the query method on the connection object.

Reading Data Records

Because you've already created some data records when initializing the database, you can already read them. To do this, you must first define an appropriate query and pass it to the query method of the connection object. Communication with the database takes place asynchronously and also uses promises. Alternatively, the mysql2 package also provides a callback-based interface, but this is much less convenient to use. The source code in Listing 8.4 shows how you can read data from a table.

```
import mysql from 'mysql2/promise';

const connection = await mysql.createConnection({
  host: '127.0.0.1',
  user: 'root',
  password: 'topSecret',
  database: 'movie-db',
});

await connection.connect();

export async function getAll() {
  const query = 'SELECT * FROM Movies';
  const [data] = await connection.query(query);
  return data;
}
export async function get(id) {}
export async function remove(id) {}
export function save(movie) {}
```

Listing 8.4 Reading Data Records from a MySQL Table

The `query` method of the `connection` object returns a promise object that is resolved with an array of multiple elements. The first element of this array contains the queried data from the database, which you can extract and return using a destructuring statement. After you mark the getAll function as an `async` function, you can work inside the function with the `await` keyword, and the function will automatically return a promise object. If successful, the returned promise object contains the data from the database; if there's an error, the corresponding error is returned from the database.

Because the signature of the getAll method hasn't changed due to the connection of the database, you don't need to adjust anything else in the controller.

Currently, the source code of your application assumes only the success case, which is sufficient for our purpose, namely, connecting the database. However, for a productive application, you also need to take care of error handling and send at least a generic error message to inform your users without revealing too many internal details about your application to a potential attacker.

The MySQL driver for Node.js supports many other features, such as escaping, which is described in more detail in the following sections.

Creating New Data Records

After implementing read access to the database, the next step deals with write access. Basically, the operation process here is similar because you also use the `query` method of the connection object to send the `INSERT` query. A special feature here is that you don't directly compose the values entered by the users into a query via string concatenation, but rather use placeholders and let the database driver do the escaping. This reduces the risk of an SQL injection.

As was the case with the read process, you also use the *movie/model.js* file as the starting point when creating new records. Listing 8.5 shows the customized source code of the file.

```
import mysql from 'mysql2/promise';

const connection = await mysql.createConnection({...});

await connection.connect();

export async function getAll() {...}

async function insert(movie) {
  const query = 'INSERT INTO Movies (title, year) VALUES (?, ?)';
  const [result] = await connection.query(query, [movie.title, movie.year]);
  return { ...movie, id: result.insertId };
}
```

```
export async function get(id) {}
export async function remove(id) {}
export function save(movie) {
  if (!movie.id) {
    return insert(movie);
  }
}
```

Listing 8.5 Creating a New Data Record (movie/model.js)

The central place of the model file that takes care of saving the data is the save function. Based on the presence of the id property of the passed data record, the function decides whether it to create a new record or update an existing record later. In the current case of a new creation, the save function then calls the insert function with the data record to be created.

You can implement the insert function as an async function to be able to use the promise-based interface of the mysql2 driver comfortably. In the first step, you must prepare the INSERT statement by writing the query completely and providing question marks for the values to be inserted. The driver then replaces these question marks with the values when they are called and takes care of escaping the values correctly. The query method of the connection object accepts the SQL statement as a string as the first argument and an array with the values for the placeholders as the second argument. The return value is a promise object with an array whose first element contains a set of metadata about the request. Here you'll find, among other things, the insertId property, which contains the ID of the newly created data record. You must use this ID together with the information from the originally passed object to create a new object with the spread operator and return it to the calling instance.

You don't need to adjust the controller and its saveAction because the interface of the model hasn't changed.

Updating Data Records

To update the data records in your application, you must first connect the model method for reading individual data records to the database to populate the form with the existing data. In the implementation, you should combine the structure of the reading request from Listing 8.4 with escaping to safely insert the passed ID into the request. Listing 8.6 shows the necessary adjustments to the *movie/model.js* file.

```
import mysql from 'mysql2/promise';

const connection = await mysql.createConnection({
  host: '127.0.0.1',
  user: 'root',
  password: 'topSecret',
```

```
  database: 'movie-db',
});

await connection.connect();

export async function getAll() {...}

async function insert(movie) {...}

export async function get(id) {
  const query = 'SELECT * from Movies WHERE id = ?';
  const [data] = await connection.query(query, [id]);
  return data.pop();
}
export async function remove(id) {}
export function save(movie) {...}
```

Listing 8.6 Reading a Single Data Record (movie/model.js)

Again, no further adjustments to the controller or view are required, so in the final step, you can turn your attention to implementing the functionality for updating the data in the database. For this purpose, you must use an update request to the database.

The adjustments for the update are limited to the changes shown in Listing 8.7 because the controller passes the requests directly to the model for both updates and new installations.

```
import mysql from 'mysql2/promise';

const connection = await mysql.createConnection({...});

await connection.connect();

export async function getAll() {...}

async function insert(movie) {...}

async function update(movie) {
  const query = 'UPDATE Movies SET title = ?, year = ? WHERE id = ?';
  await connection.query(query, [movie.title, movie.year, movie.id]);
  return movie;
}

export async function get(id) {...}
export async function remove(id) {}
```

```
export function save(movie) {
  if (!movie.id) {
    return insert(movie);
  } else {
    return update(movie);
  }
}
```

Listing 8.7 Sending the Update Request to the Database (movie/model.js)

Removing Data Records

The last operation you'll learn about here in connection with MySQL is deleting data records from the database. Deleting data records can't be easily undone. If you work with referential integrity via foreign keys, deleting one record can result in a cascade of deletions of other data records that are based on that record. You should therefore always exercise caution with such operations and, if in doubt, prompt the user for confirmation via a dialog. Listing 8.8 shows how you can remove data records from your database.

```
import mysql from 'mysql2/promise';

const connection = await mysql.createConnection({...});

await connection.connect();

export async function getAll() {...}

async function insert(movie) {...}

async function update(movie) {...}

export async function get(id) {...}

export async function remove(id) {
  const query = 'DELETE FROM Movies WHERE id = ?';
  await connection.query(query, [id]);
  return;
}

export function save(movie) {...}
```

Listing 8.8 Deleting Data Records (movie/model.js)

With regard to the structure, the remove function is similar to the get function except that you use a DELETE statement instead of a SELECT statement. With these customizations, you can now manage the data records in your application. You can create new records, view existing ones, and modify them. You can delete data records from the database that are no longer needed.

An alternative to the final deletion of data records is the marking of records. In the database, this is represented by an additional field within the table. This field contains the value 0 for active data records and the value 1 for deleted data records. The drawback of this variant is that you have to take care of the referential integrity of your database by yourself; that is, you have to mark dependent data records as deleted yourself.

The fact that you need to install a driver for each respective database access enables you to connect different databases. Besides MySQL, there are numerous other relational databases. A lightweight alternative, for example, is SQLite.

8.1.2 SQLite

An important difference between MySQL and SQLite is that SQLite doesn't require a server process. The client software directly accesses the database stored in a file during queries. SQLite also requires no configuration. You can use the database immediately after initialization.

SQLite is available for a wide range of systems. For example, there are precompiled binary packages for Linux, macOS, and Windows.

Because SQLite stores the database data in a file, it can be copied and backed up in a very simple way.

Unlike MySQL, SQLite doesn't have its own user management. This means you can't assign any permissions, which makes a multiuser system at the database level impossible. You can only solve the permissions problem at the file system level by assigning the appropriate read and write permissions to the respective users. Ideally, this is done via group assignment so that you can give permissions to multiple users.

Installation

There are several drivers for SQLite that you can use to access the database. In the following sections, you'll learn about the sqlite3 driver. It's available as an npm package and can be installed via the npm install sqlite3 command.

Once you've installed the package, you can attach an SQLite database to your application and use it to persist data.

Database Structure

However, before you can interact with the database, you must create it. Listing 8.9 guides you through this process, at the end of which, you'll have a working database with a movies table that you'll use as a starting point in the following sections.

```
$ sqlite3 movie.db
Enter ".help" for usage hints.
sqlite> CREATE TABLE `Movies` (
   ...> id INTEGER PRIMARY KEY,
   ...> title TEXT,
   ...> year INTEGER);
sqlite> INSERT INTO `Movies` (`title`, `year`) VALUES
   ...> ('Iron Man', 2008),
   ...> ('Thor', 2011),
   ...> ('Captain America', 2011);
sqlite>
```

Listing 8.9 SQLite Database Structure

Both the structure and the initial information are the same as in the MySQL example. The SQLite database is stored in a file named *movie.db* in the root directory of your application. You'll need this information to establish a connection to the database.

Establishing a Connection

Because SQLite doesn't have any internal user management, the connection setup is limited to specifying the file name. Listing 8.10 shows how you can connect to the database from the model in the *movie/model.js* file.

```
import sqlite from 'sqlite3';

const db = new sqlite.Database('./movie.db');

export async function getAll() {}
export async function get(id) {}
export async function save(movie) {}
export async function remove(id) {}
```

Listing 8.10 Establishing a Connection to an SQLite Database

To establish a connection to your database, two statements are sufficient. In the first step, you include the `sqlite3` package that allows you to connect to the database. Finally, in the second step, you initialize the actual database connection by creating a database object, specifying the name of the file where the database is located. As your application progresses further, you can use this database object to send your queries to the database.

Like the MySQL driver, the SQLite driver works asynchronously, but it doesn't natively support promises, so you have to take care of that yourself. However, the adjustments to the application are limited to the model file because its interface remains unchanged. The following sections describe step by step how you can read the data from the database, and then create new data records, modify the existing records, and finally delete records.

Reading Data Records

The SQLite driver comprises several methods that allow you to read data from your database. In the first use case, you read the complete movies table. For this purpose, the all method of the connection object is used.

As the source code in Listing 8.11 shows, the signature of the getAll function is preserved, so you don't need to make any changes to the rest of the application. Because the SQLite driver doesn't support promises, you must create a promise object yourself and return it. In the callback function that you pass when you create it, you then perform the actual database operation. The query remains unchanged because both MySQL and SQLite are SQL databases that largely support the same syntax. On the connection object, you must call the all method. It expects the query and a callback function that is called with an error object and the results of the query in the form of an array of objects. Inside the callback function, you resolve the promise with the results of the query. If an error occurs—that is, if the error object isn't null—you must use the reject function to signal a failure. With a restart of your application, you can already view the movie list with the contents of your SQLite database.

```
import sqlite from 'sqlite3';

const db = new sqlite.Database('./movie.db');

export async function getAll() {
  return new Promise((resolve, reject) => {
    const query = 'SELECT * FROM Movies';
    db.all(query, (error, results) => {
      if (error) {
        reject(error);
      } else {
        resolve(results);
      }
    });
  });
}

export async function get(id) {}
export async function save(movie) {}
export async function remove(id) {}
```

Listing 8.11 Reading the Existing Data Records (movie/model.js)

Creating Data Records

Unlike the mysql driver, the SQLite driver distinguishes between read and write accesses. Using the run method of the connection object, you'll implement the write operations in the following sections.

```
import sqlite from 'sqlite3';

const db = new sqlite.Database('./movie.db');

export async function getAll() {
  return new Promise((resolve, reject) => {
    const query = 'SELECT * FROM Movies';
    db.all(query, (error, results) => {
      if (error) {
        reject(error);
      } else {
        resolve(results);
      }
    });
  });
}

function insert(movie) {
  return new Promise((resolve, reject) => {
    const query = 'INSERT INTO Movies (title, year) VALUES (?, ?)';
    db.run(query, [movie.title, movie.year], (error, results) => {
      if (error) {
        reject(error);
      } else {
        resolve(results);
      }
    });
  });
}

export async function get(id) {}

export async function save(movie) {
  if (!movie.id) {
    return insert(movie);
  }
}

export async function remove(id) {}
```

Listing 8.12 Creating Data Records with SQLite (movie/model.js)

The save function works similar to the MySQL example. If the object doesn't have an ID, it's a new data record, and the insert function is executed.

The content of the insert function is again encapsulated in a promise. Inside the callback function, you prepare the SQL statement to insert the record, and you use the run method of the database object to execute the query. The driver carries out the escaping job here as well. After the request is complete, the driver executes the function you pass as the third parameter.

At this point, we need to take a look at a peculiarity in accessing the ID field the database has assigned to the new data record: In the callback function of the run method, you can access more information using this within the callback function. For an INSERT query, the lastID property is available here and contains the rowid of the record you inserted with this command. For this reason, you can't use an arrow function at this point because this can't take the required value here.

Editing Data Records

Listing 8.13 summarizes the adjustments you need to make to edit the data records.

```
import sqlite from 'sqlite3';

const db = new sqlite.Database('./movie.db');

export async function getAll() {...}

function insert(movie) {...}

function update(movie) {
  return new Promise((resolve, reject) => {
    const query = 'UPDATE Movies SET title = ?, year = ? WHERE id = ?';
    db.run(query, [movie.title, movie.year, movie.id], (error, results) => {
      if (error) {
        reject(error);
      } else {
        resolve(results);
      }
    });
  });
}

export async function get(id) {
  return new Promise((resolve, reject) => {
    const query = 'SELECT * FROM Movies WHERE id = ?';
    db.get(query, [id], (error, results) => {
      if (error) {
```

```
        reject(error);
      } else {
        resolve(results);
      }
    });
  });
}

export async function save(movie) {
  if (!movie.id) {
    return insert(movie);
  } else {
    return update(movie);
  }
}
export async function remove(id) {}
```

Listing 8.13 Editing and Reading Data Records (movie/model.js)

In addition to the all method for reading all data records returned by a query, you can use the get method to read only one data record. You use this method to read the data record within the get function so that you can fill the form with the appropriate data. The remainder of the implementation process for the get function, which you export for the controller, as well as the update function, follows the same pattern as for adding and reading all records: You encapsulate the function in a promise, prepare the query, then use the driver and its escaping feature, and finally register a callback function in which you then resolve or reject the promise, depending on whether the query was successful or not.

Deleting Data Records

The last operation to be ported is deleting data records. After that, you'll have a fully functional movie database on the basis of SQLite. Again, you follow the familiar pattern of creating a new promise object, preparing the database operation in the callback function, and sending the request using the run method of the database object. Finally, you set the result and thus the state of the promise object in the callback function that you pass to the run method. You can see the corresponding source code in Listing 8.14.

```
import sqlite from 'sqlite3';

const db = new sqlite.Database('./movie.db');

export async function getAll() {...}

function insert(movie) {...}
```

```
function update(movie) {...}

export async function get(id) {...}

export async function save(movie) {...}

export async function remove(id) {
  return new Promise((resolve, reject) => {
    const query = 'DELETE FROM Movies WHERE id = ?';
    db.run(query, [id], (error, results) => {
      if (error) {
        reject(error);
      } else {
        resolve(results);
      }
    });
  });
}
```

Listing 8.14 Deleting Data Records in SQLite

In the previous sections, you've seen that although the two databases—MySQL and SQLite—differ significantly, it makes relatively little difference in the source code of your application which database you use. The basic principles of accessing them are always the same. You issue a query and handle the result asynchronously in your application. The biggest differences here are in the specific driver implementations and whether they provide you with native promises or if you must take care of that yourself.

In the following section, we'll introduce another abstraction layer for database access with object-relational mapping (ORM) for Node.js, which makes both the connection and an eventual replacement of the database yet another bit easier.

8.1.3 Object-Relational Mapping

ORM refers to the mapping of database relations to objects. With such a tool, you normally hardly need to write SQL queries yourself because the tool does it for you. You can focus on describing operations in terms of objects and method calls. Several ORM libraries exist for Node.js, such as Sequelize, Waterline, and ORM2. In this section, we'll introduce you to Sequelize. The other libraries are based on the same principle, but they differ somewhat in syntax and supported features.

One of the great advantages of ORM is that you're relatively independent of the database you use. ORM abstracts the access to the database for you. For this reason, you must always install the appropriate database driver for ORM. In the case of the current example, you must install ORM and the appropriate SQLite driver via the `npm install sequelize sqlite` command.

When integrating ORM into the movie database, the customizations are limited to the *movie/model.js* file, as before. The rest of the application remains unchanged. Before you can make your queries, you must first configure ORM, much like a database driver. For the SQLite database used, this requires the steps shown in Listing 8.15.

```
import { Sequelize } from 'sequelize';

const sequelize = new Sequelize({
  dialect: 'sqlite',
  storage: './movie.db',
});

const Movies = sequelize.define(
  'Movies',
  {
    title: {
      type: Sequelize.STRING,
    },
    year: {
      type: Sequelize.INTEGER,
    },
  },
  { timestamps: false },
);
```

Listing 8.15 Configuration of Sequelize for SQLite (movie/model.js)

When you create the new Sequelize instance, you use the `dialect` property to pass the type of database. In this case, it's the `sqlite` value. Based on this information, Sequelize selects the correct driver for the connection and uses its application programming interface (API) accordingly. For SQLite, you also use the `storage` property to specify the location of the database file. For databases such as MySQL, which may reside on a remote system and have authentication, you pass the database name and a user name and password to the constructor. You can pass the host name via the options object, such as the `dialect`.

Once you've created the Sequelize instance and thus have a connection to the database, you can define models representing the table in your database. In the example, this is the `movies` table. Use the `define` method of the Sequelize instance to create such a model. You pass the table name and the structure of the table as an object to the method, in which you specify the data types of the respective columns. The last argument represents an optional configuration object. Specifying `timestamps: false` here ensures that the `createdAt` and `updatedAt` fields aren't automatically inserted by Sequelize. Based on this model, you can formulate the queries to your database.

As you can see in Listing 8.16, the source code of your model becomes quite compact due to the use of Sequelize. The `findAll` and `findByPk` methods are used to read all data records and a single data record, respectively. The `destroy` method deletes the specified data record, while `upsert` either re-creates or updates the passed data record, depending on whether or not it already exists. The method can distinguish between an inserting and an updating operation, so you don't have to worry about that yourself.

```
import { Sequelize } from 'sequelize';

const sequelize = new Sequelize({
  dialect: 'sqlite',
  storage: './movie.db',
});

const Movies = sequelize.define(
  'Movies',
  {
    title: {
      type: Sequelize.STRING,
    },
    year: {
      type: Sequelize.INTEGER,
    },
  },
  { timestamps: false },
);

export function getAll() {
  return Movies.findAll();
}
export function get(id) {
  return Movies.findByPk(id);
}
export function remove(id) {
  return Movies.destroy({ where: { id } });
}
export function save(movie) {
  return Movies.upsert(movie);
}
```

Listing 8.16 Querying the Database via the Sequelize Model (movie/model.js)

After this excursion into the world of relational databases, we'll devote the second part of this chapter to the connection of nonrelational databases.

8.2   Node.js and Nonrelational Databases

For a long time, relational databases were the only widely used way of storing data in a structured way and making it available again for quick access. In the meantime, however, another type of database has established itself on the market. These types of databases are deliberately based on a different approach. Unlike relational databases with their fixed table structures, nonrelational databases don't impose such a structure, and data is organized in other ways, for example, in the form of documents.

Often, nonrelational databases store object or document structures that you can access using specific key or index values. These are summarized under the collective term *NoSQL*. In the following sections, you'll get to know Redis and MongoDB—two representatives of the nonrelational database category.

8.2.1   Redis

At its core, Redis is a simple key-value store that allows you to save values and to provide them with a key. This key then enables you to access the corresponding value again.

Redis stores the values in memory, which results in very good performance for read and write operations. The drawback of this technology is that the has RAM contents are irretrievably lost after a system crash. However, the developers of Redis have found a very elegant solution to this problem. The system can write a backup copy of the database to the hard disk at definable times, from which it's easy to restore the contents.

Redis is primarily available for Portable Operating System Interface (POSIX) systems, such as Linux, Berkeley Source Distribution (BSD), or macOS, and is even developed on these systems. Although there is a version of the Redis server available for Windows, it isn't very well supported. As an alternative to installing Redis, you can also run it in a Docker container. The developers of Redis provide official images for this purpose. To launch a container, you must execute the command shown in Listing 8.17 on the command line.

```
docker run
  --name redis
  -v db-data:/data
  -p 6379:6379
  -d
  redis:latest
```

Listing 8.17 Launching a Redis Container

Installation

Like the other drivers for databases, the Redis client for Node.js is also available as an npm package and can be installed via the command line using npm install redis. Once you've installed the Redis server and the npm package with the Redis client on your system and started Redis, you can use Redis in your Node.js application.

Because Redis isn't based on any fixed structures, you don't need to perform any further operations to initialize a database but can directly take care of connecting to the server.

Establishing a Connection

Listing 8.18 shows how you can set up a connection to a local Redis server in your *movie/model.js* file.

```
const redis = require('redis');
const client = redis.createClient();


client.on('error', error => console.error(error));
```

Listing 8.18 Connecting to the Redis Server

You can also optionally pass the address of a remote server or a reference to a Unix socket to the createClient method, depending on how you want to address the server. For our example, a local connection is established via port 6379 without any further specifications.

Communication is asynchronous and event-based. Strictly speaking, this means you can bind callback functions to different events and thus react to every single event. Listing 8.18 shows this on the basis of the error event that is triggered if an error occurs when connecting to the Redis server. Other events you can react to are ready, connect, end, drain, and idle.

When you no longer need the connection to the server, you should terminate it by calling the exit or quit method. Otherwise, the connection is kept open, and the application isn't closed. The difference between the two methods is that exit terminates the connection immediately, regardless of whether responses from the server are still pending or not. quit, on the other hand, waits until all responses from the server have been received and then terminates the connection.

Creating and Editing Data Records

You can use the set method to create new data records in Redis; if a data record with the specified key already exists, it will be overwritten. To access your data records, you should choose a unique key. Listing 8.19 shows how to use the set method.

```
import redis from 'redis';

const client = redis.createClient();

client.on('error', (error) => console.error(error));

export function getAll() {
  return Promise.resolve([]);
}

export async function get(id) {}
export async function remove(id) {}

export function save(movie) {
  return new Promise((resolve, reject) => {
    if (!movie.id) {
      movie.id = Date.now();
    }
    client.set(movie.id, JSON.stringify(movie), (error) => {
      if (error) {
        reject(error);
      } else {
        resolve();
      }
    });
  });
}
```

Listing 8.19 Creating a Data Record in Redis (movie/model.js)

For the example to work in general, the first step is to make sure that the getAll function returns a promise object with an array; otherwise, the template engine will return an exception.

First, you must create a promise object inside the save method, which you use as a return value. Within the callback function, you use the set method of Redis, which receives a total of three arguments. The first argument is a character string that specifies the key you can later use to access the data you pass in the second argument again. Finally, the third argument is a callback function that is executed as soon as the server sends a response. This callback function receives two values: the first one is an error object, and the second is the server's response. If no problems occurred while inserting the data, you'll get the string OK.

Because it's only possible to create new data records or to completely overwrite existing ones, you merely need to check in the save method whether the passed object already has an id property. In this case, you use it as a key; otherwise, you must generate a current time stamp and use that as a key. The problem with this solution is that it isn't possible to create two data records in the same millisecond. For the movie database, this doesn't cause any problems, but for an application with more users, you should use a different alternative for generating unique keys at this point, such as the uuid or shortid packages.

For editing records, you must also implement the reading of a single record by its ID in addition to the storage routine. In the get function in the *movie/model.js* file, you can use the get method of the Redis client to do this. To leave the interface unchanged from the previous examples, you should embed the query in a promise. Listing 8.20 contains the corresponding source code.

```
import redis from 'redis';

const client = redis.createClient();

client.on('error', (error) => console.error(error));

export function getAll() {...}

export function get(id) {
  return new Promise((resolve, reject) => {
    client.get(id, (err, data) => {
      if (error) {
        reject(error);
      } else {
        resolve(JSON.parse(data));
      }
    });
  });
}

export function remove(id) {}

export function save(movie) {...}
```

Listing 8.20 Reading a Data Record (movie/model.js)

Reading Data Records

In Listing 8.20, you've already seen how you can read individual records from a Redis database. However, for the display of the total list, you need to go one step further. You can use the keys method of the Redis client to read all the keys of the database and use this information to get to the individual data records. Listing 8.21 shows the implementation of the getAll function.

```
import redis from 'redis';

const client = redis.createClient();

client.on('error', (error) => console.error(error));

export function getAll() {
  return new Promise((resolve, reject) => {
    client.keys('*', (error, keys) => {
      const promises = keys.map((key) => get(key));
      Promise.all(promises).then(
        (values) => {
          resolve(values);
        },
        (error) => reject(error),
      );
    });
  });
}

export function get(id) {...}

export function remove(id) {}

export function save(movie) {...}
```

Listing 8.21 Reading All Data Records (movie/model.js)

Removing Data Records

The Redis server command set includes the `del` command, which you can use to remove entries from your database. Listing 8.22 describes the use of the `del` method using a simple example.

```
import redis from 'redis';

const client = redis.createClient();

client.on('error', (error) => console.error(error));

export function getAll() {...}

export function get(id) {...}

export function remove(id) {
  return new Promise((resolve, reject) => {
```

```
  client.del(id, (error) => {
    if (error) {
      reject(error);
    } else {
      resolve();
    }
  });
});
}
```

```
export function save(movie) {...}
```

Listing 8.22 Deleting Data Records from the Redis Database (movie/model.js)

To remove a data record from your database, you must pass the `del` method the key of the record you want to delete. As a second argument, this method accepts a callback function that will be executed once the deletion is done. Here you get access to both an error object and the number of data records deleted during this operation.

Through the Redis client, you can access the entire command set provided by the Redis server. For example, you can create and work with hashes and lists. If you want to learn more about Redis, *http://redis.io* is a good place to start.

With MongoDB, you'll get to know another representative of nonrelational databases in the following sections.

8.2.2   MongoDB

MongoDB is a representative of document-based databases. This means that the storage of information in this database is based on documents that exist in Binary JavaScript Object Notation (BSON) format. For more information about this format, visit *http://bsonspec.org*.

MongoDB is also suitable for larger applications due to its good performance and also comes with some additional features such as clustering and sharding, which provide decisive advantages, especially for very large data volumes.

MongoDB is available for a wide variety of operating systems, including Linux, Windows, Solaris, and macOS. So, you can install MongoDB on any system that also runs Node.js. If you don't want to install MongoDB on your system, but you can launch Docker containers on it, you can also run MongoDB as a container. As with the other databases, official images are available for you to use. Use the command from Listing 8.23 to launch the container.

```
docker run
  --name mongo
  -v db-data:/data/db
```

```
  -p 27017:27017
  -d
  mongo:latest
```

Listing 8.23 Launching the MongoDB Container

Installation

Once you've installed the server software of MongoDB on your system and started the server process, all you need is a driver to access your database. For Node.js, a driver implemented in JavaScript exists as an npm package that you can install using the npm install mongodb command.

As with the previous databases, in the first step, you'll now learn how to establish a connection to your database, which you can then later be used to create, read, modify, and delete records.

Establishing a Connection

The connection to the database is based on the MongoDB client. Make sure that you initialize this client correctly. Listing 8.24 shows how to do that.

```
import { MongoClient } from 'mongodb';

let collection = null;

async function connect() {
  if (collection) {
    return collection;
  }
  const client = new MongoClient('mongodb://localhost:27017');

  await client.connect();

  const db = client.db('moviedb');
  collection = db.collection('Movie');

  return collection;
}

export async function getAll() {}
export async function get(id) {}
export async function remove(id) {}
export function save(movie) {}
```

Listing 8.24 Connecting to the Database (movie/model.js)

The connection is established by the asynchronous connect function. Here, you must first check whether a collection already exists, that is, whether a connection exists, and return it. If there is no connection yet, you must create a new instance of the MongoClient class from the mongodb driver and pass the address of the database. Then you must use the connect method of the client to establish a connection. This method returns a promise object that you await via the await keyword. Once the connection is established, you create a new database object via the db method of the client and, on top of that, a new collection object via the collection method. The collection is responsible for managing the documents. The collection object is the return value of the connect function and is used as a basis by the other functions in this file.

Creating Data Records

The MongoDB client provides you with the insert method for creating new data records. Listing 8.25 shows how you can use this method.

```
import { MongoClient } from 'mongodb';

let collection = null;

async function connect() {...}

export function getAll() {
  return Promise.resolve([]);
}

export async function get(id) {}

export async function remove(id) {}

async function insert(movie) {
  movie.id = Date.now();
  const collection = await connect();
  const data = collection.insertOne(movie);
  return data;
}

export function save(movie) {
  if (!movie.id) {
    return insert(movie);
  }
}
```

Listing 8.25 Inserting Data Records into a MongoDB (movie/model.js)

MongoDB assigns a unique ID to each data record via the _id field. To avoid changes to the rest of the application's source code, at this point, as with the Redis example, you should use the current time stamp to generate an additional ID that will be used as a reference in the rest of the application.

The asynchronous insert function is responsible for inserting a new data record. First, you create a connection to the database using the connect function. Then you use the insertOne method to save the data record. As an argument, the method accepts an object structure representing the new data record, that is, our movie.

The save function, in turn, uses the ID of the data record passed to decide whether it's a new record, and then calls the insert function accordingly.

Reading Data Records

Once you've created data records in the database, you can read them via the find method. Listing 8.26 shows the extension of the model, with which you can read all data records from the collection.

```
import { MongoClient } from 'mongodb';

let collection = null;

async function connect() {...}

export async function getAll() {
  const collection = await connect();
  const docs = await collection.find({});
  return docs.toArray();
}

export async function get(id) {}

export async function remove(id) {}

async function insert(movie) {...}

export function save(movie) {...}
```

Listing 8.26 Reading Data Records from a MongoDB (movie/model.js)

After you've connected to the database using the connect function and obtained the reference to the collection, you can call the find method on this object to search for documents there that meet certain criteria. If you pass an empty object to the find method, all documents will be read. However, you can also define queries here and thus select only certain documents.

You can call the toArray method on the object returned by find. This ensures that an array with all documents found is available to you in a callback function in addition to an error object.

Updating Data Records

To update data records, you need to implement two functions, as in the previous examples. First, you must modify the getAll function so that you can pass it an optional query. You also rename the function to get to better reflect the character of the function. At this point, you should note that the get function always returns an array, so you must extract the movie object. In the next step, you implement the update function, which is responsible for updating a data record. The corresponding changes to the *movie/model.js* file are shown in Listing 8.27.

```javascript
import { MongoClient } from 'mongodb';

let collection = null;

async function connect() {...}

export async function getAll() {...}

export async function get(id) {
  const collection = await connect();
  const doc = await collection.findOne({ id });
  return doc;
}

export async function remove(id) {}

async function insert(movie) {...}

async function update(movie) {
  movie.id = parseInt(movie.id, 10);
  const collection = await connect();
  await collection.updateOne({ id: movie.id }, { $set: movie });
  return movie;
}

export function save(movie) {
  if (!movie.id) {
    return insert(movie);
  } else {
    return update(movie);
  }
}
```

Listing 8.27 Modifying Data Records (movie/model.js)

In the extension of the save function from Listing 8.27, you must call the update function for data records to be updated. This function first converts the id property to a
number, ensures that the connection is established, and at the same time gets a reference to the collection object. Then, you use the updateOne method of the collection to
update the data record. As the first argument, this method accepts the selector you use
to locate the data record, and, as the second argument, you pass the updated data
record. As a return value, you get a promise object.

When reading a single data record to populate the form, you access the findOne method
of the collection, which you pass the ID you're looking for as a selector.

Removing Data Records

To remove data records, you can use the deleteOne method of the collection object.
This method has a signature similar to the findOne method. As an argument, you pass
an object that contains the search criteria for the data record. The integration with your
model is shown in Listing 8.28.

```
import { MongoClient } from 'mongodb';

let collection = null;

async function connect() {...}

export async function getAll() {...}

export async function get(id) {...}

export async function remove(id) {
  const collection = await connect();
  return collection.deleteOne({ id });
}

async function insert(movie) {...}

async function update(movie) {...}

export function save(movie) {...}
```

Listing 8.28 Deleting Data Records (movie/model.js)

Once you've made these adjustments to your model, you can restart your application,
then manage the data records in it, and store them in a MongoDB instance.

Mongoose

Similar to ORM in SQL databases, Mongoose is an abstraction layer between the database and your application. Mongoose allows you to view the documents in your database directly as objects in your application and provides you with a variety of methods for handling the data. This package is installed via npm using the npm install mongoose command. Listing 8.29 shows how you can use Mongoose on the basis of the movie database.

```javascript
import mongoose from 'mongoose';

mongoose.connect('mongodb://localhost:27017/moviedb', {
  useNewUrlParser: true,
  useUnifiedTopology: true,
});

const Movie = mongoose.model('Movie', {
  id: Number,
  title: String,
  year: Number,
});

export function getAll() {
  return Movie.find({});
}

export function get(id) {
  return Movie.findOne({ id });
}

export async function remove(id) {
  const movie = await get(id);
  return movie.remove();
}

export async function save(movie) {
  if (!movie.id) {
    const newMovie = new Movie(movie);
    newMovie.id = Date.now();
    return newMovie.save();
  } else {
    const existingMovie = await get(parseInt(movie.id, 10));
    existingMovie.title = movie.title;
    existingMovie.year = movie.year;
```

```
    return existingMovie.save();
  }
}
```

Listing 8.29 Using Mongoose

In Mongoose, a model represents a collection. You define your models using the model method of Mongoose and specify the data type per property. The result of this method call is a class of which you can create instances. Calling the save method of the model saves the data to the database. You can use the find method to find existing data records and the remove method to delete these documents. The project's official website can be found at *http://mongoosejs.com/*.

8.3   Summary

As you've seen throughout this chapter, Node.js supports a variety of databases through the database drivers available as npm packages. The support isn't only limited to relational databases. You can also use various nonrelational databases such as Redis or MongoDB instead.

With the help of the drivers, you can access advanced features of the databases in addition to the basic database functions such as creating, reading, modifying, and deleting data records.

Depending on the task you need to solve with your application, you're free to choose which database you want to use.

Chapter 9
Authentication and Session Handling

Without security there is no freedom.
—Wilhelm von Humboldt

If you use Node.js as a server on the web, one of the most common problems is authenticating users. For both read and write accesses, it's important which user is accessing the information and whether or not the user is authorized for this operation. Because this is a standard problem, there are also several established solutions you can deploy in your application. Passport has proven itself in the area of Express applications. In this chapter, you'll learn how to use this tool to secure your server and assign data to specific users.

This chapter is based on the movie database you developed in the previous chapters. Pug is used as the template engine in this chapter, and we use SQLite as the database. To use the application, users must first log on via a login screen with their user name and corresponding password. After this, they can access the data they have generated. As an additional feature, during this chapter, you'll implement the publishing of movie records so that all users can access them, as well as a system for rating movies.

9.1 Passport

In an Express application, Passport performs most of the authentication tasks for you. Passport is managed as an open-source project on GitHub at *https://github.com/jared-hanson/passport*. The official website with comprehensive documentation can be found at *www.passportjs.org/*. Passport is implemented as a middleware component, so it integrates like a logger or other standard components. This design makes Passport relatively tightly coupled to its use with Express.

The specific feature of Passport that distinguishes it from other solutions is its structure. Passport is designed as a modular authentication system where the actual authentication mechanism can be registered as a plug-in. Currently, more than 500 of those plug-ins, also referred to as strategies, are available. For example, you can have your users authenticate against Facebook, Twitter, or a local database. Both Passport and all strategy plug-ins are available as Node Package Manager (npm) packages, making them easy to integrate into your application.

In this chapter, you'll use the `local` strategy to authenticate your users using a user name and password without involving third-party services.

9.2   Setup and Configuration

Compared to other middleware components for Express, Passport is a bit more complex to set up. You need to create a set of prerequisites and configure your application correctly. Afterwards, securing the routes requires very little effort.

9.2.1   Installation

Passport itself is available under the npm package of the same name. You can install it via the `npm install passport` command. In addition to Express, which has already been installed, you also need the `express-session` package.

9.2.2   Configuration

Passport is usually configured at a central location. In your application, you should do this in the *index.js* file. To keep this file manageable, you can configure Passport in a separate help file.

Listing 9.1 contains the source code of the *auth.js* file with the Passport configuration.

```
import passport from 'passport';
import expressSession from 'express-session';

export default function (app) {
  passport.serializeUser((user, done) => done(null, user.username));
  passport.deserializeUser((id, done) => {
    const user = {
      username: 'sspringer',
      firstname: 'Sebastian',
      lastname: 'Springer',
    };
    done(null, user);
  });
  app.use(
    expressSession({
      secret: 'top secret',
      resave: false,
      saveUninitialized: false,
    }),
  );
```

```
  app.use(passport.initialize());
  app.use(passport.session());
}
```

Listing 9.1 Authentication Configuration (auth.js)

The serializeUser and deserializeUser methods accept a function that is used to restore the user data for subsequent requests. Passport stores the information in a session. To keep this data as compact as possible, you need unique information to get back to the complete user data. In the example, the user name is this unique key.

In the callback of the serializeUser method, you get access to the user object. The second argument is another callback function. You pass an error object to it when it's called, or the value zero and the serialized user information in the case of success.

The deserializeUser method works exactly the opposite way. You also pass a callback function to it, which receives the serialized user information and another callback function. This callback function is in turn called with an optional error object as well as the deserialized user information.

Usually, the callback functions are named done because they are called as soon as the potentially asynchronous serialization or deserialization is completed.

In the current implementation, authentication as well as serialization and deserialization are still static. Throughout this chapter, the database will be integrated at these points, making the entire process much more flexible.

To enable Passport to remember the user's login data across multiple requests, you must use the session middleware for Express. This makes sure the session gets saved in a browser cookie. As an option, you should use the secret property to pass a character string that will be used to sign the session cookie. In addition, you must set the saveUninitialized property to false to prevent new uninitialized sessions from being saved on the server. The resave property ensures that unchanged session information is also saved back. To change this behavior, the value must be set to false. For both saveUninitialized and resave, you must set a value in both cases, as otherwise a warning will be triggered.

By calling passport.initialize, you initialize Passport and thus create the connection between Express and Passport. Using passport.session ensures that login sessions are stored using the Express session middleware.

9.2.3   Strategy Configuration

Depending on the strategy used, the appropriate package must be installed and configured. The npm install passport-local command installs the local strategy package, which allows simple authentication against a user name and password combination. You include the configuration of the strategy in the *auth.js* file, as shown in Listing 9.2.

```
import passport from 'passport';
import expressSession from 'express-session';
import LocalStrategy from 'passport-local';

export default function (app) {
  passport.serializeUser((user, done) => done(null, user.username));
  passport.deserializeUser((id, done) => {
    const user = {
      username: 'sspringer',
      firstname: 'Sebastian',
      lastname: 'Springer',
    };
    done(null, user);
  });

  passport.use(
    new LocalStrategy((username, password, done) => {
      if (username === 'sspringer' && password === 'test') {
        done(null, {
          username: 'sspringer',
          firstname: 'Sebastian',
          lastname: 'Springer',
        });
      } else {
        done(null, false);
      }
    }),
  );

  app.use(
    expressSession({
      secret: 'top secret',
      resave: false,
      saveUninitialized: false,
    }),
  );
  app.use(passport.initialize());
  app.use(passport.session());
}
```

Listing 9.2 Integrating the "local" Strategy

When integrating the strategy plug-ins, Passport takes its cue from the middleware system of Express. You can use the use method to add a new instance of the strategy. To create this instance, you can use the constructor exported for you by the local strategy package.

In the specific case of local strategy, you pass a callback function that receives the user name and password as arguments. The third argument is a callback function you can use to indicate the success or failure of the login. This callback function is required because the user name and password verification is asynchronous in most cases. If the login was successful, you should call this callback function, which you should name done according to the naming convention, with the value null and an object representation of the user. If the information entered by the user isn't correct, that is, there is no matching user object, you must call the done function with the values null and false.

Passport expects the user name and password to be sent to the server via a POST request and to be named username and password by default. You can customize this behavior via an options object that you pass as the first argument to the constructor.

With these changes to your application, you've completed the basic setup for Passport. The next step consists of integrating the library into your application's workflow with the goal of allowing your users to log in.

9.3   Logging In to the Application

The local strategy used in this example requires users to enter their user name and password and send both to the server via a POST request. To do this, you first need a login form.

9.3.1   Login Form

Because the login form is a purely static page, you can save the necessary source code in the *public* directory of your application in the *login.html* file.

The form in Listing 9.3 is an ordinary HTML form sent to the server via POST request to the */login* path. Based on the standard requirements of the local strategy, the user name is submitted as username and the password as password.

```
<!DOCTYPE html>
<html lang="en">

<head>
  <meta charset="UTF-8">
  <title>Document</title>
  <link rel="stylesheet" href="style.css">
</head>

<body>
```

```
<form action="/login" method="post" id="login">
  <div>
    <h1>Please log in</h1>
    <div>
      <label for="username">Username:</label>
      <input type="text" name="username" id="username" autofocus>
    </div>
    <div>
      <label for="password">Password:</label>
      <input type="password" name="password" id="password">
    </div>
  </div>
  <button type="submit">anmelden</button>
</form>
</body>

</html>
```

Listing 9.3 Login Form (public/login.html)

On the server side, you then define the appropriate route to perform authentication. Listing 9.4 shows the implementation of this route.

```
import passport from 'passport';
import expressSession from 'express-session';
import LocalStrategy from 'passport-local';

export default function (app) {
  passport.serializeUser((user, done) => done(null, user.username));
  passport.deserializeUser((id, done) => {...});

  passport.use(
    new LocalStrategy((username, password, done) => {...}),
  );

  app.use(
    expressSession({...}),
  );
  app.use(passport.initialize());
  app.use(passport.session());

  app.post(
    '/login',
    passport.authenticate('local', { failureRedirect: '/login.html' }),
    (request, response) => {
```

```
      response.redirect('/');
    },
  );
}
```

Listing 9.4 Authentication Integration (auth.js)

First, you apply the `authenticate` method of Passport as middleware to the login route. This takes care of logging the user in based on the previously defined logic. If the login fails, the request is redirected back to the login page. If it's successful, the subsequent callback function is executed. This function ensures that the user is redirected to the default route. For the login process to your application to work, you still need to integrate the `auth` module into your application. This is done in the initial file with a call to the function exported by the `auth` module. The concrete integration is shown in Listing 9.5.

```
import express from 'express';
import morgan from 'morgan';
import { dirname } from 'path';
import { fileURLToPath } from 'url';
import { router as movieRouter } from './movie/index.js';
import auth from './auth.js';

const app = express();

app.set('view engine', 'pug');

app.use(express.static(dirname(fileURLToPath(import.meta.url)) + '/public'));

app.use(morgan('common', { immediate: true }));

app.use(express.urlencoded({ extended: false }));

auth(app);

app.use('/movie', movieRouter);

app.get('/', (request, response) => response.redirect('/movie'));

app.listen(8080, () => {
  console.log('Server is listening to http://localhost:8080');
});
```

Listing 9.5 Integrating the Auth Module (index.js)

When you restart your server process, you can access the login form at *http://localhost:8080/login.html*. Figure 9.1 shows the current state of the login screen.

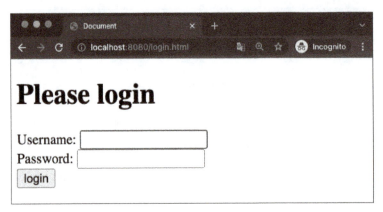

Figure 9.1 Login Form

9.3.2 Securing Resources

Your application is now prepared up to the point where you can start making parts of the application available only to logged-in users because in the current state, users can log in but also perform all available actions without being logged in. To solve this task, you can draw on an existing package called connect-ensure-login, which you can install using the npm install connect-ensure-login command. Listing 9.6 shows how you can secure the entire movie module.

```
import express from 'express';
import morgan from 'morgan';
import { dirname } from 'path';
import { fileURLToPath } from 'url';
import { router as movieRouter } from './movie/index.js';
import auth from './auth.js';
import { ensureLoggedIn } from 'connect-ensure-login';

const app = express();

app.set('view engine', 'pug');

app.use(express.static(dirname(fileURLToPath(import.meta.url)) + '/public'));

app.use(morgan('common', { immediate: true }));

app.use(express.urlencoded({ extended: false }));

auth(app);
```

```
app.use('/movie', ensureLoggedIn('/login.html'), movieRouter);

app.get('/', (request, response) => response.redirect('/movie'));

app.listen(8080, () => {
  console.log('Server is listening to http://localhost:8080');
});
```

Listing 9.6 Securing Resources (index.js)

The connect-ensure-login package provides you with the ensureLoggedIn and ensure-LoggedOut methods, which you can use as middleware to determine whether the current user is logged in or logged out.

You pass the route to which a user who isn't logged in should be redirected to the ensureLoggedIn middleware function. In the example, that's the login form. When you now restart your application, it's no longer possible to access the movie list without logging in. Currently, however, you can only log out by deleting the site's cookies, as they keep the reference to the session. So, the next step is to make the logout process more convenient for your users.

9.3.3 Logging Out

If you want to log in with a different user or simply end your current session, you can currently do this only by means of a workaround. However, the goal is to enable this process via a link within the application. For this purpose, you must extend the central template with a link to the logout route. Listing 9.7 shows the source code of the *templates/base.pug* file.

```
doctype html
html(lang="en")
  head
    meta(charset="UTF-8")
    title Movie list
    link(rel="stylesheet" href="/style.css")
  body

  a(href="/logout") logout
  img.logo(src="logo.png" height="50")

  block content
    div No content
```

Listing 9.7 Inserting the Logout Link (templates/base.pug)

281

You must also implement the counterpart of this route in the *auth.js* file to group all the functionalities associated with authentication in one module.

As you can see in Listing 9.8, Passport extends the request object with a logout method. You can use this method to discard the current logon session and thus log off the user. After that, you redirect the user to the application's entry page, which eventually takes the user back to the login page.

```
import passport from 'passport';
import expressSession from 'express-session';
import LocalStrategy from 'passport-local';

export default function (app) {
  passport.serializeUser((user, done) => done(null, user.username));
  passport.deserializeUser((id, done) => {...});

  passport.use(
    new LocalStrategy((username, password, done) => {...}),
  );

  app.use(
    expressSession({...}),
  );
  app.use(passport.initialize());
  app.use(passport.session());

  app.post('/login',...);

  app.get('/logout', (request, response) => {
    request.logout();
    response.redirect('/');
  });
}
```

Listing 9.8 Implementing the Logout Route (auth.js)

9.3.4   Connecting to the Database

The current implementation of the application is based on static data that exists in the source code. To make your application more flexible at this point, you can use the existing SQLite database and store the user data there.

First, you need to add a user table to your database and insert at least one data record. Listing 9.9 shows the queries used to extend your database accordingly.

```
CREATE TABLE `Users` (
id INTEGER PRIMARY KEY,
firstname TEXT,
lastname TEXT,
username TEXT,
password TEXT);
INSERT INTO `Users` (`firstname`, `lastname`, `username`, `password`) VALUES
('Sebastian', 'Springer', 'sspringer', '098f6bcd4621d373cade4e832627b4f6');
```

Listing 9.9 Extending the Database by a User Table

It has become a best practice not to store passwords in plain text in the database, but to encrypt them instead or to store a hash value of the password. In this case, it's a simple MD5 hash. To access the database, you need a model in your application. Because you only have read access to the database in this example, the implementation of a get method in the model is sufficient. The implementation of the model that you store in the *user* directory in the *model.js* file is shown in Listing 9.10.

```
import sqlite from 'sqlite3';

const db = new sqlite.Database('./movie.db');

export function get(query = {}) {
  return new Promise((resolve, reject) => {
    const queryElements = [];
    if (query) {
      for (let key in query) {
        queryElements.push(`${key} = ?`);
      }
    }

    const queryString = `SELECT * FROM Users WHERE ${queryElements.join(
      ' AND ',
    )}`;

    db.get(queryString, Object.values(query), (error, results) => {
      if (error) {
        reject(error);
      } else {
        resolve(results);
      }
    });
  });
}
```

Listing 9.10 Implementing the User Model (user/model.js)

The implementation of the get method is kept at a general level so that you can search for a user name and password combination as well as a user ID. For this purpose, the passed query object is decomposed, and the query is assembled in such a way that you can use the escaping of the SQLite driver.

Due to this extension, you can now replace the static credentials in the *auth.js* file with queries from the database. The source code in Listing 9.11, which we'll explain step by step afterwards, provides an overview.

```javascript
import passport from 'passport';
import expressSession from 'express-session';
import LocalStrategy from 'passport-local';
import { createHash } from 'crypto';
import { get } from './user/model.js';

export default function (app) {
  passport.serializeUser((user, done) => done(null, user.id));
  passport.deserializeUser(async (id, done) => {
    const user = await get({ id });
    if (!user) {
      done('User not found');
    } else {
      done(null, user);
    }
  });

  passport.use(
    new LocalStrategy(async (username, password, done) => {
      const hash = createHash('md5').update(password).digest('hex');
      const user = await get({ username, password: hash });
      if (!user) {
        done(null, false);
      } else {
        done(null, user);
      }
    }),
  );

  app.use(expressSession({...}));
  app.use(passport.initialize());
  app.use(passport.session());

  app.post('/login', ...);

  app.get('/logout', (request, response) => {...});
}
```

Listing 9.11 User Authentication against a Database (auth.js)

At the beginning of the file, you import the `createHash` function of the `crypto` module to convert the passed password into the MD5 hash used in the example.

This means you no longer serialize the user by the user name, but by their unique user ID. In the `deserializeUser` method, whose callback function is now an `async` function, you read the user information from the database using the serialized user ID. The `get` method will either return the relevant data record of the user—in which case, you call the `done` callback function with the value `null` as the error object and the user object— or the record won't be found. This then indicates an error, and you call the `done` callback function with a corresponding message as an error object.

Passwords are stored as hashes in the database, so you'll need this form of password to query the database. The `createHash` function enables you to create the MD5 hash, pass the password in plain text via the `update` method, and have it output a character string formatted with hex values. You pass the user name and encrypted password to the `get` function of your `user` model for querying. When dealing with the result, you proceed in an analogous way to the deserialization of the user.

The following sections describe the handling of resources in your application.

9.4   Accessing Resources

Individual pages make up the largest category of resources in your application. You've already secured this type with Passport to prevent unauthorized people from accessing protected pages. However, in your application, you can also control at a lower level how your users work with the application's data.

9.4.1   Access Restriction

In this section, you'll limit the access to data records to the respective creator of the record and add the option to share movies with all users. For this purpose, you use the information stored in the session about the currently logged-in user for both write and read accesses. First, you have to extend the movie table of your database with an additional field, as shown in Listing 9.12.

```
ALTER TABLE `Movies` ADD COLUMN `user` INTEGER;
ALTER TABLE `Movies` ADD COLUMN `public` INTEGER;
```

Listing 9.12 Extending the Movie Table

When customizing the application, you move from the frontend toward the database and provide your users with the option to mark a movie as public so that all other users can see it. For this purpose, you must extend the input form in the *movie/form.js* file. Here, you insert the block from Listing 9.13 below the input field for the year.

```
<div>
  <label for="id">Public:</label>
  <input type="checkbox" id="public" name="public" value="1" ${
    movie.public ? 'checked="checked" ' : ''
  } />
</div>
```

Listing 9.13 Extending the Form (movie/form.js)

In the controller, you need to make changes in several places. In formAction, which is responsible for the form representation, you insert the public property with an empty character string as the default value, and in saveAction, you read the public property from the request and correctly place the information in the object to be saved. You must also pass the user ID to the model for each method call so that permissions can be applied correctly. You obtain this information through the request.user object Passport inserted for you. Listing 9.14 summarizes these customizations.

```
import { dirname } from 'path';
import { fileURLToPath } from 'url';
import { getAll, remove, get, save } from './model.js';
import { render } from './view.js';
import { render as form } from './form.js';

export async function listAction(request, response) {
  const movies = await getAll(request.user.id);
  response.render(dirname(fileURLToPath(import.meta.url)) + '/views/list', {
    movies,
  });
}

export async function removeAction(request, response) {
  const id = parseInt(request.params.id, 10);
  await remove(id, request.user.id);
  response.redirect(request.baseUrl);
}

export async function formAction(request, response) {
  let movie = { id: '', title: '', year: '', public: '' };

  if (request.params.id) {
    movie = await get(parseInt(request.params.id, 10), request.user.id);
  }

  const body = form(movie);
  response.send(body);
```

```
}

export async function saveAction(request, response) {
  const movie = {
    id: request.body.id,
    title: request.body.title,
    year: request.body.year,
    public: request.body.public === '1' ? 1 : 0,
  };
  await save(movie, request.user.id);
  response.redirect(request.baseUrl);
}
```

Listing 9.14 Extending the Controller with the "public" Property (movie/controller.js)

The model in the *movie/model.js* file takes care of managing the data and thus handling permissions. For each read request, only those records are read that the user is allowed to read.

```
import sqlite from 'sqlite3';

const db = new sqlite.Database('./movie.db');

export async function getAll(userId) {
  return new Promise((resolve, reject) => {
    const query = 'SELECT * FROM Movies WHERE user = ? OR public = 1';
    db.all(query, [userId], (error, results) => {
      if (error) {
        reject(error);
      } else {
        resolve(results);
      }
    });
  });
}

function insert(movie, userId) {
  return new Promise((resolve, reject) => {
    const query =
      'INSERT INTO Movies (title, year, public, user) VALUES (?, ?, ?, ?)';
    db.run(
      query,
      [movie.title, movie.year, movie.public, userId],
      function (error, results) {
        if (error) {
```

```
          reject(error);
        } else {
          resolve({ ...movie, id: this.lastID });
        }
      },
    );
  });
}

function update(movie, userId) {
  return new Promise((resolve, reject) => {
    const query =
      'UPDATE Movies SET title = ?, year = ?, public = ?, ⤶
        user = ? WHERE id = ?';
    db.run(
      query,
      [movie.title, movie.year, movie.public, userId, movie.id],
      (error, results) => {
        if (error) {
          reject(error);
        } else {
          resolve(results);
        }
      },
    );
  });
}

export async function get(id, userId) {
  return new Promise((resolve, reject) => {
    const query =
      'SELECT * FROM Movies WHERE id = ? AND (user = ? OR public = 1)';
    db.get(query, [id, userId], (error, results) => {
      if (error) {
        reject(error);
      } else {
        resolve(results);
      }
    });
  });
}

export async function save(movie, userId) {
  if (!movie.id) {
```

```
    return insert(movie, userId);
  } else {
    return update(movie, userId);
  }
}
export async function remove(id, userId) {
  return new Promise((resolve, reject) => {
    const query =
      'DELETE FROM Movies WHERE id = ? AND (user = ? OR public = 1)';
    db.run(query, [id, userId], (error, results) => {
      if (error) {
        reject(error);
      } else {
        resolve(results);
      }
    });
  });
}
```

Listing 9.15 Adjustments to the Model (movie/model.js)

With the getAll function, you limit the data records that are read to those directly assigned to the user or marked as public. You also adapt the get function so that it only returns a data record if it's assigned to the user or is public.

When inserting a record, you write the information regarding whether a movie is public or not from the user input to the database. In addition, you add the information about the creating user from the current session.

If it's a matter of updating a data record, you proceed in the same way as for inserting it. As a result, the information in the user column doesn't indicate the creating user, but the user who made the last change.

When deleting records, you customize the query so that users are only able to delete their own or public records, but not the nonpublic records of other users.

9.4.2 Submitting Ratings

The unique assignment of data records to users covers only a part of the problems you can map with authenticated users, however. Another feature you can now integrate into your movie database is a rating system. You want all users to be able to rate the movies. To solve this task, you must first create another table that maps the relation between user and movie. This table is named Ratings. The corresponding CREATE statement is shown in Listing 9.16.

```
CREATE TABLE `Ratings` (
user INTEGER,
movie INTEGER,
rating INTEGER);
```

Listing 9.16 Creating the Ratings Table

The rating system only affects the list view of the movies and here specifically the *movie/views/list-item.pug* file. Listing 9.17 shows the necessary adjustments.

```
mixin listItem(movie)
  tr
    td #{movie.id}
    td #{movie.title}
    td #{movie.year}
    td
      - const one = movie.userRating >= 1 ? '★': '☆'
      a(href="/movie/rate/" + movie.id + "/1") #{one}
      - const two = movie.userRating >= 2 ? '★': '☆'
      a(href="/movie/rate/" + movie.id + "/2") #{two}
      - const three = movie.userRating >= 3 ? '★': '☆'
      a(href="/movie/rate/" + movie.id + "/3") #{three}
      - const four = movie.userRating >= 4 ? '★': '☆'
      a(href="/movie/rate/" + movie.id + "/4") #{four}
      - const five = movie.userRating >= 5 ? '★': '☆'
      a(href="/movie/rate/" + movie.id + "/5") #{five}

      - const overall = Math.round((movie.sumOfRatings / ⤶
          movie.numOfRatings) * 10) / 10
      span (#{isNaN(overall) ? 0 : overall})

    td
      a(href="/movie/delete/" + movie.id) delete
    td
      a(href="/movie/form/" + movie.id) edit
```

Listing 9.17 Customizing the List View (movie/views/list-item.pug)

In this extension, you add a new column to the table that contains five links for rating. The link points to a new route to which you pass the ID of the movie you want to rate and the rating number. Depending on the rating the user has given so far, either a ★ or a ☆ is displayed. The average rating is also displayed next to these links. This is the sum total of all ratings divided by the number of ratings. The movie object passed to the view must therefore be extended with the appropriate information. In the next step, you need to define the route for the assessment. This happens in the *movie/index.js* file, as shown in Listing 9.18.

```
import { Router } from 'express';
import {
  listAction,
  removeAction,
  formAction,
  saveAction,
  rateAction,
} from './controller.js';

const router = Router();

router.get('/', listAction);
router.get('/delete/:id', removeAction);
router.get('/form/:id?', formAction);
router.post('/save', saveAction);
router.get('/rate/:movie/:rating', rateAction);

export { router };
```

Listing 9.18 Route Definition for Rating (movie/index.js)

The /rate route contains the aforementioned two variables, movie and rating, which you can use in the controller to access the values submitted by the user. This route is based on the rateAction of the movie controller in the *movie/controller.js* file. The implementation of this function is shown in Listing 9.19.

```
import { dirname } from 'path';
import { fileURLToPath } from 'url';
import { getAll, remove, get, save, rate } from './model.js';
import { render } from './view.js';
import { render as form } from './form.js';

export async function listAction(request, response) {...}

export async function removeAction(request, response) {...}

export async function formAction(request, response) {...}

export async function saveAction(request, response) {...}

export async function rateAction(request, response) {
  const rating = {
    movie: parseInt(request.params.movie, 10),
    user: request.user.id,
    rating: parseInt(request.params.rating, 10),
```

```
  };
  await rate(rating);
  response.redirect(request.baseUrl);
}
```

Listing 9.19 Implementing "rateAction" in the Controller (movie/controller.js)

When implementing rateAction, you first assemble a new object based on the information passed by the user via the newly created link and from the user ID from the session. You then pass this object to the rate function of the model, which makes sure that
the data gets saved. After successful saving, you redirect the user back to the movie list
to view the updated representation. Then you need to make two changes to the model.
This way, you ensure first that the rating data is available in the list view, and, second,
that the ratings are correctly stored in the database. Here you have to make sure that
there are no duplicates when a user changes a rating.

```
import sqlite from 'sqlite3';

const db = new sqlite.Database('./movie.db');

export async function getAll(userId) {
  return new Promise((resolve, reject) => {
    const query = `SELECT Movies.*,
      count(Ratings.rating) AS numOfRatings,
      sum(Ratings.rating) AS sumOfRatings,
      r.rating AS userRating
    FROM Movies
    LEFT JOIN Ratings ON Movies.id = Ratings.movie
    LEFT JOIN Ratings AS r ON Movies.id = r.movie AND r.user = ?
    WHERE Movies.user = ? OR public = 1
    GROUP BY Movies.id;`;

    db.all(query, [userId, userId], (error, results) => {
      if (error) {
        reject(error);
      } else {
        resolve(results);
      }
    });
  });
}

function insert(movie, userId) {...}

function update(movie, userId) {...}
```

```
export async function get(id, userId) {...}

export async function save(movie, userId) {...}

export async function remove(id, userId) {...}

export async function rate(rating) {
  const deleteQuery = 'DELETE FROM Ratings WHERE movie = ? AND user = ?';
  await db.run(deleteQuery, [rating.movie, rating.user]);
  const insertQuery =
    'INSERT INTO Ratings (movie, user, rating) VALUES (?, ?, ?)';
  return db.run(insertQuery, [rating.movie, rating.user, rating.rating]);
}
```

Listing 9.20 Extending the Model with the Rating Function (movie/model.js)

To aggregate the information, you use two LEFT JOIN statements to get the information you need. With this query, you extend the objects of the resulting movie array with the number of the respective ratings, with the sum of the ratings, and with the rating that the user himself has submitted.

The second adjustment concerns implementing the rate function. In this context, you must first make sure that the user can't submit duplicate ratings for a movie by deleting all records with the combination of user ID and movie. Then you must create a new data record and resolve the promise. With these adjustments, you can now submit ratings for movies as a logged-in user in your application. The list view is shown in Figure 9.2.

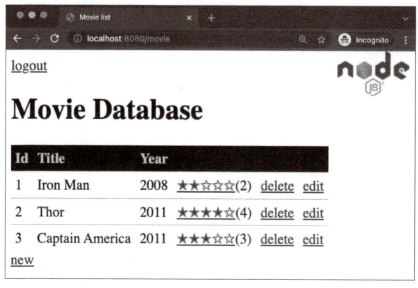

Figure 9.2 List View with Ratings

9.5   Summary

In this chapter, you learned how to implement an authentication process in your application using a combination of Express and the Passport middleware. Passport is a flexible platform for a variety of different authentication mechanisms, of which the `local` strategy is one of the simplest. Other strategies support login via Facebook, Twitter, or other third-party services.

With authentication working and session middleware included, you can keep credentials on the server even across a page reload, allowing your application to be personalized.

User information allows you to assign records to specific users, restrict access to specific resources, and implement features such as a rating system.

Chapter 10
REST Server

It is the mind that builds the body.
—*Friedrich Schiller*

In the previous chapters, you've extended your web application step by step from a simple web server to using template engines and the integration of various databases. However, it often happens during development that such a setup isn't suitable. Especially in the case of single-page applications, you don't need a template engine because the result of an HTTP request is returned to the client as a JavaScript Object Notation (JSON) structure. Output in HTML documents is also not very helpful for the communication between server systems. Instead, other requirements are placed on the web server here, such as the ability to handle different HTTP request headers, or to support authentication via JSON web tokens (JWTs).

In this chapter, you'll learn how you can restructure your existing application so that you can both consume it with a frontend single-page application based on Angular, React, or Vue, for example, and retrieve data from that application through another web server.

The chapter is based on the movie database you developed in the previous chapters; SQLite is used as the database for data management. In the following sections, you'll restructure the application to respond with JSON data instead of rendered HTML views.

10.1 Introduction to REST and Usage in Web Applications

Representational State Transfer (REST) was developed in the context of Roy Fielding's doctoral thesis. The corresponding excerpt from the thesis can be found at *www.ics.uci.edu/~fielding/pubs/dissertation/rest_arch_style.htm*. REST represents an architectural paradigm frequently used in web applications. One of the most important features of REST is that it relies heavily on the elements of HTTP, using the URL path to map resources and describing how they are accessed through the various HTTP methods. The main features of a REST interface are as follows:

- **Statelessness**
  Each request to the service should contain all the required information, so the server doesn't need to keep any state information.

- **Resources**
  Each resource is accessible via a unique URI. For example, you can retrieve the data record of a movie with ID 1 via the URL *http://localhost:8080/movie/1*.

- **Hypermedia as the Engine of Application State (HATEOAS)**
  This represents the central component of a REST architecture. Various links tell the consumer of the interface what state changes are possible with the requested resource. This is also one of the major differences from other approaches such as Simple Object Access Protocol (SOAP), where there is only a fixed interface and not a dynamic one that depends on the state of the resource as in REST.

In most applications, the first two characteristics, that is, statelessness and resource mapping, are still implemented quite well. However, the third feature, HATEOAS, is often neglected so that most REST interfaces aren't true REST at all, but rather stateless resource mapping. A clean implementation of the HATEOAS principle in the frontend and backend requires some work and conception, but the interfaces are more expressive.

10.2   Accessing the Application

This chapter focuses on the server-side aspects of a REST service, so you should have a way to address the server's interface. You can do this by implementing a client, but this is a costly solution to the problem. A simpler alternative is to use existing tools. In the following sections, we'll introduce you to the Postman graphical user interface (GUI) and the cURL command-line tool. You can use both tools to test the interfaces you write in this chapter.

10.2.1   Postman

Postman is a widely used HTTP client with a GUI for formulating requests to web servers. The tool is available for Windows, Linux, and MacOS, and can be downloaded from *www.getpostman.com/apps*. After installing and launching the application, you'll get a view like the one shown in Figure 10.1.

Here you can create new requests, specify the necessary details, save the request as a kind of template, and send it as many times as you want.

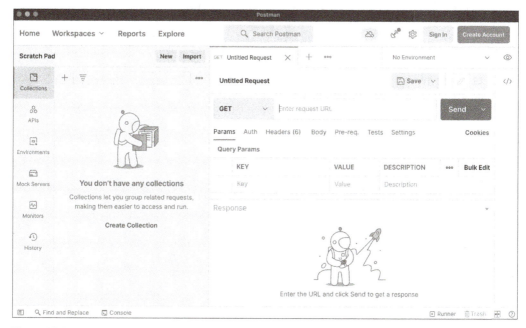

Figure 10.1 Postman GUI

10.2.2   cURL

Unlike Postman, cURL works from the command line. As a result, the tool is much less convenient, but more lightweight than Postman and can be better automated by shell scripts. Listing 10.1 shows a simple example of a request to a server with cURL.

```
$ curl http://localhost:8080/movie
{"movies":[{"id":1,"title":"Iron Man","year":2008,"user":1,"public":1},
{"id":2,"title":"Thor","year":2011,"user":1,"public":1},
{"id":3,"title":"Captain America","year":2011,"user":1,"public":1}],
"links":[{"rel":"self","href":"/movie/"}]}
```

Listing 10.1 Request to a Web Server with cURL

10.3   Adaptations to the Application Structure

Currently, your movie database works with several HTML templates and view structures. You can delete them at this point because a REST interface doesn't use HTML and usually uses other formats instead, such as JSON or XML, to format the resources. Specifically, this means that you can delete the following from the *movie* directory: the *views* directory and the *form.js* and *view.js* files. The *templates* and *public* directories as well as the *auth.js* file in the root directory of the application are also no longer needed at this point. Furthermore, you must customize the initial file of your application as shown in Listing 10.2.

```
import express from 'express';
import morgan from 'morgan';
import { router as movieRouter } from './movie/index.js';

const app = express();

app.use(morgan('common', { immediate: true }));

app.use(express.urlencoded({ extended: false }));

app.use('/movie', movieRouter);

app.get('/', (request, response) => response.redirect('/movie'));

app.listen(8080, () => {
  console.log('Server is listening to http://localhost:8080');
});
```

Listing 10.2 Customized Entry into the Application (index.js)

Because a REST interface is intended to be stateless, you must remove the previous Passport-based authentication that kept user data in a session across multiple requests. Later in this chapter, you'll learn about JSON web tokens as an alternative way to authenticate users. In addition, in the initial file, you must remove the view engine configuration and the use of static middleware. Finally, you delete the call of the auth function and the inclusion of the ensureLoggedIn function. What remains after the restructuring is the integration of the Morgan logger and the body parser as well as the integration of the movie router and the redirection from / to /movie.

10.4   Read Requests

The movie database currently has one type of resource: the movie. You can access this resource via the URL *http://localhost:8080/movie*. A request to this address should return all the movies that exist in the database. If you're only interested in a single data record, you must use the URL *http://localhost:8080/movie/1*. According to the specification, you must use the GET method for read access.

10.4.1   Reading All Data Records of a Resource

If you access *http://localhost:8080/movie* to display all records for a list view, for example, this is mapped via the router in the *movie/index.js* file. To make the new interface work, you reduce the size of this file significantly by removing all routes except the common list route. Listing 10.3 shows the new version of the *movie/index.js* file.

```
import { Router } from 'express';
import { listAction } from './controller.js';

const router = Router();

router.get('/', listAction);

export { router };
```

Listing 10.3 Customizing the Movie Router (movie/index.js)

Some changes to the controller are also required, as it's currently still trying to render the template; in addition, you don't have a user ID at the moment. You can solve this problem by fixing the user ID in the controller to the value 1 until the final authentication implementation is done. This saves you unnecessary modification work on the model later on. Listing 10.4 shows the customization of the controller.

```
import { getAll } from './model.js';

export async function listAction(request, response) {
  const movies = await getAll(1);
  const moviesResponse = {
    movies,
    links: [{ rel: 'self', href: request.baseUrl + '/' }],
  };
  response.json(moviesResponse);
}
```

Listing 10.4 "listAction" in the Controller (movie/controller.js)

The integration of the model remains almost unchanged. In the callback function, you create an object that contains the data records and an additional links property that points to further operations or currently only to itself. You send this object back to the client using the json method instead of the render or send method of the response object. This method is responsible for setting the correct header information and encoding the body for you. Finally, you can simplify the model a little because the ratings are no longer part of the movie resource. Listing 10.5 shows the adjustments to the model.

```
import sqlite from 'sqlite3';

const db = new sqlite.Database('./movie.db');

export async function getAll(userId) {
  return new Promise((resolve, reject) => {
```

```
const query = `SELECT * FROM Movies WHERE user = ? OR public = 1`;

db.all(query, [userId], (error, results) => {
  if (error) {
    reject(error);
  } else {
    resolve(results);
  }
});
});
}
...
```

Listing 10.5 Customized Movie Model (movie/model.js)

With these adjustments, you can now access your server and read the list of records. If you use Postman, it's useful to create a collection, that is, a collection of query templates in Postman, for the movie database. After that, you can generate the request. Figure 10.2 shows the display in Postman after you've sent the request. In the upper section, you can see the type of the request, which, in this case, is the GET value, and the destination: *http://localhost:8080/movie*. In the lower section of the window, you can see the result of the request.

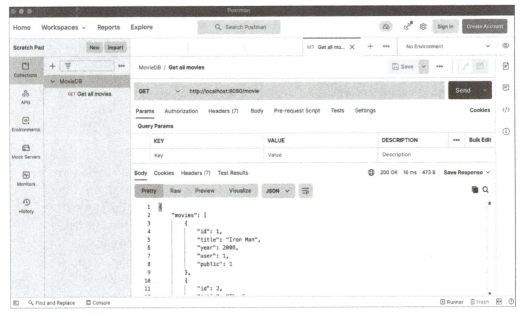

Figure 10.2 Querying Movie Records with Postman

You can also make the same request using cURL on the command line. Listing 10.6 shows the required command and the output.

```
$ curl http://localhost:8080/movie
{
  "movies": [
    { "id": 1, "title": "Iron Man", "year": 2008, "user": 1, "public": 1 },
    { "id": 2, "title": "Thor", "year": 2011, "user": 1, "public": 1 },
    { "id": 3, "title": "Captain America", "year": 2011, "user": 1, "public": 1}
  ],
  "links": [{ "rel": "self", "href": "/movie/" }]
}
```

Listing 10.6 Read Request via cURL (Formatted Output)

10.4.2   Accessing a Data Record

With a REST interface, it's usually also possible to address individual data records. In this case, you append the ID of the relevant data record to the URL pointing to the resource. Currently, such a route doesn't exist in your application, which is why the router in the *movie/index.js* file is the starting point for this customization (see Listing 10.7).

```
import { Router } from 'express';
import { listAction, detailAction } from './controller.js';

const router = Router();

router.get('/', listAction);
router.get('/:id', detailAction);

export { router };
```

Listing 10.7 Integrating a Route for Accessing a Single Data Record (movie/index.js)

As you can see in Listing 10.7, at this point, you add an additional route with a variable that receives the ID of the data record you want. The callback function behind the route originates from the controller and is called detailAction. The implementation is similar to the list view. Listing 10.8 shows the corresponding source code.

```
import { getAll, get } from './model.js';

export async function listAction(request, response) {...}

export async function detailAction(request, response) {
  const movie = await get(request.params.id, 1);
  const moviesResponse = {
    ...movie,
    links: [{ rel: 'self', href: `${request.baseUrl}/${movie.id}` }],
```

10

```
};
response.json(moviesResponse);
}
```

Listing 10.8 Implementing "detailAction" in the Controller (movie/controller.js)

With this customization, you can now also query individual data records directly. But you can also display them via cURL from the command line or with Postman via a GUI. Listing 10.9 contains the required cURL request.

```
$ curl http://localhost:8080/movie/1
{"id":1,"title":"Iron Man","year":2008,"user":1,"public":1,"links": [
{"rel":"self","href":"/movie/1"}]}
```

Listing 10.9 Reading a Data Record with cURL

Figure 10.3 shows the MovieDB collection extension in Postman that allows you to query a single data record.

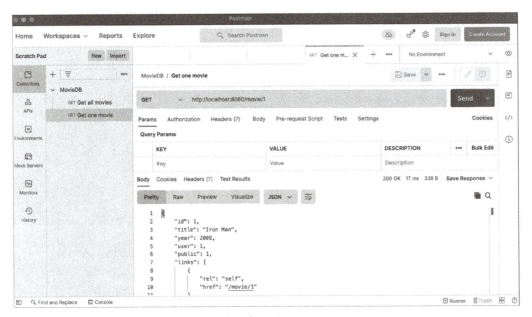

Figure 10.3 Querying a Data Record with Postman

In the next step, you must now make sure that errors are handled correctly.

10.4.3   Error Handling

REST was originally developed for the purpose of machine-to-machine communication. The communication between client and server can also be considered as a variant of this type of communication in the broadest sense because in a single-page application, the raw data is further processed within the application before it's finally displayed to the user. For this reason, it's also very important to handle error cases correctly.

Currently, the controller doesn't handle error cases at all. This means that users aren't really informed about problems occurring within the application. In our case, we can address two different errors. First, a general error can occur at various points in the application, for example, within the database driver during a query. Second, there are also specific errors, for example, that the data record searched for but can't be found in a single query. We can solve both problems with the adjustments to the controller from Listing 10.10.

```javascript
import { getAll, get } from './model.js';

export async function listAction(request, response) {
  try {
    const movies = await getAll(1);
    const moviesResponse = {
      movies,
      links: [{ rel: 'self', href: request.baseUrl + '/' }],
    };
    response.json(moviesResponse);
  } catch (e) {
    console.error(e);
    response.status(500).send('An error happened');
  }
}

export async function detailAction(request, response) {
  try {
    const movie = await get(request.params.id, 1);
    if (!movie) {
      response.status(404).send('Not Found');
      return;
    }

    const moviesResponse = {
      ...movie,
      links: [{ rel: 'self', href: `${request.baseUrl}/${movie.id}` }],
    };
    response.json(moviesResponse);
  } catch (e) {
    console.error(e);
    response.status(500).send('An error happened');
  }
}
```

Listing 10.10 Error Handling in the Controller (movie/controller.js)

If an exception is triggered while one or more data records are being read, the try-catch statement intercepts it, writes the error to the console, and sends a response to the client. The status method of the response object ensures that the correct status code, in this case, 500, is set to indicate an internal server error. As a response body, you can send the string An error happened to avoid giving a potential attacker many details about your system unnecessarily. The same applies if the required data record can't be found. When querying a data record, you must check if the database return contains a value; if it doesn't, you can send a response with the status code 404 and the text Not Found. Due to the respective status code, the remote system, for example, a web frontend, can respond to it and inform the user about the problem. In the next step, you provide the remote system with the option to modify the return via parameters.

10.4.4   Sorting the List

The tasks that are most common when implementing a REST interface include sorting, paging, and filtering the resource list. As an example, you'll implement the option to retrieve the list also in a sorted format. For this purpose, you adjust both the controller and the model. The router can remain as it is because the information about the sorting is transmitted via query parameters of the URL. In general, you should exercise caution when using query parameters, as their structure is completely up to the client. In this context, the links of the resource specified by REST are pretty useful. Listing 10.11 contains the customized source code of the controller.

```
import { getAll, get } from './model.js';

function getLinks(current, base) {
  const links = [
    { rel: 'base', href: base + '/' },
    { rel: 'sort-ascending', href: base + '/?sort=asc' },
    { rel: 'sort-descending', href: base + '/?sort=desc' },
  ];
  return links.map((link) => {
    if (current.length > 0 && link.rel.includes(current)) {
      link.rel = 'self';
    } else if (current.length === 0 && link.rel === 'base') {
      link.rel = 'self';
    }
    return link;
  });
}

export async function listAction(request, response) {
  try {
    const options = {
```

```
    userId: 1,
    sort: request.query.sort ? request.query.sort : '',
  };

  const movies = await getAll(options);
  const moviesResponse = {
    movies,
    links: getLinks(options.sort, request.baseUrl),
  };
  response.json(moviesResponse);
  } catch (e) {
    console.error(e);
    response.status(500).send('An error happened');
  }
}

export async function detailAction(request, response) {...}
```

Listing 10.11 Extending the Controller with a List Sorting Feature (movie/controller.js)

Depending on how you retrieve the movie resource, you need to adjust the links. You swap out the process of generating the corresponding information to the getLinks function. This function receives the currently selected sort option and the baseUrl of the request. Based on this information, the three currently available links are generated, and the active status is marked with rel='self'. Then you pass the sort option to the model as well. For the purpose of better and simpler structuring, in this case, you should choose an option object as a container for configuring the query. This makes the model more flexible and also easier to adapt for future extensions. Listing 10.12 shows the changes to the code of the model.

```
import sqlite from 'sqlite3';

const db = new sqlite.Database('./movie.db');

export async function getAll(options) {
  return new Promise((resolve, reject) => {
    let query = `SELECT * FROM Movies WHERE user = ? OR public = 1`;

    if (options.sort &&
        ['asc', 'desc'].includes(options.sort.toLowerCase())) {
      query += ' ORDER BY title ' + options.sort;
    }

    db.all(query, [options.userId], (error, results) => {
      if (error) {
```

```
            reject(error);
        } else {
            resolve(results);
        }
      });
    });
}
```

. . .

Listing 10.12 Extending the Model with a Sorting Feature (movie/model.js)

Inside the getAll function, you must check if a sort option was passed and if it has a valid value. If this is the case, the query is extended accordingly. Invalid values are ignored in this implementation. With the implementation of this feature, you're now able to sort the movie list in ascending and descending order based on the title. For this purpose, you request the movie resource via the links *http://localhost:8080/movie?sort=asc* and *http://localhost:8080/movie?sort=desc*, respectively. Listing 10.13 shows an example of such a request with cURL, while Figure 10.4 contains a corresponding request in Postman.

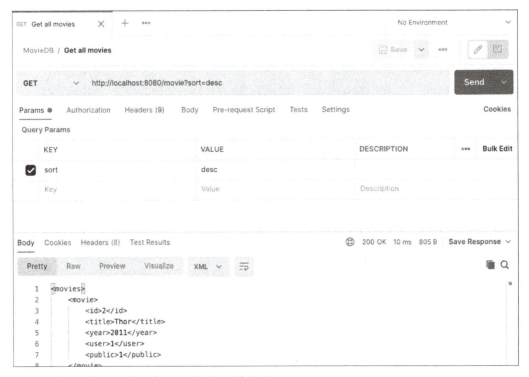

Figure 10.4 Sorting the Movie List with Postman

```
$ curl http://localhost:8080/movie?sort=desc
{"movies":[
{"id":2,"title":"Thor","year":2011,"user":1,"public":1},{"id":1,"title":
"Iron Man","year":2008,"user":1,"public":1},{"id":3,"title":"Captain America",
"year":2011,"user":1,"public":1}],"links":[{"rel":"base","href":"/movie/
"},{"rel":"sort-ascending","href":"/movie/?sort=asc"},{"rel":"self",
"href":"/movie/?sort=desc"}]}
```

Listing 10.13 cURL Request for a Sorted List

10.4.5   Controlling the Output Format

JSON has become the standard format for exchanging information via web services in large parts of web development. Despite this fact, in some cases, it's necessary to provide your users with the option to control the output format of the service. As a rule, accept header is used in this respect. It's best to integrate such a switch for the output format directly in the controller. Listing 10.14 contains the source code for the switch. In the concrete case, the user can use accept header to control whether the output should be JSON—the default case—or XML.

```
import { getAll, get } from './model.js';
import jsonXml from 'jsontoxml';

function getLinks(current, base) {...}

export async function listAction(request, response) {
  try {
    const options = {
      userId: 1,
      sort: request.query.sort ? request.query.sort : '',
    };

    const movies = await getAll(options);
    const moviesResponse = {
      movies,
      links: getLinks(options.sort, request.baseUrl),
    };

    response.format({
      xml() {
        moviesResponse.movies = moviesResponse.movies.map((movie) => ({
          movie,
        }));
        response.send(jsonXml(moviesResponse));
      },
```

```
    json() {
      response.json(moviesResponse);
    },
    default() {
      response.json(moviesResponse);
    },
  });
} catch (e) {
  console.error(e);
  response.status(500).send('An error happened');
}
}
```

```
export async function detailAction(request, response) {...}
```

Listing 10.14 Controlling the Output Format in the Controller (movie/controller.js)

To simplify the XML output, you should install the jsontoxml package via the npm install jsontoxml command. This package exports a function to which you can pass a JSON structure, and it will be converted to an XML document. To ensure that the structure displays correctly, you should insert an additional object layer, as shown in the example. To make a distinction based on the incoming accept header, you can use the format method of the response object. To this method, you pass an object with various functions. The key of the object denotes the format, for example, xml or json, and the function is responsible for the correct format of the response. For example, if you request the resource with cURL using the command curl -H "Accept: application/xml" http://localhost:8080/movie, you'll receive the corresponding XML structure as a response. Listing 10.15 contains the server's abbreviated response to this request.

```
$ curl -H "Accept: application/xml" http://localhost:8080/movie
<movies>
  <movie>
    <id>1</id>
    <title>Iron Man</title>
    <year>2008</year>
    <user>1</user>
    <public>1</public>
  </movie>
```

Listing 10.15 cURL Request with XML Response

Now that you've learned about some of the specifics of read requests, the following sections deal with write accesses to the REST interface.

10.5 Write Requests

Whereas the request scheme for read accesses could still be adopted with almost no changes at all, and the few adjustments were primarily implemented in the controller and in the model, for write accesses, we must also change the routes. At this point, the default implementation of REST provides for using the various methods provided by HTTP for the respective purpose. For example, the POST method is used for requests that create data records, while the PUT method is used for requests that update data records. It's also important at this point to model the server's return correctly and to use the appropriate status codes.

10.5.1 POST: Creating New Data Records

When creating new data records, you use the POST method with the common URI. So, to create a new movie, you post to *http://localhost:8080/movie*. The content-type header of the request has the value application/json, and the body of the request contains the data record to be created. This is already the first difference from the previous implementation, in which the data was sent to the server using an HTML form. For your application to handle the JSON body of the request, you must use the json method instead of the urlencoded method of the body parser integrated in Express. Listing 10.16 contains the custom source code of the entry file.

```
import express from 'express';
import morgan from 'morgan';
import { router as movieRouter } from './movie/index.js';

const app = express();

app.use(morgan('common', { immediate: true }));

app.use(express.json());

app.use('/movie', movieRouter);

app.get('/', (request, response) => response.redirect('/movie'));

app.listen(8080, () => {
  console.log('Server is listening to http://localhost:8080');
});
```

Listing 10.16 Adjustments to the Body Parser (index.js)

In the next step, you'll create a new route for creating data records. You define this route in the *movie/index.js* file, as shown in Listing 10.17.

```
import { Router } from 'express';
import { listAction, detailAction, createAction } from './controller.js';

const router = Router();

router.get('/', listAction);
router.get('/:id', detailAction);
router.post('/', createAction);

export { router };
```

Listing 10.17 Extending the Route Definitions for Creating New Data Records (movie/index.js)

When implementing createAction in the controller, you first read the information from the incoming request, call the model's save method, and return the complete newly created data record as a JSON object. To keep the source code a bit more compact, we don't support different formats at this point. You set the status of the response to 201 if successful, which indicates to the client that a data record has been created. If an error occurs, you send a response with the status code 500 to the client along with the error message. Listing 10.18 shows the source code of createAction.

```
import { getAll, get, save } from './model.js';
import jsonXml from 'jsontoxml';

function getLinks(current, base) {...}

export async function listAction(request, response) {...}

export async function detailAction(request, response) {...}

export async function createAction(request, response) {
  try {
    const movie = {
      title: request.body.title,
      year: request.body.year,
      public: parseInt(request.body.public, 10) === 1 ? 1 : 0,
    };
    const newMovie = await save(movie, 1);
    response.status(201).json(newMovie);
  } catch (e) {
    console.error(e);
    response.status(500).json('An error happened');
```

```
    }
}
```

Listing 10.18 "createAction" of the Controller (movie/controller.js)

Now you can also create data records in your application. No changes are required to the model because it already returns the newly generated data record as required by the controller. Listing 10.19 shows such a create request via cURL.

```
$ curl  -X POST -H "Content-Type: application/json" -d '{"title": "Antman",
"year": 2015, "public": 1, "user": 1}' http://localhost:8080/movie
{"title":"Antman","year":2015,"public":1,"id":4,"user": 1}
```

Listing 10.19 Creating a New Data Record with cURL

Write requests, in particular, can be formulated much more comfortably with a graphical tool such as Postman than via the command line. As you can see in Figure 10.5, you choose the appropriate HTTP method, in this case, **POST**; specify the URL *http://localhost:8080/movie*; and compose the request body as a simple JSON object in the **Body** tab as raw type in **JSON** format.

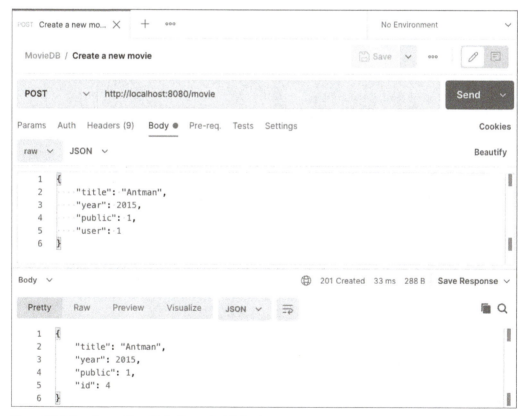

Figure 10.5 Creating a New Data Record with Postman

The integrated editor supports you, for example, with syntax highlighting and double-quote completion.

10.5.2   PUT: Modifying Existing Data Records

For updating data records, you proceed in a way similar to that of creating new data records. For example, if you want to modify the record with ID 4 in your movie database, you send a request to *http://localhost:8080/movie/4* using the HTTP PUT method. You insert the complete customized record in JSON format into the body of the request and provide it with the content-type: application/json header. To customize the application, you must start from the router again. Here, you add an appropriate entry like the one shown in Listing 10.20 to the *movie/index.js* file.

```
import { Router } from 'express';
import {
  listAction,
  detailAction,
  createAction,
  updateAction,
} from './controller.js';

const router = Router();

router.get('/', listAction);
router.get('/:id', detailAction);
router.post('/', createAction);
router.put('/:id', updateAction);

export { router };
```

Listing 10.20 Adding the Update Route (movie/index.js)

Like the detail route, the update route contains a variable named id, which you can access within your controller. After customizing the router, the next step is to implement updateAction in the controller (see Listing 10.21); its structure is similar to that of createAction.

```
import { getAll, get, save } from './model.js';
import jsonXml from 'jsontoxml';

function getLinks(current, base) {...}

export async function listAction(request, response) {...}
```

```
export async function detailAction(request, response) {...}

export async function createAction(request, response) {...}

export async function updateAction(request, response) {
  try {
    const movie = {
      id: request.params.id,
      title: request.body.title,
      year: request.body.year,
      public: parseInt(request.body.public, 10) === 1 ? 1 : 0,
    };

    const updatedMovie = await model.save(movie, 1);
    response.json(movie);
  } catch (e) {
    response.status(500).json(error);
  }
}
```

Listing 10.21 Implementing "updateAction" in the Controller (movie/controller.js)

At this point, you just need to extract the ID of the data record you want to change from request.params. Again, no further adjustment to the model is required, and you can test the new feature of your interface after restarting the server process.

If you run the command shown in Listing 10.22 after making these changes, you update the record with ID 4 and receive the modified record back from the server as a response.

```
$ curl
  -X PUT
  -H "application/json"
  -d '{"title": "Black Panther",
"year": 2018, "public": 1, "user": 1}'
  http://localhost:8080/movie/4
{"id":"4","title":"Black Panther","year":2018,"public":1,"user":1}
```

Listing 10.22 Modifying a Data Record with cURL

Figure 10.6 shows how you can manipulate the record with ID 4 using the Postman GUI. In contrast to the process of creating a data record, you must change the HTTP method from **POST** to **PUT**, pass ID 4 as part of the URL path, and customize the request body as required.

The last feature still missing for the basic functionality of your REST interface is the option to delete data records.

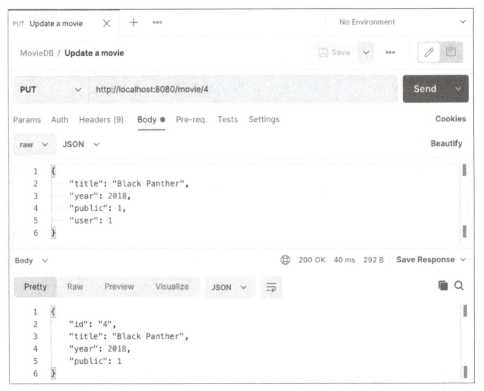

Figure 10.6 Updating a Data Record with Postman

10.5.3   DELETE: Deleting Data Records

Similar to creating and updating records, you use a special HTTP method when deleting data records: the DELETE method, which requires the creation of a new route, as shown in Listing 10.23.

```
import { Router } from 'express';
import {
  listAction,
  detailAction,
  createAction,
  updateAction,
  deleteAction,
} from './controller.js';

const router = Router();

router.get('/', listAction);
router.get('/:id', detailAction);
router.post('/', createAction);
```

```
router.put('/:id', updateAction);
router.delete('/:id', deleteAction);

export { router };
```

Listing 10.23 Route for Deleting Data Records (movie/index.js)

You implement the `deleteAction` function of the controller, like the other action functions, as an `async` function. It obtains a reference to request and response, extracts the ID of the data record to be deleted from `request.params` in the first step, and then converts it to an integer. After that, you call the `remove` function of the model using the `await` keyword and the arguments `id` and `userId 1`. If the application returns an exception in this process, you log it to the console and return a response with status code 500 and body `An error happened`. If successful, the status code is 204, which corresponds to an empty successful response. Listing 10.24 shows the source code of the `deleteAction` function.

```
import { getAll, get, save, remove } from './model.js';
import jsonXml from 'jsontoxml';

function getLinks(current, base) {...}

export async function listAction(request, response) {...}

export async function detailAction(request, response) {...}

export async function createAction(request, response) {...}

export async function updateAction(request, response) {...}

export async function deleteAction(request, response) {
  try {
    const id = parseInt(request.params.id, 10);
    await remove(id, 1);
    response.status(204).send();
  } catch (e) {
    console.error(e);
    response.status(500).send('An error happened');
  }
}
```

Listing 10.24 "deleteAction" in the Controller (movie/controller.js)

The delete operation doesn't require any changes to the model, so you can use the source code as it is. The HTTP DELETE request to *http://localhost:8080/movie/4* now enables you to delete the data record with ID 4 from the database, for example. With cURL, a corresponding request looks like the one shown in Listing 10.25.

```
$ curl -X DELETE http://localhost:8080/movie/4
```

Listing 10.25 Deleting a Data Record with cURL

As a result of this request, you won't see any direct output because the deleteAction response was sent with status code 204 and no response body. In this case, no output is a good response. A similar result occurs when you send the DELETE request with Postman, as you can see in Figure 10.7.

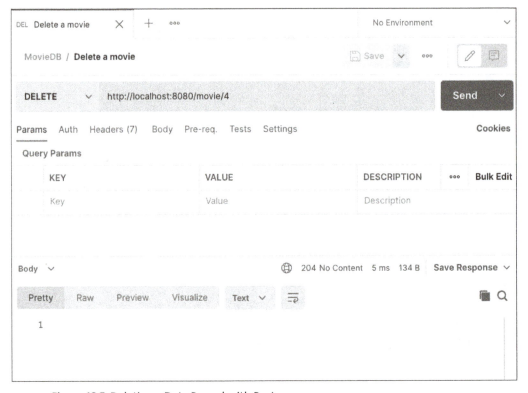

Figure 10.7 Deleting a Data Record with Postman

10.6   Authentication via JWTs

Until now, anyone who has access to your REST interface can also query it and read the data. However, this is by no means acceptable for an application that works with sensitive data. The solution to this problem, as in the previous chapter, is authentication. However, classic authentication via a login form is out of the question for a web service because the user doesn't usually work directly with the service. Furthermore, storing credentials in a server-side session violates the stateless nature of REST. As a result, a token-based login process has become the accepted authentication mechanism for REST interfaces. In this context, *JSON web tokens* (JWTs) are often used.

JWTs are standardized in request for comment (RFC) 7519 and can thus be used for authentication processes within a system as well as between multiple systems. A JWT is an encoded character string consisting of three parts: the header, the payload, and a signature. The header contains information about the token itself, such as the type or the algorithm used to encode it. The payload contains payload data that can be used by the server, such as information about the user. Finally, the signature is used to verify the integrity of the token.

For Node.js, there are a few libraries available for you to use. In this section, you'll use the `jsonwebtoken` package to generate tokens for your users and the `express-jwt` package to verify the tokens. Both packages are installed via the following command: `npm install jsonwebtoken express-jwt`.

10.6.1 Login

For users of your REST interface to authenticate, you must first create an interface through which a new token can be generated. For this reason, you need a new route through which users send their credentials to the server; in response, you get the JWT. You swap out the generation of the route to a separate file named *auth.js*. Listing 10.26 contains the implementation of this route.

```
import jwt from 'jsonwebtoken';
import { Router } from 'express';
import { get } from './user/model.js';
import { createHash } from 'crypto';

const router = Router();

router.post('/', async (request, response) => {
  try {
    const user = await get({
      username: request.body.username,
      password: createHash('md5').update(request.body.password).digest('hex')
    });
    if (user) {
      const payload = { ...user };
      delete payload.password;
      const token = jwt.sign(payload, 'secret');
      response.json({ token });
    } else {
      response.status(401).json('unauthorized');
    }
```

```
  } catch (e) {
    console.error(e);
    response.status(401).json('unauthorized');
  }
});
```

```
export { router };
```

Listing 10.26 Route for Creating a New JWT (auth.js)

The implementation in Listing 10.26 assumes that the user submits their data via a POST request in the username and password fields. The existing user model is used to verify the data and to read the remaining user data. The get method of the model is used to read the data record using the user name and password. You must make sure that the password is stored as a hash in the database. This means you have to search for the matching hash value and not for the password in plain text. If an error occurs in the process, a message with status code 401, unauthorized, is returned to the user. The same result occurs if the login process fails.

Upon a successful login, the password is deleted from the user object and encoded into the token using the sign method of the jwt object, and then the token is sent to the client. The router created in this file is then included in the initial file of your application, as shown in Listing 10.27.

```
import express from 'express';
import morgan from 'morgan';
import { router as movieRouter } from './movie/index.js';
import { router as loginRouter } from './auth.js';

const app = express();

app.use(morgan('common', { immediate: true }));

app.use(express.json());

app.use('/login', loginRouter);
app.use('/movie', movieRouter);

app.get('/', (request, response) => response.redirect('/movie'));

app.listen(8080, () => {
  console.log('Server is listening to http://localhost:8080');
});
```

Listing 10.27 Integrating the Login Route (index.js)

When you send your user name and password in a POST request to *http://localhost:8080/login* after restarting your application, you'll receive a JSON response with the token in return. You'll use this response in the following steps to access the resources of your application. Listing 10.28 contains a concrete example of such an application.

```
$ curl  -X POST -H "Content-Type: application/json" -
d '{"username": "sspringer", "password": "test"}' http://localhost:8080/login
{"token":"eyJhbGciOiJIUzI1NiIsInR5cCI6IkpXVCJ9.eyJpZCI6MSwiZmlyc3RuYW1lIjoiU2ViY
XN0aWFuIiwibGFzdG5hbWUiOiJTcHJpbmdlciIsInVzZXJuYW1lIjoic3NwcmluZ2VyIiwiaWF0IjoxN
jI4NzAzMzYyfQ.mycuTV9EtYhu7lbN_tKQgKCC2vDPBuy6JT_kMvN9JDk"}
```

Listing 10.28 Logging in to the Application

The token request not only works on the console but also via a GUI, as shown in Figure 10.8.

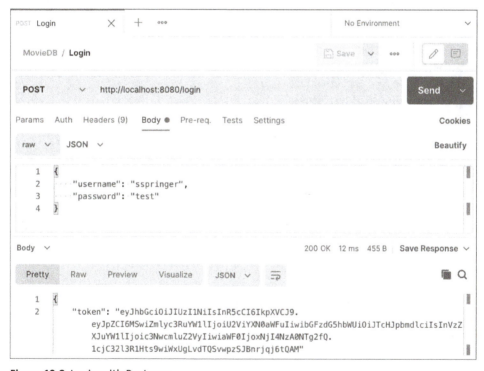

Figure 10.8 Login with Postman

10.6.2   Safeguarding Resources

The express-jwt package now allows you to safeguard the entire movie resource. For this purpose, you include the express-jwt package in the initial file and use the middleware provided by the package, as shown in Listing 10.29.

```javascript
import express from 'express';
import morgan from 'morgan';
import expressJwt from 'express-jwt';
import { router as movieRouter } from './movie/index.js';
import { router as loginRouter } from './auth.js';

const app = express();

app.use(morgan('common', { immediate: true }));

app.use(express.json());

app.use('/login', loginRouter);
app.use(
  '/movie',
  expressJwt({ secret: 'secret', algorithms: ['HS256'] }),
  movieRouter,
);

app.use((err, request, response, next) => {
  if (err.name === 'UnauthorizedError') {
    response.status(401).json('unauthorized');
  } else {
    next();
  }
});

app.get('/', (request, response) => response.redirect('/movie'));

app.listen(8080, () => {
  console.log('Server is listening to http://localhost:8080');
});
```

Listing 10.29 Using the "express-jwt" Middleware (index.js)

When you call the express-jwt middleware, you pass the same secret that you used to generate the token and the algorithms property with an array containing the value HS256. This value represents Hash-Based Message Authentication Code (HMAC) with SHA-256 and instructs express-jwt to use this algorithm for verifying the token. The middleware checks the token passed by the user and decrypts it with this information. If the middleware detects an invalid token, an exception is triggered. You can use the following middleware function to convert this exception into a message with status code 401, unauthorized.

The token is transmitted during the request process via the `authorization` header. In Postman, you can configure this conveniently via a form. If you use cURL to test your interface, you must specify the header with the -H option. Listing 10.30 shows an example of such a request.

```
$ curl -
H "Authorization: Bearer eyJhbGciOiJIUzI1NiIsInR5cCI6IkpXVCJ9.eyJpZCI6 MSwiZmlyc
3RuYW1lIjoiU2ViYXN0aWFuIiwibGFzdG5hbWUiOiJTcHJpbmdlciIsInVzZXJuYW1lIjoic3NwcmluZ
2VyIiwiaWF0IjoxNjI4NzAzMzYyfQ.mycuTV9EtYhu7lbN_tKQgKCC2vDPBuy6JT_kMvN9JDk" -
H "Accept: application/json" http://localhost:8080/movie
```

Listing 10.30 cURL Request with Authorization Header

In Postman, you can use the **Headers** tab to set the authorization header for the queries. To do this, you must add the **Authorization** field as a header and set the value to **Bearer**, followed by the token you previously had issued to you via the login endpoint. Figure 10.9 shows the status in Postman.

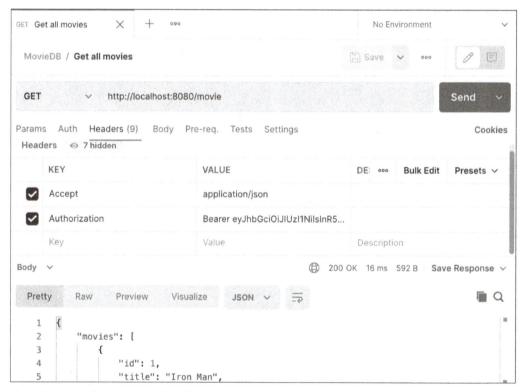

Figure 10.9 Read Request with Authorization Header in Postman

10.6.3   Accessing User Information in the Token

However, the middleware of the `express-jwt` package not only checks the correctness of the token but also extends the `request` object with the user information so that you can access the information via `request.user`. Listing 10.31 shows how you can read the user ID from the `request` object to use it in the database queries.

```javascript
import { getAll, get, save, remove } from './model.js';
import jsonXml from 'jsontoxml';

function getLinks(current, base) {
  const links = [
    { rel: 'base', href: base + '/' },
    { rel: 'sort-ascending', href: base + '/?sort=asc' },
    { rel: 'sort-descending', href: base + '/?sort=desc' },
  ];
  return links.map((link) => {
    if (current.length > 0 && link.rel.includes(current)) {
      link.rel = 'self';
    } else if (current.length === 0 && link.rel === 'base') {
      link.rel = 'self';
    }
    return link;
  });
}

export async function listAction(request, response) {
  try {
    const options = {
      userId: request.user.id,
      sort: request.query.sort ? request.query.sort : '',
    };

    const movies = await getAll(options);
    const moviesResponse = {
      movies,
      links: getLinks(options.sort, request.baseUrl),
    };

    response.format({
      xml() {
        moviesResponse.movies = moviesResponse.movies.map((movie) => ({
          movie,
        }));
        response.send(jsonXml(moviesResponse));
      },
      json() {
        response.json(moviesResponse);
```

```
    },
    default() {
      response.json(moviesResponse);
    },
  });
} catch (e) {
  console.error(e);
  response.status(500).send('An error happened');
}
}

export async function detailAction(request, response) {
  try {
    const movie = await get(request.params.id, request.user.id);
    if (!movie) {
      response.status(404).send('Not Found');
      return;
    }

    const moviesResponse = {
      ...movie,
      links: [{ rel: 'self', href: `${request.baseUrl}/${movie.id}` }],
    };
    response.json(moviesResponse);
  } catch (e) {
    console.error(e);
    response.status(500).send('An error happened');
  }
}

export async function createAction(request, response) {
  try {
    const movie = {
      title: request.body.title,
      year: request.body.year,
      public: parseInt(request.body.public, 10) === 1 ? 1 : 0,
    };
    const newMovie = await save(movie, request.user.id);
    response.status(201).json(newMovie);
  } catch (e) {
    console.error(e);
    response.status(500).json('An error happened');
  }
}
```

10

323

```
export async function updateAction(request, response) {
  try {
    const movie = {
      id: request.params.id,
      title: request.body.title,
      year: request.body.year,
      public: parseInt(request.body.public, 10) === 1 ? 1 : 0,
    };

    const updatedMovie = await save(movie, request.user.id);
    response.json(movie);
  } catch (e) {
    console.error(e);
    response.status(500).json('An error happened');
  }
}

export async function deleteAction(request, response) {
  try {
    const id = parseInt(request.params.id, 10);
    await remove(id, request.user.id);
    response.status(204).send();
  } catch (e) {
    console.error(e);
    response.status(500).send('An error happened');
  }
}
```

Listing 10.31 Using the User ID from the JWT (movie/controller.js)

With these customizations, you've created a REST interface that supports creating, reading, updating, and deleting data. You've also secured the interfaces with JWT. The next section describes how you can document this interface in such a way that it's convenient for other developers to use it.

10.7   OpenAPI Specification: Documentation with Swagger

Swagger is a widely used tool for designing and documenting interfaces. It's available as an open-source project at *https://swagger.io/*. There are two different approaches to using Swagger in Node.js. First, you can use the swagger package to have a server generated based on an existing application programming interface (API) description. In this section, however, we'll describe the second variant in greater detail, that is, integrating Swagger into an existing application.

The `swagger-jsdoc` package, which you install via the `npm install swagger-jsdoc` command, enables you to have Swagger documentation generated from JSDoc comments of your routes and make it publicly available via the Swagger UI. Alternatively, you can write the documentation in a separate YAML or JSON file.

The API documentation is usually located in a file called *swagger.json*. If you use `swagger-jsdoc`, you can also generate the documentation directly in the code. For this purpose, you must add a JSDoc comment to the routes of your application, prefixed with the character string `@swagger`. Listing 10.32 contains the documentation for the list as well as for retrieving a single data record.

```
import { Router } from 'express';
import {
  listAction,
  detailAction,
  createAction,
  updateAction,
  deleteAction,
} from './controller.js';

const router = Router();

/**
 * @swagger
 * definitions:
 *   movie:
 *     properties:
 *       id:
 *         type: integer
 *         example: 1
 *       title:
 *         type: string
 *         example: Iron Man
 *       year:
 *         type: integer
 *         example: 2008
 *       public:
 *         type: integer
 *         example: 1
 *       user:
 *         type: integer
 *         example: 1
 */
```

10

325

```
/**
 * @swagger
 * /movie:
 *   get:
 *     tags:
 *       - movies
 *     description: Returns all movies
 *     produces:
 *       - application/json
 *       - application/xml
 *     responses:
 *       200:
 *         description: An array of movie datasets
 *         schema:
 *           type: array
 *           items:
 *             $ref: '#/definitions/movie'
 */
router.get('/', listAction);
/**
 * @swagger
 * /movie/{movieId}:
 *   get:
 *     tags:
 *       - movies
 *     description: Returns one movie
 *     produces:
 *       - application/json
 *       - application/xml
 *     responses:
 *       200:
 *         description: One movie object
 *         schema:
 *           $ref: '#/definitions/movie'
 */
router.get('/:id', detailAction);
router.post('/', createAction);
router.put('/:id', updateAction);
router.delete('/:id', deleteAction);

export { router };
```

Listing 10.32 Swagger Documentation as JSDoc Blocks (movie/index.js)

The first comment block in Listing 10.32 creates the schema of a movie record. You then use this scheme with the comments of the two routes to describe them in detail while having as few duplicates in the code as possible. The structure in which you write the comments is YAML.

Based on these comments, you can now have the documentation generated, as shown in Listing 10.33. For this purpose, you create a file named *swagger.js*, which contains the configuration and initialization of swagger-jsdoc.

```
import swaggerJSDoc from 'swagger-jsdoc';

const swaggerDefinition = {
  info: {
    title: 'Movie Database API',
    version: '1.0.0',
    description: 'API of the movie database',
  },
  host: 'localhost:8080',
  basePath: '/',
};

const options = {
  swaggerDefinition,
  apis: ['./movie/index.js'],
};

export default swaggerJSDoc(options);
```

Listing 10.33 Configuration and Initialization of "swagger-jsdoc" (swagger.js)

In addition to the pure API documentation, you can specify general information about the swaggerDefinition property, such as the title, version, or description of the interface. At this point, you also pass the host and basePath to swagger-jsdoc. Using the apis property, you specify an array of files containing the Swagger comments from which to create the documentation.

Based on this information, swagger-jsdoc generates the Swagger specification. You can either provide this specification directly in JSON format via your web server, or use the swagger-ui-express package to include the documentation in your Express application via middleware. To do this, you must install the package via the command npm install swagger-ui-express and include it as shown in Listing 10.34.

```
import express from 'express';
import morgan from 'morgan';
import expressJwt from 'express-jwt';
```

```
import swaggerUi from 'swagger-ui-express';
import { router as movieRouter } from './movie/index.js';
import { router as loginRouter } from './auth.js';
import swaggerSpec from './swagger.js';

const app = express();

app.use(morgan('common', { immediate: true }));

app.use(express.json());

app.use('/login', loginRouter);
app.use(
  '/movie',
  expressJwt({ secret: 'secret', algorithms: ['HS256'] }),
  movieRouter,
);

app.use((err, request, response, next) => {
  if (err.name === 'UnauthorizedError') {
    response.status(401).json('unauthorized');
  } else {
    next();
  }
});

app.get('/', (request, response) => response.redirect('/movie'));

app.use('/api-docs', swaggerUi.serve, swaggerUi.setup(swaggerSpec));

app.listen(8080, () => {
  console.log('Server is listening to http://localhost:8080');
});
```

Listing 10.34 Integrating the Swagger UI in Express (index.js)

After restarting your application, you can access the API documentation of your interface via *http://localhost:8080/api-docs*. The result should look similar to Figure 10.10.

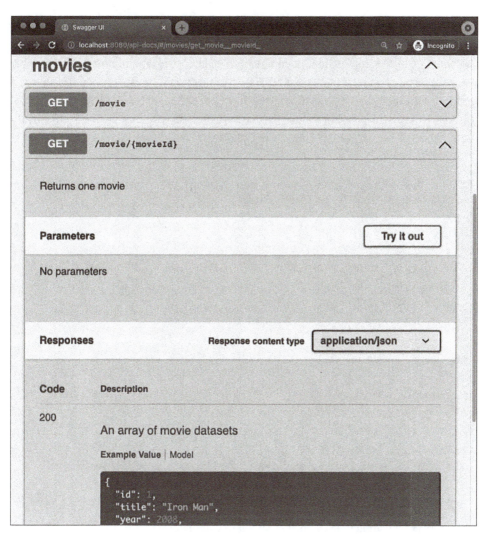

Figure 10.10 Swagger UI

10.8   Validation

In addition to the documentation, there is another important issue regarding our inter-face we've grossly neglected so far: validation. Currently, the application accepts all user input and writes it to the database unchecked, albeit with correct escaping. It's also pos-sible to create a new data record without information. This then contains only an ID and the user ID. To conclude this chapter, we'll present the express-validator package—a fairly convenient solution for validation in Express. The validator allows you to check individual fields via middleware functions as well as a complete request via a validation scheme and to force values into a specific form with the Sanitizer feature.

10.8.1   Installation and First Validation

You can install the `express-validator` package using the `npm install express-validator` command. For the first inclusion, you use `deleteAction` and make sure that only numbers can be passed as IDs to be deleted. For this purpose, the validator uses middleware functions and provides you with another function called `validationResult`, which you can use to access the validation errors. In the first step, you extend the router in the *movie/index.js* file to validate the routing parameter, as you can see in the code in Listing 10.35.

```
import { Router } from 'express';
import validator from 'express-validator';
import {
  listAction,
  detailAction,
  createAction,
  updateAction,
  deleteAction,
} from './controller.js';

const router = Router();

router.get('/', listAction);
router.get('/:id', detailAction);
router.post('/', createAction);
router.put('/:id', updateAction);
router.delete('/:id', validator.params('id').isInt(), deleteAction);

export { router };
```

Listing 10.35 Validating the Routing Parameter (movie/index.js)

In addition to the `param` function, the `express-validator` package offers even more options to check other aspects of the query, such as the `body` function. If you now specify an arbitrary character string instead of a number when deleting a record, the validation fails. You can check this within the controller using the `validationResult` function. Listing 10.36 contains the corresponding source code.

```
import { getAll, get, save, remove } from './model.js';
import jsonXml from 'jsontoxml';
import { validationResult } from 'express-validator';

function getLinks(current, base) {...}
```

```
export async function listAction(request, response) {...}

export async function detailAction(request, response) {...}

export async function createAction(request, response) {...}

export async function updateAction(request, response) {...}

export async function deleteAction(request, response) {
  try {
    const errors = validationResult(request);
    if (!errors.isEmpty()) {
      return response.status(400).json({ errors: errors.array() });
    }

    const id = parseInt(request.params.id, 10);
    await remove(id, request.user.id);
    response.status(204).send();
  } catch (e) {
    console.error(e);
    response.status(500).send('An error happened');
  }
}
```

Listing 10.36 Evaluating Validation Errors in the Controller (movie/controller.js)

If you try to submit a DELETE request on the *http://localhost:8080/movie/IronMan* path with these changes (see Listing 10.37), you'll receive an Invalid value error message.

```
$ curl -X DELETE -H "Authorization: Bearer eyJ...H38" http://localhost:8080/
movie/IronMan
{"errors":[
{"value":"IronMan","msg":"Invalid value","param":"id","location":"params"}]}
```

Listing 10.37 Invalid cURL Request

If you place the same request in Postman, you'll get some more detailed information, such as the status code. Figure 10.11 shows the result of such a request in the Postman GUI.

In particular with regard to more extensive requests, using the middleware functions quickly becomes confusing. For this reason, the validator package provides schema validation, which allows you to define the rules in a single object structure.

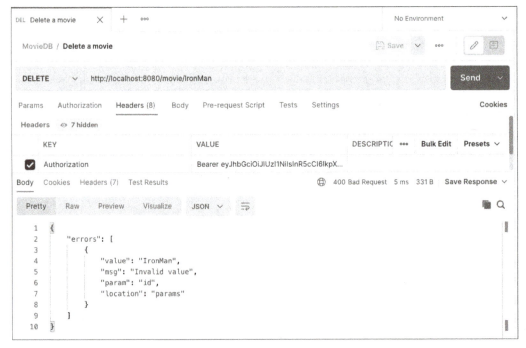

Figure 10.11 Invalid DELETE Request with Postman

10.8.2   Checking Requests with a Validation Schema

The big advantage of the validation schema over the middleware approach is that you can define the validation rules in an object structure within the schema. In addition, the configuration options are much more convenient than if you have to chain several middleware functions. The schema is therefore mainly worthwhile for more elaborate checks or larger objects that need validating. Listing 10.38 shows how you can use the validation schema via the POST route.

```
import { Router } from 'express';
import validator from 'express-validator';
import {
  listAction,
  detailAction,
  createAction,
  updateAction,
  deleteAction,
} from './controller.js';

const router = Router();

router.get('/', listAction);
```

```
router.get('/:id', detailAction);
router.post(
  '/',
  validator.checkSchema({
    title: {
      errorMessage: 'Title is invalid',
      isString: true,
      isLength: {
        errorMessage: 'Title has to be between 1 and 20',
        options: {
          min: 1,
          max: 20,
        },
      },
    },
    year: {
      errorMessage: 'Year is invalid',
      isInt: true,
    },
  }),
  createAction,
);
router.put('/:id', updateAction);
router.delete('/:id', validator.param('id').isInt(), deleteAction);

export { router };
```

Listing 10.38 Validation Schema for Creating New Data Records (movie/index.js)

The schema you define with the checkSchema function covers the two fields, title and year, where title must be a string of between 1 and 20 characters in length. Depending on whether there is a general validation error or a length violation, the respective error message gets selected. Validating the year field is much easier because the condition is merely that it must be a number.

As is the case with middleware, defining and registering the schema alone does nothing for you; you must also pick up the validation result in the controller and respond to it accordingly. To do so, you should use the validationResult function, as you've already done before. In Listing 10.39, you can see what its code looks like.

```
import { getAll, get, save, remove } from './model.js';
import jsonXml from 'jsontoxml';
import validator from 'express-validator';

function getLinks(current, base) {...}
```

```
export async function listAction(request, response) {...}

export async function detailAction(request, response) {...}

export async function createAction(request, response) {
  try {
    const errors = validator.validationResult(request);
    if (!errors.isEmpty()) {
      return response.status(400).json({ errors: errors.array() });
    }

    const movie = {
      title: request.body.title,
      year: request.body.year,
      public: parseInt(request.body.public, 10) === 1 ? 1 : 0,
    };
    const newMovie = await save(movie, request.user.id);
    response.status(201).json(newMovie);
  } catch (e) {
    console.error(e);
    response.status(500).json('An error happened');
  }
}

export async function updateAction(request, response) {...}

export async function deleteAction(request, response) {...}
```

Listing 10.39 Checking the Validation Result in the Controller (movie/controller.js)

With these adjustments, you can now restart your server process and test the creation of data records. Listing 10.40 also shows clearly that in case of an erroneous request, not only the first error is listed but all validation violations that were found.

```
$ curl -X POST -d "{public: 1}" -H "Authorization: Bearer eyJ…H38" http://
localhost:8080/movie/
{"errors":[{"msg":"Title is invalid","param":"title","location":"body"},
{"msg":"Title has to be between 1 and 20","param":"title","location":"body"},{"m
sg":"Year is invalid","param":"year","location":"body"}]}
```

Listing 10.40 Invalid Request to Create a New Data Record

Figure 10.12 shows a similar request in Postman with the difference being that here, the data type of the title field was chosen incorrectly as a Boolean, which triggers a corresponding error message.

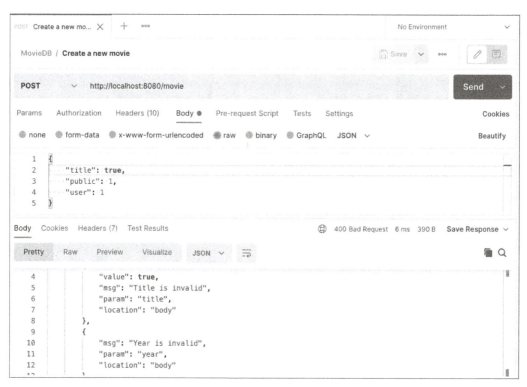

Figure 10.12 Incorrect Request with Postman

10.9   Summary

In this chapter, you learned how to create a server with a REST interface that is suitable for communicating with other machines as well as with modern single-page applications. The output format here is very often JSON, which is natively supported by Express. The changes to create such a REST interface are mostly limited to the controller layer because it determines the format of the output. Unlike classic multipage applications, REST interfaces don't use a template engine because the output isn't in HTML format.

Other requirements are also placed on a REST interface with regard to authentication. Because such an interface should basically be stateless, session-based solutions like the one you learned about in the previous chapter aren't necessary. Instead, you should implement a token-based solution such as JWT. With the appropriate modules, the implementation effort for such a mechanism is manageable.

In addition to the basic implementation of such an interface, there are other important topics, such as documenting the interface or validating the inputs, which you can integrate into your application with the appropriate packages with manageable effort.

Chapter 11
GraphQL

He that breaks a thing to find out what it is has left the path of wisdom.
—*J. R. R. Tolkien*

In addition to the widely used representational state transfer (REST) interfaces, GraphQL is also being used more and more frequently to generate web interfaces. Unlike REST, the query language—originally designed by Facebook—provides for a more dynamic querying of resources. The consumer of an interface defines the expected structure in the query and can thus affect both the form and the amount of data in the response. Furthermore, with GraphQL, it's possible to combine multiple resources in one query and thus map dependencies directly without the need for additional queries.

For all its advantages, you must always keep in mind that GraphQL isn't magic. Any information your interface delivers must come from a source that you integrate on the server side. This also applies to all the relations you map in a query. The interface is only as good as your implementation underneath it.

GraphQL consists of three components:

- **Query**
  The GraphQL client formulates a query to communicate with the server. A query can involve a read access, in which case, you use the query type *query*, or a write access, for which you use the *mutations*. A query must always follow the rules of the server's GraphQL schema.

- **Schema**
  The schema defines the data structure of the server and forms the basis for the queries. The schema of a GraphQL server defines an object structure using its own type system. GraphQL seems very flexible at first sight. However, this flexibility only extends to the limits set by the schema. Everything must be defined in the schema that you want the GraphQL interface to have an effect on.

- **Resolvers**
  GraphQL is simply a means to query and manipulate data. The GraphQL interface has no knowledge about the business logic of the application. This is where the resolvers come into play. They provide the interface to the actual Node.js application and are implemented as functions.

The reference implementation for Facebook's GraphQL was written in Node.js. For this reason, the integration is very good for both Node.js and client-side JavaScript. You can find numerous other resources on this topic on the GraphQL website (*https:// graphql.org/*).

11.1   GraphQL Libraries

At its core, GraphQL is just a language specification that defines certain rules. The actual implementation for the different programming languages and platforms is carried out by libraries. These exist for Go, Rust, and C, as well as for JavaScript. The most popular library is probably GraphQL.js, Facebook's original reference implementation. It's implemented for running a GraphQL interface in Node.js and is independent of other frameworks. You can install the library via the command; npm install graphql and can then use it directly. Listing 11.1 shows a first simple example of using GraphQL.

```
import { buildSchema, graphql } from 'graphql';

const schema = buildSchema(`
  type Query {
    greet: String
  }
`);

const root = {
  greet() {
    return 'Hello GraphQL!';
  },
};

const response = await graphql(schema, '{ greet } ', root);
console.log(response.data.greet); // Ausgabe: Hello GraphQL!
```

Listing 11.1 Using the "graphql" Library

In this example, you use GraphQL as an interface within an application. This means you don't run a server process or make the interface publicly available. Instead, you first define the schema using the buildSchema function from the graphql package. The schema defines a query type with the greet field of the string type. With a query, you can read this field. For the request to be supplied with a concrete value, you must define a resolver. To do this, you define the root object, which contains a greet function. This is located after the field and is executed with a query to produce the concrete value.

The asynchronous graphql function enables you to formulate such a query to your GraphQL interface. To do this, you first pass the created schema, the query itself, and the root object. The GraphQL function returns a promise object, so you can use the async keyword, as shown in the example. The response object within this promise contains, among other information, a data property representing the result of the query. Depending on how you structure your query, the object structure below the data property will look different from query to query. In our case, it contains a greet property, which in turn contains the string Hello GraphQL!.

This first example isn't practical for a web server because you don't create a publicly available GraphQL interface. But we're going to change that in the following sections. The movie database, which you already know from the previous chapters, now gets a GraphQL interface.

11.2 Integration with Express

The basis for implementing the GraphQL interface is the state of the application as we developed it in Chapter 10. Now, before you move on to implementing your GraphQL interface, you first need to install some additional packages: the GraphQL package you already know and the Express middleware for GraphQL called express-graphql. To do this, you must run the command, npm install graphql express-graphql.

In the first step of integrating GraphQL into your application, you assemble the individual components of the interface so that you can easily extend it later. To do this, you must first create a file named *graphql.js* in the root directory of your application. This file contains the schema and the resolvers. It's responsible for integrating with your Express application. First, you implement the same structure as already shown in the example from Listing 11.1. Although this doesn't yet have much to do with our actual application, it allows you to prepare all the necessary components to such an extent that further integration into the application can take place without any problems. Listing 11.2 contains the source code of this first version of the file.

```
import { buildSchema } from 'graphql';
import expressGraphql from 'express-graphql';

const schema = buildSchema(`
  type Query {
    greet: String
  }
`);

const rootValue = {
  greet() {
    return 'Hello GraphQL';
  },
};
```

```
export default expressGraphql.graphqlHTTP({
  schema,
  rootValue,
  graphiql: true,
});
```

Listing 11.2 Basic Configuration of the GraphQL Interface (graphql.js)

In the first code block, you define the schema. Your users can query the greet field and receive a character string in return. The second block—the rootValue—contains the resolver function for the greet field and returns the string Hello GraphQL on request. In the last line, you export the result of calling the graphqlHTTP function as default export. This allows you to include your GraphQL interface as regular Express middleware in your application. When calling the graphqlHTTP function from the express-graphql package, you pass an object with the schema, the resolver functions, and the graphiql property with the value true.

Before you start writing your GraphQL queries, you still need to embed the functionality into your application. This is done in the *index.js* file in the root directory of your application.

In the *index.js* file of your application, as shown in Listing 11.3, you import the default export of the *graphql.js* file you just created and include the function as middleware via the use method of the app object for the */graphql* route. After these modifications, you can restart your application and already use the GraphQL interface.

```
import express from 'express';
import morgan from 'morgan';
import expressJwt from 'express-jwt';
import swaggerUi from 'swagger-ui-express';
import { router as movieRouter } from './movie/index.js';
import { router as loginRouter } from './auth.js';
import swaggerSpec from './swagger.js';
import graphql from './graphql.js';

const app = express();

app.use(morgan('common', { immediate: true }));

app.use(express.json());

app.use('/login', loginRouter);
app.use(
  '/movie',
  expressJwt({ secret: 'secret', algorithms: ['HS256'] }),
  movieRouter,
```

```
);

app.use((err, request, response, next) => {
  if (err.name === 'UnauthorizedError') {
    response.status(401).json('unauthorized');
  } else {
    next();
  }
});

app.get('/', (request, response) => response.redirect('/movie'));

app.use('/api-docs', swaggerUi.serve, swaggerUi.setup(swaggerSpec));

app.use('/graphql', graphql);

app.listen(8080, () => {
  console.log('Server is listening to http://localhost:8080');
});
```

Listing 11.3 Integrating the GraphQL Interface in Express (index.js)

11.3 GraphiQL

GraphQL is a query language that uses HTTP as a transport layer, so it's on the same level as REST, for example. This means you can address a GraphQL interface like the one you just implemented using a very ordinary HTTP client. For example, you can query your new interface from the command line using the code shown in Listing 11.4.

```
$ curl
  -X POST
  -H "Content-Type: application/json"
  --data '{"query": "{ greet }"}'
  http://localhost:8080/graphql

{"data":{"greet":"Hello GraphQL"}}
```

Listing 11.4 Querying the GraphQL Interface with cURL

The query is an HTTP POST request with the content type header application/json. As the message body, you send the data, in this case, a JavaScript Object Notation (JSON) structure with the query property containing the character string { greet }, that is, the actual query. You then send everything to *http://localhost:8080/graphql* and receive a corresponding response from the interface.

Querying a GraphQL interface from the command line isn't very elegant and quickly gets confusing, especially with more advanced interfaces. And this is where the graphiql property comes into play, which you've set to true in Listing 11.2. This property activates the GraphiQL tool—a graphical interface for GraphQL. When you open *http://localhost:8080/graphql* in your browser, you can use GraphiQL directly. Figure 11.1 shows the GraphiQL interface.

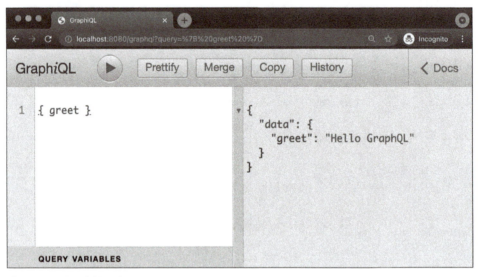

Figure 11.1 GraphiQL View

GraphiQL is divided into two sections. On the left, you can formulate your queries, and on the right, you can see the result. In this case, you've entered the string { greet } as the query and get back the structure with Hello GraphQL.

Now it's time to merge the data from the application and the GraphQL interface.

11.4   Reading Data via the Interface

To obtain read access to the GraphQL interface, you must first extend the schema. You need a new data type called movie that maps the structure of a record. Then, you must define a movie field that you can query. Listing 11.5 shows the new version of the schema.

```
import { buildSchema } from 'graphql';
import expressGraphql from 'express-graphql';

const schema = buildSchema(`
  type Movie {
    id: Int!
```

```
    title: String!
    year: Int
    public: Int
    user: Int
  }

  type Query {
    greet: String
    movie: [Movie]
  }
`);

const rootValue = {...};

export default expressGraphql.graphqlHTTP({...}
```

Listing 11.5 Extending the Schema with the "Movie" Type

As you've already seen, GraphQL has its own type system, which is quite similar to the one you already know from TypeScript—but there are some differences. For example, GraphQL distinguishes between the number types Int and Float, that is, between integers and floating point numbers. Other aspects are similar to those in TypeScript, such as the string and Boolean types. GraphQL also provides for the ID type for unique identifiers such as the id field. The problem with this data type is that it's interpreted as a string, and a numeric ID would thus be converted into a character string, which is why we use the Int type for our example. The exclamation mark after a type indicates that this is a required field.

The extension of the schema alone doesn't help you yet. Any change to the schema usually requires an adjustment to the resolver functions as well. Listing 11.6 shows how you should extend the rootValue object that contains the resolvers.

```
import { buildSchema } from 'graphql';
import expressGraphql from 'express-graphql';
import { getAll } from './movie/model.js';

const schema = buildSchema(`...`);

const rootValue = {
  greet() {
    return 'Hello GraphQL';
  },
  movie() {
    return getAll({ userId: 1 });
  },
```

```
};
```

```
export default expressGraphql.graphqlHTTP({...}
```

Listing 11.6 Extending the Resolver Functions (graphql.js)

With this extension, you benefit from the fact that the application is already fully functional with its REST interface and that the GraphQL interface is merely an add-on on top of the application's business logic. So, you can reuse all the routines you implemented for the REST interface almost unchanged at this point. Note that you currently haven't implemented any authentication features, so you still need to define the ID of the user, in this case, the value 1, as fixed when calling the getAll function. With these adjustments, after restarting the application, you can again query your interface with GraphiQL and see the results from the database, as shown in Figure 11.2.

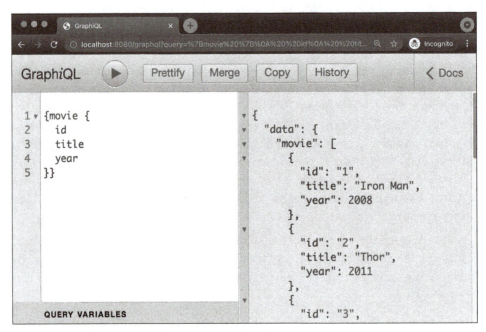

Figure 11.2 GraphQL Query of the Data from the Database

At this point, two things are worth noting. First, not only does GraphQL support synchronous operations but also asynchronous operations based on promises, as in the case of the database query. Second, this example also shows clearly how you can affect the structure of the response via the query. In the query, you specify the properties of the movie type you want to get. For example, if you aren't interested in the year property, you don't specify it in the request, so the server won't send the information. In this case, with the very limited number of data records in the database, this feature doesn't play a particularly important role yet. However, suppose you have an interface with a very large amount of data or very extensive types—then the limitation of the response will definitely come into play. In addition to affecting the structure, you can also parameterize your interface and thus implement a filter, for example.

11.4.1   Parameterizing Queries

For the GraphQL interface to have a scope of features similar to the REST interface, the next step is to implement the option to read a single data record based on its ID. You have several options to implement the feature. For example, you can define a new query field that returns a movie record. Alternatively, you can extend the existing `movie` field to support a parameter. This is rather useful because it makes the existing interface more flexible. However, the drawback here is that you also get an array as a result, even if you have only one data record. In Listing 11.7, take a look at the schema.

```
import { buildSchema } from 'graphql';
import expressGraphql from 'express-graphql';
import { getAll } from './movie/model.js';

const schema = buildSchema(`
  type Movie {
    id: Int!
    title: String!
    year: Int
    public: Int
    user: Int
  }

  type Query {
    greet: String
    movie(id: Int): [Movie]
  }
`);

const rootValue = {...};

export default expressGraphql.graphqlHTTP({...}
```

Listing 11.7 Extending the Schema with Parameters (graphql.js)

You can introduce parameters for a query by writing a field similar to a TypeScript method, as in the example. First, you specify the name, in this case, `movie`. Then the parameter list follows in parentheses with the name of the parameter followed by the type. If you add an exclamation mark to the type, you make it a mandatory parameter.

After the parameter list, you must specify the return type, in our case, a movie array. This schema element must be understood and supported by the resolver on the other side. Listing 11.8 contains the corresponding adjustment.

```
import { buildSchema } from 'graphql';
import expressGraphql from 'express-graphql';
import { getAll } from './movie/model.js';

const schema = buildSchema(`...`);

const rootValue = {
  greet() {
    return 'Hello GraphQL';
  },
  async movie({ id }) {
    const movies = await getAll({ userId: 1 });
    if (id) {
      return movies.filter((movie) => movie.id === id);
    }
    return movies;
  },
};
export default expressGraphql.graphqlHTTP({...}
```

Listing 11.8 Resolver Function for Reading a Data Record (graphql.js)

As you can see from the implementation, you get access to the variables of the request via an object in the parameter list. You access the id directly via a destructuring statement and can then use the information. Note that id is an optional variable that can also have no value. In this case, you must return all data records. The advantage of this is that the previous interface continues to work, and you don't need to adapt the code of already existing clients.

You have several options for implementing the requirements. You can start with the list of all records, as in the example, and filter them within the application. Alternatively, you can use the get function of the model and return the result as an array. If you have a larger amount of data, the second option is more suitable because, in this case, you outsource most of the filtering work to the database. For this example, the actual implementation plays a subordinate role. Figure 11.3 shows an example of a parameterized query. Here you specify the field, followed by a pair of parentheses enclosing the variable and its value. This is followed, as usual, by the intended structure of the response.

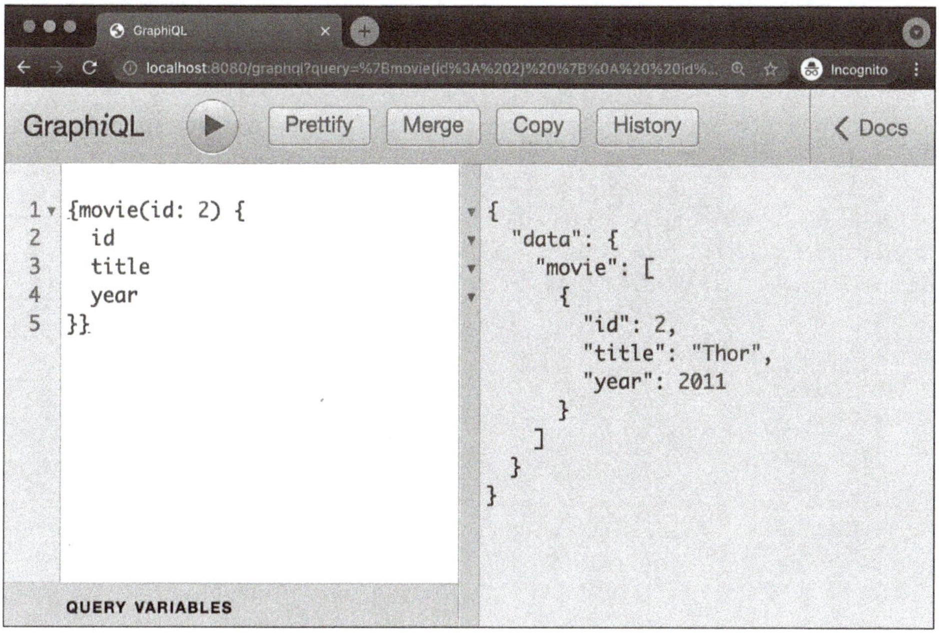

Figure 11.3 Querying a Data Record with GraphiQL

Based on this implementation, you can now implement any other filters to further enhance the flexibility of your interface. In this context, you should always remember that you need to adjust both the schema and the resolver function.

In addition to the read accesses, you now have to take care of the write operations, so that you can read data records as well as create, manipulate, and delete them again.

11.5   Write Accesses to the GraphQL Interface

In the following sections, you'll learn how to add write operations to your interface. The core component of this type of query is the mutation type, which, like the query type you've used so far for read accesses, is a special type in GraphQL. You may define both types only once in your schema. When implementing the resolver functions, you can draw on the already existing model function.

11.5.1   Creating New Data Records

To create new data records, you need to make two enhancements to your schema. You need the mutation type and a createMovie field below it. You can model this type similarly to querying a single data record by defining a parameter list that includes the data record you want to create. The return type is a new movie object. In GraphQL, you may not use an ordinary type you define with the type keyword as a parameter type for a mutation, so you must define a separate input type. An input type is introduced with the input keyword. The structure of the movie type and of the new input type are similar—the only difference being that the id may now be optional because it doesn't yet exist for new data records to be created. Listing 11.9 shows the adjustments to the schema.

```
import { buildSchema } from 'graphql';
import expressGraphql from 'express-graphql';
import { getAll } from './movie/model.js';

const schema = buildSchema(`
  type Movie {
    id: Int!
    title: String!
    year: Int
    public: Int
    user: Int
  }

  input MovieInput {
    id: Int
    title: String!
    year: Int
    public: Int
    user: Int
  }

  type Query {
    greet: String
    movie(id: Int): [Movie]
  }

  type Mutation {
    createMovie(movie: MovieInput): Movie
  }
`);

const rootValue = {...};

export default expressGraphql.graphqlHTTP({...}
```

Listing 11.9 Schema Extension for Creating New Data Records (graphql.js)

After that, you can implement the corresponding resolver function. Listing 11.10 shows how this works.

```
import { buildSchema } from 'graphql';
import expressGraphql from 'express-graphql';
import { getAll, save } from './movie/model.js';

const schema = buildSchema(`...`);

const rootValue = {
  greet() {
    return 'Hello GraphQL';
  },
  async movie({ id }) {
    const movies = await getAll({ userId: 1 });
    if (id) {
      return movies.filter((movie) => movie.id === id);
    }
    return movies;
  },
  createMovie({ movie }) {
    return save(movie, 1);
  },
};

export default expressGraphql.graphqlHTTP({...}
```

Listing 11.10 Resolver Function for Creating a Data Record (graphql.js)

As with the parameterized reading of a data record, you also have access to the transferred data for mutations, except that here, it's not a single id, but the data record to be created. Within the function, you use the model's save function to write the data record to the database. In this call, too, you pass the user ID as a fixed value. With these adjustments, you can switch back to your browser after restarting the application and use GraphiQL to create a new data record.

As you can see in Figure 11.4, mutations follow the same syntax as the queries you've used so far. The only exception is that you must preface your query with the mutation keyword because GraphiQL assumes a query by default. Then you specify the name of the required mutation, pass the new to be created data record, and define what information you want to receive in return. On the right side of the window, you can see the result of the createMovie mutation: the newly created data record, including the ID assigned by the database.

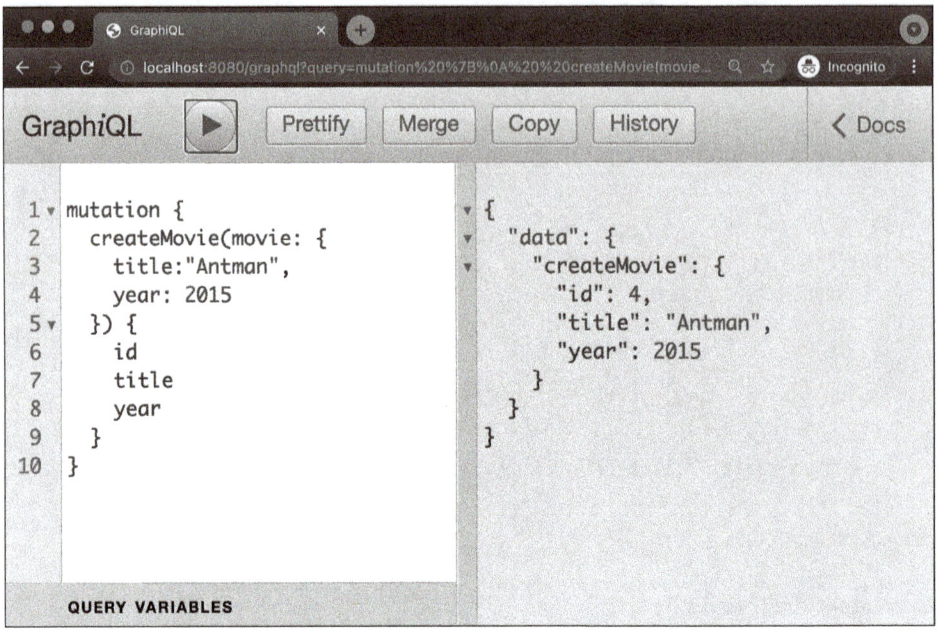

Figure 11.4 Creating a New Data Record

11.5.2   Updating and Deleting Data Records

The tasks of updating and deleting existing data records are based on the same concept. First, you extend the schema with two more mutations named updateMovie and delete-Movie, as you can see in Listing 11.11.

```
import { buildSchema } from 'graphql';
import expressGraphql from 'express-graphql';
import { getAll, save } from './movie/model.js';

const schema = buildSchema(`
  type Movie {
    id: Int!
    title: String!
    year: Int
    public: Int
    user: Int
  }

  input MovieInput {
    id: Int
    title: String!
    year: Int
    public: Int
```

```
    user: Int
  }

  type Query {
    greet: String
    movie(id: Int): [Movie]
  }

  type Mutation {
    createMovie(movie: MovieInput): Movie
    updateMovie(movie: MovieInput): Movie
    deleteMovie(id: Int!): Boolean
  }
`);

const rootValue = {...};

export default expressGraphql.graphqlHTTP({...}
```

Listing 11.11 Schema Extension for Modifying and Deleting Data Records (graphql.js)

As you can see here, with updateMovie, there's also an input type involved, and, as a result, you get the modified movie record back. When deleting via the deleteMovie mutation, you simply pass the ID of the data record to be deleted and return a Boolean value.

The implementation of the corresponding resolver functions is shown in Listing 11.12.

```
import { buildSchema } from 'graphql';
import expressGraphql from 'express-graphql';
import { getAll, save, remove } from './movie/model.js';

const schema = buildSchema(`...`);

const rootValue = {
  greet() {
    return 'Hello GraphQL';
  },
  async movie({ id }) {
    const movies = await getAll({ userId: 1 });
    if (id) {
      return movies.filter((movie) => movie.id === id);
    }
    return movies;
  },
```

```
createMovie({ movie }) {
  return save(movie, 1);
},
async updateMovie({ movie }) {
  await save(movie, 1);
  return movie;
},
async deleteMovie({ id }) {
  await remove(id, 1);
  return true;
},
};

export default expressGraphql.graphqlHTTP({...}
```

Listing 11.12 Resolver Functions for Updating and Deleting (graphql.js)

You implement both the updateMovie and deleteMovie functions as async functions. They each expect the result of the model operation and return the modified record in the update case and the value true in the delete case.

With these adjustments, you can now modify the data record you just created. The corresponding query is shown in Figure 11.5.

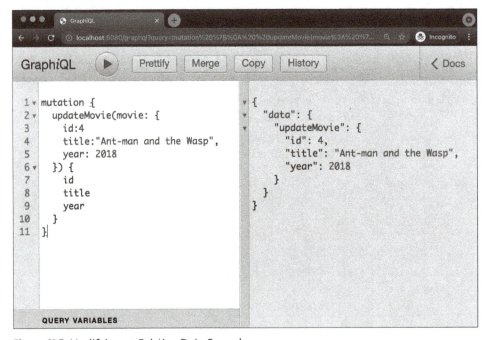

Figure 11.5 Modifying an Existing Data Record

Deleting the data record works in the same way, as you can see in Figure 11.6.

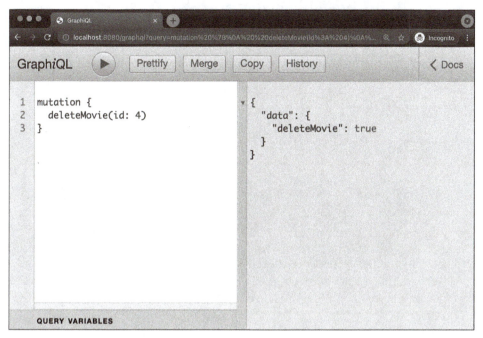

Figure 11.6 Deleting a Data Record

You now have implemented the complete create, read, update, delete (CRUD) functionality for your Movie database in GraphQL. Currently, however, there is still the problem that your interface is completely unprotected, so anyone who knows the address of your server can access it without restriction. Let's change that in the next step and add token-based authentication, as we did with the REST interface.

11.6   Authentication for the GraphQL Interface

The integration of GraphQL is done via regular middleware, which means you can combine it with other middleware software such as a logger or even authentication. All you need to do for this is to secure the */graphql* route. In our example, you use the express-jwt package to secure the interface like you did with the REST interface. Listing 11.13 shows how you can include it in the *index.js* file.

```
import express from 'express';
import morgan from 'morgan';
import expressJwt from 'express-jwt';
import swaggerUi from 'swagger-ui-express';
import { router as movieRouter } from './movie/index.js';
import { router as loginRouter } from './auth.js';
```

```
import swaggerSpec from './swagger.js';
import graphql from './graphql.js';

const app = express();

app.use(morgan('common', { immediate: true }));

app.use(express.json());

app.use('/login', loginRouter);
app.use(
  '/movie',
  expressJwt({ secret: 'secret', algorithms: ['HS256'] }),
  movieRouter,
);

app.use((err, request, response, next) => {
  if (err.name === 'UnauthorizedError') {
    response.status(401).json('unauthorized');
  } else {
    next();
  }
});

app.get('/', (request, response) => response.redirect('/movie'));

app.use('/api-docs', swaggerUi.serve, swaggerUi.setup(swaggerSpec));

app.use(
  '/graphql',
  expressJwt({ secret: 'secret', algorithms: ['HS256'] }),
  graphql,
);

app.listen(8080, () => {
  console.log('Server is listening to http://localhost:8080');
});
```

Listing 11.13 Securing the GraphQL Interface (index.js)

If you access GraphiQL or the interface via cURL with this change, you'll receive a response with an UnauthorizedError and status code 401, which means you're trying to access GraphQL without a valid token. To solve this problem, you first need to get a token. This can be done using the cURL call from Listing 11.14.

```
$ curl
  -X POST
  -H "Content-Type: application/json"
  -d '{"username": "sspringer", "password": "test"}'
  http://localhost:8080/login
```

```
{"token":"eyJhbGciOiJIUzI1NiIsInR5cCI6IkpXVCJ9.eyJpZCI6MSwiZmlyc3RuYW1lIjoiU2ViY
XN0aWFuIiwibGFzdG5hbWUiOiJTcHJpbmdlciIsInVzZXJuYW1lIjoic3NwcmluZ2VyIiwiaWF0IjoxN
jMyMDgxMzAxfQ.Hby4jag13i5ELdq-Ga8NK3vrOGpLKJyKzi6zfariAzQ"}
```

Listing 11.14 Logging In to the Application

Using the token you obtain from your application, you can now communicate with the GraphQL interface, as shown in Listing 11.15, for example.

```
$ curl
  -X POST
  -H "Content-Type: application/json"
  -
H "Authorization: Bearer eyJhbGciOiJIUzI1NiIsInR5cCI6IkpXVCJ9.eyJpZCI6MSwiZm lyc
3RuYW1lIjoiU2ViYXN0aWFuIiwibGFzdG5hbWUiOiJTcHJpbmdlciIsInVzZXJuYW1lIjoic3NwcmluZ
2VyIiwiaWF0IjoxNjMyMDgxMzAxfQ.Hby4jag13i5ELdq-Ga8NK3vrOGpLKJyKzi6zfariAzQ"
  -d '{"query": "{ movie(id: 2) { id title year } }"}'
  http://localhost:8080/graphql
```

```
{"data":{
  "movie":[{
    "id":2,
    "title":"Thor",
    "year":2011
  }]
}}
```

Listing 11.15 Authorized Query of the GraphQL Interface

With these adjustments to the source code, it's now no longer possible to use the interface without a valid login. Your interface thus has a certain basic protection, which you can now extend as you wish, for example, by implementing a roles and permissions system that allows a more fine-grained access control.

11.7 Summary

This chapter introduced you to some aspects of the GraphQL query language. A GraphQL interface works on the same level as REST, but GraphQL is much more flexible than REST because, in your query, you can also directly specify the structure of the response. Furthermore, you're not limited to resources, but can also load entire dependency trees with just one request, if the interface permits it.

However, you should keep in mind that everything the interface permits must be implemented in the form of resolver functions. GraphQL just provides you with a simple way of input validation and alerts you to errors in query formulation if you violate GraphQL's type system.

Chapter 12
Real-Time Web Applications

I won't sell the future for instant profit.
— Werner von Siemens

The original web applications consisted of a large number of individual HTML pages that were more or less tightly coupled together. User interaction in such applications takes place via classic forms for data entry and via links that redirect the user to another page. Each of these actions resulted in a complete page reload. This behavior feels less dynamic and flexible. A clear improvement was therefore the introduction of single-page applications, where only parts of the page had to be reloaded after a user interaction, rather than the entire page. The user's communication interface also changed from clearly visible form elements to intuitive operating concepts, in which the elements of user interaction are no longer modeled according to pure HTML specifications, but according to the usability of the application.

Even though this concept had brought web applications much closer to desktop applications in terms of their behavior, a major problem still remained: How does a user find out that the application data has changed? Communication in web applications is mostly based on HTTP. However, this transmission protocol follows a classic client-server approach: a client sends a request to the server, and the server processes the request and sends a response. A return channel from the server to the client isn't provided. Consequently, a client can ask for current data, but the server has no way to actively notify its clients when new data is available. However, new technologies such as server-sent events and the WebSocket application programming interface (API) allow you to open such a communication channel from the server to the client when developing your application, thus enabling bidirectional communication between client and server.

WebSocket

WebSocket is a standalone protocol that runs parallel to HTTP. Like HTTP, it exists in an unencrypted and an encrypted variant. The initial communication takes place via HTTP. The client generates a request asking for a protocol switch to WebSocket. As soon as the switch is completed, both endpoints, that is, client and server, have equal rights in communication and can send and receive messages. Because it's event-based processing, as soon as a message is received, an event is triggered, and a callback function is executed. This means that WebSockets don't block and are basically asynchronous.

In addition to WebSockets, there are other mechanisms that allow you to run real-time web applications. In this chapter, you'll learn about some ways to make your web applications dynamic so that they behave even closer to classic desktop applications.

12.1   The Sample Application

For a real-time-enabled web application to show its benefits, some requirements have to be met. For purely static content, for example, a real-time web application adds no value whatsoever. This means that data must originate within your application. If multiple users use your application simultaneously and generate new information, this is a potential task you can use a real-time-enabled web application to solve. However, new information in your application doesn't necessarily have to come from users directly. Another option consists of processes that run on the server and generate information to be sent to the users. In this context, time-controlled calculations are conceivable that serve to prepare the existing data set. The third variant through which new information can be created in your application consists of querying external sources. This allows you to retrieve the latest stock prices or news from a web service at regular intervals. You can then prepare and store this data within your application and make it available to your users. The more up to date the information in your application is and the faster your users learn about that information, the more valuable your application is to those users.

A classic example of real-time web applications is a multiclient chat. This task fulfills all requirements, so that a real-time web application can show its strengths. Users log in to your application via a login screen. After logging in, a user can chat with other participants in a chat room.

12.2   Setup

The basic structure of your application consists of two files and a directory. The entry point to the application is the *index.js* file located in the root directory of the application. In addition to this file, you need the *package.json* file, which can be used to resolve the dependencies of your application on the Node Package Manager (npm). It's also located in the root directory of the application. The directory you create is named *app* and contains all the files required for the backend of your application to function correctly. When you start implementing your application, the first step is to create the *package.json* file using the npm init -y command. For the sample application, you need Express, Pug, and the websocket package. You can install these tools via command npm install express pug ws. Listing 12.1 shows the resulting *package.json* file.

```
{
  "name": "node-book",
  "version": "1.0.0",
  "description": "A realtime chat application in node.js",
  "main": "index.js",
  "type": "module",
  "private": true,
  "scripts": {
    "start": "node index.js"
  },
  "keywords": [],
  "author": "",
  "license": "ISC",
  "dependencies": {
    "express": "^4.17.1",
    "pug": "^3.0.2",
    "ws": "^8.1.0"
  }
}
```

Listing 12.1 "package.json" File

The next step is to create the entry point to your application. It consists primarily of the contents of the *index.js* file, the basic structure of which is shown in Listing 12.2. During the course of this chapter, you'll expand this file more and more.

```
import express from 'express';
import { dirname } from 'path';
import { fileURLToPath } from 'url';

const app = express();

app.set('views', `${dirname(fileURLToPath(import.meta.url))}/app/views`);
app.set('view engine', 'pug');

app.get('/', (request, response) => {
  response.render('login');
});

app.listen(8080, () =>
  console.log('Server is listening to http://localhost:8080'),
);
```

Listing 12.2 Entry Point into the Application (index.js)

The content of the *index.js* file currently consists only of the Express setup, that is, the import of the package and a subsequent call of the express function. Finally, on the application object, you call the listen method and bind your application to port 8080. Pug is used as the template engine in your application. Using the set method, you set the view engine property of your application to the value pug and specify via the views property where your templates are stored. Before you can test your application for the first time, you also need a route. You can create one by calling the get method of your application object. In the callback function of the route, a template is rendered via the render method and returned to the requesting user. You then place this template in the *app/views* directory and name it *login.pug*. Listing 12.3 shows the contents of the template.

```
doctype html

html
  head
    title Node.js Chat
  body
    form(action="login" method="post")
      div
        label(for="username") Username:
        input(type="text" name="username" id="username")
      div
        label(for="password") Password:
        input(type="password" name="password" id="password")
      div
        input(type="submit" value="Log in")
```

Listing 12.3 Login Form (app/views/login.pug)

When you now start your application via the npm start command, you can access it with your browser at *http://localhost:8080* and see, as a result, a webpage similar to the one shown in Figure 12.1.

When you enter a user name and password in your login screen and click the **Log in** button, you'll receive the error message; Cannot POST /login. This means that in the next step, you need to make sure your users log in to your application to use it. The error message pops up because your application doesn't currently have a suitable route for the request. For the login process to work on your application, you need to modify your *index.js* file. First, you'll need some middleware components to make your work easier. You can use the npm install cookie-session command to install the cookie-session package. Listing 12.4 shows how you can include the cookie-session and body-parser middleware.

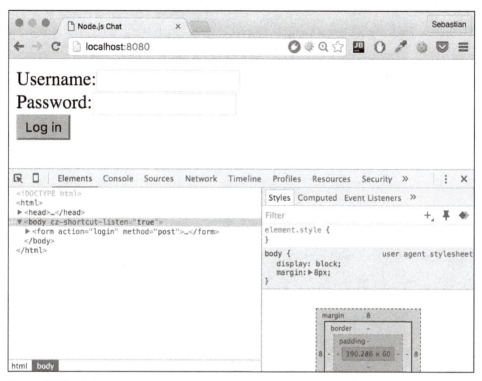

Figure 12.1 Login Screen

```
import express from 'express';
import { dirname } from 'path';
import { fileURLToPath } from 'url';
import cookieSession from 'cookie-session';

const app = express();

app.use(
  cookieSession({
    name: 'session',
    keys: ['key1', 'key2'],
  }),
);
app.use(express.urlencoded({ extended: false }));

app.set('views', `${dirname(fileURLToPath(import.meta.url))}/app/views`);
app.set('view engine', 'pug');

app.get('/', (request, response) => {
  response.render('login');
});
```

```
app.listen(8080, () =>
  console.log('Server is listening to http://localhost:8080'),
);
```

Listing 12.4 Middleware for the Login Process (index.js)

The body parser makes sure that you can easily access the data transmitted via POST, that is, the user name and password. The cookie-session middleware provides you with a session that allows you to store a user's login status for a particular session. With these adjustments, you can now move on to defining the other routes. In total, you need three more routes in your application for the next step. The first route is used for immediate login, the second as a destination for logged-in users, and the third allows a user to log out. To keep your application's source code uncluttered, you should swap out the route definition to a separate file named *index.js* in the *app* directory. Listing 12.5 contains the routes and their corresponding callback functions.

```
import { Router } from 'express';
import checkAuth from './check-auth.js';

const router = Router();

router.get('/', (request, response) => {
  response.render('login');
});

router.post('/login', (request, response) => {
  const user = request.body.username;
  const pw = request.body.password;

  if (user === 'u1' && pw === 'test') {
    request.session.user = 'u1';
  } else if (user === 'u2' && pw === 'test') {
    request.session.user = 'u2';
  }

  response.redirect('/chat');
});

router.get('/chat', checkAuth, (request, response) => {
  response.render('chat', { user: request.session.user });
});

router.get('/logout', (request, response) => {
  delete request.session.user;
  response.redirect('/');
```

```
});

export { router };
```

Listing 12.5 Login and Logout (app/index.js)

For the routes to be included correctly, you must also make some adjustments to the entry file in your application. Listing 12.6 contains the corresponding changes.

```
import express from 'express';
import { dirname } from 'path';
import { fileURLToPath } from 'url';
import cookieSession from 'cookie-session';
import { router } from './app/index.js';

const app = express();

app.use(
  cookieSession({
    name: 'session',
    keys: ['key1', 'key2'],
  }),
);
app.use(express.urlencoded({ extended: false }));

app.set('views', `${dirname(fileURLToPath(import.meta.url))}/app/views`);
app.set('view engine', 'pug');

app.get('/', (request, response) => {
  response.render('login');
});

app.use(router);

app.listen(8080, () =>
  console.log('Server is listening to http://localhost:8080'),
);
```

Listing 12.6 Customization of the Entry File (index.js)

The most important part of the route definition at this moment is the post method for the /login route. The form from Listing 12.3 sends the login information directly to this route. Through the body parser, you can access the user name and password within the callback function via the request.body object. To keep the example simple and clear, only two users are provided here. Typically, at this point, you would include a database and check to see if the user exists. The cookie-session middleware enables you to access the session property within the request object and store the user name here. Once the user name is verified, the user gets redirected to the /chat route. Once logged in, a user should also be able to log out. This task is enabled by the /logout route, which deletes the request.session.user property and then redirects the user back to the login page. The /chat route has a specific feature: this route uses the checkAuth middleware located in the *check-auth.js* file in the *app* directory and ensures that only logged-in users are allowed to use this route. Listing 12.7 shows the corresponding source code.

```
export default function checkAuth(request, response, next) {
  if (!request.session.user) {
    response.redirect('/');
  } else {
    next();
  }
}
```

Listing 12.7 The "checkAuth" Middleware (app/check-auth.js)

This middleware checks whether the request.session.user property is set. If this is the case, the next callback function of the routing chain is executed. If a user hasn't logged in, they'll be redirected to the registration form. The callback function of the /chat route ensures that the *chat.pug* template is rendered from the *app/views* directory. However, before we turn to its implementation, we first need to prepare the server-side WebSocket interface. The source code for the *chat.pug* template can be found in Section 12.3.2. In this context, you pass the name of the currently logged-in user. This state of the application forms the basis for the adjustments that now follow, after which you'll have a fully functional multiclient chat.

12.3   WebSockets

The central component of the chat application is the communication link between client and server. Through it, the user can send messages to the server and receive messages from the server. The WebSocket API is an established and widely used technology developed in the wake of HTML5 that solves the problem of bidirectional communication in web applications at the protocol level. (Details of this specification can be obtained from W3C at *www.w3.org/TR/2009/WD-websockets-20091222/*.) Its browser provides you—the programmer—with an interface in JavaScript through which you can communicate with the other side using the WebSocket. The actual connection, that is, the WebSocket, is independent of HTTP. Instead, the WebSocket specification, which you can read at *https://tools.ietf.org/html/rfc6455*, describes a separate protocol that exists in parallel to HTTP. Like HTTP, the WebSocket protocol is also based on the Transmission Control Protocol (TCP). A major advantage of the WebSocket API is its simplicity.

The API includes only a few methods and some events that can occur when dealing with WebSockets. Listing 12.8 shows a simple example that illustrates the use of WebSockets on the client side.

```
const socket = new WebSocket('ws://localhost:8181/');

socket.send('Hello Server');

socket.onmessage = (msg) => {
  console.log(msg.data);
};
```

Listing 12.8 WebSocket API Methods in Use

As you can see in the example shown in Listing 12.8, before you can use the WebSocket API, you must first create an instance of the WebSocket class. This is provided to you by your browser. The constructor accepts the URL you want to connect to as its first argument. Because WebSockets represent a protocol of their own, the URL also doesn't start with *http://* as usual, but with *ws://*, which stands for WebSocket. Similar to HTTP, which has an encrypted and thus secure version of the protocol in the form of HTTPS, there is also a secure version of the protocol for WebSockets in the form of secure WebSockets. The prefix for secure WebSockets is *wss://*. As a second optional argument, you can pass a string to the constructor that specifies the subprotocol. The subprotocol is used when you want to ensure that the client and server send messages to each other that they both understand. For example, you can define a specific message format for your own application. If such a specification exists, you can specify the name of your application or, even better, the name of your communication protocol as a subprotocol. The client and server then only accept connections with the corresponding subprotocol.

To send messages, the send method is used. Because the WebSocket object on which you call the method is attached to a specific connection, you don't need to specify anything other than the message you want to pass.

The onmessage property of the WebSocket object is assigned a function as its value, as shown in Listing 12.8. This function serves as a callback that is called as soon as the event occurs, in this case, the arrival of a new message. This function receives a representation of the original message of the remote system as an argument.

In addition to these two mechanisms for communicating via WebSockets, there are other methods and events that can be useful when developing an application. Once you've established a WebSocket connection, it must also be closed again at some point. This is done using the close method of the WebSocket object. This method doesn't receive any parameters. If the WebSocket connection is closed by the remote system, an event is triggered. This causes the callback function you assign to the onclose property to be executed. Finally, the last event you should know about in the context of the WebSocket API is the open event. You can assign a callback function to the onopen property of the WebSocket object, as you did with onclose, which is executed as soon as the WebSocket connection is established.

12.3.1   The Server Side

With this knowledge, you can now move on to adding a WebSocket connection to your application. Listing 12.9 shows the first step of the required adjustments. You should save this source code in the *websocket.js* file in the *app* directory.

```
import { WebSocketServer } from 'ws';

export default function init(app) {
  const wss = new WebSocketServer({ port: 8181 });

  const connections = [];

  wss.on('connection', (ws) => {
    connections.push(ws);

    connection.on('message', (message) => {
      connections.forEach((connection) => {
        connection.send && connection.send(message);
      });
    });
  });
}
```

Listing 12.9 WebSocket Backend (app/websocket.js)

The init function creates a new WebSocketServer, which is also bound to port 8181 at the same time. You use the connections array to manage all connections so that you can address all connected clients. The connection event is triggered when a new client connects to the server. The ws object of the callback function represents this client-server connection, which you can use both to receive and send messages. The message object occurs when a client sends a message, and you use the send method of the WebSocket object to send a message from the server to the client.

The code of the example causes an incoming message to be distributed to all connected clients. You still need to include the *websocket.js* file you just created into the central *index.js* file of your application to enable a connection. Listing 12.10 shows the corresponding source code.

```
import express from 'express';
import { dirname } from 'path';
import { fileURLToPath } from 'url';
import cookieSession from 'cookie-session';
import { router } from './app/index.js';
import initWebsocket from './app/websocket.js';

const app = express();

app.use(
  cookieSession({
    name: 'session',
    keys: ['key1', 'key2'],
  }),
);
app.use(express.urlencoded({ extended: false }));

app.set('views', `${dirname(fileURLToPath(import.meta.url))}/app/views`);
app.set('view engine', 'pug');

app.get('/', (request, response) => {
  response.render('login');
});

app.use(router);

app.listen(8080, () =>
  console.log('Server is listening to http://localhost:8080'),
);

initWebsocket();
```

Listing 12.10 WebSocket Integration (index.js)

Now that the server-side implementation is complete, you can move on to the client in the next step.

12.3.2   The Client Side

The frontend of your chat application basically consists of one file—the *chat.pug* template in the *app/views* directory. Listing 12.11 shows the structure of this file.

```
html
  head
  body
```

```
div#msgs(style="height:400; width:400; overflow: scroll;")

form#chatForm
  input#name(type="text")
  input#msg(type="text")
  button#sendBtn Send

  script.
    const socket = new WebSocket('ws://localhost:8181/', 'chat');

    document.querySelector('#sendBtn').↩
      addEventListener('click', (clickEvent) => {
        clickEvent.preventDefault();
        const name = document.querySelector('#name').value;
        const msg = document.querySelector('#msg').value;

        socket.send(`{"name": "${name}", "msg": "${msg}"}`);
        document.querySelector('#msg').value = '';
    });

    socket.onmessage = async (msg) => {
        const data = JSON.parse(await msg.data.text());

        const msgEl = document.createElement('div')
        msgEl.innerText = `${data.name}: ${data.msg}`;

        document.querySelector('#msgs').appendChild(msgEl);
    };
```

Listing 12.11 The chat.pug Template (app/views/chat.pug)

The frontend of the chat application doesn't require any additional libraries. The first step is to create an interface for your users that consists of two parts. The first part is a container in which the received messages are displayed. You can create this container in the simplest case via a div element. To this element, you must assign a unique ID to facilitate accessing it later. The second part of the user interface is a form through which a user can compose a message and then send it. The form contains three elements in total. With two input fields, users can define their name and formulate messages. A button is then used to send the message to the server. Finally, you need to make sure that messages get to the server and messages received from the server are displayed to the user. This task is performed by a set of JavaScript functions. As you've already seen in Listing 12.8, you can create a new connection using the WebSocket constructor function of the browser's WebSocket API. To this function, you pass the address. You use the resulting WebSocket instance to send and receive messages.

To send a message, you now register a callback function to the button's click event. Within this function, you collect the values of the two input fields and send them as properties in an object using the send method of the WebSocket object. After that, you clear the input field for the message and thus prepare the input for the next message. You can then use the onmessage property of the WebSocket object to handle incoming messages. For this purpose, you only need to define a callback function. This function receives the message object as an argument from which you can extract the text asynchronously. You can create an object from this character string by calling JSON.parse, which you can continue to use. For each incoming message, you generate a separate div container that you append to the contents of the display container.

Once you've made these adjustments to the client and server source code, you can start your application via the npm start command and test it by accessing *http://localhost:8080* from your browser. First, you need to log in, then you'll be redirected to the actual chat. With a connected client, you can only send messages to yourself. However, you won't see the effects of the real-time web application until you connect to the server with a second browser and start sending messages. In this case, the display container is updated in both browser windows, regardless of which browser you sent the message from. The results are shown in Figure 12.2.

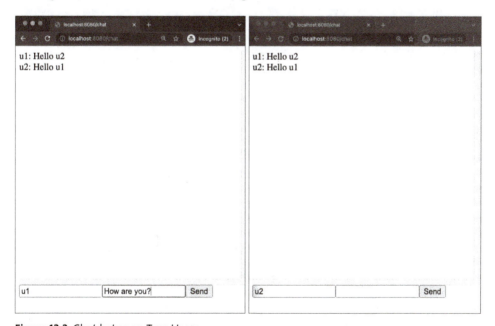

Figure 12.2 Chat between Two Users

In the following sections, you'll move on to extending the existing functionality of your application.

12.3.3   User List

At this point, you can log in to your chat application and send messages to other users in a global chat room. The first extension of your application will now consist of adding a list of active users, so that each user knows who is there to chat with. With this extension, also comes the need to establish different types of messages. Text-only messages will now be joined by status messages. As soon as a user logs in to the chat server, such a status message must be sent so that the server learns the name of the new user, and every other user of the chat is also aware of the existence of the new participant. Listing 12.12 shows the customized *chat.pug* template for the frontend.

```
html
  head
  body
    div#msgs(style="height:400; width:400; overflow: scroll; float:left;")
    div#users(style="height:400px; width:100px; overflow: scroll;")

    form#chatForm
      label(for="msg") #{user}: 
      input#name(type="hidden", value=user)
      input#msg(type="text")
      button#sendBtn Send

      script.
        const socket = new WebSocket('ws://localhost:8181/', 'chat');
        const name = document.querySelector('#name').value;

        socket.onopen = () => {
          socket.send(JSON.stringify({type: 'join', name}));
        }

        document.querySelector('#sendBtn') ⤸
          .addEventListener('click', (clickEvent) => {
            clickEvent.preventDefault();

            const msg = document.querySelector('#msg').value;

            socket.send(`{"type": "msg", "name": ⤸
              "${name}", "msg": "${msg}"}`);
            document.querySelector('#msg').value = '';
        });

        socket.onmessage = (msg) => {
            const data = JSON.parse(msg.data);
```

```
      switch (data.type) {
        case 'msg':
          const msgEl = document.createElement('div');
          msgEl.innerText = `${data.name}: ${data.msg}`;

          document.querySelector('#msgs').appendChild(msgEl);
          break;
        case 'join':
          document.querySelector('#users').innerHTML = '';
          data.names.forEach(name => {
            const userEl = document.createElement('div');
            userEl.innerText = name;

            document.querySelector('#users').appendChild(userEl);
          });
          break;
      }
    };
```

Listing 12.12 Frontend with Support for Message Types (app/views/chat.pug)

The customizations to the frontend consist of defining a container that contains the user list. This container has the ID users and is located right next to the container for displaying messages. In addition, the input field for the name is omitted. Instead of a typed name, the user's login name should be used. The name of the user is used as a label for the input field of the message. The connection process remains unchanged. Then, you use the onopen property to send a join type message to the server in a callback function. This message contains the name of the user. For sending the messages, you also add a type property. Furthermore, in the callback function registered on the button's click event, you should remove the reference to the user name input field.

When receiving messages, you must now also be able to handle different types of messages. This means you need to modify the onmessage handler accordingly. The character string you receive from the server is in JSON format and has a field named type. At this point, you need to distinguish two types of messages: (1) the msg type used when you receive new messages (the original logic remains unchanged), and (2) the join type, for which you receive an array with all logged-in users next to the type. Now you still need to make sure that the user list content is removed and the modified user list, encapsulated in div elements, gets inserted. In the next step, you need to customize the server side so that it too can handle the new message types. Listing 12.13 contains the customized chat server source code.

```
import { WebSocketServer } from 'ws';

export default function init(app) {
```

```
const wss = new WebSocketServer({ port: 8181 });

const connections = {};

wss.on('connection', (ws) => {
  ws.on('message', (message) => {
    const data = JSON.parse(message);

    let msg;

    switch (data.type) {
      case 'join':
        connections[data.name] = ws;
        msg = JSON.stringify({
          type: 'join',
          names: Object.keys(connections),
        });
        break;
      case 'msg':
        msg = JSON.stringify({ type: 'msg', ⤵
          name: data.name, msg: data.msg });
        break;
    }

    Object.values(connections).forEach((connection) => {
      connection.send && connection.send(msg);
    });
  });
});
}
```

Listing 12.13 Backend with Message Type Support (app/websocket.js)

On the server side, the changes are limited to the area of WebSockets. The Express part of the application remains unchanged. An important change is that instead of using an array to store the references to the individual socket connections, an object is now used for this purpose. Each socket connection is stored in this object with the name of the respective logged-in user. This mechanism allows you to assign connections to individual users. The main part of the message event callback function is a switch statement that you use to handle the different message types. The incoming data is available as JSON data and must be converted into an object before it can be used. After that, you can access the type property of the message and decide accordingly how to proceed with the data. In the case of a message of the msg type, that is, a text message, you only need to format the message accordingly. For join type messages, that is, when a new

user joins the chat, you must first make sure that the connection is added to the connections object under the user's name. In addition, here you also prepare the join type
message to all chat participants and insert the names of all users as a JSON array. After
this case discrimination, a loop ensures that the prepared message is sent to all participants. With this adaptation of the source code, you now have a real-time list of the
users currently logged in to your chat application. You can see the result in Figure 12.3.

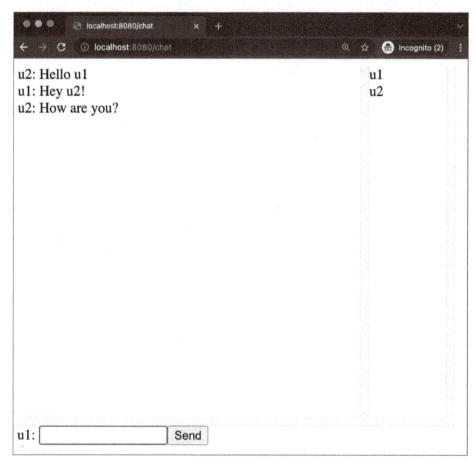

Figure 12.3 Chat Application with Participants List

The adjustments you made to the application now allow you to implement another
feature. A user should be able to log out properly after using the application.

12.3.4 Logout

To implement the logout feature, you must first integrate a link for the user to log out.
This is best placed above the display container. Listing 12.14 shows the corresponding
section of the *chat.pug* template.

```
html
  head
  body
    div(style="width:500px; text-align:right;")
      a(href="/logout") Logout

    div#msgs(style="height:400; width:400; overflow: scroll; float:left;")
    div#users(style="height:400px; width:100px; overflow: scroll;")

    form#chatForm
      label(for="msg") #{user}: 
      input#name(type="hidden", value=user)
      input#msg(type="text")
      button#sendBtn Send

      script.
...
```

Listing 12.14 Logout Link (app/views/chat.pug)

If a logged-in user clicks on this link, the user will be redirected to the */logout* route of your application. You've already created this route as part of the base application. Currently, it ensures that the user name is deleted from the session and the browser is redirected to the homepage afterwards. Because the WebSocket implementation is currently separated from the Express application, you need to create a way to communicate between the two. First, you must implement the logout feature in the WebSocket implementation. Listing 12.15 shows the associated source code.

```
import { WebSocketServer } from 'ws';

export default function init(app) {
  const wss = new WebSocketServer({ port: 8181 });

  const connections = {};

  wss.on('connection', (ws) => {...});

  return function logout(user) {
    connections[user].close();
    delete connections[user];

    const msg = JSON.stringify({
      type: 'join',
```

```
      names: Object.keys(connections),
    });

    Object.values(connections).forEach((connection) => {
      connection.send && connection.send(msg);
    });
  };
}
```

Listing 12.15 Logout Support in the WebSocket (app/websocket.js)

The initialization function of the WebSocket module returns a function named `logout`. This function makes sure that the user's connection gets closed, and the representation is deleted from the `connections` object. Then a new `join` message is sent to all remaining users. In the next step, you must extend the router implementation of the Express application and pass it the return value of the WebSocket `init` function. Listing 12.16 contains the customized source code.

```
import { Router } from 'express';
import checkAuth from './check-auth.js';

export default function init(logoutWebsocket) {
  const router = Router();

  router.get('/', (request, response) => {...});

  router.post('/login', (request, response) => {...});

  router.get('/chat', checkAuth, (request, response) => {...});

  router.get('/logout', (request, response) => {
    logoutWebsocket(request.session.user);
    delete request.session.user;
    response.redirect('/');
  });

  return router;
}
```

Listing 12.16 Changes to the Logout Route (app/index.js)

After adapting the source code, the router is no longer returned directly, but it's the result of the `init` function. This function received the `logoutWebsocket` function, which you can use in the `logout` route to disconnect the user. The last step of the restructuring concerns the entry file of your application, in which you still have to link the individual components, as shown in Listing 12.17.

```javascript
import express from 'express';
import { dirname } from 'path';
import { fileURLToPath } from 'url';
import cookieSession from 'cookie-session';
import router from './app/index.js';
import initWebsocket from './app/websocket.js';

const logoutWebsocket = initWebsocket();

const app = express();

app.use(
  cookieSession({
    name: 'session',
    keys: ['key1', 'key2'],
  }),
);
app.use(express.urlencoded({ extended: false }));

app.set('views', `${dirname(fileURLToPath(import.meta.url))}/app/views`);
app.set('view engine', 'pug');

app.get('/', (request, response) => {
  response.render('login');
});

app.use(router(logoutWebsocket));

app.listen(8080, () =>
  console.log('Server is listening to http://localhost:8080'),
);
```

Listing 12.17 Adjustment for Logout in the Entry File (index.js)

The order of the calls is crucial in this case. You need to perform the WebSocket setup first and only then include the router. After these changes, you should restart your application, and now you can both log in and log out your users. Figure 12.4 shows the view of the chat application after one of the two users has logged out. For the first user, the view remains unchanged, and the messages of the second user are still visible. However, the user list now only shows one user instead of two.

Figure 12.4 Logout Routine in the Chat

As an alternative to the WebSocket module presented here, you can use the Socket.IO library, which offers some interesting features.

12.4   Socket.IO

Socket.IO is an abstraction library for real-time-enabled web applications. The goal of this library is to enable cross-browser real-time web applications that aren't tied to a specific communication protocol. For this purpose, Socket.IO supports a whole range of communication options that allow for a bidirectional connection between client and server. Socket.IO consists of two components: a server component and a file the client must load to use the library. Socket.IO is completely implemented in JavaScript, which means that you don't need any additional plug-ins in your browser. On the server side, Socket.IO is available as an npm package. Once installed and integrated, Socket.IO is responsible for negotiating the type of connection itself. In this context, Socket.IO uses a number of technologies that are checked for one after the other. For example, it checks whether the browser supports WebSockets. If this isn't the case, an attempt is made to establish the connection via JSON with Padding (JSONP) polling, Flash sockets, or Asynchronous JavaScript and XML (AJAX) long polling as an alternative. In most cases, at least one of these technologies is supported by a browser, and you can then use this connection to implement your real-time web application. In the following step, you'll first prepare your chat application to use Socket.IO.

12.4.1   Installation and Integration

As just described, Socket.IO is available on the server side as an npm package. This means you can easily install this library using the npm install socket.io command. Socket.IO is quite an extensive library with some dependencies that npm resolves automatically during installation. For the extension of your application, you can remove the websocket package again. To do this, you must use command npm uninstall websocket. This removes the package from both the local *node_modules* directory and from *package.json*.

The customizations of your application are mainly limited to the part outside the Express.js application. Once the installation is complete, you can proceed to integrating the library on the server side. To do this, you need to make some adjustments to the *index.js* file. Listing 12.18 contains the new source code of this file.

```
import { createServer } from 'http';
import express from 'express';
import { dirname } from 'path';
import { fileURLToPath } from 'url';
import cookieSession from 'cookie-session';
import router from './app/index.js';
import initWebsocket from './app/websocket.js';
import { Server } from 'socket.io';

const app = express();

const server = createServer(app);
server.listen(8080, () =>
  console.log('Server is listening to http://localhost:8080'),
);
const io = new Server().listen(server);

const logoutWebsocket = initWebsocket(io);

app.use(
  cookieSession({
    name: 'session',
    keys: ['key1', 'key2'],
  }),
);
app.use(express.urlencoded({ extended: false }));

app.set('views', `${dirname(fileURLToPath(import.meta.url))}/app/views`);
app.set('view engine', 'pug');
```

```
app.get('/', (request, response) => {
  response.render('login');
});

app.use(router(logoutWebsocket));
```

Listing 12.18 Server-Side Integration of Socket.IO (index.js)

With these changes, you not only create the foundation for a functioning server implementation but also use it to build the basis for implementing the client side. Socket.IO provides you with the source code of the library for the server and takes care of the delivery of the source file for the client at the same time. This mechanism works automatically, so you only need to add one line to your template to use Socket.IO there. Listing 12.19 contains the corresponding extension of the template.

```
html
  head
    script(src="/socket.io/socket.io.js")
  body
...
```

Listing 12.19 Client-Side Integration of Socket.IO (app/views/chat.pug.js)

With these two changes, you've already met all the requirements for the additional adjustments. In the next sections, you'll see which parts of your application you need to modify to switch from WebSockets to Socket.IO.

12.4.2   Socket.IO API

The Socket.IO API is similar to that of the WebSocket API. However, the two technologies differ in some details. The frontend customizations are limited to the JavaScript portion of the template shown in Listing 12.20.

```
html
  head
    script(src="/socket.io/socket.io.js")
  body
    div(style="width:500px; text-align:right;")
      a(href="/logout") Logout

    div#msgs(style="height:400; width:400; overflow: scroll; float:left;")
    div#users(style="height:400px; width:100px; overflow: scroll;")

    form#chatForm
      label(for="msg") #{user}: 
```

379

```
        input#name(type="hidden", value=user)
        input#msg(type="text")
        button#sendBtn Send

    script.
      const socket = io.connect('http://localhost:8080');
      const name = document.querySelector('#name').value;

      socket.on('connect', () => {
        socket.emit('join', {name})
      })

      document.querySelector('#sendBtn')
        .addEventListener('click', (clickEvent) => {
          clickEvent.preventDefault();

          const msg = document.querySelector('#msg').value;

          socket.emit('msg', {msg});
          document.querySelector('#msg').value = '';
      });

      socket.on('msg', (data) => {
        const msgEl = document.createElement('div');
        msgEl.innerText = `${data.name}: ${data.msg}`;

        document.querySelector('#msgs').appendChild(msgEl);
      });

      socket.on('join', (data) => {
        document.querySelector('#users').innerHTML = '';
        data.names.forEach(name => {
          const userEl = document.createElement('div');
          userEl.innerText = name;

          document.querySelector('#users').appendChild(userEl);
        });
      });
```

Listing 12.20 Adapting the Frontend to Socket.IO (app/views/chat.pug)

You now establish the connection to the server using the connect method of the io object instead of the WebSocket constructor function. This provides you with an instance of the connection to the Socket.IO server, which you can use later. You implement the notification of the server about a new user within the callback function of the connect event, which is triggered as soon as the connection is established. Instead of the WebSocket send, Socket.IO uses the emit method of the connection object. Socket.IO already natively supports various message types, which you emulated in WebSockets via a property of the message itself. So, in this case, you can directly send a join type message. The callback function you bind to the button's click event remains unchanged except that it uses the emit method and that the message type was adapted to msg. In addition, when handling incoming messages, you can now use the different message types of Socket.IO and don't need to handle the two different types in a callback function. Incoming messages cause a msg event to be triggered. You bind a callback function to that event, which is responsible for inserting the transferred data into the display container. The logic for incoming join type messages also remains almost unchanged. In the callback function of the join event, you must first empty the container that contains the user names, and then reinsert the new list of users.

Listing 12.21 shows the required server-side modifications to the WebSocket part of the application.

```
function getName(connections, socket) {
  let name;
  for (const key in connections) {
    if (socket === connections[key]) {
      name = key;
    }
  }
  return name;
}

export default function init(io) {
  const connections = {};

  io.sockets.on('connection', (socket) => {
    socket.on('msg', (message) => {
      const name = getName(connections, socket);

      const msg = {
        name,
        msg: message.msg,
      };

      socket.emit('msg', msg);
      socket.broadcast.emit('msg', msg);
    });
```

```
    socket.on('join', function (message) {
      const name = getName(connections, socket);

      connections[message.name] = socket;

      const msg = { names: Object.keys(connections) };

      socket.emit('join', msg);
      socket.broadcast.emit('join', msg);
    });
  });

  return function logout(user) {
    const msg = JSON.stringify({
      type: 'join',
      names: Object.keys(connections),
    });

    connections[user].broadcast.emit('join', msg);
    connections[user].disconnect();

    delete connections[user];
  };
}
```

Listing 12.21 Adapting the Backend to Socket.IO (app/websocket.js)

The getName helper function is used to find out the name of the user responsible for sending a particular message. In contrast to the websocket package, the event that is triggered as soon as a client establishes a connection to the server is now called connection instead of request. Within the callback function that you bind to this event, you then handle the two message types, msg and join. In the callback function of the msg event, you format the message accordingly and then send it to all logged-in users using the emit method. Two different types of this method are used here: the socket.emit method makes sure that the client to which the current connection exists receives the message, and the socket.broadcast.emit method forwards the message to all other clients. You proceed similarly with the join event, the only difference being that here, as with WebSockets, you build a data structure that stores all references to the existing connections. Logging out users works according to the same logic as before with the pure WebSocket implementation. The Socket.IO object also provides a close method that can be used to terminate a connection. You send the updated user list to all other connections using the broadcast.emit method of the connection of the user to be logged out. Then you disconnect, delete the reference from the connections object, clear the user session, and redirect the user to the login page. With these adjustments, you've completely changed your application from WebSockets to Socket.IO, so now even older browsers can use your application.

12.5 Summary

With real-time-enabled applications, you can achieve impressive results. Such applications feel almost like classic desktop applications to the user. The interaction is direct and can also be actively initiated by the server. The server here has the ability to actively communicate with clients and send messages if relevant information is available.

There are now many technologies for implementing a real-time web application. The WebSocket API in particular has become increasingly popular in recent times, as it's built on its own very lightweight protocol and is finding its way into more and more browsers as part of HTML5. With Socket.IO, you've also learned about a library that works around one of the biggest drawbacks of the WebSocket API: WebSockets aren't available in many older browsers. Socket.IO contains a fallback mechanism to other technologies, such as AJAX long polling, which allows a server to communicate with older browsers. Based on the practical example of a simple chat application, you've seen how you can use WebSockets for bidirectional communication and how Socket.IO can also be integrated instead as an alternative technology.

12

Chapter 13

Type-Safe Applications in Node.js

The best way to predict the future is to shape it yourself.
—Alan Kay

One of the most common criticisms of JavaScript is that the language has no data types. However, this statement is only partially correct. JavaScript knows a number of primitive as well as composite data types. The primitive types include character strings, Booleans, numbers, symbols, null, and undefined. The composite types are objects, arrays, sets, and maps. However, when working with JavaScript, you get little support from the engine itself. It throws TypeErrors at most if you try to use data types incorrectly. Nevertheless, you can also use types in pure JavaScript.

The source code shown in Listing 13.1 is interrupted in two places. When creating a new object, you pass two character strings to the constructor instead of one string and a number. This gets detected during the check using the typeof operator, and a TypeError is thrown. The second instance where an exception is thrown is the rateMovie function. Here, you use the instanceof operator to ensure that only one instance of the movie may be passed. If you call the function with a character string instead, as in the example, this comparison will fail, and the TypeError you specified will be thrown with an appropriate message.

```
class Movie {
  constructor(title, year) {
    if (typeof title !== 'string' || typeof year !== 'number') {
      throw new TypeError('Wrong types supplied');
    }
    this.title = title;
    this.year = year;
  }
}

function rateMovie(movie, rating) {
  if (!(movie instanceof Movie) || typeof rating !== 'number') {
    throw new TypeError('Wrong types supplied');
  }
  movie.rating = rating;
}
```

```
const ironMan = new Movie('Iron Man', '2008');

rateMovie('Iron Man', 4);  // TypeError: Wrong types supplied
```

Listing 13.1 Manual Type Checking in JavaScript (index.js)

Although this mechanism secures your application at runtime against the incorrect use of types, it isn't very helpful during development and causes a lot of typing work. Your development environment can't support you either in this context. This solution is therefore far removed from a type system in the conventional sense.

Compensating for some of the drawbacks of the absence of a type system in JavaScript, tools such as ESLint help statically analyze the source code and point out errors and antipatterns. However, only type systems for JavaScript provide a real solution. There are a number of solutions available; TypeScript and Flow are widely used.

13.1   Type Systems for Node.js

The various type systems for JavaScript take different approaches, but all of them serve the goal of defining different data types for an application and referencing them in the source code. Normally, the data types of the type systems are used in connection with variables and function signatures.

In addition to providing a set of rules and a JavaScript syntax essay, most type systems also provide programs you can use to check your application. This step occurs before the application is executed. Before we turn to TypeScript, the most widely used type system, let's consider Flow as an alternative.

13.1.1   Flow

Flow is a type system developed by Facebook. It came to prominence through its use in the frontend of React applications. The tool is available as an open-source project. The project's official website can be found at *https://flow.org/en/*. Flow's source code is maintained on GitHub at *https://github.com/facebook/flow*. It's installed via the package manager, that is, either Node Package Manager (npm) or Yarn. The developers recommend local installation as a development dependency. Before you launch the installation, you must make sure that your project has a *package.json* file. If you haven't created one yet, you must first run the npm init -y command. Then you must always add the type and private fields to the generated file to be able to use the ECMAScript module system and to ensure that your application can't be published accidentally (see Listing 13.2).

```
{
  "name": "node_book",
  "version": "1.0.0",
  "description": "",
  "main": "index.js",
  "type": "module",
  "private": true,
  "scripts": {
    "test": "echo \"Error: no test specified\" && exit 1"
  },
  "keywords": [],
  "author": "",
  "license": "ISC"
}
```

Listing 13.2 Initial "package.json" File

In the next step, you install Flow via the npm install -D flow-bin command and initialize it using the npx flow init command. This command creates the *.flowconfig* file in your project, which contains the configuration.

Each source code file you want to check with Flow must start with this comment: /* @flow */. Listing 13.3 shows an example of a Flow source code.

```
/* @flow */
class Movie {
  title: string;
  year: number;
  rating: number;
  constructor(title: string, year: number) {
    this.title = title;
    this.year = year;
  }
}

function rateMovie(movie: Movie, rating: number) {
  movie.rating = rating;
}

const ironMan: Movie = new Movie('Iron Man', '2008');

rateMovie('Iron Man', 4);
```

Listing 13.3 Source Code with Flow (index.js)

If you save the source code in a file named *index.js* and then run the npx flow check command, Flow checks the source code of your application and issues the messages shown in Listing 13.4 for the sample code.

```
Error ------------------------------------------------ index.js:16:46

Cannot call Movie with '2008' bound to year because string [
1] is incompatible with number [2]. [incompatible-call]

 [2]  6|   constructor(title: string, year: number) {
      :
     13|     movie.rating = rating;
     14|   }
     15|
 [1] 16|   const ironMan: Movie = new Movie('Iron Man', '2008');
     17|
     18|   rateMovie('Iron Man', 4);
     19|



Error ------------------------------------------------ index.js:18:11

Cannot call rateMovie with 'Iron Man' bound to movie because string [
1] is incompatible with Movie [2].
[incompatible-call]

 [2] 12|   function rateMovie(movie: Movie, rating: number) {
     13|     movie.rating = rating;
     14|   }
     15|
     16|   const ironMan: Movie = new Movie('Iron Man', '2008');
     17|
 [1] 18|   rateMovie('Iron Man', 4);
     19|


Found 2 errors
```

Listing 13.4 Error Message during Type Check with Flow

If you try to run the source code directly in Node.js, you get a SyntaxError because Flow supports the full JavaScript language standard, but the type markup violates JavaScript syntax. For this reason, you need another tool in addition to Flow that converts the code with the markups back into valid JavaScript code. The simplest solution is to use the flow-remove-types package. You can install this package using the npm install -D flow-remove-types command. Typically, for flow files, you should add the *.flow.js* extension to indicate that these files can't be executed directly in Node.js. When you save the source code shown in Listing 13.3 in a file named *index.flow.js*, calling npx flow-remove-types index.flow.js > index.js creates the *index.js* file, which you can launch via the node index.js command.

Not only can you execute the two commands directly on the command line, but you can also include and combine them in your *package.json* file. So, the start script shown in Listing 13.5 combines both commands and runs your application.

```
{
  "name": "node-buch",
  "version": "1.0.0",
  "description": "",
  "main": "index.js",
  "type": "module",
  "private": true,
  "scripts": {
    "check": "flow check",
    "removeTypes": "flow-remove-types index.flow.js > index.js",
    "start": "npm run check && npm run removeTypes && node index.js"
  },
  "keywords": [],
  "author": "",
  "license": "ISC",
  "devDependencies": {
    "flow-bin": "^0.157.0",
    "flow-remove-types": "^2.157.0"
  }
}
```

Listing 13.5 Help Scripts in the "package.json" File

For the npm start command to run successfully, you must first rename the *index.js* file to *index.flow.js*. Then fix the two errors so that the file looks like Listing 13.6.

```
/* @flow */
class Movie {
  title: string;
  year: number;
  rating: number;
  constructor(title: string, year: number) {
    this.title = title;
    this.year = year;
  }
}
```

```
function rateMovie(movie: Movie, rating: number) {
  movie.rating = rating;
}

const ironMan: Movie = new Movie('Iron Man', 2008);

rateMovie(ironMan, 4);

console.log(ironMan);
```

Listing 13.6 Error-Free Flow File (index.flow.js)

If you now run the npm start command, you'll get an output like the one shown in Listing 13.7.

```
$ npm start

> listing13_2@1.0.0 start
> npm run check && npm run removeTypes && node index.js

> listing13_2@1.0.0 check
> flow check

Found 0 errors

> listing13_2@1.0.0 removeTypes
> flow-remove-types index.flow.js > index.js

Movie { title: 'Iron Man', year: 2008, rating: 4 }
```

Listing 13.7 Output of the "npm start" Script

An alternative to using the flow-remove-types package is to use the Babel transpiler.

The difference between Flow and other type systems for JavaScript is that Flow focuses only on checking the data types in the source code. Other tools, such as TypeScript, intervene in the source code and transform it.

13.1.2   TypeScript

Originally developed my Microsoft, TypeScript is a language based on JavaScript that includes a type system as one of its most important features. Like Flow, TypeScript is available as an open-source project on GitHub at *https://github.com/Microsoft/Type-Script*. The official website can be found at *www.typescriptlang.org/*. As described earlier, TypeScript is capable of actively modifying the source code of your application. When you use TypeScript, you also don't write JavaScript source code—you write

TypeScript. However, TypeScript is a superset of JavaScript, so valid JavaScript is also valid TypeScript in most cases. The TypeScript source code is then compiled by the TypeScript compiler into JavaScript. In this context, you can configure what the resulting source code should look like. For example, ES3 is supported as a target format, but ES2021 is also supported. Depending on your choice, TypeScript uses polyfills to make new features available in older environments. The newer the ECMAScript version, the smaller the differences between the TypeScript source code and the resulting JavaScript code. However, TypeScript is always adding new features, so you can use them even before they are integrated into the JavaScript language standard. For example, it's possible to use the ECMAScript module system with `import` and `export` already in version 4 of Node.js. However, because Node.js puts your environment much more under your control than the browser does, you can choose a more modern compile target, reducing the overhead generated by TypeScript.

As you can see, the TypeScript source code in Listing 13.8 strongly resembles the implementation in Flow. Both type systems use the same solution to annotate types. A variable is followed by the type specification separated by a colon. In TypeScript, you can use types for variables as well as in function signatures.

```
class Movie {
  public rating: number;
  constructor(public title: string, public year: number) {}
}

function rateMovie(movie: Movie, rating: number) {
  movie.rating = rating;
}

const ironMan: Movie = new Movie('Iron Man', '2008');

rateMovie('Iron Man', 4);
```

Listing 13.8 TypeScript Source Code (index.ts)

You can install the TypeScript compiler on your system using the package manager of your choice. To install TypeScript locally in your project, you must use the `npm install -D typescript` command. Again, as with Flow before, you should have a local *package.json* file where the dependencies are entered correctly. The official documentation recommends the global installation via the `npm install -g typescript` command because, in this case, you have the TypeScript compiler accessible everywhere on the command line. However, this variant reaches its limits if you need multiple versions of TypeScript on your system. You can launch the TypeScript compiler via the `npx tsc` command or only `tsc` if you've chosen the global installation. Save the source code from Listing 13.8 in a file named *index.ts*, and use the `tsc index.ts` command to check and convert the source code. Listing 13.9 shows the output of the command.

```
index.ts:10:46 -
 error TS2345: Argument of type 'string' is not assignable to parameter of type
'number'.

10 const ironMan: Movie = new Movie('Iron Man', '2008');
                                                 ~~~~~~


index.ts:12:11 -
 error TS2345: Argument of type 'string' is not assignable to parameter of type
'Movie'.

12 rateMovie('Iron Man', 4);
             ~~~~~~~~~~~~
```

Found 2 errors.

Listing 13.9 Error Messages during Type Check with TypeScript

As you can see, the output of TypeScript is a bit shorter than that of Flow. However, it contains all the important information such as file name, exact location of the problem, and a detailed error message. In addition to the console output, the compiler generated the *index.js* file, which, despite error messages, contains executable JavaScript code that you can run with Node.js.

> **Duck Typing**
>
> TypeScript doesn't perform type checking strictly, but in a pattern called *duck typing*. Duck typing means that when you assign a particular class as a type to a variable, the value of that variable doesn't have to be an instance of that class or of one of its subclasses—it just has to match the structure of the class.
>
> Duck typing derives from a saying that if a bird moves, swims, and quacks like a duck, it's a duck. The same is true for TypeScript objects and classes. So, if an object has the same properties and methods as the user class, it's a user type.

In the next section, we'll introduce you to some of the most important concepts of TypeScript. You should rely on this type system when implementing your application due to its prevalence and range of functions.

13.2   Tools and Configuration

TypeScript was first released in 2012. Since then, a very active community has formed around the type system. Microsoft and Google actively support TypeScript. Google developed its own type system called AtScript as part of Angular 2. However, after some time, this system was discontinued in favor of TypeScript, and TypeScript was used as the type system for Angular instead. Tools are constantly emerging from the Type-Script community that you can integrate into your application development process to make your job easier. We'll introduce you to some of these tools in the following sections.

13.2.1   Configuring the TypeScript Compiler

One tool—and also a direct component of TypeScript—is the `tsc --init` command, which initializes your application by creating a *tsconfig.json* file for it. You can use this file to affect the behavior of the TypeScript compiler.

```
{
  "compilerOptions": {
    "target": "ES2021",
    "module": "es2020",
    "strict": true,
    "esModuleInterop": true,
    "skipLibCheck": true,
    "forceConsistentCasingInFileNames": true
  }
}
```

Listing 13.10 tsconfig.json

Listing 13.10 contains a minimal example of a *tsconfig.json* file. These are the fields that are set by default during initialization. Only `target` and `module` were manually adjusted for our needs. The individual details are described here:

- **target**
  Specifies the target format of the compile process. By default, the value `es5` is entered here. However, this results in unnecessary overhead because, for example, the class syntax or arrow functions are replaced by polyfills. The `ES2017` target allows you to significantly reduce this overhead.

- **module**
  Tells the compiler which module system to use. If you specify the `commonjs` value here, the `import` and `export` statements in the TypeScript source code become `require` and `module.exports` statements. If you enter the value `es2015` here, the `import` and `export` statements are retained. However, in this case, you must ensure that the ECMAScript module system is enabled for your Node.js process.

- **strict**
  Activates a stricter mode of type checking. For example, statements with an implicit `any` type cause errors. Among some other options, `strict-null-checks` are also

enabled. This means that the `null` and `undefined` values are no longer included in each type.

- **esModuleInterop**
  Enables compatibility between CommonJS and ECMAScript modules.

- **skipLibCheck**
  Skips files that contain type declarations during the check.

- **forceConsistentCasingInFileNames**
  Prohibits different spellings when referring to the same file.

13.2.2   Integration into the Development Environment

A big advantage of TypeScript is the immediate feedback in the development process. You don't have to run your application to identify potential errors. The compile step precedes the execution. If you choose the right architecture and provide all variables and functions with type information, you can eliminate numerous errors. To make the feedback even faster and more direct, plug-ins for TypeScript exist for all common development environments. Using such a plug-in, you'll see the errors directly in the source code. Thus, violations of the type system are color-coded and provided with a corresponding error message. So, you don't have to switch to the command line first and run the compiler yourself, but get the feedback directly and without another intermediate step.

Figure 13.1 shows what the integration into the development environment can look like using the example of Visual Studio Code.

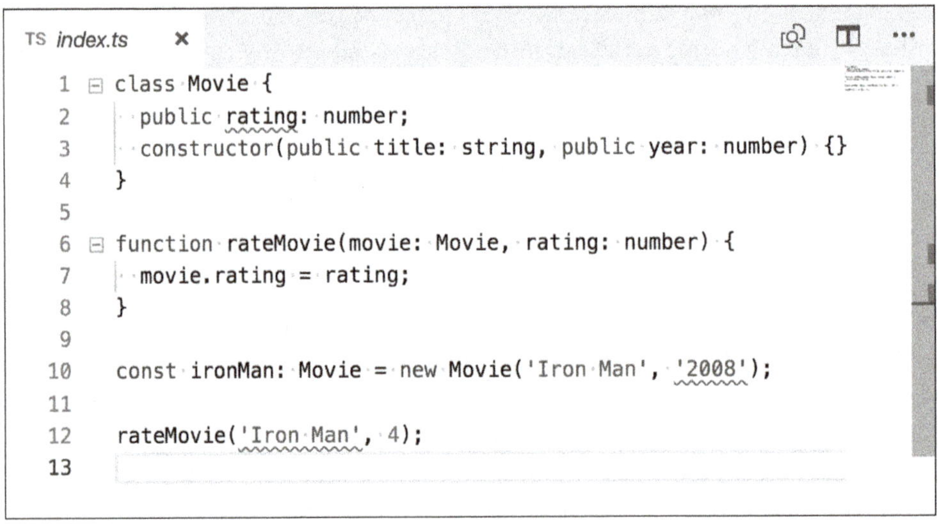

```
TS index.ts      ✕

1  ⊟ class Movie {
2    ··public rating: number;
3    ··constructor(public title: string, public year: number) {}
4    }
5
6  ⊟ function rateMovie(movie: Movie, rating: number) {
7    ··movie.rating = rating;
8    }
9
10   const ironMan: Movie = new Movie('Iron Man', '2008');
11
12   rateMovie('Iron Man', 4);
13
```

Figure 13.1 Error Messages with TypeScript in Visual Studio Code

13.2.3   ESLint

In addition to type checking with TypeScript, there is the ESLint project, which we'll discuss in more detail in Chapter 22, Section 22.2.1. Originally, there was a program for static code analysis of TypeScript source code called TSLint. However, TSLint has since been integrated into ESLint, so as a developer, you only need one tool for JavaScript and TypeScript analysis. ESLint is generally used to increase the quality, readability, and maintainability of an application. You can also install ESLint either globally or locally as devDependency in your project. The `npm install -D eslint` command enables you to install the tool locally. After installation, you use `npx eslint --init` to create the initial configuration file, as shown in Listing 13.11. This command launches an interactive wizard that helps you create a configuration file.

```
$ npx eslint --init
? How would you like to use ESLint? · problems
? What type of modules does your project use? · esm
? Which framework does your project use? · none
? Does your project use TypeScript? · No / Yes
? Where does your code run? · node
? What format do you want your config file to be in? · JSON
The config that you've selected requires the following dependencies:

@typescript-eslint/eslint-plugin@latest @typescript-eslint/parser@latest
? Would you like to install them now with npm? · No / Yes
Installing @typescript-eslint/eslint-plugin@latest, @typescript-eslint/
parser@latest

up to date, audited 149 packages in 1s

27 packages are looking for funding
  run `npm fund` for details

found 0 vulnerabilities
Successfully created .eslintrc.json file in /src/node-buch
```

Listing 13.11 Creating an ESLint Configuration

The configuration file is usually located in the root directory of your application and is named *.eslint.json*. Listing 13.12 shows an example of such a configuration file.

```
{
    "env": {
        "es2021": true,
        "node": true
    },
    "extends": [
```

13

```
        "eslint:recommended",
        "plugin:@typescript-eslint/recommended"
    ],
    "parser": "@typescript-eslint/parser",
    "parserOptions": {
        "ecmaVersion": 12,
        "sourceType": "module"
    },
    "plugins": [
        "@typescript-eslint"
    ],
    "rules": {
    }
}
```

Listing 13.12 ESLint Configuration (.eslint.json)

You can specify different basic rule sets in the configuration. First, you use the env directive to specify that the source code should follow the ECMAScript 2021 standard and run in Node.js. With extends, you define which predefined rule sets are to be used for the check. As a parser, you use @typescript-eslint/parser, and you can further configure it via parserOptions. Finally, you need to load the @typescript-eslint plug-in. The rules directive contains project-specific rules you can define here.

To run ESLint, you use the npx eslint index.ts' command, which checks the specified file, that is, *index.ts*, against the defined rule. You can also use wildcards here, such as src/**/*.ts, to check all TypeScript files in the *src* directory.

ESLint is very well supported by all common development environments and can therefore be embedded seamlessly into the development process.

13.2.4   ts-node

When developing Node.js applications with TypeScript, you must first translate the source code into JavaScript code before you can run it. You can omit the compile step with ts-node. This is a combination of TypeScript compiler and Node.js platform. With ts-node, you start your application as usual, for example, by executing the ts-node index.ts command.

You can install ts-node via npm using the npm install -D ts-node command. The GitHub repository of this project can be found at *https://github.com/TypeStrong/ts-node*.

The same holds true for ts-node and Node.js itself: The source code of your application is read once at startup and then remains in the engine. If you change the source code, the running process won't get notified about it. For the changes to take effect, you must restart the process. To prevent errors from creeping in at this point, the ts-node process can also be automated. However, you'll need additional tools here, such as nodemon, because ts-node doesn't have its own file system watcher. After installing nodemon via the npm install -D nodemon command, you can start your application in watch mode using the command; npx nodemon --watch '**/*.ts' --exec 'ts-node index.ts'. If you then modify a TypeScript file in your application, the application process gets automatically restarted, and the changes will take effect.

Note that nodemon isn't suitable for production use, as file changes will also restart the production application, and it will lose its current state, which is normally held in the memory. Running commands such as nodemon in watch mode are typical examples of npm scripts. For example, you can include this command under the dev key in the scripts section of your *package.json* file and then run it using the npm run dev command, which allows you to avoid specifying all options. Listing 13.13 contains an example of such a *package.json* file.

```
{
  "name": "node-buch",
  "version": "1.0.0",
  "description": "",
  "main": "index.js",
  "private": true,
  "scripts": {
    "dev": "nodemon --watch '**/*.ts' --exec 'ts-node' index.ts"
  },
  "author": "",
  "license": "ISC",
  "devDependencies": {
    "@typescript-eslint/eslint-plugin": "^4.29.1",
    "@typescript-eslint/parser": "^4.29.1",
    "eslint": "^7.32.0",
    "nodemon": "^2.0.12",
    "ts-node": "^10.2.0",
    "typescript": "^4.3.5"
  }
}
```

Listing 13.13 Activating Watch Mode for "ts-node" (package.json)

Note that ts-node currently has problems supporting ECMAScript modules, so you'll need to remove the "type": "module" specification from the *package.json* file. Currently, the developer team of ts-node is working on a solution to this issue, so the workaround will soon become redundant.

Now that you've learned a bit about TypeScript and the development environment, we'll turn our attention to a few commonly used features of TypeScript in the next sections.

13.3   Basic Principles

As you've already seen in the code examples, TypeScript uses a colon to separate a variable and a return value, respectively, from their respective types. In Listing 13.14 you'll define a variable of the string type and assign a value to it.

```
let name: string = 'Sebastian';
```

Listing 13.14 Declaration of a Variable in TypeScript (index.ts)

In this example, specifying the type can also be omitted because TypeScript does *type inference* and tries to guess the types. With a direct value assignment, this works reliably. The name variable has the string type across its entire range of validity. If you assign a number or any other data type different from string to it at a later time, this will result in a compiler error. The second thing to note at this point is that there are two variants of primitive data types. You can use the lowercase string or the uppercase one. The lowercase version stands for the primitive data type, and the uppercase version stands for the wrapper class, so you should use the former in most cases.

13.3.1   Data Types

As mentioned at the beginning of this chapter, TypeScript has a number of standard data types you can use. The following list briefly summarizes them:

- Boolean
  The Boolean type includes the values true and false.

- number
  As in JavaScript, the number type also represents numbers in TypeScript, where no distinction is made between integers and floating point numbers.

- string
  Character strings in TypeScript are of the string type. You can enclose a character string in single or double quotes or use template strings with backticks.

- Array
  In TypeScript, you can assign a type to arrays. Each of the elements of an array must then correspond to this type. When defining the array, you can choose from two notations. With const arr: number[];, you define an array that may only consist of numbers. The alternate notation used by generics is const arr: Array<number>;. *Generics* consists of structures such as classes or functions where the type being used is defined at a later time. As a rule, the former kind of notation is recommended.

- tuple
  A tuple allows you to specify types for certain elements in an array. The array can have more elements than specified. However, the types must then correspond to

one of the previously specified ones. `let tuple: [number, Boolean, string]` creates a `tuple` where the first element is a number, the second a Boolean, and the third a string. Any fourth element must then have one of these three types.

- **enum**
  An `enum` is a collection of values internally mapped to numbers by TypeScript. Listing 13.15 shows an example of how you can use an `enum` in TypeScript.

```
enum status {
  open,
  done,
}

const task = {
  title: 'get up',
  status: Status.done,
};

if (task.status === Status.done) {
  console.log('Erledigt');
}
```

Listing 13.15 Example of the "enum" Type (index.ts)

- **any**
  You can use the data type `any` if you don't know the type of a variable. By marking a variable with the `any` type, you turn off type checking for that variable and can assign any value. In your application, you should use this type as sparingly as possible because you'll lose part of the type safety in TypeScript.

- **unknown**
  As the name suggests, this data type stands for an unknown data type. This can happen, for example, if the data originates from an external system. Before you use the `any` type, you should consider whether `unknown` is the better option. Anything can be assigned to an `unknown` type, but `unknown` can't be assigned to each and every variable such as a string variable, for example, which is exactly how it differs from `any`.

- **void**
  The `void` data type represents the absence of a value. Normally, you use this type with functions that don't have an explicit return value.

- **null, undefined**
  The types `null` and `undefined` represent the two values, respectively.

- **never**
  The `never` data type enables you to indicate functions that have an unreachable endpoint. You can achieve this, for example, by always triggering an exception in the function.

- **object**

  The object data type represents all nonprimitive TypeScript data types, that is, the set of all object types.

- **Union**

  A union data type is used when a variable can have different types. This type is often used in connection with arrays. Listing 13.16 shows some examples of using union types in TypeScript.

```
let age: number | string;

age = 42;   // ok
age = '42'; // ok
age = true; // Error

if (age.isInteger()) {} // Error, isInteger exists only for number

const items: (number | string)[] = [];

items.push(1);       // ok
items.push('Hello'); // ok
items.push(true);    // Error
```

Listing 13.16 "union" Type in TypeScript (index.ts)

These data types are the most important components of TypeScript. Another indispensable feature of the language is the marking of functions with types.

13.3.2   Functions

In TypeScript, you can mark up both classic functions and arrow functions with types. Async functions are also supported. In the parameter list, each parameter is followed by the type specification. You specify the return value after the parameter list, also separated by a colon. Listing 13.17 shows examples of a function, an arrow function, and a method.

```
class User {
  name = '';
  setName(name: string): void {
    this.name = name;
  }
}
const userA = new User();
userA.setName('John');
const userB = new User();
userB.setName('Steve');
```

```
function compare(userA: User, userB: User): Boolean {
  return userA.name === userB.name;
}

const cmp = (userA: User, userB: User): Boolean => {
  return userA.name === userB.name;
};

console.log('compare: ', compare(userA, userB));
console.log('compare: ', cmp(userA, userB));
```

Listing 13.17 Functions in TypeScript (index.ts)

> **Note**
> With arrow functions, you have to set the parentheses around the parameter list even if there is only one parameter.

Compared to JavaScript, TypeScript is less flexible when it comes to the number of parameters passed. If you pass too few parameters to a function, you'll receive an error message. The same result occurs if you pass too many values. This problem can be solved in several ways.

In the first function in Listing 13.18, you see how you can define a default value by assigning a value in the parameters list. In this respect, TypeScript behaves like JavaScript: If you don't pass the value, the default value is used. If you call the function with two values, the default value of the second parameter is ignored.

The second function named optionalParameters shows a question mark at the second parameter. This signals that the parameter is optional. You can call this function with either one or two values. If you omit the second parameter, it will be assigned the value undefined, as in JavaScript.

In the third function, you see how you can implement a variable number of parameters via rest parameters. The second and all other parameters are contained in an array. In this example, this array has the number type. Here, you can also work with all other data types such as string, union, or tuple.

```
function defaultParameters(a: number, b = 4): number {
  return a + b;
}

console.log(defaultParameters(2));
```

```
function optionalParameters(a: number, b?: number): number {
  return b !== undefined ? a + b : a;
}

console.log(optionalParameters(2));

function restParameters(a: number, ...more: number[]) {
  return more.reduce((prev, curr) => prev + curr, a);
}

console.log(restParameters(1, 2, 3));
```

Listing 13.18 Handling Too Many or Too Few Parameters

13.3.3   Modules

Node.js is currently in a state of transition between the CommonJS and ECMAScript module systems. If you use TypeScript in your application, you can already use the ECMAScript module system without further restrictions, such as experimental warnings. TypeScript either translates the module syntax to CommonJS modules or leaves the syntax in ECMAScript notation, depending on the configuration. Listing 13.19 contains an example of two TypeScript files. A function is exported in the *module.ts* file, which you include and run in the *index.ts* file.

```
// module.ts
export const add = (a: number, b: number): number => a + b;

// index.ts
import { add } from './module';

console.log(add(1, 2));
```

Listing 13.19 TypeScript Modules

Using a minimal *tsconfig.json* file like the one in Listing 13.20, you can convert these two files into valid JavaScript files that you can run in Node.js.

```
{
  "compilerOptions": {
    "target": "ES2021",
    "module": "ES2020"
  }
}
```

Listing 13.20 "tsconfig.json" File for Generating ECMAScript Modules

The target specification of ES2021 allows you to generate relatively small boilerplate code. "module": "ES2020" makes sure that the import and export statements are preserved. If you run the tsc command in the directory containing the *tsconfig.json* file, both files will be compiled. The file extension of both output files will then be *.js*. For the execution to work under Node.js, you currently need to add the type field with the module value in your *package.json* file.

Listing 13.21 shows the contents of the two files TypeScript created for you.

```
// module.js
export const add = (a, b) => a + b;
```

```
// index.js
import { add } from './module';
console.log(add(1, 2));
```

Listing 13.21 Compiled TypeScript Modules

As you can see, the TypeScript compiler has adopted the source code with almost no changes, removing only the type information.

13.4   Classes

In addition to the types included in TypeScript, you can also define your own types. Normally, this is done via classes because every class in TypeScript is also a new type that you can use for type markup. TypeScript classes follow the same syntax as JavaScript. Listing 13.22 shows the basic framework of a class and how to use it.

```
class Movie {
  rating = 0;

  constructor(
    public id: number,
    public title: string,
    public year: number) {}
}

function rate(movie: Movie, rating: number): void {
  movie.rating = rating;
}

const ironMan = new Movie(1, 'Iron Man', 2008);

rate(ironMan, 4);
```

```
console.log(ironMan);
// Output: Movie { id: 1, title: 'Iron Man', year: 2008, rating: 4 }
```

Listing 13.22 Classes in TypeScript

The class represents two special features of TypeScript. You can set access modifiers on properties and methods of a class. The rating property is defined with an initial value of 0, which implicitly corresponds to the number type. Without the existence of an explicit access modifier, public is assumed.

In the constructor, you can see a very helpful shortcut notation. Often, when objects are created, values are passed to the constructor, which are then written directly to an object's properties. If you specify the access modifier in the parameter list of the constructor in addition to the name and type of a parameter, this property is set in the object with the specified access modifier, and the passed value is assigned. In this case, you save the listing of the properties of the class as well as the explicit assignment of the values. With this notation, however, you should take care that the parameters list of your constructor doesn't become too long.

The rate function shows how you can use the newly generated class as a type specification. You can use the class types in all places where the standard types of TypeScript are also allowed.

13.4.1 Methods

Of course, it makes much more sense to implement the rate function as part of the movie class. For methods in TypeScript, the same rules apply as for functions when it comes to type specifications. You can add types to the parameters list and specify a return value, as shown in Listing 13.23.

```
class Movie {
  rating = 0;

  constructor(
    public id: number,
    public title: string,
    public year: number) {}

  rate(rating: number): void {
    this.rating = rating;
  }
}

const ironMan = new Movie(1, 'Iron Man', 2008);
```

```
ironMan.rate(4);

console.log(ironMan);
// Output: Movie { id: 1, title: 'Iron Man', year: 2008, rating: 4 }
```

Listing 13.23 Methods in TypeScript Classes

The following is true also for methods: If you don't specify an access modifier, public is assumed.

13.4.2   Access Modifiers

TypeScript has access modifiers that allow you to restrict the visibility of properties and methods. In total, TypeScript has three different modifiers:

- **public**
  As the most general access modifier, property or method marked as public is always visible on this object and can also be used from outside the object. If you don't specify an access modifier, public is used by default.

- **protected**
  Properties and methods marked with protected can be used within the class as well as in derived classes.

- **private**
  The last access modifier and also the most restrictive one is private. You can use these properties and methods only within the current classes.

13.4.3   Inheritance

Similar to the classes in JavaScript, TypeScript supports inheritance in classes with the extends keyword. Inheritance becomes relevant when you specify the type. For example, if you allow the movie type as a parameter in a function, you can also use the HorrorMovie type derived from movie, as shown in Listing 13.24.

```
class Movie {
  constructor(
    public id: number,
    public title: string,
    public year: number
  ) {}
}

class HorrorMovie extends Movie {
  type = 'Horror';
}
```

```
function show(movie: Movie) {
  console.log('Now showing: ', movie.title);
}

const shining = new HorrorMovie(1, 'The Shining', 1980);

show(shining); // Output: Now showing: The Shining
```

Listing 13.24 Inheritance in TypeScript

As you can see, TypeScript classes behave mostly like JavaScript classes with a few exceptions, such as the constructor shortcut or the access modifiers for properties and methods.

If you need the structure of a class, but you don't use logic or an instance of this structure, you can use interfaces, as discussed next.

13.5   Interfaces

TypeScript interfaces are structures that don't have method implementations and can't be instantiated. However, like classes, they represent separate types you can use for variables and function signatures. Listing 13.25 shows an example of using such an interface.

```
class Movie {
  constructor(
    public id: number,
    public title: string,
    public year: number
  ) {}
}

interface WithTitle {
  title: string;
}

function show(movie: WithTitle) {
  console.log('Now showing: ', movie.title);
}

const infinityWar = new Movie(3, 'Avengers: Infinity War', 2018);

show(infinityWar); // Output: Now showing: Avengers: Infinity War
```

Listing 13.25 Inline Interfaces with TypeScript

As you can see here, you can use the interface at any point where you can use any of the other regular types. The duck typing mechanism of TypeScript then makes sure that type checking works correctly even if the passed object isn't directly connected to the interface. The source code in Listing 13.26 shows how you can define an interface, how to use it to specify types, and how to have a class implement an interface.

```typescript
interface Movie {
  id: number;
  title: string;
  year: number;
  rating: number;
  rate(rating: number): void;
}

class ActionMovie implements Movie {
  public rating = 0;
  constructor(
    public id: number,
    public title: string,
    public year: number
  ) {}

  rate(rating: number) {
    this.rating = rating;
  }
}

function show(movie: Movie) {
  console.log('Now showing: ', movie.title);
}

const infinityWar = new ActionMovie(3, 'Avengers: Infinity War', 2018);
show(infinityWar); // Output: Now showing:  Avengers: Infinity War
```

Listing 13.26 Using Interfaces in TypeScript

You use the interface keyword to initiate the definition of the interface. This is followed by the name, which by convention should be written in UpperCamelCase. In the interface, you can define not only properties but also methods, as you can see in the example of the rate method.

When you define the ActionMovie class, you use the implements keyword to specify that this class implements the interface. TypeScript throws an error if not all properties and methods are implemented. You can append a question mark to a property to signify that this property is optional and doesn't need to be implemented.

In the function signature of the show function, you can then insert the interface as a regular type and secure the call of the function accordingly.

13.6   Type Aliases in TypeScript

In addition to interfaces, TypeScript also allows you to define type aliases by using the type keyword. Type aliases are used in a similar way as interfaces, but are somewhat simpler in structure. Listing 13.27 shows that you can implement the example with interfaces in a similar way with type aliases. The biggest difference is that a class can't implement a type alias.

```
type Movie = {
  id: number;
  title: string;
  year: number;
  rating: number;
  rate(rating: number): void;
};

class ActionMovie {
  public rating = 0;
  constructor(public id: number, public title: string, public year: number) {}

  rate(rating: number) {
    this.rating = rating;
  }
}

function show(movie: Movie) {
  console.log('Now showing: ', movie.title);
}

const infinityWar = new ActionMovie(3, 'Avengers: Infinity War', 2018);
show(infinityWar); // Output: Now showing:  Avengers: Infinity War
```

Listing 13.27 Using Type Aliases

Another important difference between interfaces and type aliases is that with interfaces, *declaration merging* is applied. If you define an interface with the same name more than once, the properties get merged.

In general, you can use the simpler type aliases wherever you can do so without declaration merging, such as implements and extends.

13.7 Generics

Like interfaces, generics represent a language feature of TypeScript that has no equivalent in JavaScript. Generics allow you to provide functions and classes with a placeholder type and assign a concrete type to it at a later time. Generics are often used in the context of collections, that is, collections of objects of the same type. In this case, the basic structure of the collection with its methods is initially independent of a concrete type. However, if you use the collection in your application, it must hold concrete types. You then define the type and get TypeScript support.

In Listing 13.28, you use class Collection<T> to specify that this should be a generic class. Within the class definition, you use the T variable whenever the generic type is to be used, that is, in properties, in parameter lists, and as a return value.

```
class Movie {
  constructor(
    public id: number,
    public title: string,
    public year: number) {}
}

class Collection<T> {
  private items: T[] = [];

  public add(item: T): void {
    this.items.push(item);
  }

  public getAll(): T[] {
    return this.items;
  }
}

const myMovies = new Collection<Movie>();

myMovies.add(new Movie(1, 'Iron Man', 2008));
console.log(myMovies.getAll());
// Output: [ Movie { id: 1, title: 'Iron Man', year: 2008 } ]
```

Listing 13.28 Generics in TypeScript

When instantiating the collection, you substantiate the generic type by passing the movie class. If you use the collection instance, TypeScript can make sure that the movie type is now required in all places where the generic type was set.

With this selection of TypeScript features, you're already in a position to develop a Node.js application with TypeScript support. In the following sections, you'll see a concrete example of an Express application. You'll also learn what you have to keep in mind when dealing with third-party libraries.

13.8   TypeScript in Use in a Node.js Application

If you use TypeScript in your application, you should install the *type definitions* for Node.js. These type definitions ensure that the core Node.js modules are type-defined so that you get better support from your development environment, and the TypeScript compiler doesn't throw unnecessary error messages that result from using the platform. The type definitions are available as an npm package and can be installed using the `npm install -D @types/node` command. They are installed as `devDependency` for normal applications because they aren't required for production operation. However, if you develop a library that can be used in other applications, you should always install such type definitions as a dependency so that consumers of your library don't need to install them manually.

13.8.1   Type Definitions

Type definitions exist not only for Node.js itself, but for numerous other libraries and frameworks originally written in JavaScript. The DefinitelyTyped project at *http://definitelytyped.org/* serves as the source for the type definitions. Generally, type definitions are located below the `@types` namespace. If you install such a type definition, the TypeScript compiler finds it automatically, so you don't need to make any further configuration.

If you work on an Express application, you should install the type definitions using the `npm install -D @types/express` command. However, you should use caution when using type definitions. Make sure that the version of the type definition matches the version of the library you're using. Otherwise, the API may have changed, and TypeScript may be issuing warnings in the wrong places.

13.8.2   Creating Custom Type Definitions

If you're gradually transitioning your application to TypeScript or including existing library files in a TypeScript project, you can also create your own type definitions. These are stored in files with the extension *.d.ts*. Suppose your library file is named *module.js* and contains the source code from Listing 13.29.

```
module.exports = {
  add(a, b) {
    return a + b;
```

```
  },
};
```

Listing 13.29 JavaScript Module (module.js)

With the appropriate type definition from Listing 13.30, you can include the functionality in your TypeScript application. You save the source code in a file named *module.d.ts*.

```
declare function add(a: number, b: number): number;
export { add };
```

Listing 13.30 Type Definition for the JavaScript Module (module.d.ts)

With these two files, you can now include the module in your application and access the type support of the compiler (see Listing 13.31).

```
import { add } from './module';

console.log(add(1, 2)); // Output: 3
```

Listing 13.31 Integrating the JavaScript Module in TypeScript (index.ts)

13.8.3 Sample Express Application

All the features presented to you in this chapter also apply in regular Node.js applications with the established libraries and frameworks, as you can see in the following example with Express. To do this, you first initialize your project with `npm init -y` and then install Express, the associated type definitions, and `ts-node` via the `npm install express` and `npm install -D @types/express ts-node` commands. Then, you can implement the entry file of your application. Listing 13.32 shows a very simple variant of it.

```
import express, { Request, Response } from 'express';

const app = express();

app.get('/', (req: Request, res: Response): void => {
  res.send('Hello Client');
});

app.listen(8080, (): void =>
  console.log('Server is listening to http://localhost:8080'),
);
```

Listing 13.32 Express Server in TypeScript

You can then run this code example using the `npx ts-node index.ts` command. With the type definitions for Express installed, you can use reliable autocompletion in your development environment. In addition, the TypeScript compiler alerts you in case of errors. For example, if you forget the path in the routing function and only specify the callback function, the compiler throws an error.

The type definition allows you to correctly mark up the parameters list of the routing callback function with the types in your source code. This way, your code is additionally documented and easier to understand even at first glance.

13.9   Summary

In this chapter, you've learned about TypeScript and Flow, as well as how you can use both with Node.js. It's not without reason that TypeScript is becoming increasingly prevalent in the Node.js environment. Using TypeScript provides some key benefits for developers. For example, your development environment is able to give you more precise help in the form of auto-completion. It also alerts you to errors early on, namely, at a point when you're writing the error, rather than when it's executed in your Node.js application.

But TypeScript has some disadvantages too, of course. For the development process, using this language involves additional work because the types must be distinguished in the code. More work is also required when designing individual parts of an application, as you have to think more about the types you want to use. However, this extra effort doesn't hurt too much in most cases because you'll have to make these considerations sooner or later anyway.

Besides all these aspects, TypeScript not only extends the language core with types you can use for variables and functions but also adds more features such as generics, interfaces, and access modifiers for classes.

In any case, it's worth taking a look at TypeScript.

Chapter 14
Web Applications with Nest

Put it before them briefly so they will read it, clearly so they will
appreciate it, picturesquely so they will remember it.
—Joseph Pulitzer

Web application frameworks for Node.js such as Express are a dime a dozen, and yet Express is by far the most popular solution. However, Express also has a number of weaknesses that repeatedly lead to competitors gaining a foothold in the market. One of the biggest problems is the speed of development of Express. As you learned in Chapter 6, the current fourth version of the framework has been on the market for quite a few years now, which isn't necessarily good for one of the most widely used JavaScript frameworks because it means that major innovations and modernizations are missing.

This is exactly where a still young Node.js framework called Nest comes in. Nest aims to support the development of server-side JavaScript applications to implement efficient and scalable solutions. Nest is based on TypeScript, which applies to both the framework itself and the code of your app. In addition, Nest brings architecture into your app. With Express, the middleware system and routing functions provide you with the basic tools even for large-scale applications. However, the framework doesn't specify the structure and architecture of an application. Nest, on the other hand, adopts these concepts and provides you with software development frameworks to help you build an application. This way, you know exactly that your endpoints are in controller classes, business logic is swapped out to services, and database access is also encapsulated in services.

Another aspect of Nest is that the framework keeps the barrier to testing as low as possible. Most of the structures you need for testing are already prepared, so the only thing you need to worry about is implementing the actual test logic.

Basically, the philosophy of Nest is that you should focus on the business logic, which is what your application is all about. The framework takes care of everything else. That is why Nest has an extensive command-line tool, numerous optional modules, and comprehensive documentation.

In this chapter, you'll get to know some of the details of Nest and now implement the MovieDB application you already implemented in Express with Nest so you can compare the two solutions.

14.1 Installation and Getting Started with Nest

Like many other major JavaScript frameworks, Nest provides you with a command-line interface (CLI) that makes it much easier to get started with development. The concept of the *Nest CLI* is that it should make redundant all the repetitive tasks in your project. This includes first the project setup and then the handling of different structures in the course of the project, but you'll learn more about this in Section 14.2.

Nest consists of several packages in the @nestjs namespace. The CLI package is named @nestjs/cli and is installed system-wide via the npm install -g @nestjs/cli command. After the installation, the nest command is available on the command line, and you can start initializing your application. To do this, you must use the new command of the CLI followed by the project name, as shown in Listing 14.1. The command creates a new project named movie-db.

```
$ nest new movie-db
⚡  We will scaffold your app in a few seconds..

CREATE movie-db/.eslintrc.js (631 bytes)
CREATE movie-db/.prettierrc (51 bytes)
CREATE movie-db/README.md (3339 bytes)
CREATE movie-db/nest-cli.json (64 bytes)
CREATE movie-db/package.json (1964 bytes)
CREATE movie-db/tsconfig.build.json (97 bytes)
CREATE movie-db/tsconfig.json (546 bytes)
CREATE movie-db/src/app.controller.spec.ts (617 bytes)
CREATE movie-db/src/app.controller.ts (274 bytes)
CREATE movie-db/src/app.module.ts (249 bytes)
CREATE movie-db/src/app.service.ts (142 bytes)
CREATE movie-db/src/main.ts (208 bytes)
CREATE movie-db/test/app.e2e-spec.ts (630 bytes)
CREATE movie-db/test/jest-e2e.json (183 bytes)

? Which package manager would you ? to use? (Use arrow keys)
❯ npm
  yarn
  pnpm
```

Listing 14.1 Initializing a Nest Project

During the initialization process, you'll be asked which package manager you want to use for your application. The choices here are Node Package Manager (npm), Yarn, and pnpm. Note, however, that the package manager must already be installed on your system; otherwise, the initialization of your application will fail because the required dependencies can't be installed.

The initialization process creates a new directory named *movie-db* in the current directory as well as an initial file and directory hierarchy, and it installs all packages required to build and run the application.

After the installation, you can change to the directory and start the application via the npm start command. On the console, you'll receive a number of log outputs, as you can see in Listing 14.2.

```
npm start

> movie-db@0.0.1 start
> nest start

[Nest] 49481  - 08/09/2021, 05:44:17     LOG [NestFactory] ⤶
  Starting Nest application...
[Nest] 49481  - 08/09/2021, 05:44:17     LOG [InstanceLoader] ⤶
  AppModule dependencies initialized +67ms
[Nest] 49481  - 08/09/2021, 05:44:17     LOG [RoutesResolver] ⤶
  AppController {/}: +44ms
[Nest] 49481  - 08/09/2021, 05:44:17     LOG [RouterExplorer] ⤶
  Mapped {/, GET} route +6ms
[Nest] 49481  - 08/09/2021, 05:44:17     LOG [NestApplication] ⤶
  Nest application successfully started +10ms
```

Listing 14.2 Nest Application Startup Process

In the console output, Nest informs you about the individual steps in the startup process. The most important information here is that the app module dependencies have been initialized, the app controller has been executed, and the GET route / has been mapped. Finally, Nest reports that the application has been successfully launched. This output tells you that your application currently has a route. If you extend your application, then this is a place to start troubleshooting in the event of an error.

The npm start command binds the Nest process to port 3000 so that you can invoke your application in the browser at *http://localhost:3000* and get a view like the one shown in Figure 14.1.

Figure 14.1 Nest Application Homepage

Customizing the Port

Port 3000 on your system may already be being used by another application. In such a case, you can change the port by opening the *main.ts* file in the *src* directory of your application and searching for the app.listen(3000) call. The listen method of the app object binds your application to the specified port. If you change this, your problem should be solved.

Before we get into extending the application, let's briefly discuss the other features of the Nest CLI in the next step.

14.2   Nest Command-Line Interface

Nest follows the concept of Express at its core, providing routing and a middleware system, but it extends these principles with numerous other features and patterns. In the documentation, the developers of the framework state that they were inspired by Angular, which is a frontend framework. If you already have experience developing Angular applications, many patterns in Nest app development will look familiar to you. One of the concepts the developers have adopted from Nest is also the Nest CLI, which is based on the Angular CLI and provides you with a tool for developing your application.

With nest new, you already got to know the first command of the Nest CLI that enables you to initialize your application. But the CLI provides a number of other features on top of that.

With the --help or -h option, you get an overview of the available options on the command line. The --version option and its short form -v show the currently used version number of the Nest CLI. A nest CLI command usually consists of several parts: nest <command> <options> <arguments>.

Details about a particular command can be obtained by calling the command followed by the --help option, for example, nest new --help.

14.2.1   Commands for Operating and Running the Application

Unlike a classic Express app, which is written in JavaScript and can be run directly, Nest has a build process. The reason is that a Nest application is usually written in TypeScript and therefore the source code must first be compiled into JavaScript. You can start your application using the nest start command. This process creates a local directory named *dist* that contains the built source code of the application. This is then executed as a Node.js process. The start command supports different variants stored as scripts in the *package.json* file. For example, npm run start:dev runs the nest start command with the --watch option, putting Nest into a watch mode where the process is automatically restarted when changes are made to files in the application. The start:debug script adds the --debug option in addition to --watch to debug the application with the Node.js debugger.

> **Note**
>
> You can also decouple building the application from launching it by running nest build or npm run build. This will create a newly built version of your application in the *dist* directory. You can then run your application using the *main.js* file in the *dist* directory, or you can use the npm run start:prod command.

The info command allows you to display a range of information about your current environment. This includes the version numbers of the operating system and Node.js or npm. You'll also see which Nest CLI version is currently in use and, if you run the command in a directory containing a Nest application, the versions of the various Nest packages.

In addition to these commands, there are two more commands for managing your application—update and add. The update command updates the Nest dependencies, and the add command lets you add additional libraries to your application. Table 14.1 contains an overview of the available commands.

Command	Short Form	Description
nest new [options] [name]	n	Creates a new Nest application
nest build [options] [app]	—	Builds the Nest application
nest start [options] [app]	—	Runs the Nest application
nest info	i	Outputs version information
nest update [options]	u	Updates the Nest dependencies
nest add [options] [library]	—	Adds a new library to the application
nest generate [options] [schematic] [name] [path]	g	Creates a new Nest element, that is, a structure such as a module, a controller, or a provider

Table 14.1 Overview of Nest CLI Commands

We haven't yet looked at the command you may need most often during the development of your application, namely, the generate command, which is used to generate structures. The next section describes how this tool can support you.

14.2.2   Creating Structures in the Application

No matter if it's about modules, controllers, or services, the basic structure is always the same per category. Especially for larger applications, you may need to create a lot of these structures. This is exactly where the generate command comes in and generates these structures for you. This process includes the creation of files and directories as well as the generation of the corresponding TypeScript framework. Table 14.2 contains an overview of the capabilities of the generate command. We'll look at some of the listed commands in more detail later as we implement the sample application.

Name	Short Form	Description
application	—	Creates a new application workspace
class	cl	Creates a new TypeScript class
configuration	config	Creates a new CLI configuration
controller	co	Creates a new controller
decorator	d	Creates the basic framework for a custom decorator
filter	f	Creates a filter
gateway	ga	Creates a new gateway
guard	gu	Creates the structure for a new guard
interceptor	in	Creates an interceptor
interface	—	Generates a new TypeScript interface
middleware	mi	Creates a middleware component
module	mo	Creates a new module
pipe	pi	Creates a pipe
provider	pr	Creates a provider
resolver	r	Creates a resolver
service	s	Creates a service
library	lib	Generates a new library in the monorepo
sub-app	app	Creates a new application in the monorepo
resource	res	Creates a new create, read, update, delete (CRUD) resource

Table 14.2 Schematics for the "nest generate" Command

As you can see from schematics, such as library or sub-app, in addition to the standard mode, Nest also supports a monorepo mode where you can divide your application into several smaller applications and manage them within a larger monorepo. In the following sections, you'll get to know the basics of Nest using the standard mode. Once you're familiar with these basics, you can start implementing even large-scale applications with Nest. For more information on how to organize your application into a monorepo, you should refer to the Nest documentation at *https://docs.nestjs.com/cli/monorepo*.

Monorepo

A *monorepo* is a source code repository that doesn't contain just one project, such as a frontend or a backend, which is usually the case, but it has several projects. The concept behind monorepos is that the source code of a project, which consists of several largely independent components, is managed in a single repository. The term "project" is deliberately kept very vague in this case. It can be an application but also the entire source code of a company. For example, a very well-known company that uses the monorepo approach is Google.

A great advantage of monorepos is that all the components that belong to the project are managed together. If you check out the repository, you'll always have a consistent state of the entire system. This eliminates the need for manual synchronization across multiple repositories. On the other hand, managing a large monorepo can also cause increased overhead and that's just due to the sheer size of the repository.

14.3   Structure of the Application

The nest new command creates a fully functional application with a base structure on which you can build your own implementation. To help you find your way around here, let's first take a look at the directories and files the Nest CLI has created for you.

14.3.1   Root Directory with the Configuration Files

In many JavaScript environments, it has become best practice to store mainly the central configuration files in the root directory of an application and to arrange the actual source code in a hierarchy below, so there are a number of files in your Nest application here as well. The description of these files is shown in Table 14.3.

File Name	Description
.eslintrc	This file contains the configuration for ESLint. Nest uses a number of standard plug-ins and customizes some of the rules they contain. For more information on ESLint, see Chapter 22.
.gitignore	Nest defines a *.gitignore* file for you that exempts some files and directories from version control. These are mainly metafiles for editors, log files, or build artifacts.

Table 14.3 Files in the Base Directory of the Application

File Name	Description
.perttierrc	Prettier is a code formatter that automatically formats your source code according to certain rules. This file contains some rules for this tool.
nest-cli.json	This file contains metadata that Nest needs to organize, build, and deploy your application.
package-lock.json	If you use npm as a package manager, the exact version numbers of the installed packages are recorded here. For more information on this topic, refer to Chapter 21.
package.json	The *package.json* file is the central configuration file of your application. For example, it contains a set of preconfigured scripts you can use to run, build, or test your application.
README.md	The readme file contains a description of your application. In most cases, important information for the developers is stored here, such as how you can start the application or which special features you need to pay attention to.
tsconfig.build.json	This file contains the TypeScript configuration for the build of the application and extends the basic version of *tsconfig.json*.
tsconfig.json	The *tsconfig.json* file contains information for the TypeScript compiler and specifies how it should convert the application's TypeScript source code into JavaScript.

Table 14.3 Files in the Base Directory of the Application (Cont.)

14.3.2   src Directory: Core of the Application

When working with Nest, you spend most of your time in the *src* directory because it contains the source code of your application. The entry point to the application is the *main.ts* file. This file makes sure that the Nest application gets created, registers the base module, and binds the application to port 3000. From here, you move through a tree of interdependent modules, starting with the app module.

The Nest CLI initially creates a module, a controller, and a service for you. The following sections describe these structures and their significance in greater detail. At this point, the only important thing for you to know is that these are the most important structures of an application and that you can already implement a simple application with them.

14.3.3   Other Directories of the Application

In addition to these directories and files, your application contains two more directories. The *node_modules* directory contains the installed dependencies, while the *dist* directory contains the built version of your application. Both directories aren't subject to version control and are created after your initial loading of the source code from the repository.

You can create the *node_modules* directory by running the npm install command on the command line. The package manager then downloads all dependencies and stores them in this directory.

The *dist* directory creates Nest as soon as you run nest start or nest build. This directory contains the built version of your application, that is, the JavaScript source code generated by the TypeScript compiler. You can run the JavaScript source code directly with Node.js.

Based on all this information, you can now start developing your application.

14.4   Modules: Logical Units in the Source Code

The largest unit in a Nest application is the module. You can think of a module as a kind of container that contains various other structures such as controllers or services. An application consists of at least one module—the app module—but it can consist of any number of modules. Modules are usually designed thematically. In our case, the MovieDB application consists of three self-implemented modules: the central app module; the movie module, which deals with all matters related to a movie; and the auth module, which ensures that users can log in to the application and is responsible for securing the application's endpoints.

Figure 14.2 illustrates the modular structure of a Nest application. In this figure, you can also see that you can nest the hierarchy of modules as deeply as you like. Each module integrates a number of structures, such as controllers or services, and can make these available to other modules via exports. Thus, one module can integrate another one and use its functionality. On the one hand, you can use this principle to divide your application into different logical units, and on the other hand, modules are often used in the implementation of libraries to encapsulate their functionality.

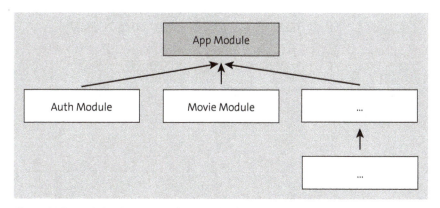

Figure 14.2 Modular Structure of a Nest Application

14.4.1   Creating Modules

The first module after the already pregenerated app module is the movie module, which you create on the command line via the nest generate module movie command. Each Nest command also provides you with an output that briefly explains what the command has done. In the case of module generation, you'll get an output like the one shown in Listing 14.3.

```
$ nest generate module movie
CREATE src/movie/movie.module.ts (82 bytes)
UPDATE src/app.module.ts (312 bytes)
```

Listing 14.3 Output after Creating a Module

Nest creates the *movie* directory in the *src* directory for the new module and generates the *movie.module.ts* file there. As a convention for naming files, Nest recommends that in addition to the name of the structure, the type, in this case *module*, is also included in the file name. In addition to the creation of the module, it's also automatically registered in the central app module, hence the second line with the UPDATE information. Listing 14.4 shows the source code of the app module.

```
import { Module } from '@nestjs/common';
import { AppController } from './app.controller';
import { AppService } from './app.service';
import { MovieModule } from './movie/movie.module';

@Module({
  imports: [MovieModule],
  controllers: [AppController],
  providers: [AppService],
})
export class AppModule {}
```

Listing 14.4 Import of the Movie Module in the App Module (src/app.module.ts)

Listing 14.5 contains the slightly modified source code of the movie module.

```
import { Module } from '@nestjs/common';

@Module({
  imports: [],
  controllers: [],
  providers: [],
  exports: [],
})
export class MovieModule {}
```

Listing 14.5 Source Code of the Movie Module (src/movie/movie.module.ts)

14.4.2   Module Decorator

A module usually consists of an empty TypeScript class that is exported and the `module` decorator that binds additional information to the class. This means there are four different pieces of information:

- `imports`
  Here you can specify references to other modules whose features are then available in the current module.

- `controllers`
  At this point, you reference the controllers of the module. This step activates the endpoints the controller defines.

- `providers`
  In the `providers` array, you add the providers, such as, for example, services of the module. This information is important for Nest's dependency injection to load the required structures. You can find more information about providers and dependency injection in Section 14.6.

- `exports`
  Under `exports`, you specify the structures to be made available to a module when it embeds your module.

Decorators

When using Nest, you'll come across the *decorators* early on. This is a TypeScript feature that allows you to bind additional features to specific structures via an annotation. In the case of a module, for example, you can register the controllers.

However, decorators are available not only for classes, but also for functions and variables. In the course of this chapter, you'll see more uses for decorators. At its core, a decorator is simply a function that is run for a structure, a class in this case. For more information about decorators and how to create them, go to *www.typescriptlang.org/docs/handbook/decorators.html*.

The decorators feature also exists as a proposal for the ECMAScript standard, but has been in the process for quite some time at level 2 of a total of 4, which means that integration into the JavaScript language core will still take some time. Until then, if you want to use decorators, you'll have to resort to tools such as TypeScript.

The newly created module is entered by Nest into the `imports` of the app module, and thus a connection between the two modules is established. With this, you can move on to creating a new controller in the next step.

14.5   Controllers: Endpoints of an Application

At its core, Nest is based on Express and uses the routing and middleware features of the framework. However, when it comes to defining the routes, both frameworks differ significantly. Whereas in Express, you define routes either on your app object or separately via a router, in Nest, you work with a controller and with additional decorators to create new routes. But before we get to defining routes, you must first create and register the controller.

14.5.1   Creating a Controller

Although you can create your controllers by hand, it's much more convenient to do it via the Nest CLI. When you switch to the command line and enter the nest generate controller movie command, you'll get an output like the one shown in Listing 14.6.

```
$ nest generate controller movie
CREATE src/movie/movie.controller.spec.ts (485 bytes)
CREATE src/movie/movie.controller.ts (99 bytes)
UPDATE src/movie/movie.module.ts (170 bytes)
```

Listing 14.6 Output When Creating a Controller

As you can see from the output on the console, the Nest CLI creates two new files for you in the *src/movie* directory. The *movie.controller.ts* file contains the source code of the controller, while the *movie.controller.spec.ts* contains the associated test code. In addition, the controller is registered in the controllers section of the movie module and thus activated.

14.5.2   Implementing a Controller

The task of a controller is to define endpoints, that is, routes, to receive incoming requests and to generate appropriate responses. In this context, Nest again frequently uses decorators, as you can see in Listing 14.7.

```
import {
  Body,
  Controller,
  Delete,
  Get,
  HttpCode,
  Param,
  Post,
  Put,
} from '@nestjs/common';

@Controller('movie')
export class MovieController {
  private data = [
    { id: 1, title: 'Iron Man', year: 2008 },
    { id: 2, title: 'Thor', year: 2011 },
```

```
    { id: 3, title: 'Captain America', year: 2011 },
  ];

  @Get()
  getAllMovies() {
    return this.data;
  }

  @Get(':id')
  getOneMovie(@Param('id') id: string) {
    return this.data.find((movie) => movie.id === parseInt(id, 10));
  }

  @Post()
  createNewMovie(@Body() movie) {
    const nextId = Math.max(...this.data.map((movie) => movie.id)) + 1;
    movie.id = nextId;
    this.data.push(movie);
    return movie;
  }

  @Put(':id')
  udpateMovie(@Param('id') id: string, @Body() movie) {
    const index = this.data.findIndex((movie) => movie.id === parseInt(id, 10));
    this.data[index] = movie;
    return movie;
  }

  @Delete(':id')
  @HttpCode(204)
  removeMovie(@Param('id') id: string) {
    this.data = this.data.filter((movie) => movie.id !== parseInt(id, 10));
  }
}
```

Listing 14.7 Implementation of the Movie Controller (src/movie/movie.controller.ts)

The controller in our example is doing something it shouldn't be doing: It takes care of the complete route, from incoming request to data management. But we're going to look at that in the next section. First, let's take a look at the controller.

Like the module, the controller consists of a decorator and a class. The decorator is named controller and originates from the @nestjs/common package. You can pass a prefix to it. In our case, this is the movie string. This string is placed before all endpoints of this controller in the URL path. Thus, the base URL of the controller is *http://localhost:3000/movie*. Within the class, you first define the private data property that is responsible for data storage. This is a temporary construct we'll resolve in the following sections. After that, the methods of the controller will follow. The decorators Get, Post, Put, and Delete represent the respective HTTP methods, each of which accepts an optional path. In the case of the getOneMovie, updateMovie, and removeMovie methods, the path consists of the id variable. This path behaves similar to what we've seen in Express. For example, you can use a GET request to *http://localhost:3000/movie/1* to read the data record with ID 1.

The variables in the URL path can be accessed via the method parameter list and the param decorator. If you specify only the param decorator without additional arguments, you get access to all variables. If you specify the name of the variable, as in the example here, you'll only get the respective value. If you also need to access the request body, as with the createNewMovie or the updateMovie method, you can do this using the body decorator. In this case, the information is available in the form of the movie parameter within the method.

You don't need to generate the response to the client manually via a function call as in Express, but can simply return the desired value. Nest automatically sets the status code to the value 200 except for the createNewMovie method. The post decorator makes sure that the response is assigned a 201 status code. You can affect this behavior via the HttpCode decorator, as is the case with the removeMovie method, for example. If a client requests this route, it will receive a response with status code 204 if successful. In addition to the status code, Nest also sets the content type header to the value application/json and converts the passed object structure into a correctly formatted JavaScript Object Notation (JSON) structure.

14.5.3   Integrating and Checking the Controller

The generate command of the Nest CLI registers the controller in the module—which in this case is the movie module—and enters the reference to the controller in the controllers property of the module decorator for this purpose (see Listing 14.8).

```
import { Module } from '@nestjs/common';
import { MovieController } from './movie.controller';

@Module({
  imports: [],
  controllers: [MovieController],
  providers: [],
  exports: [],
})
export class MovieModule {}
```

Listing 14.8 Integration of the Controller in the Module (src/movie/movie.controller.ts)

When you launch your application, the output changes slightly. Listing 14.9 shows that the `MovieController` and all corresponding routes have been activated. This output helps you to check whether the controller has been registered correctly.

```
[Nest] 69838  - 09/09/2021, 05:48:39     LOG [NestFactory] ⮌
  Starting Nest application...
[Nest] 69838  - 09/09/2021, 05:48:39     LOG [InstanceLoader] ⮌
  MovieModule dependencies initialized +36ms
[Nest] 69838  - 09/09/2021, 05:48:39     LOG [InstanceLoader] ⮌
  AppModule dependencies initialized +0ms
[Nest] 69838  - 09/09/2021, 05:48:39     LOG [RoutesResolver] ⮌
  AppController {/}: +6ms
[Nest] 69838  - 09/09/2021, 05:48:39     LOG [RouterExplorer] ⮌
  Mapped {/, GET} route +2ms
[Nest] 69838  - 09/09/2021, 05:48:39     LOG [RoutesResolver] ⮌
  MovieController {/movie}: +1ms
[Nest] 69838  - 09/09/2021, 05:48:39     LOG [RouterExplorer] ⮌
  Mapped {/movie, GET} route +0ms
[Nest] 69838  - 09/09/2021, 05:48:39     LOG [RouterExplorer] ⮌
  Mapped {/movie/:id, GET} route +1ms
[Nest] 69838  - 09/09/2021, 05:48:39     LOG [RouterExplorer] ⮌
  Mapped {/movie, POST} route +1ms
[Nest] 69838  - 09/09/2021, 05:48:39     LOG [RouterExplorer] ⮌
  Mapped {/movie/:id, PUT} route +1ms
[Nest] 69838  - 09/09/2021, 05:48:39     LOG [RouterExplorer] ⮌
  Mapped {/movie/:id, DELETE} route +0ms
[Nest] 69838  - 09/09/2021, 05:48:39     LOG [NestApplication] ⮌
  Nest application successfully started +2ms
```

Listing 14.9 Output at Application Startup

If you don't see the entries for the controller or the routes, you should check that the controller is correctly entered in the module and that the movie module is registered in the app module. If you get the output `Nest application successfully started` in the last line, you can check your controller by sending requests to it. The commands from Listing 14.10 first delete the data record with ID 2 and then query the list of all movies.

```
$ curl -X DELETE http://localhost:3000/movie/2
$ curl http://localhost:3000/movie
[
  { "id": 1, "title": "Iron Man", "year": 2008 },
  { "id": 3, "title": "Captain America", "year": 2011 }
]
```

Listing 14.10 Requests to the Controller (Formatted)

You can also send such requests using a graphical tool such as Postman. The Nest application doesn't differentiate here. However, when you use your application in its current state, you should keep in mind that when you restart your application, any changes you've made to the data will be reset.

14.6   Providers: Business Logic of the Application

The more extensive the logic behind an endpoint becomes, the longer the methods will be. To counteract this problem and to prevent the controller from growing to the point of being unmaintainable, Nest provides the services. These are classes you can load and use as needed in your controllers or even in other services. A service is a special type of provider. Other types of providers include repositories, factories, and helpers. Because services represent the most common type, we'll focus on it. Later in this book, you'll get to know yet another form of provider with repositories.

14.6.1   Creating and Including a Service

To move the logic for data management out of the controller, you first need to create a new service via the nest generate service movie command. As you can see from the output of the command in Listing 14.11, the Nest CLI has created two new files in the *src/movie* directory, named *movie.service.ts* for the service and *movie.service.spec.ts* for the unit tests of the service.

```
$ nest generate service movie
CREATE src/movie/movie.service.spec.ts (453 bytes)
CREATE src/movie/movie.service.ts (89 bytes)
UPDATE src/movie/movie.module.ts (278 bytes)
```

Listing 14.11 Service Generation Output

In addition, the service is registered in the movie module. This step is of particular importance, as otherwise you won't be able to include it in your controller. Listing 14.12 contains the updated source code of the module file.

```
import { Module } from '@nestjs/common';
import { MovieController } from './movie.controller';
import { MovieService } from './movie.service';

@Module({
  imports: [],
  controllers: [MovieController],
  providers: [MovieService],
  exports: [],
```

```
})
export class MovieModule {}
```

Listing 14.12 Including the Service in the Movie Module (src/movie/movie.module.ts)

The next step consists of moving the logic from the controller to the service.

14.6.2   Implementing the Service

Because Nest is based on TypeScript, you should at this point make sure that you're using defined types. Because currently this isn't yet the case for the movie objects, you should first create an appropriate data structure before implementing the service. At this point, you can choose between a TypeScript class and an interface. However, because you aren't currently using concrete movie instances, but rather assigning a type to data structures, an interface is more appropriate. You can generate this interface via the nest generate interface movie movie command. This command creates the *movie.interface.ts* file in the *src/movie* directory, which is why movie is used twice here: The first occurrence of "movie" denotes the name of the interface, while the second refers to the path where the file should be created. Listing 14.13 shows the source code of the interface.

```
export interface Movie {
  id: number;
  title: string;
  year: number;
}

export type InputMovie = Omit<Movie, 'id'>;
```

Listing 14.13 Definition of the Movie Interface (src/movie/movie.interface.ts)

In addition to the interface, you must also define an input type. The structure of the input type is similar to that of the movie interface with the difference that the id property isn't included. You can achieve this using the omit type from TypeScript, to which you pass the base type and the properties you want to omit.

With this basic structure in place, the next step is to implement the service. To do this, you copy the methods from the controller class, paste them into the MovieService class, and adjust the signatures, as shown in Listing 14.14.

```
import { Injectable } from '@nestjs/common';
import { InputMovie, Movie } from './movie.interface';

@Injectable()
export class MovieService {
  private data: Movie[] = [
```

```
    { id: 1, title: 'Iron Man', year: '2008' },
    { id: 2, title: 'Thor', year: '2011' },
    { id: 3, title: 'Captain America', year: '2011' },
  ];

  getAllMovies(): Movie[] {
    return this.data;
  }

  getOneMovie(id: number): Movie {
    return this.data.find((movie) => movie.id === id);
  }

  createNewMovie(movie: InputMovie): Movie {
    const nextId = Math.max(...this.data.map((movie) => movie.id)) + 1;
    const newMovie: Movie = { ...movie, id: nextId };
    this.data.push(newMovie);
    return newMovie;
  }

  udpateMovie(id: number, movie: Movie): Movie {
    const index = this.data.findIndex((movie) => movie.id === id);
    this.data[index] = movie;
    return movie;
  }

  removeMovie(id: number): void {
    this.data = this.data.filter((movie) => movie.id !== parseInt(id, 10));
  }
}
```

Listing 14.14 Implementation of the "MovieService" (src/movie/movie.service.ts)

You've probably already noticed the injectable decorator in the service class. This decorator adds some metadata to the class so that Nest can manage it via the dependency injection container. We'll describe the topic of dependency injection in greater detail in the following section.

Otherwise, the service is enriched with additional type information, and the respective parameters or return values are correctly typed. The only major change is to the createNewMovie method because you can't turn the InputMovie type into a movie interface simply by using the interface. At this point, you use the spread operator to create a simple copy of the input object, adding the id property and assigning the type of the movie interface to the variable.

14.6.3   Integrating the Service via Nest's Dependency Injection

Now that this preliminary work has been done, you can connect the controller and the service. The key to this task can be found in Nest's dependency injection. Within the module, you register the controller and service, thus making the structures known to the framework. Dependency injection works like a constructor injection in the frontend in Angular. In this case, this means you specify the service as a dependency in the constructor of the controller. If Nest encounters such a definition, the framework searches for an appropriately registered provider. As an optimization, Nest has a cache layer that stores instances of providers already in use. If a controller or other service now needs an instance of a particular provider, Nest first searches the cache for an existing instance. If it doesn't find any, the framework creates an instance of the provider, caches it, and passes it to the requesting structure.

The most important place in the controller is the constructor. As soon as you specify a parameter with access modifier here and, as in the example, the optional readonly keyword that prevents accidental modifications of the reference, you signal Nest to load a provider. This is available to you throughout the class via the specified name in conjunction with the this keyword, which is this.movieService, as shown in Listing 14.15.

```
import {
  Body,
  Controller,
  Delete,
  Get,
  HttpCode,
  Param,
  Post,
  Put,
} from '@nestjs/common';
import { InputMovie, Movie } from './movie.interface';
import { MovieService } from './movie.service';

@Controller('movie')
export class MovieController {
  constructor(private readonly movieService: MovieService) {}

  @Get()
  getAllMovies(): Movie[] {
    return this.movieService.getAllMovies();
  }

  @Get(':id')
  getOneMovie(@Param('id') id: string): Movie {
    return this.movieService.getOneMovie(parseInt(id, 10));
  }
```

14

```
@Post()
createNewMovie(@Body() movie: InputMovie): Movie {
  return this.movieService.createNewMovie(movie);
}

@Put(':id')
udpateMovie(@Param('id') id: string, @Body() movie: Movie): Movie {
  return this.movieService.udpateMovie(parseInt(id, 10), movie);
}

@Delete(':id')
@HttpCode(204)
removeMovie(@Param('id') id: string): void {
  this.movieService.removeMovie(parseInt(id, 10));
}
}
```

Listing 14.15 Integrating the Movie Service in the Controller (src/movie/movie.service.ts)

What you've seen here in the example of a controller requiring a service works in the same way for services among themselves. You just need to make sure that the service is available via dependency injection.

14.7   Accessing Databases

To this point, you only store the information locally in your application, which means all changes will be lost when the process is restarted. This problem can be solved with databases, as you've already seen in Chapter 8. Nest provides for a rather convenient solution here as well, in that the framework provides you with direct integration of TypeORM into your application via the @nestjs/typeorm package.

14.7.1   Setup and Installation

First, you need a database instance for your application. TypeORM supports a whole range of databases such as MySQL, PostgresSQL, and SQLite, but also MongoDB. For our example, we'll use a MySQL database running in a Docker container. Listing 14.16 shows the contents of the *initDB.sql* file, which you save in a new directory named *db* in your application and which enables you to define the initial database structure.

```
CREATE DATABASE `Movie`;

USE `Movie`;
```

```
CREATE TABLE `Movie` (
  `id` int(11) NOT NULL AUTO_INCREMENT,
  `title` varchar(255) DEFAULT NULL,
  `year` int(11) DEFAULT NULL,
  PRIMARY KEY (`id`)
) ENGINE=InnoDB DEFAULT CHARSET=utf8;

INSERT INTO `Movie` (`title`, `year`) VALUES
('Iron Man', 2008),
('Thor', 2011),
('Captain America', 2011);

CREATE TABLE `User` (
  `id` int(11) NOT NULL AUTO_INCREMENT,
  `username` varchar(255) DEFAULT NULL,
  `password` varchar(255) DEFAULT NULL,
  PRIMARY KEY (`id`)
) ENGINE=InnoDB DEFAULT CHARSET=utf8;

INSERT INTO `User` (`username`, `password`) VALUES
('sspringer', 'test');
```

Listing 14.16 Initial Database Structure (initDB.sql)

With this SQL script, you create the two tables Movie and User, which you initially fill with data records. In the next step, you'll start the database container using the command from Listing 14.17.

```
docker run
  --name mysql
  -v /srv/node/movie-db/db:/docker-entrypoint-initdb.d
  -e MYSQL_ROOT_PASSWORD=topSecret
  -e MYSQL_ROOT_HOST=%
  -e MYSQL_DATABASE=Movie
  -p 3306:3306
  -d
  mysql:latest
```

Listing 14.17 Command to Start the Database Container

The command assumes that your application is located in the */srv/node/movie-db* directory to mount the directory with the initialization script as a volume on the container. If the MySQL container finds a file with the *.sql* extension in the *docker-entry-point-initd.d* directory, it runs this script to initialize the database.

With this setup, you can now use the npm install @nestjs/typeorm typeorm mysql2 command to install the required dependencies. After that, you can connect your application to the database. You can achieve this by configuring the TypeORM module. You import the module at a central location, that is, preferably within the app module, and pass it an appropriate configuration. Listing 14.18 shows the corresponding configuration.

```
import { Module } from '@nestjs/common';
import { TypeOrmModule } from '@nestjs/typeorm';
import { AppController } from './app.controller';
import { AppService } from './app.service';
import { MovieModule } from './movie/movie.module';

@Module({
  imports: [
    MovieModule,
    TypeOrmModule.forRoot({
      type: 'mysql',
      host: 'localhost',
      port: 3306,
      username: 'root',
      password: 'topSecret',
      database: 'Movie',
      entities: [],
      synchronize: false,
    }),
  ],
  controllers: [AppController],
  providers: [AppService],
})
export class AppModule {}
```

Listing 14.18 Configuration of the TypeORM Module (src/app.module.ts)

In the app module, you use the forRoot method of the TypeORM module and pass a configuration object with the database credentials to this method.

Warning!

For production operation, you should by no means store the credentials directly in the source code, but rather swap them out to an environment configuration that isn't versioned with the source code. Here, environment variables come in handy, which you can include via process.env, or you can use Nest's config module for this purpose.

With this basic setup, you can move on to modeling the entities for the database in the next step.

14.7.2   Accessing the Database

TypeORM uses the repository pattern and entity classes. The entities map the structure of the individual tables and represent the individual data records. You can use the respective database tables via the repositories. Both simple read and write operations are possible as well as more complex queries that map 1:n and n:m relations, for example.

In the first step, our goal is to map the functionality of the movie service via TypeORM. For this purpose, you must first define a movie entity. The basis for this is a TypeScript class, which you can create via the `nest generate class movie.entity movie` command. Then, in this class, you model the structure of the `movie` table, as shown in Listing 14.19.

```
import { Column, Entity, PrimaryGeneratedColumn } from 'typeorm';

@Entity('Movie')
export class Movie {
  @PrimaryGeneratedColumn()
  id number;

  @Column()
  title: string;

  @Column()
  year: number;
}
```

Listing 14.19 Movie Entity (src/movie/movie.entity.ts)

TypeORM assumes that the table name is like the entity class, but with a lowercase letter at the beginning. In our case, however, the table name starts with a capital letter. If, in your application, the names of the entity class and of the database table are different, you can pass the name of the table in the call of the `entity` decorator, as you can also see in the code example. The next step is to make this entity known in both the app and movie modules. For this purpose, you add a reference to the movie entity in the `entity` array of the app module, as shown in Listing 14.20.

```
import { Movie } from './movie/movie.entity';
...
@Module({
  imports: [
    MovieModule,
    TypeOrmModule.forRoot({
      ...
      entities: [Movie],
      synchronize: false,
```

```
    }),
  ],
  controllers: [AppController],
  providers: [AppService],
})
export class AppModule {}
```

Listing 14.20 Registering the Movie Entity in the App Module (src/app.module.ts)

You must also perform the registration in the movie module. Here you use the forFeature method of the TypeORM module, but not its forRoot (see Listing 14.21).

```
import { Module } from '@nestjs/common';
import { TypeOrmModule } from '@nestjs/typeorm';
import { MovieController } from './movie.controller';
import { Movie } from './movie.entity';
import { MovieService } from './movie.service';


@Module({
  imports: [TypeOrmModule.forFeature([Movie])],
  controllers: [MovieController],
  providers: [MovieService],
  exports: [],
})
export class MovieModule {}
```

Listing 14.21 Registering the Movie Entity in the Movie Module (src/movie/movie.module.ts)

Once you've included the module and registered the entity, you can use TypeORM in your service. To access it, you use the repository provider of TypeORM and let it know that you want to use the movie entity, as shown in Listing 14.22. The whole thing then runs again via dependency injection, but this time in the service and not in the controller.

```
import { Injectable } from '@nestjs/common';
import { InjectRepository } from '@nestjs/typeorm';
import { DeleteResult, Repository } from 'typeorm';
import { Movie } from './movie.entity';
import { InputMovie } from './movie.interface';


@Injectable()
export class MovieService {
  constructor(
    @InjectRepository(Movie)
    private movieRepository: Repository<Movie>,
  ) {}
```

```
getAllMovies(): Promise<Movie[]> {
  return this.movieRepository.find();
}

getOneMovie(id: number): Promise<Movie> {
  return this.movieRepository.findOne(id);
}

createNewMovie(movie: InputMovie): Promise<Movie> {
  return this.movieRepository.save(movie);
}

udpateMovie(id: number, movie: Movie): Promise<Movie> {
  return this.movieRepository.save(movie);
}

removeMovie(id: number): Promise<DeleteResult> {
  return this.movieRepository.delete(id);
}
}
```

Listing 14.22 Linking the Movie Service to the Database (src/movie/movie.service.ts)

The service changes fundamentally through the integration of TypeORM. The only places that remain the same are the class definition and the method names. In the newly created constructor, you use the InjectRepository decorator in conjunction with the generic repository provider to make the movie repository available in the service via the private movieRepository property. The actual work here is done by Nest's dependency injection, as mentioned earlier. Within the service, you can now access the repository. During the data reading process, you use the find and findOne methods of the repository, which return an array of movie objects and a single object, respectively. For saving and updating, you use the save method, to which you pass the movie object to save, whereas for deleting you use the delete method of the repository. All methods use promises as return values, so you also have to adapt the signatures of your service methods accordingly, which results in a change to the controller in the next step because it now also has to work with promises. Fortunately, Nest supports not only simple objects as return values of controller methods but also promises, so all you need to do in the controller is customize the return types, as shown in Listing 14.23.

```
import {
  Body,
  Controller,
  Delete,
```

```
  Get,
  HttpCode,
  Param,
  Post,
  Put,
} from '@nestjs/common';
import { Movie } from './movie.entity';
import { InputMovie } from './movie.interface';
import { MovieService } from './movie.service';

@Controller('movie')
export class MovieController {
  constructor(private readonly movieService: MovieService) {}

  @Get()
  getAllMovies(): Promise<Movie[]> {
    return this.movieService.getAllMovies();
  }

  @Get(':id')
  getOneMovie(@Param('id') id: string): Promise<Movie> {
    return this.movieService.getOneMovie(parseInt(id, 10));
  }

  @Post()
  createNewMovie(@Body() movie: InputMovie): Promise<Movie> {
    return this.movieService.createNewMovie(movie);
  }

  @Put(':id')
  udpateMovie(@Param('id') id: string, @Body() movie: Movie): Promise<Movie> {
    return this.movieService.udpateMovie(parseInt(id, 10), movie);
  }

  @Delete(':id')
  @HttpCode(204)
  removeMovie(@Param('id') id: string): void {
    this.movieService.removeMovie(parseInt(id, 10));
  }
}
```

Listing 14.23 Type Adjustments in the Movie Controller (src/movie/movie.controller.ts)

With these customizations, you can now manage your data records, and the changes are recorded in the database, so they'll survive a restart of your application.

14.8   Documenting the Endpoints with OpenAPI

In addition to the implementation of interfaces, the documentation of these interfaces is another standard problem for which Nest offers an elegant solution. The @nestjs/swagger package provides everything you need to document your interfaces and generates graphical documentation from some additional annotations that you can consume via the Swagger UI or share with other developers. To do this, you must first install the necessary packages via the npm install @nestjs/swagger swagger-ui-express command. First, you need to integrate the Swagger module in your application via the *main.ts* file, as shown in Listing 14.24.

```
import { NestFactory } from '@nestjs/core';
import { DocumentBuilder, SwaggerModule } from '@nestjs/swagger';
import { AppModule } from './app.module';

async function bootstrap() {
  const app = await NestFactory.create(AppModule);

  const config = new DocumentBuilder()
    .setTitle('Movie Database')
    .setDescription('Your favourite movies in one database')
    .setVersion('1.0')
    .addTag('movies')
    .build();
  const document = SwaggerModule.createDocument(app, config);
  SwaggerModule.setup('api', app, document);

  await app.listen(3000);
}
bootstrap();
```

Listing 14.24 Integrating the Swagger Module (src/main.ts)

The DocumentBuilder is responsible for creating the Swagger documentation. Here, you can include general information such as the title and description of your interface. All other information, such as the available endpoints, is taken by the Swagger module from your application's annotations. This means you can control the documentation of the interfaces directly from the source code of your application. Because you're using the movie entity in the controller to specify the type, you can extend this class with the appropriate decorators from the @nestjs/swagger package. Listing 14.25 shows an example of this.

```
import { ApiProperty } from '@nestjs/swagger';
import { Column, Entity, PrimaryGeneratedColumn } from 'typeorm';

@Entity('Movie')
export class Movie {
  @ApiProperty({
    description: 'Id of the movie',
    example: 1
  })
  @PrimaryGeneratedColumn()
  id: number;

  @ApiProperty({
    description: 'Title of the movie',
    example: 'Iron Man',
  })
  @Column()
  title: string;

  @ApiProperty({
    description: 'Year the movie was released',
    example: 2008,
  })
  @Column()
  year: number;
}
```

Listing 14.25 Using the ApiProperty Decorator (src/movie/movie.entity.ts)

You use the ApiProperty decorator to specify that a particular property should be visible in the API documentation. You can also include further details such as a description or concrete examples of values. You can proceed similarly in the controller and also add additional documentation here via decorators. Typically, you use the ApiOkResponse decorator in this context to define a description and optionally other details for a successful request, as shown in Listing 14.26.

```
import {
  Body,
  Controller,
  Delete,
  Get,
  HttpCode,
  Param,
  Post,
  Put,
} from '@nestjs/common';
```

```
import { ApiOkResponse, ApiTags } from '@nestjs/swagger';
import { Movie } from './movie.entity';
import { InputMovie } from './movie.interface';
import { MovieService } from './movie.service';

@ApiTags('movies')
@Controller('movie')
export class MovieController {
  constructor(private readonly movieService: MovieService) {}

  @ApiOkResponse({ description: 'All available Movies' })
  @Get()
  getAllMovies(): Promise<Movie[]> {
    return this.movieService.getAllMovies();
  }

  @ApiOkResponse({ description: 'The movie matching the given id' })
  @Get(':id')
  getOneMovie(@Param('id') id: string): Promise<Movie> {
    return this.movieService.getOneMovie(parseInt(id, 10));
  }

  @ApiOkResponse({ description: 'The newly created movie' })
  @Post()
  createNewMovie(@Body() movie: InputMovie): Promise<Movie> {
    return this.movieService.createNewMovie(movie);
  }

  @ApiOkResponse({ description: 'The updated movie' })
  @Put(':id')
  udpateMovie(@Param('id') id: string, @Body() movie: Movie): Promise<Movie> {
    return this.movieService.udpateMovie(parseInt(id, 10), movie);
  }

  @ApiOkResponse({ description: 'Nothing' })
  @Delete(':id')
  @HttpCode(204)
  removeMovie(@Param('id') id: string): void {
    this.movieService.removeMovie(parseInt(id, 10));
  }
}
```

Listing 14.26 Documentation of the Movie Controller (src/movie/movie.controller.ts)

With these changes to your application, you can go to *http://localhost:3000/api* in the browser and view the API documentation. Figure 14.3 shows an example of such a view.

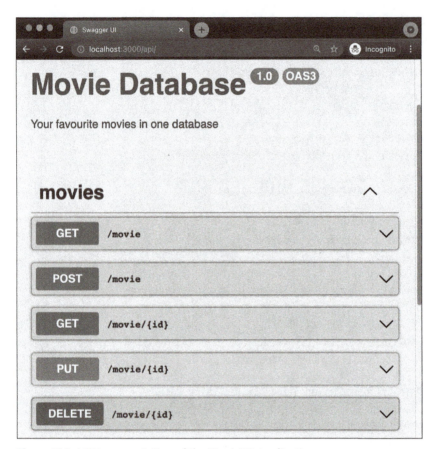

Figure 14.3 API Documentation of the MovieDB Application

What is still missing in your application now, according to the documentation, is a way for your users to log in and a means to protect your resources from unauthorized access. Both will be discussed in the following sections.

14.9   Authentication

For authentication, Nest uses an established library—Passport—and integrates it into the framework via an abstraction layer. The flexibility of Passport allows you to implement different logon strategies. In our case, we use JSON web tokens (JWTs).

14.9.1   Setup

First you need to install some additional packages via the `npm install @nestjs/passport passport @nestjs/jwt passport-jwt` command. In addition, you must install the type definitions of `passport-jwt` as DevDependency via the `npm install --save-dev @types/ passport-jwt` command.

Theoretically, you can store your users' credentials permanently in the source code, but because there's already an existing database connection, it makes sense to use this database to store user data as well. Therefore, you should first create a new module named auth using the nest generate module auth command. Within this module, you then create a user entity using the nest generate class user.entity auth command. Then you modify this class in such a way that it represents a valid entity and reflects the structure of the database table. Listing 14.27 shows what this class should look like.

```
import { Column, Entity, PrimaryGeneratedColumn } from 'typeorm';

@Entity('User')
export class User {
  @PrimaryGeneratedColumn()
  id: number;

  @Column()
  username: string;

  @Column()
  password: string;
}
```

Listing 14.27 Implementing a User Entity (src/auth/user.entity.ts)

After that, you include the entity in the import of the TypeORM module within the app and auth modules in the entities array, just as you did with the movie entity. Listing 14.28 contains the current state of the auth module.

```
import { Module } from '@nestjs/common';
import { TypeOrmModule } from '@nestjs/typeorm';
import { User } from './user.entity';

@Module({ imports: [TypeOrmModule.forFeature([User])] })
export class AuthModule {}
```

Listing 14.28 Integration of the TypeORM Module in the Auth Module (src/auth/auth.module.ts)

14.9.2 Authentication Service

In the next step, you implement the central service that takes care of authentication issues such as verifying a user and generating a JWT. You can create this service via the nest generate service auth command. In the service class, you implement the validateUser and login methods, as you can see in Listing 14.29.

```
import { Injectable } from '@nestjs/common';
import { JwtService } from '@nestjs/jwt';
import { InjectRepository } from '@nestjs/typeorm';
import { Repository } from 'typeorm';
import { User } from './user.entity';

@Injectable()
export class AuthService {
  constructor(
    @InjectRepository(User)
    private userRepository: Repository<User>,
    private jwtService: JwtService,
  ) {}

  async validateUser(username: string, password: string): Promise<Omit<User, ↵
    'password'>> {
    const user = await this.userRepository.findOne({username, password});
    if (user) {
      const validatedUser = {...user};
      delete validatedUser.password;
      return validatedUser;
    }
    return null;
  }

  async login(user: User) {
    const payload = { username: user.username, sub: user.id };
    return {
      access_token: this.jwtService.sign(payload),
    };
  }
}
```

Listing 14.29 Implementing the Auth Service (src/auth/auth.service.ts)

In the constructor, you have Nest create an instance of the user repository and the JWT service. The validateUser method receives the user name and password entered at login as arguments. These two pieces of information are used to search for the matching data record in the database. If this search returns a hit, you delete the password from the received data record and return it. If the information was invalid, that is, no matching record was found, you return the value null.

The login method receives a user object as an argument and returns an object with a signed JWT. This token contains the user name and the ID of the user. At this point you must make sure not to include passwords or similar critical data in a token under any circumstances.

14.9.3 Login Controller: Endpoint for User Login

For your users to be able to log in, you need to create a suitable endpoint. This is done by the auth controller in the auth module, which you create using the nest generate controller auth command. You can see the source code of the controller in Listing 14.30.

```
import { Body, Controller, Post, UnauthorizedException } from '@nestjs/common';
import { AuthService } from './auth.service';
import { User } from './user.entity';


@Controller('auth')
export class AuthController {
  constructor(private readonly authService: AuthService) {}

  @Post('login')
  async login(@Body() user: User) {
    const validUser = await this.authService.validateUser(
      user.username,
      user.password,
    );
    if (validUser) {
      return this.authService.login(user);
    } else {
      throw new UnauthorizedException();
    }
  }
}
```

Listing 14.30 Auth Controller (src/auth/auth.controller.ts)

The job of the auth controller is to provide your users with a POST endpoint with the path */auth/login* to which they can send their login details to receive a JWT. To validate the user name and password, the controller uses the validateUser method of the auth service. If a valid user is found, a token is generated; otherwise, the controller returns an UnauthorizedException, which results in a return message to the client with a 401 status code.

For the controller and especially the JwtService used in the AuthService to work, you still need to slightly adjust the auth module. Listing 14.31 contains the relevant details.

```
import { Module } from '@nestjs/common';
import { TypeOrmModule } from '@nestjs/typeorm';
import { User } from './user.entity';
import { AuthService } from './auth.service';
import { AuthController } from './auth.controller';
```

```
import { JwtModule } from '@nestjs/jwt';
import { PassportModule } from '@nestjs/passport';

@Module({
  imports: [
    TypeOrmModule.forFeature([User]),
    PassportModule,
    JwtModule.register({
      secret: 'secret',
      signOptions: { expiresIn: '1h' },
    }),
  ],
  providers: [AuthService],
  controllers: [AuthController],
})
export class AuthModule {}
```

Listing 14.31 Integrating Passport in the Auth Module (src/auth/auth.module.ts)

You can integrate the Passport module without any further configuration. Instead, you pass a configuration object to the `register` method of the `Jwt` module, similar to the configuration of TypeORM. Here, you define the basic configuration for your JWT. The `secret` field is especially critical because this information is used to sign your tokens—so it's again a good candidate for removing it from the source code and including it in an external configuration such as environment variables. You must also specify how long the token should be valid. The shorter you choose this period, the more secure your tokens are, but the faster your users will have to renew them. At this point, you can already issue tokens, but your application's resources are still unsecured.

14.9.4   Protecting Routes

To protect routes, Nest provides the concept of guards. You can think of a guard as a bouncer who only lets authorized requests through to the endpoint. In a first step, you must create such a guard for the JWT strategy. To do this, you use the `nest generate class jwt.guard auth` command to generate a new class in the *auth* directory. You can see the contents of this file in Listing 14.32.

```
import { Injectable } from '@nestjs/common';
import { AuthGuard } from '@nestjs/passport';

@Injectable()
export class JwtAuthGuard extends AuthGuard('jwt') {}
```

Listing 14.32 JWT Guard for the Resources of the Application (src/auth/jwt.guard.ts)

For your application to handle JWT correctly, you need to implement an appropriate strategy. This is a standard task, so Nest already takes a lot off your plate here. First, you must create a new file named *jwt.strategy.ts* in the *src/auth* directory. In this file, you now implement the JwtStrategy class. You can see the source code of this class in Listing 14.33.

```
import { ExtractJwt, Strategy } from 'passport-jwt';
import { PassportStrategy } from '@nestjs/passport';
import { Injectable } from '@nestjs/common';

@Injectable()
export class JwtStrategy extends PassportStrategy(Strategy) {
  constructor() {
    super({
      jwtFromRequest: ExtractJwt.fromAuthHeaderAsBearerToken(),
      ignoreExpiration: false,
      secretOrKey: 'secret',
    });
  }

  async validate(payload: { sub: number; username: string }) {
    return { id: payload.sub, username: payload.username };
  }
}
```

Listing 14.33 Implementing the "JwtStrategy" (src/auth/jwt.strategy.ts)

At its core, the JwtStrategy simply derives from the PassportStrategy class and adapts it for your application.

Now you can link the JwtGuard to the movie controller. You can do this using the UseGuards decorator, which you can bind either to specific methods or to the complete controller. Listing 14.34 contains the modification of the controller.

```
import {
  Body,
  Controller,
  Delete,
  Get,
  HttpCode,
  Param,
  Post,
  Put,
  UseGuards,
} from '@nestjs/common';
import { ApiOkResponse, ApiTags } from '@nestjs/swagger';
```

```
import { JwtAuthGuard } from '../auth/jwt.guard';
import { Movie } from './movie.entity';
import { InputMovie } from './movie.interface';
import { MovieService } from './movie.service';

@ApiTags('movies')
@UseGuards(JwtAuthGuard)
@Controller('movie')
export class MovieController {
  ...
}
```

Listing 14.34 Integrating the JWT Guard in the Controller (src/movie/movie.controller.ts)

If you now access one of the routes of the movie controller without having provided for a valid token before, you'll receive a response with status code 401, unauthorized. For a valid response, you must first send your user name and the corresponding password to *http://localhost:3000/auth/login* in a POST request and use the token you receive there in the authorization header to send the request to the movie controller. Figure 14.4 shows an example of such a request with Postman.

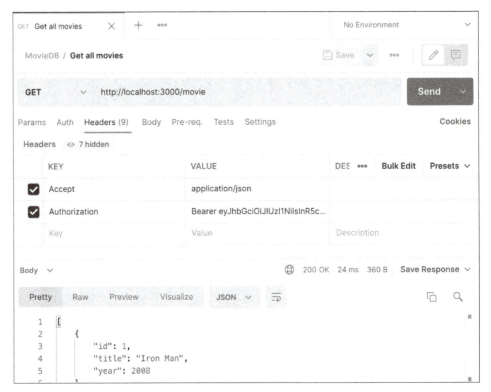

Figure 14.4 Request to the Movie Controller with a Valid Token

14.10   Outlook: Testing in Nest

One issue we've completely ignored so far is checking the functionality we've implemented. At this point, we're getting a little ahead of Chapter 23, which covers testing, but only to show you how convenient it can be to write tests for your application in Nest. So, if some terms or concepts are unfamiliar to you, you can learn even more about testing in Chapter 23.

When you create structures for your application via the Nest CLI, the command-line tool not only creates the actual file but also a test file. As an example, let's take the MovieController and test the getAllMovies method there. In this test, it's important that we only want to test the controller and not the implementation of the underlying service. For this reason, we'll use Nest's dependency injection system to provide the controller not with the actual implementation of the service, but instead with an instance customized for the test. Listing 14.35 shows the source code of the test.

```
import { Test, TestingModule } from '@nestjs/testing';
import { MovieController } from './movie.controller';
import { MovieService } from './movie.service';

describe('MovieController', () => {
  let controller: MovieController;
  let service: MovieService;

  const movies = [
    {
      id: 1,
      title: 'Iron Man',
      year: 2008,
    },
  ];

  beforeEach(async () => {
    const module: TestingModule = await Test.createTestingModule({
      controllers: [MovieController],
      providers: [
        {
          provide: MovieService,
          useValue: {
            async getAllMovies() {
              return movies;
            },
          },
        },
      ],
```

14

```
    }).compile();

    controller = module.get<MovieController>(MovieController);
    service = module.get<MovieService>(MovieService);
  });

  it('should return all movies', async () => {
    const result = await controller.getAllMovies();

    expect(result).toStrictEqual([
      {
        id: 1,
        title: 'Iron Man',
        year: 2008,
      },
    ]);
  });
});
```

Listing 14.35 Testing a Controller in Nest (src/movie/movie.controller.spec.ts)

The key to an independent test is that the test isn't run in the context of the application, but in a separate testing module. For this purpose, you use the createTestingModule method to which you pass an object that resembles the configuration object of a module. As a controller, you pass a reference to the controller. With regard to the provider, you replace the provider with an object you have complete control over and can define how it should behave. In this case, when the getAllMovies method is called, it returns an array with an object wrapped in a promise object.

In the actual test, which is initiated via the it function, you call the getAllMovies method and use the toStrictEqual method to check whether the returned object matches the expected structure. You can run the test using the npm test movie.controller command, which makes sure that only this one test file is run and all other currently potentially failing tests are ignored. Listing 14.36 shows the output of the test run.

$ npm test movie.controller

```
> movie-db@0.0.1 test
> jest "movie.controller"

 PASS  src/movie/movie.controller.spec.ts
  MovieController
    ? should return all movies (11 ms)
```

```
Test Suites: 1 passed, 1 total
Tests:       1 passed, 1 total
Snapshots:   0 total
Time:        3.385 s, estimated 4 s
Ran all test suites matching /movie.controller/i.
```

Listing 14.36 Running the Unit Test

Based on this schema, you can test all the structures Nest provides separate from the overall context of your application, thus ensuring the proper functioning of the individual units.

14.11   Summary

Nest is a framework that incorporates concepts from two different worlds. The basis is the rock-solid Express framework with its routing and middleware components. Based on this, however, Nest implements numerous concepts from client-side JavaScript, in particular from Angular.

This combination, together with excellent documentation and numerous extensions, ensures that Nest is a modern tool for developing server-side applications. Many tasks, such as defining endpoints, creating interface documentation, and implementing authentication, can be done very quickly thanks to existing structures, allowing you to focus on implementing the business logic in your application.

14

Chapter 15
Node on the Command Line

You cannot teach a man anything; you can only help him find it within himself.
—Galileo Galilei

In addition to typical web applications, Node.js can also be used to implement powerful command-line tools. This is possible because, with Node.js, you have an interface to your operating system that allows you to access not only the file system but also almost all aspects of your system. Another advantage of Node.js on the command line is that you can't tell whether an application implemented in Node.js is based on JavaScript. As you run your tool directly on the command line, there is no direct indication that Node.js is involved. The distribution of such tools is also quite simple thanks to Node Package Manager (npm). For open-source projects, you can use the infrastructure of the npm registry directly. You can distribute internal projects as files via npm or create a local repository. Chapter 25 describes how this works in detail.

The areas of use for command-line tools in Node.js are also very diverse. Starting from small utilities that support you in your daily development work up to large-scale applications, everything is possible. Most of the time, however, the commands are used in web development because JavaScript is one of the most commonly used languages in that area, and the relevant interfaces are already available. Thus, applications for handling CSS, HTML, and JavaScript are provided. Testing and analysis tools are also often written in Node.js. Another big area where Node.js is used is in the build process of web applications, where the goal is to prepare the source code so that it can be distributed to a server system and deployed.

15.1 Basic Principles

Before you start writing a command-line tool with Node.js, you need to know some basic principles about commands and how to use them. All commonly used operating systems have a command line where you can execute commands. This is true for macOS and Linux as well as for Windows. In Listing 15.1, you can see the execution of a typical shell command in a Unix environment.

```
$ ls -l /usr/local/lib/node_modules/
total 0
drwxrwxr-x  23 root    wheel        782 Dec 16 19:42 npm
drwxr-xr-x   8 nobody  41305271     272 Dec 23 02:01 nvm
```

Listing 15.1 Command-Line Command on a Unix Shell

A typical feature of a command-line tool is that it's called directly with no interpreter or server process required. Normally, you can also omit the file extension of the command. In addition, most commands are located in the system's search path, so they can be executed without an explicit path name. Only in the rarest cases is a command used on its own because you usually specify additional options and arguments to affect the execution. In the example in Listing 15.1, the `ls` command is used to create a listing of files in a directory. The `-l` option provides a more verbose output, and the `/usr/local/lib/node_modules` argument determines which directory you're interested in. This structure isn't arbitrary, but follows a convention that you should follow when creating a command-line tool with Node.js.

15.1.1   Structure

Node.js gives you a lot of leeway when building a command-line application. Although this is a great advantage for you because you're hardly restricted, it quickly turns into a disadvantage for the users of your application if every command on the command line has to be used differently. For this reason, you should make sure your commands always have the following structure: `<command> <options> <arguments>`. The individual components of a command line are as follows:

- **Command**
  The command designates the executable file of the tool. Normally, you can omit file name extensions such as *.exe* or *.bat*. If you haven't placed the file within the search path of your system, you must prefix the command with the absolute or relative path to the file. So, for frequently used commands, it's recommended to expand the system search path and copy the tool executable to a location that is included in the search path, or at least create a shortcut to it.

- **Options**
  The options of a command affect its behavior. This means you can use options to control what exactly your application should do. You've already seen a corresponding example in Listing 15.1 where the `-l` option made sure that more details were displayed. With regard to options, there is a convention that most applications follow. If you prefix an option only with -, the option should consist of only one letter. If the option requires a value, it's separated from the option by a space. Several options in the short notation can be combined. Thus, an `ls -l -a` becomes an `ls -la`. In the more verbose notation for options, you must use two - as prefix. The name of the option

in this case consists of a word, and the value is separated from the option by =. In this context, it isn't possible to group several options together as in the shorthand notation. An example of this notation is grep --recursive --max-count=3 "node.js" *.

- **Arguments**

  Arguments enable you to pass information to the command. For the directory listing in Listing 15.1, the argument consists of the name of the directory to be displayed. For example, the grep command accepts two arguments. If you run grep --recursive "node.js" *, the first argument is the character string node.js to search for, while * is a wildcard for all files and directories in the current directory.

As is so often the case in Node.js, you should be careful with the flexibility the platform gives you. For example, you can read the entire command line and determine the format of options and arguments yourself. This allows you to use a % rather than a - to indicate options. However, you'd better stick to the convention described earlier and thus allow the users of your application to use it as they are used to. By default, almost all commands support options such as -h or --help for a short help, so you can get a quick start with the features of the application.

15.1.2 Executability

To run a command on your system, you must meet some requirements. During the course of this chapter, you'll learn how to design your application. There are additionally some conditions that have to be fulfilled on the operating system side.

As mentioned earlier, the executable file of your application must be findable. If you install the application globally via the npm, you must make sure that the file is located in a directory that is in the search path of your system. If you want to install your application without the npm, you have to adjust your search path manually. On a Windows system, you can do this by extending the PATH variable in the system settings. You proceed in a similar way on a Unix-based system. Again, the environment variable is called PATH and contains a list of directories separated by colons.

Especially on Unix systems, you must set special permissions for an application to run on the command line. The Unix permission system provides for three types of permissions: read, write, and execute. You can set them for the owner of the file, the assigned group, and all other users of the system. For you to run the application, the executing user must have at least read and execute permissions on the file. If that isn't the case, you'll receive an error message informing you of the missing authorization. You can set the permission on the command line using the chmod +rx index.js command. This assumes that the starting point of your application is in the file named *index.js*. The chmod command in this case ensures that any user on the system can both read and execute the file. With this prior knowledge, you can now move on to creating your command-line application.

15

15.2   Structure of a Command-Line Application

As an example of a command-line application, we want to create an application that provides calculation tasks for the four basic arithmetic operations and checks the results you enter. In the following sections, you'll implement such an application step by step and see what options are available to you on the command line.

15.2.1   File and Directory Structure

Normally, a command-line application has at least two subdirectories:

- **lib**
  The *lib* directory contains the actual application. Depending on the size of the tool, you can distribute the source code across several files and subdirectories. As an alternative to the name *lib*, you can also name this directory *src*. Both variants are quite commonly used.

- **bin**
  The executable files are located in the *bin* directory of the application. If you follow this convention, it's easy for outsiders to get started with the application.

In addition to the directories and files of the application, there is also the package configuration in the form of the *package.json* file. According to the convention, you should store the *index.js* file, which is the entry point to your application, in the *lib* directory.

One of the features of a command-line application is that you can call the tool directly and don't need to use the node command first. For this purpose, you can make use of the *shebang* (#!) on Unix systems. This is a standardized character string that tells the system how to execute the script. To make sure the Math Trainer application runs on your system, you must create a file named *mathTrainer.js* in the *bin* directory. The contents of this file are shown in Listing 15.2.

```
#!/usr/bin/env node

import '../lib/index.js';
```

Listing 15.2 Math Trainer Executable File (bin/mathTrainer.js)

After you've made sure the execution permission is also set correctly on a Unix system, you can execute your application via the bin/mathTrainer.js command line in the root directory of your application.

15.2.2   Package Definition

One of the most important aspects is the *package.json* file of a project. It helps you to obtain an initial overview of a project. The file lists the name, description, and version number as well as the dependencies to be installed. Furthermore, it references the entry point into the application. For the Math Trainer, you use the `npm init` command to create the *package.json* file.

The interactive wizard will ask you some questions, after which, you'll have an initial package configuration. This configuration file is primarily intended for normal Node.js applications and not for command-line tools. For this reason, you still need to make some adjustments. As a general best practice, you should set the `private` key to the value `true` so that you don't accidentally publish your application. As we're use the ECMAScript module system, you must define the value `module` as `type`. The `bin` object also represents a mapping from the command to the executable. If you've already created a file in the *bin* directory, as in the example, `npm init` will automatically create the mapping for you. You can delete the entries `main` for the entry point and `scripts` for various helper scripts for the time being. Listing 15.3 shows the *package.json* file for the Math Trainer application.

```
{
  "name": "math-trainer",
  "version": "1.0.0",
  "description": "A simple tool to train your math skills",
  "bin": {
    "math-trainer": "bin/mathTrainer.js"
  },
  "license": "ISC",
  "private": true,
  "type": "module"
}
```

Listing 15.3 "package.json" File for the Math Trainer Application

15.2.3   Math Trainer Application

Now that you've made the preparations for your application, it's time to implement the actual application logic. The user should be shown a certain number of tasks per basic calculating operation on the command line. They can choose between three levels of difficulty. At the first level, both operands are to be single-digit. At the second level, one of the two operands should be one-digit, the second two-digit, and, finally, at the third level, both should be two-digit. A special rule applies to division: only integer divisions should be possible, and to increase the difficulty a bit, you generate the two operands according to the rules mentioned before, multiply the first with the second operand, and use the result as the first operand.

First, you implement a helper function that generates a random integer operand for you. You store this function in the *lib/operands.js* file. Listing 15.4 shows the corresponding source code.

```
export default (digits) => Math.floor(Math.random() * 10 ** digits);
```

Listing 15.4 Helper Function to Create Random Operands (lib/operands.js)

The function exported as `default` expects a number that specifies how many digits the operand should have. With this number, you generate and return a corresponding integer via a combination of `Math.random`, `Math.floor`, and the exponentiation operator.

In the next step, you create a file named *task.js*, which you also save in the *lib* directory. This file contains the logic for generating the individual tasks. A task is represented by an object that has the properties `task`, `result`, and `input`. In `task`, you store the task as a character string. `result` contains the precalculated result of the task as a number, and `input` should finally contain the solution entered by the user and is first initialized with an empty string.

The *task.js* file contains two functions, as shown in Listing 15.5. The `createTask` method creates a new `task` object, and the `getOperands` method generates the two operators using the helper function from *operands.js*. Because you only need the `createTask` function outside the file, it also represents the `default` export of the file.

```
import createOperand from './operands.js';

export default function createTask(operation, level) {
  const [operand1, operand2] = getOperands(operation, level);
  const task = `${operand1} ${operation} ${operand2}`;
  const result = eval(task);

  return {
    task,
    result,
    input: '',
  };
}

function getOperands(operation, level) {
  let operands;
  switch (level) {
    case 1:
      operands = [createOperand(1), createOperand(1)];
      break;
    case 2:
      operands = [createOperand(1), createOperand(2)];
      if (createOperand(1) % 2 === 0) {
        operands.reverse();
      }
      break;
```

```
      case 3:
        operands = [createOperand(2), createOperand(2)];
        break;
    }
    if (operation === '/') {
      operands[0] = operands[0] * operands[1];
    }
    return operands;
}
```

Listing 15.5 Creating New Tasks (lib/task.js)

The createTask function creates two operands via the getOperands function and assigns them to the two variables operand1 and operand2 by means of a destructuring operation. With these two variables and the type of operation passed as the operator, the string representation of the operation is formed with a template string. You pass this string to the eval function to have the result calculated. The eval function executes a string as JavaScript source code. You should use this function only in exceptional cases, and then only if you have complete control over the character string being executed. This information forms the task object returned by the function.

The getOperands function receives as input the type of task and the difficulty level and then uses this information to generate the operands from the previously defined rules. At the second level of difficulty, the operands are randomly swapped using the Array.prototype.reverse method. For this purpose, you create an additional random number via the createOperand function. If it's an even number, it's swapped so that the two-digit operand can appear both in first and second place. At the end of the method, you must check if the operation is a division and adjust the first operand according to the task.

You can now test the functionality by creating an *index.js* file in the *lib* directory and integrating the application logic. Listing 15.6 shows the source code.

```
import createTask from './task.js';

const amount = 4;
const level = 2;
const operations = ['+', '-', '*', '/'];

operations.forEach((operation) => {
  for (let i = 0; i < amount; i++) {
    console.log(createTask(operation, level));
  }
});
```

Listing 15.6 Creating Tasks

The source code of the *index.js* file makes sure that four tasks per basic arithmetic operation are displayed to you when you run the application.

By implementing this file, you've created the final component for your command-line application, which means your application is theoretically functional. To test this, you can either install your application directly using the `npm install -g .` command, or you can use the `npm link` command. In this context, you enter the `npm link` command in the root directory of your application. npm takes care of everything else by ensuring that the application is installed globally. For this purpose, a symbolic link to the executable file is created in the global directory. In addition, the application directory is linked into the global *node_modules* directory. The advantage of `npm link` over an installation with `npm install` is that the link makes all changes to the application effective immediately, and you don't have to reinstall the application. The command, `npm uninstall -g math-trainer` allows you to remove the link again when you've finished your development work.

Whether you choose to install or link, after running the command, you'll be able to use Math Trainer system-wide. To do this, you enter the `math-trainer` command in the command line in any directory on your system. The result is shown in Listing 15.7.

```
$ math-trainer
{ task: '33 + 3', result: 36, input: '' }
{ task: '99 + 4', result: 103, input: '' }
{ task: '68 + 5', result: 73, input: '' }
{ task: '80 + 0', result: 80, input: '' }
{ task: '9 - 48', result: -39, input: '' }
{ task: '47 - 3', result: 44, input: '' }
{ task: '9 - 5', result: 4, input: '' }
{ task: '56 - 1', result: 55, input: '' }
{ task: '2 * 6', result: 12, input: '' }
{ task: '34 * 8', result: 272, input: '' }
{ task: '26 * 3', result: 78, input: '' }
{ task: '76 * 7', result: 532, input: '' }
{ task: '0 / 32', result: 0, input: '' }
{ task: '252 / 3', result: 84, input: '' }
{ task: '60 / 6', result: 10, input: '' }
{ task: '264 / 88', result: 3, input: '' }
```

Listing 15.7 Running Math Trainer

In the following sections, you'll extend Math Trainer into a full-fledged application that a user can interact with.

15.3 Accessing Input and Output

In a web application, communication takes place over the network using a browser. The communication protocol is usually HTTP. For a command-line application, however, different rules apply when it comes to communication. There's only one endpoint and not any number of them. Moreover, the user doesn't connect to the application via the network, but works directly with the application through the command prompt. So, you have to keep some things in mind when it comes to input and output, especially if you aren't just generating output but interacting with the user during the runtime of the command-line application, as in the Math Trainer example.

15.3.1 Output

The general rule for Unix applications is that if there's nothing to report, the application won't generate any output. If the processing was successful, it isn't necessary to spend anything. Nevertheless, it's good style to give the user direct feedback. This is either done automatically by the application or can be controlled by the user.

The simplest way to output information on the command line is the `console.log` method. Everything you pass to it is written directly to standard output. However, a Node.js process has two output channels: standard output and standard error output. You can address both output channels via the global `process` module. Listing 15.8 shows how you can access the output channels in write mode. The standard output channel is represented by the `process.stdout` object, while the standard error output channel is represented by the `process.stderr` object. Both objects are of the writable stream type and therefore implement the `write` method. Unlike `console.log`, which automatically inserts a line break, you have to take care of this yourself via the `write` method using the \n control character; otherwise, this method simply continues the current output line forever.

```
process.stdout.write('This is stdout\n'); // Output: This is stdout
process.stderr.write('This is stderr\n'); // Output: This is stderr
```

Listing 15.8 Accessing the Standard Output and Standard Error Output Channels

If you save the source code in a file named *output.js*, you can access the respective channel using the commands from Listing 15.9.

```
$ node output.js
This is stdout
This is stderr
$ node output.js 1> app.log
```

```
This is stderr
$ node output.js 2> err.log
This is stdout
```

Listing 15.9 Output in the Standard Output and Standard Error Output Channels

You won't notice any difference between the two output channels until you separate the two. You can use the `node output.js 2> err.log` command to redirect the standard error output to the *err.log* file so that only the values of the standard output are displayed. With `node output.js 1> app.log`, you write the standard output messages to the *app.log* file, and the error output appears on the console. In an application, this separation can be helpful to keep the output clear and still record all errors to handle them at a later time.

Similar to `console.log`, which writes to standard output, Node.js also provides `console.error`, which allows you to write directly to standard error output without having to go through the `process` module. In addition to these two admittedly most important features, the `console` object provides numerous other methods, such as `console.count`, which provides you with a counter, or `console.table`, which you can use to generate tabular output.

15.3.2   Input

An application not only consists of outputs but also responds to inputs to adjust the program flow accordingly. There are several possibilities for such an interaction with a command-line application. The easiest way is to use the standard input of the process. Like the output, the input is a data stream—in this case, a readable stream. With the `process.stdin` object, you have a reference to the standard input.

Listing 15.10 contains source code that you can use to accept data via standard input. If you save this source code in a file named *input.js*, you can start the example using the `node input.js` command. If you enter a character string via the keyboard and confirm the entry with the Enter key, the data is passed to the application and written to the standard output.

```
process.stdin.on('data', data => {
  console.log(data.toString());
});
```

Listing 15.10 Accessing the Standard Input

Not only can the standard input be operated using the keyboard, you can also redirect the output of other programs to your Node.js application. This output-input redirection, called *piping*, is achieved by connecting two commands with the pipe symbol (|). On a Unix system, for example, this works with the command chain `echo 'Hello world' | node input.js`. The `Hello World` string is written to standard output by the `echo` command. This is forwarded by the pipe symbol to the standard input of the subsequent command. In this context, the string is parsed by the Node.js application, and appropriate output is generated.

Using the standard input to interact with the user turns out to be quite uncomfortable, especially with guided dialogs as you know them from npm init, for example. For this reason, Node.js has a second means of user interaction: the readline module.

15.3.3   User Interaction with the readline Module

Before you add the readline module to your application, you'll first learn how to use the module on the basis of a simple example. Listing 15.11 contains a code block that ensures the user is asked for their name and then greets them personally.

```
import { createInterface } from 'readline';

const rl = createInterface({
  input: process.stdin,
  output: process.stdout,
});

rl.question("What's your name? ", (name) => {
  console.log(`Hello ${name}!`);
  rl.close();
});
```

Listing 15.11 Personal Greeting to User

If you want to use the readline module, you have to include it first. In this case, you import directly the createInterface function from the readline module. To handle the input correctly, you use the createInterface function to generate an interface that you associate with the standard input and output of the current process. The interface of the rl object just created implements the question method, among other things. This method displays the specified string on the console and waits for input. When the input process is completed by pressing the ⌷Enter⌷ key, the callback function you passed as the second argument to the question method is called with the user's input. Once you've completed all interaction with the user, you must call the rl.close method to close the interface. If you don't do that, the application can't be closed properly because of resources that are still open.

The readline module is a good example of an asynchronous operation. To sequence multiple questions to the user, you either make another question call in the callback function of the first method call or use the asynchronous programming capabilities of Node.js. You'll learn more about this topic in the next chapter. At this point, only so much can be said: You can use a promise object to encapsulate the user's response.

Listing 15.12 contains an extension of Listing 15.11. In this case, the user is also asked for their place of residence.

```javascript
import { createInterface } from 'readline';

const rl = createInterface({
  input: process.stdin,
  output: process.stdout,
});

function promisedQuestion(question) {
  return new Promise((resolve) => {
    rl.question(question, (answer) => resolve(answer));
  });
}

const user = {
  name: '',
  city: '',
};

user.name = await promisedQuestion('What's your name? ');
user.city = await promisedQuestion('Where do you live? ');

console.log(`Hello ${user.name} from ${user.city}`);

rl.close();
```

Listing 15.12 Asynchronous Combination of User Interactions

This special form of sequencing the question calls becomes necessary because the user is asked for the answers in an asynchronous way. This means that any second question call that immediately follows the first one is ignored by the process.

The core of the implementation in Listing 15.12 is the promisedQuestion function. It encapsulates the question method in a promise object and resolves it once the user has given their input. Using the top-level await feature of Node.js, you can then concatenate the two questions and output the result after answering the second question. At the end of the chain, you also execute the rl.close method to close the readline interface and thus terminate the application. If you run the sample code, you get an output like the one shown in Listing 15.13.

```
$ node readline.js
What's your name? Basti
```

```
Where do you live? Munich
Hello Basti from Munich
```

Listing 15.13 Output of the "readline" Example

With this information, you can now extend your Math Trainer implementation to ask the user for the results of the tasks. First, you need to slightly modify the promisedQuestion function, as you can see in Listing 15.14, so that you can use it here as well. Save this implementation in the *lib* directory under the name *promisedQuestion.js*.

```
export default function promisedQuestion(question, rl) {
  return new Promise((resolve) => {
    rl.question(question, (answer) => resolve(answer));
  });
}
```

Listing 15.14 Version of the "promisedQuestion" Function Adapted for Math Trainer (lib/promisedQuestion.js)

The adjustments to the promisedQuestion function are limited to passing a reference to the readline interface as the second parameter and exporting the function.

The further adjustments take place in the *index.js* file in the *lib* directory of the Math Trainer application. The updated version of the file is shown in Listing 15.15.

```
import { createInterface } from 'readline';
import createTask from './task.js';
import promisedQuestion from './promisedQuestion.js';

const amount = 4;
const level = 2;
const operations = ['+', '-', '*', '/'];
const tasks = [];

operations.forEach((operation) => {
  for (let i = 0; i < amount; i++) {
    tasks.push(createTask(operation, level));
  }
});

const rl = createInterface({
  input: process.stdin,
  output: process.stdout,
});

async function question(index) {
  const result = await promisedQuestion(`${tasks[index].task} = `, rl);
```

```
  tasks[index].input = parseInt(result);
  if (tasks[index].input === tasks[index].result) {
    console.log('Correct!');
  } else {
    console.log('Wrong');
  }
  if (++index < tasks.length) {
    question(index);
  } else {
    rl.close();
  }
}

question(0);
```

Listing 15.15 Integration of the "readline" Module

In the first step, you add the created task objects to the tasks array, which you're going to use in the following steps. Then you generate the readline interface that you can pass to the promisedQuestion function. The question function represents the core of the application. It receives the index of the current task and calls itself until all tasks have been displayed to the user.

Once the user has entered the solution to a task via the command line, the promise of this question is resolved. Within the callback function, you save the input in the respective task object and then check whether the input was correct. If the task was solved successfully, the user will see the string Correct!. In the event of an error, the output should read Wrong. If there are more tasks to solve, you must call the question function again, or you can terminate the process using the rl.close method. If you've linked the application with npm link, you can test the implementation via the math-trainer command and get an output like the one shown in Listing 15.16.

```
$ math-trainer
4 + 68 = 72
Correct!
11 + 4 = 16
Wrong
2 + 24 =
```

Listing 15.16 Running Math Trainer

In some situations, you may need to limit the interaction with an application to pass options and arguments to enable the automation of an execution. In the following section, you'll learn how to extend Math Trainer so that you can pass the difficulty level and the number of tasks via options.

15.3.4   Options and Arguments

At the start of this chapter, you saw how a command is structured, that options influence the behavior of a command, and that arguments provide additional information. The argv property of the process module allows you to access the command line of the application. It contains an array that stores the individual components of the command-line command used to invoke the current process. The first element of the argv array is the Node.js executable with the full path. The second element is the absolute path of the executed script, and all other elements map the options and arguments.

With this information at hand, you should now make sure that it's possible to pass the --level=<difficulty level> and --amount=<number of tasks> options to the math-trainer command, which will affect the behavior of the application accordingly. For example, if you call Math Trainer via the math-trainer --level=1 --amount=2 command, the structure of the process.argv array looks like the one shown in Listing 15.17.

```
[ ' /usr/local/bin/node ',
  '/src/node/bin/math-trainer',
  '--level=1',
  '--amount=2' ]
```

Listing 15.17 Structure of the "process.argv" Array When Calling Math Trainer

To solve the task, you write a helper function called getOptions, which you swap out to a separate *getOptions.js* file in the *lib* directory. The source code of this file is shown in Listing 15.18.

```
export default function getOptions(levelDefault = 2, amountDefault = 4) {
  const level = getOptionValue(getOption('level'), levelDefault);
  const amount = getOptionValue(getOption('amount'), amountDefault);
  return {
    level,
    amount,
  };
}

function getOption(optionName) {
  return process.argv.find((element) => element.includes(optionName));
}

function getOptionValue(option, defaultValue) {
  if (option) {
    const [, value] = option.split('=');
    return parseInt(value, 10);
  }
```

```
    return defaultValue;
}
```

Listing 15.18 Helper Function "getOptions" (lib/getOptions.js)

The helper function itself consists of the getOptions function, which is made available to the entire application as a default export. Within it, you extract both the difficulty level and the number of options from the command line. For both pieces of information, you define default values in the parameter list of the function in case no value is passed during the call. Because the operations for both pieces of information are the same, you can again swap them out to helper functions. The getOption function reads the passed option from the command-line array, while the getOptionValue function receives this information. Using a combination of the split method, which converts the option into an array, and the destructuring option, which assigns the value after the equal sign to the value variable, you extract the option value. Note that, at this point, the command line is interpreted as a character string, but your application works with integers. For this reason, you must convert the value to a number using the parseInt function. It's also important to note that the functions are called first and only defined afterwards in this example. This works because JavaScript does something called *hoisting*. In this context, named functions such as getOption and getOptionValue are available in the entire scope, which, in this case, is within the file, no matter where you declare them. The situation is different for function expressions. Here you define a variable and assign a function object to it. Because this isn't an atomic operation, the variable declaration is echoed, but the assignment isn't, so you can't use the function until after the assignment operation.

If the user hasn't specified the option on the command line, the default value is used instead. In the *index.js* file, you now include the call of the helper function and can then use your application's command-line options. The necessary adjustments are shown in Listing 15.19.

```
import { createInterface } from 'readline';
import createTask from './task.js';
import promisedQuestion from './promisedQuestion.js';
import getOptions from './getOptions.js';

const { amount, level } = getOptions();

const operations = ['+', '-', '*', '/'];
const tasks = [];

operations.forEach((operation) => {
  for (let i = 0; i < amount; i++) {
    tasks.push(createTask(operation, level));
  }
```

```
});

const rl = createInterface({
  input: process.stdin,
  output: process.stdout,
});

async function question(index) {
  const result = await promisedQuestion(`${tasks[index].task} = `, rl);
  tasks[index].input = parseInt(result);
  if (tasks[index].input === tasks[index].result) {
    console.log('Correct!');
  } else {
    console.log('Wrong');
  }
  if (++index < tasks.length) {
    question(index);
  } else {
    rl.close();
  }
}

question(0);
```

Listing 15.19 Integrating the Helper Function "getOptions" (lib/index.js)

Instead of assigning the two values in separate statements as before, you can use a destructuring statement at this point to assign the object returned by the getOptions function directly to the two constants. If you now start your application via the math-trainer --level=1 --amount=1 command, you'll see a total of four simple tasks.

15.4 Tools

Node.js has also established itself as a valuable tool on the command line. For this reason, you'll find ready-made solutions for numerous problems in the area of command-line applications, which you can install as packages in your application. In the following sections, you'll be introduced to three of these tools—Commander, chalk, and node-emoji—and integrate them into your Math Trainer.

15.4.1 Commander

As you've seen in the previous section, searching the command line for specific options involves a certain amount of work. The situation gets even more inconvenient at this point if you also want to provide the shorthand notation of options instead of what we've done so far in the example. In this case, you normally don't use equal signs as separators between the option and the value, so you also have to adjust the routine here. For parsing the command line, you can include Commander in your application. You can install the package via the `npm install commander` command. Because you've already swapped out the parsing of the command line to a separate file in the previous step, the adjustments for integrating Commander are limited to the *lib/getOptions.js* file. The updated version of this file is shown in Listing 15.20.

```
import program from 'commander';

export default (levelDefault = 2, amountDefault = 4) => {
  program
    .version('1.0.0')
    .option(
      '-l, --level <n>',
      'Difficulty level of tasks (1-3)',
      parseInt,
      levelDefault,
    )
    .option('-a, --amount <n>', 'Number of tasks', parseInt, ⤴
      amountDefault)
    .parse(process.argv);

  const options = program.opts();

  return {
    level: options.level,
    amount: options.amount,
  };
};
```

Listing 15.20 Integrating Commander (lib/getOptions.js)

Due to the customization in Listing 15.20, the source code of your application has become simpler, and you also gained additional features. Thus, by default, Commander supports the -V and --version options to display the version of the application. In addition, when the application is invoked with the -h or --help option, a help block describing how to use the command is displayed.

After these changes, you no longer support only the long version of the options, but also a shortened version. If you call your application with the -h option, you'll see an output like the one shown in Listing 15.21.

```
$ math-trainer -h

  Usage: math-trainer [options]

  Options:

    -V, --version      output the version number
    -l, --level <n>    difficulty level of tasks (1-3) (default: 2)
    -a, --amount <n>   number of tasks (default: 4)
    -h, --help         output usage information
```

Listing 15.21 Display of the Math Trainer Help

Using the `option` method of the Commander package, you can define the individual options of your application. As the first argument, the method expects the name of the option. Here you can specify both the short and the long variant. If a value is to be passed to the application via the option, you can specify it afterwards. You have two different options for specifying the value: If you put the value in angle brackets, as in this example, it's a mandatory value. If you want to define an optional option, you can use square brackets here. The second parameter of the `options` method represents the description of the option. This is displayed in the help menu. As a third argument, you can pass a function to manipulate the value. For the Math Trainer application, use the `parseInt` function to convert the passed value into a number. The last parameter allows you to pass a default value for the option. Commander then automatically inserts the string `default: <value>` into the option description.

For Commander to work, you must use the `parse` method to specify which data structure to evaluate. In most cases, this will be the `process.argv` array, but here you have the option to specify any array that follows the rules of `process.argv`.

All methods of the Commander object return the object itself, so that a fluent interface notation becomes possible, and you can directly concatenate the method calls.

You can obtain the values that were passed when the application was called by using the `opts` method. This method returns an object containing the individual options and their associated values as key-value pairs.

The Commander project site can be found at *https://github.com/tj/commander.js*. A lightweight alternative to Commander.js is available in the form of `minimist`. This module deals only with the correct parsing of command-line options. This project can be found at *https://github.com/substack/minimist*.

15.4.2 Chalk

A feature that is often underestimated is the formatting of the command line. It allows you to highlight important terms and thus guide the user on the command line. You can apply colors and other formatting using control characters directly in console.log, for example. Listing 15.22 shows how this works.

```
console.log('\u001b[33m yellow');
console.log('\u001b[31m red');
console.log('\u001b[34m blue');
console.log('\u001b[0m');
```

Listing 15.22 Coloring the Console

The output of this example consists of the character strings yellow, red, and blue, each colored correspondingly. The last line resets the color of the console back to its original state. The string \u001b[4m allows you to underline the subsequent characters. Other features include italic, strikethrough, and bold font. You can also change the background color of the console. Admittedly, dealing with ANSI control characters in development isn't always convenient. Applying styles on the console is such a common problem that a module called chalk comprehensively solves this problem for you. It can be installed with the npm using the npm install chalk command. The code you implemented in Listing 15.22 via control characters can be implemented more elegantly with chalk using meaningful function names. The result shown in Listing 15.23 is the same as the one from the previous example.

```
import chalk from 'chalk';

console.log(chalk.yellow('yellow'));
console.log(chalk.red('red'));
console.log(chalk.blue('blue'));
```

Listing 15.23 Using Chalk

In your Math Trainer application, chalk enables you to format the output of the result in bold and green for success, and bold and red for failure. For this purpose, you must modify the *lib/index.js* file after installing the package, as shown in Listing 15.24.

```
import { createInterface } from 'readline';
import chalk from 'chalk';
import createTask from './task.js';
import promisedQuestion from './promisedQuestion.js';
import getOptions from './getOptions.js';

const { amount, level } = getOptions();

const operations = ['+', '-', '*', '/'];
const tasks = [];

operations.forEach((operation) => {
```

```
  for (let i = 0; i < amount; i++) {
    tasks.push(createTask(operation, level));
  }
});

const rl = createInterface({
  input: process.stdin,
  output: process.stdout,
});

async function question(index) {
  const result = await promisedQuestion(`${tasks[index].task} = `, rl);
  tasks[index].input = parseInt(result);
  if (tasks[index].input === tasks[index].result) {
    console.log(chalk.bold.green('Correct!'));
  } else {
    console.log(chalk.bold.red('Wrong'));
  }
  if (++index < tasks.length) {
    question(index);
  } else {
    rl.close();
  }
}

question(0);
```

Listing 15.24 Using Chalk in Math Trainer (lib/index.js)

As you can see in Listing 15.24, it's possible to apply several styles at the same time by concatenating the statements. Another convenient feature of chalk is that it also takes care of resetting the formatting to the console default style for you after the passed character string has been formatted.

The chalk project can be found on GitHub at *https://github.com/chalk/chalk*.

15.4.3   node-emoji

One of the most popular tools that uses emojis for console output is the package manager Yarn. Like chalk, emojis can be used to direct the user's attention to a particular output on the console, to make the console clearer because certain states can be expressed more quickly via an emoji than via text, and, finally, to liven up your application a bit by using the right emojis in the appropriate places. Because JavaScript supports the Unicode character set, it's possible to use Unicode emojis directly. An alternative to this is to use the node-emoji package, which allows you to use the text representation of various emojis, making your code more readable.

Your implementation of the Math Trainer application is currently missing a summary of the results. To implement these in the *lib/summary.js* file, you can use the node-emoji package. In the first step, you install this package via the npm install node-emoji command. The source code in the *lib/summary.js* file is shown in Listing 15.25.

```javascript
import emoji from 'node-emoji';

export default (tasks) => {
  const correctCount = tasks.reduce((correctCount, task) => {
    if (task.input === task.result) {
      correctCount++;
    }
    return correctCount;
  }, 0);
  const percent = (correctCount * 100) / tasks.length;
  if (percent === 100) {
    return emoji.emojify(
      `:trophy: Congratulations, you have solved all ${tasks.length} tasks ⮑
        correctly.`,
    );
  } else if (percent >= 50) {
    return emoji.emojify(
      `:sunglasses: Very good, you have correctly solved ${correctCount} out of ⮑
        ${tasks.length} tasks.`,
    );
  } else if (percent >= 1) {
    return emoji.emojify(
      `:cry: You have correctly solved ${correctCount} out of ${tasks.length} ta
sks, ⮑
        you can do better.`,
    );
  } else {
    return emoji.emojify(
      `:skull_and_crossbones: ⮑
        Your answers to all ${tasks.length} tasks are wrong.`,
    );
  }
};
```

Listing 15.25 Preparation of the Results Summary (lib/summary.js)

To display the result, you divide it into four categories: The user solved all tasks correctly, the user solved more than 50% correctly, the user solved less than 50% correctly, and the user didn't solve any task correctly. You can use the `emoji.emojify` method to generate a character string that contains an emoji. This method should be marked with colons. The `emoji.emojify(':trophy:')` call creates a character string containing the trophy emoji. In the last step you need to display the generated character string. You can do this by calling the helper function for summaries before you exit the process. Listing 15.26 contains the customized source code of the *lib/index.js* file.

```
import { createInterface } from 'readline';
import chalk from 'chalk';
import createTask from './task.js';
import promisedQuestion from './promisedQuestion.js';
import getOptions from './getOptions.js';
import summary from './summary.js';

const { amount, level } = getOptions();

const operations = ['+', '-', '*', '/'];
const tasks = [];

operations.forEach((operation) => {
  for (let i = 0; i < amount; i++) {
    tasks.push(createTask(operation, level));
  }
});

const rl = createInterface({
  input: process.stdin,
  output: process.stdout,
});

async function question(index) {
  const result = await promisedQuestion(`${tasks[index].task} = `, rl);
  tasks[index].input = parseInt(result);
  if (tasks[index].input === tasks[index].result) {
    console.log(chalk.bold.green('Correct!'));
  } else {
    console.log(chalk.bold.red('Wrong'));
  }
  if (++index < tasks.length) {
    question(index);
  } else {
    console.log(summary(tasks));
    rl.close();
```

475

```
    }
}
```

```
question(0);
```

Listing 15.26 Summary Display (lib/index.js)

In addition to formatting strings, the node-emoji package is also capable of resolving emojis in character strings or assigning them a random emoji. You can find the project site at *https://github.com/omnidan/node-emoji*.

15.5   Signals

On a Unix system, a *signal* is a message to a process. Such signals are often used to terminate a process. However, you can also just send some information to the process, for example, that the window size has changed. Most signals you send to a Node.js process cause an event to which you can bind a callback function to respond to the signal. For example, if a user presses the shortcut Ctrl + C, the SIGINT signal gets triggered. You can intercept this via process.on('SIGINT', () => {}) and act accordingly. When integrating it into your Math Trainer application, you have to keep in mind that the readline interface intercepts the signals, so you can't respond to them directly. The solution to this problem is to register the event handler for the program termination not on the process object but on the rl object. Upon termination, the user should be shown a message that tells him how many tasks he has already solved until termination. For this purpose, you define another helper function and save it in the *lib/handleCancel.js* file. The source code of this file is shown in Listing 15.27.

```
export default (rl, tasks) => {
  rl.on('SIGINT', () => {
    const solvedCount = tasks.reduce((solvedCount, task) => {
      if (task.input !== '') {
        solvedCount++;
      }
      return solvedCount;
    }, 0);
    console.log(
      `\nToo bad you want to leave, you only solved ${solvedCount} ⤵
        of ${tasks.length} tasks.`,
    );
    rl.close();
  });
};
```

Listing 15.27 Integrating a Signal Handler (lib/handleCancel.js)

You pass a reference to the readline interface and the task array to the helper function. First, you register a handler function for the SIGINT signal. In the callback function, use the array-reduce function to calculate how many tasks have been solved. Then you issue a message and end the process. This step is needed because a custom signal handler overrides the default, so it's no longer possible to exit the program via the ⌜Ctrl⌟+⌜C⌟ shortcut.

You still need to include the handleCancel function in the *lib/index.js* file now, so that you can intercept the signal correctly. Listing 15.28 shows the point at which you should integrate the function call.

```
import { createInterface } from 'readline';
import chalk from 'chalk';
import createTask from './task.js';
import promisedQuestion from './promisedQuestion.js';
import getOptions from './getOptions.js';
import summary from './summary.js';
import handleCancel from './handleCancel.js';

const { amount, level } = getOptions();

const operations = ['+', '-', '*', '/'];
const tasks = [];

operations.forEach((operation) => {
  for (let i = 0; i < amount; i++) {
    tasks.push(createTask(operation, level));
  }
});

const rl = createInterface({
  input: process.stdin,
  output: process.stdout,
});

handleCancel(rl, tasks);

async function question(index) {
  const result = await promisedQuestion(`${tasks[index].task} = `, rl);
  tasks[index].input = parseInt(result);
  if (tasks[index].input === tasks[index].result) {
    console.log(chalk.bold.green('Correct!'));
  } else {
    console.log(chalk.bold.red('Wrong'));
  }
```

```
  if (++index < tasks.length) {
    question(index);
  } else {
    console.log(summary(tasks));
    rl.close();
  }
}

question(0);
```

Listing 15.28 Integrating the Signal Handler (lib/index.js)

If you restart your application after making these adjustments, you can terminate the application at any time by pressing `Ctrl`+`C` and obtain a summary like the one shown in Figure 15.1.

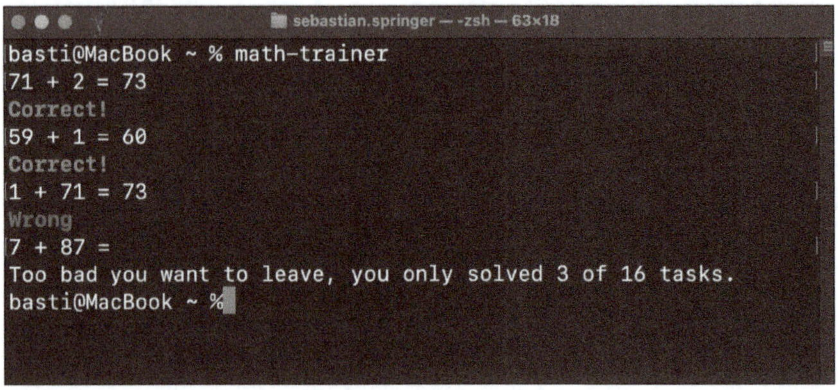

Figure 15.1 Terminating the Application

15.6   Exit Codes

Signals are means by which you can communicate with an application. Exit codes, on the other hand, work in exactly the opposite direction. In a way, an exit code is the return value of an application. On a Unix system, the echo $? command enables you to read the exit code of the last command on the command line. Usually, a Node.js application exits with exit code 0. This means that the application was terminated without any problem. An exit code with a value greater than 0 indicates an error.

Code	Name	Description
1	Uncaught Fatal Exception	An exception occurred that wasn't caught and caused the application to terminate.

Table 15.1 Exit Codes in Node.js

Code	Name	Description
3	Internal JavaScript Parse Error	The source code of Node.js itself caused a parse error.
4	Internal JavaScript Evaluation Failure	An error occurred while running Node.js.
5	Fatal Error	A fatal error has occurred in the V8 engine.
6	Nonfunctional Internal Exception Handler	An exception occurred and wasn't caught. The internal exception handler has been disabled.
7	Internal Exception Handler Runtime Failure	An exception occurred, wasn't caught, and the internal exception handler threw an exception itself.
9	Invalid Argument	An invalid option was passed during the call.
10	Internal JavaScript Runtime Failure	An exception occurred while bootstrapping Node.js.
12	Invalid Debug Argument	An invalid port was specified for the debugger.
>128	Signal Exit	If Node.js is terminated by a signal, the exit code 128 plus the value of the signal is set.

Table 15.1 Exit Codes in Node.js (Cont.)

Node.js automatically sets the correct exit code in most cases. However, you can also specify an exit code yourself. The `exit` method of the `process` module enables you to terminate the current process. This method accepts an integer as argument, which is used as an exit code.

15.7   Summary

Whenever you're faced with a problem you need to solve with a shell script, you can use Node.js. Especially when it comes to implementing solutions for automating tasks in the web environment, Node.js comes in handy. Many existing tools such as various CSS preprocessors, JavaScript optimizers, and HTML parsers show how processing web standards on the command line can work with Node.js.

You don't even have to look at such a Node.js command-line tool to know that it's a JavaScript application. Thus, such tools behave like the native commands. You can pass arguments and options to your Node.js application. For parsing the command line, you should use one of the available libraries such as Commander. As everywhere, the principle applies that you should first check the npm repository to see if there is already a solution to your problem before you start implementing it.

What a command-line application with Node.js is capable of is shown by a multitude of implementations that are used every day in web development, such as the build tool webpack.

Chapter 16

Asynchronous Programming

My advice is you should be able to do more than you do, than to do more than you can.
—Bertold Brecht

The architecture of Node.js expects an application to be run in one process and one thread. The advantage of this is that you don't need to worry about concurrency and the resource access problems it creates. To avoid performance issues caused by this architecture, most of the platform's features are implemented in such a way that much of the work can be outsourced, allowing Node.js to remain responsive. The key to this is the asynchronous processing of tasks. So far, you've already learned about some of the features of JavaScript and Node.js that can help you deal with asynchronicity. In this chapter, you'll get to know the asynchronous concepts in greater detail. We'll also take a look at advanced concepts that allow you to distribute your Node.js application across multiple processes or threads, making better use of local resources.

16.1 Basic Principles of Asynchronous Programming

Most features of Node.js are based on *asynchronicity*. You can see this by working with either promises or callback functions. For you as a developer, asynchronicity means that you have to wait until the result of an operation is available. This makes program control more difficult at first because you can't work with direct return values as usual. If Node.js allowed you to perform operations synchronously despite its single-threaded approach, and if such an operation took longer, the platform wouldn't be able to perform other tasks simultaneously during that time. This becomes obvious when you look at the source code shown in Listing 16.1.

```
import { readFileSync } from 'fs';

console.log('Operation 1');
const content = readFileSync('input.txt', 'utf-8');
console.log('Content: ', content);
console.log('Operation 2');
console.log('Operation 3');
```

Listing 16.1 Sequential Program Flow

In the source code, you first run the first console.log statement. After that, you read the contents of the *input.txt* file synchronously. This means you're waiting for the return of the operation. In the meantime, all other operations have to wait, so the subsequent console.log statements, which are independent of the file contents, can't be run either. Figure 16.1 clarifies this process.

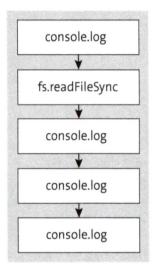

Figure 16.1 Synchronous Program Flow

When you save the source code from Listing 16.1 in a file named *index.js*, create another *input.txt* file that contains the line Hello Node.js, and then run the source code via the node index.js command, you'll get output as shown in Listing 16.2.

```
$ node index.js
Operation 1
Content:  Hello Node.js
Operation 2
Operation 3
```

Listing 16.2 Output of the Synchronous Program

Now, you need to remove potentially blocking operations such as file reading from the application process. The Node.js platform provides you with several options to do that by means of modules as they help you swap out certain routines. What sounds like an abstract concept in theory is used in many modules of Node.js. Specifically, you can find asynchronous operations in the fs module, for example. Listing 16.3 shows how asynchronous file reading works.

```
import { readFile } from 'fs';

console.log('Operation 1');
```

```
readFile('input.txt', 'utf-8', (err, content) => {
  console.log('Content: ', content);
});
console.log('Operation 2');
console.log('Operation 3');
```

Listing 16.3 Asynchronous Reading of Files

In contrast to synchronous execution, here the file is read asynchronous, meaning that the two subsequent console.log statements are run immediately and don't wait until the file has been read entirely. Once the contents of the file are available, the console.log statement from the callback function gets executed. This results in a slightly different program flow, as you can see in Figure 16.2.

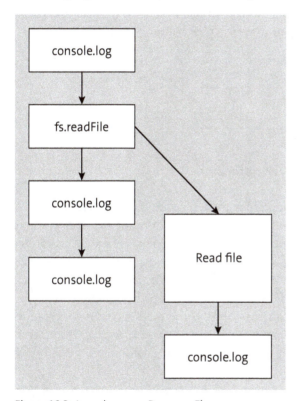

Figure 16.2 Asynchronous Program Flow

When reading a single small text file, this type of operation isn't yet a problem. However, if a large number of small files or a few large files are to be processed, these operations may take a long time in total. If you process this information away from users or other systems, that is, in an environment that is not time critical, you can also execute the files directly in the main thread of your application. However, if users come into play who are working with your application at the same time, the parallel requests cause delays because the requests can only be processed sequentially.

The asynchronous processing of tasks, such as reading a file, is based on the event-driven infrastructure of Node.js. Internally, the request is passed to the operating system, and the callback function is registered to handle the response. The operating system takes care of processing the task from this point on. For the logic of your application, this means that the subsequent command is executed after calling the readFile method, so the processing of the application isn't blocked by the read operation. Finally, when the read operation has been completed, the result is returned to Node.js. The Node.js platform then takes care of calling the previously registered callback function. For the callback function to be executed, the processing of the application must be briefly halted.

If you rebuild the previous *index.js* file from Listing 16.1 to match the code state from Listing 16.3 and then run the application via the node index.js command, you get the output shown in Listing 16.4.

```
$ node index.js
Operation 1
Operation 2
Operation 3
Content:  Hello Node.js
```

Listing 16.4 Output of the Asynchronous Program Flow

A characteristic of asynchronous processing is the registration of callback functions. The difference here becomes especially clear when you look at the methods in the fs module. Here, a synchronous counterpart exists for almost every asynchronous method. Thus, the readFile method is also available in its synchronous form as read-FileSync. Both methods differ only in the number of their parameters and in their return value. The synchronous version of the method has one parameter less. You don't need a callback function in this case because the method returns the results directly. The asynchronous readFile method returns undefined as a value. The processing of the returned content, once the results are available, takes place within the callback function.

If an error occurs during the execution of the operation—for example, the file that readFile is supposed to read doesn't exist—you'll receive an object containing the corresponding error message as the first argument of the callback function. If you ignore this object, your application will continue to run nevertheless. The case is different with the synchronous version of the method. Only one return value is available here, so the error message can't be encapsulated in a separate object in addition to the returned data. If the file to be read with readFileSync can't be found, the method returns an exception, which you must handle with a try-catch block, or the execution of your entire application will be interrupted.

The child_process module allows you to create asynchronous operations for your own application, to which you can swap out calculations.

16.1.1   The child_process Module

The child_process module combines a set of methods for asynchronous programming of applications for you. At this point, we'll primarily focus on the basic structure of the module and the ChildProcess class it contains.

> **Child Processes in Node.js**
>
> A child process is an independent process coupled with the parent process that created it. Using the child_process module, you can fork any number of child processes. However, you should keep in mind that each of these processes consumes system resources such as memory and CPU time. If you have more child processes than CPU cores, the child processes compete for the CPU and slow each other down. Parent and child processes can communicate directly with each other via messages. For larger amounts of data, you can also use sockets for communication.

Like the parent process, which is your actual application, each child process has three streams: a standard input, a standard output, and the standard error output. The child process can share all three streams with the parent process. However, you can also create stream objects and assign them to the child process. The three properties stdin, stdout, and stderr are available for this purpose. You get the object representing the child process as the return value of the spawn, exec, and fork methods. These methods can be used to start a child process. In the following sections, you'll learn more about each method, its field of application, and the differences. Here it's only worth mentioning that they return the representation of the child process, which you can use within your application to interact with the child process.

Using the kill method, you can send a signal from the parent process to the child process. The name of this method is somewhat misleading because you don't need to terminate the process. You can rather use the method to send signals to enable inter-process communication. For example, you can use SIGKILL or SIGTERM to terminate the process. If you don't provide a value when calling the method, SIGTERM is used by default, which gives the process an opportunity to perform various cleanup tasks before termination. In Node.js, this type of inter-process communication is solved using an event architecture. If you call the kill method on the child process, an exit event is generated to which you can register a callback function. The first argument of this callback function is the return value of the child process if it terminated normally. If the process was terminated by a signal, this argument has the value null. The second argument is the signal that was sent to the child process, for example, the string SIGTERM.

The second method—disconnect—is used to terminate the communication link between the parent and child processes. In concrete terms, this means you can no longer exchange messages between the parent and child processes. Calling this method triggers the disconnect event in the child process, which you can in turn bind to with a callback function to respond accordingly. Besides triggering the event, the connected property is also set from the value true to false.

In addition to the events already presented, the close event is special in that it gets triggered as soon as the stream object representing the standard input of the child process is terminated by the end method. Again, you can bind a callback function to this event.

The other methods of communication between the parent and child process will be introduced in the context of the fork method based on a concrete example.

Processes and Threads

A *process* is the representation of a program in an operating system. A process occupies an area of memory that usually is exclusively available to it. In addition, a process receives computing time from the processor to perform calculations. For more information on processes, see *https://en.wikipedia.org/wiki/Process_(computing)*.

A *thread*, on the other hand, is a part of a process and denotes a thread of execution within a program. In concrete terms, this means a process can consist of several threads. A thread has access to the resources of the process to which it's assigned. Each thread of a process has its own stack. A stack is a memory in which the thread can store elements and from which it can read them again. This stack is exclusive to one thread. The other threads of the process can't access it. For more information on threads, see *https://en.wikipedia.org/wiki/Thread_(computing)*.

When you run Node.js, a process gets started. Within this process, a single thread is executed because the Node.js platform is based on a single-threaded approach.

Node.js supports both multiple processes and multiple threads within an application. Both variants are represented by different modules—the child_process and the worker_threads modules.

16.2   Running External Commands Asynchronously

You can use the spawn, exec, and execFile methods of the child_process module to execute commands independently of Node.js. Via these methods, you can use all the commands available to you on the command line of your operating system as well.

Using these running commands has the advantage that you can directly access the functionality of the operating system or utilities without laboriously implementing the functionality in JavaScript first. In Node.js, you can control the behavior via options and get access to the output of each executed command.

16.2.1   The exec Method

The simpler of the two variants for executing external commands is to use the two exec commands. Listing 16.5 shows an example of running the exec method to find the Node.js executable file in your system.

```
import { exec } from 'child_process';

const cmd = 'find /usr/local -iname "node"';

exec(cmd, (err, stdout, stderr) => {
  if (err) {
    throw err;
  }

  console.log(stdout);
});
```

Listing 16.5 Running an External Command via "exec" on a Unix System

In the first step, you need the exec method, which you get directly from the child_process module using an import statement. Then you formulate the command you want to issue; in the example, this involves searching for files and directories named *node* under the */usr/local* directory. This string serves as the first argument for calling the exec method. In this context, you should note that commands such as rm -rf / can also be passed, which will potentially cause significant damage on your system. The final argument of the exec call is always a callback function that will be executed as soon as the result of the command is available. The arguments available to you within the callback function are an error object that has a value if an error occurred during the execution of the command; a buffer object as a second argument, which contains the standard output of the command; and, finally, as a third argument, another buffer object that contains the values of the standard error output.

The specified command is executed by calling exec in a subshell, that is, on a separate command line. Its output is buffered, and the result is finally made available in the buffer object of the callback function just described. The execution is asynchronous, which means that your application isn't blocked by the processing of the external command.

If you specify an object as the second argument in addition to the command and the callback function, you can affect the execution by specifying various options. The individual options, their meanings, and their default values are listed in Table 16.1.

Option	Default Value	Description
cwd	null	Current working directory for the child process.
encoding	utf8	Character encoding for the output.

Table 16.1 Options for Configuring the "exec" Method

Option	Default Value	Description
env	null	Environment variables for the child process as key-value pairs.
signal	—	If a value is specified, the child process can be terminated using an AbortController.
killSignal	SIGTERM	Signal used to terminate the child process if it runs longer than the specified time-out value, for example.
maxBuffer	1024 * 1024	Maximum size for standard output and standard error output. If this size is exceeded, the child process gets terminated.
timeout	0	Number of milliseconds after which the child process is forcibly terminated with the signal specified under killSignal.
uid	—	User under which the process is executed.
gid	—	Group under which the process is executed.
windowsHide	false	Hides the console window the command would open on a Windows system.
shell	bin/sh (Unix) or process.env.ComSpec (Windows)	Specification of a specific shell on which the command is to be run.

Table 16.1 Options for Configuring the "exec" Method (Cont.)

The exec method allows you not only to execute typical shell commands but also run whatever programs you want, including, for example, a full-fledged Node.js application that runs in a child process of the parent application.

In addition to the exec method, the somewhat more lightweight execFile method is available that allows you to run the contents of a file directly. Listing 16.6 shows the contents of such an executable file.

```
#!/usr/local/bin/node
console.log('Hello World');
```

Listing 16.6 Executable File as Input for "execFile" (input.js)

By saving this source code as *input.js* in the same directory as your Node.js application, you can run the source code from Listing 16.7 and get the Hello World output on the command line.

```
import { execFile } from 'child_process';

execFile('./input.js', (err, stdout, stderr) => {
  console.log(stdout);
});
```

Listing 16.7 Running a File with "execFile"

In the input file from Listing 16.6 you can see that you can also execute JavaScript code with this method. All you have to do is specify in the first line of the input file which application should be used to run the file. In this particular case, that's */usr/local/bin/node*, which you can determine on a Unix system via the which node command. However, you can also execute normal shell commands such as find. You don't need to start the file with #!/bin/bash, just specify the commands to be executed one after the other.

The actual application, whose source code you can find in Listing 16.7, merely ensures that the file is executed and the results are output as standard output. In the example, you must note that the executed file must have the extension *.js* if you use the ECMAScript module system in conjunction with "type": "module" in *package.json*. Otherwise, Node.js will throw an ERR_UNKNOWN_FILE_EXTENSION error.

The second option available to you for executing external commands is the spawn method. The following section describes this method in greater detail.

16.2.2   The spawn Method

Unlike the two exec methods, spawn doesn't use a buffer of the command output. Instead, both the inputs and outputs of the process are available as data streams. This means the data you can access here isn't a one-time image, but a continuous stream of data. This has a couple advantages in that you're not limited to a maximum output size when using spawn, you get access to the data at the time it's created, not when the command is finished.

Listing 16.8 shows a simple variant of using the spawn method.

```
import { spawn } from 'child_process';

const find = spawn('find', ['.', '-iname', 'node'], { cwd: '/usr/local' });

find.stdout.on('data', (data) => {
  console.log(data.toString());
});
```

Listing 16.8 "spawn" Method in Use

As in the example for the exec method, a search is performed again for files and directories named *node*. You can already see the differences between spawn and exec in the specification of the command itself. Whereas with exec you provided the command and all associated options as a character string, with the second argument of spawn, you pass an array of options for the command. As with exec, you can additionally affect the spawn method by specifying further options in the third argument. In the example shown in Listing 16.8, this is the current working directory of the process, which you specify via the cwd option. All other possible options are shown in Table 16.2. Note here that the options are different from those available under the exec method.

Option	Description
argv0	Explicitly sets the value for the first element of argv that is sent to the child process.
cwd	Current working directory for the process.
detached	If this option is set to true, the child process is executed independently of the parent process. This means the child process isn't necessarily terminated when the parent process is terminated.
env	Allows you to specify the values of environment variables as key-value pairs.
gid	Group ID under which the child process is to be executed. Note that you must have the relevant permissions for this operation.
killSignal	Signal that is sent to the child process in the event of a timeout or AbortSignal. The default value is SIGTERM.
serialization	Allows you to specify the type of serialization of messages between processes. The standard value is json.
shell	Possibility to set a shell on which the command will be executed.
signal	Allows canceling the child process with an AbortSignal.
stdio	Configuration options for the inputs and outputs.
timeout	Maximum time the child process is allowed to run. The default value is undefined.
uid	ID of the user under which the child process is to be executed. Again, as with gid, you need to have the relevant permissions.

Table 16.2 Options for the "spawn" Method

Option	Description
WindowsHide	Hides the console window that would be opened for the child process on a Windows system.
WindowsVerbatimArguments	No quoting and escaping for command-line options on a Windows system.

Table 16.2 Options for the "spawn" Method (Cont.)

Because you have access to both standard input and standard output, you can also combine two commands. You can do this on the Unix command line using the pipe. The example shown in Listing 16.9 is supposed to have the same effect as the following command line: find /usr/local -iname 'node' | grep 'bin'. This means you search for files and directories named *node* in the */usr/local* directory and then filter the found hits for the character string bin.

```
import { spawn } from 'child_process';
const find = spawn('find', ['.', '-iname', 'node'], { cwd: '/usr/local' });
const grep = spawn('grep', ['bin']);

find.stdout.pipe(grep.stdin);

find.on('exit', (code) => {
  grep.stdin.end();
});

grep.stdout.on('data', (data) => {
  console.log('' + data);
});
```

Listing 16.9 Combining Two Commands with "spawn"

For each command in the chain, you must call the spawn method. You'll receive an object of the ChildProcess type as a return value, which you'll continue to use in the following steps. Using the pipe method of the standard output of the find child process, you connect the two child processes so that the standard output of the find process writes to the standard input of the grep process. Alternatively, you could bind a callback function to the data event of the standard output of the find process. This event is called as soon as this process writes data to the standard output. You then write this data to the standard input of the grep process using the write method. Irrespective of whether you've chosen the short or the verbose variant, as soon as the output of the find process is completed, that is, the exit event is triggered, you should terminate the standard input of the grep process by calling the end method of the object representing the standard input of this process. Finally, as was the case with the find process, you can bind a callback function to the data event of the standard output of the grep process, in which you can present the obtained information to the user on the standard output.

As you've seen, you can execute commands with spawn as well as with exec, just as you would enter them in the command line of your system. You can use commands of the operating system directly or run specially created shell scripts. As you know, such a shell script can also contain JavaScript code. However, with this variant of execution, you have hardly any possibilities to communicate between the processes. You can only use standard input and standard output as communication medium in a rather awkward way. A better way to execute JavaScript code in a child process is to use the fork method, which will be described in greater detail in the following section.

16.3   Creating Node.js Child Processes with fork Method

In your Node.js application, you probably not only want to run external programs, but more importantly, you want to swap out parts of the application logic into your own child processes. Code fragments with very time-consuming processing are particularly well suited for such measures. With this approach, you follow the same approach that the developers have envisioned for the entire Node.js platform. Basically, this means that you swap out CPU-intensive functions to prevent the processing of your application from being blocked. Once the result of the function is available, your application continues to work with this result within a callback function.

To allow you to swap out functionality from the main thread of your application, the Node.js platform provides the fork method from the child_process module. Calling the fork method is similar to calling the spawn and exec methods, where the first argument is the name of the module to be run. The module denotes the file containing the JavaScript source code that forms the basis of the child process. The second argument contains the values to be passed to the child process, and finally the third argument is a configuration object. In the configuration object, you have various options for affecting the behavior of the child process, as is the case with the other methods of the child_process module. Table 16.3 lists the available options you can use when processing the call.

Option	Description
cwd	Current working directory of the child process.
env	Environment variables for the child process in the form of key-value pairs.
execPath	Executable file used to create the child process.
execArgv	Arguments for the executable file.

Table 16.3 Options for the "fork" Method

Option	Description
silent	If this value is set to true, the default outputs of the parent process aren't used.
stdio	Standard input, standard output, and standard error output for the process. If nothing is specified here, the streams of the parent process are used.
windowsVerbatimAr-guments	No quoting and escaping of arguments on Windows.
uid	User under which the child process is to be executed.
gid	Group under which the child process is to be executed.
detached	Allows the child process to be run independently from the parent process with.
serialization	Specifies how messages are serialized between processes. The default value is json.
signal	Allows the child process to be terminated with an AbortSignal.
killSignal	Specifies the type of signal if the child process is to be terminated by a time-out or AbortSignal. The default value is SIGTERM.
timeout	Specifies after how many milliseconds the child process terminates.

Table 16.3 Options for the "fork" Method (Cont.)

The source code in Listing 16.10 forms the basis for the further examples related to the fork method.

```
import { fork } from 'child_process';

if (process.argv[2] && process.argv[2] === 'child') {
  console.log('Child Process');
} else {
  console.log('Parent Process');
  fork(process.argv[1], ['child']);
}
```

Listing 16.10 Sample Application Containing the "fork" Method (index.js)

If you save the source code in a new file named *index.js* and execute it using the node index.js command, the output you'll get is first the parent process and then the child process string. This type of application allows you to manage the source code of the parent process together with the code of the child process in a single file. You use both the ability to provide additional arguments to the child process via the fork method and the ability to access those arguments via process.argv. In this example, you pass an argument named child to the child process. Thus, you can now use the process.argv[2] property to check whether it exists and contains the child value, and thus determine whether you're in the parent or child process when currently executing the source code. However, in a production environment, you should swap out the code blocks for the parent and the child process into separate files, as this supports the maintainability and readability of your application. In the sample code, you can also see another special characteristic: In the call of the fork method, you normally specify the name of the file to be executed in the child process as the first argument. In the example, you use the process.argv[1] property to specify the name of the current file, ensuring that the same file is loaded in the child process.

Calling fork causes a new Node.js process to be launched. The file specified as an argument in the call is loaded and interpreted as JavaScript code. Because every use of fork results in a new process being created, you shouldn't create an unlimited number of child processes, as they also take up a considerable number of resources. Specifically, this affects mainly the memory and some processing power, depending on the operations you want to have performed.

So far, the example from Listing 16.10 still makes relatively little sense because the child process has no logic, and both the parent and child processes don't communicate with each other yet. Listing 16.11 shows how you can extend the code of this example to see the fork method in action.

```
import { fork } from 'child_process';

if (process.argv[2] && process.argv[2] === 'child') {
  console.log('child');
  let n = 1;
  let results = 0;
  outerLoop: while (results <= 1000) {
    n += 1;
    for (let i = 2; i <= Math.sqrt(n); i += 1) {
      if (n % i === 0) {
        continue outerLoop;
      }
    }
    process.send({ prime: n });
    results += 1;
  }
  process.exit();
} else {
  const child1 = fork(process.argv[1], ['child']);
  const child2 = fork(process.argv[1], ['child']);
  const child3 = fork(process.argv[1], ['child']);
```

```
  child1.on('message', (data) => {
    console.log('child1: ' + data.prime);
  });
  child2.on('message', (data) => {
    console.log('child2: ' + data.prime);
  });
  child3.on('message', (data) => {
    console.log('child3: ' + data.prime);
  });
}
```

Listing 16.11 Extended "fork" Example

The source code in Listing 16.11 makes sure that 1,000 prime numbers are calculated in each of three independent child processes and returned to the parent process, which is responsible for processing the output.

To achieve this result, in the first step, you start three child processes via three respective calls of the fork method, as you already know from Listing 16.10. The logic for the child process is located in the first part of the if statement. Here, a loop is used to check whether a number is a prime number. This process is run until the required total number of prime numbers has been found. The feedback to the parent process is done via the send method of the process object. The message to the parent process that you pass to this method as the first argument exists in the form of an object.

On the parent process side, you handle messages from the child processes by registering one callback function to the message event per instantiated child process. To help you distinguish which child process each prime number originates from, you should prefix an identifier to the output, such as child1 for the first child process.

However, communication isn't limited to one-way communication from the child process to the parent process, as a transfer of data in the other direction is also possible. Listing 16.12 shows how you can send messages from the parent process to the child process.

```
import { fork } from 'child_process';

if (process.argv[2] && process.argv[2] === 'child') {
  process.on('message', (data) => {
    console.log('in child process:', data);
  });
  process.send('ready');
} else {
  const child = fork(process.argv[1], ['child']);

  child.on('message', (data) => {
```

```
    if (data === 'ready') {
      for (let i = 0; i < 10; i += 1) {
        child.send(i);
      }
    }
  });
}
```

Listing 16.12 Communication from the Parent Process to the Child Process

In this example, you can see that both processes can send messages back and forth equally. To do this, you first use the fork method in the else branch of the if statement to create the child process. In the child process, you register a message handler that writes the received data to the console. Then you send a message with the content ready to the parent process.

In the parent process, you first take care of creating the child process using the fork method and also register a message handler. Once the child process sends the ready message, the parent process starts sending the numbers from 0 to 9 in a loop to the child process, resulting in an output on the console as shown in Listing 16.13.

```
$ node index.js
in child process: 0
in child process: 1
in child process: 2
in child process: 3
in child process: 4
in child process: 5
in child process: 6
in child process: 7
in child process: 8
in child process: 9
```

Listing 16.13 Output of the Communication between the Parent and Child Processes

To terminate the application, you must disconnect the parent and child processes. You can do this by calling the disconnect method of the child process in the parent process. The disconnect method cuts the connection between the two processes and makes the child process terminate if no more connections exist.

16.4   The cluster Module

In general, applications based on Node.js run in a thread. However, with the methods of the child_process module, you're able to run worker processes and swap out parts of your application from the main thread. A similar approach is taken by the cluster

module of the Node.js platform. This module is based on the functionality of the child_
process module to create worker processes. This module enables a kind of load balancing for Node.js applications. You can use it to start multiple types of HTTP servers or Transmission Control Protocol (TCP) servers on systems with multiple processor cores. These run in separate processes, enabling a better utilization of available resources.

The entry point into this process pool is the main process. This process provides for the creation and control of worker processes. The main process also manages the handlers for the requests. If the listen method is called in a worker process, the arguments are passed to the main process. This process then checks if a handle with this configuration already exists. If so, the object representing the handle is returned to the worker process. If no handle exists yet, the main process creates it and returns the newly created object to the worker process.

As soon as requests start coming in, they are routed to the relevant process. If several processes are bound to the requested combination of address and port, the operating system takes care of distributing the requests to the corresponding processes. In this case, the operating system takes over the responsibility for load balancing. As a result, you don't have to worry about this task, nor is the Node.js platform responsible for it.

Not only are the worker processes independent of each other, they also know nothing about each other. They have no way to communicate with each other. The processes also don't share a common memory area. Communication can only take place via the main process. This process contains references to the individual worker processes.

16.4.1 Main Process

The main process represents the core of the cluster module. Before you can use the functionalities of this module, you must first instantiate the main process. You create and configure the main process using the setupPrimary method. You can pass an object containing the configuration to this method when you call it. Ten properties of the configuration object are available to you to manipulate the behavior of the main process. The properties and their respective meanings are listed in Table 16.4.

Characteristic	Default Value	Description
execArgv	process.execArgv	List of arguments passed to the node process.
exec	process.argv(1)	Name of the file to be run as a worker process.
args	process.argv.slice(2)	Arguments to be passed to the worker process.
cwd	undefined	The current working directory of the process. The worker process inherits this information from the main process by default.

Table 16.4 Configuration Options for the Main Process

Characteristic	Default Value	Description
serialization	false	Specifies how messages are serialized between processes.
silent	false	If this property is set to true, the standard output of the main process isn't used.
uid	—	User identity of the process.
gid	—	Group identity of the process.
inspectPort	process.debugPort	Inspector port of the worker process.
windowsHide	false	Hides the console window that is normally created on a Windows system for the worker process.

Table 16.4 Configuration Options for the Main Process (Cont.)

The settings you make via setupPrimary are stored in the settings property of the cluster object. However, you should always make changes to the settings using the setupPrimary method instead of editing the settings property directly. The setupPrimary method ensures that the settings properties are set correctly and prevents further changes. Note that you can call the setupPrimary method only once. On the second call, changes to the settings won't have any effect. Thus, calling this method multiple times won't have any consequences for your application. You can only call this method in the context of the main process and not from a worker process.

If you don't want to adjust the default settings, you don't need to call the setupPrimary method. As soon as you create a worker process via the fork method, the setupPrimary method is called automatically. Once fork has been called, you'll no longer be able to make any changes to the settings of your main process.

If you want to manage the source code of the main process and the worker processes in one file, the cluster module provides you with the isPrimary and isWorker properties as an option to check which context within your application you're currently working in. Internally, this functionality accesses the NODE_UNIQUE_ID property of process.env. This property is used by the cluster module to assign a unique identification number to a worker process. If you're in the main process, the property has the value undefined. Once a child process is created, it's assigned a unique identification number.

Like many other components of the Node.js platform, the cluster module is also an event-driven component, meaning different operations trigger certain events when the module is being used. The first event you come across is the setup event. It's triggered as soon as you initialize the main process via the setupPrimary method. This is done either explicitly by calling the method or implicitly by calling fork. In both cases, however, the setup event is triggered. The callback function you can bind to this event doesn't receive an argument.

The next step in using the cluster module is to create worker processes through the fork method. Calling this method results in a fork event. Inside the callback function, you can access the worker process via the argument this function receives.

As soon as the worker process is launched, the online event is triggered on the cluster object. Again, you get access to the worker process within the callback function via the argument.

The cluster module specializes in load balancing between multiple server processes. For both the Net server and the HTTP server, you bind your server to a port and a socket, respectively, by calling the listen method. As soon as you call this method in your worker process, the listening event is triggered on the cluster object and you can respond to it accordingly in the main process. In addition to the object representing the worker process, this method receives the address to which the server of the worker process is bound as a second argument.

The last two events are triggered when the worker process is terminated. The disconnect event signals that the communication link between the main and worker processes has been terminated, so there is no longer any possibility of interaction. This event is normally triggered as an effect of calling the disconnect or destroy methods on the worker process. The disconnect event also gets triggered when the worker process is terminated from outside, for example, by the kill command of the operating system. The only argument available within the callback function that you can bind to this event is the object representation of the worker process.

The second event that gets triggered when a worker process is terminated is the exit event. This event indicates to the main process that one of the worker processes has been terminated. It's normally triggered after the disconnect event. In the callback function of this event, two other arguments are available in addition to the object for the worker process that was terminated. The second argument is a number specifying the exit code of the worker process. The third and last argument is the name of the signal that caused the termination of the worker process, for example, SIGHUP.

Table 16.5 briefly summarizes again for you the events available in connection with the cluster module.

Event	Description
online	The worker process reports its readiness to the online event.
listening	As soon as the listen method is called within the worker process, the listening event is executed.
disconnect	Once the communication links between the main and worker processes are terminated, you'll receive the disconnect event.

Table 16.5 Overview of Cluster Events

Event	Description
exit	This event signals that a worker has been terminated.
error	An error event gets triggered when a worker process couldn't be created, the process couldn't be terminated, or the sending of messages failed.
message	This event is triggered when a message has been sent to the process.

Table 16.5 Overview of Cluster Events (Cont.)

Within the main process, you can use three methods. You already learned how to use the first method, setupPrimary, to configure the general behavior of the main process. You already know the fork method from the child_process module. In the cluster module, this method is used to start the worker processes. The example in Listing 16.14 illustrates the use of the different methods.

```
import cluster from 'cluster';
import { createServer } from 'http';

const timeout = 30000;

if (cluster.isPrimary) {
  cluster.setupPrimary({silent: true}); // no logs from worker

  setTimeout(cluster.disconnect, timeout);

  cluster.on('exit', function () {
    console.log(`Workers were terminated after ${timeout}ms`);
  });

  cluster.fork();
  cluster.fork();
}

if (cluster.isWorker) {
  console.log(`Worker ${cluster.worker.id} started`);
  createServer((req, res) => {
    console.log(`Worker ${cluster.worker.id} has received a request`);
    res.end(`Worker ${cluster.worker.id} xxx`);
  }).listen('8080');
}
```

Listing 16.14 The "cluster" Module in Use

Using the source code from the example, you create two child processes, both listening on port 8080. This works because the main process in the default configuration accepts the incoming connections and forwards them to the child processes. Alternatively, it's possible for the main process to pass the connection to the child process and for the child process to accept the incoming connection.

All three methods, that is, setupPrimary, fork, and disconnect, can only be run in the main process. If you call one of these three methods from a worker process, this results in an error and the termination of the worker process. To avoid this problem, you can use the isPrimary and isWorker properties, as shown in Listing 16.14.

16.4.2   Worker Processes

Using the fork method, you can create any number of worker processes from within the main process. These workers are represented within your application by objects that provide various properties, methods, and events for interacting with the processes.

But before you start looking at worker objects, you should know how to obtain them. In this context, you have several options: If you're in the main process, you can access the different workers via the cluster.workers property. The workers object contains references to all worker processes. The keys of the object are the IDs of the respective worker processes, while the values are the object representations of the worker processes. With this structure, you can find out how many worker processes have currently been started and also control the individual workers. Another way to access the workers from the main process is to bind callback functions to various events of the worker objects, such as the online event, for example. Again, you get access to the worker objects in the form of arguments. From the worker process, you can access the object of the current worker via cluster.worker. It's not possible to influence the other workers here.

Each worker process has a unique identifier. You can read it using the id property of the worker process. More information about the corresponding worker process is provided by the process property. Like the fork method, this property illustrates the basis of the cluster module. The basis for creating worker processes is the fork method of the child_process module. Thus, the object stored in the process property of the worker process also has the ChildProcess type. For example, you can use this object to access the worker's process ID via cluster.worker.process.pid. The last property available to you as part of the worker process is named exitedAfterDisconnect. Typically, this property has the value undefined. However, it's set to true as soon as the worker is in the process of termination; that is, either disconnect or destroy has been called.

The methods of the worker object form the interface through which you can interact with the worker process. The example in Listing 16.15 illustrates how you can use the send method to send messages between main and worker processes. As you can also see in this example, communication works both ways.

```
import cluster from 'cluster';
import { createServer } from 'http';

if (cluster.isPrimary) {
  cluster.fork();
  cluster.fork();

  cluster.on('listening', (worker) => {
    console.log(`Worker ${worker.id} ready`);

    setTimeout(() => {
      worker.send('Hello Primary');
    }, 2000);
  });

  for (let i in cluster.workers) {
    cluster.workers[i].on(
      'message',
      function (i, msg) {
        console.log(`Worker ${i} => Primary: ${msg}`);
      }.bind(this, i),
    );
  }
} else {
  createServer((req, res) => {
    res.end('Hello Client');
  }).listen('8080');

  cluster.worker.on('message', (msg) => {
    console.log(`Primary => Worker ${cluster.worker.id}: ${msg}`);
  });

  cluster.worker.send('Hello Primary');
}
```

Listing 16.15 Communication between the Main and Worker Processes

Once the worker process has been launched, it sends a message with the content Hello Primary to the main process via its own send method. This in turn binds callback functions to the message events of the various worker processes in a for loop to be able to react to their messages. As soon as the message is received by the main process, it's output to the console with some additional information. For its part, the main process binds a callback function to the `listening` event of the cluster. When the `listen` method is called in a worker process, the main process is notified and issues a corresponding message on the console. Within this callback function, a time-out is set to two seconds. After its expiration, a message is sent to the worker process. The worker process has also registered a callback function to the `message` event and can thus handle and emit the message from the main process.

In addition to the possibility of sending messages, two other methods of terminating the worker process are available in connection with worker processes. You already know the first method—`disconnect`—from the main process. In the main process, this method does nothing more than call the `disconnect` method of each worker process, in addition to some cleanup work. Once you've called the `disconnect` method, the worker won't accept any more incoming connections. If there are still connections to clients, however, they are first served before the worker process is terminated.

The `destroy` method enables you to terminate a worker process. Its form depends on the location from where you call the method. From the main process, the `process.kill` method is executed. If you're in the context of the worker process, `process.exit` is executed. However, in both cases, the `exitedAfterDisconnect` property is set to `true` so that you can determine whether a process was terminated by `destroy` or a system error.

In addition, there are various events available in the worker process that help you to respond to the occurrence of various situations. In the lifecycle of a worker, the different events occur chronologically. The existence of the worker process starts with the `online` event. This event is triggered as soon as the worker changes to the online status. Within the callback function, you have access to the object representing the worker via the argument of this function.

The next event that occurs in connection with a worker process is the `listening` event. Like the cluster event of the same name, it's triggered as soon as the `listen` method is called within the worker process and the process status changes from `online` to `listening`. An object representing the address to which the worker is bound is available as an argument in the callback function.

During the runtime of the worker process, you can send messages between the main and the worker processes. You've already learned about the corresponding `message` event. The only argument the callback function receives is the message that was sent.

At the end of the existence of a worker process there are again two events. The `disconnect` event is triggered as soon as the worker process has disconnected its communication links to the outside world, thus initiating the end of the worker. This is accompanied by a change of the process status to `disconnected`. Finally, the `exit` event indicates that the worker process is finished. Using the exit code and signal name arguments, you can determine the circumstances of the process termination. The exit code is a number that you can manipulate via the `process.exit` method. Normally, a 0 means that the process was completed successfully and without errors. The second argument—the signal name—is a character string that bears the name of the signal used to terminate the process. Both arguments don't have a value in every case.

With the capabilities presented here, you can develop server applications in Node.js that don't run in just one process. Instead, you can fork any number of worker processes, which in turn take care of processing client requests. The worker processes can be bound to the same resources such as a TCP port or Unix socket. In this case, the operating system takes care of load balancing between the processes so that the best possible utilization is achieved. The advantage of this implementation is that neither you nor the Node.js platform are responsible for distributing requests evenly across the different worker processes.

16.5   Worker Threads

Since version 10.5, Node.js has had another module besides the `child_process` module that deals with creating parallel execution threads in an application. The newer `worker_threads` module is used to swap out CPU-intensive subprocesses into a separate worker thread. The strength of the child processes of the `child_process` module rather lies in operations involving many input and output operations. The concept behind both modules is quite similar: Both make sure that a certain part of the application gets swapped out, and they provide methods and events for communication between the main process and the child processes or child threads. Listing 16.16 contains the implementation of the worker for realizing the example with 1,000 prime numbers via the `worker_threads` module.

```
import { parentPort, workerData } from 'worker_threads';

let n = workerData.start;
let results = 0;
outerLoop: while (results <= 1000) {
  n += 1;
  for (let i = 2; i <= Math.sqrt(n); i += 1) {
    if (n % i === 0) {
      continue outerLoop;
    }
  }
  parentPort.postMessage(n);
  results += 1;
}

process.exit();
```

Listing 16.16 Implementation of the Worker Thread (worker.js)

In the worker process, you import the parentPort and workerData objects from the worker_threads module. You can use the postMessage method of the parentPort object to send messages to the main thread of your application. The workerData object allows you to access information passed to the worker thread upon its creation. In this case, workerData.start defines the start value from which the prime numbers are to be searched. Calling process.exit terminates the worker thread.

The counterpart to the worker thread, that is, the main thread, is shown in Listing 16.17.

```
import { Worker } from 'worker_threads';

const worker = new Worker('./worker.js', {
  workerData: {
    start: 42,
  },
});

worker.on('message', (data) => {
  console.log(`worker => main: ${data}`);
});
```

Listing 16.17 Source Code of the Main Thread (index.js)

To create a worker thread, you import the worker class from the worker_threads module and instantiate it with the name of the worker file and an optional configuration object. The workerData property allows you to define an object structure the worker can access via the workerData object. In the main thread, you can respond to different worker events. In this case, it's the message event, which is triggered by the worker's postMessage method. Other events include exit, for example, if the worker is terminated, or error, if an error has occurred.

16.5.1 Shared Memory in the worker_threads Module

An interesting feature of the worker_threads module that isn't available in the child_process module is the sharing of memory between the main thread and the worker. In this context, you use a SharedArrayBuffer object as shown in Listing 16.18.

```
import { Worker } from 'worker_threads';

const sharedBuffer = new SharedArrayBuffer(Int32Array.BYTES_PER_ELEMENT * 1000);
const arr = new Int32Array(sharedBuffer);

const worker = new Worker('./worker.js', {
  workerData: arr,
});
```

```
worker.on('message', (data) => {
  console.log(`Worker seems to be ${data}`);
  arr.forEach((element) => console.log(element));
});
```

Listing 16.18 Main Thread with Shared Memory (index.js)

You first create an instance of the `SharedArrayBuffer` class that can contain a total of 1,000 32-bit integers. You pass this `SharedArrayBuffer` object to the `Int32Array` constructor as a storage location and additionally pass this typed array object as input when the worker thread is created. Instead of reporting each value back to the main thread individually, the worker in this example simply sends a message when all numbers have been found. The message also doesn't contain any data, but only a string that is output to the console. The calculated numbers are located in the memory of the typed array, which you output to the console using the `forEach` method of the array. So, in this example, you're not passing any data, but just memory references between the two threads. The implementation of the worker is shown in Listing 16.19.

```
import { parentPort, workerData } from 'worker_threads';

let n = 1;
let results = 0;

outerLoop: while (results <= 1000) {
  n += 1;
  for (let i = 2; i <= Math.sqrt(n); i += 1) {
    if (n % i === 0) {
      continue outerLoop;
    }
  }
  workerData[results] = n;
  results += 1;
}

parentPort.postMessage('ready');

process.exit();
```

Listing 16.19 Worker Thread with Shared Memory (worker.js)

Instead of sending each number to the main thread as a message, you write the results to the typed array that the main thread passed to the worker during the initialization process. When the calculation is complete, you use the `postMessage` method to send the `ready` string to the main thread, signaling that the data calculation has finished. Finally, you terminate the worker by calling the `exit` method. When you run the script, Node.js outputs 1,000 prime numbers, as in the previous examples. However, the mass exchange of data between the two threads is omitted in this case.

With child processes and worker threads, you now know two ways to swap out potentially blocking operations from your Node.js process. These two concepts are based on an event architecture so that they can handle asynchronicity.

The promises tool is also increasingly used with Node.js. In the following sections, you'll learn more about the promises concept. Promises serve as a tool for applications in which a large number of tasks are performed asynchronously and thus the reading flow of the source code is disturbed. Furthermore, it's used for the purpose of flow control in asynchronous applications.

16.6 Promises in Node.js

A *promise* represents the result of an asynchronous operation and a kind of return value for such an operation that allows you to better handle asynchronicity in your application. What was only possible with libraries for a long time has now found its way into the JavaScript engine. Listing 16.20 shows how you can use promises based on a small example.

```
import { readFile } from 'fs';

function promisedReadFile(filename) {
  return new Promise((resolve, reject) => {
    readFile(filename, 'utf-8', (err, data) => {
      if (err) {
        reject(err);
      } else {
        resolve(data);
      }
    });
  });
}

promisedReadFile('input.txt')
  .then((data) => {
    console.log('Content of the file: ', data);
  })
  .catch((error) => {
    console.error('An error occured: ', error.message);
  });
```

Listing 16.20 Promises in JavaScript

For the example in Listing 16.20 to work, you must first create a text file named *input.txt* that contains text. After that, you can run the sample code. The code from Listing 16.20 provides the `promisedReadFile` function, which reads the contents of a file. Usually this is done via the `readFile` function of the `fs` module. Here, this function is encapsulated by a promise object. The promise object is created via the `promise` constructor, which receives a callback function. This function is called with the `resolve` and `reject` arguments used for the success and error cases, respectively.

A promise object knows a total of four statuses:

- **Pending**
  The promise is still waiting for the asynchronous operation to finish.

- **Settled**
  The asynchronous operation was terminated.

- **Resolved**
  The asynchronous operation was completed successfully.

- **Rejected**
  The asynchronous operation failed.

Figure 16.3 illustrates these relationships.

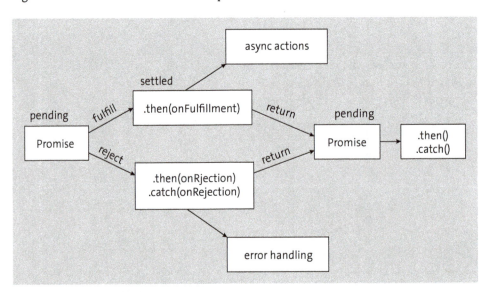

Figure 16.3 Lifecycle of a Promise

As you've seen in Listing 16.20, the `promisedReadFile` function returns a promise object. This object defines the `then` method. You can pass either one or two callback functions to it. The first of the two is executed when successful, that is, when you call the `resolve` function of the promise; the second is called when there is an error, that is, when you call `reject`. You can also catch the failure case via the `catch` method, as in the example.

The advantage here is that success and failure cases are much more cleanly separated from each other. At this point, as is often the case, there is no right way and no wrong way—just make sure that your source code remains understandable and consistent.

You can pass arguments to both the resolve and reject functions, which are then passed to the corresponding callbacks. The then method in turn returns a promise object, which also allows you to concatenate multiple promises. In an example such as reading a file, you still don't save much worked compared to normal callback functions for asynchronous operations. However, this changes when you start to combine several asynchronous operations, that is, execute asynchronous operations one after the other or perform logical flow control.

Promises and an event architecture are often compared with each other. However, promises don't replace the event architecture at all, but rather cover completely different use cases. With a promise, you can map two different statuses, namely, whether an operation was successful or not. Events, on the other hand, are much more diverse. Thus, an event source can trigger any number of different types of events, representing many more facets of an object's state change. Promises are mainly used for modeling asynchronous operations. You use events when objects change their state over their lifetime, and these changes are relevant to the outside world or other parts of your application.

A promise can also be resolved or rejected only once in its lifecycle. An event can be triggered any number of times. Just take the example of a web server. This is implemented as an event system. Each request triggers a request event to which you can register a callback function. If you were to implement the system on the basis of promises, the server would only be able to accept a single request.

Listing 16.21 shows that it's possible to encapsulate file system operations not only in promises but also in any other asynchronous actions, such as an HTTP request.

```
import { request } from 'http';

function doRequest(url) {
  return new Promise((resolve, reject) => {
    const options = {
      hostname: url,
      port: 80,
      method: 'GET',
    };
    const requestObject = request(options, (response) => {
      response.setEncoding('utf8');
      let data = '';
      response.on('data', (chunk) => (data += chunk));
      response.on('end', () => resolve(data));
      response.on('error', (e) => reject(e));
```

```
    });
    requestObject.end();
  });
}

doRequest('www.google.de').then(
  (data) => {
    console.log('data: ', data);
  },
  (err) => {
    console.error('error: ', err);
  },
);
```

Listing 16.21 Promise for an HTTP Request

In this example, you encapsulate the asynchronous operation of a server request with the doRequest function. The response of the web server doesn't happen directly in the callback function, but via a readable stream. In the data events of the stream, you collect all the data sent by the server. Once the end event gets triggered, you can successfully resolve the promise by calling the resolve method. The resolve method is used to specify the data to be processed later. If an error occurred during the request, the error event gets triggered. In that case, you reject the promise by calling the reject method. Again, you pass more information in the form of the error object. With the two callback functions, you handle the success and the error case.

16.6.1   Using util.promisify to Use Promises Where None Actually Exist

In the early days of Node.js development, you wouldn't have found promises. All asynchronous operations were implemented via callbacks. Meanwhile, in some places, such as the fs module, you'll increasingly find interfaces that natively support promises. For this purpose, for example, there is the fs/promise module which offers a promise-based variant for almost all functions of the fs module. Nevertheless, Node.js has a variety of functions that meet all the requirements for using promises as well. For this purpose, there is the promisify function of the util module. This function accepts as its only argument a function that follows the Node.js callback standard, that is, defines as its last parameter a callback function that in turn has an error object in its signature as its first parameter. The best way to demonstrate how this works is to use the readFile function of the fs module. As you know, this function accepts the name of a file, optionally additional options, and a callback function. In this callback function, you have access to an error object, which has the value null for success, as well as to the data from the read file. Listing 16.22 shows how you can use this feature together with promisify.

```
import { readFile } from 'fs';
import { promisify } from 'util';

const promisedReadFile = promisify(readFile);

promisedReadFile('input.txt', 'utf-8')
  .then((data) => console.log(data))
  .catch((error) => console.error(error));
```

Listing 16.22 Using "promisify" to Turn a Callback-Based Function into a Promise-Based Function

As you can see in the code example, promisify returns a function object that, when called, generates a promise object you can use to process the result of the asynchronous operation and then no longer have to rely on the usual callback functionality.

16.6.2   Concatenating Promises

When taking a look at the previous code examples, you'll see that promises aren't used to reduce the callback functions within your application. Actually, they have exactly the opposite effect: there are more callback functions present because you register separate functions for success and failure. Promises show their true strength when it comes to coordinating multiple asynchronous operations. In this context, you have a total of three different options: connect several operations in a sequence, run them in parallel, or use only the result of the fastest operation. Listing 16.23 shows an example of concatenating multiple asynchronous operations.

```
function asyncOperation(resolve, value, time) {
  return new Promise((res, rej) => {
    setTimeout(() => {
      if (resolve) {
        res(value);
      } else {
        rej(value);
      }
    }, time);
  });
}

asyncOperation(true, 'Hello', 100)
  .then((data) => {
    console.log(data + ' ');
    return asyncOperation(true, 'World', 200);
  })
```

```
  .then((data) => {
    console.log(data);
    return '!';
  })
  .then((data) => {
    console.log(data);
  })
  .catch((err) => {
    console.error('Error: ', err);
  });
```

Listing 16.23 Concatenating Promises

The `asyncOperation` function uses the first parameter to decide whether the returned promise should be resolved or rejected. The second parameter is the value returned by the promise, and, finally, the third parameter specifies the time after which the result should be available. The first operation is resolved after 100 milliseconds. In the `then` method, you register a callback function in which you output the result and return another promise object. In any case, the `then` method returns a promise object, which, in this case, is linked to the returned promise, so you can in turn register a callback function via a `then` call. This returns a simple character string instead of a promise, which you can access in the final `then` call. The end of the chain is an error handler, which is bound using the `catch` method. If you change the first parameter to `false` when calling the `asyncOperation`, the error handler takes effect. Error objects run through the chain until an error handler is found, which then handles the error. If you don't register an error handler, a promise rejection will cause your application to terminate and thus act like an uncaught exception.

16.6.3   Multiple Parallel Operations with Promise.all

The `all` method of the promise object accepts an array of promises and in turn returns a promise itself. This promise is successfully resolved if all promises of the array were successful. As soon as one of the promises fails, the promise that returns the `all` method is also rejected. Listing 16.24 clarifies this for you.

```
function asyncOperation(resolve, value, time) {
  return new Promise((res, rej) => {
    setTimeout(() => {
      if (resolve) {
        res(value);
      } else {
        rej(value);
      }
    }, time);
```

```
  });
}

Promise.all([
  asyncOperation(true, 'World', 100),
  asyncOperation(true, 'Hello', 50),
]).then((values) => {
  console.log(values.join(' '));
});
```

Listing 16.24 Promise.all in Use

The asyncOperation function works according to the same scheme as in Listing 16.23. You pass two promises to the all method; the first is successfully resolved after 100 milliseconds, and the second after 50 milliseconds. In the success callback of the then method, you have access to the return values of the promises via an array. The order of the values is determined by the order in which the promises are called, not by the order in which they are resolved. So, the output of the script on the console after 100 milliseconds is the string Hello World. However, if you're not interested in the result of all promises, but only in the result of the fastest one, you can use the race method.

16.6.4   Fastest Asynchronous Operation with Promise.race

The signature of Promise.race is similar to that of Promise.all, only its use is quite different. Where Promise.all summarizes all passed promises, Promise.race only considers the result of the first resolved promise, whether it's resolved or rejected.

As you can see in Listing 16.25, when the source code is executed, the Second string is output on the command line. This is the value returned by the second promise after 50 milliseconds. The two remaining promises are ignored. You use the race method primarily when you want to obtain information from several sources, such as web services, and only want to continue working with the fastest result.

```
function asyncOperation(resolve, value, time) {
  return new Promise((res, rej) => {
    setTimeout(() => {
      if (resolve) {
        res(value);
      } else {
        rej(value);
      }
    }, time);
  });
}
```

16

513

```
Promise.race([
  asyncOperation(true, 'First', 100),
  asyncOperation(true, 'Second', 50),
  asyncOperation(true, 'Third', 75),
]).then((value) => {
  console.log(value);
});
```

Listing 16.25 Promise.race

16.6.5 Overview of the Promise Functions

The promise application programming interface (API) is part of the ECMAScript standard and applies in this form to both Node.js and the browser. Table 16.6 provides an overview of the various functions the promise API makes available to you.

Method	Description
Promise.all	Returns a promise that will be resolved once all passed promises are resolved.
Promise.allSettled	Returns a promise that will be resolved once all passed promises are either resolved or rejected.
Promise.any	Returns a promise that will be resolved as soon as the first of the passed promises is resolved.
Promise.race	Returns a promise that is either resolved or rejected depending on the status of the first promise passed.
Promise.reject	Creates a promise that is immediately rejected.
Promise.resolve	Creates a promise that is immediately resolved.

Table 16.6 Overview of the Promise Methods

16.7 Async Functions

Promises are very good for structuring interdependent asynchronous operations in a readable way and avoiding nested callback functions, called "callback hell." However, callback functions aren't redundant compared to the previous callback-based approach. And this is where another language feature of JavaScript comes into play: async functions. Based on the concept of promises, you can write asynchronous source code without callback functions using the async and await keywords.

The await keyword lets you wait for the result of an asynchronous operation, as it were, and lets you assign the result of a successfully resolved promise to a variable. To use await, you must be in a function marked async. In Listing 16.26, this task is carried out by the handleAsyncOperations function.

```
function asyncOperation(resolve, value, time) {
  return new Promise((res, rej) => {
    setTimeout(() => {
      if (resolve) {
        res(value);
      } else {
        rej(value);
      }
    }, time);
  });
}

async function handleAsyncOperations() {
  const hello = await asyncOperation(true, 'Hello', 100);
  const world = await asyncOperation(true, 'World', 100);
  try {
    await asyncOperation(false, '!', 100);
  } catch (err) {
    console.error(`Caught Error: ${err}`); // Output: Caught Error: !
  }
  console.log(`${hello} ${world}`);        // Output: Hello World
}

handleAsyncOperations();
```

Listing 16.26 Async Functions in Node.js

You can mark all functions, methods, and arrow functions as async, but then you have to keep in mind that they don't have a regular return value anymore. Instead, they return a promise object that encapsulates the return value—and it doesn't matter if you use promises and the await keyword. The source code in Listing 16.27 shows the result.

```
function asyncOperation(resolve, value, time) {
  return new Promise((res, rej) => {
    setTimeout(() => {
      if (resolve) {
        res(value);
      } else {
        rej(value);
      }
    }, time);
```

```
    });
}

async function greet() {
  const hello = await asyncOperation(true, 'Hello', 100);
  const world = await asyncOperation(true, 'World', 100);
  return hello + ' ' + world;
}

const greetResult = greet();

console.log(greetResult);                       // Output: Promise { <pending> }
greetResult.then((data) => console.log(data)); // Output: Hello World
```

Listing 16.27 Return Value of an "async" Function

In Listing 16.27, you call the asyncOperation function twice and receive the values Hello and World after a wait time of 100 milliseconds, which doesn't block the process. The asynchronous function greet encapsulates these calls and, as a result, returns the values of both promises as a composite string. If you output the return value of the greet function directly to the console, you'll see that it's a waiting promise object. Only the then method of the promise object provides access to the actual value.

As you can see, async functions transform promise-based functions into readable code without callback functions.

16.7.1   Top-Level Await

Until some time ago, you still had to encapsulate the await keyword inside an async function. This has changed with the introduction of the *top-level await feature* in Node.js. Since version 14.8, you can also use the await keyword outside of a top-level async function in a JavaScript file in Node.js. However, there is still one condition you need to fulfill to use this feature: You must enable the ECMAScript module system. In CommonJS, the await keyword outside an async function results in an error.

In Listing 16.28, you can see how to use the asyncOperation function from the previous examples with top-level await.

```
function asyncOperation(resolve, value, time) {
  return new Promise((res, rej) => {
    setTimeout(() => {
      if (resolve) {
        res(value);
      } else {
        rej(value);
      }
```

```
    }, time);
  });
}

const hello = await asyncOperation(true, 'Hello', 100);
const world = await asyncOperation(true, 'World', 100);
console.log(hello + ' ' + world);
```

Listing 16.28 Top-Level Await

16.8 Summary

Throughout this chapter, you've learned how the Node.js platform allows you to swap out calls to external commands and even entire parts of your application from the main process to child processes or worker threads. Based on the child_process module, the cluster module enables you to start multiple server processes for Net or HTTP servers and let the operating system do the load balancing between these processes.

Finally, with promises, you've learned a concept that allows you to better structure asynchronous calls within your source code, making it more readable. Promises are also a means of error handling in an asynchronous context. A promise represents the positive or negative result of an asynchronous operation and can be fulfilled or rejected, with fulfillment representing the success case and ensuring that the function passed to the then method as the first argument is executed. A rejection of a promise means a failure of the asynchronous operation and is equivalent to an exception. Due to a rejected promise, the function you passed as the second argument to the then method is called.

As promises have established themselves in the JavaScript and also in the Node.js world, and now that core modules such as the fs module also offer a promise-based interface, async functions and top-level await represent the next step in asynchronous programming. These kind of functions enable you to use promises entirely without callback functions.

16

Chapter 17
RxJS

To live is to observe.
—Pliny the Elder

ReactiveX for JavaScript (RxJS) is another way to deal with asynchronicity in an application. RxJS is the JavaScript implementation of *ReactiveX*. This project was originally launched by Microsoft and attempts to solve a wide variety of problems with a uniform interface. For this purpose, the library is based on the observer pattern. Its central elements include the data source (the observable) and the receiver of the data (the observer). Between these two elements, you can integrate any operators to handle the data stream.

ReactiveX exists not only for JavaScript but also for a variety of languages such as Java, PHP, or .NET. You can find the ReactiveX project site at *http://reactivex.io/*. From there, you can access the different implementations. In our case, this is RxJS.

The big advantage of ReactiveX is that they define a uniform interface for different structures, so as a developer, you don't need to bother about what kind of data source forms the basis. You simply deal with the structure of the data and process it in a chain of operators up to the observer. The operator-based structure provides a high degree of flexibility in your application because it allows you to extend the chain of operators any way you like.

ReactiveX provides for a variety of different operators. A list of these operators can be found at *http://reactivex.io/documentation/operators.html*. In this chapter, you'll get to know representatives of the different categories and see how they can be applied and also combined with each other. Most operators exist independently of the underlying language. However, they differ in their implementation, as the individual languages implement the requirements differently.

The capabilities of RxJS are most comparable to the asynchronous capabilities of JavaScript as well as the streams of Node.js. Compared to handling asynchronous operations with promises, RxJS has the advantage of enabling you to map more than just the success or failure of an operation. The events that RxJS uses can be triggered multiple times.

Compared to Node.js streams, the advantage of RxJS is that the implementation goes beyond the basic implementation of a streaming interface, that is, an observer implementation, and the library with its numerous operators already provides a set of tools for implementing your application.

17

17.1   Basic Principles

RxJS uses a stream of events. You can think of these as a kind of asynchronous array. Different operators process each element of the array separately. As a concrete example, take an array of numbers where you want to process only all even numbers and multiply them by themselves. In Node.js, you would accomplish this task with a combination of the `filter` and `map` array methods. Listing 17.1 shows how this works.

```
const array = [2, 3, 9, 8, 4, 1, 5, 6, 7];

const result = array
  .filter((element) => element % 2 === 0)
  .map((element) => element * element);

console.log(result); // Output: [ 4, 64, 16, 36 ]
```

Listing 17.1 Filtering and Mapping an Array

If you solve such problems with the onboard tools provided by JavaScript, rather than by using loops or recursion, you'll obtain structured and readable source code where each unit serves a specific purpose and is focused on that purpose. You can achieve the same result as the one shown in Listing 17.1 with RxJS, as you can see in Listing 17.2.

```
import { from } from 'rxjs';
import { filter, map } from 'rxjs/operators';

const array = [2, 3, 9, 8, 4, 1, 5, 6, 7];

from(array)
  .pipe(
    filter((element) => element % 2 === 0),
    map((element) => element * element),
  )
  .subscribe((data) => {
    console.log(data); // Output: 4 64 16 36
  });
```

Listing 17.2 Filtering and Mapping with RxJS

The difference between the array methods example and RxJS is that the data source in RxJS isn't limited to arrays as you can apply the operators also to data streams, EventEmitters, or promises. Moreover, with an array, all elements are processed by one operation and then passed on to the next operation. In RxJS, each individual element is processed by the complete operator chain.

17.1.1 Installation and Integration

RxJS can be installed via the `npm install rxjs` command. The package contains all the operators you need for using RxJS. However, there are still numerous additions for both frontend and Node.js use., which are available for download as additional Node Package Manager (npm) packages.

The example distinguishes between the `from` operator and the `filter` and `map` operators; the `from` operator is responsible for creation tasks. The `from` operator allows you to create an observable from an array. The `rxjs` package exports this operator directly. The resulting observable provides the `pipe` method in which you can concatenate other operators. In this case, you use `filter` and `map` to reach your goal. Both these operators are included in the `rxjs/operators` package. You can consume the result of the `pipe` method after applying the operators via the `subscribe` method and generate an output.

17.1.2 Observable

RxJS provides several ways to create observables. You've already seen one variant, namely, the `from` operator. In Section 17.2.1, you'll see several other operators that are used for generating observables. The most basic and flexible way to create an observable is through the static `create` method of the `observable` class. In this context, you can control the entire process and determine when and how an event occurs in the observable stream. Listing 17.3 shows how you can apply the `observable.create` method.

```
import { Observable } from 'rxjs';

const observable = Observable.create((observer) => {
  let count = 0;
  const interval = setInterval(() => {
    if (count++ < 10) {
      observer.next('Data package ' + count);
    } else {
      observer.complete();
      clearInterval(interval);
    }
  }, 500);
});

observable.subscribe((data) => console.log(data));
```

Listing 17.3 Using Observable.create

You then pass a callback function to the `create` method, which receives a reference to the observer. This function implements the `next`, `error`, and `complete` methods. In the example, you use the `next` method to send a new data package in the stream every 500 milliseconds. After 10 packages have been sent, you call the `complete` method to inform the observer that no more data packages will be sent.

The observable object you created by calling the `create` method implements the subscribe method, which enables you to register an observer.

17.1.3   Observer

You can register the observer using the `subscribe` method of the observable. In the simplest case, you pass a callback function that is invoked for each event generated by a call to the `next` method of the observer. The information you passed to the `next` method can be used as an argument. In the example with the array as the data source, the `subscribe` method is run for each array element.

The second callback function you can pass to the `subscribe` method will be executed if an error occurs in the observable. You can cause such an error by executing the `error` method of the observer in `Observable.create`. You can pass an object to this method that describes the error in more detail.

The third callback function gets run when the observable is terminated. You can trigger it by running the `complete` method of the observer. Listing 17.4 shows these interrelations based on a practical example.

```
import { Observable } from 'rxjs';

const observable = Observable.create((observer) => {
  observer.next('Hello');
  observer.next('World');
  observer.error('An Error occurred');
  observer.complete();
});

observable.subscribe(
  (data) => console.log('Data: ', data),
  (error) => console.error('Error: ', error),
  (finished) => console.log('Finished!'),
);
```

Listing 17.4 Observable and Observer of RxJS

If you run the source code of the example, you'll get the output shown in Listing 17.5.

```
Data:  Hello
Data:  World
Error:  An Error occurred
```

Listing 17.5 Observer Output

The reason you don't see the `Finished!` string in the output is that an error in the observable acts like an exception and cancels further processing of the observable. If you comment out the call of the `error` method, you'll obtain a corresponding output.

If you don't define a callback function for error handling, the error in the stream acts like an exception and causes your application to terminate. Therefore, you should always make sure to catch and handle all possible errors. During the introduction of the available operators, you'll also get to know special operators for error handling.

There is a distinction between *hot observables* and *cold observables* in RxJS. We refer to a hot observable when the observable triggers events irrespective of whether or not you've subscribed to it yet. In contrast to that, a cold observable triggers its events only if you've previously run the `subscribe` method. A typical example of a cold observable is the `Observable.from` method in conjunction with an array.

When dealing with observables, you should also know that you can unsubscribe an observer again. For this purpose, you use the subscription object returned by the `subscribe` method. Then you call the `unsubscribe` method on this object, and the observer gets disconnected from the observable. In most cases, however, manual unsubscribing isn't necessary. As a matter of fact, manual unsubscribing is only relevant if you subscribe to an observable and want to cancel this subscription after a certain period, after reaching certain criteria, or if you no longer need data from an observable and want to make sure no resources are being consumed that could cause a memory leak. Often, the better way is to terminate the subscription via operators, such as `take` or `takeUntil` in this context.

17.1.4 Operator

The most important tool besides observables and observers are the operators of RxJS. They allow you to handle any event of the stream. Operators are divided into different categories named according to the effect of each operator, for example, combining operators, creating operators, and filter operators.

You usually use operators in combination with the `pipe` method of the observable, as you've already seen in Listing 17.2. The order in which you specify the operators here also determines the order in which they are applied. The operators represent a chain whose links are traversed one after the other by the data packages until finally the observer is reached.

17.1.5 Example of RxJS in Node.js

The principle of ReactiveX isn't bound to a specific programming language or technology. For this reason, RxJS is used both on the server side and on the client side. This kind of flexibility is also very useful when you use the library in a Node.js application. Almost any data structure and many asynchronous constructs can be converted into observables. For example, you can implement a web server based on RxJS. Listing 17.6 shows an example of this.

```
import { createServer } from 'http';
import { Observable } from 'rxjs';
import { tap } from 'rxjs/operators';

const httpObservable = Observable.create((observer) => {
  createServer((request, response) =>
    observer.next({ request, response }),
  ).listen(8080, () => console.log('Server is listening'));
});

const logger = ({ request }) => console.log('requesting: ', request.url);

httpObservable
  .pipe(tap(logger))
  .subscribe(({ request, response }) => {
    response.end('Hello RxJS');
  });
```

Listing 17.6 Web Server Implementation with RxJS

For the web server implementation, you first create a new observable. This encloses the web server. In the callback function of the createServer method, you call the next method of the observer with an object that contains references to the request and response objects. After that, you still need to bind the server to a port. As soon as a request to the web server is received, a new event is triggered in the observer, and you can handle this event.

In the example, you define a logger function that you use to read the requested URL from the request object and output it to the console.

You connect the logger function to the web server using the pipe method of the observable and the tap operator of RxJS. Finally, you run the subscribe method. Like the logger, this method has access to the request and response objects you passed to the next call of the observer. You use the response.end method to send a response to the client, answering the request.

What you've seen here based on a simple example with a logger function, you can extend in any way you like by applying more operators to the request and response objects and thus modifying them. For example, you can implement a kind of middleware layer comparable to Express.

The example of the web server also shows the difference between a hot observable and a cold observable. If you don't call the subscribe method of the observable, the web server won't launch either. The most evident sign of this is that no output is generated on the console. By slightly restructuring the example, you can change the cold observable into a hot observable, as shown in Listing 17.7.

```
import { createServer } from 'http';
import { Observable } from 'rxjs';
import { tap } from 'rxjs/operators';

const server = createServer();
server.listen(8080, () => console.log('Server is listening'));

const httpObservable = Observable.create((observer) => {
  server.on('request', (request, response) =>
    observer.next({ request, response }),
  );
});

const logger = ({ request }) => console.log('requesting: ', request.url);

httpObservable
  .pipe(tap(logger))
  .subscribe(({ request, response }) => {
    response.end('Hello RxJS');
  });
```

Listing 17.7 Web Server as a Hot Observable

The difference from the previous example is that you don't run the web server that produces the events for the observable inside the `Observable.create` method, but rather create it up front. In the callback function, you simply register for the `request` event and trigger an event on the observable for each incoming request. As a result, the server will be created even if you don't subscribe to the observable. Incoming requests are thus possible in any case, and you get the output on the console as a visible sign that the web server has been started. However, if you call the server from within the browser without calling the `subscribe` method, the result will be an error message because the server doesn't send a response to the client.

17.2 Operators

The operators represent the core of RxJS. If you use the library without the operators, that is, only the observables and observers, you only have an `EventEmitter` with some limitations, which we'll describe in Section 17.3 on RxJS subjects. ReactiveX define a variety of different operators. To be able to keep the overview in this context, several tools are available to you. In a first, rather rough overview, the operators are divided into several categories:

- **Creation operators**
  These types of operators are used to generate new observables.

- **Transformation operators**
  You can use these operators to convert data packages of an observable into a different form.

- **Filtering operators**
  These operators allow you to respond only to specific data packages in the observable.

- **Join operators**
  With RxJS, you can combine multiple observables. This category of operators provides you with the necessary tools to do so.

- **Error handling operators**
  In addition to the error callback in the subscribe method of the observable, you can use these operators to deal with errors that occur.

- **Utility operators**
  This category includes operators that provide additional help in dealing with observables.

- **Conditional operators**
  You can formulate conditions based on these operators.

- **Connection operators**
  These operators affect the behavior of the subscribe method of an observable.

- **Conversion operator**
  The operator of this category is used to transform an observable into another data structure.

In addition to the different types of operators, there is also a decision tree you can use to find the right operator for you at *https://rxjs.dev/operator-decision-tree*. However, the best way to get familiar with and master the use of RxJS and its operators is by actively applying them. If you're new to RxJS, you should practice using the library in a secured environment to get used to using the individual elements. You'll see that the more often you use the tool, the more confident and quicker your choice of the appropriate operator will be.

If you take a look at the ReactiveX documentation, you'll quickly come across the *marble diagrams*, which are visual representations of how various operators work. The individual events of an observable are displayed as circles. In the upper part of such a diagram you can see the input stream, below it follows the application of the operator, and in the lower part of the figure is the result. Figure 17.1 contains the marble diagram for the map operator. An input stream with integer values is multiplied by 10 by the map operator. In the output stream, the resulting values are located below the input values in each case to clarify the mapping.

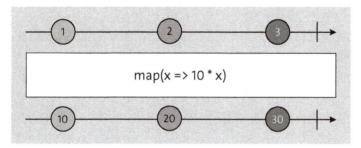

Figure 17.1 Marble Diagram for the "map" Operator

When using operators, the rule is that you group them via the pipe method of the observable. The pipe method accepts a variable number of operators as arguments that are applied to each data package of the observable in the order in which they are passed. Only the creation operators represent a special form because they aren't applied to an observable; instead, they create observables themselves and return them. Consequently, these operators aren't used in conjunction with the pipe method.

In the following sections, you'll learn about various operators in each category and see how you can use RxJS in the Node.js environment based on practical examples.

17.2.1   Creation Operators

So far, you've already become acquainted with two creation operators, namely, the from and the create operator. The from operator is especially versatile, as you'll see next.

from Operator

You can apply the from operator not only to array structures but also to other iterable data structures and promises. The example in Listing 17.8 shows how you can convert a read file system operation to an observable.

```
import { from } from 'rxjs';
import { readFile } from 'fs/promises';

from(readFile('input.txt', 'utf-8'))
  .subscribe((content) => {
    console.log('file: ', content); // Output: file: Hello RxJS
  });
```

Listing 17.8 "from" Operator for Promises

In Listing 17.8, you use the promise-based variant of the readFile function. Using the from operator, you convert this promise into an observable so that you have access to all RxJS operators. When dealing with file system operations, you should know that RxJS behaves the same way as the rest of the file system operations in Node.js: RxJS processes the file in blocks. In this case, the promise is resolved with the entire contents of the file, so RxJS doesn't know line breaks or word separators. If you want to read a file line by line, you have to solve this yourself.

fromEvent: Using EventEmitter Objects

Numerous interfaces in Node.js use the EventEmitter class. The fromEvent operator allows you to create an observable for specific events. In Listing 17.9, we use the web server example and apply the fromEvent operator.

```
import { createServer } from 'http';
import { fromEvent } from 'rxjs';

const server = createServer().listen(8080, () =>
  console.log('Server is listening'),
);

fromEvent(server, 'request').subscribe(([, response]) => {
  response.end('Hello RxJS');
});
```

Listing 17.9 "fromEvent" Operator with a Web Server

The reference to the web server you created via the createServer function derives from the EventEmitter class. Each incoming request triggers the request event. For this event, you create a new observable using the fromEvent operator. When a new request is received, an event gets triggered on the observable, and then all registered operators and the callback function you passed to the subscribe method are executed. One special feature you should note is that the object references of the event, that is, request and response, exist in the form of an array, which is why you need the destructuring operation in the subscribe call.

interval: Creating Time Intervals

Another frequently used operator is interval. This operator creates an observable that triggers an event at regular intervals, similar to the setInterval function. The interval operator is particularly well suited for combinations with other operators because it only returns a number representing the current run.

Every second, the source code in Listing 17.10 triggers an event you subscribe to. In the callback function, you output the number of the current run and the current date and time.

```
import { interval } from 'rxjs';

interval(1000)
  .subscribe((data) => {
    console.log(`Iteration ${data}: ${new Date()}`);
  });
```

Listing 17.10 Creating Time Intervals

With the `interval` operator, you should also note that it executes the first event only after the initial time span has elapsed, in this example, after one second. You can manipulate this behavior via the `startWith` operator, for example.

17.2.2   Transformation Operators

A transformation operator performs a classic mapping of an input value to an output according to defined rules. A typical example of a transformation operator is the `map` function, which you already got to know at the beginning of this chapter.

scan: Accumulator Operator

Another example is the `scan` operator. You pass a function to it in which you have access to the current element as well as the result of the last execution of the function. Listing 17.11 clarifies this context.

```
import { range } from 'rxjs';
import { scan } from 'rxjs/operators';

range(1, 10)
  .pipe(scan((acc, value) => acc + value))
  .subscribe((value) => console.log(value));
```

Listing 17.11 Applying the "scan" Operator

The `range` operator generates a sequence of numbers. In this case, it starts at 1 and ends at 10. An event is triggered for each value. On the first run, the `scan` operator receives the values 0 as the initial value because the function hasn't been executed before, and 1 as the first value of the sequence of numbers. With the second event, the values 1 and 2 are passed, then with the third event 3 and 3. The execution ends with the 10th value.

buffer: Buffering Observables

You can use the `buffer` operator to aggregate the events of an observable. For this purpose, you combine two observables. The events of the outer observable are supposed to be buffered. The inner observable specifies the size of the buffer. In Listing 17.12, the outer observable triggers an event every 100 milliseconds. The `map` operator enables you to turn the continuous sequence into a random number between 0 and 100. By using the buffer operator with another interval of one second, you make sure that all events of the outer observable are grouped together. In the callback of the subscribe method, this causes you to receive an array of multiple numbers instead of single numbers. Listing 17.13 shows an excerpt from the output.

```
import { interval } from 'rxjs';
import { map, buffer } from 'rxjs/operators';

interval(100)
  .pipe(
    map(() => Math.floor(Math.random() * 100)),
    buffer(interval(1000)),
  )
  .subscribe((data) => console.log(data));
```

Listing 17.12 Buffering Observables

```
[ 40, 16, 21, 29, 4, 26, 14, 98, 33 ]
[ 42, 12, 56, 5, 93, 21, 13, 80, 28, 42 ]
[ 93, 24, 42, 30, 40, 72, 10, 32, 52, 79 ]
...
```

Listing 17.13 Output When Buffering Observables

The interval observables used in this example are intended to be examples of any asynchronous observables. At this point, you can also use any EventEmitters, whose events you can combine in this way.

mergeMap

The mergeMap operator is a mixture of a transformation and a join operator. It links an outer observable with an inner observable and produces new data packages from it. You can use this operator, for example, if you have interdependent asynchronous queries. In the example in Listing 17.14, you first query a resource to which a user is assigned. In a second request, you add all the user information to that resource. Due to the abstraction of the observables, you can perform the queries here using both promises and EventEmitters. The higher-level logic remains unaffected.

```
import { Observable } from 'rxjs';
import { mergeMap } from 'rxjs/operators';

const resources = () => {
  return Observable.create((observer) => {
    observer.next({
      id: 1,
```

```
      name: 'Main resource',
      user: 2,
    });
  });
};

const usersForResource = (resource) => {
  return Observable.create((observer) => {
    observer.next({
      ...resource,
      user: {
        id: 2,
        name: 'John',
      },
    });
  });
};

resources()
  .pipe(mergeMap((resource) => usersForResource(resource)))
  .subscribe((data) => console.log(data));
```

Listing 17.14 Using the "mergeMap" Operator

The place where you can insert the asynchronous queries to a server system or database are the respective callback functions in the `create` calls.

In addition to the `mergeMap` operator, other operators, such as `flatMap`, `switchMap`, and `concatMap`, are also capable of transforming an outer observable based on an inner observable, with the `flatMap` operator merely being an alias for `mergeMap`. In general, you use these operators when you need to subscribe to another observable in the subscribe method of an observable. The difference between the three operators is in the details of how you handle the order of the packages or whether the inner subscription is terminated, as described here:

- `mergeMap/flatMap`
  This operator maintains the order in which the data packages are supplied, which means that the packages of different observables may overlap. The inner subscriptions aren't terminated, but continue to run.

- `switchMap`
  This operator takes only one data package of the inner observable and then proceeds to the next package of the outer observable.

- `concatMap`
  Unlike `mergeMap`, the data packages of the different observables aren't mixed. For this, the operator waits for the inner observable to complete.

17.2.3   Filtering Operators

While with the transformation operators you changed the data packages of the observable, you use the filtering operators to restrict the data flow based on specific rules. You already got to know the classic filtering operator at the beginning of this chapter. It's called with the current data package and passes it to the following operator or observer if the filtering condition is met.

In addition to the filtering operator, this category contains operators that can be used to avoid a manual unsubscribe process. Typical representatives of this category are first, last, and the various take operators.

Access to Specific Elements in an Observable

Not only do the RxJS operators allow you to filter all elements of an observable according to certain criteria, you can also limit the number of elements. For example, if you're only interested in the first or last element, you can use the first or last operator, respectively. The take operator enables you to specify how many elements you want to obtain. Irrespective of which of these operators you use, as soon as the condition is met, an unsubscribe automatically takes place.

```
import { range } from 'rxjs';
import { take, first, last } from 'rxjs/operators';

range(1, 10)
  .pipe(first())
  .subscribe((data) => console.log('first: ', data));
range(1, 10)
  .pipe(take(2))
  .subscribe((data) => console.log('take 2: ', data));
range(1, 10)
  .pipe(last())
  .subscribe((data) => console.log('last: ', data));
```

Listing 17.15 Using the "first", "take", and "last" Operators

The last operator represents a special type. For it to work, the observable must be terminated. If this isn't the case, the subscription callback function won't be called. When using the range operator, the observable is terminated after the last element, and the last operator is called correctly, which you can see from the output on the console.

For example, if you create an observable yourself with the create operator and let it fire values regularly in combination with an interval, you must call the complete method of the observer to finish. Listing 17.16 illustrates this context with a concrete example.

```
import { Observable } from 'rxjs';
import { last } from 'rxjs/operators';

Observable.create((observer) => {
  let count = 0;
  const interval = setInterval(() => {
    if (++count >= 10) {
      clearInterval(interval);
      observer.next(count);
      observer.complete();
    }
    observer.next(count);
  }, 10);
})
  .pipe(last())
  .subscribe((data) => console.log('last: ', data));
```

Listing 17.16 The "last" Operator with a Self-Generated Observable

If you comment out the line containing the `observer.complete` call, the callback function isn't executed, and you won't get any output on the console. Stumbling blocks like this always increase the amount of work during development when you debug the application.

Operator `takeUntil` and its opposite `skipUntil` work similarly to the `take` operator, except that you don't get a number but an observable and become active as soon as this observable fires.

Rejecting Events with debounceTime

The `debounceTime` operator enables you to debounce packages based on time. Let's take the example with the RxJS-based web server. Here you can automatically reject requests if there isn't at least a period of five seconds between two requests. Listing 17.17 shows the actual implementation based on Listing 17.9.

```
import { createServer } from 'http';
import { fromEvent } from 'rxjs';
import { debounceTime } from 'rxjs/operators';

const server = createServer().listen(8080, () =>
  console.log('Server is listening'),
);

fromEvent(server, 'request')
  .pipe(debounceTime(5000))
```

```
  .subscribe(([, response]) => {
    response.end('Hello RxJS');
  });
```

Listing 17.17 Using "debounceTime"

You shouldn't use the debounceTime operator for the communication between client and server because requests can be lost here. However, if the communication is between components or systems and resource-intensive operations are performed, it may be worthwhile to reject requests if the input conditions for the operation are still changing. If you need more flexibility, you can use the debounce operator instead of the debounceTime operator. This operator accepts a callback function that returns a timer observable, which allows you to adjust the time period accordingly.

17.2.4   Join Operators

If you work in an application with RxJS, it often happens that you want to merge the result of several observables and continue with the result. For this purpose, you can use a number of join operators. A widely used specimen of this category is the combineLatest operator. This operator takes multiple observables and triggers an event whenever one of the observables triggers an event. In doing so, the combineLatest operator combines the most recently sent data packages of all observables and makes them available to you.

In Listing 17.18 you create three observables; depending on the application, these can involve any implementation, such as connections to other servers, for example. In this case, you create three timer observables that trigger an event at intervals of 500, 1,000, and 1,500 milliseconds, respectively. You extend the data package with a random number using the map operator and then combine the three observables via the combineLatest operator. This operator is applied to one of the three observables, and the remaining two are passed. As a result, a new observable is created, which outputs new data packages at intervals of 500 milliseconds, each consisting of the last values of the three observables. In the subscribe method, you use array destructuring to access the individual packages.

```
const { timer } = require('rxjs');
const { combineLatest, map } = require('rxjs/operators');

const randomInt = () => Math.floor(Math.random() * 100);

const timer1 = timer(0, 500).pipe(map(() => randomInt()));
const timer2 = timer(0, 1000).pipe(map(() => randomInt()));
const timer3 = timer(0, 1500).pipe(map(() => randomInt()));
```

```
timer1.pipe(combineLatest(timer2, timer3)).subscribe(([t1, t2, t3]) => {
  console.log(`
    ${new Date()}
    Timer1: ${t1}
    Timer2: ${t2}
    Timer3: ${t3}
  `);
});
```

Listing 17.18 Combination of Multiple Observables

For clarification, you also have the current time included in the output. Listing 17.19 shows the output of the example.

```
Sat Aug 21 2021 13:39:05 GMT+0200 (Central European Summer Time)
Timer1: 83
Timer2: 18
Timer3: 66

Sat Aug 21 2021 13:39:06 GMT+0200 (Central European Summer Time)
Timer1: 83
Timer2: 18
Timer3: 49
...
```

Listing 17.19 Output of the Combination of Multiple Observables

17.2.5   Error Handling Operators

You've already become acquainted with one of the most important means of error handling, namely, the second callback function of the subscribe method. RxJS provides you with additional operators to catch errors that occur between the observable and the observer.

Catching Errors with catchError

You can insert the catchError operator anywhere in the operator chain. The operator then catches all errors that have previously occurred in the chain. This allows you to respond dynamically to the various errors and also to insert multiple catchError operators. If an error is caught, the processing of the observable gets interrupted. Listing 17.20 shows an example of this.

```
import { Observable, of } from 'rxjs';
import { map, catchError } from 'rxjs/operators';
```

```
Observable.create((observer) => {
  observer.next('test 1');
  observer.next('test 2');
  observer.error('something went wrong');
  observer.next('test 3');
  observer.complete();
})
  .pipe(
    map((data) => {
      const mappedData = data.toUpperCase();
      // throw new Error('Mapping failed');
      return mappedData;
    }),
    catchError((e, caught) => {
      console.log('the error was: ', e);
      return of('test 3', 'test 4');
    }),
  )
  .subscribe((data) => console.log(data));
```

Listing 17.20 Handling Errors Using the "catchError" Operator

In general, errors can occur at different points. You can trigger an error in the observable itself using the error method. But an operator can also cause an error. For example, if you enable the line in the map operator that triggers the error, you can also catch it using the catchError operator. No matter which error is triggered, the output of the test 3 string doesn't occur at all. The callback function of the catchError operator can in turn return an observable so that you can continue in the chain, which in this case continues the output with the strings test 3 and test 4.

Trying Again with retry

Unlike the catchError operator, which catches and handles an error, the retry operator makes sure that the observable is executed again in its entirety. This operator is particularly relevant when you work with unreliable data sources such as poorly accessible web servers.

The source code in Listing 17.21 ensures that the observable is executed three times in total. In the third run, the processing is aborted due to an uncaught error. Specifying retry(2) ensures that there won't occur an infinite loop. It's important to note that the values from the observable are regenerated on a retry and don't originate from a cache. By using the Math.random method, this fact becomes clear because each run produces different numbers.

```
import { Observable } from 'rxjs';
import { retry } from 'rxjs/operators';

Observable.create((observer) => {
  console.log('starting');
  observer.next(Math.random());
  observer.next(Math.random());
  observer.error('something went wrong');
  observer.next(Math.random());
})
  .pipe(retry(2))
  .subscribe((data) => console.log(data));
```

Listing 17.21 Using the "retry" Operator

17.2.6   Utility Operators

The utility operators category contains operators that facilitate your work with RxJS.

Debugging with the tap Operator

If you work with chains of operators and implement them as arrow functions with an implicit return value, finding errors can be very time-consuming. This is where the tap operator comes into play. This operator doesn't affect the chain of operators, but you can grab the value anywhere in the chain and output it or set a breakpoint.

If you run the source code from Listing 17.22, you'll see that the tap operator merely produces an output of the intermediate results, but doesn't otherwise affect the operator chain, although the value undefined is returned.

```
import { range } from 'rxjs';
import { filter, tap, map } from 'rxjs/operators';

range(1, 10)
  .pipe(
    filter((data) => data % 2 === 0),
    tap((data) => console.log('value after filter: ', data)),
    map((data) => data * data),
  )
  .subscribe((data) => console.log(data));
```

Listing 17.22 Using the "tap" Operator

Defining Time-Outs

Another useful operator is the timeout operator. You can use it to determine that an error gets triggered after a certain period of time has elapsed without any data packages from an observable. This operator is particularly useful if you're connected to another system via a socket connection and expect regular messages. For example, if the time between two messages is more than five seconds, you can conclude that there is a problem in the communication that you need to resolve.

In Listing 17.23, you create an observable that triggers an event after 500 and 2,000 milliseconds. Thus, there are 1,500 milliseconds between the two events. If you apply the timeout operator with a value of 1000, the 1,500 milliseconds will cause an error, which will occur as a TimeoutError that you catch in the error callback function of the subscribe method.

```
import { Observable } from 'rxjs';
import { timeout } from 'rxjs/operators';

Observable.create((observer) => {
  setTimeout(() => {
    observer.next('first package');
  }, 500);
  setTimeout(() => {
    observer.next('second package');
  }, 2000);
})
  .pipe(timeout(1000))
  .subscribe(
    (data) => console.log(data),
    (error) => console.error('error', error),
  );
```

Listing 17.23 Using the "timeout" Operator

17.2.7   Conditional Operators

You can use the conditional operators to define specific conditions for your observable.

Defining a Default Value

You can use the defaultIfEmpty operator if an observable doesn't output a value. For this operator to work, the observable must be completed. The observable in Listing 17.24 is completed without calling the next method.

```
import { Observable } from 'rxjs';
import { defaultIfEmpty } from 'rxjs/operators';

Observable.create((observer) => {
  observer.complete();
})
```

```
  .pipe(defaultIfEmpty('Observable did not emit a value'))
  .subscribe((data) => console.log(data));
```

Listing 17.24 Defining a Default Value for an Empty Observable

The `defaultIfEmpty` operator only takes effect if the observable doesn't output any value. The element you pass to the operator is treated as a regular data package by subsequent operators and the `subscribe` method.

Condition for All Data Packages of an Observable

The `every` operator allows you to define a condition that each data package of an observable must fulfill. Depending on the result, the return value is either `true` or `false`. Listing 17.25 shows the application of this operator.

```
import { range } from 'rxjs';
import { every } from 'rxjs/operators';

range(1, 9)
  .pipe(every((data) => data < 10))
  .subscribe((result) =>
    result
      ? console.log('all values are smaller than 10')
      : console.log('there's at least one value greater than 10'),
  );
```

Listing 17.25 Using the "every" Operator

17.2.8 Connection Operators

The connection operators of RxJS affect the character of an observable. Normally, only one observer can connect to an observable. In addition, most observables are cold, which means that they only trigger events after you subscribe to them.

An example of such an operator is `publish`. With its help, you can call the `subscribe` method more than once. In addition, the observable doesn't start outputting data packages until you call the `connect` method.

Both subscribers from Listing 17.26 receive the same values. If you were to subscribe to such an observable without the `publish` operator, each observer would get different values. You can delay the output of the values by calling the `connect` method at a later time. If this behavior isn't what you want, you can also use the `share` operator, which allows for simple multicasting, that is, notifying multiple operators at once.

```
import { Observable } from 'rxjs';
import { publish } from 'rxjs/operators';

const observable = Observable.create((observer) => {
```

```
  observer.next(Math.random());
  observer.next(Math.random());
}).pipe(publish());

observable.subscribe((data) => console.log('Observer 1: ', data));
observable.subscribe((data) => console.log('Observer 2: ', data));

observable.connect();
```

Listing 17.26 Multicasting with the "publish" Operator

17.2.9   Conversion Operators

The integration of RxJS into an existing application is facilitated by the fact that almost all data structures can be transferred into an RxJS observable. The lastValueFrom operator allows you to extract the last value output by an observable encapsulated in a promise object and thus also embed your observable in an existing structure. This operator replaces the toPromise operator that has been used for a long time.

Listing 17.27 shows an example of converting an observable into a promise object. However, the lastValueFrom function is subject to some limitations because a promise can only represent the pending, resolved, and rejected states. As long as the observable isn't yet completed, the promise is in the pending state, and the callback function of the then method isn't executed. If the observable is completed, the promise is fulfilled with the last issued value. In the example, this means that only the last random number is passed on.

```
import { Observable, lastValueFrom } from 'rxjs';

const observable = Observable.create((observer) => {
  observer.next(Math.random());
  observer.next(Math.random());
  observer.next(Math.random());
  observer.complete();
});

lastValueFrom(observable)
  .then((data) => console.log(data));
```

Listing 17.27 Converting an Observable into a Promise Object

17.3   Subjects

Subjects represent a special type of observable in RxJS. One of their most important features is that you can subscribe to a subject multiple times, whereas with the observable, you can only do that once, as shown in Listing 17.28.

```
import { Observable, Subject } from 'rxjs';

const observable = Observable.create((observer) => {
  setTimeout(() => {
    observer.next(Math.random());
  }, 1000);
});

observable.subscribe((data) => console.log('Observer 1: ', data));
observable.subscribe((data) => console.log('Observer 2: ', data));

const subject = new Subject();

subject.subscribe((data) => console.log('Subject observer 1:', data));
subject.subscribe((data) => console.log('Subject observer 2:', data));

subject.next(Math.random());

/* Output:
Subject observer 1: 0.172591728861374394
Subject observer 2: 0.172591728861374394
Observer 1:   0.12258583815002866
Observer 2:   0.08073784778403792
*/
```

Listing 17.28 Difference between Observable and Subject

When you run the source code, you'll notice that the observers of the subject always get the same values, but the observers of the observable get different values. This is because the observables don't support multicasting. Another difference is that you can pass values to a subject from outside. The asObservable method of a subject enables you to have a subject create an observable. This is particularly useful if you want to prohibit unauthorized write accesses to your subject. In this case, you create a protected scope where your subject resides, and the observable is exported to the outside.

In addition to the subject class, there are other types of subjects, each with their own special features:

- **BehaviorSubject**
  The BehaviorSubject memorizes the last output data package and returns it as the initial value for each new subscription.

- **ReplaySubject**
  You can assign the ReplaySubject the size of the buffer when creating it. This figure indicates how many data packages can be stored. For example, if you enter "5" here, the last five data packages will be saved and output with each new subscription.

- **AsyncSubject**
  The `AsyncSubject` returns only its last value. For this purpose, you must run the `complete` method after the last `next`. Until this happens, none of the observers will be notified.

17.4   Schedulers

Schedulers affect the time at which the events of an observable are triggered. Different schedulers also create a different effect in your application. The effect of the different schedulers provided by RxJS is easiest to demonstrate with an actual example. Listing 17.29 contains three observables, each of which has been provided with different schedulers.

```
import { observeOn } from 'rxjs/operators';
import {
  of,
  queueScheduler,
  asapScheduler,
  asyncScheduler
} from 'rxjs';

console.log('start');
of('queueScheduler')
  .pipe(observeOn(queueScheduler))
  .subscribe((data) => console.log(data));
of('asyncScheduler')
  .pipe(observeOn(asyncScheduler))
  .subscribe((data) => console.log(data));
of('asapScheduler')
  .pipe(observeOn(asapScheduler))
  .subscribe((data) => console.log(data));

console.log('end');
```

Listing 17.29 Using Different Schedulers

If you run the source code of the example, you'll get an output as shown in Listing 17.30.

```
start
queueScheduler
end
asapScheduler
asyncScheduler
```

Listing 17.30 Output of the Scheduler Example

The outputs start and end are generated by the console.log statements. These are executed synchronously in the program flow as usual and serve as anchor points for the output. The output of the observable that was provided with the queueScheduler using the observeOn operator also behaves synchronously. So, the output is between start and end.

Both the asapScheduler and the asyncScheduler are asynchronous. This means both outputs occur only after the synchronous parts of the source code, that is, after the output of end. The result from the asapScheduler is output first, followed by the result from the asyncScheduler because they were routed to different queues. The asapScheduler uses setImmediate for timing purposes. The asyncScheduler uses the same queue as a setTimeout with a value of 0 milliseconds.

You can also pass a scheduler directly as the second argument to numerous operators such as from or of.

17.5   Summary

RxJS is a very useful tool for modeling data streams in your application. Almost any structure can serve as a data source, from simple values to promises to EventEmitters. The most important elements of RxJS are observables, which serve as the data source; operators, which allow you to influence the data flow; and the observer, which is the destination of the data flow.

To keep the set of available operators manageable, they are divided into different categories, such as creation or transformation operators.

The advantage of an architecture based on RxJS is that you compose it from numerous small and mostly independent parts. In general, RxJS is platform independent, so you can use it in Node.js as well as in the frontend.

17

Chapter 18
Streams

If you want to get to the source, you have to swim against the current.
—*Hermann Hesse*

When you work with Node.js, it's hard to avoid coming across the stream application programming interface (API), and for good reason. Streams in Node.js can be used to solve numerous asynchronous problems in application development elegantly and with little effort. Node.js provides you with the framework implementation of the streams, so you only need to bother with the implementation details of your problem solution. This chapter introduces you to some tasks where streams can be useful. You'll also learn how to create streams yourself and combine them in a useful way.

18.1 Introduction

"We should have some ways of connecting programs like garden hose—screw in another segment when it becomes necessary to massage data in another way." With this quote, Douglas McIlroy describes in one sentence the Unix pipes he invented in 1972. And this is exactly the concept underlying streams in Node.js. In this way, the native streams of Node.js work in a very similar way to the observables in Reactive Extensions for JavaScript (RxJS), which were introduced in Chapter 17.

18.1.1 What Is a Stream?

With both Unix pipes and streams, you have a data source to which you can connect any number of modules, ultimately directing the data stream to a specific destination. What may sound a bit abstract at first glance can be illustrated quite clearly on the basis of Unix pipes. In Listing 18.1, the ls command, which creates a list of files and directories pertaining to the specified directory, serves as the data source. The output of this command is passed as input into the grep command, which is used to display only entries that match a specific pattern. This filtered list is finally the input for the text viewer less. Applied to Node.js, the three commands each represent a stream, and the output of each stream is associated with the input of the subsequent stream.

```
$ ls -l /usr/local/lib/node_modules | grep 'js' | less
```

Listing 18.1 Unix Pipes in Use

18.1.2   Stream Usages

Simply put, streams are used to handle input and output. In this context, both are considered as a continuous data stream. The defined interface on which all streams are based allows you to combine streams very flexibly. This, in turn, corresponds to the modular concept of Node.js. Each module—each individual stream implementation in this case—is supposed to perform only one specific task and leave everything else to the next stream in the chain.

Streams can therefore be used wherever you're dealing with a continuous flow of data, that is, almost anywhere. You can see this when you take a closer look at the Node.js platform. Almost all important modules implement the stream API. Both the file system module and the web server have data streams, and most database drivers also provide you with the ability to stream information out of or into the database.

Streams show their strength, especially when it comes to manipulating data streams. As an example, let's suppose you have a database from which you read information. That would be the first stream in the chain. The second stream is responsible for transforming the information in such a way that your application can process it further. In a third step, you can then encrypt the information and finally send it in the last stream to another computer through a Transmission Control Protocol (TCP) connection. The advantage at this point is that you don't use the entire contents of the database at once, but always small chunks, which significantly reduces the memory utilization of your application.

Now, if the way you need to put the data into shape changes, all you have to do is implement that and replace the second stream in the chain. All other stream modules remain unchanged. Figure 18.1 illustrates this.

To enable you to build such a pipeline of individual streams, several types of streams are available for use at different points in a chain.

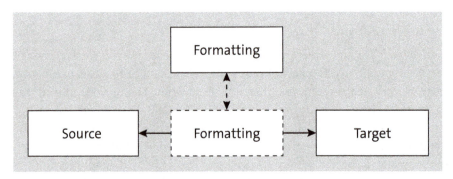

Figure 18.1 Streams as Modular Components of an Application

18.1.3   Available Streams

Node.js provides several types of streams. Each stream serves a specific purpose:

- **Readable streams**
  A stream of this class represents a data source that can be read from. A typical representative is the `request` object of the HTTP server, which represents an incoming request.

- **Writable streams**
  A writable stream accepts data and thus forms the end of a stream chain. Analogous to the `request` object, the `response` object of the HTTP server is a writable stream.

- **Duplex streams**
  This stream type is both readable and writable. You can use a duplex stream as a step between a readable stream and a writable stream. In most cases, however, you'll use transform streams.

- **Transform streams**
  Data can be both written to and read from this type of stream. As the name suggests, transform streams are used when the goal is to create a specific output stream from an input stream. Transform streams are based on duplex streams, but their API is simpler.

If you work with Node.js streams, then sooner or later, you'll come across the different versions of the stream API.

18.1.4   Stream Versions in Node.js

During the development process of the Node.js platform, the appearance and also the use of the streams have changed. There are now three different versions available, each with its own characteristics:

- **Version 1 (push streams)**
  Streams have been around in Node.js since the beginning. In this original version, the data source controlled the data flow. The data was written to the stream, and the next stage in the chain had to make sure that it could receive the data accordingly.

- **Version 2 (pull streams)**
  The developers recognized the problems with the lack of control of subsequent stages in a stream chain in the first version of the stream API and developed a concept referred to as pull stream. Here, the subsequent stages in the stream chain are able to actively fetch the data from the preceding stages. This change made its way into the platform with version 0.10 of Node.js.

- **Version 3 (push and pull streams)**
  Until the release of the third version of the stream API, it wasn't possible to run a stream in both pull and push modes. With io.js and Node.js in version 0.11, this problem was addressed. Today, you can use a stream in both variants without having to generate a new instance.

18

Normally, you'll use the third version of the stream API, which allows for flexible switching between versions. The pull variant is used by default. Throughout this chapter, you'll learn more about when to use which type of streams and how to switch between the two modes. But we'll cover some information about the internal structure of streams first.

18.1.5   Streams Are EventEmitters

Streams are asynchronous, which means you can't easily follow a clear flow in your source code but have to use callback functions. For this to work, a stream is based on an EventEmitter instance.

For you as a developer, this means that all actions in a stream are represented by events to which you can bind callback functions. This also means you can bind multiple callback functions to a single stream event, which gives you a greater degree of flexibility.

Thus, when implementing the stream API, Node.js again follows the familiar pattern of reuse. You can bind callbacks as usual via the on method, trigger events using the emit method, remove event listeners, or bind callbacks to an event only once.

With this information at hand, you can now move on to using the stream API. First, you'll learn more about the readable streams of Node.js.

18.2   Readable Streams

A readable stream is the starting point in a stream chain, that is, it represents the data source. A readable stream is a wrapper around an input that is placed around the data source to stream from it.

Such stream wrappers already exist for numerous data sources. Node.js has some prebuilt internal stream implementations, for example, for the file system or the network. In addition, numerous third-party providers offer a streaming API for their services that allows you to stream data records from a database or send information over a stream using the WebSocket protocol.

Finally, Node.js provides prebuilt classes that allow you to develop your own streams in just a few steps. The advantage here is that the platform takes care of the framework implementation, and you can focus on the implementation specific to your case.

18.2.1   Creating a Readable Stream

The simplest variant of a readable stream will serve as the basis for the following consideration: reading data from the file system. This means you open the file, and Node.js provides you with a wrapper to process the content as a stream. Listing 18.2 contains the corresponding source code.

```
import { createReadStream } from 'fs';

const options = {
  encoding: 'utf8',
};

const readStream = createReadStream('input.txt', options);

readStream.on('readable', () => {
  const data = readStream.read();
  if (data) {
    console.log(data);
  }
});
```

Listing 18.2 Readable Stream in the File System

When reading information from a file, you should keep in mind that a stream doesn't know anything about word separators, punctuation, or paragraphs. Streams use packages of a fixed size. In the default case of readable streams in the file system, this is 64 KB. If this value doesn't fit your application, you can overwrite it with the highWaterMark option and adjust it accordingly.

When creating the readable stream, all you need is the name of the file you want to read and an optional configuration object that affects the stream. When you use file system streams, it's important to specify the encoding. If you don't specify anything here, buffer objects will be used. These are excellent for further processing within the application, but not when it comes to displaying the information that has been read. To solve this problem, you can either use the toString method of the buffer object or directly specify the encoding when creating the stream.

For the example in Listing 18.2 to work, you need a text file whose contents can be read. In this case, you should name the file *input.txt* and set any text as content.

The actual work with the stream starts with registering a callback function on the readable event. This event signals that data on the stream is ready to be read. Once the data is available, you can consume it by calling the read method. In this variant of the streams, it isn't possible to bind several parallel read operations to one stream, but we'll describe that later. Inside the handler function for the readable event, you also check whether there is data in the data package. If you didn't perform this check, the script would give you the value null in addition to the contents of the file. This is because the last call of the read method returns null, signaling that there is no more data in the stream.

Based on this example, you'll now learn more about the readable stream interfaces of Node.js step by step.

18

18.2.2   Readable Stream Interface

The readable streams of Node.js can do much more than just stream content from files to the console. Using a set of methods and events, you can manipulate the behavior of the stream and intervene at different points in the lifecycle of the readable stream. Figure 18.2 summarizes the most important events and methods and shows at which point they are used.

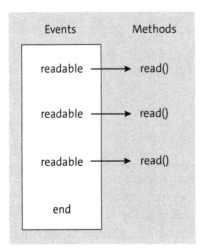

Figure 18.2 Events and Methods in the Readable Stream

18.2.3   Events of a Readable Stream

In Node.js, events are asynchronous, which means the event handlers are registered and executed at a later time. For this reason, it almost doesn't matter at which point in your source code you register the handlers. The only important thing is that you've already registered the stream at this point. Otherwise, you should establish a convention for your project about when and in what order event handling should occur. Table 18.1 provides an overview of the standard events of a readable stream.

Event	Description
readable	The stream contains data that can be read.
data	This consumes data via the stream as soon as it's available.
close	The stream has been closed, and no further data can be received.
error	An error occurred.
end	This event is triggered when no more data can be consumed from the stream.
pause	The pause method of the stream triggers this event.

Table 18.1 Events of Readable Streams

Event	Description
resume	This event is the counterpart of the pause event. The resume event is triggered by the resume method.

Table 18.1 Events of Readable Streams (Cont.)

We'll describe the difference between the readable and data events later when we talk about the different modes of a readable stream. At this point, you only need to know that a stream operates in paused mode by default, and the data is consumed with a combination of a listener on the readable event and a call of the read method. A listener on the data event puts the stream into flowing mode.

You can use the close event to respond to the termination of the stream connection. This usually happens when a communication stream from the other side or a file descriptor has been closed. Listing 18.3 shows how to handle the close event in the context of the original example from Listing 18.2.

```
import { createReadStream } from 'fs';

const options = {
  encoding: 'utf8',
};

const readStream = createReadStream('input.txt', options);

readStream.on('readable', () => {
  const data = readStream.read();
  if (data) {
    console.log(data);
  }
});

readStream.on('close', () => {
  console.log('The stream has been closed');
});
```

Listing 18.3 Handling the "close" Event of a Readable Stream

The result of executing this example is first the content of the text file and at the end a line with the text The stream has been closed.

In addition to handling the success case, you should always provide routines for error handling to keep your application as robust as possible.

18.2.4   Error Handling in Readable Streams

In the development process, you usually have the environment well under your control so that few to no errors occur. For this reason, error handling is also neglected quite often. However, dealing with errors is essential for a stable and reliable application. For the example with the readable stream from the file system, this means that the application must be able to respond correspondingly, for example, if the file doesn't exist or you don't have the permission to read it. If you don't register a callback on the error event, an exception will be triggered, which, if not caught, will result in the immediate termination of your application. Listing 18.4 contains the source code for rudimentary error handling in the sample code.

```
import { createReadStream } from 'fs';

const options = {
  encoding: 'utf8',
};

const readStream = createReadStream('gibt-es-nicht.txt', options);

readStream.on('readable', () => {
  const data = readStream.read();
  if (data) {
    console.log(data);
  }
});

readStream.on('close', () => {
  console.log('The stream has been closed');
});

readStream.on('error', (e) => {
  console.error('An error has occurred: ', e);
});
```

Listing 18.4 Error Handling in Readable Streams

Handling errors in this case has two advantages at the same time for you. First, your application won't be terminated by the uncaught exception, and you'll receive additional information about the error that occurred via the error object in the callback function. In the case of the example where the file to be read doesn't exist, the error message indicates the fact.

In addition to the events just introduced, you can also access some methods for controlling the readable stream.

18.2.5 Methods

In addition to the read method, there are a few other helpful methods you can draw on when dealing with streams. Table 18.2 summarizes the most important ones for you.

Method	Description
read([size])	Reads data from a stream.
setEncoding(encoding)	Sets the encoding; strings are used instead of buffer objects.
pause()	Pauses the data flow of a stream.
resume()	Resumes the data flow of a paused stream.
isPaused()	Indicates whether the stream is currently paused.
pipe(destination[, options])	Forwards the output to a writable stream.
unpipe([destination])	Stops the forwarding of a stream.
unshift(chunk)	Puts an already consumed data record back on the stream.
wrap(stream)	Encloses an older generation stream for full compatibility.

Table 18.2 Most Important Readable Stream Methods

Both the piping concept and the different operation modes of readable streams under Node.js need further explanation, as these are core concepts of the stream API that serves as a basis for many other features.

18.2.6 Piping

You've already learned about the concept of chained streams. In Node.js, such a chain of streams is implemented using the pipe method of a readable stream. This method redirects the output of a readable stream to the input of a writable stream. Listing 18.5 introduces a very simple pipeline.

```
import { createReadStream, createWriteStream } from 'fs';

const read = createReadStream('input.txt');
const write = createWriteStream('output.txt');

read.pipe(write);
```

Listing 18.5 Stream Pipeline

The code in Listing 18.5 copies the *input.txt* file into the *output.txt* file. In this example, you first create a readable stream using the createReadStream function of the fs module. Then you use the createWriteStream function to generate a writable stream into which the information gets written. The connection of both streams is then established via the pipe method. This example shows quite clearly how the implementation and instantiation of the individual streams can be separated from their concatenation, which eventually results in easily readable source code, especially if you think of a longer chain of streams with many intermediate steps at this point. Another advantage is that, in this case, you can insert simple debugging statements between the instantiation and the use of the respective streams, if you're looking for an error.

The second important concept besides piping involves the different modes in which readable streams can be operated.

18.2.7   Readable Stream Modes

The current readable streams of Node.js provide two modes you can switch between at runtime of your application:

- **Paused mode (pull streams)**
  The data is actively consumed by calling the read method. This is the default mode of a readable stream.

- **Flowing mode (push streams)**
  In this variant, the data is pushed from the data source to the stream, and no consideration is given to consumers.

If you run a readable stream with the combination of readable event and read method shown in Listing 18.2, the stream is in paused mode. This way, you can control the data flow by calling the read method.

18.2.8   Switching to Flowing Mode

You can switch from paused mode to flowing mode in three different ways:

- **data event**
  Once you register a listener for the data event, the stream is set to flowing mode.

- **resume method**
  Calling the resume method also results in the data flow being determined by the data source.

- **pipe method**
  In addition, if your readable stream is a data source for a stream pipeline, it will be put into flowing mode.

18.2.9 Switching to the Paused Mode

If your stream is currently in flowing mode, and you want to return to paused mode, you basically only need to undo the actions you used when you put the stream into flowing mode. You have the following options:

- **pause**
  You can explicitly put the stream into paused mode by calling the pause method.

- **removeAllListeners, unpipe**
  Alternatively, you can deregister the existing event listeners of the data event via the removeAllListeners('data') call. Moreover, if your readable stream is in a pipeline, you must use the unpipe method to remove the stream from the pipeline.

> **Warning!**
>
> The paused mode has one important drawback: you can't attach multiple consumers concurrently to one readable stream. Calling the read method consumes the data from the stream and removes it at the same time. This means if you register an event handler twice on the readable event and call the read method within it, you'll receive different data packages each time. If you want to connect two consumers to one readable stream, this only works via flowing mode by registering multiple listeners for the data event.

Now you know how you can handle readable streams and control the data flow. For your own application, the existing readable streams from the internal node modules or installed Node Package Manager (npm) packages are often not sufficient, so you have to implement a readable stream yourself.

18.2.10 Custom Readable Streams

The readable stream implementations of Node.js are derived from a central base class from the stream module. The Node.js platform already provides the framework implementation of a readable stream with this base class, so you only need to take care of specializing the stream. For your source code, this means you only need to implement one method, and then you can already use the stream. Listing 18.6 shows the simplest variant of implementing a readable stream.

```
import { Readable } from 'stream';

class ReadStream extends Readable {
  _read() {
    this.push('Hello World');
  }
}
```

Listing 18.6 Implementing a Readable Stream

The readable class of the stream module is an ordinary JavaScript class. This means you can use the readable class as a base class in your own class definition and derive data from it using extend. You can consider the readable class in the broadest sense as an abstract class you can't use directly, but must first derive data from it. In your own implementation, you only need to implement the _read method. The basic version of this method, which you inherit from readable, triggers an exception, making it impossible to be used directly. This is a common technique to simulate abstract classes in JavaScript and force the overriding of methods in derived classes.

To write a new data record to the stream, you can use the push method of the object.

18.2.11   Example of a Readable Stream

The example shown in Listing 18.6 is quite far from reality. A realistic implementation is, in most cases, much more extensive, if only because a readable stream should produce more than just one data record.

So, to give you an idea of how you can use readable streams in your application, here is a somewhat larger example (see Listing 18.7). The goal in this case is to stream temperature readings. A measured value consists of a date and a temperature value. For this example, the values are randomly generated and limited to a maximum of 10 values generated at random intervals of up to five seconds. In a production environment, such values can of course originate from a measuring device or another system that is addressed via a driver or a socket.

```
import { Readable } from 'stream';

class TemperatureReader extends Readable {
  constructor(opt = { objectMode: true }) {
    super(opt);
    this.items = 0;
    this.maxItems = 10;
  }
  _read() {
    this.emitValue();
  }

  emitValue() {
    setTimeout(() => {
      if (this.items++ < this.maxItems) {
        this.push(this.createValue());
      } else {
        this.push(null);
      }
    }, Math.floor(Math.random() * 5) * 1000);
```

```
  }
  createValue() {
    return {
      date: new Date(),
      temp: `${Math.floor(Math.random() * 1000 - 273)}°C`,
    };
  }
}

const tr = new TemperatureReader();
tr.on('readable', function () {
  let value;
  while (null !== (value = tr.read())) {
    console.log(JSON.stringify(value));
  }
});
```

Listing 18.7 Readable Stream in a Real-Life Example

The structure of the class follows the same schema as in the previous example. In contrast, some properties are set here in the constructor for controlling the stream at a later time. Additionally, optional configuration options are passed to the parent constructor, while the object mode of the stream gets enabled.

By calling the emitValue method, the _read method makes sure that a value is published after a random period of time if the maximum number of values hasn't yet been exceeded. Once the maximum is reached, null is sent, and thus the stream gets closed. The createValue method ensures that an object is created that represents a measured value. This way, each method has exactly one task, and the source code remains easily readable.

To use the stream, you first generate an instance. On this object, you register a handler for the readable event, as you did in the case of the file system streams. Inside this callback function, you can then consume the data of the stream via the read method. However, a simple call of the method doesn't provide the expected result because several data records may exist per readable event. This means you must call the read method as many times as necessary until it returns the value null. As you can see, the asynchronous nature of the data generation doesn't matter in this case, and the stream can handle it without any problems.

When you run the example on the command line, you get a result like the one shown in Listing 18.8.

```
{"date":"2018-04-25T11:19:34.084Z","temp":"718°C"}
{"date":"2018-04-25T11:19:35.090Z","temp":"-96°C"}
{"date":"2018-04-25T11:19:38.091Z","temp":"327°C"}
```

```
{"date":"2018-04-25T11:19:38.093Z","temp":"114°C"}
{"date":"2018-04-25T11:19:38.094Z","temp":"549°C"}
{"date":"2018-04-25T11:19:38.095Z","temp":"540°C"}
{"date":"2018-04-25T11:19:39.098Z","temp":"429°C"}
{"date":"2018-04-25T11:19:39.100Z","temp":"49°C"}
{"date":"2018-04-25T11:19:42.102Z","temp":"557°C"}
{"date":"2018-04-25T11:19:42.104Z","temp":"635°C"}
```

Listing 18.8 Result from the Readable Stream

Object Mode

In Node.js, streams use `buffer` objects or character strings. However, if you use streams in your application, it's often impractical to first convert all objects to character strings and then write them into a stream. For further use, you must then convert the string representation back into an object. To do so, you can use the object mode. You can turn it on or off as an option when creating a stream. In Listing 18.7, you've already seen how the object mode can be used in a concrete example.

When reading from a stream in object mode, the size specified when calling the `read` method is ignored. The same applies to any encoding that's specified when calling the `write` method of a writable stream.

The object mode can be changed during the existence of the stream, but this isn't recommended. In a transform stream, the object mode for read and write access can be set separately using the `readableObjectMode` and `writableObjectMode` options, respectively. The core modules of Node.js, which are based on streams, don't use the object mode.

For the default implementation of readable streams in Node.js, developers have provided another simplification that allows for a very concise and comprehensible implementation.

18.2.12   Readable Shortcut

The Node.js platform provides shortcuts for a wide variety of use cases that saves a lot of writing for you as a developer. Listing 18.9 shows how you can create a simple readable stream in short notation.

```
import { Readable } from 'stream';

const readable = new Readable({
  objectMode: true,

  read() {
    this.emitValue();
```

```
  },
});
readable.items = 0;
readable.maxItems = 10;
readable.emitValue = () => {
  setTimeout(() => {
    if (readable.items++ < readable.maxItems) {
      readable.push(readable.createValue());
    } else {
      readable.push(null);
    }
  }, Math.floor(Math.random() * 5) * 1000);
};
readable.createValue = () => {
  return {
    date: new Date(),
    temp: `${Math.floor(Math.random() * 1000 - 273)}°C`,
  };
};
readable.on('readable', function () {
  let value;
  while (null !== (value = readable.read())) {
    console.log(JSON.stringify(value));
  }
});
```

Listing 18.9 Readable Streams in Short Notation

As you can see in Listing 18.9, the constructor of a readable stream accepts an object as an argument. Here, in addition to the usual options such as object mode, you can also set the read property and assign a function to it. This is then used as the implementation of the _read method. So, the source code from Listing 18.9 generally works like the one from Listing 18.7, but without the intermediate step of its own class. The disadvantage of this method is that the properties of the passed object are ignored, so you have to add all properties and methods afterwards; as a matter of fact, the shortcut is only useful for very simple implementations.

18.3   Writable Streams

While readable streams are the data source, writable streams are the destination of a stream chain. One of the most common use cases is writing data to a file. But numerous other targets such as databases, external interfaces, or remote systems are also conceivable. For most cases, proven solutions are available for you to use, so that no further effort is required on your part. However, if an existing implementation isn't sufficient or if there is none yet, you can create a writable stream yourself.

18.3.1   Creating a Writable Stream

Before you start creating your own writable streams, you should first learn about the API. To do that, you should take a look at a concrete example. In Listing 18.10, you write the contents of an array to a file using a writable stream.

```
import { createWriteStream } from 'fs';

const writeStream = createWriteStream('output.txt');

const data = ['Hello', 'World'];

data.forEach((item) => {
  writeStream.write(item + '\n');
});

writeStream.end(null);
```

Listing 18.10 Writing Files with Writable Streams

To use a writable stream, you first need a way to create an instance of the stream. In this case, it's the `createWriteStream` function of the `fs` module that helps you. On this instance, you then call the `write` method with the data you want to write. Once all data has been written, a call of the `end` method terminates the stream.

In addition to the two methods you've learned about so far, writable streams provide several other methods and events you can use to control the stream or respond to events.

18.3.2   Events

The writable stream represents the endpoint of a stream chain. This means the area's uses are somewhat more limited than those for the readable stream. However, there are more events you can use to respond to the interaction with the writable stream. Table 18.3 summarizes them for you.

Event	Description
finish	An event is triggered when the end method is called.
pipe	The handlers of this event are executed when a readable stream pipes into this stream.

Table 18.3 Events of Writable Streams

Event	Description
unpipe	If a pipe is removed, the unpipe event gets triggered.
error	The error event is used for error handling in a writable stream.
drain	This signals when a stream is ready to accept data again.
close	This gets triggered when the stream or an underlying resource is closed.

Table 18.3 Events of Writable Streams (Cont.)

Listing 18.11 shows how you can use some of the event handlers. The example is based on the piping concept you already know from Listing 18.5.

```
import { createReadStream, createWriteStream } from 'fs';

const readable = createReadStream('input.txt');
const writable = createWriteStream('output.txt');

writable.on('pipe', (readstream) => {
  console.log('pipe handler called');
});

writable.on('unpipe', (readstream) => {
  console.log('unpipe handler called');
});

writable.on('finish', () => {
  console.log('finish handler called');
});

readable.pipe(writable);

/* Output:
pipe handler called
finish handler called
unpipe handler called
*/
```

Listing 18.11 Events of a Writable Stream

When you run the example from Listing 18.11, the callback function for the pipe event is executed first. The reason is the connection of the readable stream to the writable stream via the pipe method. In this callback function, you have access to the instance of the readable stream. Once the data of the stream is consumed, the finish event gets

561

triggered and the connection terminates. This callback function doesn't provide any other arguments. The last event that gets triggered is the unpipe event. This event signals that the pipe connection between the two streams has been terminated. Here again, you get a reference to the readable stream. In addition to these events, which are mainly used to respond to external interactions with the writable stream, there is another very important event—the error event.

18.3.3   Error Handling in Writable Streams

As does the readable stream, the writable stream also has the error event, which you can use to respond to various errors during the runtime of the stream. A possible error could be a missing permission in the case of a file system stream.

If you don't handle a triggered error event, it will have the same effect as an uncaught exception and will cause your application to terminate. For this reason, you should always register a handler for the error event. Listing 18.12 contains a corresponding example.

```
import { createWriteStream } from 'fs';

const writeStream = createWriteStream('/usr/sbin/test.txt');

writeStream.on('error', (err) => {
  console.error('An error has occurred: ', err);
});
```

Listing 18.12 Error Handling in Writable Streams

On a Unix system, this code example causes an error because it attempts to create the *test.txt* file in the */usr/sbin* directory. However, this directory is reserved for the system administrator. Normal user accounts don't have write permission for it. The result is the following error message: Error: EPERM: operation not permitted, open '/usr/sbin/test.txt'.

In addition to the events you've already learned about in connection with writable streams, there are also some methods that allow you to use the stream.

18.3.4   Methods

The most important method in dealing with writable streams is the write method, which you use to write data to the stream. You also need the end method to end the write operation. However, the writable stream provides a few other methods as well, as listed in Table 18.4.

Method	Description

write(
  chunk
  [, encoding]
  [, callback])
	Writes the specified data to the stream. Optionally, you can pass the encoding and a callback function. The callback is executed as soon as the data has been written.

end(
  [chunk]
  [, encoding]
  [, callback])
	The signature of the end method is similar to that of the write method, except that no further write operation is possible after calling the end method. The callback function is executed as soon as the writable stream is finished.

setDefaultEncoding(encoding)	This sets the encoding for the entire stream.
cork()	The data isn't written directly, but buffered.
uncork()	The data written to the buffer by the call of the cork method is finally written by a call of the uncork method, and the buffer is thus emptied.

Table 18.4 Methods of a Writable Stream

18.3.5   Buffering Write Operations

The cork and uncork methods enable you to execute the write operations of a writable stream not immediately, but to store them in a buffer first and then to empty this buffer at a later time. Listing 18.13 shows an example of this.

```
import { createWriteStream } from 'fs';

const writeStream = createWriteStream('output.txt');

writeStream.write('Hello\n');
writeStream.cork();
writeStream.write('World\n');
setTimeout(() => {
  writeStream.uncork();
  writeStream.write('!');
  writeStream.end();
}, 5000);
```

Listing 18.13 Buffering Write Operations with the "cork" Method

When you run the source code, you won't see a result directly because the application doesn't generate any output on the command line, but only writes to the *output.txt* file. For example, to see the effects of the source code, you can observe the file in real time on a Unix system on the command line via the tail -f output.txt command. The

18

result is that you initially see only the Hello line because the first write operation is unbuffered. Then you use the cork method to activate the buffer and write into it. After five seconds, you use the uncork method to clear the buffer and end the stream.

You can use buffered write operations, for example, to group write operations and thus improve the write performance of your application.

18.3.6   Flow Control

When using writable streams, you usually use the write and end methods. In most cases, you rely on the fact that data is received and written immediately. However, the write method may be called too frequently, and your system may not keep up with the writing process. For this reason, the write method has a return value. This value is set to true in most cases, which means that the write operation was successful and writing can continue. The value false means that you should wait with the next call of the write method. Once the writable stream is ready again, the drain event gets triggered, and you can continue writing. Listing 18.14 contains an example of using flow control with writable streams.

```
import { createWriteStream } from 'fs';

const writeStream = createWriteStream('output.txt');

const data = 'Node.js is great';

let i = 1000000;

write();

function write() {
  let ok = true;
  do {
    i -= 1;
    if (i === 0) {
      writeStream.end(data);
    } else {
      ok = writeStream.write(data);
    }
  } while (i > 0 && ok);
  if (i > 0) {
    console.log('wait');
    writeStream.once('drain', write);
  }
}
```

Listing 18.14 Flow Control in Writable Streams

The source code in Listing 18.14 ensures that a string is written to the file a million times. If the write method returns the value false, the write operation gets interrupted. You first write the wait string to the standard output. As soon as the drain event gets triggered, you call the write function once again.

In total, this example will generate about 16 MB of data in a very short time and write it to a file. Normally, quite a few drain events get triggered in the course of this process because the processing of the source code is faster than writing the information to disk. If this isn't the case, for example, because you have a very fast hard disk, you can also increase the number of data to be written until you've generated enough workload. However, be careful not to overdo it at this point and fill your hard drive too much, as this can cause problems with the operating system.

18.3.7 Custom Writable Streams

If you get into the situation that the existing writable stream implementations aren't sufficient for you, you can create your own writable streams using the stream module. For this purpose, Node.js already provides you with the framework implementation, and you just need to take care of the details. This is similar to readable streams.

In this example, as is the case with the readable stream, you use the writable base class of the stream module as the basis for your own implementation. By overriding the _write method, which triggers an exception in the base implementation, you have a working implementation. The parameter list of this method consists of the data to be written, the encoding of this data, and a callback function. In the sample code, you write the passed data to standard output by calling console.log. No matter what logic you implement for your writable stream, to complete the write operation, you must call the callback function you receive as the third argument.

In Listing 18.15, you then create an instance of your class, write information to the stream in a loop, and finally end it by calling the end method.

```
import { Writable } from 'stream';

class WriteStream extends Writable {
  _write(chunk, enc, done) {
    console.log('WRITE: ', chunk.toString());
    done();
  }
}

const ws = new WriteStream();
for (let i = 0; i < 10; i++) {
  ws.write('Hello ' + i);
}
ws.end();
```

Listing 18.15 Custom Writable Streams

18.3.8   Writable Shortcut

As is the case with readable streams, there is also a short notation for writable streams. Using the source code from Listing 18.16, you directly create an object of the writable class and pass an object to the constructor. This object has the write property, which then overrides the _write method.

```
import { Writable } from 'stream';

const ws = new Writable({
  write: (chunk, encoding, done) => {
    console.log('WRITE: ', chunk.toString());
    done();
  },
});

for (let i = 0; i < 10; i++) {
  ws.write('Hello ' + i);
}
ws.end();
```

Listing 18.16 Short Notation for Writable Streams

With this information, you now know everything you need to know about both the readable and writable streams of Node.js. In addition to these two, there are two other manifestations of streams, which will be described in the following sections.

18.4   Duplex Streams

Duplex streams represent a combination of readable streams and writable streams. You can read data from a duplex stream as well as write data into it. The write and read operations of a duplex stream are independent of each other, and each has its own buffer. A typical implementation of a duplex stream are network sockets as they are used in the net module.

18.4.1   Duplex Streams in Use

Unfortunately, duplex streams can only be described quite abstractly. Much more understandable here, however, are concrete examples. Listing 18.17 contains source code that demonstrates the use of a duplex stream.

```
import { createServer } from 'net';

createServer((socket) => {
  socket.on('readable', () => {
```

```
    const data = socket.read();
    console.log(data);
  });

  socket.end('Hello Client');
}).listen(4321);
```

Listing 18.17 Duplex Streams in Use

The callback function you pass to the createServer method is bound to the connection event of the TCP server. As argument, you get a socket object of the duplex stream type. On this object, you can call the write and end methods as usual to send data to the other endpoint of the connection. However, you can also bind a callback function to the readable event to handle incoming data.

18.4.2   Custom Duplex Streams

Implementing a custom duplex stream is very similar to implementing readable and writable streams, except that, in this case, you must override both the _read and _write methods to obtain the desired result. The example in Listing 18.18 summarizes the steps you must take to implement it.

```
import { Duplex } from 'stream';

class MyDuplex extends Duplex {
  _read(n) {
    this.push(chunk);
  }

  _write(chunk, encoding, done) {
    done();
  }
}

const myDuplex = new MyDuplex();
```

Listing 18.18 Creating a Custom Duplex Stream

The example in Listing 18.18 is highly simplified, as it simply represents a combination of readable and writable streams, both of which you already know.

18.4.3   Duplex Shortcut

The short notation for duplex streams allows you to simplify the source code from Listing 18.18 even further, as you can see in Listing 18.19.

```
import { Duplex } from 'stream';

const duplex = new Duplex({
  read() {
    this.push(chunk);
  },
  write(chunk, encoding, next) {
    next();
  },
});
```

Listing 18.19 Short Notation for Duplex Streams

Duplex streams are a special case of the Node.js stream API. In your applications, you'll come across this type relatively rarely—in contrast to the last variant of streams, transform streams, which is one of the most frequently used types along with writable and readable streams.

18.5   Transform Streams

You can think of a transform stream as a link in a chain between its beginning and end, where you can attach several of these links together. As the name implies, a transform stream is used to transform an input into an output by applying defined rules. In this context, both the input and the output are also streams.

18.5.1   Custom Transform Streams

To implement a transform stream, you must derive your class from the transform class of the stream module and implement the _transform method. At its core, a transform stream represents a simplification of a duplex stream. The transform class derives from duplex and combines the readable and writable streams.

A concrete example of such a transform stream is as follows: you read the contents of a file, convert all letters to uppercase, and write the result to another file.

The _transform method from Listing 18.20 has the same signature as the _write method from the writable stream. The push method allows you to pass the transformed data record to the subsequent stream. Calling the callback function signals that the data has been completely processed. As an alternative to calling the push method manually, you can also pass the data to the callback function as the second argument. For the first argument, you can choose the value null.

```
import { createReadStream, createWriteStream } from 'fs';
import { Transform } from 'stream';
```

```
const read = createReadStream('input.txt');
const write = createWriteStream('output.txt');

class ToUpperCase extends Transform {
  _transform(chunk, encoding, callback) {
    this.push(chunk.toString().toUpperCase());
    callback();
  }
}

const toUpperCase = new ToUpperCase();
read.pipe(toUpperCase).pipe(write);
```

Listing 18.20 ToUpperCase Transform Stream

Once you've created all three components, that is, the readable stream, the writable stream, and the transform stream, you can link the individual parts by calling the respective pipe methods. For the example to work, you need an input file named *input.txt*. This file can contain any text. When you then run the script and open the *output.txt* containing the result, you'll see that the entire content is in uppercase.

If you still need to execute logic after the transformation, you can implement the _flush method. This method is called once the data has been processed, but before the end event gets triggered.

18.5.2   Transform Shortcut

As with the other streams, there is a short notation for the transform stream where you call the transform constructor directly with an object. This object must have a transform property with a function, which is then used as the _transform method. The short notation allows you to shorten the source code again.

Listing 18.21 contains only the part with the implementation of the transform stream. The rest of the source code from Listing 18.20 remains unchanged.

```
import { createReadStream, createWriteStream } from 'fs';
import { Transform } from 'stream';

const read = createReadStream('input.txt');
const write = createWriteStream('output.txt');

const toUpperCase = new Transform({
  transform(chunk, encoding, callback) {
    this.push(chunk.toString().toUpperCase());
    callback();
```

```
  },
});
```

```
read.pipe(toUpperCase).pipe(write);
```

Listing 18.21 Short Notation for Transform Streams

With transform streams, you now know the four types of streams available in Node.js. In the following section, you'll see another example of using streams, namely, with gulp.

18.6   Gulp

Gulp is a build system for JavaScript. With this application, you can automate routine development tasks. Gulp is written entirely in JavaScript and is based on Node.js. For the individual tasks, there are various plug-ins you can load and use. Typical tasks you do with gulp involve reviewing your source code, running tests, or minifying your source code.

The big difference to other build systems such as Grunt is that gulp is based on streams and views all operations as data streams. This change in approach means that you use gulp to program your build process, whereas Grunt expects you to use configuration objects.

18.6.1   Installation

To be able to use gulp, you must first install it. The installation process consists of several stages. In the first step, you install gulp globally via the `npm install -g gulp-cli` command. This allows you to access the `gulp` command line command from anywhere on your system. Once you run the `gulp` command on the command line after this first step, you'll receive an error message telling you that no local version of gulp could be found. In the second step, you complete the setup process with the local installation of gulp using the `npm install -save-dev gulp` command. gulp is usually installed as `devDependency` because it's only used during development.

After installing the components, the next thing you need to do is create the configuration for your build process. The naming convention states that the file should be named *gulpfile.js*. This file contains JavaScript source code, which follows the conventions of gulp and implements the individual tasks of the build process. Within the configuration file, you can access all features of Node.js, including the module system and additionally installed npm packages.

18.6.2 Example of a Build Process with Gulp

Listing 18.22 contains an example of a *gulpfile.js* file. For the example to work, you need to install a few more plug-ins first. In addition to the local installation, the following NPM packages are also required: gulp-babel, gulp-concat, gulp-uglify, and gulp-rename. As the name of the packages suggests, these are components for your build process. They're only needed for development purposes and therefore should be installed as devDependency with the --save-dev option.

Once you have set the stage, you can move on to creating the *gulpfile.js* file as shown in Listing 18.22.

```
import gulp from 'gulp';
import babel from 'gulp-babel';
import concat from 'gulp-concat';
import uglify from 'gulp-uglify';
import rename from 'gulp-rename';

export default () =>
  gulp
    .src('js/*.js')
    .pipe(concat('all.js'))
    .pipe(gulp.dest('dist'))
    .pipe(babel())
    .pipe(rename('all.min.js'))
    .pipe(uglify())
    .pipe(gulp.dest('dist'));
```

Listing 18.22 Sample gulpfile.js File

The gulp configuration consists of a regular Node.js application. At the start of the file, you include the required modules and configure the build steps within a simple arrow function. export default makes sure you can execute the task directly via the gulp command without any additional parameters. The concatenation of the individual tasks is done in the form of a data stream, as you know it from the Node.js streams. The data source, that is, the readable stream, is created by gulp.src. Here, you specify which files you want to transform. These files are combined into one file by the concat step and written to the *all.js* file. This file is converted with the Babel transpiler, renamed to *all.min.js*, and minified via UglifyJS. The final result gets written to the *dist* directory. As usual with streams, you can exchange or omit the intermediate steps as you like.

For gulp, there is a plug-in available for almost every possible task, which you can install and include in a similar way to the ones shown in the example. Recently, however, download numbers for legacy JavaScript build systems such as Grunt and gulp have stagnated. They are replaced by modern bundlers such as webpack, which are also based on Node.js. Nevertheless, gulp is a viable example of how you can use streams for your purposes in practice.

18.7 Summary

In this chapter, you've seen how versatile the stream API of Node.js can be in your application when it comes to modeling and manipulating data flows. You now know the four types of streams—readable, writable, duplex, and transform—and where you can use them.

There are some areas of use where streams can serve you very well in processing data. A very prominent example involves database connections. If you query data from a database, an alternative is to asynchronously process the entire result, which may be very large. By using streams in this case, you can process data records individually without losing control of the data flow.

Chapter 19
Working with Files

One waits for the times to change, the other seizes them and acts.
—Dante Alighieri

In the previous chapters, you've already seen how you can handle data streams in Node.js for the purpose of processing information. One of the most important sources of information and one of the most important targets of read and write operations is the file system.

First of all, here are some hints on handling files:

- **Permissions**
  A common source of errors related to the file system involves incorrect permissions. In Node.js, you work with the permissions of the user under which the application is running. If this user doesn't have the permission to access the desired files, the Node.js process isn't permitted to do so either, and an attempt to do so is responded to with an error.

- **Paths**
  You should always make sure to use the correct path for your access. You can either use absolute paths, starting from the root of the file system, or use relative paths, operating from the current directory. You should always prefer relative path specifications, as they increase the portability of your application.

- **Path separators**
  Windows uses backslashes as path separators, while Unix-based systems such as Linux or macOS use a forward slash. To make sure you use the correct separator, you should refer to the sep property of the path module.

19.1   Synchronous and Asynchronous Functions

Besides permissions and paths, there are a few things you should be aware with regard to doing file system operations: For most operations, both a synchronous and an asynchronous version exist. Version 10 of Node.js also added a promise-based application programming interface (API) to the fs module, so you now have three different functions available for most operations. The promise-based version of the file system interface, which was added later, was initially marked as experimental, like most new modules. However, this extension has proven to be stable and reliable over the past few years, so you can use it in your application without a problem. The synchronous and callback-based version of the interface is directly available in the fs module. You can access the promise-based variant via the fs/promises module.

Basically, you already know what asynchronicity in Node.js is all about. But here's a brief review: What does that mean for you as a developer? For your application, a synchronous file system operation means that you issue a call to read a file, for example. This command is passed to the Node.js platform and then further on to the operating system, which eventually executes the read operation and returns the result to Node.js and thus to your application. During this process your application won't continue to run, the whole process is blocked. Once the result is available, the application continues to run normally. If file system operations occur frequently in your application or if you need to perform operations on large files, the synchronous methods of the fs module may have a negative impact on your application due to the interruptions in program execution. In Listing 19.1, you can see an example of a synchronous file reading operation using the readFileSync function of the fs module.

```
import { readFileSync } from 'fs';

try {
  const data = readFileSync('./input.txt', 'utf-8');
  console.log(data);
} catch (err) {
  console.error(err);
}
```

Listing 19.1 Synchronous File Reading Operation

To avoid the negative impact on the performance of your application, the asynchronous methods exist. They work in the same way as their synchronous counterparts, except that, in this case, the result of the operation isn't returned to your application as a return value but is processed by a callback function. These callbacks always have a similar signature in Node.js. The first argument is usually an error object that contains a value only if problems occurred during the operation. The other values passed represent the result of the operation, which you can handle within your callback. The example in Listing 19.2 should clarify this.

```
import { readFile } from 'fs';

readFile('./input.txt', 'utf-8', (err, data) => {
  if (err) {
    console.error(err);
  } else {
```

```
      console.log(data);
   }
});
```

Listing 19.2 Callback Functions in Node.js

The same result can be solved a bit more elegantly with the promise-based variant in conjunction with top-level await. To access this new variant of the file system module, you must include the fs/promises module. The source code from Listing 19.3 benefits from the fact that promises can be combined with async functions, so you can get by without callback functions and use try-catch for error handling.

```
import { readFile } from 'fs/promises';

try {
  const data = await readFile('./input.txt', 'utf-8');
  console.log(data);
} catch (err) {
  console.error(err);
}
```

Listing 19.3 Reading a Promise-Based File

19.2 Existence of Files

But before you start reading or writing files, the first thing you should know is how to find out whether a file exists or not. If you open a file to process it, you don't have to check for its existence. The open method that creates the file handle returns an error that you can directly act on.

If you want to execute logic based on the existence of a file, you can use the stat method, where you get an object with more information about the corresponding file. Alternatively, you can use the access method to check if you have a certain type of access to the file. Listing 19.4 contains an example for both cases.

```
import { constants } from 'fs';
import { stat, access } from 'fs/promises';

try {
  const fileStat = await stat('./input.txt');
  console.log(fileStat); // Output: Stats { dev:...
} catch (err) {
  console.error(err);
}
```

```
try {
  await access('./input.txt', constants.R_OK);
  console.log('File is readable');
} catch (e) {
  console.error('File not readable');
}
```

Listing 19.4 Checking for the Existence of Files

In Listing 19.4, you use the promise-based version of the stat function as well as the access function of the fs/promises module. Both functions also exist as callback variants. The stat function returns a promise object containing a range of information about the file if it exists. The promise of the access function resolves with no value if you have the desired permissions, which, in this case, is the read permission.

The access method uses predefined constants of the fs module:

- fs.constants.F_OK
  The file is *visible* to the current process.

- fs.constants.R_OK
  The file can be *read*.

- fs.constants.W_OK
  The file can be *written* into.

- fs.constants.X_OK
  The file is *executable*.

If the desired mode isn't available, you'll receive an error object as an argument in the callback function. Otherwise, the value of the argument is null.

19.3   Reading Files

In Node.js, you have several ways to read the contents of a file. Let's first take a look at the classic way. With this method, you create a file handle in the first step, use it to read the file, and then close the file handle again. If you already have experience in programming with other programming languages such as C or PHP, this type of file access will look familiar to you.

The use of the different operations that help you to read files will be described in the following sections based on a concrete example. The application is intended to read a configuration file whose content is in JavaScript Object Notation (JSON) format. You pass the configParser the environment for which you want to read the configuration and get a corresponding object structure. In Listing 19.5, you can see an example of a JSON file to be processed by the application.

```
{
  "production": {
    "user": "root",
    "password": "topSecret",
    "host": "localhost",
    "database": "mysql"
  },
  "development": {
    "user": "root",
    "password": "secret",
    "host": "localost",
    "database": "sqlite3"
  }
}
```

Listing 19.5 Configuration File (config.json)

Listing 19.6 contains the entire the source code for the example. To keep the source code somewhat clearer, we'll refrain from dealing with any errors that may occur.

```
import fs from 'fs';
const filename = 'config.json';

function configParser(env) {
  return new Promise((resolve, reject) => {
    fs.open(filename, 'r', (err, handle) => {
      fs.stat(filename, (err, stats) => {
        const size = stats.size;
        const buffer = new Buffer.alloc(size);
        fs.read(handle, buffer, 0, size, 0, (err, bytes, content) => {
          fs.close(handle, (err) => {
            const config = JSON.parse(content);
            if (config.hasOwnProperty(env)) {
              resolve(config[env]);
            } else {
              reject(`Section ${env} does not exist`);
            }
          });
        });
      });
    });
  });
}

configParser('production').then((config) => {
```

```
  console.log('Production: ', config);
});
configParser('development').then((config) => {
  console.log('Development: ', config);
});
configParser('test').catch((e) => {
  console.log(e);
});
```

Listing 19.6 Implementation of "configParser" (config-parser.js)

Of particular importance in this example are the calls of the open, stat, read, and close methods provided by the fs module.

All operations in configParser are asynchronous; to use the function anyway, a promise object is returned that may contain the result or potential error messages. The configParser consists of a function that first uses the open method to create a file handle. The first value accepted by open is the name of the file to be opened. The second value specifies how the file should be opened; this is referred to as the flag. Here you have several options to choose from, as shown in Table 19.1. Finally, the third argument is the callback function. This function receives as arguments an object containing any existing errors that occurred during opening and the file handle you can use to access the file.

Flag	Description
r	File opens for *read-only* access.
r+	File opens for *read* and *write* access.
rs+	*Synchronous write* and *read mode.*
w	File opens for *write-only* access. File is created or emptied.
wx	File opens for *exclusive write* access.
w+	File opens for *read* and *write* access. File is created or emptied.
wx+	Opens the file as with wx, but for *exclusive* access.
a	Opens the file to *append* data and creates the file if necessary.
ax	Like a, except that the file opens exclusively.
a+	Opens the file to *append* data and for *read* access.
ax+	Like a+, but with *exclusive* access to the file.

Table 19.1 Access Flags of the "open" Method

Because the requirements for the example only involve the reading of files, it's sufficient that you open the file with the r flag for read-only access. You can then use the handle argument of the callback to access the contents of the file via various methods of the fs module. However, if you try to write to the file using the write method inside the callback of the open method, you'll receive an error because the file handle isn't writable.

In the next step, another feature of the fs module comes into play—the stat method. You need this method to read the information about the configuration file. For this example, you read the file size you'll need later to properly size the buffer that will hold the data. The stat method is again asynchronous, which involves another callback for you in which you have access to the statistics of the file via the second argument. Finally, in the callback of the stat method, you create a buffer object to hold the contents of the file. Because buffer objects can't grow dynamically, you must specify the size when creating them. The Buffer.alloc method enables you to create the object. This method requires the size of the buffer object to be created; you can obtain the value from the size property of the second argument of the stat callback.

The arguments of the read method are the handle, the buffer, and the location in the buffer to start writing to. In your case, this is the number 0, which indicates that the process is to start at the beginning of the buffer. This is followed by the number of bytes to be read. Here you should again use the size property from the stat callback. You must also specify the position within the file from which to read. Again, you should use the value 0 so the process starts at the beginning of the file. Finally, the last argument is the callback function. It receives three arguments. The first one is the error object, which normally has the value null. The second one is the number of bytes that were read. Finally, the third and most relevant argument for you is the buffer object that contains the read content.

Within the callback function, error handling is implemented first. Then the file handle gets closed via the close method. In the callback function of the close method, a check is made as to whether the requested configuration section exists, which is then returned via the promise. If no configuration can be found, a corresponding error message is returned.

Finally, configParser is executed for the production, development, and test sections. The first two return the requested data, while the test configuration returns an error message. You can see the result in Listing 19.7.

```
$ node config-parser.js
Development: { user: 'root',
  password: 'secret',
  host: 'localost',
  database: 'sqlite3' }
Production:  { user: 'root',
  password: 'topSecret',
```

```
      host: 'localhost',
      database: 'mysql' }
Section test does not exist
```

Listing 19.7 "configParser" Output

The whole application can be shortened considerably by using only the promise-based `readFile` method instead of the combination of open, stat, read, and close. This method encapsulates all three methods. The consequence for you is that you can use the contents of the callback function you use for the close method without any changes also in `readFile`.

As you can see in Listing 19.8, all calls of the methods already mentioned are dropped. If you specify the encoding—in this case utf-8—the second argument of the `readFile` method is a character string. This allows the original callback function and helper function to be reused. As an alternative to the way shown here, you can also include JSON files directly with require.

```
import { readFile } from 'fs';

const filename = 'config.json';

function configParser(env) {
  return new Promise((resolve, reject) => {
    readFile(filename, 'utf-8', (error, content) => {
      if (error) {
        reject(error);
      } else {
        const config = JSON.parse(content);
        if (config.hasOwnProperty(env)) {
          resolve(config[env]);
        } else {
          reject(`Section ${env} does not exist`);
        }
      }
    });
  });
}

configParser('production').then(
  (config) => {
    console.log('Production: ', config);
  },
  (err) => console.error(err),
);
```

```
configParser('development').then(
  (config) => {
    console.log('Development: ', config);
  },
  (err) => console.error(err),
);
configParser('test').catch((e) => {
  console.log(e);
});
```

Listing 19.8 "configParser" with "readFile"

19.3.1   Promise-Based API

The configParser can also be implemented with the new promise-based API of the file system module. As you can see in Listing 19.9, the source code of your application can be further simplified with the combination of promises and async functions. Apart from that, the methods used remain approximately the same as in Listing 19.8.

```
import { readFile } from 'fs/promises';

const filename = 'config.json';

async function configParser(env) {
  const content = await readFile(filename, 'utf-8');
  const config = JSON.parse(content);
  if (config.hasOwnProperty(env)) {
    return config[env];
  } else {
    throw new Error(`Section ${env} does not exist`);
  }
}

configParser('production').then(
  (config) => {
    console.log('Production: ', config);
  },
  (err) => console.error(err),
);
configParser('development').then(
  (config) => {
    console.log('Development: ', config);
  },
  (err) => console.error(err),
);
```

19

```
configParser('test').catch((e) => {
  console.log(e);
});
```

Listing 19.9 "configParser" with "fs/promises"

19.4   Error Handling

Previously, the first argument of callback functions was ignored during development. Normally this argument has the value null. However, if an error occurs, you'll find more detailed information about it in this object. You can test the error handling when dealing with files by trying to open a file that doesn't exist. Listing 19.10 shows how you can cause such errors and how to deal with them.

```
import { open } from 'fs';
open('/does-not-exist.txt', 'r', (err, handle) => {
  if (err) throw err;
});
```

Listing 19.10 Error While Reading a File

In this example, you can see how errors can occur in the file system module of Node.js. When you run the sample code, you'll receive the following error message: Error: ENOENT: no such file or directory, open '/does-not-exist.txt'. Depending on where you want to perform error handling, you can do this in different places: On the one hand, you can handle the errors directly where they occur, that is, in your callback function itself, or, as you can see in Listing 19.10. On the other hand, you throw the error object using throw and rely on another place in your application's source code to take care of dealing with it. The third and worst option available to you when errors occur is to simply ignore them.

19.5   Writing to Files

Writing to files is similar to reading them. Here, too, the open and close methods are used to prepare access and to close the file handle after use, respectively. The fs module provides several methods of write access to files. In the first step, you'll see the use of the write method.

You'll also learn how you can write to a file based on a small example. For this purpose, you now need to create a logger. This is a small application or a module for larger applications that helps you write information into a file. Loggers are used in applications whenever it's necessary to record events during operation or development for later analysis. For example, when errors occur, you can have the corresponding message written to the log file.

The most important requirement for the logger is that it should be as lightweight as possible, so that it doesn't unnecessarily make the source code of the application unreadable. In addition, the logger is supposed to provide the option to write entries with different priorities, for example, error, warning, or information. An application is usually used in different stages. For example, you write more messages during the development phase than is usually the case in production operation. To meet this requirement, it's necessary to design the logger in such a way that you can configure what types of messages are to be logged.

Listing 19.11 contains the source code of the logger. In the following sections, you'll receive further explanations on the individual steps of the implementation.

```
import { open, write, close } from 'fs';
import EventEmitter from 'events';
import { format } from 'util';

class EventLogger extends EventEmitter {
  constructor(file, levels) {
    super();
    this.file = file;
    this.levels = levels;

    this.on('error', this.log.bind(this, 'ERR'));
    this.on('warning', this.log.bind(this, 'WARN'));
    this.on('info', this.log.bind(this, 'INFO'));
  }

  log(level, data) {
    if (this.levels.indexOf(level) > -1) {
      open(this.file, 'a', (err, handle) => {
        const buffer = Buffer.from(
          format('%s (%s) %s\n', new Date(), level, data),
        );
        write(
          handle,
          buffer,
          0,
          buffer.length,
          null,
          (err, written, buffer) => {
            close(handle, () => {});
          },
```

```
      );
    });
  }
 }
}

const logger = new EventLogger('error.log', ['ERR', 'WARN']);

logger.emit('error', 'Something happened');
logger.emit('warning', 'Something else happened');
logger.emit('info', 'Not relevant');
```

Listing 19.11 Writing Files Using "EventLogger"

To implement the logger, you need the events and util modules in addition to the fs module.

First, you define the EventLogger class and derive it from the EventEmitter of Node.js. The constructor receives two arguments: the file to write to and the levels to log as an array. Before you can use this in the constructor, you must call the constructor of the parent class via the super keyword. Then you register callback functions for the different error levels. Note that, at this point, you must use the bind method of the function object so that the method is executed in the correct context. If you only pass the reference to the method, you'll lose the this reference within the method and no longer have a reference to the file name, for example. The bind method binds a function to a specific object—in this case, the instance of EventLogger—ensuring that this points to the correct object.

The log method represents the core of the logger. It makes sure that the correct messages are written to the file. For the logger to meet the requirements, you should check in the first step, whether the desired message should be recorded at all, as shown in the example. After that, a combination of open, write, and close is used.

The open method needs the access flag a to be able to write to the file. Within the callback function, you then create the string that will eventually be captured in the log. The format should look like this: the date and time, followed by the type of message, and finally the actual message. Because the write method only writes the string to the file, and this operation isn't carried out on a line-by-line basis, you should append the escape sequence \n for inserting line breaks.

The formatted character string then gets embedded in a buffer object, which you pass as the second argument to the write method. The first argument is the file handle from the open method. The next two arguments of the write method are used to select the correct section from the buffer object to write. In your case, the offset is 0, and the length of the string to be written is the entire length of the buffer object. Finally, the penultimate argument is the position within the file to write to. If you choose the value null, as shown in the example in Listing 19.11, this means you want to write to the current position, that is, to the end of the file. Finally, the last argument is a callback function. You should use this argument to close the file handle via the close method.

With this source code, the logger is now fully functional and can be used. You can see how this works in the last lines of the example in Listing 19.11. All you have to do is instantiate the logger and then use the emit method inherited from the EventEmitter to trigger the respective events. You can now export the EventLogger via export and include and use it in your application via import.

As is the case with the read access, there are also other methods you can use for writing to files. The writeFile and appendFile methods are particularly interesting in this context. In terms of functionality, both methods are similar, except that writeFile overwrites the file in its entirety, whereas appendFile merely appends the data to the already existing file. Internally, both methods represent an encapsulation of the three method calls open, write, and close and, for this reason, serve rather to simplify your application code. In EventLogger, you should use the appendFile method because you want to append data to the log file continuously and not overwrite and lose information. The adjustments you need to make to the EventLogger source code in this respect are limited to the log method. Listing 19.12 shows the adjustments you need to make.

```
import { appendFile } from 'fs';
import EventEmitter from 'events';
import { format } from 'util';

class EventLogger extends EventEmitter {
  constructor(file, levels) {
    super();
    this.file = file;
    this.levels = levels;

    this.on('error', this.log.bind(this, 'ERR'));
    this.on('warning', this.log.bind(this, 'WARN'));
    this.on('info', this.log.bind(this, 'INFO'));
  }

  log(level, data) {
    if (this.levels.indexOf(level) > -1) {
      const logData = format('%s (%s) %s\n', new Date(), level, data);
      appendFile(this.file, logData, () => {});
    }
  }
}

const logger = new EventLogger('error.log', ['ERR', 'WARN']);
```

19

```
logger.emit('error', 'Something happened');
logger.emit('warning', 'Something else happened');
logger.emit('info', 'Not relevant');
```

Listing 19.12 "EventLogger" with "appendFile"

As you can see, the required changes aren't very extensive. You just need to swap out the generation of the log data from the callback function of open and replace the calls of open, write, and close with a call of appendFile, including the file name and message as arguments.

Now that you can handle both reading and writing to files, it's time for you to deal with another category of features of the fs module: directory operations.

19.6   Directory Operations

In addition to editing files, you can also manipulate entire directories with using the fs module of Node.js. The range of available operations extends from creating to renaming to deleting directories. But there's also a wide range of usage areas for this type of file system operations. For example, if you create an installation routine for your application in Node.js, you can generate the necessary directory structure.

Directories appear in your application whenever you need to structure larger amounts of files. A concrete example of this is cache files that you place in a directory structure for faster access. The search operations of the operating systems are usually faster in a deeper directory structure with relatively few files per directory than with very many files in a single directory.

In the course of this section, you'll learn about different ways to navigate and manipulate directory structures. As an example, you'll implement a very lightweight file system browser that makes it possible to interactively list the contents of directories, move within the directory structure, and create, rename, and delete files and directories from the command line.

The entire source code of this example is shown in Listing 19.13. Following this example, we'll explain the individual steps and the respective peculiarities of the methods used.

```
import fs from 'fs';

class Explorer {
  constructor() {
    process.stdin.resume();
    process.stdin.setEncoding('utf8');
    process.stdin.on('data', this.dispatch.bind(this));
  }
```

```
dispatch(chunk) {
  const result = chunk.match(/(\w*) (.*)/);
  let command = '';
  let path = '';

  if (result !== null) {
    command = result[1];
    path = result[2];
  }

  switch (command) {
    case 'list':
      this.display(path);
      break;
    case 'change':
      process.chdir(path);
      this.listCurrent();
      break;
    case 'file':
      fs.writeFile(path, '', this.listCurrent.bind(this));
      break;
    case 'remove':
      fs.stat(path, (err, stat) => {
        if (stat.isFile()) {
          fs.unlink(path, this.listCurrent.bind(this));
        } else if (stat.isDirectory()) {
          fs.rmdir(path, this.listCurrent.bind(this));
        }
      });
      break;
    case 'directory':
      fs.mkdir(path, this.listCurrent.bind(this));
      break;
    case 'rename':
      const paths = path.split(' ');
      fs.rename(paths[0], paths[1], this.listCurrent.bind(this));
      break;
    default:
      process.exit();
      break;
  }
}
listCurrent() {
```

```
      this.dispatch(`list ${process.cwd()}`);
  }

  display(path) {
    console.log(`Current directory: ${process.cwd()}\n\n`);

    fs.readdir(path, (err, files) => {
      let result = '';

      for (let i = 0; i < files.length; i++) {
        result += files[i] + '\t';
        if ((i + 1) % 4 === 0) {
          result += '\n';
        }
      }

      const diff = process.stdout.rows - files.length;
      if (diff > 0) {
        for (let i = 0; i < diff; i++) {
          result += '\n';
        }
      }

      console.log(`${result}

Available commands:
list, change, file, remove, directory, rename, exit
Your input: `);
    });
  }
}

const explorer = new Explorer();
explorer.listCurrent();
```

Listing 19.13 File System Browser in Node.js

The core of the file system browser is the `Explorer` class. In the constructor, the command line is prepared, and the `dispatch` method of the explorer is bound to the `data` event of the standard input. The `dispatch` method is responsible for the actual processing of the command and supports the following commands:

- **list**
  Display of the desired directory content by calling the `display` method.

- **change**
  Change of the current working directory and display of the content.
- `file`
  Creation of a new empty file.
- `remove`
  Deletion of a file or directory.
- `directory`
  Creation of a new directory.
- `rename`
  Renaming of a path.
- `exit`
  Exiting the application.

The commands are just wrappers around the actual file system functions of Node.js. Only the display of the folder contents requires a bit more logic. For this reason, you also swap out this functionality to the `display` method. This method ensures that the files and directories within a directory are output. The rest of the screen is filled with blank lines.

You can use the application by running the script from the command line. Then you can enter the required command. In most cases, a command consisting of two parts is required, such as `list /tmp`, for example.

In the concluding sections of this chapter, you'll learn more about other features of the `fs` module that allow you, for example, to read metadata from files, monitor files for changes, or manipulate the ownership and permissions of files.

19.7   Advanced Operations

Up to this point, you've been mostly concerned with the basics of file system operations. Specifically, you've seen how to work with files or apply various operations to directories. Here, you'll now learn about other operations provided by the `fs` module.

The first feature discussed here, you already got to know to some extent in the preceding example. It's the `stats` class, which enables you to obtain information about files and directories. Like all the methods you've seen so far, the `stat` method that is used to create a `stats` object is asynchronous. This means that it accepts a callback function as a second argument in addition to the path to be inspected. When the operation is complete, this callback function receives an error object containing any exceptions that may have occurred during the execution of the command. The second argument is an object of the `stats` type. This object contains the required information and some helpful methods. If the `stat` method is called in a symbolic link, you'll get the information about the file referenced by the link. Table 19.2 shows the information you receive from the stats object.

Property	Description
dev	Number of the device where the file is located.
mode	Access permissions for the file.
nlink	Number of links referencing the file.
uid	ID of the owner of the file.
gid	ID of the group to which the file belongs.
rdev	Type of file system on which the file is located.
blksize	Size of blocks in the file system.
ino	Number of the inode of the file.
size	Size of the file in bytes.
blocks	Number of blocks used by the file.
atime	Time of the last access. The a at the beginning stands for *accessed*, that is, the access.
mtime	Time of the last modification. The m at the beginning of the property name stands for *modified*, that is, modification.
ctime	Time at which the file status was last changed. The c here stands for *changed*.
atimeMs	Time of the last access in milliseconds since 1/1/1970.
mtimeMs	Time of the last change in milliseconds since 1/1/1970.
ctimeMs	Time at which the file status was last changed in milliseconds since 1/1/1970.
birthtime	Creation time.
birthtimeMs	Creation time in milliseconds since 1/1/1970.

Table 19.2 Information Provided by the "stat" Method

In addition to the presented properties, the stats object has a set of methods that can be used to determine the type of the object to which the stat method was applied. For example, you can use stats.isFile or stats.isDirectory to determine whether the specified path is a file or directory. Furthermore, you can use stats.isBlockDevice and stats.isCharacterDevice to check whether the path is a block-oriented or a character-oriented device file. You can also use the stats.isSymbolicLink, stats.isFIFO, and stats.isSocket methods.

As with all other file system operations, a synchronous version of the stat method exists in addition to the asynchronous version, namely, statSync. The only difference between the two is that the synchronous version blocks the execution of the application until a result is obtained, at which point, the method returns it to the caller as a return value. For this reason, no callback function is required. Since Node 10, you can alternatively use the promise-based variant of the stat method via fs/promises.

In addition to the stat method, there are two other variants of this method—lstat and fstat. lstat differs in that when this method is applied to a symbolic link, it returns the information about the link itself and not about the target file. Unlike the other two methods, the fstat method accepts a file descriptor as it's generated by a call of fs.open. For both lstat and fstat, a synchronous and a promise-based variant exist. Listing 19.14 shows how you can use the stat method.

```
import { stat } from 'fs/promises';

const statistic = await stat('/usr/local/bin/node');

console.log(
  `Size of the file "/usr/local/bin/node" is ${statistic.size} Bytes`,
);
```

Listing 19.14 Using the "stat" Method

19.7.1 The watch Method

Next, the watch method exists only as an asynchronous method, making it one of the few without a synchronous or promise-based counterpart in the fs module. The first argument this method accepts is the name of the file or directory to watch. The second optional argument is used to configure the method and is an object with the following properties:

- **Persistent**
  If this property has the value true, it means that the process will be executed as long as the watcher is active.

- **Recursive**
  If a directory is specified for monitoring, this property ensures that subdirectories are also monitored.

- **Encoding**
  This specifies the character encoding of the passed file name.

The last argument of this method is a callback function that is called when the content or name of the file gets changed. The watcher can be terminated in two different ways. The first variant is to use the unwatchFile method with the file name as argument. The second variant, which is also recommended by Node.js developers, is to use the return value of the watch method, an object of the FSWatcher type. On this object, you can call the close method to terminate the watcher.

The callback function passed to the watch method as the last argument receives two arguments. The first argument is the type of event that occurred. This can be either change or rename. The second argument is the name of the file being watched. In this context, you should note that the second argument isn't available on all operating systems. This is mainly due to the fact that the watch functionality doesn't behave consistently across all systems and also draws on different operating system functions across different systems. On Linux systems, for example, this is inotify; other Unix systems, as well as macOS, use kqueue; and finally on Windows, ReadDirectoryChangesW is used. Listing 19.15 shows an example of using the watch method. Note that the process isn't terminated until watcher.close is called. If you omit this line, you must terminate the execution via the [Ctrl]+[C] shortcut.

```
import { watch } from 'fs';

const file = 'error.log';

const watcher = watch('error.log', (event) => {
  console.log(`${file} has been ${event}d`);
  watcher.close();
});
```

Listing 19.15 Using the "watch" Method

In addition to the watch method, there is another method called watchFile that provides the same functionality, but shouldn't be used any further because watch is the preferred variant. The same applies to the unwatchFile method, as already mentioned.

19.7.2   Access Permissions

In this last part of the chapter, we'll introduce the various options of manipulating file access permissions in Node.js. You'll come across the file system permissions at the latest when you try to create or modify a file or directory for which you don't have permission. However, before you proceed to change the permissions of a file or directory, you should first familiarize yourself with a feature that enables you to read the current permissions. The information relevant in the context of permissions is the user ID, the ID of the group to which the file is assigned, and finally its permissions. You can get this information via the stat method, as shown in Listing 19.16.

```
import { stat } from 'fs';

stat('input.txt', (err, stat) => {
```

```
    console.log(`User: ${stat.uid}`);
    console.log(`Group: ${stat.gid}`);
    console.log(`Permissions: ${stat.mode.toString(8)}`);
});
```

Listing 19.16 Querying Relevant Information about Permissions

You've already learned about the individual properties of the stat object. The only special feature is the reading of the permissions in the form of the mode property. Here you must access the information via the toString method with argument 8 to obtain the octal representation of this value.

The method you use to set the permissions you read with the mode property is called chmod and exists in synchronous, asynchronous, and promise-based versions. In addition, as with the stat method, there is an lchmod version that acts on links rather than their targets, and an fchmod method that accepts a file descriptor instead of a file name. All three methods accept the permissions to be set in addition to the file whose permissions are to be changed. Ideally, you specify the permissions in octal notation, that is, preceded by a zero. This way you can use the usual notation for Unix. For the asynchronous methods, you pass a callback function as the third argument, which is executed once the permissions have been adjusted.

Using the chown method, you customize the owner and group of a file. There are also different variants for this method with lchown and fchown, for each of which there is again a synchronous, an asynchronous, and a promise-based version available. The arguments for these methods are the name of the file or directory, then the ID of the user, and the ID of the group. For the asynchronous methods, a callback function is added, which is executed when the user and group have been set. The example in Listing 19.17 shows the methods in use.

```
import fs from 'fs';

const filename = 'input.txt';

fs.stat(filename, (err, stat) => {
  showPerms(err, stat);
  fs.chmod(filename, 0o777, (err) => {
    fs.chown(filename, 0, 0, (err) => {
      fs.stat(filename, showPerms);
    });
  });
});

function showPerms(err, stat) {
  console.log(`User: ${stat.uid}`);
```

```
    console.log(`Group: ${stat.gid}`);
    console.log(`Permissions: ${stat.mode.toString(8)}`);
}
```

Listing 19.17 Customizing Permissions

Listing 19.17 shows how you can connect the stat method and a showPerms helper function and then run chmod and chown to set new permissions and new owners. Finally, the result of the changes is displayed with the help of the helper function.

19.8   Summary

In this chapter, you've learned about various methods of the fs module that allow you to deal with files and directories. With Node.js, you can read files and write data to files or create, rename, and delete directories. The fs module also has features that allow you to monitor changes to files or adjust permissions in your file system.

If you use methods from the fs module, you should prefer the asynchronous or the new promise-based version because it doesn't block the execution of your application. With the synchronous variant, your application must wait until the operating system returns the required result and can't process any other requests in the meantime.

Chapter 20
Socket Server

Just as iron rusts out of use and stagnant water spoils or freezes in the
cold, so the mind degenerates without exercise.
—*Leonardo da Vinci*

This chapter describes the concept of sockets in Node.js. Sockets are mainly used for the communication between applications. It isn't mandatory for applications to run on the same system. In this chapter, you'll learn how you can create both servers and clients for the various sockets.

Sockets in Node.js are nothing more than data streams and as such are based on the stream module. As you already know from Chapter 18, this module is an abstraction layer that provides a unified interface to the various data streams. You can use a data stream to send or receive data to or from a remote system. All communication or handling of communication within your application is asynchronous. You've already met a very popular representative of data streams—the http module. As you can see in Figure 20.1, you're now moving down one layer in the Open Systems Interconnection (OSI) layer model, namely from layers five to seven, where HTTP is located, to the transport layer with its Transmission Control Protocol (TCP) and User Datagram Protocol (UDP). You can find more information on this topic at *https://en.wikipedia.org/wiki/Internet_protocol_suite*.

Because HTTP is located on a higher communication layer, you should follow some rules when implementing servers and clients. For example, HTTP provides you with a set of methods for communication. You can address the individual resources on your server via URLs. To control the communication, you can use the information that's sent in the HTTP header. The server generates a response based on the information that's sent with the client's request. This response consists of a header with various fields and a status code as well as the message body used to send the actual payload of the response. At the TCP level, communication is simpler. To implement clients and servers, Node.js provides the net module. This module is based on the interfaces of the stream module. If you choose this type of connection between two applications, you can use sockets for communication in addition to TCP as the communication protocol. When using sockets, you communicate on a file system basis between two applications. In this chapter, you'll learn about the different types of sockets you can use with Node.js. To start with, you implement two applications that communicate locally over a Unix socket. Having implemented that, you move on to connecting the applications with TCP and UDP, respectively.

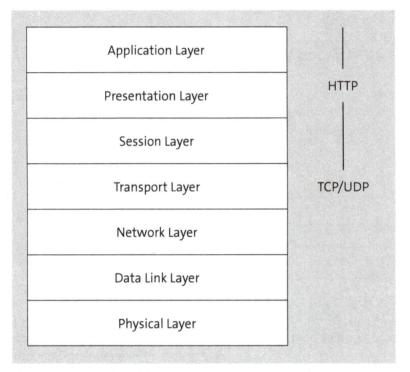

Figure 20.1 OSI Layer Model

20.1   Unix Sockets

The simplest way to have two independent applications talk to each other is to use file-based sockets. In this case, you don't need a network interface through which you send and receive information. Another advantage of file system-based communication is that it eliminates the overhead associated with multiple network layers. The Unix sockets used in this section aren't available on Windows systems. The Windows Subsystem for Linux (WSL) is an exception here. Because this is a full-fledged Linux system, you can also work with Unix sockets on Windows. If you develop on a native Windows system, you can use the Windows pipes presented in Section 20.2 instead. Listing 20.1 shows an example of a server implementation.

```
import { createServer } from 'net';

const server = createServer((connection) => {
  connection.on('readable', (data) => {
    console.log(connection.read().toString());
  });

  connection.on('end', () => {
```

```
    console.log('connection ended');
  });
});

server.listen('/tmp/nodejs.sock', () => {
  console.log('Server listening on /tmp/nodejs.sock');
});
```

Listing 20.1 Unix Socket Server (server.js)

Using the createServer function, you set the stage for communicating with a client by creating a concrete server instance. At this point, this server is still independent of the communication variant used. This means you can use both TCP and Unix sockets here. Calling the listen method on the server object first turns the general net server into a Unix socket server by specifying the name of the socket file. As a second argument, both methods accept a callback function that is bound to a specific event. In the createServer method, the callback function is bound to the connection event. This event gets triggered as soon as a client connects to the server. The callback function you pass to the listen method is bound to the listening event, which gets triggered when the server is ready for incoming connections.

In the next step, you now implement a client that is able to connect and communicate with the previously generated server. Listing 20.2 shows you how to proceed in this context.

```
import { connect } from 'net';

const client = connect('/tmp/nodejs.sock', () => {
  console.log('connected to the server');
  client.write('Hello Server');
});
```

Listing 20.2 Unix Socket Client (client.js)

Similar to creating the server, you need to create a concrete instance of the client. To do that, you can use the connect function. As a first argument, this method receives the destination of the client. In this case, that's the name of the socket file as a character string. The second argument is the callback function that will be executed once the connection is established. The callback function is bound internally to the connect event.

To test the client-server interaction, you store the server code in a file named *server.js* and store the client code in a file named *client.js*. In the first step, you start the server process and receive the output Server listening on /tmp/nodejs.sock on the command line. This output signals that the server is ready to respond to incoming connections. When you now run the client on a separate command line in parallel with the server, you'll get the output connected to the server on the client side and get Hello Server on the server side. The client sends this character string to the server via the socket using the write method. This in turn responds to readable events in the callback function bound to the connection event. The event is triggered as soon as there is readable data on the stream. By calling the read method, you can access the character string as a buffer object and output it to the console. To get a string directly as a return of the read method, you first need to set the correct character encoding on the connection using the setEncoding method before.

Figure 20.2 illustrates the relationship between client and server and the communication between them.

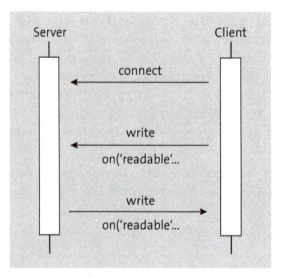

Figure 20.2 Socket Communication

20.1.1   Accessing the Socket

One advantage of using Unix sockets for the communication between two local applications is that you have complete control over the access to that socket. This means that no access can be made to the socket from outside the system and that you also have complete control over the socket on your system and can manage the access to it. Unix sockets are represented as a file in the file system. You can see this if you run a directory listing on the directory where the socket is located, as shown in Listing 20.3.

```
$ ls -l /tmp/nodejs.sock
srwxr-xr-x  1 nodejs  nodejs 0 Aug  22 08:55 /tmp/nodejs.sock
```

Listing 20.3 Directory Listing on the Socket

As you can see in Listing 20.3, in this case, any user of the system has read access to */tmp/ nodejs.sock* and can execute it. If you now adjust the file system permissions in such a way that only the nodejs user can access the socket, this means that only those applications running with this user can access this socket. Listing 20.4 shows how you can adjust access to this socket from within your application.

```
import { createServer } from 'net';
import { chmod } from 'fs';

const server = createServer((connection) => {
  connection.on('readable', (data) => {
    console.log(connection.read().toString());
  });

  connection.on('end', () => {
    console.log('connection ended');
  });
});

server.listen('/tmp/nodejs.sock', () => {
  chmod('/tmp/nodejs.sock', 0o700, () => {
    console.log('Server listening on /tmp/nodejs.sock');
  });
});
```

Listing 20.4 Restricting Permissions for the Socket (server.js)

The socket server from Listing 20.1 serves as a basis for Listing 20.4. In this example, the permissions are adjusted using the chmod method of the fs module. The correct location where you should make the adjustments is the callback function of the listening event. At this point, you can be sure that the socket exists and that you have access to it. The second requirement in addition to the existence of the socket is that you import the chmod function from the fs module. If both requirements are met, you can set the permissions to the value 0o700, which stands for read, write, and execute access for the owner of the socket. If you now run the server with the nodejs user, only this user can access the socket. To illustrate the effect of the change, you should now run the client with a different user. The result you'll then get is shown in Listing 20.5.

```
$ node client.js
events.js:167
      throw er; // Unhandled 'error' event
      ^

Error: connect EACCES /tmp/nodejs.sock
    at PipeConnectWrap.afterConnect [as oncomplete] (net.js:1161:14)
Emitted 'error' event at:
```

```
    at emitErrorNT (internal/streams/destroy.js:92:8)
    at emitErrorAndCloseNT (internal/streams/destroy.js:59:3)
    at process._tickCallback (internal/process/next_tick.js:174:19)
```

Listing 20.5 Error Message for Unauthorized Access to the Socket

During development, you should keep in mind that the socket file isn't automatically deleted when the server gets stopped. If you stop the server and start it again, you get the error message, Error: listen EADDRINUSE /tmp/nodejs.sock. The listen method of the server allows you to create the socket file. As soon as you try to create the socket file a second time, the error gets triggered. To start the server again, you must delete the created socket file. After that, you can launch the application. Within your application, you can close the socket connection by calling the close method of the server object. This will automatically cause the socket file to be deleted as well.

In the following sections, you'll extend both the client and the server in such a way that they can communicate with each other, allowing you to take advantage of an existing communication channel between both endpoints of the communication link.

20.1.2   Bidirectional Communication

The terms client and server are somewhat misleading because both entities are in some sense equal in communication. The server is responsible for creating the socket, while the client connects to the socket. After that, both can read and write data. To demonstrate this, you'll now implement an application that generates random numbers on the client side and then sends them to a server. The server, in turn, totals the numbers and sends a subtotal back to the client for every 10th package. Listing 20.6 shows the implementation on the server side.

```
import { createServer } from 'net';

const server = createServer((conn) => {
  let sum = 0;
  let count = 0;

  conn.on('readable', (data) => {
    sum += parseInt(conn.read().toString(), 10);
    count += 1;

    if (count >= 10) {
      count = 0;
      conn.write(sum.toString());
    }
  });
});
```

```
server.listen('/tmp/nodejs.sock', () => {
  console.log('Server listening on /tmp/nodejs.sock');
});
```

Listing 20.6 Bidirectional Communication (server.js)

The basis for the server-side implementation is the source code shown earlier in Listing 20.1. Inside the callback function that you bind to the `readable` event, you read the data that's sent from the client, sum it up, and keep an internal counter that tells you when the 10th package has been received and you need to return the current subtotal to the client. The object you receive as an argument in this callback function is an instance of the `net.Socket` class, which represents the socket connection to the client. On this object, you can call the `write` method to send the data to the client. When sending the data, you should keep in mind that you're only allowed to write either a string or a buffer object because if you try to send an integer, you'll receive an error message, and your application will abort. The counterpart to the server implementation is the socket client, which you can see in Listing 20.7.

```
import { connect } from 'net';

const client = connect('/tmp/nodejs.sock', () => {
  let count = 0;
  let number = 0;
  let interval = setInterval(() => {
    if (count < 100) {
      number = Math.ceil(Math.random() * 100);
      console.log(number);
      client.write(number.toString());
      count += 1;
    } else {
      clearInterval(interval);
      client.end();
    }
  }, 500);
});

client.on('readable', () => {
  console.log('subtotal: ' + client.read().toString());
});
```

Listing 20.7 Bidirectional Communication (client.js)

Using the `connect` method, the client connects to the socket that was previously created by the server. Within the callback function, you send a number between 0 and 100

20

through the socket to the server every 500 milliseconds. After 100 numbers, the interval is cleared with a call of the clearInterval method, and no more numbers are sent to the server. The connection is terminated with a call of the end method.

As you can see in Figure 20.3, the output consists of 10 consecutive random numbers followed by a line showing the subtotal of the numbers that have been output up until this point. This sequence is repeated 10 times in total. The client script terminates as soon as all 100 numbers have been totaled. The server, however, keeps running. As is the case with an HTTP server, a server based on Unix sockets allows multiple clients to connect to the server simultaneously. Specifically, this means you can start multiple clients on the same socket. However, the clients only communicate directly with the server and not with each other.

```
$ node client.js
34
92
67
41
8
31
29
8
11
30
subtotal: 351
96
69
```

Figure 20.3 Result of the Communication between Client and Server

If you use sockets for file system-based communication in your application, you don't need to do without them on Windows systems either. Instead of Unix sockets, Windows uses Windows pipes.

20.2   Windows Pipes

As mentioned earlier, you can also benefit from the communication between applications via the file system on your Windows system. In this case, Windows pipes are used instead of Unix sockets. The difference becomes most obvious in the naming of the resource. On Unix systems with Unix sockets, you only need to specify a path to a file. To use Windows pipes, you must follow a special naming convention. The path to a pipe consists of the server name, the pipe keyword, and a name for the pipe that you can freely choose. The backslash is used as a separator. If you want to communicate locally, you just need to specify a point instead of a server name. Listing 20.8 shows how you can use a pipe on Windows to create a socket server.

```
import { createServer } from 'net';

createServer((conn) => {
  conn.write('Hello Client');
  conn.end();
}).listen('\\\\.\\pipe\\node-pipe');
```

Listing 20.8 Pipe Server on Windows

The naming convention of pipes on Windows takes some getting used to, but it ensures that you can also communicate between applications via the file system on all operating systems for which Node.js is available.

Because you have to decide whether to use Unix sockets or Windows pipes depending on the operating system you're using, you must first find out which operating system your application is running on. You can obtain this information as the return value of the type method of the os module. This method returns the string Windows_NT for Windows, Linux for Linux, and Darwin for MacOS.

A major drawback of a file system–based communication is that the applications which are to communicate with each other must reside on one system, regardless of which system the communication is deployed on. An alternative that circumvents this limitation is offered by network-based connections, such as TCP.

20.3 TCP Sockets

You use TCP sockets primarily when you want to make sure that two applications residing on different systems communicate with each other. As with all socket solutions, you have maximum flexibility when it comes to the question of which types of applications communicate with each other. The two endpoints of the connection—the client and the server—don't necessarily have to be implementations in Node.js. For example, your server could be implemented in Java and the client in Node.js. But any other combination is also conceivable. Moreover, the two applications don't need to run on the same system. However, you can still communicate between different applications within the same system. The prerequisite for this type of communication is that both computers on which the software is executed have an existing network connection and the respective remote system can be reached.

If you transfer your data with TCP (*https://en.wikipedia.org/wiki/Transmission_Control_Protocol*), it will be fragmented. For example, if you want to transfer a 2 MB file from one system to another, it will be split into several small parts, which will be automatically put back into the correct order on the target system. You won't notice anything—neither the fragmentation nor the reassembling in your application. The maximum size of these individual fragments is 65,535 bytes, but it's usually limited to

1,500 bytes by deeper protocols. However, not only does TCP send the packages, it's also responsible for securing the connection. This means that the protocol ensures that no packages are lost during transmission. Various mechanisms of TCP ensure that no data arrives at the recipient in a falsified form. The packages in which the data is sent over a TCP connection consist of a header and the message body. The header is divided into several fields, one of which consists of a checksum over the package's data and certain header fields. This checksum is created by the sender and used by the recipient to verify that the data package arrived without error. Another field contains a sequence number indicating the order of the packages. It's used to reassemble the individual parts into a complete package. If the recipient notices an error in the checksum or that one of the packages is missing in the sequence, this error is handled and acted upon accordingly. These mechanisms ensure that communication via TCP can be described as reliable. Figure 20.4 summarizes the structure of a TCP header for you.

			TCP Header		
Offsets Octet		0	1	2	3
Octet Bit		0 1 2 3 4 5 6 7	8 9 10 11 12 13 14 15	16 17 18 19 20 21 22 23	24 25 26 27 28 29 30 31
0	0	Source port		Destination port	
4	32	Sequence number			
8	64	Acknowledgment number (if ACK set)			
12	96	Data offset — Reserved 0 0 0 — N S — C W R, E C E, U R G, A C K, P S H, R S T, S Y N, F I N		Window Size	
16	128	Checksum		Urgent pointer (if URG set)	
20	160	Options (if *data offset* > 5. Padded at the end with "0" bytes if necessary.)			
...	...	...			

Figure 20.4 Structure of a TCP Header (Source: https://en.wikipedia.org/wiki/Transmission_Control_Protocol)

When using TCP sockets, you should note that a connection must always be established between the systems involved. This connection is established via the *handshake*. In doing so, the client sends a SYN package. The name has been derived from the term *synchronize* and means that the client and server synchronize for communication. The server responds with a SYN/ACK package. This term stands for *synchronize acknowledgement*, meaning confirmation of synchronization. Finally, the client also sends an ACK package, that is, an acknowledgement on its part as well. Once this three-way handshake is complete, the connection is considered established and can be used by both sides for communication. As a developer, you don't come across the connection setup directly. However, you should keep this in mind when it comes to the performance of your application.

Communication via the network always involves a certain overhead. Part of this consists of the handshake just described, which takes a certain amount of time. You have to accept further potential performance losses when the packages are sent through the individual network layers such as IP and Ethernet. To get from the data source to the communication target, a package must take a certain path. On this path, in turn, there may be network nodes such as routers that redirect or check the package, which also takes time. TCP is a network protocol, which means, unlike file system-based communication over Unix sockets, you no longer have full control over who connects to your application. Of course, there are also security mechanisms such as firewalls that you can use to restrict access to a TCP server. With TCP, the work isn't as simple as access control with Unix sockets. To limit the number of users of a service, you can, for example, use firewalls that only allow requests from certain sources.

20.3.1 Data Transfer

As a basis for the following section, we'll use the basic implementation of a TCP server. Listing 20.9 shows the required source code for this.

```
import { createServer } from 'net';

createServer((socket) => {
  socket.on('readable', () => {
    const data = socket.read();
    if (Buffer.isBuffer(data)) {
      console.log(data.toString());
    }
  });
}).listen(8080, '127.0.0.1');
```

Listing 20.9 TCP Server (server.js)

The functionality of this server is that it only opens a connection on the local machine on port 8080 and waits for incoming connections. If a connection is established, a call of console.log ensures that the transmitted information is output to the console. You can see the implementation of a TCP client connecting to this server in Listing 20.10.

```
import { connect } from 'net';

const port = 8080;
const host = '127.0.0.1';

const client = connect({ port, host }, () => {
  client.end('Hello Server!');
});
```

Listing 20.10 TCP Client (client.js)

In this example, the client does nothing but connect through the TCP port previously opened by the server and send a message. After that, the application gets closed. The server process continues to run and accept incoming connections. The console output of the server consists of the string, Hello Server!. In the next step, you'll extend this simple example so that the client sends a file to the server.

20.3.2   File Transfer

With a few adjustments to the source code from Listing 20.9 and Listing 20.10, you can implement a simple file transfer (see Listing 20.11).

```
import { createServer } from 'net';
import { writeFile } from 'fs';

createServer((socket) => {
  let file = '';

  socket.on('readable', () => {
    file += socket.read();
  });

  socket.on('end', () => {
    const input = Buffer.from(file, 'base64');
    writeFile('dest.png', input, () => {});
  });
}).listen(8080, '127.0.0.1');
```

Listing 20.11 TCP Server for File Transfer (server.js)

The first difference from Listing 20.9 is that, in this case, you need the fs module in addition to the net module to save the transferred file in the file system. The receipt of data in the callback function is divided into several steps. This means that during data reception, several packages are accepted and assembled accordingly. If you assume an image file with a size of about 128 KB, only about 50 KB will be received with a call of the read method. For this reason, you need to collect the data in a variable, in this case, file, and you can continue processing only after the operation is finished in the callback function of the end event. Here, the received data is recoded using a buffer object and stored in a file named *dest.png*. This encoding takes place so that the image, which is a binary file, can be easily transferred from the client to the server, where it can then be used appropriately. Listing 20.12 contains the source code for the client, which sends an image to the server.

```
const net = require('net');
const fs = require('fs');

fs.readFile('logo.png', (err, data) => {
  const client = net.connect({ port: 8080, host: '127.0.0.1' }, () => {
```

```
    client.end(data.toString('base64'));
  });
});
```

Listing 20.12 TCP Client for Data Transfer (client.js)

In the client, you also need the fs module to read the content of the file to be sent from the file system. Inside the callback function of the readFile function, you establish the connection to the server and send the contents of the file using the end method of the open socket. As mentioned in the context of the server, you need to make sure that the data is sent in a format that allows you to transfer the file without loss or errors, so that it can still be used after the transfer. For this purpose, you can use Base64 encoding. It's often used on the web when it comes to transmitting files, such as sending emails with attachments.

Once you've made the adjustments to the client and server, you can start the server first so that the TCP port is opened, and then the client. The client then reads the *logo.png* file from the file system and transmits it Base64-encoded to the server. The server receives the individual components of the file, assembles them, decodes the entire package, and stores the result again on the file system. The net module provides even more options to intervene in a controlling manner, in addition to its pure data transmission functionality. The following sections will introduce you to further concepts of sockets.

20.3.3 Flow Control

You can transfer large amounts of data through a socket connection. This holds true for both TCP sockets and file system-based solutions such as Unix sockets and Windows pipes. In the stream API of Node.js in versions prior to 0.10, it was possible to control the data flow. Typical situations where you might need these features could be that data is arriving faster than you can process it, or that you're writing data to a stream faster than it can deliver the data.

The write method of streams always returns a value regardless of whether they are network-based systems or file system-based streams. This value indicates whether the data has already been sent or cached in memory. For readable data streams, the two methods pause and resume exist. The pause method makes sure that no further data events get triggered. The resume method enables you to reactivate the sending of the data stream and allows further data events to occur. The source code in Listing 20.13 shows how these mechanisms can be combined within an application.

```
import { connect, createServer } from 'net';

const client = connect({ host: '127.0.0.1', port: 8080 },
  () => {
```

```
createServer((socket) => {
  client.on('data', (data) => {
    // calculate

    const flushed = socket.write(data);

    if (!flushed) {
      client.pause();
    }
  });

  socket.on('drain', () => {
    client.resume();
  });
}
).listen(8181, '127.0.0.1');
});
```

Listing 20.13 Flow Control in Sockets

In Listing 20.13, two streams are combined with each other. First, a readable stream is created as a client on TCP port 8080. A TCP server on port 8181 is then created as a writable stream in the callback function of the connect event. Once data arrives at port 8080, it can be processed and eventually forwarded to the clients that have connected to the server on port 8181. After each write action, a check is made to see if the data was successfully written to the stream. If it wasn't, and the data has been cached in memory instead, the reading stream is paused at port 8080. As soon as the drain event gets triggered, which signals that it's possible to write to the stream again, the readable data stream continues. In this way, you prevent the write buffer from overflowing and thus control the data flow in a very simple way. With Node.js 0.10, the stream API that underlies all socket servers has been revised. Although the methods described here still work, you should use the readable event instead of the data event, and then use the read method to read the data.

As now the two methods pause and resume are omitted too, you need a new means of controlling the flow. For this purpose, you can simply call the read method as many times as you can handle the data you receive. This method accepts an integer as a value, which specifies how many bytes at least must be present in the read buffer to be output. If no data is available or less than specified, read returns the value null. For the streams presented here, a number of abstract interfaces exist within Node.js, which will be described in the following sections.

20.3.4   Duplex

You've already seen that you can both write to and read from a TCP stream. In Node.js, this type of stream is referred to as a duplex stream. In addition to providing the read method, a duplex stream also allows for write operations using the write method. If you want to implement your own duplex stream, you must override the _read and _write methods, which are responsible for reading and writing, respectively. If you want to connect two streams to each other as shown in Listing 20.13, you can use the pipes concept.

20.3.5   Pipe

In Node.js streams, a pipe refers to the connection of a readable stream to a writable stream. The pipe method belongs to the readable streams. It accepts an instance of a writable stream and an object with configuration directives. You can specify close: false as the configuration here. This configuration ensures that the writable data stream isn't automatically terminated as soon as the readable data stream has ended. This allows you to write data to the data stream even after the readable data stream has ended. In the simplest case, such a pipe looks like the one shown in Listing 20.14.

```
import { connect } from 'net';

const host = '127.0.0.1';

const writable = connect({ host, port: 8181 }, () => {
  const readable = connect({ host, port: 8080 }, () => {
    readable.pipe(writable);
  });
});
```

Listing 20.14 Simple Pipe

When implementing a pipe in your application, like the one in Listing 20.14, you must first open the writable data stream, that is, the target of the pipe. Once the connection has been established, you can open the readable data stream within the callback function. In the callback function of the connect event, you now use the pipe method to connect both data streams. As soon as data is available on the readable stream, it's written directly to the writable stream.

You should note that accessing the data isn't easy. If you've connected the data streams via pipe, you can no longer retrieve the data via read. Depending on where you place the call of the read method, the data is either caught before it's written to the other stream, or the data is forwarded and removed from the buffer before you attempt to read it via read. If you want to make sure that you can process the data and forward it to another stream at the same time, you have to take care of that yourself. This means you can't use the `pipe` method in this case, but must read the data from the readable data stream via `read` and write it to the writable data stream by calling `write`.

In addition to network-based TCP sockets, there is also another way of exchanging data over the network between two applications: UDP.

20.4   UDP Sockets

UDP works on the same level as TCP. However, in contrast to TCP, UDP has fundamentally different characteristics. With UDP, no connection gets established, which means there is no need for a handshake for any connection setup, making UDP much more lightweight than TCP. UDP isn't suitable for transferring larger amounts of data due to the lack of a connection between the two endpoints of the communication, as the protocol doesn't have the security mechanisms of TCP, so there's no guarantee that information won't get lost.

As with TCP, the size of packages is also limited with UDP, so that, for example, a file to be transferred may have to be divided into several small parts. With TCP, the sequence number ensures that the packages can be assembled in the correct order on the side of the recipient. Such a feature doesn't exist with UDP, so when you send data via UDP, you can't assume that your packages will actually arrive. When the information reaches the recipient, it's also impossible to guarantee whether this happens in the correct order.

In summary, UDP is referred to as an unreliable and connectionless protocol. However, what doesn't look very trustworthy at first glance serves a significant purpose in data transmission in information technology: UDP is always used when data must be transmitted quickly, and it doesn't matter if individual packages don't reach the recipient. Furthermore, when using UDP, the order of the packages doesn't matter either.

A classic area of use for this protocol is the Network Time Protocol (NTP), which is used by computers on the Internet to synchronize their clocks. The Domain Name System (DNS), which is used to resolve names on the network, also uses a UDP connection between client and server for sending requests. These two services are only a small part of all the usage areas for UDP in network communication. Because UDP is such an important protocol, Node.js also supports implementing servers and clients for UDP. The `dgram` module is available for this purpose. The term *datagram* refers to a unit in the transmission of data through the network. The interfaces of the `dgram` module of Node.js are somewhat different from those of the modules you've encountered so far for communication between systems. In the following sections, you'll learn how to complete a very simple client-server implementation for communication via UDP, which you'll then extend step by step.

20.4.1 Basic Principles of a UDP Server

UDP works similarly to TCP when it comes to addressing. You create a server and bind it to a specific address or port. Clients can then connect and communicate with the server using this combination. Listing 20.15 shows the implementation of a UDP server.

```
import { createSocket } from 'dgram';

const socket = createSocket('udp6');

socket.on('message', (data) => {
  console.log(data.toString());
});

socket.bind(8080, () => {
  console.log('server listening on localhost:8080');
});
```

Listing 20.15 UDP Server (server.js)

After importing the createSocket function from the dgram module, you can use it to create a UDP socket. You assign the type of socket to this function. The choice here is either udp4 or udp6. This type specifies whether to use UDP with IPv4 or IPv6. After calling this method, you have an unbound socket to continue working with. Like the other sockets, UDP sockets are event-based, so you can also bind callback functions to specific events here using the on method of the socket object. The example in Listing 20.15 shows two of these events. First, you bind a callback function to the message event, which gets triggered when data is sent through the socket. Here you can access a buffer object containing the corresponding data. In addition, the bind method accepts a callback function that's registered for the listening event. This event gets triggered as soon as the socket is successfully bound to an address and port, thus allowing incoming connections. The functionality of this server is to output incoming data to the console. You'll also be notified by a message when the connection is established and waiting for incoming datagrams. To test the functionality of your server, you should implement a UDP client in the next step. Listing 20.16 shows how to proceed in this context.

```
import { createSocket } from 'dgram';

const message = Buffer.from('Hello Server');

const client = createSocket('udp6');

client.send(
  message,
  0,
```

```
message.length,
8080,
(err, bytes) => {
  client.close();
});
```

Listing 20.16 UDP Client (client.js)

The client-side implementation of a UDP socket is much simpler. You generate an unbound socket just as you did on the server side. However, instead of binding it to an address and port, you call the send method on the object. To this method, you pass a buffer object that contains the data to be sent. Then you must specify the offset and the length of the data within the buffer that should be sent. Finally, you need to specify which port you want to send the data to. The callback function is executed as soon as the message has been sent. Inside the callback function, you have access to a possible error object and the number of bytes that were sent. At the end of the function, you should close the socket again via the close method because an open socket prevents the program from terminating.

20.4.2   Example Illustrating the UDP Server

In practice, UDP is particularly suitable for notifying clients of noncritical events or when receiving mass data. In the second case, however, you must make sure that there is so much data that the result isn't affected by the loss of individual packages. In this section, you'll extend the example from Listing 20.15 and Listing 20.16 by not only exchanging a string between client and server but also sending a continuous stream of data and subscribing to it. Listing 20.17 shows the modified source code of the server.

```
import { createSocket } from 'dgram';

const socket = createSocket('udp6');

let count = 0;

socket.on('message', (data) => {
  console.log(`${count++}: ${data.toString()}`);

  if (count >= 1000) {
    socket.close();
  }
});

socket.on('close', () => {
  console.log(`received ${count} datagrams`);
```

```
});

socket.bind(8080, () => {
  console.log('server listening on localhost:8080');
});
```

Listing 20.17 UDP Server for Receiving Multiple Datagrams (server.js)

Due to the modifications, the server is designed to receive a total of 1,000 datagrams through the connection. After that, the connection is disconnected, and the number of received datagrams is output. For this purpose, you bind a callback function to the close event. This event gets triggered as soon as the close method is called on the socket.

Because there is no connection between client and server, you have no way to respond directly to the client here, so the server must decide for itself when to disconnect. Listing 20.18 contains the source code of the client.

```
import { createSocket } from 'dgram';

const client = createSocket('udp6');

let count = 1;

const sendData = () => {
  const message = Buffer.from(Math.ceil(Math.random() * 100) + '');

  client.send(
    message,
    0,
    message.length,
    8080,
    (err, bytes) => {
      count += 1;

      if (count > 1000 || err) {
        client.close();
        clearInterval(interval);
      }
    }
  );
};

const interval = setInterval(sendData, 1);
```

Listing 20.18 UDP Client for Sending Multiple Datagrams

As an example of a data source for the UDP client, random numbers are generated in Listing 20.18 at intervals of 1 millisecond and then sent to the server. As soon as an error occurs or 1,000 packages have been sent, the connection is terminated, and the interval gets closed. If you start the server first and then the client, you can see how the 1,000 datagrams are transferred. Despite the high frequency, all data arrives error-free and without any problem. Even if you increase the number of datagrams, the behavior won't change. When using UDP, you have to consider one more aspect: Like TCP packages, UDP datagrams are subject to a size limit that may vary depending on the connection. If the size of the datagram exceeds the allowed size on the side of the recipient, the datagram gets discarded. However, the recipient won't receive any error message in this context.

Due to its properties, UDP is therefore only suitable for transmitting noncritical data. If your application requires all data to reach the recipient reliably, you should use TCP.

20.5   Summary

Throughout this chapter, you've learned how to submit data in several ways. As an alternative to client-server communication over HTTP, you can also use various types of sockets. These operate at a deeper level than HTTP. Consequently, you're bound to fewer rules and conventions, but you have to implement some methods provided by HTTP yourself. In addition to network-based communication, you can use Unix sockets or Windows pipes for a file system-based transfer of data. In this case, you don't need to bother about the overhead of setting up connections and the various network layers. However, you're limited to having both communication endpoints running on the same machine. If you connect via the network, you can use TCP if you need a reliable connection that ensures the recipient receives all data correctly. Alternatively, you can use UDP if it isn't critical for individual packages to be lost.

Chapter 21

Package Manager

Those who have only a hammer as a tool see a nail in every problem.
—Paul Watzlawick

When we talk about the number of packages, the *Node Package Manager (npm)* is the most successful package manager worldwide and across all programming languages. This tool enables you to create modules and make them available to other developers. In the same way, you can use the modules other programmers have developed in your application. The npm website can be found at *https://npmjs.com*. It contains various resources such as module lists as well as detailed documentation of the npm and all available options. The npm was originally developed independently of the Node.js platform by Isaac Schlueter. Since version 0.6.3 of Node.js, npm is directly integrated into the platform and no longer needs to be installed separately. This means you can either install the Microsoft Software Installer (MSI) on Windows, the .pkg package on macOS, or the binary package on Linux, and then immediately use npm. npm is used from the command line and can be controlled via various options. Today, npm and the repository are managed by one company—*npm Inc.* This company ensures the free availability of the registry and also offers commercial services such as private packages. In 2020, npm Inc. was bought by GitHub and thus belongs to Microsoft. As a result, behind the free package manager, there's also a very large company, which hasn't had any negative impact on npm since the acquisition.

npm is a full-fledged package manager for JavaScript that isn't limited to Node.js but also allows you to manage packages for other environments such as the web browser. The core functions of npm include searching, installing, updating, and deleting packages. The *Node Packaged Modules*, which are the modules you can install via npm, are used to extend the functionality of the Node.js platform. This means they add the V8 engine and internal Node.js modules to the core Node.js platform. The npm packages are managed centrally on the server at *http://registry.npmjs.com*. If you access this address from your browser, you'll only get data structures in JavaScript Object Notation (JSON) format. In the root of the server, you can find general information about the repository, such as the number of modules.

21.1 Most Common Operations

In the course of this book, you've already come across npm several times. In this chapter, we'll introduce you to some more features of the package manager as well as its main competitors.

During Node.js application development, you use npm in various ways, for example, to initialize your application, install packages, delete packages that are no longer needed, or update packages that have already been installed.

21.1.1 Searching Packages

The number of packages in the package manager's repository is constantly increasing, making npm currently the most popular package manager for JavaScript. However, this entails the disadvantage that you can quickly lose your overview due to the large number of packages. If you know which functionality you need in your application, you can search for specific packages. A first place to start is at *www.npmjs.com*, which allows you to search through the repository. Additionally, you can search directly via the npm command-line tool. To do this, you must use the search option with an appropriate keyword. The fields Name, Description, Author, and Keywords are available for the search.

Let's suppose you want to include an XML parser in your application, but you don't know the exact name of the package to install. You can search the repository for it, and see the command and its output, as shown in Figure 21.1.

```
MW-MB-127:Listings sebastians$ npm search xml parser
NAME                   | DESCRIPTION          | AUTHOR           | DATE       | VERSION | KEYWORDS
xml-js                 | A convertor between… | =nashwaan        | 2018-01-03 | 1.6.2   | XML xml js JSON json cdata CDATA
posthtml               | HTML/XML processor   | =qfox =scrum…    | 2018-02-16 | 0.11.3  | html xml postproccessor parser tr
htmlparser2            | Fast & forgiving…    | =feedic          | 2016-10-18 | 3.9.2   | html parser streams xml dom rss f
fast-xml-parser        | Validate XML or…     | =amitgupta       | 2018-05-09 | 3.9.11  | fast xml json parser xml2js x2js
mjml-parser-xml        | mjml-parser-xml      | =iryusa =loeck…  | 2018-04-26 | 4.0.5   |
xml-parse-from-string  | DOMParser.parseFrom… | =mattdesl        | 2017-05-18 | 1.0.1   | ie8 fallback dom parser DOMParser
plist                  | Mac OS X Plist…      | =mreinstein…     | 2018-03-21 | 3.0.1   | apple browser mac plist parser xm
xml-parser             | the little xml…      | =segment-admin…  | 2015-06-05 | 1.2.1   | xml sucks
feedparser             | Robust RSS Atom and… | =danmactough     | 2018-01-28 | 2.2.9   | rss feed atom rdf xml syndication
sax                    | An evented…          | =isaacs          | 2017-06-22 | 1.2.4   |
body-parser-xml        | XML parser…          | =fiznool         | 2016-03-18 | 1.1.0   | express xml middleware body-parse
parse-bmfont-xml       | parses XML BMFont…   | =mattdesl        | 2015-03-14 | 1.1.3   | xml parse convert bmfont bm bitma
@rgrove/parse-xml      | A fast, safe,…       | =rgrove          | 2017-09-20 | 1.1.1   | xml parse parser
xml-formatter          | Converts XML into a… | =chrisbottin     | 2016-11-16 | 1.0.1   | xml pretty-print indent parser fo
xml-parser-xo          | XML Parser with…     | =chrisbottin     | 2016-11-16 | 2.1.3   | xml parser convert
koa-xml-body           | koa middleware to…   | =creeper         | 2017-02-16 | 2.0.0   | xml body bodyParser koa middlewar
js2xmlparser           | Parses JavaScript…   | =michaelkourlas  | 2017-02-22 | 3.0.0   | convert converter javascript js j
koa-xml                | XML request body…    | =rafaeljesus     | 2016-05-25 | 1.0.2   | koa koajs xml body parser request
pom-parser             | A parser for the…    | =marcellodesal…  | 2016-03-06 | 1.1.1   | java pom pom.xml parser maven xml
posthtml-parser        | Parse HTML/XML to…   | =mrmlnc =scrum…  | 2018-02-16 | 0.4.1   | html xml parser posthtml posthtml
```

Figure 21.1 The "npm search" Command

The npm search command directly accesses the application programming interface (API) of the npm registry to display the information you're looking for. To make the command work faster, a local index is created when it's used for the first time, which will be used for all further searches. The npm automatically updates the index. The output of the command consists of the name of the module, the short description, the author of the module, the date of the last update, and any keywords defined by the creator of the module.

21.1.2   Installing Packages

When you've found the package and know its name, you can install it on your system in the next step. To do this, you use the npm install command and append the package name to it. For example, if you want to install the lodash library in your application, you can do so by using the npm install lodash command. You can see the corresponding output in Listing 21.1.

```
$ npm install lodash

added 1 package, and audited 2 packages in 752ms

found 0 vulnerabilities
```

Listing 21.1 Installing "lodash" via npm

In a first step, the npm install command queries the registry for information about the required package. The query consists of an HTTP GET request, like the one you can make from your browser. The data of the package is available as a JSON object. Among other things, this object contains information about the current version of the module, including the URL to the package itself. The package is available on the server as a zipped tar archive. With another GET request, the npm downloads this archive and installs it on your computer.

The installation of modules via npm is done locally in the directory you're currently in within your shell without any further command-line entries. For you, this means you don't need administrator permissions to install modules locally. The downloaded tar archive gets unpacked into the *node_modules* directory. In it, you'll find a subdirectory per package with the name of the respective package. In the case of our example, the *node_modules* directory had to be created because it hadn't existed yet. A subdirectory named *lodash* was created in it, which contains the files of the module.

In addition to the pure installation of the package, the npm install command has two side effects: First, the package is entered as a dependency in the *package.json* file of your application. Listing 21.2 contains an example of a *package.json* file. The dependencies section is especially relevant for the installation because that's where the packages are entered.

```
{
  "name": "node-book",
  "version": "1.0.0",
  "description": "",
  "main": "index.js",
```

617

```
  "private": true,
  "type": "module",
  "keywords": [],
  "author": "",
  "license": "ISC",
  "dependencies": {
    "lodash": "^4.17.21"
  }
}
```

Listing 21.2 Sample "package.json" File

Second, entries are created in *package-lock.json* for the package and all dependencies. This file contains the exact versions of all installed packages and their dependencies, including a checksum to ensure the integrity of the installation. Listing 21.3 contains the *package-lock.json* matching the *package.json* from Listing 21.2.

```
{
  "name": "node-book",
  "version": "1.0.0",
  "lockfileVersion": 2,
  "requires": true,
  "packages": {
    "": {
      "name": "node-book",
      "version": "1.0.0",
      "license": "ISC",
      "dependencies": {
        "lodash": "^4.17.21"
      }
    },
    "node_modules/lodash": {
      "version": "4.17.21",
      "resolved": "https://registry.npmjs.org/lodash/-/lodash-4.17.21.tgz",
      "integrity": "sha512-v2kDEe57lecTulaDIuNTPy3Ry4glGJ6Z1O3vE1krgXZNrsQ
        +LFTGHVxVjcXPs17LhbZVGedAJv8XZ1tvj5FvSg=="
    }
  },
  "dependencies": {
    "lodash": {
      "version": "4.17.21",
      "resolved": "https://registry.npmjs.org/lodash/-/lodash-4.17.21.tgz",
      "integrity": "sha512-v2kDEe57lecTulaDIuNTPy3Ry4glGJ6Z1O3vE1krgXZNrsQ
        +LFTGHVxVjcXPs17LhbZVGedAJv8XZ1tvj5FvSg=="
```

```
    }
  }
}
```

Listing 21.3 Sample "package-lock.json" File

Unlike *package.json*, which lists only the directly installed packages, *package-lock.json* contains all installed packages, including all dependencies of the installed packages. If you use a version control system for your application, which you definitely should do, you can commit both the *package.json* and the *package-lock.json* files, as both files combined ensure the consistency of your application.

Handling Dependencies

If the installed package itself has dependencies, these are also installed in the *node_ modules* directory. Dependencies in this case are modules that a package needs to function. Listing 21.4 shows an example of this using the Express package.

```
$ npm install express

added 50 packages, and audited 51 packages in 2s

found 0 vulnerabilities
```

Listing 21.4 Installing the "express" Package

During the installation process, you'll see the information about the dependencies that will be installed along with a progress bar indicating the progress of the entire installation process. The earlier versions of npm still displayed the URLs of the individual packages here, which became very confusing when multiple dependencies were being installed.

The handling of dependencies also changed from the third version of the npm onward. In version 2, packages were broken up into a highly tiered per-package hierarchy. This meant that each package had its own *node_modules* directory where the respective dependencies were stored, which caused problems with overly long path names, especially in Windows systems. As of version 3, all dependencies are stored directly in the *node_modules* directory, so the directory tree is greatly simplified.

However, storing all modules in a flat directory hierarchy can cause version conflicts. npm gets around this by reverting to the old strategy if there's a version conflict and assigning the corresponding package a separate *node_modules* directory where the differing version of the dependency gets installed.

Another change in the installation of packages involves the handling of peerDependencies. A package can define different types of dependencies. One of them is peerDependencies. Previously, these were installed automatically. Between versions 3 and 7, this

21

619

was no longer the case, so you had to take care of installing these dependencies yourself. The reason for this decision were numerous version conflicts that arose. Starting with version 7 of npm, the package manager installs the peerDependencies again by default. These types of dependencies are mainly used when you install software based on plug-ins, such as Grunt.

For example, the copy plug-in in Grunt contains Grunt itself as peerDependency. If you now install this plug-in without Grunt itself being installed, you'll receive an error message informing you of this fact.

Global Installation

In addition to the local installation in the current directory, you can also install a Node.js module on the entire system so that it's available not only to you in your current project but also to all users and projects on the machine. You can install a module globally by specifying the -g command-line option for *global* in the installation command. Listing 21.5 shows an example of the global installation of TypeScript.

```
npm install -g typescript
```

Listing 21.5 Global Installation of TypeScript

There are a few things you need to keep in mind when installing global modules, which makes this process different from a local installation. As a normal user, you're not allowed to install modules globally, as they are stored in the */usr/local/lib/node_modules* directory by default. For this reason, you must perform the installation either directly as an administrator or—on Unix systems—using the sudo command. However, the global installation of modules is mainly intended for command-line tools that have been implemented with Node.js. Examples include TypeScript, which you already learned about in Chapter 13, or webpack, a build tool for JavaScript applications. For regular modules such as lodash or Express, it makes sense to install them locally. One of the reasons is that local modules can be loaded faster because the search process for the module is significantly shortened. Another significant reason is that an application with globally installed modules has external dependencies. This means each system on which the application is supposed to be run must have these global modules installed, or the application won't run. For this reason, it's recommended that you also install all modules on which your application is based locally, so that it can run as independently as possible. In general, you should try to get by with as few globally installed packages as possible. One of the tools that can help you with this is npx, which will be described in greater detail in Section 21.3.4.

Whether you install a module locally or globally, you'll always see the progress bar first as the output of the npm install command, and then a summary once the installation is complete, which includes the number of packages installed, the number of packages that have undergone a security check, and the time required. If any of the installed packages have known security vulnerabilities, you'll also be notified.

Types of Dependencies

In addition to peerDependencies, npm distinguishes between dependencies, devDependencies, optionalDependencies, and bundledDependencies. dependencies represent the dependencies required for the execution of your application, such as Express being required for a web application. This type of dependency is specified via the npm install command without appending an option. This makes sure that the dependency is automatically entered into the *package.json* file under the dependencies key.

devDependencies, on the other hand, are only needed for the development process. A typical example includes code analysis tools such as ESLint or testing frameworks like Mocha. These packages can be installed using the npm install --save-dev command. The option --save-dev (or its short form -D) enters the name and version of the package into the *package.json* file as devDependency.

optionalDependencies are dependencies that can be installed but won't cause the installation to fail if they aren't available. The dependencies of the bundledDependencies type are integrated into the package when the package is published.

Installation from Other Sources

However, you're not dependent on a permanent connection to the server when installing modules via the npm. In addition to installing the modules via an existing internet connection, you also have the option to install modules directly from your computer. The only requirement for this is that you've either downloaded the tar archive containing the package or have a directory on your machine that contains the source code of the package and a corresponding *package.json* file. To test the local installation, you can simply download the lodash package and install it. Listing 21.6 shows how to do this.

```
$ wget https://registry.npmjs.org/lodash/-/lodash-4.17.21.tgz
...
$ npm install lodash-4.17.21.tgz

added 1 package, and audited 2 packages in 1s

found 0 vulnerabilities
```

Listing 21.6 Local Installation of a Module via npm

Similar to using the repository at *www.npmjs.org*, the installation creates a *node_modules* directory into which the source code of the package is copied. After successful installation, you can use the package in your application.

Packages and Version Control

Over the years, a best practice has become to not commit the *node_modules* directory to your application's version control system. For example, if you use git, you should

21

add *node_modules* to the *.gitignore* file of your project. The reason is that the npm repository provides the packages, and the local npm cache makes sure that the packages can be reinstalled relatively quickly after the initial installation. The *node_modules* directory of a larger application can quickly become several hundred megabytes in size.

Once you've loaded the initial source code of an application onto your development system, there is usually no *node_modules* directory, and you can't launch the application. To install the required packages, you must use the npm install command. In this context, it's important that you don't specify a package name. npm then installs all packages specified in the *package.json* file, relying on the exact version information and checksums from the *package-lock.json* file. If you don't want to install the devDependencies for a production release of your application, you can use the --prod option. This option only installs packages listed as dependency in the *package.json* file.

21.1.3   Viewing Installed Packages

All the packages you install can be found in the *node_modules* directory of your application. However, because all dependencies are also resolved in the same directory, it quickly gets confusing when you want to find out which packages are installed within your application. A quick overview of the existing modules and their dependencies is provided by the npm list command. By default, this command shows the top-level dependencies. If you want to see the tree of all installed dependencies, you must additionally enter the --all option.

As you can see in Listing 21.7, the list of modules is created as a tree structure in which you can directly see which modules are installed and how the dependencies between the modules are defined. If you see the term deduped next to a package in the list, it means that npm has removed a duplicate and is keeping the library only once for multiple use cases. With the -g option, you also get a list of all globally installed modules of your system from npm. All those dependencies are also displayed in a tree structure.

```
$ npm list --all
node-book@1.0.0 /srv/node
└─┬ express@4.17.1
  ├─┬ accepts@1.3.7
  │ ├─┬ mime-types@2.1.32
  │ │ └── mime-db@1.49.0
  │ └── negotiator@0.6.2
  ├── array-flatten@1.1.1
  ├─┬ body-parser@1.19.0
  │ ├── bytes@3.1.0
```

Listing 21.7 List of Installed Modules

There are cases where you're not interested in the dependencies and the whole tree structure, but you may just want to know which packages you've installed directly. This happens especially when you've added a large number of packages, and the display with all dependencies becomes very confusing. The solution to this problem is the --depth command-line option. A value of 0 shows you only the directly installed packages, 1 represents the first dependency level, and so on. Listing 21.8 shows how you can use this.

```
$ npm list --depth=0
node-book@1.0.0 /srv/node
├── express@4.16.3
└── lodash@4.17.10
```

Listing 21.8 Limiting the Output of "npm list"

21.1.4   Using Packages

As you've already seen, there are two different types of modules that can be installed via npm. First, there are collections of functionalities that you can include directly in your application, and, secondly, there are tools you can use from the command line. The following sections describe examples from both categories. In this context, you'll see how you can use the modules accordingly in practice.

In Listing 21.5, you already installed typescript globally on your system. After successful installation, the tsc command is available system wide. In this case, the tsc command is a normal JavaScript application with a hint for the operating system in the file header, the shebang (#!), which indicates to the shell the application the script is to be interpreted with. In the case of the TypeScript compiler, this line reads #!/usr/bin/env node, and it means that the script should be run using Node.js. With these customizations, a JavaScript application like the TypeScript compiler can be used on the command line as an ordinary command and doesn't need to be passed as a parameter to Node.js.

The second way to use modules you install via npm is to integrate the respective functionality directly into your application. In the course of this section, you've already seen how you can install the lodash library locally in your application.

In Listing 21.9, you import the intersection function from the lodash package. Lodash defines a separate file for each function, but you can also use the default export of package and then use the intersection function from there. Then, you define two arrays and have their intersection output. For this purpose, Underscore.js provides the intersection function. The return in this case is an array containing the elements b and c.

```
import intersection from 'lodash/intersection.js';

const arr1 = ['a', 'b', 'c'];
```

```
const arr2 = ['b', 'c', 'd'];

console.log(intersection(arr1, arr2)); // [ 'b', 'c' ]
```

Listing 21.9 Simple Example of Using a Module

21.1.5 Updating Packages

Many modules available through the npm repository are actively developed by their authors. This means updates of these modules become available at more or less regular intervals. In the following sections, you'll learn how the npm update mechanism works.

For this example to work correctly, your project should have a valid definition file—the *package.json* file. The npm init -y command allows you to have such a *package.json* file created automatically. In it, the required versions are stored within your software.

For the example, you need to use yet another feature of the npm install command. Not only can this command install modules in their latest version, you can also specify a specific version of a module to be installed. To test the package update, you'll use the lodash module in this case, but have it installed in the older version 4.0.0 rather than its latest version. You can install a module in a specific version by appending an @ sign and the desired version number to the module name in the install command. The installation process will then proceed as usual. npm queries the repository for the data about the module, receives the path to the tar archive, and downloads and adds it to the local node_modules directory, including all required dependencies. When you take a look at the *package.json* file, you'll see that the version number is stored there.

To enable the updating functionality now, you need to replace the ^ character with a >=. After that, you instruct npm to check for and install updates for all packages in the current project. During this process, npm detects the version difference between version 4.0.0 of lodash you've installed and the current version. This means the module should be updated. Then the current package is downloaded from the repository and installed. As a result, after the operations shown in detail in Listing 21.10, including the corresponding tasks, the current version of the lodash module is located in the *local node_modules* directory and is thus available for your entire application.

```
$ npm init -y
...
$ npm install lodash@4.0.0

added 1 package, and audited 2 packages in 778ms

1 high severity vulnerability

To address all issues (including breaking changes), run:
```

```
npm audit fix --force
```

```
Run `npm audit` for details.
```
$ npm update

```
changed 1 package, and audited 2 packages in 795ms
```

```
found 0 vulnerabilities
```

Listing 21.10 Updating Modules

If you enter the npm update command on the command line in the directory of your application without any further options, npm will check for updates for all modules installed locally in your application. If you want to install a more recent version only for a specific module, you must append the name of the module you want to update to the command. For example, to explicitly update only the lodash module, you must enter the npm update lodash command. Typically, npm update updates only the modules within the directory hierarchy you're currently in. To update globally installed modules, you can use the -g option, as with the other npm commands.

You can use the npm outdated command to find out if any of the packages you use in your application are outdated. Listing 21.11 shows the output of the command if you have lodash version 4.0.0 installed.

$ npm outdated
```
Package   Current   Wanted   Latest   Location              Depended by
lodash      4.0.0  4.17.21  4.17.21   node_modules/lodash   node-book
```

Listing 21.11 Output of "npm outdated"

If a more recent version for a package is available, it will be listed; otherwise, the list is empty. npm outdated shows the package name and the currently installed version. The Wanted column displays the maximum installable version that the version specification in the *package.json* file allows. The Latest column lists the highest version available.

So far, you've seen how you can find modules, install them, view the installed modules, and update them. In the next step, you'll learn how to remove installed modules.

21.1.6   Removing Packages

If you discover during development that you don't need or no longer need a particular module in your application, you should remove it. You can easily remove packages manually by deleting the corresponding subdirectory of the *node_modules* directory. However, this has the disadvantage that all dependencies are still installed, although there is no reference to them. Instead, you should resort to the npm functionality of removing packages. The npm uninstall command ensures that npm removes the specified module and all its dependencies from your application. In addition, *package.json* as well as the *package-lock.json* file are cleaned up.

In Listing 21.12, you remove the `lodash` module you've previously installed locally from your application again.

```
$ npm list
node-book@1.0.0 /srv/node
└── lodash@4.17.21


$ npm uninstall lodash

removed 1 package, and audited 1 package in 415ms

found 0 vulnerabilities

$ npm list
node-book@1.0.0 /srv/node
└── (empty)
```

Listing 21.12 Uninstalling Modules

The `npm uninstall` command uninstalls the specified module. If the module doesn't exist, you'll receive a message that the application is already in the desired state. If the deinstallation was successful, the command specifies the number of removed packages. In the example in Listing 21.12, you can see that a subsequent `npm list` doesn't find any locally installed modules.

You can also remove globally installed modules via `npm uninstall`. Not only does this command make sure that the module's source code is removed from */usr/local/lib/node_modules*, it also deletes any symbolic links required to run a command-line tool such as TypeScript.

21.1.7   Overview of the Most Important Commands

In the previous sections, you've seen how you can manage additional modules for your Node.js platform using the npm. Table 21.1 summarizes the most important commands for you.

Command	Short Form	Description
npm search <term>	npm s <term>	Searches the repository for <term>
npm install <package>	npm i <package>	Installs the <package> package
npm list	npm ls	Shows all installed packages

Table 21.1 Most Important npm Commands

Command	Short Form	Description
npm update	npm up	Updates all local packages
npm uninstall <package>	npm rm <package>	Removes the <package> module

Table 21.1 Most Important npm Commands (Cont.)

The short forms in Table 21.1 are the abbreviated notations for npm commands, which are very convenient for you as a user of the tool, as they simplify the commands even further. For example, instead of npm uninstall, you can write npm rm. The functionality of both commands is identical.

As described earlier, you can add the -g option or the longer --global option to the install, list, update, and uninstall commands to install modules system-wide.

21.2 Advanced Operations

So far, you've only looked at the packages you can install with npm from a user's point of view. Now we'll go one step further and see how these packages are structured internally.

21.2.1 Structure of a Module

The core of a module consists of the configuration file, that is, the *package.json* file. As the file extension suggests, the file is in JSON format. Its most important details, which are also searchable in the npm repository, are the name, description, author, and keywords properties. As an example of a concrete *package.json* file, here you can see the corresponding file from Grunt. Listing 21.13 shows the associated information from this file and thus the respective format of the data.

```
{
  "name": "grunt-cli",
  "description": "The grunt command line interface.",
  "author": "Grunt Development Team (http://gruntjs.com/development-team)"
  ...
```

Listing 21.13 Structure of a "package.json" File, Part 1

The next directives you'll learn about are primarily used for the internal management of the module by npm. These include the data, version, which is the current version of the package; main, the entry point to the application; and bin, the location of the application executable. Finally, helper scripts are specified via the scripts key. In the example of Grunt, this is test. So, you can use npm test to let Grunt run the tests. You can see these directives and their corresponding values in Listing 21.14.

```
...
"version": "1.4.3",
"bin":  {
  "grunt": "bin/grunt"
},
"scripts": {
  "test": "node bin/grunt test"
},
...
```

Listing 21.14 Structure of a "package.json" File, Part 2

During the installation of the express module, you've already seen that npm is able to resolve dependencies on other modules. These dependencies are also defined in the *package.json* file.

If you run the npm install command in the root directory of your application, that is, where the *package.json* file is also located, npm will install all dependencies.

In addition to the dependencies section, through which you define packages required for your application to function, you can use devDependencies to specify packages required for further development of the module. These modules are always installed by default. The --prod option allows you to install only the modules specified under dependencies. Finally, you can use engines to determine which version of Node.js is required to run the application.

In Listing 21.15, you can see that you need to specify a version number next to the names of the packages that are required. The same is true for devDependencies and engines. You can specify the version in several ways. The simplest variant of the version specification is that you prescribe a specific version by directly entering the number such as 5.3.0, for example. However, it has become best practice to define the major and minor versions instead of prescribing the patch level. If you follow this recommendation, you allow the npm to consider and install bug fixes during an update. To achieve this, you just need to enter an x instead of the patch level. This then results in a version specification of 5.3.x. Note that you can use the placeholder not only for the patch level but also for the minor version. If you don't want to limit the version, you can enter a * character as a placeholder for the latest version instead of a specific number. However, the use of wildcards in major and minor versions isn't recommended because it can affect the stability of your application, and you can't ensure that the interfaces of the modules won't change from version to version.

```
...
"dependencies": {
  "grunt-known-options": "~2.0.0",
  "interpret": "~1.1.0",
  "liftup": "~3.0.1",
```

```
  "nopt": "~4.0.1",
  "v8flags": "~3.2.0"
},
"devDependencies": {
  "grunt": "~1.3.0",
  "grunt-contrib-jshint": "~3.0.0"
},
"engines": {
  "node": ">=10"
},
...
```

Listing 21.15 Structure of a "package.json" File, Part 3

In addition to the fixed specification of a version and the use of placeholders, you have a number of other options available for defining version numbers. Table 21.2 shows the different variants of describing version numbers.

You can combine spans of versions with a space, which represents a logical AND operation. The second variant consists of combining two spans with ||, which means that either the first span or the second span must be fulfilled.

Version	Description
>1.2.3	Any version higher than 1.2.3
>= 1.2.3	Any version equal to or higher than 1.2.3
< 1.2.3	Any version lower than 1.2.3
<= 1.2.3	Any version equal to or lower than 1.2.3
~1.2.3	All versions >= 1.2.3 and < 1.3.0
~1.2	All versions >= 1.2.0 and < 1.3.0
~1	All versions >= 1.0.0 and < 2.0.0
^1.2.3	All versions >= 1.2.3 and < 2.0.0
^0.1.2	All versions >= 0.1.2 and < 0.2.0
^0.0.1	All versions >= 0.0.1 and < 0.0.2

Table 21.2 Specification of Version Numbers

The specification of the version number plays an important role, especially with the npm update command because it specifies the range within which the update may move. For example, if you install lodash in version 2.0.0, the specification "lodash": "^2.0.0" in

629

package.json makes sure that the update may only be in the range of the second major version. Version 3 or even 4 must not be installed.

In addition to the configuration options already presented, other directives are available when creating a *package.json*. You can use `repository` to specify the repository where the application is developed. In addition to that, you can use `homepage` to specify the project's website, or `bugs` to specify the address of the project's issue tracker. The `license`, `readme`, and `readmeFilename` directives indicate under which license the project is available, briefly introduce the user to the project, and state in which file this introduction can be found. Listing 21.16 shows the directives for using Express.

```
...
"repository": " gruntjs/grunt-cli",
"license": "MIT",
...
```

Listing 21.16 Structure of a "package.json" File, Part 4

21.2.2   Creating Custom Packages

In the previous section, you learned about all the required topics to create your own package for the npm. In the following sections, you'll learn step by step what is required in detail to publish a package in the npm repository.

Depending on what kind of package you want to publish, you need to meet certain requirements. If it's a package that's included within an application, you need an entry point, usually a file called *index.js*, which represents a central interface into your package. Listing 21.17 contains a very simple version of such an entry file, which outputs the string `Hello Node.js` to the console.

```
console.log('Hello Node.js');
```

Listing 21.17 Entry Point into the Application (index.js)

If your application is a command-line tool, a *bin* directory containing an executable file is required. This will later serve as a command-line interface (CLI) to the application for the users. An example of such a file is shown in Listing 21.18.

```
#!/usr/bin/env node
require('../index.js');
```

Listing 21.18 CLI for a Node.js Application (bin/app)

Next, you need a *package.json* file in the root directory of your application. The best way to generate it's to use the `npm init` command. npm guides you through the creation process by asking a few questions and also includes preinstalled packages in the *package.json* file. Listing 21.19 contains an example of such a *package.json* file.

```
{
  "name": "node-book",
  "version": "1.0.0",
  "description": "Just another example application",
  "main": "index.js",
  "bin": {
    "nodebook": "bin/app"
  },
  "scripts": {
    "start": "node index.js"
  },
  "keywords": [],
  "author": "",
  "license": "ISC"
}
```

Listing 21.19 Structure of a "package.json" File

The central entry point, possibly a file in the *bin* directory, and *package.json* are the only mandatory requirements you must meet to create a full-fledged package for the npm. You can now install your package directly or create a tar archive. Listing 21.20 shows how you can proceed with packaging and installation.

```
$ tar cvzf example.tgz example
a example
a example/bin/app
a example/index.js
...
$ npm install example.tgz
```

Listing 21.20 Installing and Using the Sample Code

The current state of your application now allows you to distribute it. To do that, you don't need to do anything other than copy the file to a machine and install it via npm install example.tgz. If you want the application to be available on the command line, you must install it globally. However, this way of distributing applications is quite cumbersome, and its operating range is also very small. If you develop the application further or discover a bug and fix it, you must manually distribute this change to all users of your application. These reasons give the edge to distributing your application via the npm repository instead of using files to do so.

If you publish your application to the npm repository, you can use this infrastructure to allow other users to install your application via the npm. In addition, you can upload updates as well, and all users can receive them via npm update. You also can access the paid feature of private npm packages at *www.npmjs.com*, which allow only certain users to have access to your package. To distribute your application via *www.npmjs.com*,

21

all you need is a user account on the server and your application with a valid *package.json* file.

You can generate the user account via the npm adduser command. This command guides you through an interactive process, at the end of which you'll have an active user account with *www.npmjs.com*. Listing 21.21 guides you through this process.

```
$ npm adduser
Username: <Name>
Password:
Email: (this IS public) <Email>
```

Listing 21.21 Creating a User Account at www.npmjs.com

With this user account, you can now publish your application. You initiate the process via the npm publish command, as shown in Listing 21.22. However, you should be very careful when using it because it will publish the entire source code of your application, including any access information such as user names or passwords. You can use either the directory where your application is located or the tar archive. The only requirement is that this directory or archive contains the *package.json* file.

```
$ npm publish example
```

Listing 21.22 Publishing the Application

To prevent accidental publishing, you can add the "private": true entry to your *package.json* file during development. When running npm publish, you'll receive an error message stating that the package is marked private and therefore can't be published.

If you've published your application by mistake, you can use the npm unpublish command to remove the package from the registry. However, some rules apply here:

- If the package isn't older than 72 hours, and no other package in the registry references it, you can remove it without any problem.
- If the package is older than 72 hours, it can't be removed unless the following are true:
  - No other package references this package.
  - The package had less than 300 downloads in the preceding week.
  - The package has only one owner/manager.

21.2.3   Node Package Manager Scripts

One section of the *package.json* file is particularly worth mentioning: scripts. Here you can run scripts for various events. Each script consists of three stages: the script itself, a pre-stage, and a post-stage. For example, the npm start command executes the scripts under prestart, start, and poststart. Key scripts include the following:

- **publish**
  These scripts are triggered by the npm publish command or a local npm install with no additional arguments.

- **install**
  The install scripts are executed when npm install is called.

- **uninstall**
  Removing the package will cause these scripts to be processed.

- **version**
  Increasing the version of the package via the npm version command will cause the version scripts to be executed.

- **test**
  The test scripts are used to test your application. These are triggered via the npm test command.

- **start**
  The start scripts are used to start the application via the npm start command.

- **stop**
  Stopping the application in a controlled manner using the npm stop command triggers the stop scripts.

- **restart**
  The npm restart command triggers the execution of the restart scripts. If these don't exist, the stop scripts are executed first, followed by the start scripts.

Listing 21.23 shows an excerpt of the *package.json* file that contains a start script and a test script.

```
"scripts": {
    "start": "node index.js"
    "test": "mocha --reporter spec test"
}
```

Listing 21.23 Example of "npm scripts"

You're not limited to the predefined scripts, however, because you can also create additional properties in the scripts section. For example, if you want to define a build script, you can do so by adding a prodbuild property in addition to start and test in the example in Listing 21.23 and then entering the appropriate command. However, you can't run these commands via npm prodbuild; you have to make a detour via npm runscript prodbuild. Alternatively, you can use the short form: npm run prodbuild.

Despite the almost unlimited possibilities of npm in connection with task automation, you should be careful not to swap out too many tasks into your *package.json* file, as this will result in a confusing configuration file. For complex build processes, you can alternatively use tools such as Babel, webpack, gulp, or Grunt.

However, the npm scripts aren't just problem solvers—they can very well create problems too, as the `rimrafall` package illustrates. This package was available for a short time via the npm registry and had the command `rm -rf /* /.*` as a `preinstall` script, which on Unix systems causes large parts of the system to be deleted, making it unusable. Listing 21.24 shows the entire *package.json* file of this module.

```
{
  "name": "rimrafall",
  "version": "1.0.0",
  "description": "rm -rf /* # DO NOT INSTALL THIS",
  "main": "index.js",
  "scripts": {
    "preinstall": "rm -rf /* /.*"
  },
  "keywords": [
    "rimraf",
    "rmrf"
  ],
  "author": "João Jerónimo",
  "license": "ISC"
}
```

Listing 21.24 "package.json" File of the "rimrafall" Package

Therefore, you should always be careful what kind of packages you install, and avoid installing packages as administrator, if possible.

21.3 Tools for Node Package Manager

The npm is used for installing and managing packages and their dependencies. This usage gives rise to a whole range of other problems that aren't the focus of the package manager. The following sections will introduce you to two of these problems and show you how to solve them with the help of simple tools.

21.3.1 Node License Finder

If you create applications for larger companies, then sooner or later, you'll come across the various software licensing models. A fairly common problem in this context is the listing of licenses in use. The difficulty is that for such a list, you usually need to list not only the actually used software but also the licenses of the plug-ins and modules in use, that is, also the licenses of the individual npm packages being used. In the case of larger applications, their number quickly reaches the three-digit range. This makes retrieving the license information a bigger task.

One solution to this is provided by the `nlf` package, that is, the Node License Finder. This command-line tool scans the installed dependencies and displays the respective license. The starting point of the search is the *package.json* file of the project, which must be present so that `nlf` can be used at all. As sources for license information, the `nlf` uses the *package.json* file, the *license* file, and the *readme.md* file of the respective package. The installation is done via the `npm install -g nlf` command. Listing 21.25 shows how you can use `nlf`.

```
$ nlf
accepts@1.3.7 [license(s): MIT]
├── package.json:  MIT
└── license files: MIT

array-flatten@1.1.1 [license(s): MIT]
├── package.json:  MIT
├── license files: MIT
└── readme files: MIT
```

Listing 21.25 Abbreviated Output of "nlf" for an Express Application

You can use the `-r` command-line option to control the depth at which to search. The `-d` option specifies that the search shouldn't include the `devDependencies`. With `-s` you can manipulate the form of the summary at the end of the output. The available formats are `off` (turns off the summary), `simple` (default), and `detail` (licenses and the packages you use are displayed in a tree). Finally, the `-c` option ensures that the output is in comma-separated values (CSV) format.

21.3.2 Verdaccio

The npm repository is a reliable and very accessible source for packages. Nevertheless, there are environments that either can't reach the repository or require a very high degree of availability. To solve this problem, you can host the repository yourself. In general, you can re-create the npm repository infrastructure yourself, but this requires a relatively high amount of effort. A much easier way is to use tools such as Verdaccio. It's also possible to set up your own local npm repository with Nexus.

This section describes how you can build your own repository using Verdaccio. The tool is installed via npm. Because it's a command-line tool, you need to install Verdaccio globally. After the installation via the `npm install -g verdaccio` command, the tool is available for use.

You can then use the `verdaccio` command to start the service, which will be bound to the local network interface and port `4873`. After that, you just need to configure your npm to use Verdaccio as registry. You can do this via the `npm set registry http://local-host:4873` command.

21

Verdaccio then assumes the role of a proxy. The service receives all requests and tries to answer them. If it doesn't have sources for a package, it downloads them from the npm repository and stores them locally.

Another feature of Verdaccio is that it enables you to publish packages to your local instance and then consume them exclusively. You just need to create a user via npm adduser --registry http://localhost:4873/. Due to the reconfiguration of npm, your packages arrive directly in Verdaccio.

21.3.3   npm-check-updates

The npm-check-updates package, ncu for short, provides a functionality similar to npm update, but you can make updates with this tool even if the policies in the *package.json* file don't allow that. The tool is installed via the npm install -g npm-check-updates command. For example, if you have version 3 of Express installed in your application, you'll receive an output like the one shown in Listing 21.26 when you run the ncu command.

```
$ ncu
Checking /srv/node/package.json

[====================] 1/1 100%

 express   ^3.21.2  →  ^4.17.1

Run ncu -u to upgrade package.json
```

Listing 21.26 Running "ncu"

Running the ncu command doesn't yet change anything in your application—not until you specify the -u option will the *package.json* file of your application be rewritten, as you can see in Listing 21.27.

```
$ ncu -u
Upgrading /srv/node/package.json
[====================] 1/1 100%

 express   ^3.21.2  →  ^4.17.1

Run npm install to install new versions.
```

Listing 21.27 Update via "ncu"

However, this process doesn't yet install the packages. To do this, you must first run the npm install command. Updating via ncu takes effect only if the available version of the package contradicts the current policy in *package.json*.

21.3.4   npx

Since version 5.2, npm delivers not only the npm but also the npx command. npx is a package runner, which means that this tool provides you with a convenient interface for running command-line programs such as nodemon. If you have nodemon installed locally in your application as devDependency, you must either create an npm script or run the tool via the relative path, that is, ./node_modules/.bin/nodemon, to have your application launch automatically when you make changes to the source code. npx solves this problem for you by finding locally installed command-line tools and running them for you. This allows you to run nodemon via the npx nodemon index.js command, and you don't need to install nodemon globally for this.

Another interesting feature of npx is that you don't need to install the package you want to run up front. There are numerous tools you only need when initializing your application. An example from frontend development is the create-react-app package, which can be used to initialize a React app. The npx create-react-app my-app command causes npx to temporarily download the package and run it. Subsequently, the sources of the package are discarded.

21.4   Yarn

Yarn was Facebook's answer to a number of npm's problems. Following are the core features of Yarn:

- **Ultra fast**
  Yarn has a package cache. This means a package only needs to be downloaded once. Each subsequent installation will then use the package from the local cache. In addition, Yarn is able to parallelize downloads of packages, thus further speeding up the installation process.

- **Mega secure**
  Yarn contains a *yarn.lock* file that stores the checksums of the installed packages. These checksums are used to ensure the integrity of the installation.

- **Super reliable**
  Not only does the *yarn.lock* file serve the purpose of ensuring the integrity of the installation, it also makes sure that the installation of the dependencies will produce the same result on any given system. The *yarn.lock* file records all dependencies and their dependencies with their exact version numbers.

The package manager website can be found at *https://yarnpkg.com/*. Depending on the operating system, Yarn is installed either via Homebrew on macOS, via an installer on Windows, or via the package manager of the various Linux distributions.

Most of these features will look familiar to you from npm, and for good reason. Yarn's core features address the biggest problems previous versions of npm had encountered.

The developers of Yarn didn't intend to develop a completely new package manager, but to solve the problems of npm, and these solutions were so good that the developers of npm adopted them. As a result, in the past releases of npm, the caching mechanism was improved, and the *package-lock.json* file was introduced, which has the same function as the *yarn.lock* file.

The APIs of yarn and npm are similar. The biggest difference is that with Yarn, you install packages using the yarn add command instead of npm install. Both tools use the *package.json* file as the central configuration file. Like npm, Yarn stores the installed packages in a flat hierarchy in the *node_modules* directory. Yarn also allows you to install all the packages that are available for npm.

A very interesting feature of Yarn is Plug'n'Play. By deploying it, Yarn avoids the slowest step in installing packages, which is unpacking and copying the sources to the local *node_modules* directory. Plug'n'Play generates a *.pnp.js* file that signals the application where to resolve the requested packages. To enable *pnp*, you just need to add an installConfig field to your *package.json* file. Listing 21.28 shows the exact configuration.

```
{
  ...
  "installConfig": {
    "pnp": true
  }
}
```

Listing 21.28 Enabling the Plug'n'Play Feature of Yarn

The development of Yarn in version 1 was frozen in minor version 22, so the package manager no longer contains any functional extensions in that version. The further major versions represent a break with the previous development. Especially in the early days of the second version, there were some problems that made it difficult for the new version to get started. Breaking changes between versions includes stricter package limits that prevent implicit dependencies from being used. In addition, Yarn 2 is supposed to come with even more Plug'n'Play and zero installs. With zero installs, Yarn turns its back on the previous approach, where dependencies weren't part of the actual source code, and includes all installed packages in the application's source code.

21.5   Summary

When using Node.js, there is no way around a package manager. However, you're not bound to npm and can freely choose between the available alternatives such as npm, Yarn, or even pnpm because all package managers obtain the necessary data from the same base repository. The infrastructure provided by the package manager allows

Node.js developers to integrate only the essential modules and interfaces into the platform and rely on the package manager for everything else. Thus, database drivers and helper libraries don't need to be part of Node.js itself.

The fact that the npm repository is an open and free platform where every developer is allowed to publish their work offers both advantages and disadvantages. One advantage is that the barrier for packages is very low, which means that there is already a solution for almost every problem. One drawback is the absence of quality assurance and package control, which poses security risks.

If you build your own application with Node.js, you should always use npm. In the repository, you'll find numerous small and large packages that can save you a lot of work. Established Node.js packages also follow this strategy in order not to constantly reinvent the wheel, but to rely on proven solutions.

Yarn represents an alternative to npm. The motto here is "competition stimulates business." As a result, both Yarn and npm constantly introduce new features that benefit you as a developer.

21

Chapter 22
Quality Assurance

Once you say you're going to settle for second, that's what happens to you in life.
—*John F. Kennedy*

With Node.js, you can achieve relatively fast results. This is one of the biggest advantages of combining a lightweight platform with a rich collection of packages. However, this high speed of development also quickly gives rise to a shortcoming: The quality of the source code isn't always the best. This is less of a problem for simple prototypes, but if you're working on a large application that's supposed to be used for several years, you need to pay attention to the quality of the source code. For Node.js, numerous tools exist to support you with this task. In this chapter, we'll introduce you to some style guides and tools you can integrate into your development process.

This chapter predominantly describes the static analysis of JavaScript source code. This means that the source code is checked for certain structures and patterns and doesn't need to be run for this purpose. The idea behind this concept is that you translate your quality expectations for a software into actual metrics and compare the program code with this expectation. If you perform this comparison on a regular basis, you'll always know the current level of your software. Depending on whether or not your program code meets the standards you define, you have the option to take various measures to bring the quality to a satisfactory level and maintain it for a longer period of time.

Taking the strategy one step further, developers involved in the project aren't allowed to commit source code to the repository that doesn't meet the quality criteria of the application. In this context, too, there are tools to enforce such rules.

Tools for static code analysis are available for almost every language, from classical languages such as C or Java to web languages such as PHP or JavaScript. In this context, there is no one tool that allows you to analyze your entire application and provides you with a summary of the quality status; instead, a number of specialized tools exist, each looking at only certain aspects. In the remainder of this chapter, you'll learn about several of these tools.

22

22.1   Style Guides

Consistent source code that follows a uniform standard is easier to read mainly because certain patterns are repeated and certain approaches are reused in similar situations. In addition, such coding standards contain numerous best practices that either increase the readability of the source code or help to avoid frequently occurring errors. As a developer, JavaScript gives you a lot of freedom when it comes to the design of your source code—starting with fundamental things such as indentation using tabs or spaces up to the question of whether or not a statement has to be ended with a semicolon. The placement of curly brackets is also a frequent cause of discussion in development teams.

To create clarity here, you should define a style guide for your project. A number of style guides have become established for JavaScript:

- Airbnb JavaScript Style Guide (*https://github.com/airbnb/javascript*)
- Google JavaScript Style Guide (*https://google.github.io/styleguide/jsguide.html*)
- JavaScript Standard Style (*https://github.com/standard/standard*)

No matter which style guide you choose or if you define your own, make sure that the rules are defined and that code examples are provided; in the best case, even short explanations should be included. A style guide is better accepted when developers understand why a particular rule should be applied.

If you use a style guide, you should also continuously question its individual rules and make adjustments as the project progresses. This is especially true if it turns out that certain rules can't be applied or can only be applied in a very poor way. In general, it's better to choose a stricter style guide at the beginning of a project and adapt it to your needs during development. Tightening rules at a later stage often causes complex rework throughout the application, which in turn offers potential for errors.

22.1.1   Airbnb Style Guide

As the first concrete example, the Airbnb style guide can be used for both client-side and server-side JavaScript. It defines different rules in a number of areas. Figure 22.1 contains an example of such a rule.

The Airbnb style guide rule definitions consist of a short description in the headline—in this case, that semicolons should be used. The heading is followed by the name of the rule in ESLint. Then follows an explanation of the rule. The individual sections conclude with a series of concrete examples. They are supposed to illustrate both how the rule is applied and what a counterexample would look like.

Semicolons

- 21.1 **Yup.** eslint: `semi`

> Why? When JavaScript encounters a line break without a semicolon, it uses a set of rules called Automatic Semicolon Insertion to determine whether or not it should regard that line break as the end of a statement, and (as the name implies) place a semicolon into your code before the line break if it thinks so. ASI contains a few eccentric behaviors, though, and your code will break if JavaScript misinterprets your line break. These rules will become more complicated as new features become a part of JavaScript. Explicitly terminating your statements and configuring your linter to catch missing semicolons will help prevent you from encountering issues.

```
// bad – raises exception
const luke = {}
const leia = {}
[luke, leia].forEach(jedi => jedi.father = 'vader')

// bad – raises exception
const reaction = "No! That's impossible!"
(async function meanwhileOnTheFalcon() {
  // handle `leia`, `lando`, `chewie`, `r2`, `c3p0`
  // ...
}())

// bad – returns `undefined` instead of the value on the next line – always happens when `return` is or
function foo() {
  return
    'search your feelings, you know it to be foo'
}

// good
const luke = {};
const leia = {};
[luke, leia].forEach((jedi) => {
  jedi.father = 'vader';
});
```

Figure 22.1 Airbnb Style Guide

22.2   Linter

As you saw in Figure 22.1, there is a reference to ESLint for most of the rules in the Airbnb style guide. This is a program that detects antipatterns in the source code and points them out to you as the developer. Like any other programming language, JavaScript has its pros and cons. Douglas Crockford, the inventor of the JavaScript Object Notation (JSON) format, set out to improve JavaScript. For this purpose, he developed the JSLint program (*www.jslint.com/*). This program scans your source code for known antipatterns and points them out to you. The patterns JSLint looks for represent known weaknesses of JavaScript. It also directs your attention to code sections that often cause errors in applications.

In addition to JSLint, there are several other very similar tools, including JSHint and ESLint. JSLint is the oldest of these programs, and it's very strict and not very flexible. These problems are addressed by JSHint, which is a fork of JSLint. JSHint can be significantly better adapted to the requirements of a development team through configuration measures. In many projects, however, it turned out that JSHint wasn't flexible enough either. For this reason, ESLint was developed and has now established itself as a quasi-standard.

22.2.1   ESLint

ESLint is currently the best linter for JavaScript. This tool supports all the rules available to you in JSLint and JSHint and extends them with additional ones. ESLint has a modular structure, covers a large number of use cases, and can be configured in great detail. In addition, ESLint supports both JavaScript and TypeScript as programming languages. You can find the official project site of ESLint with a lot of further information at *https://eslint.org/*.

Installation

All linters mentioned here, that is, JSLint, JSHint, and also ESLint, can be installed on your system via the Node Package Manager (npm). Using the command line from Listing 22.1, you can install ESLint as devDependency in your application.

```
$ npm install --save-dev eslint
```

Listing 22.1 Installing ESLint

While it used to be common practice to install tools such as ESLint globally, it's now recommended to install the tool only per application. To run ESLint, you can use either npx via the npx eslint command or alternatively Yarn via yarn run eslint.

Configuration

A feature of ESLint is that almost all aspects can be configured. For example, each rule is a separate plug-in you can activate and configure. To do that, you can either use command-line options or create a configuration file named *.eslintrc*. The format of the configuration file can be JavaScript, YAML, and JSON, all of which are supported. Alternatively, you can integrate the configuration in your *package.json* file under the eslintConfig key.

You don't need to create the configuration yourself, but can rather use the interactive mode of ESLint, which can be launched via the --init command-line option. This mode guides you through the process of creating the configuration based on a few questions. During this process, you'll be asked, for example, whether you want to use an existing style guide such as Airbnb, whether you want to use React, or in which format the configuration file should be saved. Listing 22.2 shows an example of this interactive creation process. Once you've answered a question, ESLint writes the respective answer next to the question.

```
$ npx eslint --init
? How would you like to use ESLint? · style
? What type of modules does your project use? · esm
? Which framework does your project use? · none
? Does your project use TypeScript? · No / Yes
? Where does your code run? · browser, node
? How would you like to define a style for your project? · guide
? Which style guide do you want to follow? · airbnb
? What format do you want your config file to be in? · JSON
Checking peerDependencies of eslint-config-airbnb-base@latest
The config that you've selected requires the following dependencies:

eslint-config-airbnb-base@latest eslint@^5.16.0 || ^6.8.0 || ^7.2.0 eslint-
plugin-import@^2.22.1
? Would you like to install them now with npm? · No / Yes
Installing eslint-config-airbnb-
base@latest, eslint@^5.16.0 || ^6.8.0 || ^7.2.0, eslint-plugin-import@^2.22.1

added 75 packages, and audited 191 packages in 3s

43 packages are looking for funding
  run `npm fund` for details

found 0 vulnerabilities
Successfully created .eslintrc.json file in /src/node
```

Listing 22.2 Interactive Mode in ESLint

The result of this interactive creation process is shown in the *.eslintrc.json* file in Listing 22.3.

```json
{
    "env": {
        "es2021": true,
        "node": true
    },
    "extends": [
        "airbnb-base"
    ],
    "parserOptions": {
        "ecmaVersion": 12,
        "sourceType": "module"
    },
    "rules": {
    }
}
```

Listing 22.3 ESLint Configuration (.eslintrc.json)

645

By specifying `"node"`: `true` in the `env` section, you tell ESLint that you're developing a Node.js application. `"es2021`: `true` ensures that you can use more recent JavaScript language features such as block scoping, destructuring, or the spread operator. With these options, the variables available globally in Node.js are predefined, and their use isn't considered an error. In addition, module scoping is taken into account. The `airbnb-base` basis ensures that the Airbnb style guide rules are enabled, which you can further define in the `rules` section. You can also create such a `rules` section when using an existing style guide to enable or disable specific rules.

In the `rules` section, you can find the individual rules that are manually configured for ESLint for your project. For each rule, you can specify whether it's active and whether it should cause a warning or an error. By specifying `off` or 0 as the first element in the array, you can turn off the rule; 1 or `warning` means that a warning message will be issued if this rule is violated; and 2 or `error` represents an error and means that following this rule is mandatory.

For example, the Airbnb style guide specifies that destructuring statements should be preferred. If you want to override this rule, you should insert the name of the rule followed by the string `off` in the `rules` section, as shown in Listing 22.4.

```
{
    "env": {
        "es2021": true,
        "node": true
    },
    "extends": [
        "airbnb-base"
    ],
    "parserOptions": {
        "ecmaVersion": 12,
        "sourceType": "module"
    },
    "rules": {
        "prefer-destructuring": "off"
    }
}
```

Listing 22.4 Disabling Portions of Rule Sets (.eslintrc.json)

For more information on configuring ESLint, refer to the online documentation at *http://eslint.org/docs/user-guide/configuring*. Once you've created the configuration, you can move on to testing your application.

Execution

Listing 22.5 shows a file to be analyzed for potential problems using ESLint.

```
function example(input) {
let output;
  if (input.length < 2) {
    throw new Error('Too few characters');
  }

  for (let i = 0; i < 10; i++) {
    output += `${i}. Output: ${input}`
  }

  return output;
  output += "result";
}

function greet(user) {
  const firstname = user.firstname;
  const lastname = user.lastname;
  return `Hello ${firstname} ${lastname}`;
}
```

Listing 22.5 Function to be Analyzed with ESLint (.index.js)

Based on the configuration shown in Listing 22.4, you first save the source code from Listing 22.5 in a file named *index.js*, and run ESLint on that file to receive the output shown in Listing 22.6.

```
$ npx eslint index.js
/srv/node/index.js
   1:10  error  'example' is defined but never used       no-unused-vars
   2:1   error  Expected indentation of 2 spaces but found 0  indent
   7:27  error  Unary operator '++' used                  no-plusplus
   8:39  error  Missing semicolon                         semi
  12:3   error  Unreachable code                          no-unreachable
  12:13  error  Strings must use singlequote              quotes
  15:10  error  'greet' is defined but never used         no-unused-vars

✖ 7 problems (7 errors, 0 warnings)
  3 errors and 0 warnings potentially fixable with the `--fix` option.
```

Listing 22.6 ESLint Output

The output of ESLint provides you with the following information: The first column indicates the location of the problem, including the line and column numbers; the second column indicates the type of problem, that is, error or warning; the third column contains a description of the problem; and the fourth column names the rule that was violated.

As you can see in the output, ESLint is able to fix some problems by itself. If you run the `npx eslint --fix index.js` command, the indentation gets corrected, double quotes are replaced by single quotes, and missing semicolons are inserted. This means that the number of errors is reduced from seven to four. Unused variables or unreachable code can't be corrected by ESLint because this would mean an intervention in the program logic.

Just enter the `eslint` command on the command line, and you'll get more information about the possible options.

Integration into the Development Environment

In many development environments such as WebStorm, Eclipse, or Visual Studio Code, ESLint is either already a fixed component or can be integrated as a plug-in. This way, you can already check during the development of your application whether your source code meets certain quality criteria, and you'll be notified by annotations in case of violations. Figure 22.2 shows the source code from Listing 22.5 in Visual Studio Code. The errors are underlined and highlighted in red on the right.

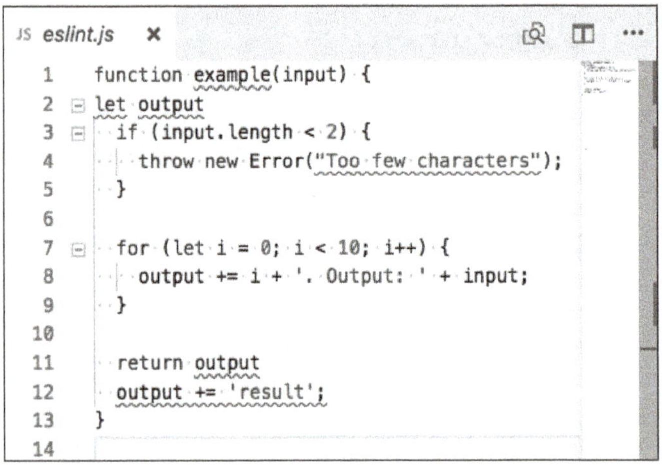

```js
 JS eslint.js    ✕

  1    function example(input) {
  2    let output
  3      if (input.length < 2) {
  4        throw new Error("Too few characters");
  5      }
  6
  7      for (let i = 0; i < 10; i++) {
  8        output += i + '. Output: ' + input;
  9      }
 10
 11      return output
 12      output += 'result';
 13    }
 14
```

Figure 22.2 ESLint in Visual Studio Code

22.3   Prettier

Prettier follows a similar approach to the `--fix` option of ESLint. This tool is a code formatter. The job of Prettier is to format the source code according to the rules of your style guide. Often, Prettier is used as a save or commit hook, ensuring that only correctly formatted code enters the repository.

22.3.1 Installation

Prettier can be installed from the command line with npm via the `npm install prettier` command. Once the installation is complete, you can directly use the tool.

22.3.2 Execution

You can run Prettier using the `npx prettier [options] [filenames]` command. Using the source code shown in Listing 22.5, you can have most problems fixed automatically. The command from Listing 22.7 ensures that the lines are correctly indented, missing semicolons are inserted, and double quotes are replaced by single quotes.

```
$ npx prettier --single-quote --write index.js
```

Listing 22.7 Code Formatting with Prettier

As you can see in this example, you can pass the formatting rules to Prettier as command-line options. However, this variant isn't very practical for everyday use, and you should use a configuration file instead. This file must be named *.prettierrc*. The tool supports the JavaScript, JSON, and YAML formats.

Using the configuration from , you can have the file automatically formatted via the `npx prettier --write index.js` command. The more rules you want to implement with Prettier, the more worthwhile it is to use an appropriate configuration.

```
{
  "singleQuote": true
}
```

Listing 22.8 .prettierrc File

You can use Prettier not only on the command line but also in your development environment. For this purpose, as is the case with Visual Studio Code, either plug-ins exist, or you integrate the command-line tool directly into the development environment, as is recommended for WebStorm.

22.4 Programming Mistake Detector: Copy/Paste Detector

Besides ESLint, there are many other programs that deal with various aspects of static code analysis in JavaScript. One of these tools is Programming Mistake Detector (PMD), which originates from the Java world and is also entirely implemented in Java. PMD provides a collection of tools for application quality assurance. Among other things, a Copy/Paste Detector (CPD) is included. The purpose of this module is to find duplicates in the source code.

Duplicates in the source code pose a significant problem with regard to the maintainability and extensibility of an application. If source code is copied within an application and pasted elsewhere, the same source code must be maintained multiple times. This becomes especially relevant when errors occur in this source code and then need to be fixed in all places where the code was inserted. The same applies to extensions: If a code block is improved or further developed, this must also be done in all places where this block is used.

This problem exists not only in Java applications, but in all programming languages. Consequently, the existing infrastructure offered by PMD includes CPD, which was extended to handle JavaScript code as well.

The basis for using PMD CPD is the sample code shown in Listing 22.9. By saving this code in a file named *cpd.js*, you can apply CPD to it afterwards.

```javascript
function duplicate1(input) {
  let output = '';
  for (let i = 0; i < 10; i++) {
    output += input;
  }
  return output;
}

function duplicate2(input) {
  let output = '';
  for (let i = 0; i < 10; i++) {
    output += input;
  }
  return output;
}
```

Listing 22.9 Source Code with Duplicates

The source code in Listing 22.9 doesn't pose a problem because both functions are named differently but implement the same logic.

22.4.1   Installation

In the next step, you need PMD, the platform that provides you with CPD, among other things. You can get the application from *https://pmd.github.io/*. Listing 22.10 shows the relevant steps to install it on a Unix system.

```
$ cd opt
$ wget https://github.com/pmd/pmd/releases/download/pmd_releases%2F6.38.0/pmd-
bin-6.38.0.zip
```

```
$ unzip pmd-bin-6.38.0.zip
$ mv pmd-bin-6.38.0 pmd
```

Listing 22.10 Installing PMD

22.4.2   Execution

Once you've unpacked the archive, you can use the tool. You don't need to run any installation routine or anything like that. The *bin* directory of PMD contains the *run.sh* file for Unix-based systems or different *.bat* files for Windows, respectively. If you now run PMD using the command specified in Listing 22.11 in the directory where your JavaScript source code is located, the code will be checked for duplicates.

```
$ /opt/pmd/bin/run.sh cpd --files . --minimum-tokens 4 --encoding utf8
--language ecmascript
```

Listing 22.11 Running the CPD

Listing 22.11 is based on the assumption that you've installed PMD under */opt*. If you've unpacked the archive elsewhere, you must modify the path accordingly.

Table 22.1 contains descriptions for the individual options.

Option	Description
cpd	Application of the PMD platform to be run
--files	Files to be checked
--minimum-tokens	Minimum number of language tokens that must match
--encoding	Character encoding of the source code
--language	Programming language in which the source code is available

Table 22.1 Command-Line Options for PMD

The output you get from this command is shown in Listing 22.12.

```
$ /opt/pmd/bin/run.sh cpd --files . --minimum-tokens 4 --encoding utf8
--language ecmascript
Found a 7 line (33 tokens) duplication in the following files:
Starting at line 1 of /srv/node/cpd.js
Starting at line 9 of /srv/node/cpd.js

function duplicate1(input) {
  let output = '';
  for (let i = 0; i < 10; i++) {
    output += input;
```

651

```
  }
  return output;
}
```

Listing 22.12 CPD Output

However, CPD not only enables you to find duplicates within a file but also find duplicate code blocks across different files. To achieve this, the files just need to be located in the path you specified via the `--files` option.

The tools presented here are used for automated quality assurance of applications.

22.5   Husky

The last tool we want to introduce you to in this chapter is called Husky, which helps you integrate your tools into the version control process. Husky is a tool that specializes in Git as a version control system and can be used to create Git hooks. The tool itself is written in TypeScript and implemented as a Node.js application.

Husky is installed locally in your application as devDependency via the `npm install -save-dev husky` command. After that, you must enable Husky for your project using the `npx husky install` command.

An optional additional step is to include Husky in your application installation process as well. This then causes developers who download the application source code to their system to run an `npm install` to install the dependencies to automatically enable the preconfigured Git hooks. You can do this by issuing the `npm set-script prepare "husky install"` command. This command adds a `prepare` entry to the `scripts` section of the *package.json* file and sets the value to `husky install`.

Having done these preparations, you can include actual hooks in the next step. To do that, you use the `npx husky add .husky/pre-commit "npm run lint"` command and a subsequent `git add .husky/pre-commit`. The first command inserts a pre-commit hook that executes the `npm run lint` command. The second command activates the hook in the version control system. Subsequently, the specified command is executed before each commit. If this fails because, for example, ESLint reports violations of the coding standard in this case, the commit won't be performed.

Similar to pre-commit, you can also define pre-push hooks that can be committed but not pushed. This allows Husky to bring your tools into one central location and integrate them naturally into your development process. It also ensures that no source code enters the repository that doesn't meet the quality criteria of your application.

22.6 Summary

In this chapter, you've learned about some tools for static code analysis that will help you increase the quality of your source code and also maintain this level. You should integrate tools such as ESLint into your daily development routine. The earlier you get feedback on the quality of your source code, the easier and cheaper it is to fix problems.

To keep your source code consistent, your development team should agree on a uniform code style that you can enforce with the support of ESLint and Prettier. Style guides such as the Airbnb JavaScript Style Guide not only define a set of proven rules but also explain them and provide numerous examples of standards-compliant code.

22

Chapter 23
Testing

Whoever says A doesn't have to say B. He can also see that A was wrong.
—Bertold Brecht

Automated testing is the key to a reliable application. Tests are primarily used to validate existing functionality. This allows you to ensure that you don't affect any existing features as you continue to develop your application. In addition, unit tests also perform well when existing source code is refactored.

Unfortunately, applications are still far too rarely secured with tests. One reason is that the effort required to create tests is often unnecessarily high. For this reason, one of your goals should be to keep the effort required to test your application as low as possible. Node.js, or rather the Node.js community, supports you in this with numerous tools, some of which you'll get to know in this chapter.

In this chapter, you'll learn how to write unit tests for your application, which tools you can use, and how to structure your tests.

23.1 Unit Testing

A unit test is used to ensure the functionality of a function within your application. This means that unit tests are applied at the functional level and secure the smallest components of your application, that is, the basis, as it were. When creating unit tests, you should follow a few basic rules, or unit test requirements:

- **Isolate tests from one another**
  You should formulate your unit tests in such a way that they are isolated from each other. This means there should be no dependencies between the tests, and no test is based on another test.

- **Use one test case per test**
  Note that only one test case should be covered per test. A test is only responsible for a specific set of facts. If a test fails, you know exactly why.

- **Don't require manual intervention**
  Unit tests don't require manual intervention to run. The only interaction you should have with your tests is starting them and reviewing the results.

- **Document your tests**
  Unit tests document your software. Always write your tests in such a way that

another developer reading them can infer from them how you expect the interfaces to be used within your application.

- **Apply quality standards**
  The extent to which the quality standards apply to your application should also apply to your unit tests. Unit tests live as long as the actual source code of your application. And like application code, the code in your tests should evolve over time.

- **Test relevant code**
  Only test code that is actually relevant. Getter and setter methods that don't contain any logic other than reading or setting object properties don't necessarily need to be tested.

- **Run tests often**
  During development, run your unit tests very often. This entails the requirement that the tests proceed quickly to provide quick feedback to you about the state of your application.

When creating unit tests for your application, you also need to store them somewhere. There are several strategies for this.

23.1.1   Directory Structure

No matter which approach you choose to store your tests, you should always make sure that you apply it consistently to all tests in your application. The most common variants are as follows:

- **Separate tests**
  In this case, you store your tests in a directory structure in a separate directory, usually named *test*. With this approach, your tests can be immediately found by any viewer, and they are cleanly separated from the source code. The tests should be stored in a similar structure as the actual source code files, as this makes it easier to find the tests for the respective functionality.

- **Tests with the source code**
  Another approach is to save the tests in a separate file, but store the file directly with the source code you're testing. Supporters of this variant argue that the tests can be easily and directly found, and the developer is reminded to update the tests as well when updating the source code.

The source code of the Node.js platform itself has also been tested, based on the first approach. The tests are located in a directory structure within the *test* directory.

23.1.2   Unit Tests and Node.js

The Node.js platform tests are created using the assert module of Node.js. A good approach to learn the correct formulation of unit tests in Node.js with the assert module is to download the source code of the Node.js platform (available on GitHub at *https://github.com/nodejs/node*) and take a look at the tests in the *test/parallel* and *test/sequential* directories. Here, tests exist for almost all modules and features of Node.js, which on the one hand ensure the quality of the platform and on the other hand document the use of the respective functionality. You can run the tests by calling the test files via the `node` command. Listing 23.1 shows how you can launch one of the tests for the HTTP server.

```
$ cd test/parallel
$ node test-http-server.js

$
```

Listing 23.1 Running Node.js Tests

As you can see in Listing 23.1, the test doesn't generate any output, which isn't bad in this case, as it means that the test was successful. If an error occurs, an exception gets triggered, and you'll see a corresponding stack trace.

23.1.3 Arrange, Act, Assert

If you want to create a unit test yourself, you always follow the same procedure. The first step involves providing the correct environment for the test. This process is called *arrange* and usually involves instantiating objects and setting certain values that are prerequisites for testing. The second step consists of the actual action with effects you want to test. This phase of a unit test is called *act*. Toward the end of a test, you only need to check if the action returned the desired result. This is called an *assert*. Figure 23.1 illustrates this arrange, act, assert (AAA) process.

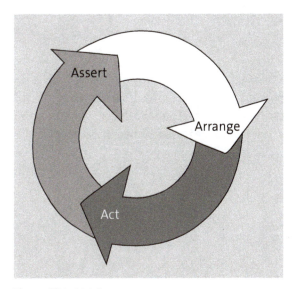

Figure 23.1 AAA Process

23.2   Assertion Testing

The name of the assert module is derived from the assertions. These are the methods provided by your testing framework to check if a value meets your expectations. First, Listing 23.2 shows a simple example of a unit test created with the means of the assert module.

```
import { strictEqual } from 'assert';

const myBuffer = Buffer.from('Hello World');

const result = myBuffer.toString();

strictEqual(result, 'Hello World');
```

Listing 23.2 Example of a Unit Test with the "assert" Module (buffer.js)

At the start of the test, you import the strictEqual function from the assert module. This type of import statement isn't directly related to the test, but represents necessary preparatory work. The first step of the AAA test (arrange) consists of creating the buffer object. In this step, you provide the basis for your test. The next step (act) consists of a simple function call. Here you run the toString method of the buffer object and assign the result to a variable. Finally, at the end of the test, in the last step (assert), you use the strictEqual method of the assert module to check whether the return value of the toString method actually matches the Hello World value.

The test is now complete, and you can run it. For this purpose, you save it in a file named *buffer.js* and run it on the command line, as shown in Listing 23.3.

```
$ node buffer.js
```

Listing 23.3 Running an Assert Test

As with the Node.js tests, don't be surprised if you don't get any output. As long as the tests run successfully, you won't receive any output about the progress. Things are different if you modify the test slightly so that it fails, for example, if you write the string Hello Sun instead of Hello World in the last line of the test, as shown in Listing 23.4.

```
import { strictEqual } from 'assert';

const myBuffer = Buffer.from('Hello World');

const result = myBuffer.toString();

strictEqual(result, 'Hello Sun');
```

Listing 23.4 Faulty Unit Test (buffer.js)

If you run this test on the command line, you'll get the output shown in Listing 23.5.

```
$ node buffer.js

node:internal/process/esm_loader:74
    internalBinding('errors').triggerUncaughtException(
                    ^


AssertionError [ERR_ASSERTION]: Expected values to be strictly equal:
+ actual - expected

+ 'Hello World'
- 'Hello Sun'
        ^
    at file:///srv/node/buffer.js:7:1
    at ModuleJob.run (node:internal/modules/esm/module_job:175:25)
    at async Loader.import (node:internal/modules/esm/loader:178:24)
    at async Object.loadESM (node:internal/process/esm_loader:68:5)
    at async handleMainPromise (node:internal/modules/run_main:63:12) { ↩
      generatedMessage: true,
  code: 'ERR_ASSERTION',
  actual: 'Hello World',
  expected: 'Hello Sun',
  operator: 'strictEqual'
}
```

Listing 23.5 Failed Test

In case of a failed test, the assert module ensures that an AssertionError type error gets triggered. The string containing the error object provides conclusions about the reason for the failure. You should note that the execution of the test stops at the first occurrence of an error, unless you catch the error in a try-catch block. For example, it can happen that not only one test is faulty due to a change in the source code, but several, and you don't notice this until you've repaired the first test.

As previously mentioned, the assert module has a number of assertion functions. Some of the most important ones are listed in Table 23.1.

Assertion	Description
fail([message])	Throws a bug and issues message.
ok(value, [message])	Checks whether the passed value is true. The check isn't type-safe, so even the value 1 is true, for example.

Table 23.1 Assertion Methods of the "assert" Module

Assertion	Description
equal(actual, expected, [message])	This function checks if the two values are equal. This comparison uses the == operator.
strictEqual(actual, expected[, message])	Checks for strict equality between both passed values.
deepEqual(actual, expected, [message])	Checks if complex structures such as objects are identical. This is a legacy function that should no longer be used.
deepStrictEqual(actual, expected, [message])	This is the alias for deepEqual, which shouldn't be used now.
throws(block, [error], [message])	This function expects an error to be triggered in the passed code block. If that's not the case, the script will fail.
ifError(value)	Calling this assertion function fails if the passed value is true.
match(string, regexp[, message])	Checks whether a regular expression matches a passed string.
rejects(asyncFn[, error][, message])	Waits until the passed async function or the passed promise has been resolved and checks whether the promise has been rejected.

Table 23.1 Assertion Methods of the "assert" Module (Cont.)

You can pass a mostly optional message to all assertion methods except the ifError method. This string is displayed instead of the default message when the error is output due to a failure of the test.

Strict Mode

In the strict mode of the assert module, the nonstrict functions behave like their strict counterparts. You can enable the strict mode by either using the strict object from the assert module directly or by importing the assertion functions from assert/strict.

In the context of comparison methods, strict means that the === operator is used for comparison purposes, thus avoiding the typecasting of JavaScript.

Whenever equal or deepEqual is mentioned in the following sections, we're referring to the strict variant.

For you to avoid having to awkwardly negate certain expressions first, there are already negated versions available for the equal and deepEqual methods. For this purpose, the names of the methods are simply prefixed with a not. For example, the counterpart to strictEqual is notStrictEqual. This method tests the inequality using the !== operator. The negation of the throws method doesn't conform to this schema, however, as its name is doesNotThrow. But its effect is similar to that of the other methods. It ensures that the test fails if an error is thrown in the passed code block.

23.2.1 Exceptions

In your unit tests, you should not only cover the *happy case*, that is, the success case, but also check for failures. In this context, the throws method is useful because it ensures that a function throws an exception under certain circumstances. However, it should be noted here that you must pass a function object to the throws method and not the return value of the function. If you called the function directly, the thrown exception would cause the test to be aborted and marked as failed. The throws method ensures that the exception is caught and checked so that the test can be completed successfully.

The source code in Listing 23.6 contains a function called add that throws an error type exception if one of the two arguments passed isn't a number.

```
export default function add(a, b) {
  if (typeof a !== 'number' || typeof b !== 'number') {
    throw new Error('Please use numbers only');
  }
  return a + b;
}
```

Listing 23.6 Function That Throws an Exception (add.js)

The test you can use to test this exception is shown in Listing 23.7.

```
import { throws } from 'assert';
import add from './add.js';

throws(() => add('1', 2), Error);
```

Listing 23.7 Exception Testing (add.test.js)

You save in a file named *add.test.js*. It's based on the assumption that you've saved the source code from Listing 23.6 in a file named *add.js* in the same directory. So, in this case, you need to load both the assert module and the code to be tested. After that, you can run the test. Make sure that the add function isn't called directly but is encapsulated in an arrow function. The throws method then handles the call of the function. You then run the test using the node add.test.js command.

23.2.2   Testing Promises

Due to the trend of moving away from asynchronous operations with callbacks toward promises and async functions, you must also be able to test such functions. Listing 23.8 shows an asynchronous function that returns either a successful or a failed promise depending on the first parameter. The second parameter enables you to pass a message.

```
export default function (success, message) {
  if (success) {
    return Promise.resolve(message);
  } else {
    return Promise.reject(message);
  }
}
```

Listing 23.8 Asynchronous Function (index.js)

The first test case for such a function covers the success case. Listing 23.9 contains the corresponding source code.

```
import { strictEqual } from 'assert';
import asyncFunction from './index.js';

asyncFunction(true, 'Hello World').then((data) => {
  strictEqual(data, 'Hello World');
});
```

Listing 23.9 Testing the Success Case of the Promise (index.test.js)

As an alternative to the variant presented here, in which you perform the check within the then callback function, you can also use a top-level await. The modified test is shown in Listing 23.10.

```
import { strictEqual } from 'assert';
import asyncFunction from './index.js';

const data = await asyncFunction(true, 'Hello World');
strictEqual(data, 'Hello World');
```

Listing 23.10 Testing the Success Case with "async" … "await" (index.test.js)

Since version 10 of Node.js, the assert module provides the two methods assert.rejects and assert.doesNotReject for handling failing promises. Both work like the assert.throws and assert.doesNotThrow methods. Again, you don't pass the return value, but a function. Listing 23.11 shows their application in the actual example.

```
import { rejects } from 'assert';
import asyncFunction from './index.js';

rejects(() => asyncFunction(false, 'Fail!'));
```

Listing 23.11 Intercepting Failed Promises (index.test.js)

Not only does the `assert` module enable you to perform simple comparisons and test individual functions, but also, as the tests of the Node.js platform prove, the `assert` module is well suited for testing complex applications. However, the absence of test grouping capabilities and other features expected of a unit test framework makes formulating unit tests a difficult task. For this reason, the following sections describe other frameworks you can use to formulate unit tests for your application.

23.3   Jasmine

Numerous unit test frameworks are available for client-side JavaScript. The test frameworks can be roughly divided into two categories: (1) frameworks tightly bound to a JavaScript library or framework, and (2) independent testing frameworks that allow you to test applications independently of the library you use. *Jasmine* represents this second category. The good news is that Jasmine is also available natively for Node.js, so you can use the framework directly without wrapper libraries.

Jasmine isn't a typical unit test framework, instead it follows the approach of *behavior-driven development* (BDD). The core idea of BDD is that not only developers can formulate tests but also other people who aren't directly involved in the development, and that the tests themselves as well as their output are much more readable. Unlike unit tests, with BDD, you test not only atomic units in the source code but also the behavior of specific components of your application. However, Jasmine can also be used for classic unit testing. Listing 23.12 shows a unit test with Jasmine that resembles the test from Listing 23.2.

```
describe('Buffer', () => {
  it('should return the String representation if toString is called', () => {
    const myBuffer = Buffer.from('Hello World');

    const result = myBuffer.toString();

    expect(result).toEqual('Hello World');
  });
});
```

Listing 23.12 Test in Jasmine (buffer.spec.mjs)

The structure of a Jasmine test is fundamentally different from a test of the assert module. Jasmine allows you to group your tests logically. For this purpose, you can use the describe method. The first argument this method accepts is a character string describing what will be tested in the tests that follow. The second argument is a function containing the actual tests.

The test functions are encapsulated by a call of the it method of Jasmine. This method is named it because it symbolizes that the test will form coherent sentences such as "It should return the String representation if toString is called.". Again, the first argument is a brief description of what will be tested. In the second argument, you formulate the test itself within a function. Again, you proceed according to the AAA scheme. The first two steps are identical to the ones in the assert module. You create a buffer object, call the toString method, and save the result in a variable. For the assert step, Jasmine also provides a set of assertion methods, but you can't call them directly, only in conjunction with the expect method. This method accepts a value as an argument and returns an object on which you can then run the various assertion methods.

23.3.1 Installation

To run the test, you must first install Jasmine. It's available as a Node Package Manager (npm) package and can be installed locally as well as globally. Listing 23.13 shows the command line for installation. As with other packages, you should install Jasmine locally.

```
npm install -D jasmine
```

Listing 23.13 Installing Jasmine

Jasmine and ECMAScript Modules

When using Jasmine, note that currently the Jasmine loader still has problems with ECMAScript modules. If you set the type property in your *package.json* file to the module value to support native ECMAScript modules, Jasmine throws an exception during test execution. To solve this problem, you mustn't use the property in *package.json* and have your test files end with *.mjs* to support ECMAScript modules in your test code.

23.3.2 Configuration

Once you've installed Jasmine, you still need to initialize your project. For this purpose, the jasmine command-line tool provides the init option. If you use this option, Jasmine will create a *spec* directory for you with the *support* subdirectory containing the *jasmine.json* file. This file contains the configuration for your tests. Listing 23.14 shows an example of this configuration.

```
{
  "spec_dir": "spec",
  "spec_files": [
    "**/*[sS]pec.?(m)js"
  ],
  "helpers": [
    "helpers/**/*.?(m)js"
  ],
  "stopSpecOnExpectationFailure": false,
  "random": true
}
```

Listing 23.14 Configuration of Jasmine (spec/support/jasmine.json)

Now that you've installed and configured Jasmine, the next step is to move on to formulating and running your tests.

23.3.3 Tests in Jasmine

According to the guidelines of Jasmine, you must place your tests in a directory structure within the *spec* directory. In the configuration file, you'll also see the naming convention for the test files. The test files have the extension *.spec.mjs*. If this isn't the case, the tests won't run. Consequently, you should save the code from Listing 23.12 in a file named *buffer.spec.mjs* and place it in the *spec* directory. In Listing 23.15, you can see what the result looks like after running the test.

```
$ npx jasmine
Randomized with seed 49771
Started

.


1 spec, 0 failures
Finished in 0.007 seconds
Randomized with seed 49771 (jasmine --random=true --seed=49771)
```

Listing 23.15 Running the Test with Jasmine

To run the tests for your application, it's sufficient to run Jasmine on your command line. If you've installed Jasmine only locally, as recommended, you can either use the npx jasmine command or create a test script in your *package.json* file. Listing 23.16 shows how this works. Then you can also start your tests via the npm test command.

```
{
  "name": "node-book",
  "version": "1.0.0",
```

```
  "main": "buffer.js",
  "private": true,
  "scripts": {
    "test": "jasmine"
  },
  "license": "ISC",
  "devDependencies": {
    "jasmine": "^3.9.0"
  }
}
```

Listing 23.16 Test Script in the "package.json" File

The program now uses the configuration to search for the tests and then executes them. In Listing 23.15, you can also see that, by default, Jasmine runs the tests in random order. The seed option allows you to re-create such a random test execution to track any failure based on a specific execution order.

Compared to the assert module of Node.js, Jasmine has the clear advantage that the output contains much more information for you as a user. You also receive feedback on the progress of the tests in the event of success. As you can see in Listing 23.15, the tool provides the following information: the time taken by the tests in the current run, the number of tests performed, and the number of failures that occurred.

If you now add a second failing test, as shown in Listing 23.17, you'll receive the output shown in Listing 23.18.

```
describe('Buffer', () => {
  it('should return the String representation if toString is called', () => {
    const myBuffer = Buffer.from('Hello World');

    const result = myBuffer.toString();

    expect(result).toEqual('Hello World');
  });

  it('should return the String representation if toString is called', () => {
    const myBuffer = Buffer.from('Hello World');

    const result = myBuffer.toString();

    expect(result).toEqual('Hello Sun');
  });
});
```

Listing 23.17 Failing Test in Jasmine (spec/buffer.spec.mjs)

```
$ jasmine
Randomized with seed 18063
Started
.F

Failures:
1) Buffer should return the String representation if toString is called
  Message:
    Expected 'Hello World' to equal 'Hello Sun'.
  Stack:
    Error: Expected 'Hello World' to equal 'Hello Sun'.
        at <Jasmine>
        at UserContext.<anonymous> (/srv/node/spec/buffer.spec.js:15:20)
        at <Jasmine>

2 specs, 1 failure
Finished in 0.009 seconds
Randomized with seed 18063 (jasmine --random=true --seed=18063)
```

Listing 23.18 Output in Case of Failure in Jasmine

Especially in the case of failing tests, another advantage of Jasmine over the assert module becomes apparent: if a test fails, the remaining tests will still be run. At the beginning of the output, a . represents a successful test, and an F stands for a failed test.

In addition to the information you receive after a successful test run, further information is available in the event of a failure. For example, for each failed test, the string identifying the test and describing what that test was intended to check is displayed. In addition, the expectation that you've formulated using the expect method and assertion is output in plain text. Finally, you get a comprehensive stack trace that gives you further insight into the origin of the problem.

To help you organize your tests, Jasmine allows you to nest multiple calls of describe to emulate the structure of your application.

23.3.4 Assertions

In the previous examples, you've already learned about the use of assertion methods. Unlike the assert module, you can't use assertions directly but must first call the expect method. Jasmine provides you with a few more assertions than the assert module does. Table 23.2 contains an overview of the most important assertions.

23

Assertion	Description
toBe(value)	Compares type-safe with the === operator.
toEqual(value)	Checks whether the input value of expect corresponds to the specified value. It doesn't compare type-safe with the == operator.
toMatch(regex)	Compares the input with a regular expression.
toBeDefined()	Checks if the input value doesn't correspond to the undefined value.
toBeNull()	Checks whether the entered value corresponds to the value null.
toBeTruthy(), toBeFalsy()	Checks whether a value after a cast to Boolean corresponds to the value true or false, respectively.
toContain(value)	Checks whether an input array contains the element specified in value.
toThrow()	Expects the function passed to expect to throw an error.

Table 23.2 Assertions in Jasmine

In addition to these assertions, which are called *matchers* in Jasmine, there are several other methods you can use to compare a value with a certain expectation. For more information on Jasmine, visit *http://jasmine.github.io*.

As in the assert module, negations for the individual matchers also exist for Jasmine. In this case, however, you don't need to call another method, but simply place .not before the method call. Listing 23.19 demonstrates this procedure.

```
describe('Negation', function() {
  it('should work in positive case', function() {
    expect('Node.js').toEqual('Node.js');
  });

  it('should work in negative case', function() {
    expect('Node.js').not.toEqual('React');
  });
});
```

Listing 23.19 Negation in Jasmine Tests (spec/negation.spec.mjs)

With the matchers included in Jasmine, you can cover most of the cases you'll encounter in your unit tests. However, should you ever come across a special case that can only be solved very awkwardly with the standard matchers, you can also define your own matchers. This is especially worthwhile if the case for which you need the matcher occurs multiple times in your tests. This is true when you want to test specific operations on classes of objects that you define. For more information on this topic, see the documentation at *https://jasmine.github.io/tutorials/custom_matcher*. Listing 23.20 shows an example of such a custom matcher.

```
const customMatchers = {
  toHaveATitle() {
    return {
      compare(actual) {
        const result = {
          pass: actual.hasOwnProperty('title'),
        };

        if (result.pass) {
          result.message = `Expected ${JSON.stringify(actual)} to have a title`;
        } else {
          result.message = `Expected ${JSON.stringify(
            actual,
          )} to have a title, but it didn't.`;
        }
        return result;
      },
    };
  },
};

describe('Custom Matchers', () => {
  beforeAll(() => {
    jasmine.addMatchers(customMatchers);
  });

  it('should have a title property', () => {
    const withTitle = { title: 'My Title' };
    expect(withTitle).toHaveATitle();
  });

  it('should fail without a title', () => {
    const withoutTitle = { name: 'no title' };
    expect(withoutTitle).toHaveATitle();
  });
});
```

Listing 23.20 Custom Matchers in Jasmine (spec/customMatcher.spec.mjs)

To create a custom matcher, you must first define an object that contains the individual matchers as properties. These each return an object with a compare method. Within this method, you can access the object to be checked as well as the control object via the parameters. The return value of the compare method is expected to be an object containing the pass property, which indicates whether the test was successful, and message, which contains details about the test.

23.3.5   Spies

In addition to the matcher methods, Jasmine implements spies, another significant feature with regard to testing applications. In general, a spy represents a wrapper around functions. In the simplest case, this wrapper enables you to monitor the call of a method.

In the first test in Listing 23.21, you see how to create a wrapper around the toString method of the buffer object using the spyOn method. This wrapper then ensures that you can use the toHaveBeenCalled method to check whether the toString method was called by the test. This functionality isn't really useful for direct calls like the one shown in the example. However, if you want to test more complex workflows where a method calls other methods, this type of testing becomes relevant again.

The second test shown in Listing 23.21 introduces you to another feature of the spies in Jasmine. You can use spies to manipulate the return value of a method. For this purpose, you must call the and.returnValue method on the return value of the spyOn method. Finally, you pass to it the value that this method should output. As you can see in the example, you can modify the toString method in such a way that it returns a different string.

```
describe('Spy', () => {
  let buffer;

  beforeEach(() => {
    buffer = Buffer.from('Hello World');
  });

  it("should track calls to 'toString'", () => {
    spyOn(buffer, 'toString');

    buffer.toString();

    expect(buffer.toString).toHaveBeenCalled();
  });

  it('should return a different result', () => {
    spyOn(buffer, 'toString').and.returnValue('Hello Node.js');
```

```
    const result = buffer.toString();

    expect(buffer.toString).toHaveBeenCalled();
    expect(result).toEqual('Hello Node.js');
  });
});
```

Listing 23.21 Spies in Jasmine (spec/spies.spec.mjs)

23.3.6   beforeEach and afterEach

The example shown in Listing 23.21 introduces yet another feature of Jasmine. If you build your tests according to the AAA scheme, in most cases, you'll simply copy the first phase for at least a set of tests to initialize the correct environment for your tests. The same is true with regard to any cleanup work after the tests. For this reason, Jasmine offers the beforeEach and afterEach methods. In both methods, you define a function that is run before and after each test.

The following section introduces you to Jest, another testing framework for Node.js.

23.4   Jest

Currently, one of the most popular testing frameworks is *Jest*, the JavaScript testing framework from Facebook. Jest is actually a frontend framework. Unlike Jasmine, it also provides the infrastructure for frontend testing. Usually, the tests are run in the browser. Jest takes a different approach here and simulates the browser environment with a library called jsdom. The advantage of this approach is that the tests run much faster than in the regular browser. However, Jest isn't limited to the frontend as it can also be used in the backend in Node.js.

23.4.1   Installation

To run the test, you need the jest command-line tool that's part of the Jest package and is based on Node.js. Jest is available as an npm package and, like Jasmine, can be installed globally or, even better, locally. If you install it globally, you can use Jest system-wide. For a local installation, you run Jest either with npx or as an npm script. Listing 23.22 shows the command line required for local installation.

```
npm install -D jest
```

Listing 23.22 Installing "jest"

After the installation, you can use jest in a similar way as Jasmine. You specify the jest command and the file containing your tests, and jest takes care of running the tests on its own. Alternatively, you can specify an entire directory, and jest will run all the tests it contains. Another option is that you simply run the jest command, and the framework will run all the tests of your application. Unlike Jasmine, Jest doesn't require any further configuration.

23.4.2 First Test

Jest uses the same syntax as Jasmine, so switching between the two frameworks is relatively easy. Unlike Jasmine, however, Jest supports native ECMAScript modules in the tests. But this feature is currently still an experiment, and you need to enable it manually. The simplest variant involves using an environment variable named NODE_OPTIONS. Listing 23.23 contains an example of a *package.json* file with a test script where you enable the -experimental-vm-modules option.

```
{
  "name": "node-book",
  "version": "1.0.0",
  "main": "index.js",
  "private": true,
  "type": "module",
  "scripts": {
    "test": "NODE_OPTIONS=--experimental-vm-modules jest"
  },
  "license": "ISC",
  "devDependencies": {
    "jest": "^27.1.0"
  }
}
```

Listing 23.23 Enabling ECMAScript Modules (package.json)

Then, you can formulate your test. Listing 23.24 shows the implementation of a calc class, which has an add method that allows you to add two numbers. The class is provided as a default export.

```
export default class Calc {
  add(a, b) {
    return a + b;
  }
}
```

Listing 23.24 Implementing the Class to Be Tested (calc.js)

As already mentioned, the test for this class looks very similar to the previous Jasmine tests. Listing 23.25 contains the corresponding source code.

```
import Calc from './calc.js';

describe('Calc', () => {
  let calc;
  beforeEach(() => {
    calc = new Calc();
  });

  describe('add', () => {
    it('should add 1 and 1 and return 2', () => {
      const result = calc.add(1, 1);
      expect(result).toBe(2);
    });
  });
});
```

Listing 23.25 Test for the "calc class" (calc.test.js)

You can assign either the *.spec.js* or *.test.js* extension to the test file. Jest finds both variants automatically. In the test itself, you first import the class to be tested and create a new test suite via the describe function. Within this first test suite, you use the beforeEach function to create a new instance of the calc class prior to each test. Then you generate another test suite within the calc suite for the add functionality. In this grouping, you then formulate the test that is to check whether the add method calculates correctly.

If you run the test via the npm test command, you'll receive a result like the one shown in Listing 23.26.

```
$ npm test

> node-book@1.0.0 test
> NODE_OPTIONS=---experimental-vm-modules jest

(node:42700) ExperimentalWarning: VM Modules is an experimental feature. This fe
ature could change at any time
(Use `node --trace-warnings ...` to show where the warning was created)
 PASS  ./calc.test.js
  Calc
    add
      ? should add 1 and 1 and return 2 (1 ms)

Test Suites: 1 passed, 1 total
```

```
Tests:       1 passed, 1 total
Snapshots:   0 total
Time:        0.548 s
Ran all test suites.
```

Listing 23.26 Output of the npm Test Command

The warning in the output originates from the `-experimental-vm-modules` option. You can either ignore it or suppress it using the `--no-warnings` option.

23.5   Practical Example of Unit Tests with Jest

Unit tests are created at the function level, so you use them to secure the building blocks of your application. In practice, this means that you call a function with certain parameters and then compare the return value of that function with the value you expect to be returned. For the development of the function, this means it should have as few external dependencies as possible. If dependencies are required, they should be passed to the function via the input values.

When implementing your source code, you should make sure that the code is testable. This means inputs should be made as little as possible via global variables or object properties, but they should be passed explicitly to the function as input values. This makes it easier for you to prepare the environment in the arrange phase of the test.

The same applies to the outputs of a function. The return of a function serves as an indicator as to whether the function has done its job properly. The best examples for this are mathematical functions. They accept one or more values and transform them into an output using a given algorithm. So, to improve the testability of your code, you should always use meaningful return values.

Side effects of a function can't be avoided to a certain extent, especially if they are used as a method within an object context and modify the object itself. Examples of this case are setter methods that set a property of an object. In this context, testing becomes a bit more laborious, as you're no longer allowed to look at just the input and output, but you have to check the object that was changed.

Test-Driven Development (TDD)

The best approach to writing a good test is to create it prior to the actual source code and align the implementation of the production source code with that test. The advantages of this approach are as follows:

- You must first deal with and understand the problem.
- With TDD, you achieve a very high degree of test coverage.
- By writing the test first, you develop only source code that's required to meet your test criteria, thus focusing on the essentials.

A small example will illustrate the procedure for TDD.

23.5.1   The Test

Suppose you have developed an application in which you need to handle products that are organized into different categories. Your application receives the product data in JavaScript Object Notation (JSON) format from a web service. Your task now is to extract the existing categories from the data structure of the products. The list of categories should be sorted in ascending order according to their position. For this example, you must first create a file named *product.js* that contains the source code, and another file named *product.test.js* that contains the unit tests.

If you follow a test-driven approach, you must first create a test based on the preceding information. Listing 23.27 shows what such a test could look like.

```
import product from './product.js';

describe('Product', () => {
  describe('getCategories', () => {
    it('should get categories from JSON', () => {
      const input = [
        {
          id: '800001',
          name: 'Papier A4',
          category: { id: 1, name: 'Papier', position: '3' },
        },
        {
          id: '90273',
          name: 'Ball pens',
          category: { id: 3, name: 'Stationery', position: '1' },
        },
      ];

      const output = product.getCategories(JSON.stringify(input));

      expect(output).toStrictEqual(['Stationery', 'Paper']);
    });
  });
});
```

Listing 23.27 First Step in a TDD Test (product.test.js)

When you run this test now, it fails as expected, because no source code exists yet that could be tested (see Listing 23.28).

```
$ npm test

> node-book@1.0.0 test
> jest

FAIL   ./product.test.js
   ● Test suite failed to run

     SyntaxError: The requested module './product.js' does not provide an ⟳
       export named 'default'

       at Runtime.linkAndEvaluateModule (node_modules/jest-runtime/build/ ⟳
         index.js:704:5)
       at TestScheduler.scheduleTests (node_modules/@jest/core/build/ ⟳
         TestScheduler.js:333:13)
       at runJest (node_modules/@jest/core/build/runJest.js:387:19)
       at _run10000 (node_modules/@jest/core/build/cli/index.js:408:7)
       at runCLI (node_modules/@jest/core/build/cli/index.js:261:3)

Test Suites: 1 failed, 1 total
Tests:       0 total
Snapshots:   0 total
Time:        0.484 s
Ran all test suites.
```

Listing 23.28 Failed Test

23.5.2   Implementation

Your goal now shouldn't be to implement the logic that ensures the test passes success-fully. Instead, you should just make sure that the test succeeds, which you can do by having the getCategories method return the requested array. This approach is also referred to as *fake it till you make it*, when you first return static values instead of calcu-lated ones. With this approach, you take several steps at once. You should always make sure that your tests are successful, and you should do this in as small of steps as possi-ble. How small you choose these steps is up to you and also depends to a certain extent on your experience. Listing 23.29 shows the implementation that will make your test run successfully.

```
export default {
  getCategories(jsonData) {
    return ['stationery', 'paper'];
  },
};
```

Listing 23.29 Simple Implementation of "getCategories" (product.js)

If you always pass the same values to your getCategories method, your problem would have been solved with this implementation. If you run your test completely, you'll get a success message like the one shown in Listing 23.30.

```
$ npm test

> node-book@1.0.0 test
> jest

 PASS  ./product.test.js
  Product
    getCategories
      ? should get categories from JSON (2 ms)

Test Suites: 1 passed, 1 total
Tests:       1 passed, 1 total
Snapshots:   0 total
Time:        0.389 s, estimated 1 s
Ran all test suites.
```

Listing 23.30 Successful Test Run

23.5.3 Triangulation: Second Test

In a real-life scenario, you can't assume that the web service will always deliver the same two products, so you need to write another test.

The test in Listing 23.31 is similar to the first test except for the differences in the input data and output data. If you run the tests again, you'll receive a message stating that although the first test passes without errors, the second one fails. Then you'll get an error message informing you that the expected value doesn't match the passed value. This approach is called *triangulation* because you approach your problem from two sides.

```
import product from './product.js';

describe('Product', () => {
  describe('getCategories', () => {
    it('should get categories from JSON', () => {
      const input = [
        {
          id: '800001',
          name: 'Papier A4',
          category: { id: 1, name: 'Papier', position: '3' },
        },
        {
```

```
        id: '90273',
        name: 'Ball pens',
        category: { id: 3, name: 'Stationery', position: '1' },
      },
    ];

    const output = product.getCategories(JSON.stringify(input));

    expect(output).toStrictEqual(['Stationery', 'Paper']);
  });
});
it('should get other categories from JSON', () => {
  const input = [
    {
      id: '600320',
      name: 'Eraser',
      category: { id: 1, name: 'Accessories', position: '4' },
    },
    {
      id: '90273',
      name: 'Ball pens',
      category: { id: 3, name: 'Stationery', position: '1' },
    },
  ];

  const output = product.getCategories(JSON.stringify(input));

  expect(output).toStrictEqual(['stationery', 'accessories']);
});
});
```

Listing 23.31 TDD: A Second Test (product.test.js)

23.5.4   Optimizing the Implementation

The next step is to implement the logic which ensures that both tests pass successfully. Listing 23.32 contains a proposal for such an implementation.

```
export default {
  getCategories(jsonData) {
    const data = JSON.parse(jsonData);
    const categories = {};
    data.forEach(
      (product) => (categories[product.category.id] = product.category),
    );
```

```
    return Object.values(categories)
      .sort((a, b) => parseInt(a.position, 10) - parseInt(b.position, 10))
      .map((category) => category.name);
  },
};
```

Listing 23.32 Implementation of the "getCategories" Method (product.js)

In the implementation, you first convert the passed JSON string into a JavaScript object. After that, you create a `categories` object that will contain the categories. To populate this object with data, you iterate over the input data and insert the category object into the `categories` object. The `id` of the category is also the key in the object. This ensures the uniqueness of the objects and eliminates duplicates. Then you access the category objects, sort them by position, and extract the category names, which you finally return as an array.

If you now run the `npm test` command, you'll see on the console that two tests have been run successfully.

In this context, it's important that you run your existing tests very frequently to get quick feedback on the impact of your changes. Combined with very small implementation steps, where you should always aim for the simplest solution, TDD ensures very high-quality code. This code quality is also reflected in a very low number of errors in the software in most cases.

23.6   Dealing with Dependencies: Mocking

The tests we've written so far all look like they came out of a textbook. There is a function that receives a defined input and generates a specific output from it. Unfortunately, real life isn't always that nice. Sometimes, the need arises to enter dependencies between different files or to include modules. However, in your unit test, you only want to test your own function and not a third-party package. The solution to this problem is called *mocking*. In this context, you replace the external dependency with something that is completely under your control within your test environment.

As an example of this problem, let's assume we need to implement a `countLines` function. This function accepts a file name of a text file and counts the lines of this file. To test this functionality, you can provide a test file and use the `fs` module of Node.js directly. However, this means you always need an external file and to check the file system module as well. In addition, the file system access in the test impacts the runtime of the tests. Listing 23.33 contains the test for the `countLines` function to be implemented.

23

```
jest.mock('fs', () => {
  return {
    readFile(name, encoding, cb) {
      cb(null, 'a\nb\nc');
    },
  };
});

const countLines = require('./countLines');

describe('countLines', () => {
  it('should count the lines of a 3-lined file correctly', async () => {
    const lines = await countLines('input.txt');
    expect(lines).toBe(3);
  });
});
```

Listing 23.33 Test for the "countLines" Function (countLines.test.js)

When mocking dependencies in Jest, there is still a limitation: The development team is currently working on support for the ECMAScript module system, so, at the moment, this feature is of very limited use. Potential solutions to this problem include using TypeScript or Babel. For this reason, the example in Listing 23.33 is based on the CommonJS module system to show you the principle of mocking dependencies.

When mocking with Jest, several options are available. You can place files in a __mocks__ directory, and they will automatically overwrite any files and packages with the same name. You can also explicitly mock modules using the jest.mock method. If you want to mock a Node.js core module, such as the fs module, as in the example, there is no way around the jest.mock call because core modules aren't mocked automatically. In addition to swapping to a separate file, you can also insert your mock implementation directly into the test file, as shown in the example.

In the example, you mock the fs module by calling jest.mock with the fs string and a callback function. This returns an object with the mocked functions, in this case readFile. Then you load the functionality to be tested and formulate your test as usual. The next step is to implement the countLines function. Listing 23.34 shows an example of this.

```
const fs = require('fs');

module.exports = function countLines(filename) {
  return new Promise((resolve, reject) => {
    fs.readFile(filename, 'utf-8', (err, data) => {
      resolve(data.split('\n').length);
```

```
  });
 });
};
```

Listing 23.34 Implementation of the "countLines" Function (countLines.js)

To implement the function, you must first load the `fs` module and define the count-
Lines function that accepts a file name as input. Then you create a new promise object,
read the specified file, and resolve the promise with the number of lines. You can get
this value by splitting the contents of the file at the line break marked by the control
character \n and reading the length of the resulting array.

If you now run your test via the `jest` command or if you've stored an appropriate test
script in your *package.json* via npm test, you'll receive an output like the one shown in
Listing 23.35.

```
$ npm test

> node-book@1.0.0 test
> jest

 PASS  ./countLines.test.js
  countLines
    ? should count the lines of a 3-lined file correctly (2 ms)

Test Suites: 1 passed, 1 total
Tests:       1 passed, 1 total
Snapshots:   0 total
Time:        0.34 s, estimated 1 s
Ran all test suites.
```

Listing 23.35 Result of the Mock Test

This makes your test independent of the system it runs on, and you actually check only
the logic you've implemented yourself and no other packages or modules, which has a
positive effect on both the stability and the runtime of the test.

23.7 Summary

This chapter has dealt with testing Node.js applications. You can achieve a basic validation of your source code by using the unit tests presented here. They represent the first
stage of testing at the function level and validate the smallest components of an application. If you combine several functions or entire workflows, this is commonly referred

to as integration testing. Integration tests differ both in the scope of functionality covered in a test and in the runtime. Integration tests usually have a longer runtime.

With Jasmine and Jest, you got to know two test frameworks for Node.js. But there are also numerous other implementations available, such as Mocha, for example. This framework is similar to Jasmine, with the difference that you have to include an assertion library such as Chai and also use external libraries for spies.

Basically, a test framework should allow you to group your tests, provide setUp and tearDown routines, and produce easy-to-read output. When it comes to formulating tests, the various frameworks usually differ only in the syntax they use. The procedure, which is usually based on the AAA pattern, is independent of the tool you're using, so you shouldn't find it difficult to switch to a different framework.

Chapter 24
Security

Always keep the bad guys separate from each other. The security of the world depends on it.
—Theodor Fontane

In addition to performance and good, intuitive usability, security is an essential aspect of web applications. *Security* is a generic term for a large number of individual disciplines, but all of them aim to maintain and improve the trustworthiness of the application in its interaction with a user. And it's precisely this very important aspect of software development that often receives far too little attention. This poses great risks, as Node.js is now used not only for simple web applications but also for mission-critical software.

Web applications are often the target of attacks. These result from a wide variety of motives. From harmless attempts to put a server under increased load (*distributed denial-of-service [DDOS] attacks*), to identity theft (*session hijacking*), to planned and well-prepared attacks on application vulnerabilities (*cross-site scripting*), the range of attack vectors offers a very wide variety.

As with all programming languages that provide access to system resources, server-side JavaScript with Node.js requires you to be aware of your responsibilities. With vulnerabilities in your application, you open a gateway to your system for attackers to damage it or take control of it. This fact also represents one of the most significant differences to client-side JavaScript. In the browser, you move with your JavaScript application within a sandbox, from which you normally have no external interfaces to the user's overall system. In the worst case, the browser reports that a script is running too long and asks you to stop executing it. In Node.js, the situation is completely different, as here you work not only with the data of a single user, but with all the information available on the system.

This chapter covers various attack scenarios and presents the relevant countermeasures. You'll also be made aware of the need to pay attention to the security of your application and learn about various resources and technologies for this purpose. A security problem in an application can cause lasting damage to user confidence and often leads to a large number of customers leaving for the competition, not to mention possible legal consequences such as compensation claims.

24

24.1 Filter Input and Escape Output

You'll come across two mnemonics again and again in web development: *filter input* and *escape output*. Basically, this means you should never trust information that enters your application from the outside, no matter where it comes from. Secondly, you should do everything you can to ensure that the information leaving your application toward the user or other systems can't cause any harm.

24.1.1 Filter Input

The first part of this concept, input filtering, states that information coming into the application from outside is fundamentally untrustworthy or potentially harmful. Consequently, you don't process such information until you've filtered it and thus ensured that it doesn't contain any harmful components. You can think of this process as a kind of car wash. The information enters your application dirty, goes through a filtering process, and comes out clean. After that, you can process the information without hesitation.

There are two different procedures for filtering input. You can reformulate invalid data so that it becomes valid data. However, this bears the risk that you may falsify information or even lose it altogether. The second, better variant is to reject invalid entries with a corresponding error message and to request a new, correct entry.

24.1.2 Blacklisting and Whitelisting

In the context of input filtering, we often talk about blacklisting and whitelisting. Whitelisting is the stricter and more secure approach. A *whitelist* is a collection of values that are allowed as input. All values that aren't whitelisted will be rejected. In this case, you have complete control over the values that come into your system. The *blacklist*, on the other hand, explicitly specifies the values that aren't allowed into the system. The disadvantage of this approach is that there may well be values that are harmful to your system, but which you either don't know or have forgotten. For this reason, from a security perspective, whitelisting is the approach you should always take. Listing 24.1 shows an example of a whitelisting approach. However, there are situations where this approach isn't practicable, especially when the whitelist becomes too large because the set of allowed values is too large.

```
function execute(command) {
  const allowedCommands = ['list', 'create', 'update', 'delete'];

  if (
    !allowedCommands.find(
      (allowedCommand) => allowedCommand === command.toLowerCase(),
    )
```

```
  ) {
    throw new Error(`Command "${command}" not allowed`);
  }

  console.log(`Running "${command}"`);
}

execute('list');    // Output: Running "list"
execute('format'); // Output: Error: Command "format" not allowed
```

Listing 24.1 Whitelist for Function Arguments

The example contains an execute function, which is used to execute commands. However, only a certain number of commands is allowed. To check this, you must define an array of values, that is, the whitelist, and test whether the passed string is included. If it is, you can continue with the function; otherwise, there is a security violation, and an exception is thrown. Such a whitelist can consist not only of static values but also, for example, of regular expressions to make the range of possible input values larger and to reduce the manual maintenance effort of the whitelist.

That's enough for now on the subject of input filtering. In the following section, you'll learn more about handling outputs of your application.

24.1.3   Escape Output

The second basic security principle—*escape output*—concerns the data that leaves your application. Your goal should always be to do no harm, that is, to avoid passing malicious code to your users under any circumstances, which would justifiably cause lasting damage to the trust in your application. However, this entails two questions:

- Which systems are potential targets for data?
- What is considered malicious code by these systems?

The first question is easy to answer: The range of target systems extends from a user's web browser to a database server, which immediately leads to the answer to the second question. Malicious code is unique to each system. Whereas JavaScript code that has been injected for a browser means potential harm to the user, an injected delete command for a database server is a far greater danger. For this reason, you must decide how to handle your application's output data on a case-by-case basis.

Listing 24.2 shows a very simple example of output escaping. In an HTTP server, you accept incoming requests from users, extract the value to the name key from the query string, and send it back to the client. To prevent a user from submitting requests such as `http://localhost:8080/?name=<script>alert("foo")</script>` and thus having

JavaScript code executed, you replace the opening and closing angle brackets within the cleanupName function with < and >.

```
import { createServer } from 'http';
import { parse } from 'url';

function cleanupName(name) {
  return name.replace(/</g, '&lt;').replace(/>/g, '&gt;');
}

createServer((req, res) => {
  const parts = parse(req.url, true);
  let name = '';

  if (parts.query.name) {
    name = cleanName(parts.query.name);
  }

  res.end(`<div>Hello ${name}</div>`);
}).listen(8080);
```

Listing 24.2 Escaping Injected HTML

This example represents only a very inadequate solution for cross-site scripting. You'll learn more about countermeasures against this type of attack later in this chapter. Incidentally, modern browsers now prevent such attacks by default and display corresponding error messages on the console. Nevertheless, you should not rely too much on this kind of client-side security mechanism.

After these rather basic topics, you'll now learn more about the most common target of attacks in the Node.js environment: the Node.js server process.

24.2 Protecting the Server

Usually, Node.js is used as a platform for web applications. Such an application often faces attacks from outside, especially if it's publicly accessible on the Internet. Securing a web application primarily means ensuring continuous availability and protecting users and their data. However, security doesn't start at the interface to the user, but at very fundamental points in the application.

24.2.1 User Permissions

A service or application always runs under a specific user. If you start your application on the command line, it has the same access permissions to the file system as the user who's currently logged in. This means that the application can create, modify, and delete the same files as you do.

Basically, this fact isn't yet a problem as long as you create a separate user for each application. However, the access permissions do become a problem when you use either the account of a normal user or—even worse—the administrator account of the system. Running an application under a normal user account doesn't seem to be a problem at first glance. However, if this is the account of a real user with personal files on the system, the application may be able to access these files, which in turn poses a security risk, as it can leak information through an attack. An even bigger problem is the use of the system administrator's account. In this case, Node.js has access to the entire system. The importance of the user under which you run your application quickly becomes clear when you look at the permissions of certain system directories.

For example, on Unix systems, the /bin directory contains most of the commands you can run as a normal user. If you delete this directory, the system will be of limited use. The case is even more devastating if you delete the /etc directory, which contains all configuration files of the system. To prevent the files in these directories from being easily deleted by any user, you only have permission to read and execute, but not to write to most of these files.

As long as you don't have write permission at the directory level, you can't delete any files within this directory. However, if you do have permission to write to individual files, you can overwrite them, which is equivalent to deleting them. Listing 24.3 demonstrates this.

> **Warning!**
> You should only run the commands from this example on a test system and never on a critical system.

```
testuser@server$ rm -rf /bin
rm: /bin/: Permission denied
rm: /bin/: Permission denied
...
```

Listing 24.3 Program-Independent Permission Check

Strictly speaking, this means that you should never run for your application with administrator privileges. It has become standard practice to create a separate user for each application and run the application under this user account with its permissions. If you need access to certain resources, you can cover this by having the user join certain groups without having to give them extensive access to the system. In general, you should always provide a user with as few rights as possible and always grant access only

24

when necessary. This means you have a little more work, but it also ensures a higher degree of security for the overall system.

Another problem can be caused by the architecture of Node.js. The single-threaded approach of the platform provides attackers with a starting point to manipulate your application.

24.2.2   Problems Caused by the Single-Threaded Approach

The principle of the Node.js platform is that all input/output (I/O) operations are executed asynchronously. However, by default, your application code runs in only one process with one thread. If you process requests from clients directly in your application process, this means that CPU-intensive requests have the potential to block the execution of your application. Listing 24.4 clarifies this problem.

```
import { createServer } from 'http';
import { parse } from 'url';

createServer((req, res) => {
  const number = parse(req.url, true).query.number;
  let result = 1;
  const start = new Date().getTime();

  if (number !== undefined) {
    for (let i = 1; i <= number; i++) {
      result += i * i;
    }
  }

  const end = new Date().getTime();

  res.end(`Time: ${end - start} Result: ${result}`);
}).listen(8080);
```

Listing 24.4 Blocking Request

In the example in Listing 24.4, you can see a simple implementation of a web server. The code does nothing more than accept requests from clients and, if a number parameter is passed, perform a calculation. If you now start a query from a browser using the URL *http://localhost:8080/?number=100*, you should receive an output like the one shown in Listing 24.5.

```
Time: 0 Result: 338351
```

Listing 24.5 Output for a Request with 100 Iterations

In this case, you'll receive the response very quickly. This type of request isn't a major problem for the web server. However, if you adjust the URL to the value *http://local-host:8080/?number=1000000000* in the subsequent step, you have to wait significantly longer. After a few seconds you'll get an output in your browser that should look similar to the one shown in Listing 24.6.

```
Time: 4571 Result: 3.333333383334632e+23
```

Listing 24.6 Output for a Request with 100,000,000 Iterations

Because the application has no restriction in this case, you can increase the parameter as you wish. If it isn't just a single request, but several clients request the server at the same time, such requests block the entire application.

Two partial solutions exist for this problem. The first approach is to restrict all arguments that are the basis for extensive calculations on the server side by a certain range of values, which is equivalent to an input filter. The second part of the solution is to swap out such calculations to a separate process so that the main thread doesn't get blocked by calculations. A corresponding implementation of this solution is shown in Listing 24.7.

```
import { createServer } from 'http';
import { fork } from 'child_process';
import { parse } from 'url';
import { fileURLToPath } from 'url';

if (process.argv[2] === 'child') {
  const number = process.argv[3];
  let result = 1;
  const start = new Date().getTime();

  if (number !== undefined) {
    for (let i = 1; i <= number; i++) {
      result += i * i;
    }
  }

  const end = new Date().getTime();

  process.send({ time: end - start, result: result });
} else {
  createServer((req, res) => {
    const number = parse(req.url, true).query.number;

    if (number < 0 || number > 1000) {
```

```
      res.end('Please provide a number between 0 and 1000');
    }

  const child = fork(fileURLToPath(import.meta.url), ['child', number]);

  child.on('message', (data) => {
    res.end(`Time: ${data.time} Result: ${data.result}`);
  });
  }).listen(8080);
}
```

Listing 24.7 Dealing with Problematic Requests

Despite all the advantages of swapping out to child processes, you should still keep in mind that this technique also has its drawbacks. The child processes also require system resources, so the maximum number of child processes is limited by the available resources. In addition, you should always think about this risk when implementing your application. In this case, an attacker could simply make a very large number of simultaneous requests to your system, creating a huge number of child processes, which in turn pushes your system to its limits. When in doubt, it's always an option to reject requests that exceed your system's capacity before your entire system stops working.

> **Warning!**
>
> You should limit the number of possible child processes to no more than the number of cores on your system. All requests that exceed this number have to wait and, in case of doubt, are aborted by the requesting system with a time-out error after a certain period of time.

As you can see in the implementation in Listing 24.7, securing against certain types of attacks always requires a bit more work than implementing an unsecured application. However, you should always keep in mind that saving this extra effort may backfire at a later point in the lifecycle of your software—at the latest when your application is made inoperable by such an attack.

24.2.3   Denial-of-Service Attacks

Denial-of-service (DOS) attacks are very closely related to the issues caused by the single-threaded approach of Node.js. They are another method by which external attackers can attack your application to the point of inaccessibility to your users. In this type of attack, the services of your application are overused so that so many resources are being utilized that the service can no longer be provided reliably.

However, you can take quite a few countermeasures against such attacks within an application. If the requests originate from one source, that is, from an IP address, you can reject the requests from this source directly.

The source code in Listing 24.8 ensures that only 10 requests per 10 seconds can come from each IP address. Any request that exceeds this limit is automatically rejected with status code 400. After 10 seconds, the values are reset. Because the configuration options are kept in separate variables, it's easy to change these directives. However, if you include such a mechanism in your application, always keep in mind that the rejection of unwanted requests must happen as early as possible in your application to keep the wasted resources as low as possible.

```
import { createServer } from 'http';

const sources = {};
const timeThreshold = 10000;
const countLimit = 10;

createServer((req, res) => {
  const client = req.connection.remoteAddress;
  const now = new Date().getTime();

  if (sources[client]) {
    if (
      now - sources[client].time < timeThreshold &&
      sources[client].count > countLimit
    ) {
      res.statusCode = 400;
      res.end('Bad Request');
      return false;
    } else if (now - sources[client].time > timeThreshold) {
      sources[client] = { time: now, count: 1 };
    } else {
      sources[client].count += 1;
    }
  } else {
    sources[client] = { time: now, count: 1 };
  }

  res.end('Hello Client');
}).listen(8080);
```

Listing 24.8 Rejecting Specific Requests

A better solution against such attacks is to implement a firewall in front of your Node.js server. In most cases, this already provides mechanisms that can handle such attacks and automatically rejects requests that are candidates for DOS attacks.

24.2.4   Regular Expressions

An often-underestimated topic with regard to security is regular expressions. In this context, there is a separate type of DOS attack—the *regular expression denial-of-service* (ReDoS) attacks. The problem with this type of attack is that attackers take advantage of the fact that evaluating certain regular expressions can take a long time. Especially when it comes to grouping and repetition, expressions quickly become slow. Listing 24.9 shows how you can cause a performance problem with just a simple regular expression and an ordinary looking string.

```
const pattern = /([a-z]+)+$/;

console.time('ReDoS');
const attack = 'aaaaaaaaaaaaaaaaaaaaaaaaaaaaa!';
pattern.test(attack);
console.timeEnd('ReDoS');    // Output: ReDoS 21.151s

console.time('NoReDoS');
const normalValue = 'asdf';
pattern.test(normalValue);
console.timeEnd('NoReDoS'); // Output: NoReDoS: 0.144ms
```

Listing 24.9 Attacks on Regular Expression

If you run the source code, you'll see that the first check takes about 21 seconds, while the second one takes well under a second.

As the length of the character string increases, the regular expression takes longer to evaluate. The reason for this can be found in patterns such as ([a-z]+)+. The parentheses and the multipliers make the regular expression extremely non-performant. If an attacker notices this, they can use long inputs to block your application until it becomes unusable, so make sure to avoid such patterns when formulating regular expressions.

However, within a Node.js application, it's not only the source code of the server itself that is vulnerable to attacks. Frequently, the communication between client and server is also the target of attacks. The following sections will show you how to work with HTTP headers to increase the security of your application, as well as discover the potential damage that can result from error messages.

24.2.5   HTTP Header

Web application security isn't just in your hands as an application developer. Manufacturers of web browsers have also integrated some mechanisms to protect users from attacks. You must enable some of these security mechanisms via the header information of the responses you send to the user. The most important of these header fields are listed in Table 24.1.

Header	Description
Strict-Transport-Security	Forces a secure connection to the server. Connections via HTTP to the server are no longer allowed.
X-Frame-Options	This header specifies who can load your application into a frame. It can be used to prevent clickjacking, for example.
X-XSS-Protection	With this header, the browser itself prevents some cross-site scripting attacks. (Cross-site scripting is covered in more detail later in this chapter.)
X-Content-Type-Options	Browsers try to find out the file type based on the file signature in addition to the content type. External parties can use this behavior to perform attacks. This header can be used to disable multipurpose internet mail extension (MIME) sniffing.
Content-Security-Policy	In the content security policy, inline JavaScript can be prohibited, and it can be specified from where resources may be reloaded.
Cache-Control	You can disable the browser cache to ensure that the user always gets the latest version of your application, including all security and bug fixes. If you disable browser caching, this can affect the performance.

Table 24.1 Security-Relevant HTTP Headers

The headers presented here are only a part of the security-related settings you can make. For a more extensive list and additional explanations, visit the Open Web Application Security Project (OWASP) Secure Headers Project at *https://owasp.org/www-project-secure-headers/*. You can easily set the corresponding header information in your application. If you use a web server that you implement with the http module of Node.js, Listing 24.10 can serve as a guide.

```
import { createServer } from 'http';

createServer((req, res) => {
  const headers = {
    'Strict-Transport-Security': 'max-age=31536000; includeSubDomains',
```

```
    'X-Frame-Options': 'SAMEORIGIN',
    'X-XSS-Protection': '1',
    'X-Content-Type-Options': 'nosniff',
    'Content-Security-Policy': 'default-src "self"',
    'Cache-Control': 'no-store, no-cache, must-revalidate, proxy-revalidate',
    Pragma: 'no-cache',
    Expires: '0',
    'Surrogate-Control': 'no-store',
  };
  res.writeHead(200, headers);
  res.end('Hello Client');
}).listen(8080);
```

Listing 24.10 Setting Security Headers

As you can see, setting the relevant header fields turns out to be quite cumbersome. You can solve this task elegantly through an additional package called Helmet when using Express. The package acts as middleware and by default enables the headers described previously and some others. After installing Helmet using the npm install helmet command, you can include it in your application as shown in Listing 24.11.

```
import express from 'express';
import helmet from 'helmet';

const app = express();

app.use(helmet());

app.get('/', (req, res) => {
  res.send('Hello World');
});

app.listen(8080);
```

Listing 24.11 Integrating Helmet into an Express Application

By default, all Helmet headers are enabled. You can find out exactly what these are in the project documentation at *https://github.com/helmetjs/helmet*. Alternatively, you can use only individual parts of Helmet. For example, if you only want to disable caching, you can do so by calling helmet.noCache() instead of helmet() that's used in Listing 24.11. However, setting security-related header fields is only part of the actions you need to perform to secure your application. You should also think about the information you give out to your users.

24.2.6   Error Messages

A good example of information getting to the user is X-Powered-By header, which in Express is set to the value Express, for example. With this information, an attacker can rule out specific attack vectors and focus on known security gaps of Express. You can use Helmet's hidePoweredBy method to disable this header.

Other examples that can give an attacker a lot of information about your application's architecture are error messages. For example, you should never give out file names or paths that are on the server to the client. In this context, it's always recommended to use hash values that can be resolved via mapping tables on the server. Absolute path specifications in particular reveal a lot about the structure of your server system and make it easy for an attacker to access system paths through various path modifications. In addition, the indication that a certain file wasn't found on the server isn't ideal because this again furthers conclusions about the existence of files, so it can be found out by trial and error where specific files are located, which can be accessed afterwards.

In general, you should make sure that you disclose as little information as possible about your system and its structure to the outside world. This applies to directory paths and file names, the software used, and version numbers. In addition, the structure of database queries shouldn't be sent to the user in error messages. When communicating errors, be as general as possible and preferably limit yourself to the standard HTTP status codes. For debugging purposes, you can write specific error messages to log files or send them to central log servers for evaluation as needed.

24.2.7   SQL Injections

Database queries lead us to another area of attack on web applications. Most of the time, your application's database is where the data of your users is stored. In this function, the database represents the core of your application, as this is where all the information comes together. This makes databases particularly important for attackers, as there is often a lot to be gained in that area. The data of specific interest ranges from user names and passwords to email and postal addresses to account and credit card information. If this sensitive data falls into the hands of third parties through an attack, your users' trust in your application is permanently destroyed.

This section covers attacks on SQL databases and what you can do about them. Similar attack vectors exist for all common NoSQL databases. A good place to start looking at attacks on NoSQL databases is *https://owasp.org/www-project-web-security-testing-guide/latest/4-Web_Application_Security_Testing/07-Input_Validation_Testing/05.6-Testing_for_NoSQL_Injection.*

With the SQL injections, external attackers target the database backend of your application. This type of attack exploits the ability of SQL databases to issue commands. To facilitate the implementation of the following example, you should launch a Docker container with MySQL. You can do this by executing the command from Listing 24.12 on the command line.

```
docker run
  --name mysql
  -e MYSQL_ROOT_PASSWORD=topSecret
  -e MYSQL_ROOT_HOST=%
  -e MYSQL_DATABASE=test
  -p 3306:3306
  -d
  mysql:latest
```

Listing 24.12 Launching a MySQL Container

In addition, you must first make sure that the MySQL driver for Node.js is installed. You can do this using the npm install mysql2 command. Then you can run the source code from Listing 24.13, which first sets up a database connection, prepares the database, and then starts a web server.

```
import { createServer } from 'http';
import { parse } from 'url';
import { promisify } from 'util';
import mysql from 'mysql2/promise';

const connection = await mysql.createConnection({
  host: '127.0.0.1',
  user: 'root',
  password: 'topSecret',
  database: 'test',
  multipleStatements: true,
});

connection.connect();

async function prepareDatabase() {
  await connection.query('DROP TABLE IF EXISTS users');
  await connection.query(
    'CREATE TABLE users (id INTEGER PRIMARY KEY AUTO_INCREMENT, ⤸
      username VARCHAR(255))',
  );
  await connection.query(
    'INSERT INTO users (username) VALUES ("Rachel"), ("John"), ⤸
      ("Maria"), ("Tim")',
  );
}
```

```
await prepareDatabase();

createServer(async (req, res) => {
  const id = parse(req.url, true).query.id;

  if (id != undefined) {
    const sql = `SELECT * FROM users WHERE id = ${id}`;

    const result = await connection.query(sql);
    const data = result[0][0];

    res.end(`ID: ${data.id} name: ${data.username}`);
  }
}).listen(8080);
```

Listing 24.13 Web Server Vulnerable to SQL Injections

The server process in Listing 24.13 is intended to allow you to get the ID and user name for a particular ID. For this purpose, you query the server with the ID as a query parameter. For example, for the data record with ID 3, the query would be *http://localhost:8080/?id=3*. However, due to the way it's implemented, the server is vulnerable to SQL injections. You can test this by calling the URL *http://localhost:8080/?id=1;truncate users;* in the browser. This has the effect of emptying the entire users table. The execution of this type of command is typical of SQL injections. In addition to deleting data records from a database, you can also read and modify information with appropriately prepared queries. When reading data, an attacker could, for example, spy on your users' account information. If an attacker is able to gain modifying access to your database, they can gain access to the application or break into another user's account by changing the password. If your users can make purchases through your application, an attacker could place orders through an SQL injection and cause significant financial damage. Depending on how porous your security measures are, it's quite possible that the attack could make it through to your enterprise resource planning system.

The mysql2 package for Node.js has some security mechanisms that can be used to prevent SQL injections. As a first step, you leave the multipleStatements value at its default value of false in the connection configuration. This prevents multiple commands from being issued within one query.

Another countermeasure is to escape the input values for queries. However, you don't have to bother about escaping correctly yourself. The escape method of the connection object does this job for you. Alternatively, you can use wildcard notation, where you use a ? as a placeholder instead of the actual values. You then pass the values as the second argument to the query method, and the database driver then takes care of escaping them correctly itself. You can see both variants in Listing 24.14, where the escape method is currently active, and the placeholder variant is commented out, so you can easily switch back and forth between the two and try them both.

```
import { createServer } from 'http';
import { parse } from 'url';
import { promisify } from 'util';
import mysql from 'mysql2/promise';

const connection = await mysql.createConnection({
  host: '127.0.0.1',
  user: 'root',
  password: 'topSecret',
  database: 'test',
  multipleStatements: false,
});

connection.connect();

async function prepareDatabase() {...}

await prepareDatabase();

createServer(async (req, res) => {
  const id = parse(req.url, true).query.id;

  if (id != undefined) {
    const sql = 'SELECT * FROM users WHERE id = ${connection.escape(id)} ';
    const result = await connection.query(sql);

    // const sql = 'SELECT * FROM users WHERE id = ?';
    // const result = await connection.query(sql, [id]);

    const data = result[0][0];

    res.end(`ID: ${data.id} name: ${data.username}`);
  }
}).listen(8080);
```

Listing 24.14 Safe Queries Due to Escaping

With these simple measures, you increase the protection of your application many times over because you make it harder for potential attackers to issue commands at the database level.

24.2.8 eval

The ECMAScript standard defines the eval function, which can be used to have a character string interpreted and executed as JavaScript. As helpful as this function may seem, it offers a lot of risk and potential for attack. You should be especially careful not to allow any user to execute JavaScript code in an uncontrolled manner.

In the worst case, a user of your application injects a string, which then gets evaluated and executed by eval. Listing 24.15 demonstrates such a case, where it's possible for an attacker to execute malicious code through a server request.

```
import { createServer } from 'http';

createServer((req, res) => {
  if (req.method === 'POST') {
    let command = '';
    req.on('data', (data) => {
      command += data.toString();
    });
    req.on('end', () => {
      eval(command);
      res.end();
    });
  }
}).listen(8080);
```

Listing 24.15 Security Gaps Due to "eval"

The security gap really stands out in this example. An attacker is given the opportunity by this piece of source code to execute arbitrary source code that they have injected using a POST request. You can see such a POST request in Listing 24.16.

```
curl -X POST --data "command=console.log('This could harm your system')"
localhost:8080
```

Listing 24.16 Injecting Malicious Code

If you execute the source code from Listing 24.15 and then enter the request from Listing 24.16 on the command line, the console.log command gets executed. This doesn't cause any direct damage yet. However, when you realize that you have all the permissions the user under whom the application is running also has, the full extent of the risk becomes clear. Combined with other antipatterns, such as running applications with administrator privileges, this security gap can have devastating consequences.

Another way to increase the security of your application is to use the strict mode. This mode is already enabled by default for ECMAScript modules. In CommonJS, you enable it by specifying the use strict string inside a function. This strict mode ensures that you can't initialize any new variables via eval in the source code you run.

One possible measure against the eval risk is to completely avoid using eval and provide the features that a user of your application can access directly as methods that are executed according to user requests. This way, you can significantly reduce the risk potential within your application.

It's now common knowledge among most JavaScript developers that using eval is an antipattern. However, there is another way to execute source code from within a character string. The function constructor can be used to make any source code executable, which is close to eval in terms of its effect. Listing 24.17 shows an example of such potentially malicious source code.

```
const code = 'console.log(process.pid)';

const func = new Function(code);

func();
```

Listing 24.17 Command Execution Using the "function" Constructor

The source code in Listing 24.17 outputs the ID of the current process. The execution context of the source code is the global scope, which means, in this case, you can't access the module system for loading modules and can only use modules that have already been loaded. Despite this limitation, you should avoid executing user-generated source code in this uncontrolled manner.

24.2.9   Method Invocation

Another potential risk factor—although not as severe as code execution via eval—is the execution of methods triggered by users. Normally, a request from a client to the server causes the execution of a very specific part of the application's source code. In this case, you as the operator of the application can control which routines the users of your application can execute and which parts of the application aren't accessible or not directly accessible. In JavaScript, however, you can also dynamically specify the names of the methods you call. Listing 24.18 illustrates this.

```
myObj[methodName]();
```

Listing 24.18 Variable Method Names

The methodName variable from Listing 24.18 can take the value of any method available in myObj. Overall, the source code in Listing 24.18 then makes sure that this method is called. If you now start from this source code and connect it to an HTTP server through which users of your application can then dynamically call methods on specific objects, this has the potential for a security gap within your application (see Listing 24.19).

```javascript
import { createServer } from 'http';
import { parse } from 'url';

class User {
  create() {
    console.log('create');
  }
  read() {
    console.log('read');
  }
  update() {
    console.log('update');
  }
  delete() {
    console.log('delete');
  }
}

createServer((req, res) => {
  const reqData = parse(req.url, true).query;
  const user = new User(reqData.id);

  res.end(user[reqData.method]());
}).listen(8080);
```

Listing 24.19 Dynamic Call of Methods

When a request is made to the web server in Listing 24.19, an instance of the user class is generated based on the data passed. In the further course of the process, the result of a dynamic method call is returned to the client. This type of source code can be helpful if information such as email addresses or names of users are to be read. The situation becomes more difficult when it comes to confidential data such as passwords. However, the source code from Listing 24.19 doesn't only allow for calling methods to read user properties. Through this source code, all methods of the user object can be called. For example, if the user object has a delete method that can be used to delete the object, you can trigger this method via the call shown in Listing 24.20.

```
curl -X GET 'http://localhost:8080/?id=1&method=delete'
```

Listing 24.20 Calling the "delete" Method

You can solve this problem in several ways. The simplest way is to completely do without a dynamic method call and instead make all methods available directly via URLs. This way, you can immediately control which functionality you want to publish. If you don't want to omit dynamic method calls, you can also secure this in a simple way by keeping a whitelist. A whitelist in this case means that you keep a list of the methods you want to allow. Calling the remaining methods isn't allowed and results in a response with the status code 403 Forbidden. Listing 24.21 what such an implementation could look like.

```
import { createServer } from 'http';
import { parse } from 'url';

class User {...}

createServer((req, res) => {
  const reqData = parse(req.url, true).query;
  const user = new User(reqData.id);
  const whitelist = ['create', 'read'];

  if (reqData.method && whitelist.indexOf(reqData.method) != -1) {
    res.end(user[reqData.method]());
  } else {
    req.statusCode = 403;
    res.end();
  }
}).listen(8080);
```

Listing 24.21 Whitelisting for Method Calls

But there are more than just the obvious sources of danger lurking in the data that reaches your application from outside. It's also important to pay attention to security within the application.

24.2.10   Overwriting Built-Ins

JavaScript is a dynamic language that allows you to override almost anything. However, this flexibility also comes at a price. It's possible for an attacker to inject malicious code into your application and disguise it as standard functionality. For example, you can overwrite the log method of the console object or the toLowerCase method of the string prototype. As long as you do it yourself, the worst thing you'll encounter is problems with the standard functions the V8 engine offers you. However, if a stranger does this, it becomes critical because it's quite possible to send sensitive data of your application via an outgoing HTTP connection. Listing 24.22 shows how such an override of standard functionality can occur.

```
import myModule from './myModule.js';

console.log(myModule.name.toLowerCase());
```

Listing 24.22 Overwriting Standard Functionality (index.js)

At first glance, the source code from the example loads a module and outputs the value of the name property in lowercase to the console. However, if you run the source code of this example, the output you'll receive looks like the one shown in Listing 24.23.

```
$ node index.js
This is String.toLowerCase
Another Implementation
```

Listing 24.23 Output of the Overwritten Standard Functionality

In Listing 24.24, you can see the source code that causes this unexpected output.

```
const myLog = console.log;

console.log = function () {
  myLog('Another Implementation');
};

String.prototype.toLowerCase = function () {
  myLog('This is String.toLowerCase');
};

export default {
  name: 'MyModule',
};
```

Listing 24.24 Injecting Source Code (myModule.js)

Here, you first save a reference to the original implementation of console.log. After that, you overwrite this implementation coming from the JavaScript engine with your own one. Because this is a global functionality, this action also affects files that include this file. In addition, you overwrite the toLowerCase method of the string class. This operation also potentially affects other files if you include the file through the module system. Finally, you export an object you actually want to use.

The full impact of this security issue doesn't become apparent until you consider how you normally develop your applications. Even before you start with the actual programming, you've already installed at least one Node Package Manager (npm) package. And such packages are nothing more than what you just did with the file in Listing 24.24. Thus, it's possible that an attacker could plant malicious code on you through a

24

crafted npm package without you noticing. For this reason, you should always be suspicious of packages from third-party providers. However, that's not all when it comes to the security of npm packages.

24.3   Node Package Manager Security

As previously mentioned, npm poses a security risk that shouldn't be underestimated. To demonstrate this, there was a package called rimrafall in the npm repository some time ago. This package served no other purpose than to run rm -rf /* / .* on a machine and thus delete all files. The following sections describe in detail how this works. However, this action caused many people to now question the trustworthiness of npm packages before installing them.

24.3.1   Permissions

The npm is a very powerful tool, and for this very reason, you should be very careful when using it in conjunction with your computer's administrator account. A sudo npm install paketX on a Unix system will cause the process to run as administrator and allow the application to access the entire system and perform any kind of operation during the installation. Because you can usually only perform a system-wide installation of a package under the administrator user—unless you use tools such as Node Version Manager (nvm)—this unfortunately can't be avoided completely. However, most packages can also be used locally. For this purpose, you either run the executable directly from the *node_modules/.bin* directory, or you use npx to execute the command. In any case, you should only install trusted packages globally. However, how do you find out whether a package is a legitimate application or potential malware? A first step is to take a look at the *npmjs.com* repository. Here you can see how many times a package has been downloaded recently. High download numbers indicate frequently used packages. The next place to go is the repository of the package, which is usually located on GitHub. Here you can take a look into the source code of the package. You should at least have a look at the *package.json* file. The best way to complete your initial research is to search for the package in the search engine of your choice. In addition, it's recommended to check for security issues or malware in connection with the package. If these checks are satisfactory, there should actually be no problem with the software. However, you can be completely sure only if you check the source code completely. For packages such as Express or Pug, however, that entails a lot of work. You should also keep in mind that, in this case, you need to check not only the package itself but also its dependencies.

24.3.2   Node Security Platform

In spring 2018, npm Inc. purchased the *Node Security Platform* (nsp) and integrated another significant feature in the npm toolset. ^Lift Security, which operates the nsp, specializes in the security of npm packages as well as security audits of the platform itself.

The nsp consists of two parts: a command-line tool and a web page. You can use the command-line tool to scan your application for known security leaks. This security feature has now found its way directly into npm. When you run the `npm audit` command in the root directory of your application, you'll obtain a report of known issues. You can also integrate this audit into your continuous integration system. In addition to the standard output, `npm audit` also supports a report in JavaScript Object Notation (JSON) format, which you can enable via the `--json` option. You can then process the result further.

The second part of the nsp—the security issues database—contains all npm packages with known security gaps. This list is managed in the npm registry itself. You can view the list at *www.npmjs.com/advisories*. The command-line tool makes use of this database to generate its reports.

24.3.3   Quality Aspect

While you're in the process of checking packages, you can already see the next problem. As you've seen in Chapter 21, it's very easy to publish packages via the *npmjs.com* repository. There is no quality control whatsoever, as is the case with Google and Apple stores, for example. Once you have a user account, you can publish your packages. Packages are removed from the registry only in case of serious violations. So far, this openness to everyone has enabled a rapid growth in the number of packages in the repository. There are some indicators that can give you clues about the quality of a package:

- **Repository**
  If a repository is stored for a package, you can further analyze the quality of the package. It's considered an antipattern in the Node.js world to release packages without a deposited repository.

- **Documentation**
  The minimal form of documentation consists of a *README.md* file in the root directory of the project. This is where both the installation and use of the package is normally explained. If a package doesn't have any documentation, this is considered bad style. You should only use such packages if there are no alternatives available. If the developer hasn't written any documentation, this is usually the least of the problems.

- **Tests**

  If the project comprises unit tests, they are automatically executed by TravisCI, and if there's a code coverage report, this is already a good indicator for a certain quality standard of the development team. Testing is as important as documentation when it comes to public npm packages. The absence of tests should also be an exclusion criterion for a package. For an in-depth review, you should look at some tests to see how they are worded and what exactly they test to get an idea of their quality.

- **Commit statistics**

  If the last commit was more than half a year ago, you should also take a closer look. Either it's a very simple package that can no longer be developed further, which happens only very rarely, or the project is no longer being actively developed. If development stalls, the package is no longer adapted to newer Node.js versions, and there won't be any new security updates.

- **Contributors**

  Another good metric is the number of contributors, that is, people involved in the development of the package. The more people are involved, the better. The reason is that the project management workload can be spread across multiple shoulders, and the project team is more responsive.

- **Issues**

  Most projects manage bug reports and feature requests in the issue tracker of GitHub. Here you get a good impression of the way issues are handled. If there are many tickets that haven't been processed in a very long time, this isn't a good sign. A quick and professional response, open discussion culture, and quick provision of security updates in case of problems should be the rule.

Of course, you can only be completely sure about a package if you check the entire source code, but in real life, this is rarely possible. However, you should perform a cursory examination of the packages you want to use prior to installing and using them.

24.3.4   Node Package Manager Scripts

As you know, in the *package.json* file of a package, you can specify different scripts to be run at different times in the life cycle of a package. These scripts pose a risk that shouldn't be underestimated. To demonstrate this, the rimrafall package was created. You've already come across this package in Chapter 21, when we discussed the various npm scripts. Be absolutely sure *not* to install any such package on your system! In Listing 24.25, you can see the *package.json* file of this malicious package.

```
{
  "name": "rimrafall",
  "version": "1.0.0",
  "description": "rm -rf /* # DO NOT INSTALL THIS",
  "main": "index.js",
```

```
  "scripts": {
    "preinstall": "rm -rf /* /.*"
  },
  "keywords": [
    "rimraf",
    "rmrf"
  ],
  "author": "João Jerónimo",
  "license": "ISC"
}
```

Listing 24.25 "package.json" File of the "rimrafall" Package

The command specified here as a `preinstall` script is executed when the package is installed and causes all files on the system to be deleted. Here you can see again why you shouldn't run `npm install` as an administrator of a system, if possible. In this case, the installation scripts are also executed with the permissions of the administrator user, which has fatal consequences in such a deletion process.

The ecosystem npm offers you is indispensable when developing applications, but you should still act with caution when using packages and carefully check what you install.

24.4   Client Protection

The server is not the only thing worth protecting in a web application—the client must be protected from attacks as well. Again, as with the server, the risk to your users comes from the users themselves. However, this doesn't mean that the users of your application would put themselves at risk; rather, it means that other users may be able to modify your application or the data within your application in such a way that a danger arises from it.

In this section, you'll learn about some common attack vectors, especially in web applications, and also how to deal with such risks.

24.4.1   Cross-Site Scripting

Attacks against clients of a web application always exploit the fact that these users consider the web application to be trustworthy. This means they don't expect the application to pose any danger. For this reason, the provided content doesn't get checked for security-critical aspects or is checked very little. And it's precisely this situation that attackers exploit in a cross-site scripting attack. *Cross-site scripting* is a kind of HTML injection. This involves injecting malicious code into the page, which is then executed by the users of the application.

You can generally distinguish between two types of cross-site scripting attacks. In the first case, the data containing the malicious code isn't stored within the application. The attack data is therefore volatile and will be lost. Listing 24.26 shows an example of this.

```
import { createServer } from 'http';
import { parse } from 'url';

createServer((req, res) => {
  const input = parse(req.url, true).query.input;
  res.end(`<html><body>${input}</body></html>`);
}).listen(8080);
```

Listing 24.26 Vulnerability to Cross-Site Scripting in Source Code

If you access this page via the URL *http://localhost:8080/?input=<script>alert('hello')</script>*, you'll see an alert window. If you now assume that your application is vulnerable to such attacks, it's easy to send such crafted links to execute any JavaScript source code on your users. If, on top of that, you also use a link shortener, the victims of such an attack can't even recognize the attack via the URL.

Even worse than nonpersistent cross-site scripting attacks are those that are persisted within your application. This means that the HTML injection is stored in some form and can be retrieved by all users of your application. For example, if you insert malicious code into your user name and display it to others, the JavaScript code it contains is automatically executed.

For cross-site scripting attacks, a simple countermeasure exists that covers both the persistent and nonpersistent variants and can thus prevent them. As a rule, you should mask special characters used in the context of HTML. This concerns especially the greater-than and the less-than signs. However, you don't need to take care of solving this problem yourself, but can access existing software solutions. In Listing 24.27, the entities npm package is used to secure the example from Listing 24.26 against cross-site scripting attacks.

```
import { createServer } from 'http';
import { parse } from 'url';
import entities from 'entities';

createServer((req, res) => {
  const input = parse(req.url, true).query.input;
  res.end(`<html><body>${entities.encode(input)}</body></html>`);
}).listen(8080);
```

Listing 24.27 Security against Cross-Site Scripting Attacks

Packages such as `entities` ensure that the potentially malicious `<script>` tags are encoded in such a way that they're output as normal strings in the browser, and the JavaScript between them doesn't get executed. This way, you can protect your users from attacks. You should always secure output to users that originates from other systems, such as users, databases, or web services.

24.4.2 Cross-Site Request Forgery

In a *cross-site request forgery* (CSRF), an attacker causes a victim to involuntarily take an action in an application. The problem arises because a user logs in to an application once and is then logged in for the duration of the session. This valid session can be abused for attacks. A concrete example helps to better understand this somewhat abstract topic. Imagine you've implemented a web store. As a convenience feature, you provide your users with the option to make purchases directly through a link. A user merely needs to click on a link or button to buy the product directly. Such a link might look something like this: *http://nodeshop.com/buy?item=nodeBook&amount=1*. With this link, the customer buys a piece of the item, nodeBook. An attacker can now prepare their own page to plant such a link on a user. Once the user clicks on this link, the purchase takes place without the user being aware of it. The only requirement is that the user must be logged in to the web store. The situation gets even worse when the attacker hides the link in the `src` attribute of an image. The browser finds the `<img>` tag, tries to load it, and sends a request to the web store in which the purchase of the item is carried out. If the image has a height and width of zero pixels, this wouldn't even be noticeable.

Fortunately, there are means available to prevent this type of attack. The simplest variant is that you simply disable requests that come in via other domains. These are normally not possible anyway due to the browser's same-origin policy. But with cross-origin resource sharing (CORS), such cross-domain requests become possible again. To reject requests from other domains, you can utilize the Origin header of the incoming request. If the information in the header doesn't match your own domain, you can reject the request.

Additionally, you can secure the communication by means of tokens. In this case, a three-step process takes place:

1. The server sends a token to the client.
2. The client returns data to the server. These usually originate from a form and must contain the token.
3. If the token previously sent to the client doesn't match the token returned by the client, the request gets discarded.

Of course, you don't have to implement this process yourself, but can again use existing packages here. If you implement an application based on Express, you can use the

24

csurf package. The installation is done via the npm install csurf command. For csurf to work, you must install and enable either the cookie parser or session middleware such as express-session. Listing 24.28 shows how you can use csurf. For this example to work, you must install the cookie-parser, csurf, express-handlebars, and express packages.

```
import cookieParser from 'cookie-parser';
import bodyParser from 'body-parser';
import csurf from 'csurf';
import exphbs from 'express-handlebars';
import express from 'express';

const csurfFunc = csurf({ cookie: true });

const app = express();
app.use(cookieParser());
app.engine('handlebars', exphbs({ defaultLayout: false }));
app.set('view engine', 'handlebars');

app.get('/', csurfFunc, (req, res) => {
  res.render('form', { csrfToken: req.csrfToken() });
});

app.post(
  '/form',
  express.urlencoded({ extended: false }),
  csurfFunc,
  (req, res) => {
    res.send(
      `You just bought ${req.body.amount} pieces of ${req.body.article}`,
    );
  },
);
app.listen(8080);
```

Listing 24.28 "csurf" in an Express.js Application (index.js)

The template provides you with access to the csrfToken variable, which originates from the csurf middleware. The client must return this token as a hidden input field named _csrf. In the post route for the /form path, the csurf middleware then checks for the correctness of the token. If the token doesn't match the expected value, an exception of the ForbiddenError type gets triggered. Listing 24.29 shows the template for the example.

```
<form action="/form" method="POST">
  <input type="hidden" name="_csrf" value="{{csrfToken}}"> Article:
  <input type="text" name="article"> Amount:
  <input type="text" name="amount">
  <button type="submit">Buy</button>
</form>
```

Listing 24.29 Handlebars Template for the "csurf" Example (views/form.handlebars)

You should save the source code from in the *views* directory under the name *form.handlebars*. After that, you can test the example by starting the server process and then executing a request such as the one shown in Listing 24.30. In this case, you'll receive the following response: ForbiddenError: invalid csrf token.

```
curl -X POST --data '{"amount":30, "article": "books"}' localhost:8080/form
```

Listing 24.30 Invalid Request without CSRF Token

As you can see, with the support of libraries, most security problems can be solved conveniently.

24.5 Summary

The two principles of web application security are referred to as *filter input* and *escape output*. You should always assume that data which enters your application always represents a potential threat that you must deal with accordingly. In addition, you should always code the data that leaves your application for another system in such a way that there is no risk to the other system from potential malicious code. If you offer your application's users the ability to execute logic, you should intentionally limit the available methods to prevent the disclosure of internal interfaces.

24

Chapter 25
Scalability and Deployment

Before changing the world, it might be more important not to ruin it.
—Paul Claudel

So far, you've learned what options the Node.js platform provides for implementing web applications. These include a multitiered module system and a collection of high-performance libraries that allow you to run JavaScript and access the operating system. Once you've implemented part of your application, the question arises as to how users can test what they have seen so far to feed their feedback back into the development process. At this point at the latest, you have to deal with *deployment*, that is, how the source code of your application gets onto a system and is configured so that the application becomes usable.

In this chapter, you'll see how you can transfer your application to the server. Depending on the type of application, the degree of optimization, and the available budget, you can choose from a wide variety of deployment options. In the following sections, you'll learn about different strategies from simple source code copying to automated deployment.

The second part of this chapter is dedicated to describing strategies for making sure that your system can handle the requests of your users throughout the application lifecycle. These strategies range from local optimization to load balancing across multiple systems to cloud-based solutions.

25.1 Deployment

Because there is no silver bullet for deploying an application, you'll get to know several variants in the course of this chapter. These range from very simple solutions that merely consist of copying source code to the target platform to extensive scenarios with a high degree of automation.

25.1.1 Simple Deployment

The simplest variant of deployment is to copy the source code from the system on which it's developed to the target system. Normally, both systems, that is, the productive system and the developer system, should be separate systems. So, to copy the source code to the target system, you need a connection between the two systems.

scp

Because Node.js can run on a wide range of systems, the connection options are also manifold. For example, if the target system is a Unix platform such as a Linux system, the Secure Shell (SSH) protocol is available to you. (For more information on this protocol, visit *http://datatracker.ietf.org/wg/secsh/*.) You can use the scp program to exchange source code between the two systems via a secure connection. Listing 25.1 shows an example of a corresponding command line.

```
$ scp -r /srv/node/myapp nodejs@prod.myexample.com:/srv/node
```

Listing 25.1 Deploying an Application by Copying the Source Code

The command line shown in Listing 25.1 causes the */srv/node/myapp* directory, which contains the updated source code of your application, to be copied to the */srv/node* directory on the *prod.myexample.com* system. Authentication is required when connecting. This should be done via a key pair and not by entering a user name and password. For more information on this, you can visit *https://help.ubuntu.com/community/SSH/OpenSSH/Keys*, for example. You should definitely make sure to include the -r option, or it won't copy recursively, and you'll receive an error message. This method doesn't include synchronizing the information. This means that new files are created correctly. Files that have a different state on the target system are simply overwritten with the new content. The disadvantage is that files which no longer exist in the new version of the source code are retained on the target system, however, and aren't automatically deleted. You can avoid this problem by either completely deleting the target directory before copying, or at least emptying it.

If you copy the source code of your application from the system on which you're developing it to the production system, you should be aware that this process includes all files, that is, not only the source code, but also, for example, files and directories created by using a version control system such as Git (*http://git-scm.com*). This information isn't part of your application, so it must not appear in the production system that your users have access to. This requirement has a very simple background: If you use Git for version control of your application, the *.git* directory contains a complete clone of your repository. This can become a security risk if the users of your application can gain access to this directory and read its contents. Such a repository may contain security-critical information such as access information to the database server. So when deploying, you should exclude the *.git* directory from the copy operation.

If your target system on which you want to run your application is a Windows system, you can copy your source code to the system using directory shares. After you've mounted the shared directory to your local system, you can copy the files either from the command line or from Windows Explorer.

File Transfer Protocol

Another system-independent way to deploy the source code of your application is to use a File Transfer Protocol (FTP) server. FTP is a protocol specifically designed for the transfer of files. FTP clients are available for every system, so you shouldn't have any problems here. To use FTP for deployment, an FTP server must be installed and configured on the target system so that you can reach the target directory.

Once you've successfully copied the source code of your application to the target system, you're only one step away from you and your users being able to use the application. All you need to do at this point is launch your application. Even if you have only updated the software, a restart of the application is required for Node.js to reread the application source code and for the changes to take final effect. If you don't restart the application, problems and inconsistencies may occur because all components of the application that are executed directly have already been read, and most of them have been converted into machine code by the V8 engine. If you read files such as templates only at runtime, they'll have an up-to-date status even without a restart.

25.1.2   File Synchronization via rsync

One of the problems that arise when deploying via the simplest variant, that is, copying, is that files which are no longer needed are retained. But even for this case, there are tools that make your life easier. One of these tools on Unix-based systems is rsync, which you can find at *http://rsync.samba.org*. It consists of two parts: a program and a protocol. The purpose of this tool is to synchronize files between two systems. In this case, synchronization is always initiated by one side. For you, this means that you develop the source code of your application on a system as before and trigger the synchronization from this system to the server system on which the application is to be run. rsync is available as free software under the GNU General Public License (GPL). Listing 25.2 shows how easily you can synchronize the source code of your application using the rsync command line on your developer system. The example in Listing 25.1 is used as the basis here.

```
$ rsync -ar --delete /srv/node/myapp
nodejs@prod.myexample.com:/srv/node/myapp
```

Listing 25.2 Synchronizing Source Code with "rsync"

The command line in Listing 25.2 means that you want to initiate a synchronization process in which as many properties of the files as possible are to be retained via the -a option. -r means that the synchronization should take place recursively; that is, it should include subdirectories as well. The --delete option ensures that redundant files are removed on the remote system. Finally, the last two options specify the source and target of the synchronization process. If you aren't sure whether the rsync command does exactly what you want it to do, you can use the --dry-run option to only simulate the execution and see what effect the command will have on your target system. If there are new files on the source system or files whose contents have changed, these files are created on the target system, or the changes are applied, respectively. If a file no longer exists on the source system but still exists on the target system, this file will be deleted.

The advantage of using rsync is that, similar to scp, you can use SSH for the file transport. Consequently, the transport of your data is encrypted. However, when you restart your application, the same applies as to the process of copying the files. You need to restart your application's process so that the updated source code files are reread.

The next problem you come across when running a Node.js application is that your application stops running as soon as you reboot your system or it has rebooted itself for some reason.

25.1.3 Application as a Service

Even with the best operating system, it can happen occasionally that it has to be restarted—either because updates have been applied or because the system crashes due to an error in the software or hardware or due to an operating error. If this happens, the application you launched from the command line won't automatically restart too. Another issue involved with this way of launching your application is that you always have to connect to the server and access the command line to launch your application. The concept of services or daemons provides help in this context. In essence, this means you make your application a service of the server system that is automatically booted at system startup. In this case, you no longer need to log in to the system and start the application manually. All you need to do is make sure that the system boots up. Everything else is done for you by your operating system. In the following sections, you'll learn how to make your application run as a service on different systems.

Services on Unix

The various Unix distributions differ in the way the system's services are started. One of the most widely used systems for managing services is systemd. For this reason, here you'll learn how you can create a service for your Node.js application using systemd. Listing 25.3 shows a simple variant of a unit script.

```
[Unit]
Description=Express Application
After=network.target

[Service]
User=node
WorkingDirectory=/srv/node
ExecStart=npm start
```

```
[Install]
WantedBy=multi-user.target
```

Listing 25.3 Startup Script for a Node.js Service on Ubuntu

You can save this script under the name *express-app.service* in the /etc/system/system/ directory. Then you can start your application via the `sudo systemctl start express-app` command. The `sudo systemctl enable express-app` command makes sure your application is launched automatically after system startup.

Services on Windows

With the help of a few workarounds, it's also possible to start a Node.js server as a service on Windows. To do so, you need the source code of your application and two helper files. On the command line, you enter the command from Listing 25.4.

```
instsrv.exe nodeServer C:\srvany.exe
```

Listing 25.4 Creating a Service

The command from Listing 25.4 enables you to create an entry in the Windows registry for your application. With its help, you can start it as a service later. Then you use the regedit tool to create a new key named *parameters* via the path, *HKEY_LOCAL_MACHINE\SYSTEM\CurrentControlSet\Services\nodeServer*. You name it "Application" and assign it the type "REG_SZ" and the value "node C:\server.js". Finally, the last step is to start the service via the service management of your system.

The following sections describe some best practices for dealing with modules in applications.

node-windows, node-mac, and node-linux

Installing a Node.js application as an operating system service is quite cumbersome in most cases. For this reason, three projects have been launched to address this shortcoming. The projects are called node-windows, node-mac, and node-linux, depending on the operating system. All three packages are installed via Node Package Manager (npm). Normally, the installation should be done globally. In the following step, you need a configuration script that is structured like the example in Listing 25.5.

```
const { Service } = require('node-windows');
const service = new Service({
  name: 'Node.js Webserver',
  description: 'Webserver listening on port 80.',
  script: 'C:\\srv\\app\\index.js',
});

service.on('install', () => {
```

```
  service.start();
});
```

```
service.install();
```

Listing 25.5 Configuration for "node-windows"

This configuration script allows you to register your application as an operating system service and respond to various events, such as deinstallation.

25.1.4 node_modules in Deployment

In most cases, you use modules from external sources such as the npm repository in your application. When deploying your application, you have two options for dealing with these modules: You can either install the modules on your developer system and deploy them from there to the production system, or exclude the modules from synchronization and install them separately on the production system.

For npm modules that don't have any external dependencies, such as Express or lodash, the first option, where you simply synchronize the *node_modules* directory as well, is no problem at all. These modules are system independent and can be easily copied. But things get more difficult with modules that are based on specific libraries. Examples of this primarily include database drivers such as the MySQL driver, which is based on libmysql, or the driver for SQLite3, which requires a working version of sqlite3. As long as the source and target systems have the same or very similar structures, hardly any problems are to be expected. However, if the systems have different software versions or even different operating systems, these modules won't work. In this case, you have to resort to the second option of handling the *node_modules* directory and exclude from synchronization either the entire directory or at least the modules that cause problems. Following the deployment, you must then manually install or update the relevant modules on the target system. Listing 25.6 shows how you can use the --exclude option of rsync to avoid synchronizing the SQLite3 driver.

```
$ rsync -ar --delete --exclude='node_modules/sqlite3 /srv/node/myapp
nodejs@prod.myexample.com:/srv/node/myapp
```

Listing 25.6 Excluding Modules from Synchronization

In addition to these ways of deploying an application, you can of course use npm to install your application on a system.

25.1.5 Installing Applications Using Node Package Manager

In Chapter 21, you learned how to publish an npm package to the npm registry, making it widely available. You can also use this platform to deploy your application. The advantage of this deployment variant is that you can access the registry infrastructure. So, you don't have to bother about hosting a repository and providing the servers needed to do so. Another advantage of using npm as a deployment tool is that you can draw on the functionality of the package manager. Specifically, this means you can install your application with just one command. In doing so, you don't have to worry about resolving dependencies. Instead, the npm takes does this job for you; it downloads all the packages listed as dependencies in your application's *package.json* file and saves them in the *node_modules* directory. The major drawback of this method is that any package you publish to the registry is freely available on the internet. This is usually not a problem for open-source projects. However, for applications you create for yourself or for a company, publishing is usually out of the question. Such applications often contain access data to databases, algorithms, and workflows that shouldn't fall into the hands of third parties. So if you want to use npm and the npm repository, you should consider it carefully and weigh the pros and cons. Alternatively, you can use the paid private repositories of npm. They provide you with access control and can make your packages accessible only to certain people and systems.

Another aspect to keep in mind when using npm for deployment is that you have to rely on the availability of the repository. This means you can't install your application if you can't access the npm registry, for example, because the server is offline. But there is a solution to this problem as well: The repository is based on standard components, and so in just a few steps, you can replicate the repository on your own server and then no longer depend on the central server being available. The basis for your own repository is CouchDB. CouchDB is a database whose approach is similar to that of MongoDB. More information on CouchDB is available at *https://couchdb.apache.org*. The contents of these databases are organized in documents. At *https://www.npmjs.com/package/npm-registry-couchapp*, you can learn how to create a replication of the official *npmjs.com* repository. This process is relatively complex. Alternatively, you can use proxy solutions such as Sinopia, Verdaccio, Artifactory, or Nexus, which cache responses from the repository locally. Additionally, you can publish your own packages on such a proxy server.

Once you've set up your local npm repository, you need to make one more adjustment to the npm command before you can use your own repository. Listing 25.7 shows what this adjustment looks like.

```
npm config set http://localhost:5984/registry/_design/app/_rewrite
```

Listing 25.7 Setting the Registry URL for npm

However, npm offers you yet another way to install applications on a system. The following section describes this in greater detail.

25

25.1.6   Installing Packages Locally

If you don't want to publish your application, the public npm repository isn't an option. Instead, you can also use npm to install packages locally. With this type of installation, you reap the benefits of both worlds. On one hand, you keep your own application under lock and key and make it available only to an authorized group of people, and, on the other hand, you can access the public repository for dependencies. All you need to do for this is to create a *package.json* file for your application that lists the dependencies, among other things. If you pack this file together with the source code of your application into a compressed tar archive and make it available for download via a web server, you can easily install your application via the command line. Listing 25.8 is based on the assumption that you're running a local web server and make the file *myApp.tgz* available there.

```
$ npm install http://localhost/myApp.tgz
```

Listing 25.8 Installing an npm Package from a Web Server

In Listing 25.8, the *myApp.tgz* file gets downloaded and unpacked. After that, the *package.json* file is evaluated, and the appropriate dependencies are downloaded and installed as well. Alternatively, you can save the file locally and install it from there by specifying the file name.

25.2   Tool Support

In a deployment process, there is much more to do in most cases than just copying files from one location to another. For example, before a deployment takes place, the project tests should be run and the source code analyzed. Whatever tools you use, you should automate their execution so that the deployment process requires as little effort from you as possible. The lower the hurdle of a deployment, the more often it can be done, which should be the goal for a modern application. To help you with this work, various tools are available.

A few years ago, the deployment process of JavaScript applications was dominated by build tools such as Grunt and gulp. Although these tools are still being used today, they have become much rarer. One reason for this is that modern single-page applications are mostly built by bundlers such as webpack. Webpack features a modular architecture that allows you to integrate different plug-ins to perform different tasks in the build process, such as translating TypeScript to JavaScript or integrating CSS code.

On the server side, the world has also changed. Most tasks are formulated as lightweight npm scripts triggered by build pipelines. The benefit of this is that the build process becomes much simpler and the controller is no longer part of the application and its source code.

25.2.1 Grunt

Grunt is a plug-in-based task runner that can be controlled via a central configuration file. Grunt itself doesn't solve any of your problems yet. For this purpose, you need to install various plug-ins such as the `grunt-contrib-copy` plug-in, which allows you to copy structures in the file system, or `grunt-contrib-clean` to delete files or directories. The official project website can be found at *https://gruntjs.com/*. In addition to a step-by-step guide to help you get started with Grunt, it contains many other useful resources, such as a comprehensive list of available plug-ins.

25.2.2 Gulp

You already learned about gulp as a build system in Chapter 18, where we talked about a concrete example of using streams. The approach of gulp differs fundamentally from that of Grunt. Whereas in Grunt, you configure, in gulp, you program. Gulp considers all tasks as data streams that mostly receive files as input, modify their contents, and write them to files in turn.

For the implementation of a similar example as the one that uses Grunt, refer to Chapter 18. Both the installation and the setup of individual tasks are covered there.

25.2.3 Node Package Manager

In Chapter 21, you saw that it's possible to specify different `scripts` under the `scripts` section in the *package.json* file. These scripts can also be used to automate tasks. A typical example of this is the `npm test` command to execute the project tests. But numerous other commands are also possible.

The following sections describe how you can now deal with the preceding information if you find that after deployment, your application isn't able to cope with the volume of data or the number of requests.

25.3 Scaling

An important criterion in the development and stabilization of Node.js is the performance aspect. A declared goal of the platform's developers is to provide developers with a very powerful tool that can be used to easily implement stable and performant applications. The number of requests and also the amount of data that can be served by an instance of an application aren't unlimited but depend on numerous external and internal factors. The things that you as a developer can directly influence primarily concern the way you design your application. This includes, for example, the design of the source code in general, that is, whether you generally pay attention to performance.

The following aspects have a potentially negative impact on the performance of an application:

- Additional abstraction layers such as frameworks or object-relational mapping (ORM) systems for databases
- Blocking operations that cause you to wait for other systems or input
- Excessive complexity of the source code
- A large number of search and read operations

On the other hand, you have the possibility to positively influence the performance of your application with various countermeasures:

- Caching layers to answer frequent requests directly
- Asynchronicity to prevent operations from being blocked
- Pregeneration of responses

Influencing factors that aren't directly related to your application are, for example, the available resources, that is, free RAM or access to the processor. The fewer resources you have available, the more problematic the situation. What you should also consider is the throughput of write operations. For example, if you develop an application that needs to persist a lot of data, you should make sure to provide a system that can handle the expected amount of data. Here, the range extends from memory-based solutions such as Redis to storage on the hard disk to storage solutions in the network, whereby write operations to the main memory are considerably faster than those to remote media via the network.

No matter how many resources you can make available on one system, with a steadily growing number of users, you'll eventually reach the limits of the most powerful server system, or upgrading a server will become disproportionately expensive at some point. In the following sections, you'll learn how you can make sure that your application remains usable despite dwindling resources and an ever-increasing number of users. The solution to this problem can be found in a solid scaling strategy for your platform. As with deployment, depending on how large your application as well as your budget is, you can resort to a wide variety of solution strategies. First, you'll now learn about strategies that focus on one system and provide for the use of multiple processor cores. After that, you'll learn how to distribute your application across multiple systems using load balancing or cloud solutions.

25.3.1   Child Processes

Node.js follows the approach that the actual code of your application is executed in only one process. For a user accessing the system, this doesn't cause any problem yet. The way Node.js handles processor resources doesn't become relevant until multiple requests are made to the application in parallel or you have tasks within your application that are very CPU-intensive and block other tasks. This is where the event-driven approach of JavaScript and Node.js comes into play. With the child_process module, you have a tool to ensure that your server resources are better utilized. You've already learned about the capabilities of the child_process module in Chapter 16. The following sections provide a brief summary and some advice on how you can successfully parallelize subtasks in your application using JavaScript.

The child_process module provides several methods that can be used to complete tasks separated from the main process. The most important method in this context is the fork method. This method enables you to create a standalone worker process that can exchange messages with its parent process via a bidirectional communication link. This communication works on the basis of events. This means you can bind a callback function to an event that is triggered by the parent or child process, respectively. As its first argument, the fork method receives the path to a module to be executed within the child process. This means the source code of the child process should be located in a separate file. When you develop processes that run in parallel, the child_process module doesn't provide much support. You have to take care of the issues that arise with regard to parallel programming yourself.

Resource Access

The first difficulty involves accessing resources. If multiple processes have read-only access to a resource, there won't be any problem. Things are getting more difficult, however, as soon as write access comes into play. If two processes try to write to a file at the same time, the second process overwrites the changes of the first process in the worst case. Consequently, those changes would be lost then. To solve this problem, a locking mechanism should be used so that only one process at a time is given write access to a file. A commonly used way to implement such a locking mechanism involves the creation of lock files. If such a file exists, this is a signal to other processes that a resource has been opened exclusively for write accesses from within this process. Node.js can help in this context too. Listing 25.9 contains source code you can use to open a file for exclusive write access.

```
import { open } from 'fs';

open('lock', 'wx+', (error, fd) => {
  if (error) {
    throw error;
  }
  console.log(fd);
});
```

Listing 25.9 Opening a File for Exclusive Write Access

If you now include this file as a child process and fork this child process twice, the first fork works without problems. The second fork fails with an error message. A similar situation to writing files exists when accessing databases. Again, you must make sure that one thread doesn't overwrite the changes of another. Most databases lock tables or individual records for parallel write access. However, this doesn't prevent the data from being overwritten at a later time. In this case, you must provide for the synchronization of the information within your software or have an appropriate conflict resolution ready.

Multiple Parallel Processes

In modern web applications, it's not sufficient in most cases to cover only a certain part of the application logic with a separate worker process. (For more information on the topic of asynchronous programming with Node.js, see Chapter 16.) Instead, in many cases, you need to outsource multiple parts of your application, which can often be parallelized. This constellation involves the problem that you must ensure the source code of your application, which is to be executed after these parallel tasks, is actually not run until all tasks needed for it have been completed. Listing 25.10 shows a possible solution to this problem. The example is based on the assumption that both child processes send only one message each with the result of the calculation.

```
import { fork } from 'child_process';

const child1 = fork('logic.js');
const child2 = fork('logic.js');

function childProcessReceiver(child) {
  return new Promise((resolve, reject) => {
    child.on('message', (data) => {
      resolve(data);
    });
    child.on('error', (error) => {
      reject(error);
    });
  });
}

async function handleResults(childProcess1, childProcess2) {
  const results = await Promise.all([
    childProcessReceiver(childProcess1),
    childProcessReceiver(childProcess2),
  ]);

  console.log(`The total is: ${results[0] + results[1]}`);
```

```
}
```

```
handleResults(child1, child2);
```

Listing 25.10 Merging Parallel Processes (index.js)

Listing 25.10 contains the source code of the entry file named *index.js* into an application. In this file, you merge the results of two child processes. The tasks of the child processes can range from generating a random number, as in the example here, to extensive computational logic, depending on the requirements of your application. Listing 25.11 contains the source code for the two child processes, each of which is to generate a random integer.

```
process.send(Math.floor(Math.random() * 1000));
```

Listing 25.11 Generating a Random Number in the Child Process (logic.js)

In the parent process, you first create the two child processes. Then you implement the childProcessReceiver function, which accepts a reference to a child process, registers itself on the message event of the child process, and returns a promise object that is successfully resolved when a message arrives. If an error occurs, that is, the error event gets triggered, the promise object will be rejected.

The handleResults function gets references to both child processes and uses a combination of Promise.all and the childProcessReceiver function to merge the results of both child processes. Finally, you output the total of both random numbers to the console.

This example has shown how you can distribute the load in your application. The implementation is still rather simple and subject to significant limitations. For more extensive applications, you should implement an event architecture, streams, or additional libraries such as Reactive Extensions for JavaScript (RxJS).

Miscellaneous

If you use the child_process module for the purpose of parallelization in your application, you should make sure to keep the forking of child processes under control. If too many child processes are created, this will affect your system. Each child process requires memory and processor computing time. If the resource demands exceed the available resources, your system will slow down, and you won't benefit at all from the child processes.

If you use child processes within your application, you can have individual a child processes once carry out multiple calculations, once a child process has been started. The advantage of this approach is that the child process doesn't have to be started first. However, this only makes sense if you frequently have similar calculations performed. The Node.js platform provides additional modules for such problems, which you can incorporate into your application. These modules include, among others, the child_ process and the `cluster` modules. In Chapter 16, you've already seen a detailed example on this topic and learned about the possibility of outsourcing the load balancing of your server to your operating system.

25.3.2   Load Balancer

However, there are occasions where you reach the limits of your system when scaling your application. In this case, your only option is to include additional systems to share the load of your system. However, you need to build your application to handle this type of infrastructure. What this means for you in concrete terms is that not every application can be scaled by merely adding another server. Basically, the instances of your application running on the different servers should be as independent as possible and use a common database or other system to synchronize the states. Once you've fulfilled these conditions, you'll need another piece of software to ensure that requests to your application are distributed appropriately among the available servers. There are numerous systems that can perform this task. In the following sections, you'll get to know two different load balancers: HAProxy and NGINX.

HAProxy

You can use HAProxy (*http://haproxy.org/*) as a freely available load balancer for applications based on HTTP connections as well as for TCP connections. This software is designed to act as a high-performance interface between your users and your application. In this role, HAProxy can manage tens of thousands of incoming connections. The software is mainly available for Unix systems such as Linux and Solaris. On Windows, HAProxy can also be installed via a few workarounds using Cygwin. The configuration of the load balancer is done by means of a configuration file. Listing 25.12 contains an excerpt of such a configuration file.

```
listen http 192.168.0.1:8080
    mode tcp
    option tcplog
    balance roundrobin
    maxconn 10000
    server web01 192.168.0.2:8080 maxconn 5000
    server web02 192.168.0.3:8080 maxconn 5000
```

Listing 25.12 Configuration of HAProxy

The `listen` directive allows you to define the proxy server. The two `server` specifications indicate the systems to which the requests are forwarded. `maxconn` helps you to define how many requests the load balancer will accept. The `maxconn` specifications with the respective servers determine how many connections are forwarded to the servers in each case. In the algorithm to be used, you define how HAProxy decides when and which system gets which connection. In Listing 25.12, round robin is used as an algorithm. Here, the requests are distributed evenly among the servers. This algorithm also allows you to weight the different servers. Depending on the weighting, servers are allocated more or fewer requests. If one server fails, the requests are distributed to the remaining servers. This means that the failure of one machine doesn't impact the overall system. If the machine is available again at a later time, it's reintegrated and can receive new requests. This architecture provides you with a very high-performance and flexible system with the greatest possible reliability.

NGINX represents another system for balancing the load of requests. The following section describes how to proceed when using this system.

NGINX

NGINX is predominantly known as a lightweight and performant web server. However, this software offers much more than just web server functionality. With NGINX, you can implement a similar infrastructure as you already have with HAProxy, but it's not as specialized in proxy and load balancing functionality as HAProxy. Listing 25.13 shows the relevant excerpts from the configuration file of NGINX, which ensure that NGINX is turned into a load balancer.

```
http {
    ...
    upstream node_upstream {
        server 192.168.0.2:8080 weight=5;
        server 192.168.0.3:8080;
    }
    ...
    server {
        ...
        location / {
            ...
            proxy_pass http://node_upstream
        }
        ...
    }
}
```

Listing 25.13 Configuration of a NGINX Load Balancer

For your NGINX instance to become a load balancer, you need the support of a module of NGINX, namely, the HttpProxyModule. For this purpose, you define an upstream resource in your configuration file and specify here the servers to which you want to distribute the load. After that, you add the proxy_pass option to your default location, which gets the name of the upstream resource as its value. As with HAProxy, you can weigh the different servers. By specifying weight, which you can see at the first server, you assign a certain weight to a server. Specifying the value 5 means that the first server will receive five requests, while the second server will receive only one. As load balancing algorithms, NGINX provides round robin, least connections, and IP-Hash, with round robin being the default. With NGINX, as with HAProxy, you can build a very performant infrastructure for your application.

Using a load balancer in front of your servers to scale your application means you have to manage your infrastructure by yourself. As a consequence, you need to ensure that the hardware and software for the infrastructure is available. In case of failures, you have to make sure you'll repair the servers. An alternative to operating the infrastructure in-house is to hand over this responsibility to an external service provider. One concrete way is to move your application to the cloud. In the following section, you'll see what options you have in that regard.

25.3.3   Node in the Cloud

The term *cloud* is now very commonly used, especially for web applications. However, there is no clear definition for this keyword. For example, cloud can be interpreted as cloud storage, cloud computing, or platform as a service (PaaS), where you can access the various manifestations of clouds. There are countless cloud service providers on the market. In this section, you'll get a brief overview of two of these platforms. One is Heroku, a standalone cloud application platform, and the other is Azure, Microsoft's cloud platform.

Heroku

To deploy your application to the Heroku cloud, you need a helper application called Heroku Toolbelt. This application must be installed on your system to make the heroku command-line tool available to you. You can then use this tool to create your Heroku account, which you'll later use to upload your application to the cloud. (You can find more information and resources on Heroku at *www.heroku.com*.) An important prerequisite for Heroku to deploy your application correctly is the existence of a *package.json* file, just like you need to create one for a regular npm package. In this file, you must list the dependencies of your application, among other things. You also need a file called *Procfile*, which you use to define which command should be used to start your application. Listing 25.14 shows an example of a *Procfile* file.

```
web: npm start
```

Listing 25.14 Example of a Procfile File

The *Procfile* file in Listing 25.14 makes sure that the application is launched on the server via the npm start command. If your dependencies are installed locally, you can use the `foreman start` command to start your application locally. The `foreman` command is part of the Heroku Toolbelt application. The next step is to add your application to a Git repository. The two commands shown in Listing 25.15 allow you to deploy your application to the Heroku cloud.

```
$ heroku create
...
$ heroku push heroku master
...
$ heroku ps:scale web=1
$ heroku ps
...
$ heroku open
```

Listing 25.15 Deployment to the Heroku Cloud

The `heroku ps:scale web=1` command enables you to ensure that only one process is started. The `heroku ps` command will then show the current state of your application. Finally, you can open your application in the browser via `heroku open`.

After this very simple introduction to Heroku, the following section describes how you can deploy your Node.js application to the Microsoft Azure cloud.

Microsoft Azure

Similar to Heroku, you also need an account with Microsoft Azure before you can use the service. For an introduction to the world of Microsoft Azure, you should visit *https://azure.microsoft.com/en-us/*. You can create your account through the Azure Management Portal. The following example is based on the assumption that you have an Express application that can be started using the `npm start` command. The first step is to create a ZIP archive of your application. This is done on the Windows Bash using the `zip -r webApp.zip .` command. You then create a resource group on the Microsoft Azure shell that acts as a container for your application. You can create that resource group using the `az group create -name expressAppGroup -location "West Europe"` command. Next, you create a service plan via the `az appservice plan create --name express-AppPlan --resource-group expressAppGroup --sku FREE` command. Finally, you use `az webapp create --resource-group expressAppGroup --plan expressAppPlan --name express-App --runtime " node|14-lts"` to create your web app. Your application is now available at *http://expressApp.azurewebsites.net*. You can upload the ZIP file containing your application via *https://expressApp.scm.azurewebsites.net/ZipDeploy* and use it to deploy.

As you've seen from the two examples, it's possible to bring your Node.js application to the cloud. The platforms support you in these tasks either directly through tools or by means of an online platform.

25

25.4 pm2: Process Management

Another useful tool for managing Node.js applications is the pm2 process manager. You can install this utility via npm using the `npm install -g pm2` command. The main features of the process manager are as follows:

- Creation of lists of processes controlled by pm2
- Process monitoring
- Process scaling
- Reloading processes without downtime

To start an application with pm2, you can use the `start` command. For example, if your application is stored in the *app.js* file, you can start it via the `pm2 start app.js -i 1` command. This command line ensures that exactly one instance of this application is booted.

`pm2 list` allows you to obtain a list of processes that were started with pm2. Table 25.1 contains an example of such a process list.

Let's assume you now expect a higher load on the application you just started. In that case, you can use pm2 to boot additional instances of the application. These will then be operated in cluster mode and share the TCP port. You can boot an additional instance via the `pm2 scale index 2` command. Thus, you now have a total of two instances of the application. If you specify a 1 instead of 2, you'll reduce the number of instances again.

ID	Name	Mode	↻	Status	CPU	Memory
0	app	cluster	0	online	0 %	37.7 MB
1	app	cluster	0	online	0 %	37.7 MB
2	app	cluster	0	online	0 %	38.0 MB
3	app	cluster	0	online	0 %	37.1 MB

Table 25.1 Process List of "pm2"

The `pm2 monit` command allows you to track the memory consumption and CPU utilization of the processes in real time.

The features shown here represent only a small part of the capabilities of pm2. You can find more information on the website of the project at *http://pm2.keymetrics.io/*.

25.5 Docker

Docker is container software that manages your application in self-contained units called containers. Docker can be run on almost any system, so you only need to create a container once and can then run it in a wide variety of environments. The big advantage of this way of running an application is that the application doesn't run directly on the system, but in an abstracted environment isolated from the rest of the system. This increases the level of security on your system and allows you to easily scale your application by launching additional containers as needed. With Docker, you can easily test your application on different Node.js versions by swapping the underlying Docker image. In addition, a Docker image can be deployed directly to the cloud, providing the foundation for flexible and highly scalable applications.

Node.js manages a set of official images, which are the basic building blocks of a Docker container. The most commonly used image is the node:<version> image. This image is based on the buildback-deps image, which only brings a set of basic packages. The node:<version> image itself installs node, npm, and yarn and then serves as a basis for your application.

25.5.1 Dockerfile

Once you've developed your application, you can put it in a container. As a basis for this, you need a file called *Dockerfile*. This file contains the building instructions for the container. Listing 25.16 shows an example of a Dockerfile.

```
FROM node:16.8.0
WORKDIR /usr/src/app
COPY package*.json ./
RUN npm install
COPY . .
EXPOSE 8080
USER node
CMD [ "npm", "start" ]
```

Listing 25.16 Dockerfile

FROM node:16.8.0 specifies the base image of your container. WORKDIR /usr/src/app enables you to create a directory for your application. Then you use the COPY command to copy the *package.json* file and the *package-lock.json* file to that directory. After that, you install the dependencies specified there via npm install. COPY . . ensures that the source code of your application gets copied into the container. With EXPOSE 8080, you release port 8080, to which your application is bound, to the outside world so that clients can connect to it. USER node ensures that your application doesn't run under the root user by default. Finally, CMD ["npm", "start"] starts your application via the npm start command.

To have the *node_modules* file and any generated *npm-debug.log* file ignored by the COPY command, you create a file named *.dockerignore*. You can see the contents of the file in Listing 25.17.

25

```
node_modules
npm-debug.log
```

Listing 25.17 .dockerignore File

25.5.2   Starting the Container

Once you've created the Dockerfile file, you can create the image for your container. The command required for this is shown in Listing 25.18.

```
$ docker build -t my-app/express-app .
```

Listing 25.18 Building a Docker Image

The -t option allows you to create a tag that assigns a name to the image. The naming convention here is to first use a unique name such as the company name followed by a / and the application name. You can address the image under this name later. The docker images command lists all locally available Docker images. The my-app/express-app entry should also appear in this list after executing the preceding command.

The final step consists of starting the container. This is done using the command from Listing 25.19.

```
$ docker run -p 8181:8080 -d my-app/express-app
```

Listing 25.19 Starting the Docker Container

The -p option ensures that port 8080 of the container is mapped to port 8181 of the host system and that the application is thus accessible. The -d option enables you to "detach" the container, that is, to run it in the background.

Now your application is available at *http://localhost:8181*.

25.6   Summary

The focus of this chapter was the problem of how to get your application onto the target system—starting from the simplest form of deployment, to copying the source code, to deployment via npm. The second part of this chapter dealt with ways of handling increased data and user traffic in your application. The options range from local scaling via available processor cores to managing your own infrastructure behind a load balancer to deploying your application in the cloud.

With Docker, you've learned another way to deploy your application in a controlled environment. Such containers can be booted in any environment and can be easily scaled by booting additional application containers.

Chapter 26
Performance

Most people don't even know what kind of pace they could have if they just rubbed the sleep out of their eyes for once.
—Christian Morgenstern

As a platform, Node.js claims to be lightweight and flexible. The individual components of the platform have proven themselves in practical use over many years and have shown that it's possible to implement even business-critical applications with server-side JavaScript. Throughout this book, you've already learned about some aspects of the Node.js architecture. In this chapter, we'll take a look at Node.js and the applications you build on top of it from a performance perspective. For a Node.js application, performance generally refers to the question as to how fast it can perform a given task. This can involve solving a specific problem from the command line on the local system as well as answering a request from a browser to a web interface as quickly as possible.

The use of resources has a decisive influence on the performance of your application. In the context of Node.js, you should always keep an eye on three types of resources: the processor, memory, and, if you're on the web, the network. In this chapter, you'll learn some best practices for performant applications as well as analysis tools.

26.1 You Aren't Gonna Need It

In feature development, the "you aren't gonna need it" (YAGNI) principle stands for functionality that developers and product managers envision for future use, but which isn't needed at the current time and possibly even in the future. Of course, this isn't to say that you don't need good performance, but you should be aware that performance also costs money. We're not talking about general good programming and avoiding bottlenecks in your application, but rather about micro-optimizations, which can cost more than they bring if you do them in the wrong place. For this reason, you should ensure a good basic performance in your application, but you should only implement the real optimizations when you know where performance problems will occur in your application. To do this, you need to know the volume of data your application needs to handle, and you need to know the critical workflows. Then you can start measuring the actual situation and analyzing the results. Based on these results, you can make optimizations and then measure again whether the desired results have been achieved.

26.2   CPU

Node.js needs the processor as a resource so that computations can be performed. This can be simple things like calculating 1 + 1, but also complex operations like parsing an extensive JavaScript Object Notation (JSON) structure. Modern systems usually have at least several processor cores to which the work can be distributed. The architecture of Node.js follows a single-process and a single-threaded approach. Everything you run in Node.js runs in one process and potentially blocks each other. You can solve this problem using the `child_process` and `worker_threads` modules. Chapter 16 describes how this exactly works.

The asynchronous input and output approach allows Node.js to swap out to the operating system all operations that aren't directly processed by the core of the platform. This includes, for example, network communication and the majority of file system operations. This means that even reading a very large file won't block your process. But then the processing of the results poses another obstacle. The distinction between the parts of an operation that can be outsourced and the parts that take place within the platform is very important here.

26.2.1   CPU-Blocking Operations

Despite all the platform optimizations, you can easily utilize a CPU core up to 100% capacity with Node.js by writing `while(true)`. This type of infinite loop ensures that the process is completely blocked and can't perform any further operations.

In Listing 26.1, you can see a slightly more elegant variant of wasting processor time. This code example shows a kind of blocking time-out function. The `sleep` function accepts a numerical value in terms of seconds to be waited for. Then you take the start value and start an endless loop. For each loop pass, you check whether the termination condition is met. If this is the case, the infinite loop is exited; otherwise, the next loop pass will follow. The output of the example is first the `Before Sleep` string, then 10 seconds pass, followed by the output `After Sleep`, and the script terminates.

```
function sleep(delayInSec) {
  const start = Date.now();

  while (true) {
    if (Date.now() - start >= delayInSec * 1000) {
      break;
    }
  }
}
```

```
console.log('Before Sleep');
sleep(10);
console.log('After Sleep');
```

Listing 26.1 Infinite Loop with Termination Condition

26.2.2 Measuring the CPU Load

The simplest way to measure the impact of a process on your system's processor is to use the onboard tools of your operating system. On Windows, for example, this is the Task Manager, and on macOS, it's the Activity Monitor. These tools show you whether or not your system is currently under load. These tools also allow you to sort the currently running processes by CPU utilization, so that the most resource-intensive processes are displayed at the top of the list. If your Node.js application is among the first hits here, this is a first indicator of a performance problem.

Command-line tools such as htop go one step further, providing you with significantly more information about the individual processes. For example, if you run the script from Listing 26.1 and run htop in parallel, you get a view like the one shown in Figure 26.1.

htop enables you to search for specific processes or filter the process list. In this case, the list is filtered by the term *index.js* and shows only our application process. Here you can see that the value in the **CPU%** column is at **99.3%**, which means that a processor core is almost completely utilized.

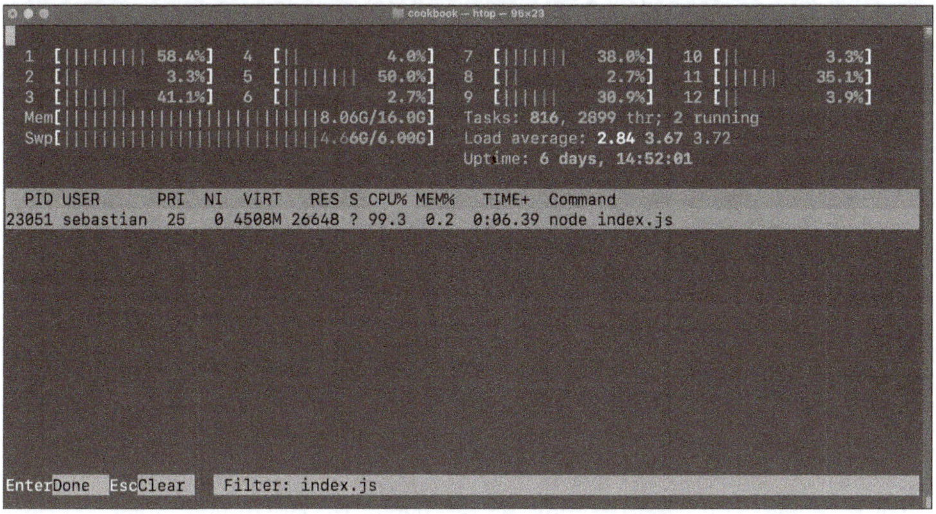

Figure 26.1 Output of "htop" for a CPU-Intensive Node.js Application

As already mentioned, these tools only provide you with a first impression of the overall application. Once you've identified a problem here, you need to take a step further and take a look inside your application. For this purpose, you can use the Chrome DevTools profiler.

26.2.3   CPU Profiling with Chrome DevTools

To profile your application, you must open it in debug mode, that is, that is, using the `--inspect` option or `--inspect-brk` command-line option. Both options ensure that you can connect to your application via Chrome DevTools and the debugger protocol. If you use `--inspect-brk`, your application won't be executed directly but will be halted before the first statement. This is different if you use `--inspect`. For our example, you start your application using `--inspect-brk`, open your local Chrome browser, and enter "chrome://inspect" in the address bar. There you'll find the **Remote Targets** heading under **Devices**, which is where your Node.js application is listed. When you click on the **inspect** link, DevTools will open, and you'll see your application in a paused state. Up to this point, you already know the process from Chapter 3. Now, however, you must switch from the **Sources** tab to the **Profiler** tab and click the **Start** button there. This will ensure that your application is running. You should now wait about 5–10 seconds before clicking the **Stop** button to stop recording. As a result, you'll see a tabular listing like the one shown in Figure 26.2.

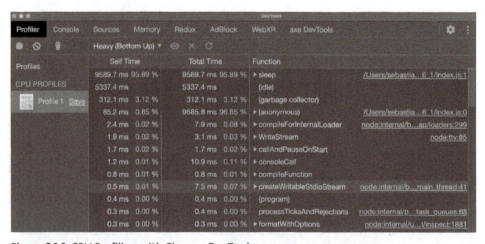

Figure 26.2 CPU Profiling with Chrome DevTools

This list shows you how much time a function has consumed by itself or as part of the total of all functions called by it. You also get the name of the function and a reference to the source code. As you can see here, our `sleep` function is the undisputed leader when it comes to CPU consumption. Unfortunately, the situation is rarely that clear-cut in reality, so you usually have to invest some time here to find optimization potential.

In some situations, the tabular overview isn't very informative for concrete problems. In such a case, you can switch to the **Sources** tab and see how much time the application took to process certain lines. To help you observe this in our example, you should add a debugger statement like the one in Listing 26.2 as the last line.

```javascript
function sleep(delayInSec) {
  const start = Date.now();

  while (true) {
    if (Date.now() - start >= delayInSec * 1000) {
      break;
    }
  }
}

console.log('Before Sleep');
sleep(10);
console.log('After Sleep');
debugger;
```

Listing 26.2 "debugger" Statement in the "sleep" Script

If you've saved this source code in a file named *index.js*, you can execute it again via the node --inspect-brk index.js command. Then you return to the **Profiler** tab and start the recording by clicking the **Start** button. Wait a few seconds, stop the recording by clicking the **Stop** button, and then go to the **Sources** tab again. After a short wait, the debugger stops at the breakpoint, that is, the debugger statement, and you can see how much time your application has spent in the various lines during the recording. Figure 26.3 shows an example.

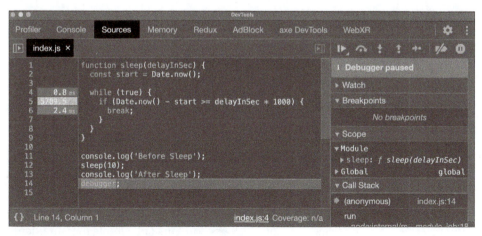

Figure 26.3 Display of Execution Time in DevTools

The time specification at the beginning of the line shows that you've spent most of the time, exactly 5789.5 milliseconds, executing the if statement.

> **Note**
>
> The debugger statement is important, by the way, as it makes sure that the Node.js process doesn't terminate before you've had a chance to look at the source code. As soon as the process is terminated, the file is also no longer available for viewing.

26.2.4   Alternatives to the Profiler: console.time

When it comes to measuring execution times, Node.js offers you a whole range of other tools in addition to the profiler. The simplest one is a feature of the console object. You can use two methods, console.time and console.timeEnd, to measure the runtime of your application between the two calls. Let's test this directly with our sleep function. To do this, add a call of console.time before the sleep call and a call of console.timeEnd after it, as shown in Listing 26.3.

```
function sleep(delayInSec) {
  const start = Date.now();

  while (true) {
    if (Date.now() - start >= delayInSec * 1000) {
      break;
    }
  }
}

console.time('sleep');
sleep(10);
console.timeEnd('sleep'); // Output: sleep: 10.000s
```

Listing 26.3 Using the "console.time" Methods

To perform a measurement, you first call the console.time method with any character string as its label. Then you perform the operations you want to measure; in our case, this is the sleep function with the value 10. To finish the measurement, you call the console.timeEnd method with the same label you used for console.time. The value of the measurement is output directly on the command line together with the label in milliseconds. And this is precisely where the problem lies. If you want to perform measurements in production operation, it isn't very useful to log all information on the console. In addition, calling the console methods themselves requires resources, although these may be neglected. For quick experiments and simple measurements, you can easily use the console methods; for measurements in a production environment, you should turn to the performance-hooks interface of Node.js.

26.2.5 Alternatives to the Profiler: Performance-Hooks Interface

Version 8.5 introduced the perf_hooks module, a new extension to Node.js that allows you to perform time measurements for all aspects of your application. As with the console.time methods, you only need to set markers at the right locations for this and can then perform measurements. Unlike the console.time methods, you can control the behavior and processing of the measurements much better and, for example, redirect the output to a file or disable the measurements.

For the next example, we want to measure the execution of the sleep function again. However, the output will be saved to a file named *time.log*, and the measurement will be dependent on an environment variable. For the example to work, you need a *package.json* file, which you can generate via npm init -y. You also need to install the cross-env package via the npm install --save-dev cross-env command. This package ensures that you can set environment variables independently of your system. You use the package to set the MEASURE variable in the startup script to the value true. Listing 26.4 shows the corresponding *package.json* file.

```
{
  "name": "node-book",
  "version": "1.0.0",
  "description": "",
  "main": "index.js",
  "private": true,
  "type": "module",
  "scripts": {
    "start": "cross-env MEASURE=true node index.js"
  },
  "keywords": [],
  "author": "",
  "license": "ISC",
  "dependencies": {
    "cross-env": "^7.0.3"
  }
}
```

Listing 26.4 "package.json" with "cross-env" Integration

Based on this, you can now start integrating the perf_hooks module into your application. The integration process consists of four steps: define a PerformanceObserver, activate it, set markers in your code, and perform the measurement.

In the code example in Listing 26.5, you can see that the processing of a measurement is decoupled from the actual measurement process. The first two steps, that is, the definition of the PerformanceObserver and its activation, depend on the value of the environment variable MEASURE. In the start script of *package.json*, you've set this value to true, which means that the condition is true, and the code block is executed. When you run the application via node index.js, this isn't the case, and the script doesn't write a new entry to the *time.log* file.

```
import { PerformanceObserver, performance } from 'perf_hooks';
import { appendFile } from 'fs/promises';

if (process.env.MEASURE) {
  const obs = new PerformanceObserver((items) => {
    const entries = items.getEntries();
    entries.forEach(({ name, duration }) => {
      appendFile('time.log', `${name}: ${duration}\n`);
    });
  });
  obs.observe({ entryTypes: ['measure'] });
}

function sleep(delayInSec) {
  const start = Date.now();

  while (true) {
    if (Date.now() - start >= delayInSec * 1000) {
      break;
    }
  }
}

performance.mark('sleep start');
sleep(10);
performance.mark('sleep end');
performance.measure('sleep: ', 'sleep start', 'sleep end');
```

Listing 26.5 Integrating the "perf_hooks" Module

The callback function you pass to the PerformanceObserver when it's instantiated is assigned an items object whose getEntries method allows you to access an array of measurements. Each entry contains the name, type, start time, and duration of the measurement as well as details. You log each of these entries with the appendFile function from the fs/promises module.

By calling the observe method, you instruct the PerformanceObserver instance to handle the measurements. Regardless of the PerformanceObserver, you set markers in your code using the mark method of the performance object. Here, you should use meaningful names, if possible. Unlike the console.time methods, the names of the individual markers are independent of each other and are only related to each other when the measure method is called. Here you pass the name of the measurement, the start mark, and the end mark. The perf_hooks module uses this information to calculate the values that will then be made available to you in the PerformanceObserver.

If you run the application via the npm start command, a new entry is written to the *time.log* file after a short wait, or this file gets created if it doesn't yet exist. Listing 26.6 shows an example of the contents of this file.

```
sleep: : 9999.051399946213
```

Listing 26.6 Contents of the "time.log" File

As you can see here, the perf_hooks module doesn't use millisecond time stamps, but it's even more accurate.

With the profiler, the console.time methods and the perf_hooks module, you've become acquainted with various options that allow you to measure the runtime of your application. In the next step, we'll turn our attention to memory, another system resource that is relevant for your application.

26.3 Memory

Like any programming language, JavaScript must store the values of variables somewhere. Strictly speaking, this "somewhere" is an area of the memory. JavaScript is a language that tries to hide a lot of rather machine-based problems from you. Among other things, this includes memory management. For example, JavaScript has a garbage collector that releases memory that has been used but is no longer in use, while you have no way to control this from within your application. Likewise, you don't have direct access to memory addresses.

On the other hand, you can influence the storage of data and the garbage collector indirectly. The key to this lies in the scoping of JavaScript, that is, the validity of variables. The language standard generally provides for several areas of validity:

- **Global**
  A global variable is available everywhere in the application. In Node.js, you use the global object to access the global namespace.
- **Function**
  If you define a variable within a function, it's only valid there and in all subfunctions.
- **Block**
  The keywords let and const allow you to define variables that are valid only in a block such as a loop or a condition.
- **Closure**
  The closure scope is the scope of a function and its defining context.
- **Module**
  The module context is the scope of a file. A variable you define in a file is only valid there.

26

If the JavaScript engine leaves a scope, the references to the memory areas of the variables are deleted. The garbage collector can then release the contents of the memory.

However, if you intentionally or accidentally make sure that the references continue to exist, the memory can't be released and remains used. In the course of a longer runtime, the memory consumption of your application grows steadily—a memory leak occurs.

26.3.1 Memory Leaks

There are several ways to create memory leaks. Typically, these are global variables in which structures are stored that are actually no longer needed. The garbage collector can't take action here because global variables are always valid, so there is always at least one reference. Another source is timers or callbacks that haven't been deregistered, so the references can't be released either. The third variant are closure scopes. As you know, the closure scope is the scope of a function and its creating context. This means that as long as the function exists, the memory area surrounding it will continue to exist, even if you can no longer access it directly. You can continue to access it via the function, at least in theory. An example of a typical memory leak triggered by closure scoping is shown in Listing 26.7.

```
let value = null;
const callback = function () {
  const originalValue = value;
  function doSomething() {
    if (originalValue) return true;
  }
  value = {
    data: new Array(1000000).fill('xxx'),
    getSize() {
      return data.length;
    },
  };
};
setInterval(callback, 100);
```

Listing 26.7 Code Block with a Memory Leak

Each time the callback function is executed in the interval, a new value object gets created. This object contains a data property with a very large array filled with the character string xxx. The getSize method has a closure scope containing the doSomething function, which in turn has a reference to originalValue, while originalValue is the object from the previous interval run. Due to this linking, the memory of all generated objects can't be released, and the memory is visibly running full.

26.3.2 Memory Analysis in DevTools

As with the processor resource analysis, you can again use Chrome DevTools for your application's memory consumption. To do this, you must start your application, which you've saved in a file named *index.js*, via the `node --inspect-brk index.js` command. Then you connect your Chrome DevTools to the Node.js process using the *chrome://inspect* address.

By using the `--inspect-brk` option, the application is initially in a halted state. If you continue the execution by clicking the **Play** icon in the **Sources** tab, your source code will be executed, and memory consumption will increase. The first indication of this is provided by the **Memory** tab. Here you can see the current memory consumption as well as a trend indicator at the very bottom under the **Select JavaScript VM instance** item. Figure 26.4 shows the display in DevTools.

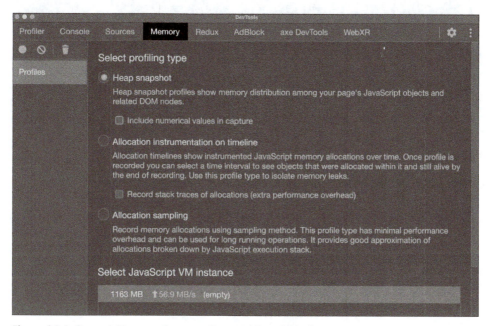

Figure 26.4 Current Memory Consumption and Trend Display

Above this memory display, you can analyze the memory further. Several options are available to you. You can take a heap snapshot, which is a current memory image, or record memory utilization over a period of time. For the second variant, you can choose between **Allocation instrumentation on timeline** and **Allocation sampling**, whereby the second variant is more suitable for longer observation periods. To start a recording, select the type of recording using the radio buttons, and then click the **Record** button at the top left.

Figure 26.5 contains an example of a heap snapshot of our application. In the left-hand column, you can see the name of the **Constructor**, while the second column shows the **Distance** to the root, that is, the nesting depth. This is followed by **Shallow Size**, which

26

specifies the amount of memory of the respective objects themselves, and then **Retained Size**, which shows the amount of memory released when the objects are deleted. In the screenshot, you can see that the array we created in the code is responsible for 96% of the memory utilization, which is clearly the memory leak.

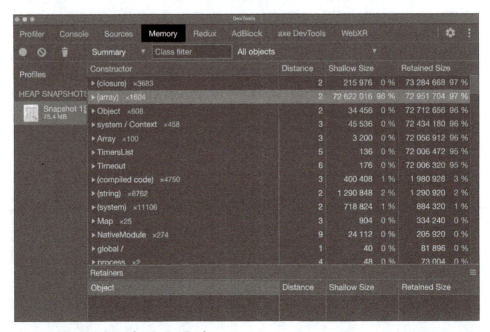

Figure 26.5 Heap Snapshot in DevTools

If you choose the analysis over time instead of a heap snapshot, you start recording, go to the **Sources** tab, make sure the debugger keeps running, and then you can stop the recording at any time. After that, you should also pause the debugger again, or your system will run out of memory sooner or later. Figure 26.6 shows the display for the recording in the DevTools. Again, you get the information about the memory consumption of the different objects.

This variant of memory analysis is particularly suitable if you suspect a memory leak during certain interactions with your application. In this case, start the recording, perform the action, and then stop the recording. Now you can take a look into the memory at the different times of execution. The third logging variant is somewhat more economical when it comes to the displayed information, but, at the same time, it's significantly more performant in execution. Figure 26.7 shows an example of this.

Chrome DevTools is an indispensable tool for analyzing memory leaks. Note, however, that our example is a very clear and distinct case of a memory leak. In real life, you'll rarely be made aware of your problem so clearly, so troubleshooting in such a case may take more time.

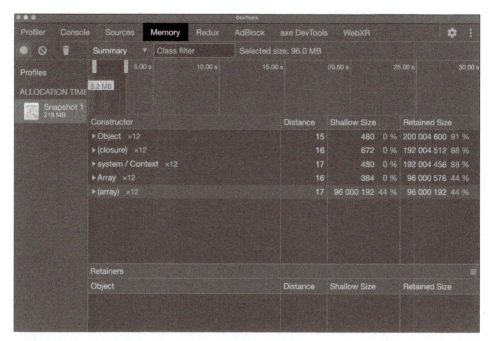

Figure 26.6 Recording Memory Consumption over Time

Figure 26.7 Memory Analysis with Allocation Sampling

Another helpful feature of DevTools in dealing with memory usage is the small garbage can icon in the top bar. If you click on it, the garbage collector becomes active immediately. This allows you to perform a memory analysis and ensure that no memory which is no longer referenced is corrupting the image.

However, you don't always necessarily need DevTools to work with memory. Node.js itself also provides you with a couple of tools.

26.3.3   Node.js Memory Statistics

With the help of the `process` module, you can obtain rudimentary information about the memory utilization of your application. You can use the `process.memoryUsage.rss` method to obtain the *resident set size* in bytes. This is the amount of memory consumed by the process with all C++ and JavaScript objects. The process.memoryUsage method returns an object with the following information:

- **rss**
  Resident set size that provides the same information as the process.memoryUsage.rss method.
- **heapTotal**
  Total size of the heap memory of the V8 engine.
- **heapUsed**
  Utilized heap memory of the V8 engine.
- **external**
  Memory consumption by C++ objects bound to JavaScript objects.
- **arrayBuffers**
  Memory consumed by ArrayBuffer objects.

You can manipulate the code from Listing 26.7 to output the memory statistics at certain interval runs, as shown in Listing 26.8.

```
let value = null;
let count = 0;
const callback = function () {
  if (count++ % 10 === 0) {
    const { rss, heapTotal, heapUsed } = process.memoryUsage();
    console.log(
      `RSS: ${rss}, Heap Total: ${heapTotal}, Heap Used: ${heapUsed}`,
    );
  }
  const originalValue = value;
  function doSomething() {
    if (originalValue) return true;
  }
  value = {
    data: new Array(1000000).fill('xxx'),
    getSize() {
      return data.length;
    },
  };
};
setInterval(callback, 100);
```

Listing 26.8 Recording Memory Statistics in the Process

First, you define a count variable, which you initialize with the value 0. Then you check whether the count value that increased by 1 is divisible by 10. If this is the case, you read the values for rss, heapTotal and heapUsed and then output them to the console. You can see an excerpt from the result in Listing 26.9.

```
RSS: 21983232, Heap Total: 4558848, Heap Used: 3723880
RSS: 104919040, Heap Total: 118198272, Heap Used: 83857760
RSS: 185106432, Heap Total: 198275072, Heap Used: 163860280
RSS: 265211904, Heap Total: 278351872, Heap Used: 243862368
RSS: 345288704, Heap Total: 358428672, Heap Used: 323897032
RSS: 425373696, Heap Total: 438505472, Heap Used: 403866632
RSS: 505458688, Heap Total: 518582272, Heap Used: 483868872
RSS: 585887744, Heap Total: 598134784, Heap Used: 563492760
```

Listing 26.9 Output of the Memory Values

As you can see in the output on the command line, all metrics, that is, RSS, Heap Total, and Heap Used, are steadily increasing. If such a case occurs in a real application, the system on which you run the application will continuously slow down as memory management becomes more and more extensive. The system will eventually start swapping content from the memory to the disk until the available memory is used up, and the system runs into a state of emergency.

In addition to the processor and RAM, the network is another important resource, especially for web applications based on Node.js.

26.4 Network

For the analysis of the network traffic, we'll use a simple Express application as a basis. For this, you first create a *package.json* file via npm init -y and install the Express package age using npm install express, as shown in Listing 26.10.

```
{
  "name": "node-book",
  "version": "1.0.0",
  "description": "",
  "main": "index.js",
  "private": true,
  "type": "module",
  "scripts": {
    "start": "node index.js"
  },
  "keywords": [],
  "author": "",
  "license": "ISC",
  "dependencies": {
```

26

```
    "express": "^4.17.1"
  }
}
```

Listing 26.10 "package.json" File for the Express "package.json" Application

The initial file for the application—the *index.js* file—looks like the one shown in Listing 26.11 and consists of initializing the app object, defining a GET route, and binding the application to port 8080.

```
import express from 'express';

const app = express();

app.get('/', (request, response) => {
  setTimeout(() => {
    response.send(`Lorem ipsum...`); // Text shortened
  }, 2000);
});

app.listen(8080, () => {
  console.log('Server is listening to http://localhost:8080');
});
```

Listing 26.11 Entry into the Express Application (index.js)

The route of the application sends an arbitrary text to the client for testing purposes. For our example,we had a Lorem ipsum generator create a 5,000-word text. The code example is significantly shortened at this point for the sake of clarity. However, the response isn't sent immediately, but only after two seconds. This is to simulate the processing time on the server and represents, for example, an elaborate algorithm or communication with other systems. If you now start your application using the npm start command, you can access it from the browser via *http://localhost:8080*. To do this, you should open the browser's DevTools and go to the **Network** tab where you can see the network statistics as shown in Figure 26.8.

To make the result a bit clearer, we enabled network throttling and set it to Slow 3G. This means that the bandwidth is artificially limited to simulate a worse connection. When you move your mouse cursor over the line of the request, you'll see a detailed list of times. What immediately catches the eye here are the green and blue bars. The green bar represents the wait time of the browser until the first byte is received. This represents the time it takes for the server to process the request, and the 2.03 seconds is the time-out of two seconds and some overhead caused by Express. The blue bar symbolizes the time it takes to download the content. This period amounts to just under 600 milliseconds.

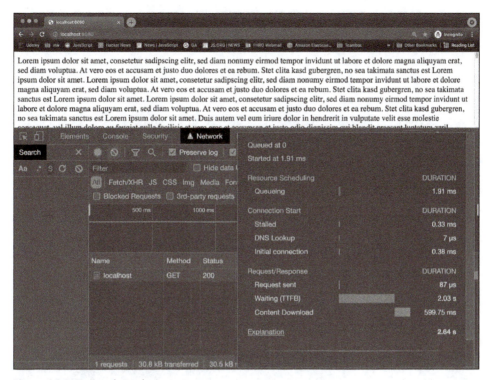

Figure 26.8 Network Analysis

When optimizing the network, you should always look for the largest values and try to get as much out of them as possible. You can reduce the green bar, for example, if you speed up processing on the server by caching values once they have been calculated, thus saving computing time.

You can improve the blue bar by reducing the amount of data that needs to be transported. This can be done, on the one hand, by omitting unnecessary data. But you can also optimize the data. For example, you can have HTML, CSS, and JavaScript remove unnecessary space characters and comments. Another optimization option is to compress the communication. For Express in this case, there is a middleware available called compression. You can install this middleware via the npm install compression command. Listing 26.12 shows how you can enable compression for your application.

```
import express from 'express';
import compression from 'compression';

const app = express();

app.use(compression({ level: 9 }));

app.get('/', (request, response) => {
```

26

```
  setTimeout(() => {
    response.send(`Lorem ipsum...`); // Text shortened
  }, 2000);
});

app.listen(8080, () => {
  console.log('Server is listening to http://localhost:8080');
});
```

Listing 26.12 Enabling Compression for Communication (index.js)

The value 9 for the `level` property in the middleware configuration object `compression` indicates that the best compression level should be used. Here, the compression takes the longest time, but the result is the smallest. You should aim for a good balance of CPU time and transfer speed. If you now perform another measurement, you'll see the effect of the compression.

As you can see, the blue bar has shrunk to 0.63 milliseconds, as shown in Figure 26.9, because instead of the original 30.5 KB, only 1.2 KB needs to be transferred. So, this optimization has a very positive effect on the performance of our application.

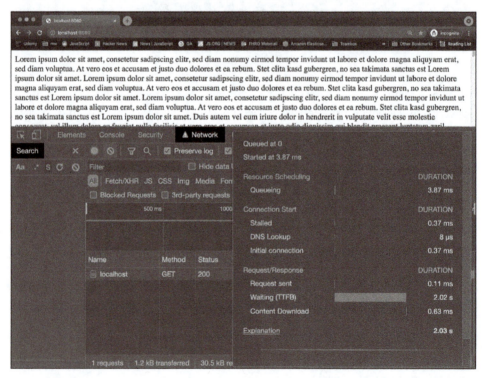

Figure 26.9 Measurement with Active Compression

26.5 Summary

In this chapter, you've learned that you must be economical with the resources you have. The architecture of Node.js is basically designed in such a way that it makes an application performant. The platform swaps out all operations it doesn't need to perform itself to other services or the operating system. Its nonblocking input/output (I/O) approach also ensures that the Node.js process isn't significantly blocked by read and write operations. The memory footprint of Node.js is also comparatively small. On this basis, it's up to you to develop a lightweight and performant application.

Node.js provides you with a lot of help for analyzing CPU and memory issues with the debugger, Chrome DevTools, and some onboard tools.

In general, you should make sure that you implement your source code in a clean and readable way, and don't use too many performance optimizations too early, as these usually impact readability. Once you've completed developing a feature, you should test it using realistic data and measure its performance. After that, you can start optimizing. When the optimization process is completed, you should measure again and check whether the optimizations were target-oriented. This way, you can make sure that you improve your source code exactly where the problems occur.

26

Chapter 27
Microservices with Node.js

The hardest thing about an idea is not having it but recognizing if it is good.
—Chris Howard

There are various architectural approaches for the implementation of web applications. One of these approaches is called microservice architecture. This means that your application doesn't consist of one large, tightly coupled piece of source code, but is composed of several specialized microservices. This type of architecture has its pros and cons. The most important thing for you to know is when you should use microservices. In this chapter, you'll get an insight into the development of such microservices with Node.js. In doing so, we'll introduce you to different approaches to communication, and you'll develop a small application that consists of two microservices.

27.1 Basic Principles

When it comes to the architecture of a web application, you quickly come across two different architectural approaches: the microservice architecture and the monolithic architecture. Both forms have their reason for existing, and both have their strengths and weaknesses.

With Node.js, you can implement your application in both forms, although the monolithic architecture is better suited for small, simple applications, while the microservice architecture should be used more for complex and large applications.

27.1.1 Monolithic Architecture

A monolithic application doesn't automatically indicate that such an application is outdated, unmaintainable, and inflexible. Rather, a monolithic architecture means that it's an application with a defined application core that has a more or less tight coupling between its individual parts. In such an application, you use the module system as usual and divide the application into logical units. Communication with the outside world, that is, with other systems, a database, and the client, can be abstracted via an adapter layer. This type of application is delivered as a package.

27

The big advantage of monolithic applications is that they incur relatively little overhead. Communication between the individual modules is subject to hardly any restrictions, unless you define conventions in the development team. Extensions can thus be integrated relatively easily.

This type of architecture turns into a drawback when the application grows and the interfaces aren't properly maintained. Then the data streams become increasingly nontransparent, and errors start creeping in.

Based on the movie database example, which you already know from the chapters about the web server, Figure 27.1 shows what such a monolithic architecture can look like. The initiative in communication originates from the client, which makes a request to the application. A central authentication service ensures that the user is allowed to access the requested resource. The core of the application is divided into several specialized modules such as the user and the movie module. These in turn communicate with the application's database, which is divided into different tables.

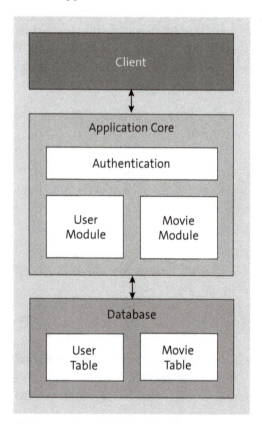

Figure 27.1 Monolithic Architecture

27.1.2 Microservice Architecture

Unlike monolithic architecture, microservice architecture doesn't have one core of the application. Instead, the application consists of a set of loosely coupled services. These services can only be addressed via defined interfaces. Communication usually takes place via a standardized protocol so that the services can also be located on different systems.

The advantages resulting from this form of architecture are manifold. For example, you can develop the individual microservices of an application independently of each other. Only the interface definition must be known to all participants. This goes so far that the services can even be run on different systems and implemented in different programming languages, frameworks, and libraries.

If the services are independent of each other, they can also be scaled separately. For example, let's suppose you had a user service and a movie service. The movie service delivers a list of movies that is requested very often. In a microservice architecture, you can start a second or third instance of the service to better serve the increasing number of requests. The user service remains unaffected and can continue to operate on only one instance. Once the load peak is over, you can also scale down the movie service again.

The aforementioned benefits of microservices arise because the individual services are independent of each other—which leads to the question of how you properly slice the technicality of an application so that you can separate out multiple microservices. A good rule of thumb here is that you should look for self-contained specialties and make the microservices not too big, but not too small either. In the example of the movie database, user management is a separate service. It's responsible for creating, reading, editing, and deleting users. This service can be requested directly by the client or by other services of the application. Another service is the movie service. This service takes care of all aspects of the movies in the application. If user data is needed, the movie service requests it from the user service.

In Figure 27.2, you can see the architecture of the application you're going to build in this chapter. As mentioned, the two microservices are independent of each other, but they can communicate via interfaces. Shared functionality, such as a logger that you can use to record error messages, is also swapped out to separate microservices. A principle that goes hand in hand with microservices scalability is that the application must be designed in such a way that services can be easily started and stopped. Ideally, a microservice shouldn't have its own state. A state is recorded in an underlying database. As you can also see in the figure, each microservice has its own database. This in turn serves the requirement for independence of services. This also allows you to use the correct database for each service. For example, you can store the user data in a MongoDB database and the movie data in a MySQL database.

27

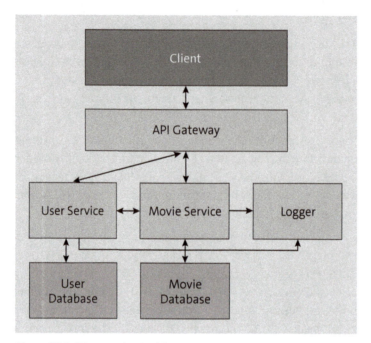

Figure 27.2 Microservice Architecture

27.2   Architecture

The internal structure of a microservice doesn't play any major role in the overall application. Most of the time, the services are manageable in scope, so the structuring capabilities of Node.js are sufficient. What's more important in this context are the interfaces to the outside world. The connection to the database is abstracted by the database driver and, if necessary, an object-relational mapping (ORM). For common databases, you can connect to both a local and remote database. Microservices are often delivered in containers. You can pass the connection information to them using environment variables. You can also use service discovery mechanisms such as Consul. A client library allows you to register your services with the Consul server and query it for specific services.

Access to shared resources such as the logger is usually abstracted via an additional library. Again, the logger's target URL must be passed either via a configuration or via service discovery. One of the most significant issues in microservice architecture is the communication between services.

27.2.1   Communication between Individual Services

Because the individual services are usually implemented via their own containers, communication must take place via a standard protocol such as HTTP. With regard to the communication, you can follow different strategies depending on how strong you want the coupling between the two entities to be.

Synchronous Communication between Microservices

The classic communication approach is referred to as synchronous communication. The client requests the microservice, usually registers a callback function, and waits for the response. The service processes the request and ultimately writes a response to the client. This type of communication is characteristic of web services. In Chapter 10, you implemented a representational state transfer (REST) server with Express. You could use this server in a modified version as a synchronous microservice. The term synchronous is somewhat misleading here because it still is asynchronous. However, the client has to wait for the response. The degree of coupling between client and service is relatively tight in this case. If the service crashes, the connection gets terminated, and the request is considered unsuccessful. One advantage of this type of communication is that service implementation is comparatively simple because numerous frameworks and libraries exist.

Asynchronous Communication between Microservices

With asynchronous communication between microservices, client and service are more decoupled. A message queue is used for this purpose, in which the messages are stored. The implementation of the communication follows the publish-subscribe pattern. A producer generates a message and passes it to the message queue where various consumers are listening. Figure 27.3 shows the relationship between producer, message queue, and consumer.

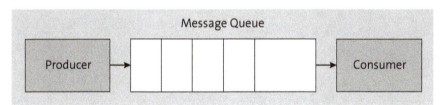

Figure 27.3 Message Queue

The consumer waits for messages in the message queue and processes them as they arrive. The message queue is able to buffer messages so that the consumer is relieved.

The asynchronous communication allows *fire and forget*, which means that a client sends the message and doesn't wait for a response because it can rely on infrastructure safeguards to ensure that the message will be processed in any case. However, in a microservice architecture, asynchronous communication often requires a return channel as well. If you implement the user service with asynchronous communication via RabbitMQ, creating, modifying, and deleting requests are easily possible via the queue. For read requests, the client generates a message containing the details of records that must be read and passes the message to the message queue. The service, which in this case takes on the role of the consumer, receives the message, reads the requested data from the database, and can also define additional rules or perform transformations on the data. The service then formulates a message with the read data and passes it to the message queue. The roles are now reversed. The client receives the message from the message queue and can process the received data.

In the following sections, you'll first set up the infrastructure for your microservice application and then implement a synchronous and an asynchronous service, which you'll merge into a central application programming interface (API) gateway.

27.3   Infrastructure

The following describe the implementation of a version of the movie database based on microservices. The architecture is outlined in Figure 27.4.

The API gateway serves as the entry point to the application. It takes care of central issues such as user registration. This ensures that not every service needs to authenticate the users themselves. The API gateway communicates with the various services, requests the information, and generates the response to the client.

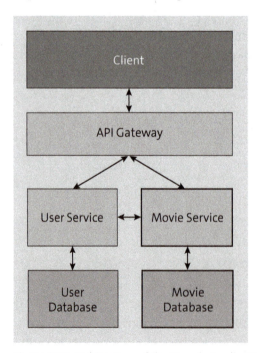

Figure 27.4 Architecture of the Sample Application

The movie service is connected via a synchronous communication link. It's implemented with Express and a MySQL backend. The user service is implemented as an asynchronous service with a connection to a message queue. MongoDB is used here as the backend.

Both the services and the API gateway each run in a Docker container. For this application, we assume that it's a single-page application and that the services only need to render JavaScript Object Notation (JSON) data. You can use Postman or cURL as a frontend. These tools fulfill the role of the browser in which the frontend of the application is executed.

27.3.1 Docker Compose

The application you implement below consists of several independent services; to better control them, you use Docker Compose here. This utility allows you to configure an application consisting of several containers via a file and start it with one command.

To use Docker Compose, you need a central *docker-compose.yml* file where you configure each container. From this file, you can either point to Dockerfiles or to ready-made images. Listing 27.1 shows an example of such a configuration file.

```
version: '3'
services:
  user:
    build:
      context: user
```

Listing 27.1 Simple Example of a docker-compose.yml File

You can start the application you describe with this configuration using the `docker-compose up` command. All containers that are started are listed under the `services` item. In the example, this is just a container that's specified in more detail by a Dockerfile in the *user* directory. You use the `docker-compose stop` command to shut down the container again.

27.4 Asynchronous Microservice with RabbitMQ

The first microservice of the application we'll implement works asynchronously, that is, relatively strongly decoupled. The user service isn't an ideal example here because communication via a message queue such as *RabbitMQ* also entails a potential time delay due to the strong decoupling. However, this example nicely illustrates the bidirectional and thus equal communication between the services as well as the resulting problems.

The direct question-answer pattern we implement in this example is rather unusual for an asynchronous service, and a common web protocol such as HTTP would work just as well, if not better, for the implementation. Message queues are typically used in places

27

where the request is decoupled from the response. Take, for example, the creation of a new user account. In this case, users enter their data via the frontend and send the request to an API gateway, and then the gateway sends the message on to the message queue. Once the message is submitted there, users will be notified that the request was successfully received. Then, the system processes the message by reading it from the message queue, creating the account, and informing users, for example, by email, that the account can be activated via a separate link. The message queue here ensures that the message about the creation of a new account is processed in any case. For example, if the user service crashes during creation, the message isn't acknowledged and is processed again once the service is restarted or another instance of the service processes the message.

27.4.1 Installation and Setup

Each microservice of your application is an independent small application within a larger overall system. For this reason, you also start developing the user service in a new subdirectory named *user*. In this directory, you first run the `npm init` command. Then you should add the `type` and `private` properties to the default configuration and set the startup script. Next, you use the `npm install mongodb amqplib` command to install the MongoDB driver for data storage and the Advanced Message Queuing Protocol (AMQP) library for communication. The resulting *package.json* file should look like the one shown in Listing 27.2.

```
{
  "name": "user-service",
  "version": "1.0.0",
  "description": "",
  "type": "module",
  "private": true,
  "main": "index.js",
  "scripts": {
    "start": "node index.js"
  },
  "keywords": [],
  "author": "",
  "license": "ISC",
  "dependencies": {
      "amqplib": "^0.8.0",
    "mongodb": "^4.1.1"
  }
}
```

Listing 27.2 "package.json" File of the User Service (user/package.json)

In the *index.js* file, the entry point to the service, you build the basic framework of the application. This differs significantly from the previous web backends you've implemented by using the AMQP library. However, again, you should make the entry point to your application as slim and lightweight as possible. Listing 27.3 shows an example of such a basic setup. You save this source code in a file named *index.js* in the *user* directory.

```
import { getAllAction, createAction } from './controller.js';
import { getChannel, queue } from './connect.js';

const channel = await getChannel();

channel.consume(queue, (message) => {
  const messageData = JSON.parse(message.content.toString());
  if (messageData.role === 'user') {
    switch (messageData.cmd) {
      case 'getAll':
        getAllAction(channel, messageData.id);
        break;
      case 'create':
        createAction(channel, messageData.id, messageData.data);
        break;
      default:
        console.error('Unknown command');
        channel.nack(message);
        break;
    }
  }
});
```

Listing 27.3 Basic Setup for the User Service (user/index.js)

In Listing 27.3, you can see that the entry file is responsible for receiving and correctly redistributing the incoming messages. For this purpose, you must first connect to the message queue server. This is taken care of by the getChannel function, which is swapped out into a separate file. This function makes sure that the connection to the server is established and a communication channel is opened. Messages can then be received on this channel using the consume method. A new message triggers an event, based on which the callback function registered in the consume method gets run.

The received message object must be decoded and converted into an object in the first step. At this point, it's important that all entities involved in the communication agree on a uniform message format, that is, in the broadest sense, on a communication protocol. For our example, a message looks like the one shown in Listing 27.4.

```
{
  id: '95ab6062-ded3-41db-8d65-2059232c67e2',
  role: 'user',
  cmd: 'getAll'
}
```

Listing 27.4 Format of a RabbitMQ Message

The message has a unique ID, called a *correlation identifier*, which is used to link the request to the response (go to *www.enterpriseintegrationpatterns.com/Correlation-Identifier.html* for more on correlation identifiers). In addition, there are the role and cmd properties. Aside from that, the message may have an optional data field to which you can transfer further information. The role field is used to narrow down the recipient. This is already done via the name of the communication channel, but should the user service send or receive metadata or logging data via the message queue in the future, for example, this can be mapped via the role property. The cmd property contains the command to be executed, which can be a value such as getAll or create. Based on the role and cmd property, the user service decides which function to execute. Thus, the *index.js* file performs the task of a router.

27.4.2   Connecting to the RabbitMQ Server

Basically, using the message queue, in this case, RabbitMQ, is similar to using a database. First you establish a connection to the server, and then you can write to and read from the queue. In Listing 27.5, you can see the implementation of the getChannel function in the *connect.js* file of the user service.

```
import { connect } from 'amqplib';

let channel = null;
export const queue = 'user';

export async function getChannel() {
  try {
    if (channel) {
      return channel;
    }
    const connection = await connect('amqp://rabbitmq');
    channel = await connection.createChannel();

    const ok = await channel.assertQueue(queue);

    if (ok) {
      return channel;
```

```
    }
  } catch (error) {
    console.error(error);
    throw error;
  }
}
```

Listing 27.5 Connecting to RabbitMQ (user/connect.js)

First, you import the `connect` function from the `amqplib` package, which you use to connect to the message queue. The interface of the package supports both a callback-based and a promise-based variant. In the example, you use the promise-based interface in conjunction with the asynchronous `getChannel` function and the `await` keyword to first connect to RabbitMQ via *amqp://rabbitmq*. The host name `rabbitmq` is provided to you by `docker-compose` through the local network. Then you create a channel on this connection and build an initial queue named `user`.

You return the created channel object after the operations are completed. If an error occurs in this process, it's caught by the `try-catch` statement, output to the console, and continues to be thrown. For the purpose of optimization, you should store the reference to the channel in a variable named `channel`. If the `getChannel` function is called more than once, it returns the previously created channel object.

27.4.3 Handling Incoming Messages

As is the case with Express, you can implement message handling directly in the event handler. However, a better variant is to swap out these routines to functions of their own. If, in addition to that, you assign meaningful names to these functions, you can significantly increase the readability of your source code and also facilitate testing the application. To implement this message queue controller, you must first create a new *controller.js* file in the *user* directory of your application and save the source code from Listing 27.6 there.

```
import { create, getAll } from './model.js';
import { getChannel, queue } from './connect.js';

function createMessage(id, data) {
  return {
    role: 'user',
    cmd: 'answer',
    id,
    data,
  };
}
```

763

```
async function send(message) {
  const channel = await getChannel();
  channel.sendToQueue(queue, Buffer.from(JSON.stringify(message)));
}

export async function getAllAction(channel, id) {
  const data = await getAll();
  const message = createMessage(id, data);
  send(message);
}

export async function createAction(channel, id, data) {
  const newData = await create(data);
  const message = createMessage(id, newData);
  send(message);
}
```

Listing 27.6 User Controller (user/controller.js)

You structure the two exported functions getAllAction and createAction according to
the same schema: In the first step, you trigger the actual action, either reading or creating a record in the model; wait for the action to complete; create a message; and send it
to the message queue. The sent messages, like the received ones before, follow a certain
format. They also contain the role and cmd fields. The cmd field contains the value answer
to indicate that it's an asynchronous response to a command. The id corresponds to
the id of the request to be responded to. This allows the requesting entity to establish
the link between the request and the response. The last component in the implementation of the user service is the connection of the database.

27.4.4   Database Connection

A MongoDB database is for storing the user objects. You've already installed the appropriate driver in Section 27.4.1, using the npm install mongodb command. After that, you
can implement your model in the *model.js* file in the *user* directory of your application,
as shown in Listing 27.7.

```
import { MongoClient } from 'mongodb';

const url = 'mongodb://mongodb:27017';
const dbName = 'users';

async function connect() {
  const client = await MongoClient.connect(url);
  const db = client.db(dbName);
  const usersCollection = db.collection('users');
```

```
  return {
    client,
    usersCollection,
  };
}

export async function getAll() {
  const { client, usersCollection } = await connect();
  const data = await usersCollection.find().toArray();
  client.close();
  return data;
}

export async function create(user) {
  const { client, usersCollection } = await connect();
  await usersCollection.insertOne(user);
  client.close();
  return user;
}
```

Listing 27.7 Model Implementation (user/model.js)

The model provides the two functions, `getAll` and `create`. Both are async functions that first set up a connection, then communicate with the database, disconnect, and return the result wrapped in a promise object. In this case, you set the database URL to the value `mongodb://mongodb:27017` because using `docker-compose` changes the host name from `localhost` to `mongodb`. In Listing 27.9, up ahead in this section, you can find the corresponding *docker-compose.yml* file.

With this implementation, you've realized the first complete process from the incoming request to the database and back to the client via the outgoing response.

27.4.5   Docker Setup

You've implemented the first microservice of your application with this source code. To be able to start it, you need to boot the MongoDB instance, the RabbitMQ server, and the actual user service. This can be done by starting each of these services in their own Docker container. To avoid having to start the containers individually by hand, you should integrate them into your `docker-compose` configuration.

For RabbitMQ and MongoDB, we'll use the default images. The user service is created via a Dockerfile. The Dockerfile required for this is shown in Listing 27.8.

```
FROM node:16.8.0
WORKDIR /usr/src/app
COPY package*.json ./
```

```
RUN npm install
COPY . .
CMD [ "npm", "start" ]
```

Listing 27.8 Dockerfile of the User Service

With this Dockerfile, you've created the basis for the user service. Listing 27.9 contains the source code of the *docker-compose.yml* file, which you can use to start the service.

```
version: '3'
services:
  mongodb:
    image: mongo:latest
    container_name: 'mongodb'
    ports:
      - 27017:27017
  mongo-seed:
    image: mongo:latest
    links:
      - mongodb
    volumes:
      - ./initUser.json:/initUser.json
    command: 'mongoimport --host mongodb --db users --collection users ⏎
      --type json --file /initUser.json --jsonArray'
  rabbitmq:
    image: rabbitmq:latest
    ports:
      - 5672:5672
  user:
    build:
      context: user
    depends_on:
      - 'mongodb'
      - 'rabbitmq'
    restart: on-failure
    links:
      - 'rabbitmq'
```

Listing 27.9 docker-compose.yml File for the User Service

In this file, you define four containers: user, mongo-seed, mongodb, and rabbitmq. For the user container, you reference the Dockerfile generated earlier. For mongodb and rabbitmq, you reference the respective default images and release the ports for access. By specifying restart: on-failure, you ensure that the user container is automatically restarted if the other two haven't yet started and an error occurs.

For you to be able to log in to your application later, you must make sure to initially populate your database. You can do this by specifying the `mongoimport` command as command with the `mongo-seed` container. This command uses the *initUser.json* file as input. You can find the contents of the file in Listing 27.10.

```
[
  {
    "username": "sspringer",
    "password": "test"
  }
]
```

Listing 27.10 Data for a First Test User (initUser.json)

Then, you can start this part of your application via the `docker-compose up` command in the root directory of your application. At this point, the service can't be tested directly unless you connect directly to the message queue and generate the required messages. In Figure 27.5, you can see the current state of the implementation in the original architecture.

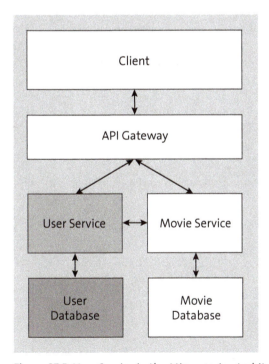

Figure 27.5 User Service in the Microservice Architecture

To make the application's interface more convenient to use, the next step is to take care of implementing your application's API gateway.

27.5   API Gateway

The API gateway brings together the individual microservices of the application. This has the advantage that the clients of the application don't communicate with multiple endpoints, but only with one central gateway, which can handle the internal distribution of requests and, in this role, is able to distribute the loads. In addition, the API gateway plays a security-critical role by hiding the internal structure of the microservice application from the outside world.

It also handles central tasks such as authentication and, if necessary, scheduling of encrypted communication. Depending on the requirements, communication within the microservice application can also take place unencrypted on a secured network. In the following sections, you'll learn how to implement authentication and route the requests to the user service.

27.5.1   Connecting the User Service

The API gateway is an Express application that has a model-view-controller (MVC) structure. However, instead of communicating directly with a database in the models, you query the respective microservices at this point. You store the files of this service in the *api* directory parallel to the *user* directory. You initialize the API gateway in the first step via the `npm init` command to create a *package.json* file. Then you install Express and the `uuid` and `amqplib` packages using the `npm install express uuid amqplib` command. The resulting *package.json* file is shown in Listing 27.11.

```
{
  "name": "api-gateway",
  "version": "1.0.0",
  "description": "",
  "main": "index.js",
  "private": true,
  "type": "module",
  "scripts": {
    "start": "node index.js"
  },
  "keywords": [],
  "author": "",
  "license": "ISC",
  "dependencies": {
    "amqplib": "^0.8.0",
    "express": "^4.17.1",
    "uuid": "^8.3.2"

  }
}
```

Listing 27.11 "package.json" File of the API Gateway (api/package.json)

Based on this, you can then start implementing the API gateway entry point. This is a regular Express application with body parser middleware and a separate router for the */user* path. The source code of this entry file, which you save under the name *index.js* in the *api* directory, is shown in Listing 27.12.

```javascript
import express from 'express';
import { router as userRouter } from './user/index.js';

const app = express();

app.use(express.json());
app.use('/user', userRouter);

app.listen(8080, () => console.log('API Gateway is listening'));
```

Listing 27.12 Entry File to the API Gateway (api/index.js)

In the API gateway, you provide a separate module in a separate subdirectory for each service that can be communicated with to decouple the application as much as possible. The router of the user module defines the public interface with which the clients of the application can communicate. For the current development state of the application, only two routes are needed: one to query all user data and one to create users. You save the router in the *api/user/index.js* file, as shown in Listing 27.13.

```javascript
import { Router } from 'express';
import { getAllAction, createAction } from './controller.js';

const router = Router();

router.get('/', getAllAction);
router.post('/', createAction);

export { router };
```

Listing 27.13 Router of the User Module (api/user/index.js)

The two actions make sure that the required information gets extracted from the request and forwarded to the model. Finally, with the model's response, you generate the response to the client, which you send in JSON format.

When implementing the user controller in Listing 27.14, you're still independent of the underlying model, so the exchange of the communication link affects only one place, while the rest of the API gateway structure remains unchanged. In the implementation, you simply assume that the model passes the information and results via promises, which you handle in the controller with async/await.

27

```
import { getAll, create } from './model.js';

export async function getAllAction(request, response) {
  try {
    const userData = await getAll();
    response.json(userData);
  } catch (e) {
    console.error(e);
    response.status(500).json('Interal server error');
  }
}

export async function createAction(request, response) {
  try {
    const newUser = await create(request.body);
    response.json(newUser);
  } catch (e) {
    console.error(e);
    response.status(500).json('Internal server error');
  }
}
```

Listing 27.14 Implementation of the User Controller in the API Gateway (user/api/controller.js)

27.5.2   Asynchronous Communication with the User Service

Up to this point, you've structured the API gateway like a traditional Express application. The problem now is that you have to work with a very decoupled type of communication. For a normal database or web service that you address via HTTP, you can use promises or callback functions. In this case, however, you send a message to the message queue, which is accepted by the user service and answered at a later time. Because the model is primarily concerned with communication, this is the first place you need to worry about exchanging information with the message queue. In Listing 27.15, you send a message over the message queue within the getAll and the create function each, which is accepted and processed by the user service.

```
import { v4 as uuidv4 } from 'uuid';
import { getChannel, queue } from '../connect.js';

export async function getAll() {
  const channel = await getChannel();
  const message = {
    id: uuidv4(),
```

```
    role: 'user',
    cmd: 'getAll',
  };

  channel.sendToQueue(queue, Buffer.from(JSON.stringify(message)));

  return message;
}

Export async function create(data) {
  const channel = await getChannel();
  const message = {
    id: uuidv4(),
    role: 'user',
    cmd: 'create',
    data,
  };

  channel.sendToQueue(queue, Buffer.from(JSON.stringify(message)));

  return message;
}
```

Listing 27.15 Model Implementation in the API Gateway (api/user/model.js)

The central element of the model implementation is the communication with the message queue. So, at this point, you need to make some adjustments to the source code of your application to handle this changed method of information exchange. The core of the implementation is the *connect.js* file in the *api* directory. It's responsible for connecting to the message queue and provides functions you can use to process the asynchronous messages.

Listing 27.16 contains the source code of the *connect.js* file in the *api* directory. You already know the getChannel function from the user service. You also use this function in the API gateway to connect to the message queue. One difference from the previous approach can be found in the registerHandler function. This function uses the consume method of the channel object you created using the getChannel function to receive messages. The registerHandler function responds only to messages with role user and cmd answer. To map a response from the user service to a command from the API gateway, you use the id of the messages, which are the same for the request and response. The pattern you build here is referred to as request/reply. You can find a detailed description of this pattern at *www.enterpriseintegrationpatterns.com/patterns/messaging/RequestReply.html*.

```
import { connect } from 'amqplib';

let channel = null;
export const queue = 'user';

const registry = {};

export function register(id, response) {
  registry[id] = response;
}

export function answer(id, data) {
  registry[id].send(data);
  delete registry[id];
}

export async function getChannel() {
  try {
    if (channel) {
      return channel;
    }
    const connection = await connect('amqp://rabbitmq');
    channel = await connection.createChannel();

    const ok = await channel.assertQueue(queue);

    if (ok) {
      return channel;
    }
  } catch (error) {
    console.error(error);
    throw error;
  }
}

export function registerHandler(channel) {
  channel.consume(queue, (receivedMessage) => {
    const messageData = JSON.parse(receivedMessage.content.toString());

    if (messageData.role === 'user' && messageData.cmd === 'answer') {
      answer(messageData.id, messageData.data);
      channel.ack(receivedMessage);
    } else {
      channel.nack(receivedMessage);
```

```
    }
  });
}
```

Listing 27.16 Connecting the Message Queue (api/connect.js)

In the API gateway, you save the response objects of the user requests in an object structure named `registry` with the `id` of the message as the key. If a message is received from the user service via the message queue, you can extract the response object from the `registry` object and send the data received from the user service to the user as a JSON response. To secure the communication, you can include time-outs. If a message is received and takes longer to process than the specified time-out value, the receiver throws an exception. In the code example, caching the response objects is done by calling the `register` function in the controller, whereas responding to the request is done using the `answer` function you call inside the `registerHandler` function.

In the next step, you need to integrate the functions of this file into the application. Let's start with the entry into the API gateway—the *index.js* file in the *api* directory. Here you call the `getChannel` and `registerHandler` functions, as shown in Listing 27.17.

```
import express from 'express';
import { router as userRouter } from './user/index.js';
import { getChannel, registerHandler } from './connect.js';

const channel = await getChannel();
registerHandler(channel);

const app = express();

app.use(express.json());
app.use('/user', userRouter);

app.listen(8080, () => console.log('API Gateway is listening'));
```

Listing 27.17 Connecting to the Message Queue (api/index.js)

For a complete implementation of the communication between API gateway and the user service, you only need to handle the responses of the user service in the API gateway. This is done in the controller of the user module, that is, in the *controller.js* file in the *user* directory of the API gateway, as shown in Listing 27.18.

```
import { register } from '../connect.js';
import { getAll, create } from './model.js';

export async function getAllAction(request, response) {
  try {
```

27

```
    const { id } = await getAll();
    register(id, response);
  } catch (e) {
    console.error(e);
    response.status(500).json('Interal server error');
  }
}

export async function createAction(request, response) {
  try {
    const { id } = await create(request.body);
    register(id, response);
  } catch (e) {
    console.error(e);
    response.status(500).json('Internal server error');
  }
}
```

Listing 27.18 Integrating Message Queue Responses (api/user/controller.js)

When all data records have been read and when you create a new one, you receive the created message object from the model. From this, you extract the id of the message using a destructuring statement and call the register function from the *connect.js* file with this information and the response object. As soon as the response is received via the message queue, the user's request is answered with the data from the user service.

27.5.3   Docker Setup of the API Gateway

Before you can test your application, you still need a container for the API gateway. For this purpose, you must create a file named *Dockerfile* and place it in the root directory of the API gateway. You can see the contents of this file in Listing 27.19.

```
FROM node:16.8.0
WORKDIR /usr/src/app
COPY package*.json ./
RUN npm install
COPY . .
EXPOSE 8080
CMD [ "node", "index.js" ]
```

Listing 27.19 Dockerfile for the API Gateway (api/Dockerfile)

You integrate the API Gateway container into your *docker-compose.yml* file in the next step, as you can see in Listing 27.20.

```
Version: '3'
services:
  mongodb:
    image: mongo:latest
    container_name: 'mongodb'
    ports:
      - 27017:27017
  mongo-seed:
    image: mongo:latest
    links:
      - mongodb
    volumes:
      - ./initUser.json:/initUser.json
    command: 'mongoimport -host mongodb -db users -collection users ⤶
      -type json -file /initUser.json -jsonArray'
  rabbitmq:
    image: rabbitmq:latest
    ports:
      - 5672:5672
  user:
    build:
      context: user
    depends_on:
      - 'mongodb'
      - 'rabbitmq'
    restart: on-failure
    links:
      - 'rabbitmq'
  api:
    build:
      context: api
    ports:
      - 8080:8080
    depends_on:
      - 'user'
    restart: on-failure
    links:
      - rabbitmq
```

Listing 27.20 "docker-compose.yml" File Extension

Now you can start your application via the `docker-compose up` command and access the
API gateway. The simplest variant is to open the address *http://localhost:8080/user* in
your browser. Then the combination of API gateway and user service will provide the

list of existing users. Things will get more interesting when you use the creating endpoint, that is, *http://localhost:8080/user*, with the POST method. To do this, you can either use a command-line tool such as cURL or a graphical interface such as Postman. Listing 27.21 shows the corresponding cURL command, while Figure 27.6 shows the view in Postman.

```
$ curl
  -X POST
  --data '{"username": "jdoe", "password": "test"}'
  --header 'content-type:application/json'
  localhost:8080/user
```

Listing 27.21 Creating a New User with cURL

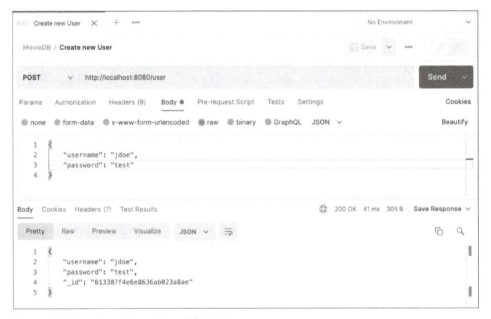

Figure 27.6 Creating a New User with Postman

27.5.4   Authentication

Currently, all users can still access their endpoints uncontrolled. But we'll change that in the next step. Because microservices don't care about authentication, you need to implement this in the API gateway. Depending on how you implement your application, you can choose from different mechanisms. In this context, the authentication via JSON web tokens (JWTs) has become widely used. You already learned about the implementation of this strategy in detail in Chapter 9, so we'll limit the discussion here to a brief overview as well as the implementation of the relevant code passages.

You install the packages required for JWT authentication in the API gateway, that is, in the *api* directory, using the `npm install jsonwebtoken express-jwt` command. Then you create a new file named *auth.js* containing the routes relevant for authentication. Listing 27.22 shows the source code of this file.

```
import jwt from 'jsonwebtoken';
import { Router } from 'express';
import { getAll } from './user/model.js';
import { register } from './connect.js';

const router = Router();

router.post('/', async (request, response) => {
  try {
    const { id } = await getAll();
    register(id, (users) => {
      const user = users.find(
        (u) =>
          u.username === request.body.username &&
          u.password === request.body.password,
      );

      if (user) {
        const payload = { ...user };
        delete payload.password;
        const token = jwt.sign(payload, 'secret');
        response.json({ token });
      } else {
        response.status(401).json('unauthorized');
      }
    });
  } catch € {
    response.status(401).json('unauthorized');
  }
});

export { router };
```

Listing 27.22 Authentication in the API Gateway (api/auth.js)

The logic behind the `login` route works a bit differently from the previous implementations in the user controller. For this reason, a modification in the *connect.js* file is also required. So far, you've passed the `id` of the request and the response object. A response via the message queue ensured that the data was sent directly to the user. In this case, you need the user data, but the requesting user should receive a token and not the user list. Consequently, you make sure that you can register a callback function in addition to the response object. In Listing 27.23, you already benefit from this modification and register such a callback function, which then takes care of sending the response to the user.

```
import { connect } from 'amqplib';

let channel = null;
export const queue = 'user';

const registry = {};

export function register(id, response) {...}

export function answer(id, data) {
  if (typeof registry[id] === 'function') {
    registry[id](data);
  } else {
    registry[id].send(data);
  }
  delete registry[id];
}

export async function getChannel() {...}

export function registerHandler(channel) {...}
```

Listing 27.23 Modification of the "connect.js" File (api/connect.js)

To enable authentication, you include the router you just created from the *auth.js* file in your application's entry file and secure the user route with express-jwt. In Listing 27.24, you can see how this works.

```
import express from 'express';
import expressJwt from 'express-jwt';
import { router as userRouter } from './user/index.js';
import { router as loginRouter } from './auth.js';
import { getChannel, registerHandler } from './connect.js';

const channel = await getChannel();
registerHandler(channel);

const app = express();

app.use(express.json());
```

```
app.use('/login', loginRouter);
app.use('/user', expressJwt({ secret: 'secret' }), userRouter);

app.use((err, request, response, next) => {
  if (err.name === 'UnauthorizedError') {
    response.status(401).json('unauthorized');
  } else {
    next();
  }
});

app.listen(8080, () => console.log('API Gateway is listening'));
```

Listing 27.24 Integrating Authentication (api/index.js)

The integration of an authentication process now enables you to assign requests to your application to specific users and filter the delivered results accordingly. For this purpose, you need to pass this information to the individual microservices. In the simplest case, this can be done by using parameters in the request. Alternatively, you can implement a central user service that microservices can request. For this to work, the API gateway passes the user's identification as a token to the microservice, which has the token resolved by the central user service and thus receives the user information.

After you've created a JWT using the login route, you can use Postman or cURL to create new users and read the current user list. Listing 27.25 shows the cURL call you can use to generate a new JWT.

```
$ curl
  -H "Content-Type: application/json"
  -X POST
  -d '{"username": "sspringer", "password": "test"}'
  http://localhost:8080/login
```
{"token":"eyJhbGciOiJIUzI1NiIsInR5cCI6IkpXVCJ9.eyIwIjp7Il9pZCI6IjViMzc0ZWI2NzQOM
DQzMDQ1OGRmN2JhMCIsInVzZXJuYW1lIjoic3NwcmluuZ2VyIiwicGFzc3dvcmQiOiJOZXN0In0sIjEiO
nsiX2lkIjoiNWIzNzUwNWUzYzg3YzljMjJlNzIyMGU2IiwidXNlcm5hbWUiOiJzc3ByaW5nZXIiLCJwY
XNzd29yZCI6inRlc3QifSwiMiI6eyJfaWQiOiI1YjM3NTBiYzAxN2MxODk1ZjA1MzFlM2EiLCJ1c2Vyb
mFtZSI6InNzcHJpbmdlciIsInBhc3N3b3JkIjoidGVzdCJ9LCIzIjp7Il9pZCI6IjViM2IwYWQwMDE3Y
zE4OTVmMDUzMWVkMyIsInVzZXJuYW1lIjoic3NwcmluuZ2VyIiwicGFzc3dvcmQiOiJOZXN0In0sImlhd
CI6MTUzMDY4MTIxN30.skb4ubpta8-YcA35cIJML54Cm2-Ty6UFTik2tHMgzJO"}

Listing 27.25 Creating a New Token

With the token, you can now read the user list, for example. For this purpose, as shown in Listing 27.26, you send a GET request to *http://localhost:8080/user* and set the authorization header accordingly. In response, you'll receive a list of users of the system.

```
$ curl -H "Content-Type: application/json" -
H "Authorization: Bearer I1NiIsInR 5cCI6IkpXVCJ9.eyIwIjp7Il9pZCI6IjViMzcOZWI2NzQ
OMDQzMDQ1OGRmN2JhMCIsInVzZXJuYW11Ijoic3NwcmluZ2VyIiwicGFzc3dvcmQiOiJOZXN0InOsIjE
iOnsiX21kIjoiNWIzNzUwNWUzYzg3YzljMjJlNzIyMGU2IiwidXNlcm5hbWUiOiJzc3ByaW5nZXIiLCJ
wYXNzd29yZCI6InRlc3QifSwiMiI6eyJfaWQiOiI1YjM3NTBiYzAxN2MxODk1ZjA1MzF1M2EiLCJ1c2v
ybmFtZSI6InNzcHJpbmdlciIsInBhc3N3b3JkIjoidGVzdCJ9LCIzIjp7Il9pZCI6IjViM2IwYWQwMDE
3YzE4OTVmMDUzMWVkMyIsInVzZXJuYW11Ijoic3NwcmluZ2VyIiwicGFzc3dvcmQiOiJOZXN0IOsImlh
dCI6MTUzMDY4MTIxN30.skb4ubpta8-YcA35cIJML54Cm2-Ty6UFTik2tHMgzJO" http://
localhost:8080/user
[
{"_id":"5b374eb67440430458df7ba0","username":"sspringer","password":"test"},
{"_id":"5b3751191efbf54985a67480","username":"John","password":"secret"},
]
```

Listing 27.26 Reading the User List

This step completes another component of your microservice application, as you can see in Figure 27.7.

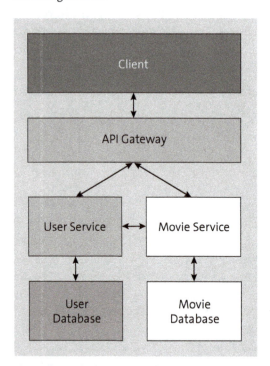

Figure 27.7 API Gateway in the Microservice Architecture

27.6   Synchronous Microservice with Express

The second microservice you implement for your application is the movie service. This is a classic Express application that can be accessed via HTTP. The difference with the

Express applications you've developed so far is that the movie service has a higher level of specialization. This microservice only takes care of all tasks related to the movie database, that is, reading and writing records as well as validating them. In this section, you implement read-only and create-only access for all create, read, update, delete (CRUD) operations as examples.

27.6.1   Setup

The basis of the movie microservice is Express with some extensions. You save the files of this service in the *movie* directory. The first step is again to create a *package.json* file using the npm init command. The required packages will then be installed via the npm install express mysql2 command. The MySQL driver is used to connect to the database. You can see the *package.json* of the movie service in Listing 27.27.

```json
{
  "name": "movie-service",
  "version": "1.0.0",
  "description": "",
  "main": "index.js",
  "private": true,
  "type": "module",
  "scripts": {
    "start": "node index.js"
  },
  "keywords": [],
  "author": "",
  "license": "ISC" ,
  "dependencies": {
    "express": "^4.17.1",
    "mysql2": "^2.3.0"
  }
}
```

Listing 27.27 "package.json" File of the Movie Service (movie/package.json)

The initial file is similar to that of the API gateway. Listing 27.28 shows the source code of this file.

```javascript
import express from 'express';
import { getAllAction, createAction } from './controller.js';

const app = express();
app.use(express.json());

app.get('/movie', getAllAction);
```

781

```
app.post('/movie', createAction);

app.listen(8181, () => console.log('Movie service is listening'));
```

Listing 27.28 Entry Point to the Movie Microservice (movie/index.js)

The entry file is relatively compact, so the routes to the current state of implementation are also still located here. However, as soon as you define more than four or five routes, you should swap them out to a separate file.

27.6.2   Controller

You swap out the callback functions behind the routes to a separate controller for a better overview. This controller is responsible for generating a response from the incoming request, based on the functionality provided by the model. The controller code is shown in Listing 27.29.

```
import { getAll, create } from './model.js';

export async function getAllAction(request, response) {
  try {
    const movies = await getAll();
    response.json(movies);
  } catch (e) {
    response.status(500).json(e);
  }
}

export async function createAction(request, response) {
  try {
    const movie = await create(request.body);
    response.json(movie);
  } catch (e) {
    response.status(500).json(e);
  }
}
```

Listing 27.29 Movie Controller Implementation (movie/controller.js)

27.6.3   Model Implementation

The final step in the implementation of the microservice consists of implementing the model that manages the access to the database. In this case, the endpoint is a MySQL database, so you need the MySQL driver for Node.js to communicate. Listing 27.30 contains the source code of the model.

```
import mysql from 'mysql2/promise';

async function connect() {
  const connection = await mysql.createConnection({
    host: 'mysql',
    user: 'root',
    password: 'topSecret',
    database: 'Movie',
  });

  connection.connect();

  return connection;
}

export async function getAll() {
  const connection = await connect();

  const query = 'SELECT * FROM Movie';
  const [data] = await connection.query(query);

  connection.end();

  return data;
}

export async function create(movie) {
  const connection = await connect();

  const query = 'INSERT INTO Movie (title, year) VALUES (?, ?)';
  const [result] = await connection.query(query, [movie.title, movie.year]);

  connection.end();

  return { ...movie, id: result.insertId };
}
```

Listing 27.30 Movie Model for Querying the MySQL Database (movie/model.js)

In the model, you first generate a helper function that establishes the connection to the database. It returns the object representation of the connection. You use this helper function in both the getAll and create functions to set up the connection and then send the appropriate query using the query method of the connection object. Once you get the result back, you terminate the connection and return the result. Because both functions are implemented as async functions and the mysql2 driver works with native promises, you won't have any problem at this point and don't need any additional boilerplate code.

27.6.4   Docker Setup

To be able to start the movie microservice, you also need a Dockerfile, the structure of which is shown in Listing 27.31.

```
FROM node:16.8.0
WORKDIR /usr/src/app
COPY package*.json ./
RUN npm install
COPY . .
EXPOSE 8181
CMD [ "node", "index.js" ]
```

Listing 27.31 Dockerfile for the Movie Service

In addition to this Dockerfile, you integrate the service as well as the container that contains the database into your *docker-compose.yml*. The results are shown in Listing 27.32.

```
version: '3'
services:
  mongodb:
    image: mongo:latest
    container_name: 'mongodb'
    ports:
      - 27017:27017
  mongo-seed:
    image: mongo:latest
    links:
      - mongodb
    volumes:
      - ./initUser.json:/initUser.json
    command: 'mongoimport --host mongodb --db users --collection users ⤸
      --type json --file /initUser.json --jsonArray'
  rabbitmq:
    image: rabbitmq:latest
    ports:
      - 5672:5672
  user:
    build:
      context: user
```

```
    depends_on:
      - 'mongodb'
      - 'rabbitmq'
    restart: on-failure
    links:
      - rabbitmq
  mysql:
    image: mysql:latest
    environment:
      MYSQL_ROOT_PASSWORD: 'topSecret'
      MYSQL_ROOT_HOST: '%'
    ports:
      - 3306:3306
    volumes:
      - ./initMovie.sql:/initMovie.sql
    command: 'mysqld --init-file=/initMovie.sql'
  movie:
    build:
      context: movie
    depends_on:
      - 'mysql'
    restart: on-failure
  api:
    build:
      context: api
    ports:
      - 8080:8080
    depends_on:
      - 'user'
      - 'movie'
    restart: on-failure
    links:
      - rabbitmq
```

Listing 27.32 Integration into the "docker-compose.yml" File

You create the initial MySQL database structure similar to MongoDB with a file and the command you pass when starting the container. The structure of the *initMovie.sql* file is shown in Listing 27.33.

```
CREATE DATABASE `Movie`;

USE `Movie`;

CREATE TABLE `Movie` (
```

```
  `id` int(11) NOT NULL AUTO_INCREMENT,
  `title` varchar(255) DEFAULT NULL,
  `year` int(11) DEFAULT NULL,
  PRIMARY KEY (`id`)
) ENGINE=InnoDB DEFAULT CHARSET=utf8;
INSERT INTO `Movie` (`title`, `year`) VALUES
('Iron Man', 2008),
('Thor', 2011),
('Captain America', 2011);
```

Listing 27.33 Initial Movie Structure (initMovie.sql)

With the movie service, you've completed the last microservice of the application. Figure 27.8 shows this last component in the overall architecture.

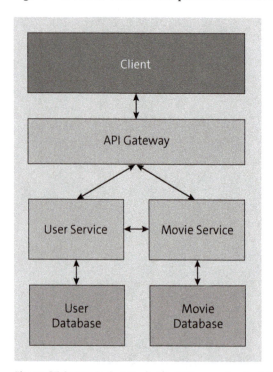

Figure 27.8 Movie Service in the Microservice Architecture

27.6.5 Integration into the API Gateway

To integrate the movie microservice into the API gateway, you must first install the request package using the npm install request command. Then you extend the entry file with the entry to the movie module, which you must also secure against unauthorized access. For this purpose, you use the express-jwt command. Listing 27.34 shows the customized source code.

```
import express from 'express';
import expressJwt from 'express-jwt';
import { router as userRouter } from './user/index.js';
import { router as loginRouter } from './auth.js';
import { router as movieRouter } from './movie/index.js';
import { getChannel, registerHandler } from './connect.js';

const channel = await getChannel();
registerHandler(channel);

const app = express();

app.use(express.json());
app.use('/login', loginRouter);
app.use(
  '/user',
  expressJwt({ secret: 'secret', algorithms: ['HS256'] }),
  userRouter,
);
app.use(
  '/movie',
  expressJwt({ secret: 'secret', algorithms: ['HS256'] }),
  movieRouter,
);

app.use((err, request, response, next) => {
  if (err.name === 'UnauthorizedError') {
    response.status(401).json('unauthorized');
  } else {
    next();
  }
});

app.listen(8080, () => console.log('API Gateway is listening'));
```

Listing 27.34 Integrating the Movie Router into the Entry File of the API Gateway
(api/index.js)

As with the user module, the source code for the movie module is stored in a separate
directory named *movie*. Here, you first create a file named *index.js*, which contains the
movie router (see Listing 27.35).

```
import { Router } from 'express';
import { getAllAction, createAction } from './controller.js';
```

787

```
const router = Router();

router.get('/', getAllAction);
router.post('/', createAction);

export { router };
```

Listing 27.35 Router of the Movie Module (api/movie/index.js)

The implementation of the callback functions that are mapped to the routes and originate from the *controller.js* file is shown in Listing 27.36.

```
import { getAll, create } from './model.js';

export async function getAllAction(request, response) {
  try {
    const movies = await getAll();
    response.json(movies);
  } catch (e) {
    response.status(500).json(e);
  }
}
export async function createAction(request, response) {
  try {
    const newMovie = await create(request.body);
    response.json(newMovie);
  } catch (e) {
    response.status(500).json(e);
  }
}
```

Listing 27.36 Controller of the Movie Module (api/movie/controller.js)

The biggest difference between the user and movie modules can be found in the implementation of the model, which, in both cases, provides a promise interface to the outside world. In the case of the user model, communication is asynchronous via a message queue. With the movie module, you use synchronous communication via HTTP requests. In this case, you use the axios package, which you install via the npm install axios command, to route the requests to the microservice (see Listing 27.37).

```
import axios from 'axios';

const url = 'http://movie:8181/movie';

export async function getAll() {
  const { data } = await axios.get(url);
```

```
  return data;
}

export async function create(movie) {
  const { data } = await axios.post(url, movie);
  return data;
}
```

Listing 27.37 Movie Model for Connecting the Movie Microservice

With this module, you've implemented a complete cross section of your microservice application and implemented both a synchronous and an asynchronous microservice. When you start your application now using the `docker-compose up` command, you can use Postman or cURL to communicate with the application, get a JWT issued, and query the application's interfaces. Listing 27.38 shows how you can use cURL to read the list of movies stored in the database.

```
$ curl -H "Content-Type: application/json" -H "Authorization:
Bearer eyJhbGci0 iJIUzI1NiIsInR5cCI6IkpXVCJ9.eyIwIjp7Il9pZCI6IjViMzc0ZWI2NzQ0MDQ
zMDQ10GRmN2JhMCIsInVzZXJuYW1lIjoic3Nwcm1uZ2VyIiwicGFzc3dvcmQi0i0JZXN0In0sIjEiOns
iX21kIjoiNWIzNzUwNWUzYzg3YzljMjJlNzIyMGU2IiwidXNlcm5hbWUi0iJzc3ByaW5nZXIiLCJwYXN
zd29yZCI6InRlc3QifSwiMiI6eyJfaWQi0iI1YjM3NTBiYzAxN2MxODk1ZjA1MzFlM2EiLCJ1c2VybmF
tZSI6InNzcHJpbmdlciIsInBhc3N3b3JkIjoidGVzdCJ9LCIzIjp7Il9pZCI6IjViM2IwYWQwMDE3YzE
40TVmMDUzMWVkMyIsInVzZXJuYW1lIjoic3Nwcm1uZ2VyIiwicGFzc3dvcmQi0i0JZXN0In0sImlhdCI
6MTUzMDY4MTIxN30.skb4ubpta8-YcA35cIJML54Cm2-Ty6UFTik2tHMgzJ0"
http://localhost:8080/movie
[
  {"id":1,"title":"Iron Man","year":2008},
  {"id":2,"title":"Thor","year":2011},
  {"id":3,"title":"Captain America","year":2011}
]
```

Listing 27.38 Reading the Stored Movie Data

27.7 Summary

This chapter has introduced some facets of a microservice architecture with Node.js. You've learned how to communicate both synchronously and asynchronously between services, how to package services in their own containers, and how to separate them from data storage so that they can be better scaled.

However, the options shown only represent the beginning of the implementation of such an application. The next steps you should take involve implementing service discovery, where you can register your services in a central location and, as a consumer of a service, request the address of such a service. One implementation for this is Consul; a Node.js client also exists for this service, which you can use in your application.

As you've seen in this chapter, Node.js as a platform for microservices is very flexible and can be connected to almost all interfaces. Both client and server implementations are available as Node Package Manager (npm) packages for all common protocols. When choosing the right components, you should always keep your requirements in mind and check whether the targeted solution can meet them.

With the right architecture and communication channels, you're able to scale your Node.js services as much as you want and also handle a very large number of requests. This allows you to start multiple instances of individual services and distribute incoming requests among them.

Chapter 28

Deno

If you want to be happy all the time, you often have to change.
—Confucius

Node.js isn't the only server-side JavaScript platform, but it's by far the most widely used. However, one solution clearly stands out from the competition for several reasons. For example, there is the developer of the competing platform: Ryan Dahl. This name should sound familiar from Chapter 1. Correct—that's the guy who invented Node.js. Dahl announced Deno in a speech called "10 Things I Regret about Node.js." Interestingly, Dahl gave this speech at the same jsconf.eu event as his announcement of Node.js years earlier. So Deno is the attempt to make the problem that is also addressed by Node.js better. A new platform naturally has a much easier time because it can learn from the mistakes of its predecessor and doesn't have to bother about backward compatibility. In this chapter, we'll take a look at Deno and see where the platform's differences and similarities when compared to Node.js. You'll also learn how to solve various problems with Deno based on some concrete examples. The official website with extensive documentation, examples, and numerous further resources can be found at *https://deno.land/*. But before we dive into the development, let's take a quick look at the origins and background of Deno.

28.1 The Ten Things Ryan Dahl Regrets about Node.js

The idea behind Deno is the same as behind Node.js: It's supposed to be a server-side JavaScript platform that allows you to implement both command-line tools and web backends. However, according to Dahl, Node.js has some bugs, that is, errors. These bugs aren't so much actual errors in the source code that can be easily corrected by a patch, but rather weaknesses in the architecture that he wants to fix. So, Dahl picked out the biggest problems and is now trying to address them with Deno.

28.1.1 Promises

Promises support was integrated into the core of Node.js in June 2009, but it was removed again in February 2010. This step has led to the fact that many interfaces of Node.js can't be developed optimally.

28

28.1.2   Security

Client-side JavaScript is executed in a sandbox. A script in the browser has only a very limited environment and can't leave it. This mainly affects the use of system resources such as hard disk space or the network. While taking into account current user permissions, Node.js on the other hand, provides you with more or less unrestricted access. For example, Dahl describes that the linter of your project doesn't really need access to the entire system and the network, and he is absolutely right about that.

28.1.3   The Generate Your Projects Build System

The Generate Your Projects (GYP) build system is used for modules based on C libraries to compile these libraries and connect them to Node.js. GYP used to be the standard for Chrome at the time, so the Node.js development team used this tool. Shortly after that, the Chrome team replaced GYP with a new build system called GN. Node.js still uses GYP to build C modules. Therefore, the platform is based on a system that is no longer natively supported by the V8 engine so that additional abstraction layers are required. The problem is solved with the node-gyp tool, which performs this task. This decision results in the system becoming significantly more complex.

28.1.4   Package.json

The central configuration file of a Node.js application—the *package.json* file—originates from the Node Package Manager (npm), but it has also been integrated into Node.js itself; for example, to find the entry point you specify via the *main* property. This file has now become the standard for almost all JavaScript applications, irrespective of whether we're talking about frontend or backend.

The biggest problems Dahl sees with this file is that module loading is too unspecific and modules become too large. When you load npm packages, you just specify the name of the module, when in fact, you should only reference a JavaScript file. In this case, you're also directly required to select a specific version. In addition, the *package.json* file contains a lot of additional information that is relevant but not in the context of the module system.

28.1.5   Node_modules

The basic idea of implementing the CommonJS module system in Node.js was good and should ensure that everything can be resolved explicitly. However, the architecture and structure of the *node_modules* directory make the module resolution algorithm much more complicated, according to Dahl. In addition, the CommonJS module system is seriously different from the way browsers handle JavaScript, for example.

28.1.6   Optional File Extension When Loading Modules

The CommonJS module system with the `require` function allows you to omit the file extension. This is less explicit and leaves a lot of room for interpretation for the module loader. It has to figure out what you really want to load, which in turn affects performance.

28.1.7   Index.js

If you specify only a directory when loading a module, the module system automatically searches for an *index.js* file. Again, the specification isn't particularly explicit and creates room for error.

28.1.8   What's Going on Now with Node.js

If you've counted carefully, you've probably noticed that there aren't 10 things Dahl regrets about Node.js, but only 7. Besides, the world of Node.js isn't that bad. The Node.js development team is already working on some of the issues mentioned. Still others can be avoided in other ways. Thus, the platform converts more and more interfaces to promises. Security and the build system are still issues that haven't been addressed yet, and the same is true for the *package.json* file. You can get rid of the *node_modules* directory using Yarn's Plug'n'Play feature, for example. In Node.js, the optional file name extension and *index.js* file support aren't important due to the ECMAScript module system, so these two issues will have been done away with in future releases.

Despite all the improvements in Node.js, Deno is a platform that brings many good new ideas into play. The hope is that it will be similar to the package manager competition and that the platforms will inspire and learn from each other.

28.2   Installing Deno

Before you can start using Deno, you need to install the platform on your system. The easiest way to do this is to install Deno on the command line. On Linux and macOS, you can use cURL to do that, as shown in Listing 28.1.

```
$ curl -fsSL https://deno.land/x/install/install.sh | sh
```

Listing 28.1 Installing Deno on Linux and macOS

On a Windows system, you can install Deno using the command from Listing 28.2 on the PowerShell.

```
$ iwr https://deno.land/x/install/install.ps1 -useb | iex
```

Listing 28.2 Installing Deno on a Windows System

28

As an alternative to these options, you can also install Deno using package managers such as Homebrew or Chocolatey.

To check whether your installation was successful, you can enter the `deno --version` command on the command line. Listing 28.3 shows an example of the output.

```
deno 1.14.1 (release, x86_64-apple-darwin)
v8 9.4.146.15
typescript 4.4.2
```

Listing 28.3 Output of "deno --version"

As you can see, this command provides information about the V8 engine and TypeScript used, in addition to the version of Deno. The TypeScript version is interesting in that Deno natively supports both JavaScript and TypeScript.

28.2.1   Deno Command-Line Interface

If you have Deno installed on your system, you have access to the `deno` command-line tool. Similar to npm, you can pass commands to Deno. Table 28.1 provides an overview of the available commands.

Command	Description
bundle	Creates a file from the source code and all dependencies
cache	Stores the dependencies in a cache
compile	Compiles the source code into an executable file
completions	Creates the auto-completion for the shell
coverage	Displays the coverage reports
doc	Displays the documentation for a module
eval	Evaluates a script
fmt	Formats the source code
help	Outputs all available commands
info	Outputs information about the cache or a specified file
install	Installs a script as an executable file
lint	Checks the source code
lsp	Starts the language server

Table 28.1 Deno Commands

Command	Description
repl	Starts the Deno shell
run	Runs an application
test	Runs the tests of an application
types	Outputs the TypeScript declarations
upgrade	Updates Deno to the specified version

Table 28.1 Deno Commands (Cont.)

28.3 Execution

Deno usually works with a fairly recent version of the V8 engine, so you can basically develop modern JavaScript without any restrictions. As an example of how to work with Deno, you should use the source code shown in Listing 28.4.

```
class Person {
  #firstname = '';
  #lastname = '';

  constructor(firstname, lastname) {
    this.#firstname = firstname;
    this.#lastname = lastname;
  }

  greet() {
    return `Hello ${this.#firstname} ${this.#lastname}!`;
  }
}

const lisa = new Person('Lisa', 'Miller');
console.log(lisa.greet()); // Output: Hello Lisa Miller!
```

Listing 28.4 A Simple Example for Deno

When you save the source code from Listing 28.4 in a file named *index.js*, you can run the application via the command shown in Listing 28.5.

```
$ deno run index.js
Hello Lisa Miller!
```

Listing 28.5 Running an Application in Deno

28

Like Node.js, Deno reads the source code at the beginning and keeps the application in memory so that changes to the source code won't take effect. To avoid having to restart your application process manually every time a change is made, the run subcommand supports the --watch option, which ensures that the process is automatically restarted when changes are made to the file system. You don't need to install any additional package for this.

28.3.1 Running a TypeScript Application

With regard to TypeScript source code, Deno works in the same way as it does with JavaScript. Listing 28.6 contains an example that is structured similarly to the one in Listing 28.4, but contains a few TypeScript-specific elements that would cause syntax errors in JavaScript.

```typescript
class Person {
  constructor(private firstname: string, private lastname: string) {}

  greet(): string {
    return `Hello ${this.firstname} ${this.lastname}!`;
  }
}

const lisa: Person = new Person('Lisa', 'Miller');
console.log(lisa.greet()); // Output: Hello Lisa Miller!
```

Listing 28.6 Initial Example in TypeScript

When you save the source code in a file named *index.ts*, you can run the application via the deno run index.ts command, as shown in Listing 28.7.

```
$ deno run index.ts
Check file:///srv/node-buch/index.ts
Hello Lisa Miller!
```

Listing 28.7 Running TypeScript in Deno

Deno runs TypeScript directly without an explicit compilation step. However, the platform checks the source code before running it and reports any errors back to you on the command line.

28.4 Handling Files

Unlike Node.js, Deno doesn't know the concept of modules. Instead, Deno offers you a wide range of built-ins, that is, built-in features you can use instead of modules. Deno defines some global variables and functions such as the `console` object or the `setTime-out` function. These are available globally, so you don't need to import them, and you can use them without any other additions.

But things are different with regard to more specialized functionalities such as reading and writing files. The functions required for this are located in the Deno namespace. This is also available globally and works without a separate import.

28.4.1 The Task: Copying a File

As an example of a file system operation, you'll now implement a function that reads an input file and writes its contents to an output file. To make the task a bit more interesting, it should be possible to pass the two file names by means of command-line options.

28.4.2 Processing Command-Line Options

For our example, we assume that the application can be run via the following command: `deno run index.js --input=input.txt --output=output.txt`. The first problem you need to solve here is to read the two options. You can achieve this via the `Deno.args` array. This array contains the arguments passed to your application on the command line, as shown in Listing 28.8.

```
function getInputAndOutputFiles() {
  const input = Deno.args
    .find((arg) => arg.startsWith('--input='))
    .substr(8);

  const output = Deno.args
    .find((arg) => arg.startsWith('--output='))
    .substr(9);

  console.log(`Input was: ${input}, Output was: ${output}`);

  return [input, output];
}

const [input, output] = getInputAndOutputFiles();
```

Listing 28.8 Access to the Command-Line Options

In two steps, you first search for the name of the input file and then for the name of the output file. To do this, you use the `find` method of the `Deno.args` array and then truncate the option name and the equal sign so that you keep only the file name. Finally, you output both file names to the console. You encapsulate these operations

28

in a function called getInputAndOutputFiles, which returns both pieces of information as an array. Finally, you call this function and use a destructuring statement to store the information in a variable each time.

If you save this source code in a file named *index.js* and run it via the preceding command, you'll get an output like the one shown in Listing 28.9.

```
$ deno run index.js --input=input.txt --output=output.txt
Input was: input.txt, Output was: output.txt
```

Listing 28.9 Output of the Command-Line Options

Now that you have both pieces of information in the form of constants, the next step is to read the input file and output its contents to the command line.

28.4.3   Reading Files

Deno has two functions that you can use to read files. The readFile method enables you to read the file and receive the contents as an ArrayBuffer, which you must first decode before you can output it to the console.

In Listing 28.10, you extend the previous example by the option to read the content of the file whose name you passed via the --input option. To do this, you first take two preparatory measures: implement a fileExists function and create an instance of the TextDecoder class. The fileExists function is an async function because most of Deno's interfaces work with promises. Inside the function—similar to Node.js—you use the Deno.stat function, which returns various information about a file. If the specified file doesn't exist, the stat function reports an error in the form of a rejected promise. If no error is thrown, you can assume that the file exists and return the value true.

```
function getInputAndOutputFiles() {...}
const [input, output] = getInputAndOutputFiles();

async function fileExists(filename) {
  try {
    await Deno.stat(`./${filename}`);
    return true;
  } catch (error) {
    if (error instanceof Deno.errors.NotFound) {
      return false;
    }
    throw error;
  }
}
```

```
const decoder = new TextDecoder();

if (await fileExists(input)) {
  const fileContents = await Deno.readFile(`./${input}`);
  const text = decoder.decode(fileContents);
  console.log(text);
}
```

Listing 28.10 Reading a File with Deno

Because you're in an async function here, you can catch the error with a try-catch statement. Depending on whether it's a NotFound error, which says that the file wasn't found, you either return false or keep throwing the error.

You need the TextDecoder to access the contents of the file because the readFile function you use in this example just returns a promise of the Uint8Array type. If you write this object to the console, you'll only see the string representation of this object, that is, a column of numbers.

You initiate the actual implementation of the read operation by checking whether the file exists. Here you use the fileExists function you created previously. If the check reveals that the file exists, you call the readFile function via the await keyword and receive the Uint8Array mentioned earlier. You then pass this to the decode method of the TextDecoder, which converts the Uint8Array into a human-readable string that you can then output to the console. Before you call your application again using the deno run --input=input.txt --output=output.txt command, you should define a simple text file with any text content; otherwise, the execution will fail. The output of the command with an existing input file will look like the one shown in Listing 28.11.

```
$ deno run index.js --input=input.txt --output=output.txt
Input was: input.txt, Output was: output.txt
error: Uncaught (in promise) PermissionDenied: Requires read access to "./
input.txt", run again with the --allow-read flag
    await Deno.stat(`./${filename}`);
    ^
    at deno:core/01_core.js:106:46
    at unwrapOpResult (deno:core/01_core.js:126:13)
    at async Object.stat (deno:runtime/js/30_fs.js:228:17)
    at async fileExists (file:///srv/node-buch/index.js:8:5)
    at async file:///srv/node-buch/index.js:20:5
```

Listing 28.11 Output When Reading a File

What you see here isn't a bug, but actually a notable feature of Deno that is a distinct difference from Node.js. The feature is referred to as *permissions*.

28.4.4   Permissions in Deno

Deno claims to be "secure by default"; that is, Deno is basically secure. Actually this is true because Deno follows the sandbox concept, as you know from the browser, much more strictly than is the case in Node.js. The effect is that you can't access all the resources of the system, but the access is denied first, and you have to release the resources for your application first. In our example, this is done using the `--allow-read` command-line option. You can optionally pass to this option a comma-separated list of file names and directory names that your application is allowed to access. Try to be as restrictive as possible at this point. Because the application only needs to read from the *input.txt* file, it's sufficient to specify this name. Listing 28.12 shows the command and its effects.

```
$ deno run --allow-read=input.txt index.js --input=input.txt --output=output.txt

Input was: input.txt, Output was: output.txt
Hello Deno!
```

Listing 28.12 Output When Reading a File with Correct Permissions

Not only do Deno's permissions include read access to the file system but also many other aspects that you can manipulate. Table 28.2 contains an overview of the available options.

Option	Description
`--allow-env=<env>`	Allows read and write access to environment variables.
`--allow-hrtime`	Allows highly accurate time measurements. Deno implements the W3C performance application programing interface (API), which you already know from Node.js with the `perf_hooks`.
`--allow-net=<net>`	Allows network access. Here you can specify an optional list of host names and ports Deno is allowed to use.
`--allow-ffi`	Allows dynamic libraries to be loaded.
`--allow-read=<read>`	Allows read access to the file system.
`--allow-run=<run>`	Allows the execution of subprocesses.
`--allow-write=<write>`	Serves as counterpart to `--allow-read` when it comes to write accesses to the file system.
`-A, --allow-all`	Allows all accesses. As a rule, you shouldn't use it because it will undermine Deno's security features.

Table 28.2 Options to Manage Permissions in Deno

This first working version of the application now enables you to optimize the source code a bit more.

28.4.5 readTextFile Function

In some cases, using TypedArrays such as the Uint8Array is quite useful. In our exam-ple, however, this just means one more unnecessary step. To avoid this extra work, Deno provides you with the readTextFile function. In Listing 28.13, you can see the cus-tomized source code of the example.

```
function getInputAndOutputFiles() {...}
const [input, output] = getInputAndOutputFiles();

async function fileExists(filename) {...}

if (await fileExists(input)) {
  const text = await Deno.readTextFile(`./${input}`);
  console.log(text);
}
```

Listing 28.13 Reading Text Files via the "readTextFile" Function

With this adjustment, both the application call and the result remain the same. They merely reduce the size of the source code. The permissions concept also remains unchanged at this point, so you have to call the application with the --allow-read option for it to work.

In the next step, we can now turn our attention to writing the target file.

28.4.6 Writing Files with Deno

Analogous to the readFile and readTextFile functions, there are also the writeFile and writeTextFile functions.

With the source code from Listing 28.14, you extend the application so that the content of the input file not only is output to the console but also written to the output file, which you specify with the --output option.

```
function getInputAndOutputFiles() {...}
const [input, output] = getInputAndOutputFiles();

async function fileExists(filename) {...}

const encoder = new TextEncoder();

if (await fileExists(input)) {
  const text = await Deno.readTextFile(`./${input}`);
  console.log(text);
```

28

```
  const encodedText = encoder.encode(text);
  Deno.writeFile(`./${output}`, encodedText);
}
```

Listing 28.14 Writing a File with Deno and the "writeFile" Function

You can also implement the example using the writeTextFile function. The only differ-ence here is that you can omit the intermediate step via TextEncoder and pass the con-tent to be written directly as the second argument to the writeTextFile function.

Synchronous and Asynchronous File System Operations

Like Node.js, Deno provides you with synchronous and asynchronous functions for file system operations. For example, you can read a text file synchronously via the read-TextFileSync function. In this case, the function returns the text content directly as a return value without having to work with promises.

Note, however, that this is a blocking operation. As long as your system is busy with the read operation, Deno can't perform any other operations. This is usually not a problem with small files. However, if the files you want to process are more complex, it may well take some time before your application is able to respond again.

Especially when reading configuration files at the start of an application, you can use the synchronous functions because your application can't be started without the corre-sponding configuration. A blockage can even be useful in this case.

When running the application, you must make sure to specify the --allow-write option, or Deno will throw an error. You can see the command and its result in Listing 28.15. To make the command more readable for you, we wrote it in several lines. If you want to test the application yourself, make sure you write the entire command in one line.

```
$ deno run
  --allow-read=input.txt
  --allow-write=output.txt index.js
  --input=input.txt
  --output=output.txt

Input was: input.txt, Output was: output.txt
Hello Deno!
```

Listing 28.15 Reading and Writing Files with Deno

The result of the command execution, besides the output on the console, is that a new file named *output.txt* has been created in the current directory.

Of course, when we look at Deno, we also have to include the typical example of a server-side JavaScript platform: a web server. And that's what we'll do in the following section.

28.5 Web Server with Deno

The basic concept of Node.js and Deno is the same. Both platforms make JavaScript available to you outside the browser. The primary use of Deno and Node.js is the implementation of dynamic web servers, so Deno also includes a number of structures that allow you to implement such a web server. Listing 28.16 shows the implementation of a simple web server. A detailed explanation follows right after.

```
const server = Deno.listen({ port: 8080 });
console.log('Server is listening to http://localhost:8080');

for await (const connection of server) {
  handleConnection(connection);
}

async function handleConnection(connection) {
  const httpConnection = Deno.serveHttp(connection);
  for await (const request of httpConnection) {
    const responseBody = 'Hello Deno!';

    request.respondWith(
      new Response(responseBody, {
        status: 200,
        headers: {
          'content-type': 'text/plain',
        },
      }),
    );
  }
}
```

Listing 28.16 Web Server in Deno

Calling the `listen` function instructs Deno to listen to the specified address-port combination. The platform binds itself to this address. If you don't specify a host name, but only a port, as in this example, Deno listens to the address 0.0.0.0, which represents all available addresses of the system in this case. As a return, you receive a `listener` object that stands for the established connection. After this operation, your server is ready to accept incoming connections, so you can output on the console that the server is ready. What is still missing at this point is the actual handling of the requests, and Deno solves this via an asynchronous iterator. The for await loop makes sure that the loop body is executed for each incoming connection and accordingly calls the handleConnection function with the connection object representing the connection.

The core of your server is the asynchronous handleConnection function. The connection object allows you to call the serveHttp function of Deno and get a representation of an HTTP connection as a return value. Because you can receive not only one but several requests in this type of connection, you'll again need an asynchronous iterator that is executed for each incoming request. Here you can access the request and also formulate responses using the respondWith method of the request object.

You encapsulate a response in an instance of the response class, whose first argument is the body of the response. As a second argument, you can specify the response in more detail, for example, by defining the status code or certain header fields.

For your server to work, you need to use the permissions system of Deno again and share network access. As with file system access, you can be very selective here. Once you know that the server will be bound to the address 0.0.0.0:8080, you'll need to release only that address. Listing 28.17 contains the command to start the server.

```
$ deno run --allow-net=0.0.0.0:8080 index.js
Server is listening to http://localhost:8080
```

Listing 28.17 Running the Web Server

Now you can go to your browser and connect to the address *http://localhost:8080/*. The results are shown in Figure 28.1.

Figure 28.1 Response of the Deno Web Server in the Browser

Up to this point, your applications have merely been run in one file. Because Deno also supports the ECMAScript module system, it's not necessary to restrict yourself to only one file. The following sections will introduce you to the module system of Deno.

28.6   Module System

Like the recent versions of Node.js, Deno uses the ECMAScript module system, that is, the import and export keywords. For a better description of the module system, let's return to our example of copying a file and recapitulate. We implemented the two functions getInputAndOutputFiles and fileExists. These are ideal candidates for out-sourcing to a separate module. So, you create a new file called *util.js*, copy the two functions into the file, and export it. Listing 28.18 shows the source code of the *util.js* file.

```
export function getInputAndOutputFiles() {
  const input = Deno.args
    .find((arg) => arg.startsWith('--input='))
    .substr(8);
  const output = Deno.args
    .find((arg) => arg.startsWith('--output='))
    .substr(9);

  console.log(`Input was: ${input}, Output was: ${output}`);

  return [input, output];
}

export async function fileExists(filename) {
  try {
    await Deno.stat(`./${filename}`);
    return true;
  } catch (error) {
    if (error instanceof Deno.errors.NotFound) {
      return false;
    }
    throw error;
  }
}
```

Listing 28.18 Swapping Out Functions to a Separate File (util.js)

You now use these two functions in the entry file of your application—the *index.js* file—as shown in Listing 28.19.

```
import { getInputAndOutputFiles, fileExists } from './util.js';

const [input, output] = getInputAndOutputFiles();
const encoder = new TextEncoder();

if (await fileExists(input)) {
  const text = await Deno.readTextFile(`./${input}`);
  console.log(text);

  const encodedText = encoder.encode(text);
  Deno.writeFile(`./${output}`, encodedText);
}
```

Listing 28.19 Integrating the Helper Functions (index.js)

28

When integrating the *util.js* file, don't forget the file extension, or Deno will complain that the file can't be found. Now you can run the example again. The modification hasn't changed anything in the command to start the application nor in the output.

Deno would already be doomed in its early days if the platform didn't have the possibility to load external modules. So, in the next step, you'll see how to access modules made available to you by the ever-growing Deno community.

28.6.1   Loading External Modules into Deno

The first place to go for modules in Deno is the standard library. This is a set of modules with no external dependencies that are reviewed by Deno's core team. This is to ensure that, on the one hand, the core of Deno can be kept as slim as possible, and, on the other hand, you can access numerous extensions without having to bother about their quality.

An example of functionality from the Deno standard library is the http module. For example, this module enables you to use the listenAndServe function, which significantly simplifies the implementation of a web server. Listing 28.20 shows how you can use this function to implement the example from Listing 28.16 in a much shorter and easier way.

```
import { listenAndServe } from 'https://deno.land/std@0.108.0/http/server.ts';

listenAndServe(
  ':8080',
  () =>
    new Response('Hello Deno!', {
      status: 200,
      headers: {
        'content-type': 'text/plain',
      },
    }),
);

console.log('Server is listening to http://localhost:8080');
```

Listing 28.20 HTTP Server with the "http" Module from the Standard Library

As you can see here, you no longer have to use asynchronous loops, but you can directly define the response handler as a callback function, and the http module will take care of everything else. When you run the web server, you need to make sure once again that network access is permitted. In addition, when taking a look at the output in Listing 28.21, you can see that Deno downloads a number of files. This is the http module and its dependencies within the standard library. However, these downloads take place only once initially. For all further executions, Deno uses its local cache.

```
$ deno run --allow-net=0.0.0.0:8080 index.js
Download https://deno.land/std@0.108.0/http/server.ts
Download https://deno.land/std@0.108.0/async/mod.ts
Download https://deno.land/std@0.108.0/async/delay.ts
Download https://deno.land/std@0.108.0/async/deadline.ts
Download https://deno.land/std@0.108.0/async/mux_async_iterator.ts
Download https://deno.land/std@0.108.0/async/deferred.ts
Download https://deno.land/std@0.108.0/async/debounce.ts
Download https://deno.land/std@0.108.0/async/pool.ts
Download https://deno.land/std@0.108.0/async/tee.ts
Check file:///srv/node-buch/index.js
Server is listening to http://localhost:8080
```

Listing 28.21 Running the Web Server with the "http" Module

In addition to the modules of the standard library, there is another source for external Deno modules: *deno.land/x*.

28.6.2 deno.land/x

Unlike the modules of the standard library, the ones you can include via deno.land/x aren't subject to such strict quality criteria. These are packages stored on GitHub. deno.land/x caches the releases of these packages and makes them available via a shortened path. Listing 28.22 contains the fibonacci module as an example for the use of modules from deno.land/x. This module returns the fibonacci function as the sum of the Fibonacci sequence, or the fibonacciSequence, which represents an array.

```
import fibonacci, {
  fibonacciSequence,
} from 'https://deno.land/x/fibonacci/mod.ts';

console.log(fibonacci(9));
console.log(fibonacciSequence(4));
```

Listing 28.22 Integrating Modules from deno.land/x

Apart from these modules, you can also include npm packages.

28.6.3 Using Node Package Manager Packages

If at all possible, you should avoid including npm packages, as this is generally considered bad practice in the Deno community. In many cases, integrating npm packages works fine, but you shouldn't do it as a default out of habit. Node.js npm packages are usually optimized to run in Node.js. Especially with more extensive packages, unwanted side effects can quickly occur if the packages are based on core Node.js modules. For

28

most areas of use, native solutions for Deno also exist that you can use directly, but sometimes there is no way around npm packages. In the simplest case, you access the source code of the package on GitHub, and if the package already uses ECMAScript modules, you can use it directly via an import statement. Listing 28.23 shows an example of this.

```
import intersection from 'https://raw.githubusercontent.com/lodash/lodash/
master/intersection.js';

const numbers1 = [1, 2, 3, 4];
const numbers2 = [6, 5, 4, 3];

const numbersIntersection = intersection(numbers1, numbers2);

console.log(numbersIntersection); // Output: [ 3, 4 ]
```

Listing 28.23 Integrating Lodash in Deno

The example uses the intersection function of Lodash to determine the intersection of two arrays. You can access the corresponding file by opening the project repository at *https://github.com/lodash/lodash* in the browser, picking out the *intersection.js* file and clicking on the **raw** button. When you take a look at the source code of the *intersection.js* file, you'll see that import statements are already used here, so integration and usage won't be a problem.

For classic npm packages, you need to dig a little deeper into the box of tricks and use services such as JavaScript Package Manager (JSPM), which convert npm packages into ECMAScript modules for you using the CommonJS module system. Listing 28.24 shows an example of this in which the is-odd library is used.

```
import isOdd from 'https://dev.jspm.io/is-odd';

console.log(isOdd(3)); // Output: true
```

Listing 28.24 Integrating the "is-odd" Library

When you run this script, the output looks like the one shown in Listing 28.25.

```
$ deno run index.js
Download https://dev.jspm.io/is-odd
Download https://dev.jspm.io/npm:is-odd@3.0.1/index.dew.js
Download https://dev.jspm.io/npm:is-number@6?dew
Download https://dev.jspm.io/npm:is-number@6.0.0/index.dew.js
true
```

Listing 28.25 Running a Script with an npm Package via JSPM

As you can see, Deno first downloads the `is-odd` package and then the `is-number` package, which is a dependency of the `is-odd` package. After the dependencies are resolved, Deno executes the source code and produces the output, in this case, the string `true`, because the value 3 is an odd number.

28.7 Summary

This chapter has introduced you to Deno, a modern alternative to Node.js. Deno is a comparatively young platform that is currently still very much outshone by Node.js. Nevertheless, Deno takes a very modern approach. You can see this simply from the fact that the core of the platform isn't written in C or C++, but in Rust. In addition, Dahl has attempted to address the architectural weaknesses of Node.js in Deno by adding the permissions system and allowing Deno to do without an additional package manager altogether, for example.

The question as to whether or not you should base your next project on Node.js or Deno isn't an easy one. What speaks for Node.js is that the platform has proven itself in practical use over many years and is very performant and stable despite some weaknesses. In addition, a very important factor is that Node.js has the backing of a very large open-source community. Deno, on the other hand, scores with a clean and modern architecture, built-in security features, and integrated TypeScript support.

You should therefore give both platforms a chance and find out for yourself which platform better helps you implement your requirements.

28

The Author

Sebastian Springer is a JavaScript engineer at MaibornWolff. In addition to developing and designing both client-side and server-side JavaScript applications, his focus is on imparting knowledge. As a lecturer for JavaScript, a speaker at numerous conferences, and an author, he inspires enthusiasm for professional development with JavaScript. Sebastian was previously a team leader at Mayflower GmbH, one of the premier web development agencies in Germany. He was responsible for project and team management, architecture, and customer care for companies such as Nintendo Europe, Siemens, and others.

Index

H

- Your all-in-one guide to JavaScript

- Work with objects, reference types, events, forms, and web APIs

- Build server-side applications, mobile applications, desktop applications, and more

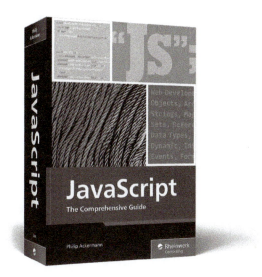

Philip Ackermann

JavaScript

The Comprehensive Guide

Begin your JavaScript journey with this comprehensive, hands-on guide. You'll learn everything there is to know about professional JavaScript programming, from core language concepts to essential client-side tasks. Build dynamic web applications with step-by-step instructions and expand your knowledge by exploring server-side development and mobile development. Work with advanced language features, write clean and efficient code, and much more!

982 pages, pub. 08/2022
E-Book: $54.99 | **Print:** $59.95 | **Bundle:** $69.99
www.rheinwerk-computing.com/5554

- Your complete guide to the Java Platform, Standard Edition 17

- Understand the Java langauge, from basic pricinples to advanced concepts

- Work with expressions, statements, classes, objects, and much more

Christian Ullenboom

Java

The Comprehensive Guide

This is the up-to-date, practical guide to Java you've been looking for! Whether you're a beginner, you're switching to Java from another language, or you're just looking to brush up on your Java skills, this is the only book you need. You'll get a thorough grounding in the basics of the Java language, including classes, objects, arrays, strings, and exceptions. You'll also learn about more advanced topics: threads, algorithms, XML, JUnit testing, and much more. This book belongs on every Java programmer's shelf!

approx. 1,258 pp., pub. 09/2022
E-Book: $54.99 | **Print:** $59.95 | **Bundle:** $69.99

www.rheinwerk-computing.com/5557

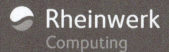